The Media Guide
1999

Edited by Paul Fisher

& Steve Peak

Researched by Jo Wallace

& Emma Johnson

Fourth Estate • London

Published in Great Britain by:
Fourth Estate Ltd, 6 Salem Road, London W2 4BU
The seventh annual edition

Copyright 1998 Guardian News Service Ltd and Steve Peak
119 Farringdon Road, London EC1R 3ER

A catalogue record for this book is available from the British Library: ISBN 1-85702-872-4

Publisher: Gerald Knight

Picture research: Judith Caul

Picture credits

16 Kelvin MacKenzie, Graham Turner	113 Tony Blair, John Reardon	170 John Birt, Garry Weaser
18 Marjorie Scardino, Pearson	122 James Eisen, Frank Baron	171 Rupert Murdoch, Frank Martin
18 Rosie Boycott, Frank Baron	146 Peter Salmon, Sean Smith	196 Dave Rushton, Channel 6
18 Simon Kelner, The Guardian	148/283 Chris Smith, Sean Smith	285 Alistair Campbell, Martin Argles
19 Hugh Cudlipp, Michael Peto	150 John Birt, David Sillitoe	327 Civil War mock-up, The Guardian
27 Ian Hargreaves, David Sillitoe	150 Michael Jackson, Martin Argles	329 Margaret Thatcher, Neil Lidden
27 Peter Wilby, New Statesman	150 David Elstein, E Hamilton West	333 Rockers, Sally Soames
36 Chris Oakley, Newspaper Society	152 Robin Biggam, E Hamilton West	337 M1, The Guardian
38 Freddie Johnston, The Guardian	163 Brain Redhead, Sean Smith	340 Phone, David Sillitoe
78 Trevor Phillips, BBC	163 James Naughtie, David Sillitoe	363 European Parlt., Garry Weaser
78 Trevor McDonald, Frank Baron	169 Diana funeral, Frank Baron	374 British soldier, The Guardian

Advertisement manager: Kassandra Farrington

Advertisement index

Acknowledgements: Graham Brown, Mathew Clayton, Michael Foley, Ian Garland, Roger Harrison, Andrew Hillier, Rosy Lyne, Amanda Kelly, Eoin McVey, Dave Rushton

Designed by Gary Phillips and produced on Apple computers using Quark Express by Paul Fisher and Emma Johnson. Based on an idea of Steve Peak. Set in Scala and Helvetica

Printed in Great Britain by WBC Book Manufacturers, Bridgend

OLSWANG

Unanimously voted 'Law Firm of the Year' [1]
Awarded 'Media Team of the Year' [2]

Telephone no: 0171 208 8888   Fax: 0171 208 8800   http://www.olswang.co.uk   Email: olsmail@olswang.co.uk
1 The Lawyer/HIFAL Awards   2 Legal Business Awards

SOCIETY

ACTION

Foreword

Welcome to this year's Media Guide which launches us into yet another rich media year. Because of the rapid - and sometimes breathtaking - expansion of the industry, it is always possible to see new revolutions on the horizon. This time the revolution is right upon us.

With the launch of digital television finally here, the talking, arguing and general one-up manship will stop and at last the consumers get to have their say. Who will win this most important of media battles? Will we all rush out and buy our digital televisions complete with surround sound and pin-sharp pictures? Or will we remain on the sofa, flicking through the same old options and declaring ourselves "very happy indeed" with the present five terrestrial options. Predictions are awkward things, liable to come back and haunt you when you wish they would go and die somewhere quietly by themselves. It is not exactly bold to say that digital television will take off. But who will win the intriguing series of guerilla wars which will ensue throughout the year? Sky Digital and On Digital have been at each other's throats from the outset and the battle will continue, rich and varied. Expect huge marketing and advertising campaigns, the like of which we have not seen since Sky first launched against British Satellite Broadcasting or VHS took on Betamax in the video wars.

I say, after taking a brave swallow, that Sky will have the upper hand as long as they can sort out their problems with ITV. For the losers it will be a humbling experience and some people, most with very large reputations, are bound to be caught up in the maelstrom. Embarrasments will be legion. It will be the leading issue of the year, but by no means the only one.

Just a quick run through the pressing subjects in any media person's in-tray reveals how much there is still to debate. Is there a Diana effect? Has her death really changed the way journalists work or has the year simply been marked by a series of gestures? On the surface, the Mirror's decision to return the James Hewitt letters to Buckingham Palace or the Sun's decision to warn Buckhingham Palace about the Camilla-meets-Prince-William story appear to say that Diana still stalks the media world. But what about naked pictures of Kylie Monogue on a beach? Or Nicole Kidman in a wheelchair, leaving hospital after an operation? Diana is a developing issue. As is the law.

The incorporation of the European Convention on Human Rights into British law will bring fundamental changes to the way newspapers and journalists work. The government has moved some of the way to allay fears that judges will have the power to put the interests of privacy over the public's right to know. But there will be still be the issue of how the judicial process will balance the essentially conflicting Articles 8 and 10 of the Convention, the protection of privacy and the protection of free speech. At stake is the freedom of the press.

Other essential elements in 1999's media mix are: sport and TV; the relationship between the independent and the terrestrial broadcasters; truth and TV; the royal family and the press; whether radio is dumber and duller or better for being more accessible; and the role of regional and local newspapers, which are enjoying a circulation surge.

The media is a complicated subject to find your way around. Who is the features editor of the Observer? Who does what, where and why? The answers are here in an updated and expanded Media Guide. Along with the usual forensic detail on Britain's media industry, there are extra sections on digital television and restricted licences, on radio producers and media analysts and a whole new section on the Republic of Ireland. Here is the handbook we all need on our desks.

Kamal Ahmed, Media Editor, The Guardian

Big media numbers

UK media owners ranked by turnover

COMPANY	1996	1997
1 Granada	£3817m	£4091m
2 Reed Elsevier	£3381m	£3417m
3 Pearson	£2186m	£2294m
4 United News & Media	£1046m	£1971m
5 Carlton	-	£1750m
6 BSkyB	£1008m	£1270m
7 D Mail & General Trust	£1007m	£1200m
8 EMAP	£705m	£768m
9 Mirror Group	£538m	£559m
10 Channel 4	£519m	£553m
11 Guardian	£302m	£326m
12 Trinity	£332m	£325m
13 Newsquest	£366m	£279m
14 Scottish Media Group	£127m	£197m

Data taken from individual research, company reports and Media Map Datafile. The Telegraph and News International are not UK owned and so do not appear. To be classed as media turnover, the commercial company's revenue must come from advertising, publishing, broadcasting, TV & film production, subscription fees, government grants, etc. Contract printing, music production, retail distribution and the like are not included. In addition, miscellaneous income that cannot be clearly linked to media activity has not been included in the total.

Source: Campaign for Press & Broadcasting Freedom

1997 change in share value

COMPANY	%CHANGE
1 Home Counties Newspapers	97.75
2 Midland Ind. Newspapers	59.25
3 Daily Mail 'A'	51.22
4 News Corp Pref Ord	37.68
5 Independent Newspapers	34.23
6 Goodhead Group	30.51
7 Ulster TV	29.59
8 News Corp	27.71
9 EMAP	25.27
10 Southern Newspapers	19.85
11 Portsmouth & Sunderland	15.67
12 Elsevier	14.04
13 Euromoney Pub	12.83
14 Reed International	12.76
15 Scot Radio HDG	11.62
16 Johnston Press	10.84
17 Pearson	9.27
18 Trinity	5.62
19 Adscene Group	4.65
20 United News & Media	2.08

Source: Datastream

World's largest media owners

COMPANY	REVENUES $MILLION
1 Walt Disney Company	$18,739
2 Bertelsmann AG	$14,728
3 Viacom Inc	$12,084
4 Time Warner Inc	$10,064
5 The News Corporation	$9,935

Top European media owners revenue

COMPANY	TOTAL REV '95 $M	MEDIA REV '95
1 Reed Elsevier	$5,702m	$3,367m
2 CLT-UFA	$3,272m	$3,166m
3 Havas	$8,716m	$2,950m
4 Bertelsmann	$14,353m	$2,923m
5 Axel Springer	$2,764m	$2,395m
6 United News & Media	$2,955m	$2,295m
7 Lagardere	$10,269m	$2,209m
8 Heinrich Bauer	$1,924m	$1,895m
9 Mediaset	$1,915m	$1,804m
10 Canal Plus	$1,984m	$1,687m
11 WAZ	$2,000	$1,617m
12 TF1	$1,785m	$1,461m
13 DMGT	$1,366m	$1,354m
14 VNU	$1,806m	$1,261m
15 BSkyB	$1,216m	$1,170m
16 RCS Editori	$1,620m	$1,102m
17 Sat 1	$1,083m	$1.083m
18 Carlton Comms	$2,468m	$1,407m
19 Holtzbrinck	$1,828m	$1.015m
20 ProSieben	$978m	$978m
21 Pearson	$2,860m	$962m
22 Emap	$1,102m	$947m
23 Granada	$3,721m	$877m
24 RAI	$2,598m	$864m
25 Burda	$1,136m	$846m
26 Mirror Group	$783m	$783m
27 Bonnier	$1,434m	$719m
28 Channel 4	$725m	$700m
29 De Telegraf	$681m	$681m
30 Hersant	$670m	$670m
31 Sebaldus	$660m	$659m
32 Marieberg	$1,456m	$643m
33 DuMont Schauberg	$587m	$587m
34 Mondadori	$1,395m	$580m
35 Suddeutscher Verlag	$746m	$578m

Source: Zenith Media. From 1995 trading figures

National newspapers

MAD TABS

8 AUGUST 1997: Tabloid references to nutters and loonies were "stigmatising mental illness", claimed a Health Education Authority report.

"TOSSER ... PRAT"

15 AUGUST: The Mirror editor Piers Morgan said he'd acted like "a complete tosser and a total prat". And why? He'd decided he'd been over-critical of Sun coverage of alleged match fixing by John Fashanu, Bruce Grobbelaar, and Hans Segers. "I've been a juvenile delinquent," Morgan continued.

FAREWELL TO SUBS

22 AUGUST: The European announced plans to get rid of sub-editors and have its journalists writing straight into page. Andrew Linnane, a European executive editor, said correspondent's copy would have to be word-perfect and carry a suggested headline: "If the copy is good enough, it will wurk. Wot we's trying to achive very quickly isnotoer paper has ever, eliminating pruction and writers writieng direclty to page."

PRINT OUTSTRIPS TV

28 AUGUST: Newsprint emerged as the most profitable part of News Corporation's global operation with their contribution to turnover increasing 26 per cent to £300 million in 1996/97. The Sun, News of the World, Times and Sunday Times reported a 33 per cent increase in profits, while BSkyB's profits grew by 22 per cent. JP Morgan, a New York stockbroker, said: "Murdoch's UK titles constitute the world's most profitable editorial franchise - The Times remains the most influential paper in Europe and The Sun and NoW remain the voice of John Bull."

SNODDY TO TIMES

1 SEPTEMBER: Ray Snoddy, the Financial Times' main media man for a decade, became a Murdoch employee and started his new career at the Times. In March 1998, at the height of the row about Murdoch/Harper Collins' rejection of Chris Patten's book, Snoddy wrote a winsome defence of his position. "Trying to write about the affairs of one's own newspaper or, even worse, the other business interests of the proprietor, is never easy - and may actually be impossible." Well, he took a job which has pushed him toward this feeble irony: "Why, even the Times has been known, occasionally, to appear to avert its gaze when some activity of Mr Murdoch is being criticised by some ill-informed soul." Snoddy's FT replacement is John Gapper.

FT IN AMERICA

9 SEPTEMBER: The Financial Times started a £100 million American sales drive by making the paper a give-away on Wall Street. The FT's owner, Pearson, aims to dent the Wall Street Journal's 1.8 million circulation with a US edition featuring a new table of contents, much colour and the McPaper approach of easily digested stories, analysis - and comment. Half the paper's 300,000+ circulation is outside Britain. Six months later the paper exceeded city expectations when it reported a £35 million profits for 1997, a 138 per cent increase, largely attributed to success in America.

NEW BOSS

12 SEPTEMBER: Bob Phillis, the deputy general of the BBC, was appointed as Guardian Media Group chief executive. At the BBC he had headed BBC Worldwide, the division which negotiated deals to launch subscription channels with Flextech and Discovery.

DAILY MAIL SUCCESS

12 SEPTEMBER: Paul Dacre, the Daily Mail editor since 1992, was credited with boosting circulation from 1.7 million to 2.2 million without price cutting except in Scotland. A Mail spokesman said: "There is a real prospect of the Daily Mail replacing The Mirror as the second biggest-selling newspaper in the UK. Public taste is moving more towards where Today sat and where the Mail and Express now sit, away from the rabid ranting of the red-tops."

the perfect party

THROWING A PARTY?

We spent years looking for the best party organisers, finally the ultimate company Capital VIP provided the answer.

Don't even think about throwing a party until you've consulted Justin Etzin and his team at Capital VIP. From the moment you call them you just know that you've come to the right people. Capital VIP is London's leading party organiser, with a list of private clients reading like the pages of Who's Who.

Even fashion gurus like *Gucci, Louis Vuitton, MTV* and *Harrods* are turning to Capital VIP in recognition of its outstanding ability to organise the ultimate party. Capital VIP provides every ingredient for the perfect party, including catering, marquees and entertainment. They are particularly noted for their stunning interiors, imaginative theming and attention to detail. Rumour has it that the head Honcho of Gucci said that the recent party that Capital VIP organised to launch their diamond G watch was a total success, but all for the wrong reasons. Why? Because all his guests were heard to be commenting on the wonderful food, and not the extravagant watch displays!

Capital VIP is renowned for organising spectacular events. Two recent film premiere parties organised by Capital VIP were held at the famous Café de Paris. Justin Etzin explains that choosing the right venue is paramount to the success of a party.

Capital VIP has earned its title as "The Ultimate Party Organiser". I'll let you into a little secret - when you call Capital VIP (0171) 495 7070 - would you believe that they send you their company brochure hand-delivered by a black-tie messenger? With attention to detail like this, it's no wonder that everyone is turning to Capital VIP to have their party organised.

CAPITAL VIP

INDIE REDESIGN

16 SEPTEMBER 1997: The redesigned Independent declared: "Big, hoarsely shouting headlines are out. This should make the paper easier to read, but it also means more words per page than before. If the opposite of dumbing-down in smartening up, then that is what we are doing." The relaunch came with a week of price cutting to 20p (before rising to 45p) and the pledge of a £12 million budget. "Strong papers evolve, weak ones keep on relaunching themselves," said the ex-Indie man Stephen Glover. There were rumours the Barclay Brothers would buy the paper and acrimony following the sacking of Barbara Gunnell, assistant editor on the Independent on Sunday.

PHOTOCOPYING

1 OCTOBER: After long delay, News International joined other newspaper publishers as a member of the Newspaper Licensing Agency. The NLA collects fees to permit photocopying of cuttings. "NI's participation means that organisations will be able to buy a single licence covering all nationals," said Guy MacNaughton, the NLA managing director.

READERS' EDITOR

3 OCTOBER: The Guardian appointed Ian Mayes as readers' editor and assigned editorial space to carry corrections and clarifications. Mayes said: "I've never understood why we as journalists should be coy about the way we work and think - or about our fallibility. We're living in a more open age, and the Guardian and its readers are part of it."

DEMPSTER FACTS

13 OCTOBER: Nigel Dempster, the Daily Mail's chief gossip merchant since 1973, was fined for contempt of court after repeating a libel first punished in 1995. Judge Richard Walker said Dempster's crime was either deliberate - in which case there would have been a "significant" jail sentence - or inept. The following April Dempster was convicted of drinking and driving, having said that fear of syringes meant he couldn't give a blood test. After the hearing he said: "Never complain, never explain."

STANDARD FINED

31 OCTOBER: The Evening Standard was fined £40,000 for an article that halted the trail of IRA terrorists accused of escaping from Whitemoor Prison. The judge called the article a "negligent mistake".

WITNESS PAYMENTS

5 NOVEMBER: Lord Irvine the Lord Chancellor told the House of Commons media select committee of his intention to ban newspapers from paying witnesses. Some 20 witnesses in the Rosemary West trial were paid for their stories. In March Lord Irvine confirmed the intention to legislate when he endorsed the Press Complaints Commission's view that the self-regulation favoured by the press is not enough.

HAMILTON "TOOK THE CASH"

6 NOVEMBER: Neil Hamilton, the former Tory MP who had tried to sue the Guardian for libel, was rebuked by Parliament's Standards and Privileges Committee. Its chairman Robert Sheldon said: "There is compelling evidence he took cash from Mohamed Al Fayed. And that was agreed by nine votes to nil. You can't get a better verdict than that from a jury."

LORD MCGREGOR DIES

10 NOVEMBER: Lord McGregor, the first chairman of the Press Complaints Commission, died aged 76. When Andrew Morton published his first Princess Di book, McGregor criticised "journalists who dabbled their fingers in the stuff of other people's souls".

LIAR

4 DECEMBER: Publication of The Liar - a book about Jonathan Aitken by Guardian journalists Luke Harding, David Leigh and David Pallister - revealed how the former cabinet minister had launched his libel action against the Guardian with money provided by his Saudi backer, Prince Mohammed bin Fahd. In February 1998 Aitken took a job as an arms salesman for GEC, a post he lost the next month when questioned by the police in connection with allegations of conspiracy to pervert the course of justice.

CAMERA PRESS LONDON

One of the World's Great Picture Agencies

Top Photographers ..... Top Images

Editorial * * ** * Publishing * ** *.* Advertising ** * * * Archive

Visit our Website at www.camerapress.com

Camera Press Ltd
21 Queen Elizabeth Street
London SE1 2PD
Telephone: 00 44 (0) 171 378 1300
Fax: 00 44 (0) 171 278 5126
UK Sales Fax: 00 44 (0) 171 357 0885

DAILY MAIL PROFITS UP

11 DECEMBER 1997: The Daily Mail and General Trust reported a 68 per cent profits increase to £143.7 million on a £1.2 billion turnover. While its newsprint costs fell by 18 per cent, advertising across the group was up by 12 per cent. Looking to the future, DMTG said: "Much will depend on the well-being of the UK economy and especially of recruitment advertising, which, while currently buoyant, has been known to turn down very quickly."

ANDREAS THE CENSOR

18 DECEMBER: Andreas Whittam Smith, the Indie's founding editor, was appointed president of the British Board of Film Classification.

BIG SALARY

18 DECEMBER: Richard Littlejohn (who lives next door to Arsenal's Denis Bergkamp) transferred from the Daily Mail back to the Sun in a deal that had him committed to a Sky TV chat show as well as his column. Littlejohn's annual salary of £800,000 makes him Britain's best-paid working journalist way ahead of the sad quarter millions reputedly earned by Lynda Lee Potter (Daily Mail) and Anne Robinson (Express).

A CHRISTMAS TALE

24 DECEMBER: The Mirror bolstered the cause of those who favour privacy legislation by revealing that an unnamed cabinet minister's son smoked dope. In fact he'd even supplied a tenner's worth to the Mirror's intrepid Dawn Alford. William Straw, the home secretary's son, emerged as the dope fiend in the Scottish press and on the Internet and then, by 3 January, throughout the rest of the British press. Alford was arrested for buying drugs, Straw Jnr received a police caution. Neither was prosecuted and the non-story came to an end.

MACKENZIE'S MOVES

13 JANUARY: Kelvin MacKenzie, former Sun editor and latterly the boss of Live TV, became deputy chief executive and group managing director of the Mirror Group. "Clearly the Mirror is in such trouble they need a real

journalist to take over. They've tried everything else - relaunches, new magazines, bulk sales. Kelvin's job title masks his real title: editor-in-chief," commented Stuart Higgins, MacKenzie's successor at the Sun. "My job?" MacKenzie asked. "Look, there are financiers out there who are unutterably brilliant. But they can't do what I can do. I push numbers. I believe in the audience, I push lots of people to watch television or to read newspapers."

Kelvin MacKenzie

9 June: MacKenzie, former deputy chief executive and group managing director of the Mirror Group, left his long job title behind him to form a consortium to bid for Talk Radio. A friend explained the move to a new medium by saying MacKenzie wanted "his own train set".

MARR SACKED

30 JANUARY: The Independent editor Andrew Marr was sacked for refusing to implement further budget cuts. Rosie Boycott took Marr's place and continued editing the Independent on Sunday. Hers was the 21st editor's job to be awarded during David Montgomery's five year leadership of Mirror Group Newspapers. Polly Toynbee resigned from the Indie and defected back to the Guardian. She said: "I don't think Mr Montgomery has any idea what the real values of the Independent are. He seems to think it should be positioned between the Times and the Daily Mail but does he really think he can battle with the big sharks on a policy of no resources and no promotion?" Meanwhile Daily Mail sales crept up on the Mirror.

SUNDAY BUSINESS

15 FEBRUARY: The new Sunday Business relaunched under the editorship of Jeff Randall and the guidance of Andrew Neil (Randall's mentor when both were at the Sunday Times). Sales did not reach the 80,000 target and within six weeks the paper's owner, the Barclay Brothers, had to invest a further £1 million.

MARTHA GELLHORN DIES

17 FEBRUARY 1998: Martha Gellhorn - whose D-Day, Cuban and Vietnam war reporting made her more famous even than her five year marriage to Ernest Hemingway - died aged 89. John Pilger, who in many ways is her inheritor, paid tribute. "She was undoubtedly one of the greatest of all war correspondents - if not the greatest - because she reported wars from the point of view of people, not power."

ROUNDED AND DEDICATED SUN

27 FEBRUARY: A £2.5 million ad campaign to present the Sun as a "more rounded product" sought to get back women readers who had defected to the Mirror and the Mail. It was its first general image building TV campaign and didn't push a competition or particular bit of editorial. The two big red tops are both seeking the newly coined mezzo brow readers - the contemporary twentysomethings who don't quite fit old stereotypes. Two weeks earlier "Dedicated to the people of Britain" appeared under the Sun's title.

MAXWELL BACK IN THE NEWS

1 MARCH: Robert Maxwell made a posthumous return to front page news when the Sunday Times alleged that Lord Donoughue, a former Maxwell director and the Labour food and farming minister, "may have known more than previously thought about the business practices that led to the loss of millions of pounds from the Mirror Group Newspapers' pension fund".

MORNING STAR STRIKE

6 MARCH: A five week strike ended in victory to the workers when management reinstated John Haylett. The editor had been sacked with no written or verbal warning.

INDEPENDENT SALE

11 MARCH: Tony O'Reilly, the Irish media and food millionaire, took control of the two Independents when his Dublin-based Independent Newspapers paid Mirror Group Newspapers £29 million for MGN's 40 per cent holding in Newspaper Publishing. Three million pounds went to MGN, the remaining £26 million represented loans and debt. "Vanity publishing by an ambitious man," said one media analyst in commenting on O'Reilly' plans to up the circulation to even 250,000. Andrew Marr, who had parted company with MGN in January, was back as co-editor with Rosie Boycott. They were dubbed the "dream team" and spoke in dream-like soundbites.

Andrew Marr: "We know what each other is doing all the time ... we talk the whole time about everything. We have a constant conversation."

Rosie Boycott: "We both really love books, we both really love science. We both really love particular kinds of writing."

THE TIMES' INDEPENDENCE

16 MARCH: MPs presented Rupert Murdoch with calls for his ownership of the Times to be challenged for the newspaper's partiality in reporting Chinese news. Paddy Ashdown, the Lib Dem leader, said Murdoch had broken pledges made when he took over the Times and recommended a referral to the Monopolies and Mergers Commission. The Labour MP Robin Corbett spoke in the Commons to demand a Press Complaints Commission enquiry into alleged interference in editorial independence. Chris Smith, the culture secretary, said: "Editorial independence in the press is a matter for proprietors and editors. Any interference by the government in this relationship would, of course in a democracy, be inappropriate."

DAILY GETS MUCH FROGGIER

18 MARCH: The Express, Sunday Express and Daily Star doubled 1997 profits to nearly £20 million. They were still branded as "frogs" by Goldman Sachs in a report which dubbed United News and Media's Miller Freeman magazine division as a "prince" and said that, in its opinion, the company would not sell Express Newspapers. UNM as a whole was valued at £4.7 billion and Express Group at £218 million. UNM bade farewell to chief operating officer David Arculus and MD Stephen Grabiner. Arculus left to become chairman of IPC and Grabiner to run BDB.

PEARSON/SCARDINO

18 MARCH 1998: Pearson's 1997 profits were £232.2 million on a £2.3 billion turnover with the Financial Times contributing a £35 million profit, 138 per cent up on 1996. Since Marjorie Scardino (below)became Pearson chief executive in January 1997 she has sold at a pace and has now got rid of her "peripheral businesses".

The Pearson/Scardino progress

Feb '97: Sold 10% of TVB in Hong Kong for £111.1m. Profit £4.1m

Jun '97: Sold Flextech shares. Profit £23.9m

Jul '97: Sold stake in Troll for £55m. Profit £12.5m

Jul '97: Bought McClanahan educational publisher

Aug '97: Bought into Red Storm Entertainment

Aug '97: Bought Resource Data International for £57m.

Aug '97: Sold Livingstone for £57m. Profit £30.4

Sep '97: Alliance with Pecoletos and Telefonica in Spain

Oct '97: Bought All American Communications (Baywatch) for £233m

Feb '98: Sold holding in SES satellite firm for £159.5m. Profit £132.2m

Mar '98: Sold legal and tax publishing firms for £70m. Profit £61m

Mar '98: Sold Mindscape for $150m. Loss £212m

April '98: Sold Future Publishing for £142 million. Profit £89.5 million

July '98: Madame Tussauds, Alton Towers, plus other roadside attractions on sale for £400m

AUTOMATED PUZZLES

30 MARCH: A six month labour saving exercise began on the Daily Telegraph with a database of crossword clues used to supplement compilers' efforts. Their pay-per-puzzle dropped from £140 to an estimated £60. Their complaints led to a victory against technology for the computer plan was dropped. "In spite of the advantages the computer possesses, the machine has been condemned for a fatal lack of soul," said Boris Johnson, the Telegraph's deputy editor. "The crossword will remain a duel of wits between individual composer and solver."

TIMES EDITORS' SHARE VALUE

3 APRIL: News Corporation accounts showed that the Sunday Times editor John Witherow had been given share options with a notional profit of £560,000. Over at The Times, Peter Stothard's editorial bonus was worth £143,000.

BOYCOTT AT EXPRESSES

24 APRIL: Rosie Boycott quit as editor of both Independents to start as editor of both Expresses. The consensus was that Boycott, ex-editor of Spare Rib and latterly a campaigner for the legalisation of cannabis, was an odd choice for the Express' middle-England/Tory leaning readership. Richard Addis, the departing Express editor who'd been there since January 1996 and halted the radical decline in circulation, said: "I told her she would have a lovely staff and people will be very loyal. I couldn't think of a better person to hand it over to really. I'm glad it's not somebody I don't like." Boycott: "He was very sweet. He's a lovely man."

Rosie Boycott (see above)   **Simon Kelner (below)**

KELNER AT INDEPENDENT

1 MAY: Simon Kelner was appointed Independent editor reportedly on a £250,000 annual salary. One of the founding Independent staff in 1986, Kelner moved from two years of editing the Mail on Sunday's Night and Day supplement. On taking up his new job he said: "The [Independent's] founding principles have been eroded in the past few years." Andrew Marr resigned.

PRESS COMPLAINTS

6 MAY: The Press Complaints Commission's annual report for 1997 revealed that seven out of ten complaints related to accuracy in reporting. The PCC boss Lord Wakeham said: "We resolved more complaints than ever before. We also did so more quickly. It took an average of 44 days to resolve a complaint in 1997 - a speed which the law or any statutory system could never match." A balloon of press self-satisfaction was pricked in the furore after the publication of Gita Sereny's book about the child murderer Mary Bell, about payments to Bell for her contribution to the book and newspapers all but identifying where she had rebuilt her life. The PCC stressed its commitment to self-regulation as the best way of dealing with complaints - and issued a warning to tabloids that they should avoid peddling offensive national stereotypes during the World Cup. Wakeham called an inquiry into the naming of paedophiles by local and national papers.

FREELANCE RATES: NATIONALS

8 MAY: Brian Whittle, the founder of Cavendish press agency, wrote a Press Gazette column complaining of declining freelance rates. "At the News of the World, an exclusive page lead is fetching just £750 - half the going rate of ten years ago. As a comparison, I recall the Sunday Mirror paying me £2,000 for a well-researched spread on the then American phenomenon of down-sizing. Not bad. But that was 20 years ago." At the end of May Alan Rusbridger, the Guardian editor, wrote to 500 regular freelances saying "there should be no bar on freelances writing for the Guardian, regardless of their views". See also local events, beginning of May.

CHEQUES FOR SAUDI NURSES

21 MAY: Chequebook journalism caused a diplomatic row between Britain and Saudi when two nurses convicted of murder were released by Saudi courts. Reportedly, the Mirror paid Lucille McLauchlan £100,000 and the Express Deborah Parry £60,000. "Criminals are not supposed to profit from their crimes," said George Galloway, the Labour MP who lodged a complaint with the PCC.

HUGH CUDLIPP DIES

17 MAY: Hugh Cudlipp (above), Fleet Street's youngest ever editor at 24, died aged 84. He pioneered tabloid journalism on the Mirror and edited it during its sixties pomp when it had a five million daily circulation. He founded the Sun and ended his career as chairman of IPC. Geoffrey Goodman, Cudlipp's friend and colleague said: "He was the greatest tabloid journalist. He helped build up the Mirror into what people thought was the most outstanding popular newspaper in the world."

JONATHAN AITKEN

21 MAY: Jonathan Aitken, the disgraced former Conservative cabinet minister whose libel case against the Guardian collapsed when his case was proved to rest on a lie, was charged with perjury, conspiracy to pervert the course of justice and perverting the course of justice. The charges ended an 11 month investigation by Scotland Yard's Special Operations Unit. The Telegraph said Aitken had lied for his country. Aitken said: "I have no intention of using it as a defence to the allegation that I told a lie on oath during my libel case" [against the Guardian and Granada TV].

MOS APOLOGY

31 MAY 1998: The Mail on Sunday published a front page apology to the actress Brooke Shields admitting its story about her being searched for drugs at Nice airport was "wholly without foundation". The size of the apology - which came with a "six figure sum" - is matched only by the Sun's sorry to Elton John and the Sunday Times' apology over the fake Hitler diaries.

HIGGINS QUITS THE SUN

4 JUNE: Stuart Higgins left his job as Sun editor, after having been in charge five years. His resignation followed disputes with management who want to take the paper upmarket. His replacement, 35 year old David Yelland, was a Sun financial reporter who been with Rupert Murdoch's New York Post since 1993.

STAR POSHES UP

8 JUNE: The redesigned Daily Star altered its written style with an editorial directive banning such clichés as "raunchy ... page three stunner ... curvy ... mad-cap ... motor-mouth ... mega ... lesbo."

MACKENZIE QUITS MIRROR

8 JUNE: Kelvin MacKenzie's short stay as the Mirror's editor in chief ended with his resignation to form a consortium to bid for Talk Radio.

SIR DAVID ENGLISH DIES

10 JUNE: Sir David English, the editor behind the Daily Mail's success, died aged 67. Praise was fulsome. Tony Blair: "He was a truly outstanding journalist. He never lost his eye for a good story." Peter Preston: "A great editor in the sense that, over decades, he rebuilt the fortunes of a paper which seemed to sliding towards oblivion when he took its chair nearly 27 years ago." Kelvin MacKenzie: "David has been a fabulous friend to journalists. If there has been a greater journalist, I've not met him."

NO BUYER FOR MGN

15 JUNE: The German publisher Axel Springer Verlag withdrew from preliminary negotiations to buy the Mirror. The rumour machine switched to stories that the deal was scuppered after Rupert Murdoch had promised the Sun would mount a "bloody fight" against a German owned Mirror and that the Barclay Brothers might be potential buyers.

ROYAL CRUMPET DENIAL

18 JUNE: Buckingham Palace complained to the Press Complaints Commission about Mail on Sunday allegations that staff in the Prince of Wales' office vet girls who have caught Prince William's eye. A spokesman said: "This is grossly intrusive, and gruesomely embarrassing to a boy who is not yet 16; above all it is completely untrue."

MAXWELL INQUEST REOPENED

20 JUNE: Spanish authorities decided on another inquiry into the drowning of Robert Maxwell in November 1991 following the dismissal of the inquest judge on grounds of mental illness. Food for conspiracy theorists who have long dwelt on procedural irregularities after Maxwell's corpse was pulled from the sea.

GUARDIAN PROFITS

23 JUNE: Guardian Media Group declared record £53 million profits in the year to the end of March. The 76 per cent increase over the previous year was attributed to "ad growth, lower newsprint prices and tight cost control".

MET VS GUARIDAN

8 JULY: The Court of Appeal rejected a Metropolitan Police bid to reopen a libel trial against the Guardian on the grounds the first case had ben mishandled by the judge. The police argued that the Guardian had suggested five officers had planted drugs on suspects. The Guardian denied it had made the suggestion. Lord Chief Justice Bingham was "not of the opinion that any miscarriage has been occasioned". Alan Rusbridger, the Guardian editor, said: "This is significant victory for newspapers. Until the Guardian fought this case the Police Federation had won 95 cases in a row. Rank-and-file police officers might like to ask whether millions of pounds on these actions is a proper use of union funds."

Local newspapers

SUNDAYS UP, DAILIES DOWN

8 AUGUST 1997: Paid for local Sundays increased their readership share while their sister weekly and daily titles had declining readership, according to a Mintel survey of local newspaper trends since 1993. However Mintel predicted a bright future with an 8 per cent real terms increase in ad and circulation revenue by 2001.

BRISTOL BUYS WESSEX

10 SEPTEMBER: Newsquest sold its Wessex newspapers subsidiary to Bristol United Press for £35 million. The six newspapers involved include the Bath Chronicle and made a £1 million profit on a £4.3 million turnover in the six months to June.

NEW NATION, NEW OWNER

15 SEPTEMBER: Southnews bought New Nation, a tabloid weekly for aspiring black people launched by Rupert Murdoch's daughter in 1996. New Nation joined Eastern Eye, Caribbean Times and Asian Times in Southnews' Ethnic Media Group.

QUEST FOR READIES

29 SEPTEMBER: Newsquest (and its main shareholder Kohlberg Kravis Roberts) announced a stock market flotation and said it expected to raise £100 million, possibly to fund a bid for UNM's local titles. Newsquest, formed after a management buyout from Reed International, owns 173 titles including the world's oldest paper, the Berrows Worcester Journal. Jim Brown, the Newsquest chairman, is another paper millionaire and worth some £4 million through the deal.

FRONT PAGE STORY

3 OCTOBER: The Darlington and Stockton Times finally bowed to modern pressures and put news as well as advertising on its front page. The paper - which is also known as the Dalesman's bible - took the design leap to mark its 150th anniversary

BUSINESS BUDDIES

10 OCTOBER: A closer relationship between local papers belonging to the Guardian Media Group and United Newspapers was suggested by UNM's chief exec Stephen Grabiner. He wanted national arrangements for print and distribution to be extended to regional titles and sought to quash speculation he'd been attempting to buy GMG's Manchester Evening News.

YORKSHIRE POST FOR SALE

1 DECEMBER: United News and Media put its portfolio of 61 papers on sale. The reason for the sale of United Provincial Papers, which includes the Yorkshire Post, was to allow UNM to concentrate more on TV and national papers.

BIGGIES BUY FAMILY BUSINESSES

22 DECEMBER: Concentration of local ownership continued with Southern Newspapers buying the Bailey Newspaper Group for £35 million and Johnston Press buying Home Counties Newspapers for £52 million.

POWER OF THE PRESS

23 JANUARY: "Have you seen the Evening Argus?" said one police officer to another. The officers - less well briefed by their press office than local journalists - were waiting to raid a pub in Eastbourne when they read of details of the bust they were about to do.

TV CATCHES LOCALS

4 FEBRUARY: Research commissioned by the ITC showed growing numbers of people say TV, not local papers, is their main source of news.

MASS STORAGE, BIG NUMBERS

3 MARCH: The London Press Club proposed a £15 million scheme to get Lottery money for an immutable digital archive. Project Newsplan had suitably mad statistics: "3,460 locals are at risk, comprising some 26 per cent of all titles, or 86,000 reels of microfilm. That's equivalent to 52 million broadsheet pages which would stretch almost halfway round the Equator."

UNM DESERTS THE REGIONS

FEBRUARY 1998: The Express owner, United News and Media, sold United Provincial Papers in two lots. The smaller tranche of southern titles went to Southnews for £47.5 million. UNM's 44 northern titles - which include the Yorkshire Post, Yorkshire Evening Post and Lancashire Evening Post - went to Candover, a venture capital firm, for £360 million. Candover appointed Chris Oakley as chief executive of UNM's northern titles, which was renamed Regional Independent Media. In 1991 Oakley headed a £125 million Midland Independent management buyout and, in 1997, sold MIN on to Mirror Group for £297 million. "If you look at the history of MIN," Oakley said, "we have developed, grown, become more efficient. But there isn't a bloody trail of redundancies behind us. What I'll be looking at in United is to make sure we are the best and most efficient company in the regional newspaper industry, but I don't go there with a list of targets for execution."

DIVERSIFY OR FADE

20 APRIL: John Griffith, the Liverpool Echo editor, told a Guild of Editor's conference that local editors should consider themselves as newsroom leaders rather than merely heading up their newspapers. He said: "The existing newsroom is a very expensive commodity and one we don't fully exploit. If it remains dependent on one existing product, which is in long-term decline, then it will inevitably decline."

FREELANCE RATES: LOCALS

8 MAY: Brian Whittle, the founder of Cavendish press agency, wrote a Press Gazette column complaining of declining freelance rates. "Not that the national discovered parsimony first; the regionals and local have been at it for years. Take our local evening, the Manchester Evening News. A half page of advertising will cost £4,554. A page lead occupying the same space pays just £23.46 plus VAT. And it's not just freelances. Experienced old hands on many regionals are being bought off and replaced with badly trained kids, many of whom can't report their way out of a paper bag." See also national press events for May.

LOCAL NEWSPAPER WEEK

27 APRIL: The start of the first Local Newspaper Week, a Newspaper Society PR wheeze to ensure a repetition of such copy as "nine out of 10 people read one of the 1,400 regional and local papers in the UK every week - around 4,000 are sold every minute".

PRESCOTT ON PRIVACY

7 MAY: The deputy prime minister John Prescott criticised "editors [who] are reluctant to apologise when they're found to be wrong or even to consider the same prominence for such acknowledgements". Prescott, whose son's involvement in a Hull housing project attracted wide publicity, deplored "mass picketing [of] innocent citizens". Speaking to local publishers at the Newspaper Society annual lunch, he said he remained a firm advocate of self-regulation.

TRAINING

3 JUNE: Brian Wilson, the then Scottish Office minister for education and industry, said that while "media education has come of age as a fully-fledged topic of study" its quality was iffy. "It seems to me these courses produce a lot of people who can hold a microphone and who can produce a story in a certain way. But they seem to have thought very little about the ethos or ethics of what they are doing. How many people coming out of courses in media education have thought about issues such as the role of the media in manipulating public opinion, who owns the media and what is its purpose?"

TINDLE PROFITS

17 JUNE: Tindle reported a £10.73m profit for the year to March, up from last year's £4m.

MIRROR EXPANDS IN N. IRELAND

8 JULY: The Mirror Group bought the Derry Journal for £18.25 million, thus putting a notable nationalist paper under the control of David Montgomery. "He's very much a Unionist," said one of the Derry Journal's staff. "It's like Gerry Adams taking over the News Letter." (The News Letter is a Loyalist paper also owned by the Mirror Group.) Montgomery pledged he would "respect the paper's traditions and ethos".

Magazines

NO SMOKE WITHOUT MONEY
4 AUGUST 1997: Style mags like Loaded and The Face encourage smoking among the young, claimed the Health Education Authority. In 1996, 28 per cent of boys by the age of 15 and 33 per cent of girls are smokers compared with 24 per cent and 25 per cent in 1982. In November Labour earned its first bad publicity when, having decided not to ban tobacco advertising on Formula One racing cars, it was revealed it had received a £1 million donation from the F1 boss Bernie Ecclestone. The money was returned but the fags sponsorship remained. In December 1997, the PPA distributed a press release quoting FAEP (the European magazine publishers' federation) support of tobacco advertising: "The European Health Council has decided to follow the cheap politically expedient measure of banning advertising for a product legally on sale ..." and so on and so forth.

GLOSSY SEX WAR
15 AUGUST: FHM overtook Cosmopolitan when the glossy chap's mag sold over 500,000 copies and the chappess's under 500,000. Good news for Emap, the FHM publisher, with a single issue's copy sales generating £1.6 million and annual ad revenue heading for £6 million. Within weeks, Chanel withdrew an ad campaign in FHM because of its high nipple count.

EYE SHOCK
17 AUGUST: Lin Cooke, widow of the Private Eye founder Peter Cooke, said she wanted to sell her 40 per cent holding in the magazine. The Eye editor Ian Hislop said: "Legally she can't, as I understand that she is bound by the articles of association. And practically she can't, because I'll burn down the building."

FUTURE OF IPC
26 AUGUST: Rumours emerged of Reed Elsevier's intention to sell its IPC consumer magazine group (including Woman's Own, Marie Claire and TV Times) to concentrate on electronic and business information ventures.

A DOZEN LAUNCHES
SEPTEMBER: Twelve new mags hit the newsstands: a revamped Modern Review; Frank, a women's mag from the publishers of The Face; a transatlantic Condé Nast Traveller; Beautiful Homes; Promise, a christian title "for women who believe in family"; So; Good Health; Neon; Cult TV; GMTV; B; and Cake Decoration.

TRADE MAG PURCHASE
1 SEPTEMBER: United News and Media paid £81 million for Telecom Library, an American trade magazine publisher. Miller Freeman, UNM's business publishing division, ruled out any further acquisitions.

NEW MEDIA MAG
11 SEPTEMBER: The launch of Channel 21, a staff-owned monthly mag for TV and news media people in competition with TV World and Television Business International.

RACIST JAILED
15 SEPTEMBER: Mark Atkinson, of Stormer magazine, was jailed for 21 months for publishing material likely to stir up racial hatred. Judge George Bathurst-Norman said: "I have never encountered such vile outpourings of hatred and incitement to violence." Among the magazine's targets were Frank Bruno and his mother, Anna Ford and Paddy Ashdown.

INFLATED READERSHIPS
26 SEPTEMBER: Reed Elsevier's share price fell by half a billion pounds as it faced compensation bills for overstating circulation figures on hotel and airline directories belonging to Reed Travel Group. At the end of January, just after Reed merged its magazine division with Wolters Kluwer, Reed announced the cost of advertiser refunds was likely to be £200 million.

CUT PRICE MAGS
28 SEPTEMBER: Tesco knocked 20 per cent off cover prices of women's mags like Bella, That's Life, Take a Break and Eva.

MEDIA MAGS' MOVES

OCTOBER 1997: Quantum Publishing, which bought the Press Gazette and Media Week from Emap, said goodbye to both editors of its leading media titles. Roy Farndon, editor of Press Gazette, was pushed and Media Week editor Susannah Richmond pledged to work through her notice. Quantum also told staff they would have to say goodbye to their central London offices. Hello Croydon. Lucy Rouse, the Media Week associate editor, resigned. "It's not just a media luvvie thing about not wanting to work from the suburbs," she said. Quantum's managing director Richard Flaye said: "Media is no longer a central London phenomenon, hence there's no perfect place to be."

OLD BOY NETWORKS

4 DECEMBER: Clive Harold - a former pupil of Hill House prep school, ex-Woman's Own staff writer and currently a Big Issue vendor - bumped into another ex-Hill Houseian when Prince Charles visited the Big Issue. "I only remember him because we both had big ears," Harold said. Another Big Issue salesman, the ex-Observer editor Andrew Jaspan, announced he would leave his job as Big Issue publisher to work for Scottish Media Group.

NEW STATESMAN OWNER

8 DECEMBER: Geoffrey Robinson, who paid £375,000 to take over the New Statesman in 1996 and then became Labour's Paymaster General, threatened the Observer and Sunday Times with legal action. The Sundays had discovered portions of Robinson's wealth were salted away in offshore tax havens of the kind his boss, the chancellor Gordon Brown, wants to regulate. The stories compromised Robinson's plans to curb tax breaks for middle class savers and prompted questions about his dealings with Robert Maxwell. In January it emerged that Robinson, who resigned as Statesman director after the election, was paying staff via an offshore company called Stenbell.

REED: MULTI-MILLION SELL OFF

5 JANUARY: Reed Elsevier sold IPC Magazines for £860 million to a management team backed by Cinven venture capitalists. Bid speculation for 74 consumer titles - which include Woman's Own, Marie Claire and TV Times - had mounted since August with interest also shown by Bauer, Bertelsmann, Hachette and Emap. It was among the biggest of management buyouts in British corporate life.

REED: MULTI-BILLION MERGER

13 JANUARY: Reed Elsevier, the Anglo-Dutch publisher, announced its intention to merge with Wolters Kluwer - another Dutch company. The deal involved £20 billion worth of share transfers and the likelihood of job losses among a new combined workforce of 42,000. Nigel Stapleton, Reed Elsevier's co-chairman, said: "This will give us a better position to exploit new media. In the context of content-ownership, big is beautiful; if we really want to get the attention of software providers like Microsoft and the delivery channels, then we must get bigger." On 9 March the deal unravelled after Wolters' had cold feet about US and European regulators threats to make it sell off some of its interests.

AD GROWTH

1 FEBRUARY: The Advertising Association predicted consumer magazine advertising would grow by 9.2 per cent in 1998 and business and professional magazine advertising by 5.8 per cent with a slowing in the expansion of job ads.

"TITILLATION" TO EDUCATION

26 MARCH: The teenage girls' mags which a Tory MP had tried to ban for their "squalid titillation", were targetted by the health minister Tessa Jowell to play a part in helping cut teenage pregnancies. Jowell said: "I think an important focus of that group will be to help pupils to understand what it means to have children ... so they do not have children while they are children themselves."

PROG MAGS

24 APRIL: The Independent Television Commission responded to years of magazine publisher lobbying by allowing magazines to be turned into Channel 3, 4 and 5 TV programmes.

Ian Locks, head of the Periodical Publishers' Association and a leading proponent of masthead programming, said: "We've never been able to understand why it should be acceptable for programme makers and channel owners to produce magazines while publishers were not allowed to develop television programming from their magazines. "

FUTURE SALE

24 APRIL: Pearson sold Future Publishing - the Bath publishing firm whose best-selling titles include Classic CD and Total football and many computer titles - for £142 million. In 1994 Pearson bought Future from its founder Chris Anderson for £52.5 million. Anderson has returned to the company with "a significant minority stake" in a management buyout largely funded by Apax Partners, the same group which is behind Chris Evans' rise as media mogul.

READER'S DIGEST GOES FOR YOOF

MAY: Reader's Digest relaunched itself by knocking the contents list off the cover and pitching for a younger readership. "We certainly won't be calling for legislation of cannabis," its UK editor Russell Twisk said. With a global circulation of 27 million, Reader's Digest is the world's best selling mag but British sales have fallen from 1.8 million in 1993 to 1.5 million. Reader's Digest is a Lottery victim in that those of its readers who aren't dead and dying have had a bigger prize draw than even the world's biggest magazine can offer.

NEW STATESMAN EDITORS

1 MAY: Peter Wilby, former Independent on Sunday editor, was appointed to edit the New Statesman. He replaced Ian Hargreaves, who resigned from his £100,000 a year job saying he wanted to spend more time with his family.

OUT: Ian Hargreaves

IN: Peter Wilby

HIGH COVER PRICES INHIBIT SALES

11 MAY: Sales figures of consumer magazines revealed 1997 to have been a year of "wild launch activity", a 7 per cent increase in revenue and a 1.1 per cent fall in the number of copies actually sold. Wessenden Marketing issued a report recommending publishers ought to look at how far they can raise magazine prices before seriously affecting their volume of sales.

SPORTING LIFE REBIRTH

12 MAY: Sporting Life's existence as a racing-only paper ended with its owners, Mirror Group Newspapers, announcing an October relaunch as a general sporting title, with a £20 million budget and 120 staff. John Mulholland, the editor, moved from an eight year stint on the Guardian where he set up Media Guardian as a separate supplement. Of his new job, he said: "There are no end of people telling me this has no chance. I wouldn't have taken on this job if I didn't have in mind something which I think will appeal to sports fans. But we'll see." On 5 August MGN announced the project had been delayed and Mulholland lost his job. Kamal Ahmed became Media Guardian editor.

REED: £1BN US PURCHASES

27 MAY: Following the fiasco of its proposed merger with Wolters Kluwer, Reed Elsevier paid £988 million for two American legal publishers. The purchase of Matthew Bender and Company plus 50 per cent of Shepard's Company puts Reed level-pegging with Thomson Corp as the world's biggest legal publisher.

PPA AND NEWSPAPER SOCIETY

1 JULY: Magazine and local newspaper trade bodies announced an alliance to lobby on four main issues: representations in Brussels; UK public affairs; the establishment of a national Training Orgfanisation; and the provision of legal advice. In a joint statement the NS director David Newell and PPA chief executive Ian Lock said: "Regional newspapers, magazines and business information publishing represent well over half the print media sector - with combined revenues of £9 billion - and it makes sense for us to work together in the future."

The nationals

Good news about national newspapers was in a report called The Future of Newspapers, a crisis-what-crisis document written by the Henley Centre for Forecasting. Like the best such reports, it takes what was often thought and expresses it in market-speak with a smattering of statistics. Did you know, for example, that 55 per cent of the population say they often debate what they read in the paper and that 34 per cent agree very strongly that they would miss their daily newspaper? To summarise the prose: newspapers are embedded in our culture and are a cohesive force in society; newspapers - being portable, easy to read, easy to store and accessible - will continue playing a central role in our lives; they allow people to turn dead time on a train, say, into fruitful time; they help people define an identity; they still set the news agenda, shape debate and allow the "discursive space" where the news gets its interpretation. "Rather than merely mediating reality, for many the newspaper seems to be an anchor of it, despite all the other media sources currently available."

Jargon, maybe, but carrying an optimism to counter standard issue gloom. Try this from Lachlan Murdoch, executive chairman of News Corporation's Australian interests, who says: "Many of my friends who should read a morning paper don't bother. These are young, intelligent ambitious people who understand the power of information. They should be natural newspaper readers and yet they aren't." While it is surprising the rapidly promoted 26 year old son of Rupe has any friends of his own age, it's unremarkable he should be preoccupied with a global decline in newspaper circulations. Newsprint is the most profitable part of News Corp's operation. However, Lachlan - along with nearly every other newspaper executive - may grow to temper their preoccupation with youth. Census predictions for the next decade say the number of retired people in the UK will grow, that life expectancy will increase and the number of under 16s will fall. Assuming pensions don't fail entirely, there are many readers with a newspaper habit who are here for a while yet.

However, circulation is a sure measure of prosperity and a gentle decline accounts for the editorial musical chairs shown on page 32 and the diminishing percentage of advertising that the nationals attract. The figures have been given constant repetition: since 1988 daily UK sales have dropped by nearly 10 per cent from 15 million to about 13.5 million today; meanwhile ad revenue, which typically accounts for half a newspaper's turnover, has fallen from 13.3 per cent of all advertising in 1990 to some 12 per cent in 1998. This decline of the nationals will continue with the rise and rise of the Internet plus the rise of local radio, the proliferation of TV channels and aggressive marketing from local giveaways. The response has been more colour, more pages, more sections, more price cuts, more lifestyle, more sport, more columns - more and more of more or less everything except hard news. John Pilger gives a moralist's spin to these changes in the Cultural Chernobyl chapter of his book Hidden Agendas. It is recommended reading.

National newspaper circulations

DAILIES	JAN-JUN 98	JAN-JUN 97	CHANGE
1 Sun	3,713,476	3,894,007	-4.64%
2 Mirror	2,320,670	2,366,434	-1.93%
3 Daily Mail	2,295,791	2,152,874	+6.64%
4 Express	1,168,598	1,227,300	-4.78%
5 D. Telegraph	1,073,822	1,124,640	-4.52%
6 Times	787,788	747,710	+5.36%
7 Daily Star	579,516	657,040	-11.80%
8 Guardian	402,842	408,790	-1.46%
9 F. Times	353,928	312,723	+13.18%
10 Independ't	220,534	257,010	-14.19%
SUNDAYS			
1 News o'World	4,334,115	4,469,884	-3.04%
2 Mail on S'day	2,211,804	2,129,089	+3.88%
3 S'day Mirror	2,070,804	2,284,985	-9.37%
4 S'day People	1,745,868	1,956,977	-10.79%
5 S'day Times	1,354,285	1,322,988	+2.37%
6 S'day E'press	1,085,804	1,163,150	-6.65%
7 S'day T'graph	841,062	892,630	-5.78%
8 Observer	412,632	456,496	-9.61%
9 Ind on S'nday	257,601	275,810	-6.60%

Source: ABC

Circulation decline has been patchy. The Daily Mail has bucked all trends with Paul Dacre, its editor since 1992, having boosted circulation from 1.7 million to 2.2 million without price cutting except in Scotland. Lord Rothermere, chairman of Associated Newspaper explains the success in socio-political terms. "People who used to be working class now think of themselves as middle class," he says. "This is one of the things Tony Blair realised and which enabled him to create New Labour. The party appeals to the lower middle class, which is fast becoming the majority in this country. And the Daily Mail is right in there with them which is why we're growing." And growing and growing to the point where the Mail's circulation is likely to outstrip the Mirror's before the millennium.

Red top tabloids have suffered most in an era of increasing educational standards, the dissolution of old class boundaries and the emergence of twenty-something mezzo brow readers who don't quite fit old stereotypes. Blair's Britain isn't the place for the Sun to pass itself off as the Daily Zeitgeist and we have the comedy of publicity campaigns presenting the Sun as a "more rounded product" rather than a source of exclusives and soaraway competitions. More comical is the Star, whose main merit was blowing raspberries in an updated Donald McGill fantasia, issuing a sub editor's guide banning such clichés as "raunchy ... page three stunner ... curvy ... mad-cap ... motor-mouth ... mega ... lesbo."

As for the broadsheets, only the Independent is in serious difficulty but still living in hope that its brand new proprietor, Tony O'Reilly, can pull off another of his marketing tricks. Meanwhile the Telegraph keeps its circulation above the magic million, the Times has bought a number one heavyweight slot with price cutting and the Financial Times builds on a successful foray into America. The Guardian circulation remains above 400,000. A report in Campaign says: "The Guardian would seem to have benefitted from its strong record on political exclusives and its clear brand positioning, and it has steered clear of discounting."

Sunday papers lose readers at twice the rate of the dailies, having mislaid 1.25 million purchasers since the early nineties. There are several reasons for this: their sister dailies put out multi-section Saturday editions which are as fat as any Sunday; the Saturday papers contain the next week's TV listings; shops

National newspaper circulations

DAILIES	1958	1968	1978	1988
Express	4,062,587	3,819,674	2,458,792	1,658,252
Financial Times	84,858	159,536	181,678	282,675
Guardian	177,962	274,638	283,494	454,038
Herald	1,513,217			
Independent				381,210
Daily Mail	2,104,932	2,067,468	1,973,580	1,775,695
Mirror	4,527,208	4,991,616	3,806,003	3,119,365
News Chronicle	1,255,233			
Record	523,748	721,796	770,589	
Sketch/Graphic	1,213,184	900,336		
Daily Star				990,110
Sun		1,037,577	3,960,076	4,182,848
Daily Telegraph		1,393,094	1,358,875	1,133,173
Times	248,338	408,300	295,863	443,462
Today				478,220
SUNDAYS	1958	1968	1978	1988
Empire News	2,155,132			
Mail on Sunday				1,926,047
NoW	6,716,258	6,161,138	4,919,905	5,287,190
Observer	642,588	878,266	712,712	735,826
The People	4,906,019	5,479,878	3,901,314	2,746,348
Reynolds News	356,676			
S. Dispatch	1,752,101			
S. Express	3,412,333	4,221,914	3,260,600	2,088,086
S. Graphic	933,214			
Sunday Mirror			3,865,926	2,866,007
S. Pictorial	5,378,189	5,076,344		
Sunday Sport				551,377
S, Telegraph		729,942	855,803	704,737
Sunday Times	813,924	1,450,694	1,399,073	1,338,623

Source: ABC

National newspaper circulations by type

DAILIES	1958	1968	1978	1988
1998				
Qualities	511,158	2,235,568	2,119,910	2,295,458
Mid-market	8,635,936	6,787,478	4,432,372	3,912,167
Popular	6,564,173	6,750,989	8,536,668	8,292,323
TOTAL	15,711,267	15,774,035	15,088,950	14,499,948

SUNDAYS	1958	1968	1978	1988
1998				
Qualities	1,456,512	3,058,902	2,967,588	2,779,186
Mid-market	6,097,648	4,221,914	3,260,600	4,014,133
Popular	19,512,274	16,717,360	12,687,145	11,450,922

The top topics for media exposure

SUBJECT MATTER	PERCENTAGE OF COVERAGE IN FULL YEAR	HALF YEAR
Accidents/disasters	approx 28%	25%
Sport	10%	23%
The economy	9%	15%
Politics	8%	10%
Crime (approx 32% female)	8%	8%
Overseas interest	6%	9%
Royalty	5%	1%
Entertainments/arts	4%	5%
Health and medicine	3%	4%
Europe	2.5%	2.25%
Legal issues	2.25%	3.5%
Education	2%	2%
Charities/lottery	2%	0.5%
Transport	2%	1.75%
Environment/energy	1.5%	1.5%
Science/technology	1.25%	2%
Sex	1.25%	1.25%
The media	1%	3%
Fashion	0.5%	0.25%
The weather	0.25%	0.2%
Religion	0.2%	1%

Source: Durrants

Time spent reading

NEWSPAPERS	
Sunday newspapers	45.6 mins
Daily newspapers	39.3 mins
Newspaper suplements/sections	25.3 mins

Source: IPA, ISBA, PPA

are open on Sunday and so are football grounds, which means that the full soccer league tables are not available until Monday - which is the day when nearly every daily puts out a sports section.

Despite the importance of national newspapers to national and personal life, it is still undeniably a market in gentle decline. Such a market becomes the preserve of accountants and marketeers and they tend to be much drawn to new tech. They reason that the computers which have saved money in production might now be turned to saving readers and much investment therefore goes into web sites and inter-activity. The Henley report gives these ideas short shrift, commenting: "The Daily Me concept in practice is not really a newspaper at all but a piecemeal collection of articles without any coherent editorial focus. Already the vision behind it seems part of an outmoded eighties dream of ever-extending customisation and choice." Whatever happens with the net, we can expect more in the way of focus groups and readers' panels. The most extreme example is on the Johannesburg Star, where readers' vote on the first edition to find their preferences reflected in the second.

It's a long way from the normal autocratic hierarchy of a newspaper and certainly anathema to the late Sir David English who said: "You can have marketing men by the barrelful ... but if you don't have a good editor, all that amounts to nothing." Most journalists would agree and ask why it's editors, rather than marketing staff, who get sacked with such regularity.

Newspaper price wars

In mid-December 1997 the Guardian Media Group, Telegraph Publishing and Newspaper Publishing came together in anticipation of the Competition Bill. A spokesperson for this ad hoc cartel said: "At the moment the only way to prove predatory pricing is when you go under. The rules are not strong enough and, in our opinion, this can't continue." The then Independent editor Andrew Marr joined the fray by calling the government "gutless", an odd remark given that in September the Indie had boosted its relaunch with a price cut to 20p. Since the Times started price cutting in 1993, its sales have nearly doubled to 800,000 while the Independent's have fallen from nearly 400,000 to 256,840.

Murdoch, who wasn't about to lose *his* job, wasn't going to budge from the front line of the price war either. He'd already told the annual BSkyB meeting: "No way will I call a truce. No one else wants to call a truce. They insult me every day, so they can go to hell." In the next instalment of price cuts the Guardian, billing itself as "the only truly independent newspaper", offered Independent readers a week's free subscription to the Guardian and Observer. Rosie Boycott, the new Independent editor, said: "Here you are, supposedly standard-bearers for liberalism, using underhand tactics with one intention in mind, to put us out of business."

In February the House of Lords defeated the government when it voted by 121 votes to 93 to amend the Competition Bill to stop newspapers abusing "a dominant market position" to eliminate rivals. Tony Blair emerged in the Commons in all his laissez faire splendour. "The amendment that was supported in the Lords is wrong," he said. "It would end up with the situation where it would actually - and it's bizarre that it is being supported by the Conservative Party as well - end up preventing newspapers competing against each other."

Raymond Snoddy, recently installed as the Times' media editor, dropped out of his normal crisp style into passive-voice market-speak. "The amendment was seen as being aimed at the price promotion policy of the Times," he said. And so it was, if not by Labour's front bench

then by Labour Lords. "Anything to curb Murdoch's power is OK by me," Baroness Castle declared. Lord McNally put the amendment forward saying: "The present policy of the Times does not make sense unless to clear the field of two competitors: the Telegraph and the

This Times from January showed several signs of the times: a multi-section paper; loss leader price; and a website address beneath the masthead.

Independent. What is good business for Rupert Murdoch is not necessarily good sense for a healthy democracy or a healthy press."

About 50 Labour back bench MPs made their disgruntlement known through off message quotes. Margaret Beckett, president of the board of trade, assured MPs the Competition Bill was tougher than they thought and that it would effectively prohibit predatory price cutting. Tony Blair asserted the McNally amendment "would actually mean that newspapers weren't allowed to compete against each other at all" and that the Bill "will allow us to investigate predatory pricing in a full way that the present legislation does not". A week later, on 12 May, Blair met Rupert Murdoch at 10 Downing Street. A spokesman said: "Mr Blair regularly meets newspaper proprietors." But he wouldn't say what had been discussed at the meeting. Some Labour MPs remained unconvinced and in July, in one of the biggest revolts since Labour came to power, 23 Labour MPs voted against the Bill. Chris Mullin accused News International of "dragging down other newspapers" by using the Times and occasionally the Sun as loss leaders

Editors' chairs

THE PEOPLE	December 1997
Out: **Len Gould**	
In: **Brendon Parsons**	

THE PEOPLE January 1998
Out: **Brendon Parsons**
In: **Neil Wallis**

SUNDAY MIRROR January 1998
Out: **Bridget Rowe**
In: **Brendon Parsons**

THE INDEPENDENT January 1998
Out: **Andrew Marr**
In: **Rosie Boycott**

SUNDAY BUSINESS February 1998
In: **Jeff Randall**

THE INDEPENDENT March 1998
Back In: (as Editor-in-chief) **Andrew Marr**

MORNING STAR January-March 1998
Out then back in: **John Haylett**

SPORT FIRST March 1998
In: **Bob Harris**

THE INDEPENDENT April 1998
Out: **Rosie Boycott and Andrew Marr**
In: **Simon Kelner**

THE EXPRESS April 1998
Out: **Richard Addis**
In: **Rosie Boycott**

SUNDAY MIRROR April 1998
Out: **Brendon Parsons**
In: **Colin Myler**

NEW STATESMAN May 1998
Out: **Ian Hargreaves**
In: **Peter Wilby**

THE SUN June 1998
Out: **Stuart Higgins**
In: **David Yelland**

THE OBSERVER July 1998
Out: **Will Hutton**
In: **Roger Alton**

NATIONAL DAILIES

Some entries will have changed since this book went to press in mid-August 1998.

Daily Mail
2 Derry Street, Kensington, London W8 5TT
Fax 0171-937 3251 Tel 0171-938 6000
News fax 0171-937 4463 Tel 0171-938 6372
Web site: www.dailymail,co.uk
Editor-in-chief: Paul Dacre, since 1992.
Deputy editor: Peter Wright
News editor: Ian Macgregor
Features editor: Veronica Wadley
Deputy foreign editor: Gerry Hunt
Picture editor: Paul Silva
City editor: Andrew Alexander
Diary editor: Nigel Dempster
Advertising director: Mike Ironside
Managing director: Guy Zitter
Financial director: Guy Morgan
Founded: 1896. Owner: Daily Mail & General Trust

Daily Star
245 Blackfriars Road, London SE1 9UX
Fax 0171-620 1644 Tel 0171-928 8000
News Tel 0171-922 7070
Editor: Phil Walker
Deputy editor: Peter Hill
Associate editor: Kay Goddard
Assistant editor, news: Hugh Whittow
Features editor: Linda Duss
Picture editor: Mark Moylan
Sports editor: Jim Mansell
Managing editor: Denise Fraser
Managing director: Nicholas Rudd-Jones
Marketing director: Paul Woolfenden
Circulation director: Don Gray
Advertisement manager: Andy Whelan
Founded: 1978. Owner: United News and Media

Daily Telegraph
1 Canada Square, Canary Wharf, London E14 5DT
Fax 0171-538 6242 Tel 0171-538 5000
News fax 0171-513 2506 Tel 0171-538 6355
E-mail: corprels@telegraph.co.uk
Web site: www.telegraph.co.uk
Editor: Charles Moore, since 1995
Deputy editor: Sarah Sands
Home editor: Neil Darbyshire
Arts editor: Sarah Crompton
Foreign editor: Stephen Robinson
Business editor: Roland Gribben
City editor: Neil Collins
Education editor: John Clare
Picture editor: Bob Bodman
Advertising director: Len Sanderson
Editorial director: Brenda Haywood
Managing director: Jeremy Deedes
Financial director: Niamh O'Donnell-Keenan
Marketing director: Hugo Drayton
Founded: 1855. Owner: The Telegraph

The Express

245 Blackfriars Road, London SE1 9UX
Fax 0171-6201654   Tel 0171-928 8000
News   Tel 0171-922 7070
E-mail newsdesk@dailyexpress.co.uk
Editor: Rosie Boycott since April 1998
Deputy editor: Chris Blackhurst
Executive editors: John Murray, Chris Williams
Assistant editor, news: Michael Streeter
Assistant editor, comment: John Price
Head of features : Albert Read
Head of City: Robert Miller
Diary: John McEntee
Head of pictures: Chris Djukanovic
Foreign editor: Jacqui Goddard
Group managing editor: Lindsay Cook
Managing director: Nicholas Rudd-Jones
Marketing director: Peter Woolfenden
Circulation director: Don Gray
Deputy md/advertising director: Andy Jonesco
Founded: 1900.   **Owner:** United News and Media

Financial Times

1 Southwark Bridge, London SE1 9HL
Fax 0171-873 3076   Tel 0171-873 3000
News fax 0171-407 5700   Tel 0171-873 3616
Website: http://www.ft.com
Editor: Richard Lambert, since 1991
Acting editor: Andrew Gowers
Managing editor: Robin Pauley
News editor: Lionel Barber
Foreign editor: Quentin Peel
Finance director: Richard Leishman
Founded: 1888.
Owner: Pearson

The Guardian

119 Farringdon Road, London EC1R 3ER
Fax 0171-837 2114   Tel 0171-278 2332
Website: http://www.guardianunlimited.co.uk
Editor: Alan Rusbridger, since 1995
Deputy editor: Georgina Henry
Managing editor: Brian Whitaker
Deputy editor (news): Paul Johnson
Home editor: Harriet Sherwood
News editor: Clare Margetson
Features editor: Ian Katz
Political editor: Michael White .
Economics editor: Larry Elliot
Arts editor: Claire Armitstead
Media editor: Kamal Ahmed
Women's editor: Sally Weale
Weekend magazine editor: Katharine Viner
Picture editor: Eamonn McCabe
Sports editor: Michael Averis
Internet editor: Simon Waldeman
Executive finance editor: Ben Clissitt
Managing director: Caroline Marland
Marketing director: Stephen Palmer
Finance director: Paul Naismith
Commercial director: Carolyn McCall
Founded: 1821
Owner: Guardian Media Group

Independent

1 Canada Square, Canary Wharf, London E14 5DL
Fax 0171-293 2435   Tel 0171-293 2000
E-mail letters@independent.co.uk
Website: www.independent.co.uk
Editor: Simon Kelner since April 1998
Deputy editor: Ian Birrell
Associate editors: Hamish McRae, Jack O'Sullivan
News editor: David Felton
Arts editor: Chris Maume
Foreign editor: Ray Whitaker
Picture editor: David Swanborough
Sports editor: Paul Newman
Advertising director: Guy Griffiths
Managing director: Brendan Hopkins
Founded: 1986.   **Owner:** Newspaper Publishing

The Mirror

1 Canada Square, Canary Wharf, London E14 5AP
Fax 0171-293 3843   Tel 0171-510 3000
News fax 0171-510 3409   Tel 0171-293 3831
Editor: Piers Morgan, since 1995
Deputy editor: Tina Weaver
News editor: Eugene Duffy
Foreign editor: Mark Dowdney
Features editor: Mark Thomas
Picture editor: Ron Morgans
Advertisement director: Mark Pritchett
Managing director: Roger Eastoe
Marketing director: Jill Playle
Founded: 1903.   **Owner:** Mirror Group Newspapers

The Sun

1 Virginia Street, Wapping, London E1 9BD
Fax 0171-488 3253   Tel 0171-782 4000
Editor: David Yelland, since June 1998
Deputy editor: Rebekah Wade
City editor: Isabelle Murray
Political editor: Trevor Kavanagh
Picture editor: Jeff Webster
Features editor: Sam Carlisle
Sports editor: Ted Chadwick
Women's page: Vicki Grimshaw
Commercial director: Camilla Rhodes
Founded: 1912 Daily Herald; in present form since '69.
Owner: News International

The Times

1 Pennington Street, Wapping, London E1 9XN
Fax 0171-488 3242   Tel 0171-782 5000
Website: www.the-times.co.uk
Editor: Peter Stothard, since 1992
News editor: Graham Duffill
Deputy editor: John Bryant
Homes news editor: Graham Duffill
Business/city/financial editor: Patience Wheatcroft
Diary editor: Jasper Gerard
Environment: Nick Nuttall
Saturday editor: Brian MacArthur
Political editor: Phil Webster
Sports editor: David Chappell
Features editor: Sandra Parsons
Founded: 1785.   **Owner:** News International

NATIONAL SUNDAYS

Express on Sunday
245 Blackfriars Road, London SE1 9UX
Fax 0171-620 1654   Tel 0171-928 8000
    Tel 0171-922 7070
Editor: Rosie Boycott since April 1998
Deputy editor: Chris Blackhurst
Executive editors: John Murray, Chris Williams
Executive editor (Sunday): Amanda Platell
Assistant editor, news: Ian Walker
Assistant editor, comment: John Price
Head of features : Albert Read
Head of City: Robert Miller
Diary: John McEntee
Head of pictures: Chris Djukanovic
Foreign editor: Tom McGhie
Group managing editor: Lindsay Cook
Managing director: Nicholas Rudd-Jones
Marketing director: Peter Woolfenden
Circulation director: Don Gray
Deputy md/advertising director: Andy Jonesco
Founded: 1900.
Owner: United News and Media

Independent on Sunday
1 Canada Square, Canary Wharf, London E14 5DL
Fax 0171-293 2043   Tel 0171-293 2000
Newsfax 0171-293 2043   Tel 0171-293 2480
Editor: Kim Fletcher, since 1998
Deputy editor: Rebecca Nicolson
News editor: Adam Leigh
Sunday Review editor: Laurence Earle
Commissioning editor (features): Simon O'Hagan
Political editor: Rachel Sylvester
Foreign editor: Ray Whitaker
Picture editor: Victoria Lukens
Sports editor: Neil Morton
Ad manager: Guy Griffiths
Managing director: Brendan Hopkins
Founded: 1990.
Owner: Independent Newspapers

Mail on Sunday
2 Derry Street, London W8 5TT
Fax 0171-937 3745   Tel 0171-938 6000
Tape Room Fax 0171-937 7896/3829
Editor: Jonathan Holborow, since 1992.
Deputy editor: Rod Gilchrist
Executive editor: Peter Dobbie
News editor: Paul Henderson
Features editor: Sian James
City editor: William Kay
Assistant editor (news & pictures): Jon Ryan
Assistant editor (features): Sian James
Picture editor: Andy Kyle
Sports editor: Dan Evans
Advertising director: Simon Barnes
Managing director: Kevin Beatty
Founded: 1982.
Owner: Daily Mail & General Trust

News of the World
1 Virginia Street, Wapping, London E1 9XR
Fax   Tel 0171-782 4000
Editor: Phil Hall
Assistant editor: Bob Bird
Assistant editor (news): Greg Miskiw
Features editor: Ray Levine
Art director: Danny Fox
Picture editor: Lynn Cullen
Production editor: John Mellowdrew
Associate editor: Robert Waren
Sports editor: Mike Dunn
Colour supplement editor: Judy McGuire
Advertising director: Richard Webb
Managing editor: Stuart Kuttner
Chairman: Rupert Murdoch
Founded: 1843.
Owner: News International

Observer
119 Farringdon Road, London EC1R 3ER
Fax 0171-837 2114   Tel 0171-278 2332
Editor: Roger Alton, since 1998
Editor-in-chief: Will Hutton
Deputy editor: Paul Webster and John Mulholland
Home news editor: Paul Dunn
Political editor: Patrick Wintour
Arts editor: Jane Ferguson
Foreign editor: Leonard Doyle
Economics editor: William Keegan
Science editor: Robin McKie
Review editor: Tim Adams
Business editor: Ben Laurence
Picture editor: Greg Whitmore
Executive editor: Alan Rusbridger
Managing director: Caroline Marland
Marketing director: Stephen Palmer
Finance director: Paul Naismith
Commercial director: Carolyn McCall
Founded: 1791.
Owner: Guardian Media Group

The People
1 Canada Square, Canary Wharf, London E14 5AP.
News fax 0171-293 3810   Tel 0171-293 3201
Editor: Neil Wallis since January 1998
Political editor: Nigel Nelson
Arts editor: Bruce Preston
Foreign editor: Danny Buckland
Technology editor: Danny Buckland
Sports editor: Ed Barry
Business editor: Cathy Gunn
Picture editor: Martyn Spaven
Advertising manager: Phil O'Hara
Founded: 1881.
Owner: Mirror Group Newspapers

Sunday Business

200 Gray's Inn Road, London WC1X 8XR
Fax 0171-418 9605   Tel 0171-418 9600
E-mail: sundaybusiness@the-european.com
Editor-in-chief: Andrew Neil
Editor: Jeff Randall, since 1998
Deputy editor: Richard Northedge
Associate editor: Martin Baker
News editor: Frank Kane
Political correspondent: David Cracknell
Science & technology correspondent: Carl Franklin
Features editor: Vivien Goldsmith
Leisure industries reporter: Matthew Goodman
Transport & construction correspondent: Dominic O'Connell
City editor: Nils Prately
Re-launched: February 1998
Owner: Barclay Brothers

Sunday Mirror

1 Canada Square, Canary Wharf, London E14 5AP
Fax 0171-293 3405   Tel 0171-293 3000
News fax 0171-293 3939   Tel 0171-293 3601
Website: www.sundaymirror.co.uk
Editor: Brendon Parsons
Executive editors: Paul Bennett & Mike Ryder
Assistant editor (news): John Meshan
Assistant editor (features): Fiona Wyten
Associate editor: Michael Ryder
Magazine editor: Fiona Wingett
Picture editor: Paul Bennett
Sports editor: Steve McEnlay
Group sales director: Mark Pritchett
Managing director: Roger Eastoe
Finance director: Steve Barber
Founded: 1915 as Sunday Pictorial.
Owner: Mirror Group

Sunday Sport

19 Great Ancoats Street, Manchester M60 4BT
Fax 0161-236 4535   Tel 0161-236 4466
Editor: Mark Harris
Deputy editor: Jon Wise
News editor: Paul Carter
Features editor: Sarah Stevens
Picture editor: Paul Currie
Advertising manager: Alan Pollock
Managing director: John Gibbons
Founded: 1986.
Owner: Sport Newspapers (David Sullivan).

Sunday Telegraph

1 Canada Square, Canary Wharf, London E14 5DT
Fax 0171-538 6242   Tel 0171-538 5000
News fax 0171-513 2504   Tel 0171-538 7350
Editor: Dominic Lawson, since 1995
Deputy editor: Matthew d'Ancona
News editor: Chris Anderson
Features editor: tba
Arts editor: John Preston
Literary editor: Miriam Gross
City editor: Neil Bennett
Foreign editor: Con Coughlin
Political editor: David Wastell
Picture editor: Nigel Skelsey
Advertising director: Len Sanderson
Chairman: Conrad Black   **MD:** Jeremy Deedes
Finance director: Niamh O'Donnell-Keenan
Founded: 1961.   **Owner:** The Telegraph

Sunday Times

1 Pennington Street, London E1 9XW
Fax 0171-782 5658   Tel 0171-782 5000
Editor: John Witherow since 1994
Deputy editor: Martin Ivens
News review editor: Sarah Baxter
News editor: Mark Skipworth
Associate editor (politics): Michael Jones
Political editor: Andrew Grice
Managing editor, business news: John Jay
Picture editor: Ray Wells
Insight editor: David Leppard
Arts editor: Helen Hawkins
Music critic: Hugh Canning
Design editor: Gordon Beckett
Travel editor: Christine Walker
Economics editor: David Smith
Education: Judith O'Reilly
Environment/transport correspondent: Jonathan Leake
Literary editor: Geordie Greig
Style editor: Jeremy Langmead
Colour supplement, editor: Robin Morgan
Chairman: Rupert Murdoch
Founded: 1822.   **Owner:** News International

The European

200 Grays Inn Road, London WC1X 8NE
Fax 0171-713 1840   Tel 0171-418 7777
E-mail: letters@the-european.com
Website: http://www.the-european.com
Editor-in-chief: Andrew Neil, since 1997
Executive editor: Susan Douglas
Assistant editor (politics): Victor Smart
News editor: David Meilton
Assistant features editor: Nicola Davidson
Picture editor: Jeanette Downing
Sports editor: Dominic O'Reilly
Advertising manager: Julie Ferguson
Chief executive: Bert Hardy
Head of finance: Stan Walczak
Founded: 1990.   **Owner:** The European (Barclay twins)
(The European publishes on Thursdays, but is included here because it is a weekly.)

Local papers

The cliché about constant change out there in the global village is at its most true in local papers, the most village-like part of the media. Local might sound naff and small and parochial but it's no longer a synonym for decline, depression and career graveyard. Community is the new buzz word, as in the comment of Jim Brown, chairman of Newsquest, who said: "People are going back into community activities because they are weary of turgid programmes on television. And while national newspapers are increasingly falling into disregard, people still feel they can trust the regional dailies."

Much of the change is due to shifts in ownership, with almost half the 1,500 local papers having moved from multi-media multinationals like Thomson, Reed, Pearson and Emap. All those companies - Northcliffe,

NEW LOCALS

The Regional Independent Media chief executive Chris Oakley (above) could have been writing an Oxdown Trumpeter leader when he told Newspaper Society members: "The regional press had been riven by dissent and more interested in competing against each other than in presenting an attractive image to those whose votes we are trying to win when it comes to influencing their advertising spend. Just like Labour, we were seen as old fashioned and irrelevant, a smokestack industry standing for the outdated values of the past in a microchip age. Just like old Labour, at a point where figures were telling us we were facing rejection by our previous supporters, we finally got our act together. In the last three years we've had a change of leadership etc etc"

the Guardian Media Group and Mirror Group Newspapers still remaining as exceptions to a new rule - saw locals as a peripheral activity and subscribed to a received wisdom which said locals were mature products in a declining market, a market moreover which would grow increasingly irrelevant in a zippy new world of Internet and electronic publishing. Their financial geniuses advised sell, sell, sell and so they sold.

Latest to follow this way of thinking was the Express owner, United News and Media which, in February 1998, sold United Provincial Papers in two lots. The smaller group of southern titles went to Southnews for £47.5 million and UNM's 44 northern titles - including the Yorkshire Post, Yorkshire Evening Post and Lancashire Evening Post - went to Candover, a venture capital firm, for £360 million. Arise the Yorkshire Post Group.

Ownership has now consolidated into the hands of managements like YPG, Trinity, Newsquest and Johnston Press which, though backed by City money, depend on their local markets. Local papers are now being run by specialists with a sense for the 300 year old tradition in which many of them began their careers, and the new mood - along with new technology, lower newsprint prices and a healthy economy - has helped circulations.

Sales figures for the second half of 1997 showed that 56 per cent of papers had increased their circulations The weeklies did best with 60 per cent of them recording an increase in their ABC figures. In fairness, the whole picture was of a slowing in the rate of decline because, overall, there was a 0.5 per cent annual drop in sales. However, compare that with the 2.2 per cent circulation drop in 1995 and it's good news. Anthony Peachem, head of operations at the Audit Bureau of Circulation, summarised. "It has been another good year for the regional press, with 275 titles showing a sustained period-on-period growth."

Success shows itself in a number of other ways. For a start it makes people feel that it is

Top 20 regional press publishers

GROUP NAME	TITLES	WEEKLY CIRCULATION
1 Trinity International Holdings	121	8,301,337
2 Northcliffe Newspapers Group	56	8,040,969
3 Newsquest Media Group	124	7,653,088
4 Johnston Press	141	4,269,973
5 Mirror Group Newspapers	42	4,219,914
6 Regional Independent Media	33	3,275,611
7 Eastern Counties Newspapers Group	70	3,145,719
8 Southern Newspapers	63	2,749,509
9 Guardian Media Group	36	2,708,407
10 Southnews	54	2,655,744
11 Midland News Association	20	2,204,597
12 Portsmouth & Sunderland N'papers	23	1,963,748
13 Bristol United Press	14	1,436,506
14 Adscene Group	44	1,378,916
15 Scotsman Publications	6	1,378,662
16 Scottish Media	2	1,335,210
17 Yattendon Investment Trust	21	850,639
18 Independent Newspapers	28	814,910
19 DC Thomson & Co	2	782,874
20 Kent Messenger Group	17	716,551

Source: The Newspaper Society

worthwhile to innovate, the best example being a defensive move to hold on to classified advertising - the river of gold which has kept the locals alive - by popping it on the Internet. The Adhunter web site contains nearly three-quarters of job, house and car ads and is funded by a consortium of owners.

Financial brains - except of course the ones employed by the multinational sellers - reckon that newspapers are a good bet. When Trinity reported an 18 per cent profit rise to £74 million, analysts at Panmure Gordon said: "The outlook for regional newspaper publishers remains promising. Near term, display and classified advertising looks reasonably robust and newsprint prices have subdued." Financiers at the US investment bank Salomon Smith Barney talked of "a number of years ahead of good earning growth" and reckon that new monopolies could emerge as some of the new players merge. Already, Salomon points out, the more concentrated ownership of titles makes locals more attractive to national advertisers.

Locals also look more attractive to young journalists who recognise a good place to start a career. The pay is still lousy but tyros can recognise that personal success is more likely to flow from institutional success, an about turn from two decades during which old local apprenticeships disappeared and the ambitious turned to magazines for a start in life. And perhaps it has something to do with communitarian values as well, for here the locals are way ahead of most nationals. While it would be wrong to picture the new owners as community-oriented philanthropists, their papers - when it comes to old fashioned journalistic verities of accuracy, fair presentation and respect for both sides of an argument - have kept a certain integrity. They are good because they have to be, surviving, as they do, close to the people they write about. Lies, damned lies, distortions and sensational exclusives might shift papers in the global village but they don't carry so much weight in local villages.

As ever in writing of local papers, there is the nomenclature debate with owners and those who cuddle up to them preferring the aggrandised, multi-syllabic "regional" to describe their prized possessions. We've stuck to the rule that "local" isn't a rude word, and that it describes the reach of most of the papers in this sector The large exception is the large circulation titles which are defined as "regional".

Takeover times

Newsquest's WESSEX NEWSPAPERS to BRISTOL UNITED PRESS

Elisabeth Murdoch's NEW NATION to SOUTHNEWS

BAILEY NEWSPAPER GROUP to SOUTHERN NEWSPAPERS

HOME COUNTIES NEWSPAPERS to EASTERN COUNTIES NEWSPAPERS

The southern titles of United News and Media's UNITED PROVINCIAL PAPERS to SOUTHNEWS

The northern titles of United News and Media's UNITED PROVINCIAL PAPERS to CANDOVER under the name of REGIONAL INDEPENDENT MEDIA

Freddie Johnston (above), the chairman of Johnston Press, said his company is "constantly seeking suitable opportunities for further sensible expansion". Speaking last April in anticipation of a Monopolies Commission ruling on his deal to buy Home Counties papers, Johnston predicted further consolidations, saying these are "surely in the public interest".

Sir Ray Tindle, the owner of Tindle Newspapers, had a similar message when he told delegates at a Newspaper Society meeting that all was well in their business. "Are takeovers such a bad thing?" he asked. "Well, it doesn't indicate the industry is in any trouble, that's for sure. Revenue is up. Circulations are holding. Bottom lines look pretty good. For every seller there have been four or five buyers and prices have been high. The time to be concerned is surely when there are few buyers and prices are low."

LOCAL PAPER OWNERS

Adnews
Albert Chambers, Canal Street, Congleton CW12 4AA
Fax 01260-299324   Tel 01260-281012

Adscene Group
Newspaper House, Canterbury, Kent CT1 3YR
Fax 01227-470308   Tel 01227-767321
74 titles.
The group publishes titles in Kent, Greater London, Lincs, Notts, Leics, South Yorks and Hereford. It bought Tamworth Herald & Co, SC Publishing, Lichfield Mercury and Associated Kent Newspapers from EMAP in December 1995 for a total of £29.39 million.

Advertiser & Times (Hants)
62 Old Milton Road, New Milton, Hants BH25 6EH
Fax 01425 638635   Tel 01425-613384
Publishes New Milton Advertiser & Lymington Times.

Alpha Newspaper Group
56 Scotch Street, Armagh, N Ireland BT61 7DQ
Fax 01861-527029   Tel 01861-522639

Anderstown News
Nuachtan, 301 Glen Road, Anderstown, Belfast, County Antrim BT11 8ER
Fax 01232-620602   Tel 01232-619000
E-mail: nuachtan@iol.ie

Anglia Advertiser
The Precinct, High Street, Great Yarmouth NR31 6RL
Fax 01493-652082   Tel 01493-601206
5 titles. Norwich Advertiser, Great Yarmouth & Gorleston Advertiser, Waveny Advertiser, Suffolk Advertiser, Ipswich Advertiser.

Angus County Press
Craig O'Loch Road, Forfar DD8 1BT
Fax 01307-466923   Tel 01307-464899
Publishes 9 papers.

The Arbroath Herald
Burnside Drive, Arbroath DD11 1NS
Fax 01241-878789   Tel 01241-872274

Arran Banner Printing & Publishing
Brodick, Isle of Arran KA27 8AJ
                    Tel 01770-302142

Associated Newspapers
Northcliffe House, 2 Derry Street, London W8 5TT
Fax 0171-937 3745   Tel 0171-938 6000
Evening Standard. See also Northcliffe Newspapers

Bailey Newspaper Group
Reliance House, Long Street, Dursley GL11 4LS
Fax 01453-540212   Tel 01453-544000
Now taken over by Southern Newspapers.

Banbridge Chronicle Press
14 Bridge Street, Banbridge, County Down BT32 3JS
Fax 018206-24397   Tel 018206-62322

Barnsley Chronicle
47 Church Street, Barnsley, South Yorkshire S70 2AS
Fax 01226-734444   Tel 01226-734734
E-mail: editorial@barnsley-chronicle.co.uk
3 titles.

Baylis & Co
48 Bell Street, Maidenhead, Berkshire SL6 1HX
Fax 01628-419523   Tel 01628-798048
E-mail: maidads@maidenhead-advertiser.co.uk
Website: http://www.maidenhead-advertiser.co.uk
1 title.

Bristol Evening Post & Press
Temple Way, Bristol BS99 7HD
Fax 0117-934 3570   Tel 0117-934 3000
Web: www.epost.co.uk
E-mail: mail@epost.co.uk
10 titles.

Bute Newspapers
10 Castle Street, Rothsay, Bute PA20 9HB
Fax 01700-505159   Tel 01700-502931

CN Group
PO Box 7, Newspaper House, Dalston Road, Carlisle,
Cumbria CA2 5UA
Fax 01228-612601   Tel 01228-612600

Caledonian Newspaper Publishing
195 Albion Street, Glasgow G1 1QP
Fax 0141-552 1344   Tel 0141-552 6255
2 titles.
A company formed in 1992 by the management buyout
of The Herald and The Evening Times from Lonrho
and George Outram and Co. Now owned by Scottish
Newspapers. Two titles, The Herald and The Evening
Times, part of the Scottish Media Group. Acquired in
October 1996 from Caledonian Publishing.

Cambrian News
Publishing Centre, Unit 7, Cefn Llan Science Park,
Aberystwyth, Dyfed SY23 3AH
Fax 01970-624699   Tel 01970-615000
5 titles.

Candover
20 Old Bailey, London, EC4M 7LN
Fax 0171-248 5483   Tel 0171-489 9848
A venture capitalist group and the new owners of the
Yorkshire Evening Post as of March '98.

Champion Newspapers
Clare House, 166 Lord Street, Southport, Merseyside
PR9 0QA
Fax 01704-531327   Tel 01704-531302

Cheadle & Tean Times
18 Tape Street, Cheadle, Staffordshire ST10 1BD
Fax 01538-754465   Tel 01538-753162
3 titles.

Chester Standard Newspapers
Linen Hall House, Stanley Street, Chester CH1
2LR
Fax 01244-351536   Tel 01244-351234
3 titles.

Chew Valley Publications
Wellington Place, Tunbridge Road, Chew Magna,
Bristol BS40 8SP
Fax 01275-333067   Tel 01275-332266

Chronicle Publications
102 Boothferry Road, Goole, Yorkshire DN14 6AE
Fax 01405-720003   Tel 01405-720110
E-mail: gooletimes@btinternet.com
Publishers of The Goole Times.

City of London & Docklands Times
Suite 23, Salisbury House, London Wall, London
EC2M 5QQ
Fax 0171-628 2842   Tel 0171-628 2841

Clyde & Forth Press
Pitreavie Business Park, Dunfermline, KY11 5QS
Fax 01383-737040   Tel 01383-728201

Coates & Parker
36 Market Place, Warminster, Wiltshire BA12 9AN
Fax 01985-217680   Tel 01985-213030
Publishes the Warminster Journal.

The County Press
North Wales series, County Press Buildings, Bala,
Gwynedd LL23 7PG
Fax 01678-521262   Tel 01678-520262

Courier Newspapers (Oxford)
2-4 Ock Street, Abingdon, Oxon OX14 5AH
Fax 01235-554465   Tel 01235-553444
E-mail: 106314.653@compuserve.com
6 titles. The 3 best sellers are: The Oxford Journal;
Oxford Courier series; Reading's Thames Valley Weekly.

SR & VI Crane
30 Queen Street, Redcar, Cleveland TS10 1BD
Fax 01642-477143   Tel 01642-480397
Publishes The Clarion.

W Y Crichton & Co
2-4 Church St, Downpatrick, Co Down BT30 6EJ
Fax 01396-614624   Tel 01396-613711
E-mail: downr@sol.co.uk

D & J Croal
18 Market Street, Haddington, East Lothian EH41 3JL
Fax 01620-826143   Tel 01620-822451
E-mail: courier@croal.demon.co.uk

Cumberland & Westmorland Herald
14 King Street, Penrith, Cumbria CA11 7AH
Fax 01768-890363   Tel 01768-862313

Derry Journal Co
Buncrana Road, Londonderry BT48 8AA
Fax 01504-272218/272260   Tel 01504-272200
5 titles. The 3 best sellers are: Derry Journal (Friday);
Derry Journal (Tuesday); Donegal Democrat.

Dimbleby Newspaper Group
14 King Street, Richmond, Surrey TW9 1NF
Fax 0181-332 1899   Tel 0181-940 6030
11 editions.

Dumfriesshire Newspapers Group
96 High St, Annan Dumfriesshire DG12 6DW
Fax 01461-205659   Tel 01461-202078

Dunfermline Press
A Romanes & Son, Pitreavie Business Park,
Dunfermline, Fife KY11 5QS
Fax 01383-737040   Tel 01383-728201

Dungannon Development Association
1 Savings Bank Street, Dungannon, County Tyrone
BT70 1DT
Fax 018687-24666   Tel 018687-25445

Eastern Counties Newspapers Group
Prospect House, Rouen Road, Norwich, Norfolk NR1
1RE
Fax 01603-612930   Tel 01603-628311
E-mail: ecnmail@ecn.co.uk

Echo Press
Echo House, Jubilee Drive, Belton Park,
Loughborough, Leicestershire LE11 5TQ
Fax 01509-238363   Tel 01509-232632
E-mail: postmaster@echoweb.demon.co.uk
Website: http://www.loughborough-echo.co.uk
12 titles, the best seller is: Loughborough Echo.

Ellerman Investment (aka Barclay Bros)
200 Gray's Inn Road, London WC1X 8NE
                    Tel 0171-418 7850
6 titles. Ellerman Investment bought The Scotsman
Publications off Thomson Regional Newspapers for
£90 million in November 1995.

Ellesmere Press
The British School, Otley Street, Skipton BD23 1EW
Fax 01756-799766   Tel 01756-799765
E-mail: rupert@epltd.demon.co.uk

Eskdale & Liddesdale Newspapers
Commercial House, High Street, Langholm,
Dumfriesshire DG13 0JH
Fax 013873-80345   Tel 013873-80012

Fletcher Newspapers
38-46 Harmer Street, Gravesend, Kent DA12 2AY
Fax 01474-353758   Tel 01474-363363
Now owned by Independent Newspapers.

Forest of Dean Newspapers
Woodside Street, Cinderford, Gloucestershire GL14
2NN
Fax 01594-826213   Tel 01594-822126
The Forester, incorporating Dean Forest Guardian,
Dean Forest Mercury and the Lydney Observer.

Friday Ad Group
Eastbourne Road, Uckfield, E Sussex TN22 5ST
Fax 01825-766318   Tel 01825-766000
E-mail: sales@friday-ad.co.uk

Galloway Gazette
71 Victoria Lane, Newton Stewart, Wigtownshire DG8
6PS
Fax 01671-403391   Tel 01671-402503

Garnett Dickinson Publishing
Eastwood Works, Fitzwilliam Road, Rotherham S65
1JU
Fax 01709-820588   Tel 01709-364721
E-mail: info@gdpublishing.co.uk

Guardian Media Group
164 Deansgate, Manchester M60 2RD
Fax 0161-832 5351   Tel 0161-832 7200
Around 100 titles.
The Guardian Media Group's national titles are The
Guardian and The Observer. Its local papers are
published by the Greater Manchester Division, and by
the Surrey and Berkshire Division. Autotrader
publishes regional editions in conjunction with Hurst
Publishing All ordinary shares of the Guardian Media
Group are owned by the Scott Trust and any dividends
"shall be devoted towards building up the reserves of
the company and expanding, improving and increasing
the circulation of its newspapers."

The Guernsey Press Co
Braye Road, Guernsey, Channel Islands GY1 3BW
Fax 01481-43393   Tel 01481-45866
E-mail: gp@guernsey-press.com
Website: http://guernsey-press.com
2 titles.

Hawick News
24 High Street, Hawick TD9 9EH
Fax 01450-370706   Tel 01450-372204
E-mail: david@hawicknews.demon.co.uk

Heads (Congleton)
11 High Street, Congleton, Cheshire CW12 1BW
Fax 01260-280687   Tel 01260-273737
E-mail: 100554.1443@compuserve.com
Web:
http://ourworld.compuserve.com/homepages/Jeremy
_Condliffe
Last independent newspaper in Cheshire.

Heathrow Villager
260 Kingston Road, Staines, Middlesex TW18 1PG
Fax 01784-453196   Tel 01784-453196

Herald Observer Newspapers
Webb House, 20 Church Green East, Redditch B98
8BP
Fax 01527-584371   Tel 01527-67714

Higgs Group (Henley Standard)
Caxton House, 1 Station Road, Henley-on-Thames,
Oxon RG9 1AD
Fax 01491-419401   Tel 01491-419444
E-mail: webmaster@higgsgroup.co.uk
Website: http://www.henley-on-thames.com

Hill Bros (Leek)
Newspaper House, Brook Street, Leek, Staffordshire
ST13 5JL
Fax 01538-386975   Tel 01538-399599
Publishes the Post Times series in North Staffordshire.

John H Hirst & Co
1 Market Street, Cleckheaton, W Yorks BD19 3RT
Fax 01274-851304   Tel 01274-874635
Part of Dewsbury Reporter series which is owned by
UPN.

Hirst, Kidd & Rennie
172 Union Street, Oldham, Lancashire OL1 1EQ
Fax 0161-627 0905   Tel 0161-633 2121
E-mail: hjhirst@oldham-chronicle.co.uk
Publishes 1 daily and 1 free weekly: Oldham Evening
Chronicle; Chronicle Weekend.

Edward Hodgett
4 Margaret Street, Newry, Co Down BT34 1DF
Fax 01693-63157   Tel 01693-67633

Holderness Newspapers
1 Seaside Road, Withernsea, E Yorkshire HU19 2DL
Fax 01964-615303   Tel 01964-612777

Home Counties Newspapers (Holdings)
63 Campfield Road, St Albans, Hertfordshire AL1 5HX
Fax 01727-833484   Tel 01727-811911
24 titles.
Bought the Herald Newspaper Group for £7 million in
November 95.

Horley Publishing
76a Victoria Road, Horley, Surrey RH6 7PZ
Fax 01293-409653   Tel 01293-409649
Independent Newspapers (UK)
Newspaper House, 2 Whalebone Lane South,
Dagenham, Essex RM8 1HB
Fax 0181-592 7407   Tel 0181-517 5577
43 titles. The 3 best sellers are: East London Advertiser;
Barking & Dagenham Post; Islington Gazette.
E & R Inglis
219 Argyll Street Dunoon, Argyll PA23 7QT
Fax 01369-703458   Tel 01369-703218
Irish News
113-117, Donegall Street, Belfast BT1 2GE
Fax 01232-337505   Tel 01232-322226
E-mail: s.simpson@irishnews.com
Website: http://www.irishnews.com
Isle of Wight County Press
Brannon House, 123 Pyle Street, Newport, Isle of
Wight PO30 1ST
Fax 01983-527204   Tel 01983-521333
E-mail: adman@iwcpress.demon.co.uk
1 paid for weekly.
J & M Publishing
13-15 West Curch Street, Buckie, Banff AB56 1BN
Fax 01542-834316   Tel 01542-832265
E-mail: ba@moray.com
Website: http://www.moray.com
3 titles.
Jacob & Johnson
57 High Street, Winchester, Hampshire SO23 9BY
Fax 01962-842313   Tel 01962-841772
Jersey Evening Post
W E Guiton & Co, PO Box 582, Five Oaks, St Saviour,
Jersey CI, JE4 8XQ
Fax 01534-611620   Tel 01534-611611
E-mail: jepdaily@itl.net
Johnston Press
53 Manor Place, Edinburgh EH3 7EG
Fax 0131-225 4580   Tel 0131-225 3361
E-mail: j.brads@johnstonpress.co.uk
Website: http://www.johnston.co.uk
150 titles with a four million weekly circulation. The
three best sellers are: Derbyshire Times; Falkirk Herald;
Kettering Evening Telegraph. Johnston is the fourth
largest regional newspaper publisher. Has expanded
over recent years with several acquisitions, the major
one being Emap Newspapers in 1996 costing £211
million. In April 1996 it bought Doncaster Newspapers
from Newsquest Media.
Journal Publishing Co
50a Warwick Street, Leamington Spa CV32 5JS
Fax 01926-313487   Tel 01926-832789
32 titles. The 3 best sellers are: Cty of London Journal;
Reading & Thames Valley Guardian; Oxford Gazette.
Kent Messenger
Messenger House, New Hythe Lane, Larkfield
Aylesford ME20 6SG
Fax 01622-719637   Tel 01622-717880
20 titles. The 3 best sellers are: the Kent Messenger;
Kentish Gazette; Kentish Express.

Leigh Times Co
34a The Broadway, Leigh-on-Sea SS9 1AJ
Fax 01702-478710   Tel 01702-477666
Lichfield Mercury
Graphic House, 17 Bird Street, Lichfield, Staffordshire
WS13 6PX
Fax 01543-415814   Tel 01543-414414
Local Publications (Bourne)
Newspaper House, 17 Abbey Road, Bourne,
Lincolnshire PE10 9EF
Fax 01778-394087   Tel 01778-425876
Local Publications (Saffron Walden)
10 Emson Close, Saffron Walden, Essex CB10 1HL
Fax 01799-520561   Tel 01799 516161
Local Sunday Newspapers Group
22 Mill Street, Bedford MK40 3HD
Fax 01234-304404   Tel 01234-304403
Loot
Loot House, 24-32 Kilburn High Road, Kilburn,
London NW6 5TF
Fax 0171-625 7921   Tel 0171-625 0266
E-mail: freeads@lootlon.loot.co.uk
The Manchester Reporter Group
24 School Lane, Didsbury, Manchester M20 6RG
Fax 0161-434 9921   Tel 0161-446 2212
2 titles. South Manchester Reporter; Heatows &
Reddish Reporter.
G W McKane & Son
Reliance Works, 32-34 Station Street, Keswick,
Cumbria CA12 2HF
Fax 017687-71203   Tel 017687-72140
Midland Independent Newspapers
28 Colmore Circus,Queensway, Birmingham B4 6AX
Fax 0121-233 3958   Tel 0121-236 3366
30 titles.
Midland Independent was formed in 1991 and
concentrates activites on local papers in the West and
East Midlands. Now part of the Mirror Group.
Midland News Association
51-53 Queen Street, Wolverhampton, West Midlands
WV1 3BU
Fax 01902-319721   Tel 01902-313131
E-mail: feedback@expressandstar.co.uk
Montrose Review Press
59 John Street, Montrose DD10 8QU
Fax 01674-676232   Tel 01674-672605
Morton Newspapers Group
2 Esky Drive, Portadown, Craigavan BT63 5YY
Fax 01762-393940   Tel 01762-393939
25 titles. The 3 best sellers are: East Antrim series;
Ulster Star, Portadown Times. Bought by Scottish Radio
Holdings for £11.2 million in 1995.
Mortons of Horncastle
Newspaper House, Morton Way, Horncastle,
Lincolnshire LN9 6JR
Fax 01507-527840   Tel 01507-523456
E-mail: 100765.1777@compuserve.com
Mourne Observer
The Roundabout, Castlewellan Road, Newcastle, Co
Down BT33 0JX
Fax 013967-24566   Tel 013967-22666

NW Ireland Printing & Publishing Co
10 John St, Omagh, Co Tyrone, Ireland BT7 1DT
Fax 01662-242206   Tel 01662-243444

Nairnshire Telegraph Co
10 Leopold Street, Nairn IV12 4BG
Fax 01667-455277   Tel 01667-453258

New Journal Enterprises
40 Camden Road, London NW1 9DR
Fax 0171-209 1322   Tel 0171-419 9000
E-mail: letters.cnj@cablenet.co.uk

New Rutland Times
Times House, 16b Mill Street, Oakham, Rutland LE15 6EA
Fax 01572-755599   Tel 01572-757722

Newark Advertiser Co
Appletongate, Newark, Notts NG24 1JX
Fax 01636-681122   Tel 01636-681234

Newbury Weekly News (Printers)
Newspaper House, Faraday Road, Newbury, Berkshire RG14 2DW
Fax 01635-522922   Tel 01635-564525
E-mail: paulj.nwn@pop3.hiway.co.uk
Website: http://www.newburynews.co.uk

Newsquest Media Group
Newspaper House, 34-44 London Road, Morden, Surrey SM4 5BR
Fax 0181-646 3997   Tel 0181-640 8989
173 titles. 7.8 million weekly circulation.
Newsquest Media was formed by a management buyout of Reed Regional Newspapers for £205 million in November 1995. Much of the funding was supplied by the American financier Kohlberg Kravis Roberts. Newsquest bought the Bury Times from Johnston in April 1996 at the same time selling it Doncaster Newspapers. In August 1996 it bought Westminster Press. in October 1997 the company floated on the Stock Exchange and in March 1998 it bought Property Weekly.

Newtownards Chronicle
25 Frances Street, Newtownards, Co Down BT23 3DT
Fax 01247-820087   Tel 01247-813333

Normanton Advertiser
4 West Street, Normanton, W Yorks WF6 2AP
Fax 01924-215327   Tel 01924-892117
E-mail: norad@demon.co.uk

North Derbyshire Newspapers
Blenheim Court, Newbold Road, Chesterfield S41 7PG
Fax 01246-200177   Tel 01246-234920

North Devon Gazette & Advertiser
16 Tuly Street, Barnstable, Devon EX31 1DH
Fax 01271-324608   Tel 01271-344303

North Edinburgh News
6 West Pilton Crescent, Edinburgh EH4 4HP
Fax 0131-343 3911   Tel 0131-332 1236

North Wales Newspapers
Mold Business Park, Wrexham Road, Mold, Flintshire CH7 1XY
Fax 01352-752180   Tel 01352-707707
E-mail: nwnfd@netwales.co.uk

Northcliffe Newspapers Group
31 John Street, London WC1N 2QB
Fax 0171-400 1207   Tel 0171-400 1100
57 titles. including Evening Standard.
Northcliffe Newspapers is part of the Daily Mail and General Trust of which Associated Newspapers is the overall management company. The group publishes the Daily Mail and Mail on Sunday. Northcliffe is the second largest regional newspaper publisher and operates from 23 centres. It bought Aberdeen Journals form Thomson Regional Newspapers in 1995.

Northern Newspaper Group
20 Railway Road, Coleraine, Northern Ireland BT51 1PD
Fax 01265-43606   Tel 01265-43344
3 titles and 1 free. Coleraine Chronicle; Ballymena Guardian; Northern Constitution.

Nuneaton & District Newspapers
Newspaper House, 11-15 Newtown Road, Nuneaton, Warwickshire CV11 4HR
Fax 01203-353481   Tel 01203-353534

Oban Times Group
John Street, Oban, Argyll PA34 5PY
Fax 01631-565470   Tel 01631-563058
E-mail: editor@obantimes.co.uk

Observer Newspapers (NI)
Ann Street, Dungannon, Co Tyrone BT70 1ET
Fax 01868-727334   Tel 01868-722557

The Orcadian
Hatston Industrial Estate, Kirkwall, Orkney KW15 1DW
Fax 01856-879001   Tel 01856-879000

Outlook Press
Castle Street, Rathfriland, Co Down BT34 5QR
Fax 018206-31022   Tel 018206-30202

P M Publications
The Messenger, 2 Kings Road, Haslemere, Surrey GU27 2QA
Fax 01428-661658   Tel 01428-653999

John Penri Press
11 St Helens Road, Swansea SA1 4AL
Fax 01792-650647   Tel 01792-652092

W Peters & Son
16 High Street, Turriff, Aberdeenshire AB53 4DT
Fax 01888-563936   Tel 01888-563589
3 titles.

Portsmouth & Sunderland Newspapers
37 Abingdon Road, London W8 6AH
Fax 0171-590 6611   Tel 0171-590 0640
19 titles.
A family firm founded in 1873 by the great-grandfather of the present chairman. The groups main activities are in central, southern and north east England.

Powys Newspapers
11 Bulwark, Brecon, Powys LD3 7AE
Fax 01874-624097   Tel 01874-622932
E-mail: b&rexpress@netwales.co.uk

Recorder (Wales)
Cambria House, Wyndham Street, Bridgend, Mid Glamorgan CF31 1EY
Fax 01656-656894   Tel 01656-669330
E-mail: recorder@globalnet.co.uk

Regional Independent Media
PO Box 168, Wellington Street, Leeds, West Yorks
LS1 1RF
Fax 0113-242 1814   Tel 0113-243 2701
Website: www.upn.co.uk
64 titles. Formerly the northern division of United
Provincial Newspapers until taken over by the Candover
ventrue capital group. It operates from centres in
Yorkshire and the North West.

Review & Advertiser Newspaper Group
Kinetic Business Centre, Theobald Street,
Borehamwood, Hertfordshire WD6 4PJ
                              Tel 0181-953 9119

Review Free Newspapers
The William Henry Building, Porters Wood, St Albans,
Hertfordshire AL3 6PQ
Fax 01727-852770   Tel 01727-834411

Ross Gazette
35 High St, Ross-on-Wye, Herefordshire HR9 5HE
Fax 01989-768023   Tel 01989-562007

SC Publishing Co
14b-14c Birmingham Road, Sutton Coldfield, West
Midlands B72 1QG
Fax 0121-355 0600   Tel 0121-355 6901
6 titles. The 3 best sellers are: Sutton Coldfield
Observer; Geat Barr Observer; Walsall Advertiser.

The Scotsman Publications
20 North Bridge, Edinburgh EH1 1YT
Tel 0131-225 2468

Scottish and Universal Newspapers
                              Tel 01786 459426

Scottish County Press
Sherwood Industrial Estate, Bonnyrigg, Midlothian
EH19 3LW
Fax 0131-663 6863   Tel 0131-663 4606

Scottish Daily Record & Sunday Mail
40 Anderston Quay, Glasgow G3 8DA
Fax 0141-242 3545   Tel 0141-248 2727
E-mail: editor@features.dailyrecord.co.uk
Website: http://www.record-mail.co.uk/rm

Scottish Media Newspapers
195 Albion Street, Galsgow G1 1QP
Fax 0141-552 3050   Tel 0141-552 6255
Owns Caledonian Magazines and Caledonian
Newspapers.

Scottish Provincial Press
13 Henderson Road, Inverness, Scotland IV1 1SP
Fax 01463-221251   Tel 01463-713700

Sheffield Mercury Newspaper (Baycro)
PO Box 70, Sheffield, South Yorkshire S8 0QA
Fax 0114-274 6444   Tel 0114-274 6555
E-mail: j603180406@aol.com

The Shetland Times Co
Prince Alfred Street, Lerwick, Shetland ZE1 0EP
Fax 01595-694637   Tel 01595-693622
E-mail: editorial@shetland-times.co.uk
Website: http://www.shetland-times.co.uk

Slough Observer Group
Upton Court, Datchet Road, Slough, Berkshire SL3
7NR
Fax 01753-693895   Tel 01753-523355

G H Smith & Son
Market Place, Easingwold, York YO61 3AB
Fax 01347-822576   Tel 01347 821329
E-mail: ghsmith@globalnet.co.uk

Southern Newspapers
Newspaper House, Test Lane, Redbridge,
Southampton, Hampshire SO16 9JX
Fax 01703-424969   Tel 01703-424777
Website: http://www.southern-newspapers.co.uk

Southnews
326 Station Road, Harrow, Middlesex HA1 2DR
Fax 0181-863 0932   Tel 0181-424 0033
32 titles.
A company formed in 1986 by a management team
which had previosuly worked for Westminster Press or
Reed Regional Newspapers. Bought the Croydon
Advertiser for £12.95 million from Portsmouth and
Sunderland Newspapers in November 95. Its most
recent purchase was the southern part of United
Provincial.

Southwark News
Unit J104, Tower Bridge Business Complex,
Clement's Road, London SE16 4DG
                              Tel 0171-231 5258

Spalding & South Lincs Herald
3 St Thomas Road, Spalding, Lincs PE11 2XY
Fax 01775-713714   Tel 01775-713723

Spectator Newspapers
109 Main Street, Bangor, Co Down BT20 4AF
Fax 01247-271544   Tel 01247-270270
E-mail: spectator@dial.pipex.com

The St Ives Printing & Publishing Co
High Street, St Ives, Cornwall TR26 1RS
Fax 01736-795020   Tel 01736-795813
E-mail: times@echo.clara.net

Star Publishing
The Maidstone Press Centre, Bank Street, Maidstone,
Kent ME14 1PZ
Fax 01622-675071   Tel 01622-678556

Star Newspapers (Camberley)
192 Victoria Road, Aldershot, Surrey GU11 1JZ
Fax 01252-343042   Tel 01252-316311
                              Tele-ads: 01252-317171

Starbuys
3 Kings Arcade, Lancaster LA1 1LE
Fax 01524-843649   Tel 01524-66902

The Tamworth Herald Co
Ventura Park Road, Bitterscote, Tamworth,
Staffordshire B78 3LZ
Fax 01827-848488   Tel 01827-848586

Teesdale Mercury
24 Market Place, Barnard Castle, County Durham
DL12 8NG
Fax 01833-638633   Tel 01833-637140

DC Thomson & Co
2 Albert Square, Dundee, Tayside DD1 9QJ
Fax 01382-322214   Tel 01382-223131
E-mail: dct@dcthomson.co.uk
2 titles.
A family owned company which also publishes the
Beano and the Dandy.

Tindle Newspapers
114 West Street, Farnham, Surrey GU9 7HL
Fax 01252-723950 Tel 01252-723938
Website: http://www.tindlenews.co.uk
80 titles. A family-owned company which publishes in the South West, Surrey, Hampshire, Kent, Lancashire and South Wales.

Topper Newspapers
Maychalk House, 8 Musters Road, Notts NG2 7PL
Fax 0115-982 6565 Tel 0115-982 6974

Trident Midland Newspapers
Bridge Road, Coalville, Leicester LE67 3QP
Fax 01530-811361 Tel 01530-813101

William Trimble
8-10 East Bridge Street, Enniskillen, N Ireland BT74 7BT
Fax 01365-325047 Tel 01365-324422

Trinity International Holdings
Kingsfield Court, Chester Business Park, Chester, Cheshire CH4 9RE
Fax 01244-687100 Tel 01244-687000
E-mail: TIHMail@tih.co.uk
120 titles. The Liverpool Daily Post and Echo until 1985, Trinity expanded by buying Argus Newspapers in London and the home counties plus titles in Wales and Scotland. It became the largest regional paper publisher in Britain with the £327.5 million purchase, in November 1995, of the Thomson Regional Newspaper titles: Belfast Telegraph, Chester Chronicle and Assoc. Newspapers, Newcastle Chronicle and Journal, North Eastern Evening Gazette and Western Mail and Echo.

The Tweeddale Press Group
PO Box 10, 90 Marygate, Berwick Upon Tweed, Northumberland TD15 1BW
Fax 01289-307377 Tel 01289-306677
E-mail: Tweeddale@aol.com
Website: www.tweeddalepress.co.uk
The 3 best sellers are: Southern Reporter; Berwick Advertiser; Berwickshire News.

Tyrone Constitution Group
25-27 High Street, Omagh, Co Tyrone BT78 1BD
Fax 01662-243549 Tel 01662-242721

United Advertising Publications
Alexander House, 94-96 Talbot Road, Old Trafford, Manchester M16 0PG
Fax 0161-877 9134 Tel 0161-872 6996

United Provincial Newspapers
Sold by UNM to Candover and Southnews. See entries for Regional Indpenedet Media and Southnews

West Highland Publishing Co
Broadford, Isle of Skye IV49 9AP
Fax 01471-822694 Tel 01471-822464
E-mail: newsdesk@whsp.co.uk

Westminster Press
Now owned by Newsquest

Wigtown Free Press
St Andrew Street, Stranraer, Wigtownshire DG9 7EB
Fax 01776-706695 Tel 01776-702551

Yattendon Investment Trust
Barn Close, Yattendon, Berkshire RG18 0UX
Fax 01635 202564 Tel 01635-202909

TOP REGIONAL DAILIES

Belfast Telegraph
124-144 Royal Avenue, Belfast BT1 1EB
Fax 01232-554506 Tel 01232-264000
E-mail: editor@belfasttelegraph.co.uk
Websote: http://www.belfasttelegraph.co.uk
Editor: Edmund Curran
Deputy editor: Jim Flanagan
News editor: Janet Devlin
Features editor: John Caruth
Arts editor: Neil Johnston
Picture editor: Gerry Fitzgerald
Sports editor: John Laverty
Advertising director: John Leslie
Managing director: Derek Carvell
Financial director: Ken Simpson
Founded: 1870
Owner: Trinity International Holdings

Birmingham Evening Mail
28 Colmore Circus, Birmingham B4 6AX
Fax 0121-233 0271 Tel 0121-236 3366
Editor: Ian Dowell
Deputy editor: Tony Dickens
News editor: Norman Stinchcombe
Features editor: Paul Cole
Picture editor: Roland Rowley
Sports editor: Leon Hickman
Advertising director: Patrick Sexton
Managing director: Roger Chappell
Financial director: John Whitehouse
Founded: 1857
Owner: Mirror Regional Newspapers

Bristol Evening Post
Temple Way, Bristol BS99 7HD
Fax 0117-934 3575 Tel 0117-934 3000
Editor: Mike Lowe
News editor: Rob Stokes
Features editor: Matthew Shelley
Picture editor: Peter Watson
Sports editor: Chris Bartlett
Advertising director: Nick Weston
Managing director: Paul Kearney
Owner: Bristol United Press

Coventry Evening Telegraph
Corporation Street, Coventry, West Midlands, CV1 1FP
Fax 01203-631736 Tel 01203-633633
E-mail: editorial@coventry-telegraph.co.uk
Website: http://www.coventry-telegraph.co.uk
Editorial director: Dan Mason
Deputy editor: Alan Kerby
News editor: John West
Business editor: Andrew Macleod
Features editor: Paul Simoniti
Women's editor: Barbara Argument
Picture editor: Malcolm Hepple
Sports editor: Roger Draper

Advertisement manager: Andrew Haddow
Managing director: Michael Hutchby
Finance director: Neil Appleton
Founded: 1857   Owner: Mirror Regional Newspapers

Courier & Advertiser
80 Kingsway East, Dundee DD4 8SL
Fax 01382-454590   Tel 01382-223131
E-mail: courier@dcthomson.co.uk
Website: http://www.dcthomson.co.uk/courier
Editor: Adrian Arthur
Deputy editor: Alastair Fyfe
News editor: Steve Bargeton
Features editor: Shona Lorimer
Arts editor: Joy Watters
Sports editor: Graeme Dey
Advertisement manager: A McEwan
Owner: DC Thomson & Co

Daily Record
Anderston Quay, Glasgow, Strathclyde G3 8DA
Fax 0141-242 3340   Tel 0141-248 7000
E-mail editor@dailyrecord.co.uk
Editor: Terry Quinn
Deputy editor: Charles McGhee
News editor: Murray Morse
Features editor: Allan Rennie

Arts director: Lucy Allsopp
Picture editor: Stuart Nicol
Sports editor: Andy Swinburne
Sales director: Jim Park
Managing director: Liam Kane
Financial controller: Graham McCall
Founded: 1847.
Owner: Mirror Regional Newspapers

Eastern Daily Press
Prospect House, Rouen Road, Norwich, Norfolk NR1 1RE
Fax 01603-612930   Tel 01603-628311
E-mail: edp@ecn.co.uk
Website: http://www.ecn.co.uk
Editor: Peter Franzen
Assistant editor: Roy Strowger
News editor: Paul Durrant
Business editor: Ken Hurst
Arts editor: Charles Roberts
Features editor: Derek James
Picture editor: Dennis Whitehead
Sports editor: David Thorpe
Managing director: Tom Stevenson
Advertising director: Stephen Phillips
Founded: 1870
Owner: Eastern Counties

Top 25 regional dailies

DAILIES	CIRCULATION	OWNER
1 Glasgow Daily Record	714,636	Mirror Regional Newspapers
2 London Evening Standard	454,016	London Evening Standard
3 Birmingham Evening Mail	192,188	Mirror Regional Newspapers
4 Express and Star	191,869	The Midland News Association
5 Manchester Evening News	173,191	Guardian Media Group
6 Liverpool Echo	159,800	Trinity
7 Belfast Telegraph	129,204	Trinity
8 Glasgow Evening Times	119,853	Scottish Media
9 Newcastle Evening Chronicle	111,466	Trinity
10 Leicester Mercury	110,975	Northcliffe Newspapers Group
11 Aberdeen Press and Journal	105,176	Northcliffe Newspapers Group
12 Glasgow The Herald	102,682	Scottish Media
13 Yorkshire Evening Post	100,384	Regional Independent Media
14 Dundee Courier and Advertiser	97,727	DC Thomson & Co
15 Stoke The Sentinel	91,307	Northcliffe Newspapers Group
16 Shropshire Star	90,323	The Midland News Association
17 Nottingham Evening Post	89,726	Northcliffe Newspapers Group
18 Sheffield Star	89,045	Regional Independent Media
19 Hull Daily Mail	85,809	Northcliffe Newspapers Group
20 Edinburgh Evening News	82,846	Scotsman Publications
21 Coventry Evening Telegraph	81,876	Mirror Regional Newspapers
22 The Scotsman	81,330	Scotsman Publications
23 Bristol Evening Post	80,025	Bristol United Press
24 Norfolk Eastern Daily Press	78,484	Eastern Counties Newspapers Group
25 Yorkshire Post	75,825	Regional Independent Media

Source: The Newspaper Society

Edinburgh Evening News
20 North Bridge, Edinburgh, EH1 1YT
Fax 0131-225 7302   Tel 0131-225 2468
Editor: John McLellan
Deputy editor: Simon Reynolds
Associate news editor: David Lee
Associate editor (features): Helen Martin
Associate editor (news): David Lee
Picture editor: Tony Marsh
Sports editor: Paul Greaves
Business editor: Ian Burrell
Managing director: Michael Jones
Advertising director: Stephen Tait
Finance director: Gordon Affleck
Founded: 1873
Owner: Scotsman Publications

Evening Chronicle
Groat Market, Newcastle-upon-Tyne NE1 1ED
Fax 0191-230 4144   Tel 0191-232 7500
E-mail: chron@ncjchronicle.demon.co.uk
Executive editor: Neil Benson
Editor: Alison Hastings
Deputy editor: Roger Borrell
Assistant editor: Paul Robertson
News editor: David Bourn
Features editor: Jane Pickett
Production editor: Barbara Waite
Picture editor: Rod Wilson
Sports editor: Paul New
Sales director: Shaun Bowron
Managing director: Stephen Parker
Founded: 1885
Owner: Trinity International Holdings

Evening Standard
2 Derry Street, London W8 5EE
Fax 0171-937 3193   Tel 0171-938 6000
Editor: Max Hastings
Deputy editor: Andrew Bordiss
News editor: Stephen Clackson
Features editor: Bernice Davison
Picture editor: David Ofield
Sports editor: Simon Greenberg
Advertising director (classified): Sally Smith
Advertising director (display): Sue Minnikin
Managing director: Jonathan Harmsworth
Financial: Karen Dyson
Founded: 1827
Owner: Associated Newspapers

Evening Times
195 Albion Street, Glasgow G1 1QP
Fax 0141-553 1355   Tel 0141-552 6255
Editor: John Scott
Deputy editor: Ewan Watt
News editor: Ally McLaws
Features editor: Russell Kyle
Picture editor: Alistair Stairs
Sports editor: David Stirling
Commercial director: Christine Costello

Managing director: Andrew Flanagan
Financial director: Gary Hughes
Founded: 18th century
Owner: Scottish Media Group

Express and Star
51-53 Queen Street, Wolverhampton, West Midlands
WV1 1ES
Fax 01902-319721   Tel 01902-313131
Editor: Warren Wilson
Deputy editor: Richard Ewels
News editor: Dave Evans
Features editor: Gary Copeland
Picture editor: Geoff Wright
Sports editor: Steve Gordos
Advertising manager: Brian Clarke
Managing director: Tony Witts
Financial director: David Allatt
Founded: 1874
Owner: Midland News Association

The Herald
195 Albion Street, Glasgow G1 1QP
Fax 0141-552 2288   Tel 0141-552 6255
E-mail: lettersheraldmail@cims.co.uk
Website: http://www.theherald.co.uk
Editor: Harry Reid
Deputy editor: Alf Young
News editor: Bill McDowall
Features editor: Jackie McGlone
Arts editor: Keith Bruce
Picture editor: Jim Connor
Sports editor: Iain Scott
Commercial director: Christine Costello
Managing director: Andrew Flanagan
Financial director: Gary Hughes
Founded: 18th century
Owner: Scottish Media Group

Hull Daily Mail
Blundells Corner, Beverley Road, Hull HU3 1XS
Fax 01482-584353   Tel 01482-327111
E-mail: hdm@dial.pipex.com
Website: http://www.hulldailymail.co.uk
Editor: John Meehan
Deputy editor: Mel Cook
Community & campaigns editor: Stan Szecowka
Head of news: Marc Astley
Women's page: Jo Davison
Arts editor: Tracy Fletcher
Picture editor: Dave Barker
Sports editor: Mark Woodward
Advertising director: Steve Hollingsworth
Managing director: Ken Thompson
Financial director: Jonathon Wells
Founded: 1885
Owner: Northcliffe Newspapers Group

Leicester Mercury
St George Street, Leicester LE1 9FQ
Fax 0116-262 4687   Tel 0116-251 2512
Website: http://www.leicestermercury.co.uk
Editor: Nick Carter
Deputy editor: Simon Crane
News editor: Simon Orrell
Features editor: Mark Clayton
Arts editor: Mark Clayton
Picture editor: Richard Elliott
Sports editor: Alan Parr
Advertising director: Phil Brewin
Managing director: Tony Hill
Financial director: Christine Dooley
Founded: 1874
Owner: Northcliffe Newspapers Group

Liverpool Echo
Old Hall Street, Liverpool L69 3EB
Fax 0151-236 4682   Tel 0151-227 2000
E-mail: letters@liverpoolecho.co.uk
Website: http://www.liverpool.com
Editor: John Griffith
Deputy editor: Tony Storey
News editor: John Thompson
Picture editor: Stephen Shakeshaft
Arts editor: Joe Riley
Picture editor: Stephen Shakeshaft
Sports editor: Ken Rogers
Advertising director: Heather Vasco
Managing director: Leo Coligan
Financial director: Philip Hoyle
Founded: 1879
Owner: Trinity

Manchester Evening News
164 Deansgate, Manchester M60 2RD
Fax 0161-832 5351   Tel 0161-832 7200
Website: http://www.manchesteronline.co.uk
Editor: Paul Horrocks
Deputy editor: Brian Rhodes
News editor: Lisa Roland
Features editor: Maggie Henfield
Arts editor: Rachel Pugh
Picture editor: Dave Thomas
Sports editor: Peter Spencer
Deputy managing director: Mark Dodson
Managing director: Ian Ashcroft
Financial director: Neil Canetty-Clarke
Owner: Guardian Media Group

Nottingham Evening Post
Canal Wharf House, Nottingham NG1 7EU
Fax 0115-964 4032   Tel 0115-948 2000
E-mail: nep.editorial@dial.pipex.com
Editor: Graham Glen
Deputy editor: Jon Grubb
Assistant editor: Duncan Hamilton
Features editor: Jeremy Lewis
Picture editor: Scott Riley
Sports editor: Kevin Pick

Advertising director: Kevan Weeds/David Waghorne
Managing director: Steve Anderson-Dixon
Financial director: Jonathan Persent
Founded: 1878
Owner: Northcliffe Newspapers Group

Press and Journal
Lang Stracht, Mastrick, Aberdeen AB15 6DF
Fax 01224-663575   Tel 01224-690222
E-mail: editor@pj.ajl.co.uk
Editor: Derek Tucker
Assistant editors: Ron Knox, Kay Drummond
News editor: David Knight
Features editor: Kay Drummond
Sports editor: Jim Dolan
Advertising director: Janis Gallon Smith
Managing director: Alan Scott
Founded: 1747
Owner: Northcliffe Newspaper Group

The Scotsman
20 North Bridge, Edinburgh H1 1YT
Fax 0131-226 7420   Tel 0131-225 2468
Editor in chief: Andrew Neil
Editor: Martin Clarke
Deputy editor: Alan Taylor
Business news editor: Mark McSherry
Sports editor: Daniel Evansl
Assistant editor (features & arts): Jane Johnson
Literary editor: Catherine Lockerbie
Local government: David Scott
News editor: Ian Stewart
Political editor: John Penman
Scottish political editor: Peter MacMahon
Supplements editor: Ken Houston
Owner: Barclay Brothers
Founded: 1817

The Sentinel
Sentinel House, Stoke-on-Trent, Staffs ST1 5SS
Fax 01782-280781   Tel 01782-289800
Editor: Sean Dooley
Deputy editor: Roger Clift
News editor: Michael Woods
Features editor: Roy Coates
Arts editor: Roy Coates
Picture editor: Trevor Slater
Sports editor: Nigel Wiskar
Advertising directors: Graham White, Rudd Apsey
Managing director: Peter Keller
Financial director: John Adams
Founded: 1873
Owner: Northcliffe Newspapers Group

Shropshire Star
Ketley, Telford, Shropshire TF1 4HU
Fax 01952-254605   Tel 01952-242424
Editor: Andy Wright
Deputy editor & news editor: Sarah Jane Smith
Features editor: Alun Owen
Arts editor: Alun Owen
Picture editor: Ken Done
Sports editor: Pete Byram
Advertising director: Alan Harris
Managing director: Keith Parker
Financial director: Roger Glews
Founded: 1964
Owner: Claverley Co

The Star
York Street, Sheffield, South Yorks S1 1PU
Fax 0114-272 5978   Tel 0114-276 7676
Editor: Peter Charlton
Features editor: Bob Rae
Picture editor: Dennis Lound
Sports editor: Martin Smith
Advertising director: Paul Bentham
Managing director: David Edmonson
Founded: 1889
Owner: Regional Independent Media

Yorkshire Evening Post
Wellington Street, Leeds, West Yorks LS1 1RF
Fax 0113-238 8536   Tel 0113-243 2701
E-mail: eped@tpn.co.uk
Editor: Chris Bye
Assistant editor: Adrian Troughton
Features editor: Anne Pickles
Womens editor: Carmen Bruegmann
Picture editor: Mike Fisher
Sports editor: Steve White
News editor: David Helliwell
Advertising director: Mike Pennington
Managing director: Steve Auckland
Financial director: Katherine Armitage
Founded: 1890
Owner: Regional Independent Media

Yorkshire Post
Wellington Street, Leeds, West Yorks LS1 1RF
Fax 0113-244 3430   Tel 0113-243 2701
E-mail: yp.newsdesk@ypn.co.uk
Editor: Tony Watson
Deputy editor: Nick Jenkins
Womens editor: Jill Armstrong
Features editor: Michael Hickling
Business editor: Peter Curtain
Sports editor: Bill Bridge
Managing director: Steve Auckland
Advertising director: Mike Pennington
Finance director: Kathryn Armitage
Founded: 1754
Owner: Regional Independent Media

TOP REGIONAL SUNDAYS

Scotland on Sunday
20 North Bridge, Edinburgh EH1 1YT
Fax 0131-220 2443   Tel 0131-225 2468
Editor: John McGurk
Deputy editor: Mark Douglas-Home
News editor: William Paul
Features editor: Aaron Hicklin
Picture editor: Neil Hanna
Sports editor: Kevin McKenna
Owner: European Press Holdings

Sunday Independent
Burrington Way, Plymouth, Devon PL5 3LN
Fax 01752 206164   Tel 01752 206600
Editor: Anna Jenkins
Deputy editor: Nikki Rowlands/John Collings
Features editor: Stuart Fraser
Picture editor: Steve Porter
Sports editor: Harley Lawer
Owner: Southern Newspapers

(Belfast) Sunday Life
124-144 Royal Avenue, Belfast BT1 1EB
Fax 01232-554507   Tel 01232-264300
E-mail: barnold@belfasttelegraph.co.uk
Editor: Martin Lindsay
Deputy editor: Dave Culbert
News editor: Martin Hill
Features editor: Sue Corbett
Picture editor: Fred Hoare
Sports editor: Jim Gracey
Advertising manager: Alastair Hunter
Managing director: Derek Carvell
Owner: Trinity International

Sunday Mail
Anderston Quay, Glasgow G3 8DA
Fax 0141-242 3587   Tel 0141-248 7000
Editor: Jim Cassidy
Assistant editor: Andy Sannholm
Assistant editor (news): Brian Steel
Features editor: Rob Bruce
Women's editor: Melanie Reid
News editor: Alan Crow
Picture editor: Dave McNeil
Sports editor: George Cheyne
Magazine editor: Janette Harkness
Advertising director: Pat Moore
Managing director: Mark Hollinshead
Owner: Mirror Group

Sunday Mercury
28 Colmore Circus, Birmingham B4 6AZ
Fax 0121-234 5877   Tel 0121-236 3366
Editor: Fiona Alexander
Deputy editor: Alf Bennett
Assistant editor: James Windle
News editor: Bob Haywood
Assistant editor (sport): Lee Gibson
Advertising sales manager: Denize McNeish
Managing director: Roger Chappell
Owner: Midland

Sunday Post
2 Albert Square, Dundee DD1 9QJ
Fax 01382-201064   Tel 01382-223131
E-mail: post@dcthomson.co.uk
Website: http://www.dcthomson.co.uk
Editor: Russell Reid
Deputy editor: David Pollington
News editor: Tom McKay
Features editor: Brian Wilson
Picture editor: David Burness
Sports editor: David Walker
Magazine editor: Maggie Dun
Advertising manager: Ian Foggie
Managing director: Brian Thomson
Owner: DC Thomson & Co

Sunday Sun
Thomson House, Groat Market, Newcastle-upon-Tyne NE1 1ED
Fax 0191-230 0238   Tel 0191-201 6330
E-mail: office@SundaySun.demon.co.uk.
Editor: Peter Montellier
Deputy editor: David Bellew
Assistant editor: Mike McGiffen
Associate editor: Carole Watson
Chief reporter: Jim Oldfield
Feature writer: Emma Nugent
Sports editor: Dylan Younger
Chief photographer: Paul Forrest
Advertising manager: Phil Young
Newspaper sales manager: Sandy Gamlin
Managing director: Stephen Parker
Owner: Trinity

Wales on Sunday
Havelock Street, Cardiff CF1 1XR
Fax 01222-583725   Tel 01222-583720
E-mail: WOSMAIL@wme.co.uk
Editor: Alan Edmunds
Senior assistant editor: Mike Smith
Assistant editor (production): Andrea Jones
Assistant editor: Mark Dawson
News editor: Alastair Milburn
Sports editor: Richard Morgans
Advertising director: Geraldine Aitken
Managing director: Mark Haysom

Paid for Sunday regional newspapers

TITLE	CIRCULATION	OWNER
1 Glasgow Sunday Mail	818,081	Mirror Regional Newspapers
2 Dundee Sunday Post	791,400	DC Thomson & Co
3 Sunday Mercury (Birmingham)	145,548	Mirror Regional Newspapers
4 Newcastle upon Tyne Sunday	118,493	Trinity
5 Scotland on Sunday	113,516	Scotsman Publications
6 (Belfast) Sunday Life	104,641	Trinity
7 Wales on Sunday	61,541	Trinity
8 Plymouth Sunday Independent	38,758	Southern Newspapers

Free Sunday regional newspapers

TITLE	CIRCULATION	OWNER
1 Luton on Sunday	98,198	Local Sunday Newspaper Group
2 Milton Keynes Sunday Citizen	88,774	Johnston Press
3 Bedfordshire on Sunday Borough	60,238	Local Sunday Newspaper Group
4 Bedfordshire on Sunday Mid	46,477	Local Sunday Newspaper Group
5 Bedfordshire on Sunday L Buzz	14,811	Local Sunday Newspaper Group

Source: The Newspaper Society

Local paper listings d=daily, w=weekly, s=Sunday, f=free

BEDFORDSHIRE

Ampthill & Flitwick Herald wf
Eastern Counties Newspapers
01234-364221
Bedford Citizen series wf
Johnston Press
01234-363101
Bedford & Kempston Herald wf
Herald Newspapers
01234-364221
Bedfordshire On Sunday s
Local Sunday Newspapers
01234-345191
Biggleswade & Sandy Herald wf
Eastern Counties Newspapers
01727-846866
Biggleswade Chronicle w
Johnston Press
01767-313479
Dunstable Gazette w
Eastern Counties Newspapers
01582-212222
Dunstable Leader wf
Eastern Counties Newspapers
01582-212222
Leighton Buzzard Citizen wf
Johnston Press
01908-371133
Leighton Buzzard Herald wf
Eastern Counties Newspapers
01727-846866
Leighton Buzzard Observer w
Eastern Counties Newspapers
01582-212222
Luton Leader wf
Eastern Counties Newspapers
01582-212222
Luton News w
Eastern Counties Newspapers
01582-212222
Luton/Dunstable Herald & Post wf
Trinity International Holdings
01582-401234
Luton On Sunday s
Local Sunday Newspapers
01582-484836
MidBed Times w
Johnston Press
01234-363101

BERKSHIRE

The Advertiser wf
Newbury Weekly News
01635-550444
Ascot News w
Reading Newspaper Co
01344-56611

Ascot & Sunningdale Observer wf
Slough Observer
01753-523355
Berks & Bucks Observer wf
Frank Lawrence
01753-523355
Bracknell & Ascot Times w
Berkshire Press
0118-957 5833
Bracknell & Wokingham News wf
Trinity International Holdings
01344-56611
Bracknell & Wokingham Std wf
Guardian Media Group
0118-957 5833
Bracknell News w
Trinity International Holdings
01344-56611
Crowthorne, Sandhurst Newsweek w
Reading Newspaper Co
01344-56611
Crowthorne & Sandhurst Times w
Berkshire Press
0118-957 5833
Maidenhead Advertiser w
Baylis & Co
01628-771100
Newbury/Thatcham Chronicle wf
Trinity International Holdings
01734-503030
Newbury Local Mart wf
Local Mart Publications
01635-31855
Newbury Weekly News w
Newbury Weekly News
01635-550444
Reading Chronicle w
Trinity International Holdings
01734-503030
Reading Chronicle Midweek wf
Trinity International Holdings
01734-503030
(Reading) Evening Post d
Guardian Media Group
01734-575833
Reading Standard wf
Berkshire Press
01734-575833
Sandhurst/Crowthorne News wf
Guardian Media Group
01252-28221
Slough & Langley Observer w
Frank Lawrence
01753-523355
Slough,Windsor&Eton Express w
Southnews
01753-825111

Windsor/Maidenhead Leader wf
Southnews
01753-825111
Windsor & Maidenhead Obs wf
Frank Lawrence
01753-523355
Wokingham & Bracknell Times w
Guardian Media Group
01734-782000
Wokingham News w
Reading Newspaper Co
01344-56611
Woodley Chronicle w
Reading Newspaper Co
0118-950 3030

CITY OF BRISTOL

Bristol Evening Post d
Bristol Evening Post
0117-926 0080
Bristol Journal wf
Southern Newspapers
0117-923 1153
Bristol Observer wf
Bristol Evening Post
0117-926 0080
(Bristol) Western Daily Press d
Bristol Evening Post
0117-926 0080
Clevedon Mercury wf
Bristol Evening Post
01275-874248
Glos & Avon Gazette w
Bailey Newspapers
01453-320111
Keynsham & District Adv wf
Southern Newspapers
0117-923 1154
Northavon Gazette w
Southern Newspapers
01453-544000
Portishead Admag wf
Southern Newspapers
0117-923 1153
Thornbury Gazette w
Southern Newspapers
01453-544000

BUCKINGHAMSHIRE

Bletchley Citizen wf
Johnston Press
01908-371133
Buckingham Advertiser w
Johnston Press
01280-813434
Buckinghamshire Advertiser w
Southnews
01895-233133

Top 50 paid weekly local newspapers

TITLE	CIRCULATION	OWNER
1 West Briton	50,391	Northcliffe Newspapers Group
2 Essex Chronicle	49,598	Northcliffe Newspapers Group
3 Surrey Advertiser	45,419	Guardian Media Group
4 Chester Chronicle	44,765	Trinity
5 Western Gazette	43,510	Bristol United Press
6 South London Press (Fri ed)	43,252	Trinity
7 Kent Messenger	43,085	Kent Messenger Group
8 Derbyshire Times	41,896	Johnston Press
9 Kent & Sussex Courier	40,550	Northcliffe Newspapers Group
10 Croydon Advertiser series	40,266	Southnews
11 Hereford Times	39,547	Newsquest
12 Barnsley Chronicle	39,256	The Barnsley Chronicle
10 Iolo of Wight County Press	37,517	Isle of Wight County Press
14 Cornish Guardian	37,001	Northcliffe Newspapers Group
15 Cumberland News	36,686	CN Group
16 North Devon Journal	35,316	Northcliffe Newspapers Group
17 Warrington Guardian	34,680	Newsquest
18 Surrey Mirror series	34,477	Trinity
19 Falkirk Herald	33,724	Johnston Press
20 Aldershot News series	33,664	Guardian Media Group
21 Harrogate Advertiser series	33,218	Regional Independent Media
22 Herts Mercury series	33,157	Yattendon Investment Trust
23 Westmorland Gazette	32,980	Newsquest
24 Darlington & Stockton Times	32,110	Newsquest
25 Farnham Herald series	31,840	Tindle Newspapers
26 Mansfield Chronicle Advertiser	31,802	Johnston Press
27 Somerset County Gazette	31,135	Southern Newspapers
28 South London Press (Tues ed)	29,783	Trinity
29 Doncaster Free Press	29,746	Johnston Press
30 Reading Chronicle	29,512	Trinity
31 Maidenhead Advertiser	28,716	Baylis & Co
32 Oxford Times	28,689	Newsquest
33 Tamworth Herald series	28,656	The Adscene Group
34 Wakefield Express	28,635	Johnston Press
35 Bury Free Press	28,389	Johnston Press
36 Dyfed Western Telegraph	27,866	Southern Newspapers
37 Rotherham & S Yorkshire Adv	27,754	Garnett Dickinson
38 Rochdale Observer (Sat)	27,586	Guardian Media Group
39 Bucks Free Press	27,284	Newsquest
40 Hamilton Advertiser	27,157	Trinity
41 Derry Journal (Fri)	26,531	Derry Journal
42 Salisbury Journal	26,517	Southern Newspapers
43 Ayrshire Post	26,446	Trinity
44 Dewsbury Reporter Group	26,245	Regional Independent Media
45 Eastbourne Herald	26,143	Johnston Press
46 Newbury Weekly News	26,131	Newbury Weekly News
47 Lynn News (Fri)	25,882	Johnston Press
48 Derry Journal (Tues)	25,844	Derry Journal
49 Thanet Times	25,741	The Adscene Group
50 Basingstoke Weekend Gazette	25,694	Southern Newspapers

Source: The Newspaper Society

Bucks Advertiser
Johnston Press
01296-24444
Bucks Examiner w
Southnews
01494-792626
Bucks Free Press w
Newsquest Media Group
01494-521212
Bucks Herald
Johnston Press
01296-24444
(High Wycombe) Midweek w
Newsquest Media Group
01494-521212
High Wycombe Leader wf
Southnews
0181-424 0044
Milton Keynes Citizen wf
Johnston Press
01908-371133
Milton Keynes Herald wf
Eastern Counties Newspapers Group
01727-846866
Milton Keynes & District Observer w
Eastern Counties Newspapers
01727-866166
Newport P & Olney Citizen wf
Johnston Press
01908-371133
South Bucks Star wf
Newsquest Media Group
01494-535911
Stony Stratford/Woburn Citizen wf
Johnston Press
01908-374033

CAMBRIDGESHIRE

Cambridge Evening News d
Yattendon Investment Trust
01223-358877
Cambridge Weekly News wf
Yattendon Investment Trust
01223-358877
Cambs Times/March Adv w
Eastern Counties Newspaper Group
01603-628311
Cambs Town Crier East wf
Johnston Press
01223-69966
Cambs Town Crier West wf
Johnston Press
01223-69966
Ely Standard w
Eastern Counties Newspaper Group
01603-628311
Ely Weekly News wf
Yattendon Investment Trust
01223-358877
Fenland Citizen wf
Johnston Press
01945-584372

Huntingdon Weekly News wf
Yattendon Investment Trust
01223-358877
Huntingdon Town Crier w
Peterborough Evening Telegraph
01480-407555
The Hunts Post wf
Eastern Counties Newspaper Group
01480-411481
Peterborough Citizen wf
Johnston Press
01733-555111
Peterborough Evening Telegraph d
East Midlands Newspapers
01733-555111
Peterborough Herald & Post wf
Midland Independent Newspapers
01733-318600
St Ives Weekly News wf
Yattendon Investment Trust
01223-358877
St Neots Weekly News wf
Yattendon Investment Trust
01223-358877
Wisbech Standard w
Eastern Counties Newspaper Group
01603-628311

CHANNEL ISLANDS

Guernsey Evening Press & Star d
The Guernsey Press Co
01481-45866
Guernsey Weekly Press w
Guernsey Press Co
01481-45866
Jersey Evening Post d
Jersey Evening Post
01534-73333
Jersey Weekly Post w
Jersey Evening Post
01534-73333

CHESHIRE

Bramhall & District Courier wf
Courier Group
01625-586140
Chester & District Standard wf
Chester Standard Newspapers
01244-351234
Chester Chronicle w
Trinity International Holdings
01244-340151
Chester Herald & Post wf
Trinity International Holdings
01244-340151
Congleton Adnews wf
Adnews (Midlands)
01260-281012
Congleton Chronicle series w
Heads (Congleton)
01260-273737

Congleton Guardian wf
Newsquest Media Group
01260-280686
Crewe & District Herald Post wf
Trinity International Holdings
01244-340151
Crewe & Nantwich Guardian wf
Newsquest Media Group
01270-258858
Crewe Chronicle w
Trinity International Holdings
01244-340151
Didsbury & District Courier wf
Courier Group
01625-586140
Ellesmere Port Pioneer w
Trinity International Holdings
01244-340151
Ellesmere Port Standard wf
Chester Standard Newspapers
01244-351234
High Peak Reporter w
United Provinicial Newspapers
0161-303 1910
Knutsford Express Advertiser wf
Guardian Media Group
0161-480 4491
Knutsford Guardian w
Newsquest Media Group
01565-634114
Macclesfield Express Adv. w
Guardian Media Group
0161-480 4491
Macclesfield Messenger wf
Newsquest Media Group
01625-618830
Macclesfield Times wf
Guardian Media Group
0161-480 4491
Middlewich Chronicle w
Chronicle Newspapers
01244-340151
Northwich Chronicle w
Trinity International Holdings
01244-340151
North Cheshire Herald w
Ashton Weekly Newspapers
0161-303 1910
Northwich Guardian w
Newsquest Media Group
01606-43333
Northwich Herald & Post wf
Trinity International Holdings
01606-43762
Poynton Times wf
Guardian Media Group
0161-480 4491
Runcorn Herald & Post wf
Trinity International Holdings
01244-340151

Top 25 free weekly local newspapers

TITLE	CIRCULATION	OWNER
1 Manchester Metro News	300,149	Guardian Media Group
2 The Glaswegian	279,523	Mirror Regional Newspapers
3 Lverpool Weekly Nwprs Group	191,005	Trinity
4 Nottingham Recorder	186,267	Northcliffe Newspapers Group
5 Bristol Observer series	182,908	Bristol United Press
6 SE Hants Property Guide	181,363	Portsmouth & Sunderland Newspapers
7 Edinburgh Herald & Post	175,669	Scotsman Publications
8 Nottingham Topper	167,770	Topper Newspapers
9 Portsmouth Journal series	165,698	Portsmouth & Sunderland Newspapers
10 Advertiser series (Hull)	164,080	Northcliffe Newspapers Group
11 Dorset Advertiser series	162,477	Southern Newspapers
12 Leeds Weekly News	160,147	Regional Independent Media
13 Birmingham Metronews	160,102	Mirror Regional Newspapers
14 Bex'heath/Dart/Sid News Shopper	142,846	Newsquest
15 Wirral Globe	141,035	Newsquest
16 Leicester Mail series	140,702	Northcliffe Newspapers Group
17 Wirral News Group	140,118	Trinity
18 Southampton Advertiser	138,251	Southern Newspapers
19 North Staffs Advertiser	125,495	Northcliffe Newspapers Group
20 Sheffield Weekly Gazette	122,723	Regional Independent Media
21 Derby Express series	121,685	Northcliffe Newspapers Group
22 Coventry Citizen series	121,378	Mirror Regional Newspapers
23 Hendon Times series	121,057	Newsquest
24 Kingston Guardian series	116,455	Newsquest
25 Newcastle Herald & Post	116,089	Trinity

Source: The Newspaper Society

Runcorn Weekly News w
Trinity International Holdings
01244-340151
Runcorn World wf
Newsquest Media Group
0151-424 7711
Sandbach Chronicle w
Heads (Congleton)
01260-273737
South Cheshire Mail wf
Chronicle Newspapers
01244-340151
South Wirral Herald wf
Trinity International Holdings
01244-340151
Warrington Guardian w
Newsquest Media Group
01925-633033
Warrington Mercury wf
Kinsman Reeds
01925-417727
Widnes Weekly News w
Trinity International Holdings
01244-340151
Widnes World wf
Newsquest Media Group
0151-424 7711

Wilmslow Express Advertiser wf
Guardian Media Group
0161-480 4491
Wilmslow Messenger wf
Newsquest Media Group
01625-527695

CORNWALL

Bude & Stratton Post w
Cornish & Devon Post
01566-772424
Camelford & Delabole Post w
Cornish & Devon Post
01566-772424
Camborne & Redruth Packet wf
Tindle Newspapers
01326-373791
Cornish and Devon Post w
Tindle Newspapers
01566-772424
Cornish Guardian w
Northcliffe Newspapers Group
01208-781338
Cornish Times w
Tindle Newspapers
01579-342174
The Cornishman w
Northcliffe Newspapers Group
01736-62247

Falmouth Packet w
Packet Newspapers
01326-370500
Hayle Times w
St Ives Printing & Publishing Co
01736-795813
Helston & District Gazette wf
Packet Newspapers
01326-370500
Launceston Gazette wf
Tindle Newspapers
01566-772424
Liskeard Gazette wf
Tindle Newspapers
01579-47444
Mid Cornwall Advertiser wf
North Cornwall Advertiser
01208-815096
North Cornwall Advertiser wf
North Cornwall Advertiser
01208-815096
Packet Series w
Southern Newspapers
01326-373791
Penwith Pirate wf
Packet Newspapers
01326-370500

Redruth & Camborne Tinner
Packet Newspapers
01326-370500
St Austell, Newquay Packet wf
Southern Newspapers
01326-373791
St Ives Times & Echo w
St Ives Printing & Publishing
01736-795813
Truro Packet wf
Southern Newspapers
01326-373791
West Briton w
Northcliffe Newspapers Group
01872-71451

CUMBRIA

The Advertiser wf
CN Group
01229-821835
(Barrow) N West Evening Mail d
CN Group
01229-821835
(Carlisle) News & Star d
CN Group
01228-23488
Cumberland Herald w
Cumberland & Westmorland Herald
Newspapers
01768-862313
Cumberland News w
CN Group
01228-23488
East Cumbrian Gazette wf
CN Group
01228-41151
Keswick Reminder w
G W McKane & Son
01768-72140
Lakeland Echo wf
United Provinicial Newspapers
01539-730630
Lakes Leader wf
Newsquest Media Group
01539-720555
W Cumberland Times & Star w
CN Group
01900-601234
West Cumbrian Gazette wf
CN Group
01228-41151
Westmorland Gazette w
Newsquest Media Group
01539-720555
Whitehaven News w
CN Group
01946-691234

DERBYSHIRE

Alfreton & Ripley Echo wf
Johnston Press
01773-834731

Alfreton Chad wf
Johnston Press
01623-26262
Ashboourne News Telegraph w
Yattendon Investment Trust
01335-300200
Belper Express wf
Northcliffe Newspapers Group
01332-292222
Belper News w
Johnston Press
01773-820971
Bolsover Advertiser wf
Derbyshire Times
01246-200144
Buxton Advertiser w
Johnston Press
01298-22118
Buxton Times wf
Derbyshire Times
01246-200144
Chesterfield Advertiser wf
Johnston Press
01246-202291
Chesterfield Express wf
North Derbyshire Newspapers
01246-234620
Chesterfield Gazette wf
Johnston Press
01246-200144
Derby Evening Telegraph d
Northcliffe Newspapers Group
01332-291111
Derby Express wf
Northcliffe Newspapers Group
01332-291111
Derby Journal wf
Journal Publishing
01332-369162
Derby Trader wf
Midland Independent Newspapers
01332-253999
Derbyshire Times w
Johnston Press
01246-200144
Dronfield Advertiser wf
Johnston Press
01246-202296
Eckington Leader wf
Johnston Press
01246-434343
Glossop Chronicle w
United Provinicial Newspapers
0161-303 1910
High Peak Courier wf
Johnston Press
01457-855385
Ilkeston & Ripley Trader wf
Midland Independent Newspapers
01332-253999

Ilkeston Advertiser w
Johnston Press
0115-932 4285
Ilkeston Express wf
Northcliffe Newspapers Group
01332-292222
Matlock Mercury w
Johnston Press
01629-582432
Ripley & Heanor News w
Johnston Press
01773-742133
Swadlincote Times w
Trident Midland Newspapers
01530-813101

DEVON

Axminster News wf
Eastern Counties Newspapers Group
01392-447766
Dartmouth Chron/S Hams Gazette w
Tindle Newspapers
01803-832724
Dawlish Gazette w
Tindle Newspapers
01626-779494
Dawlish Post wf
Devon & Cornwall Newspapers
01626-864161
East Devon News series wf
Eastern Counties Newspapers Group
01392-447766
(Exeter) Express & Echo d
Northcliffe Newspapers Group
01392-442211
Exeter Leader wf
Northcliffe Newspapers Group
01392-442450
(Exeter) Midweek Herald wf
Eastern Counties Newspapers Group
0117-923 1153
Exmouth Herald wf
Eastern Counties Newspapers Group
0117-923 1154
Exmouth Journal w
Eastern Counties Newspapers Group
0117-923 1153
Holsworthy Post w
Conish & Devon Post
01566-772424
Honiton & Ottery News wf
Eastern Counties Newspapers Group
01392-447766
Ivybridge Gazette w
Tindle Newspapers
01752-893255
Kingsbridge Gazette w
Tindle Newspapers
01548-853101
Mid-Devon Advertiser series w
Tindle Newspapers
01626-55566

Mid-Devon Express & Star wf
Southern Newspapers
01823-335261
Mid Devon Gazette w
Northcliffe Newspapers Group
01884-252725
Newton Abbot Weekender wf
Northcliffe Newspapers Group
01803-213213
North Devon Gazette & Adv wf
Eastern Counties Newspapers Group
01271-76677
North Devon Journal w
Northcliffe Newspapers Group
01271-43064
Okehampton Times w
Tavistock Newsapers
01822-613666
(Plymouth) Evening Herald d
Northcliffe Newspapers Group
01752-765500
Plymouth Extra wf
Northcliffe Newspapers Group
01752-765500
Plympton News wf
Tindle Newspapers
01752-893255
Pulmans Weekly News w
Bristol Evening Post
01935-74551
Sidmouth Herald w
Eastern Counties Newspapers Group
0114-923 1153
South Devon & Plymouth Times w
Devon & Cornwall Newspapers
01803-862585
Sunday Independent w
West of England Newspapers
01752-206600
Tavistock Times Gazette w
Tindle Newspapers
01822-613666
Teignmouth News wf
Tindle Newspapers
01626-779494
Teignmouth Post w
Devon & Cornwall Newspapers
01626-53555
Torbay Weekender wf
Northcliffe Newspapers Group
01803-213213
(Torquay) Herald Express d
Northcliffe Newspapers Group
01803-213213
Totnes Times Series w
Tindle Newspapers
01803-862585
Western Morning News d
Northcliffe Newspapers Group
01752-765500

DORSET

Avon Adv (Hants & Dorset) wf
Southern Newspapers
01722-337466
Bournemouth/Christchurch/
Poole Advertiser wf
Southern Newspapers
01202-666633
(Bournemouth) The Daily Echo d
Southern Newspapers
01202-554601
Bridport News w
Southern Newspapers
01823-335361
Christchurch Advertiser wf
Advertiser Series
01202-411411
Dorset Evening Echo d
Southern Newspapers
01305-784804
Poole Advertiser wf
Advertiser Series
01202-411411
Stour Valley News wf
Southern Newspapers
01258-456067
Swanage & Wareham Adv wf
Southern Newspapers
01929-427428
West Dorset Express & Star wf
Southern Newspapers
01823-335361
Weymouth Advertiser wf
Southern Newspapers
01305-776101

COUNTY DURHAM

Chester le Street Advertiser wf
Newsquest Media Group
01325-381313
The Clarion wf
SR & VI Crane
01642-480397
Consett & Stanley Advertiser wf
Newsquest Media Group
01325-381313
Darlington Advertiser wf
Newsquest Media Group
01325-381313
Darlington & N Yorks Herald wf
Trinity International Holdings
01642-245401
Darlington & Stockton Times w
Newsquest Media Group
01325-381313
Durham Advertiser wf
Newsquest Media Group
01325-381313
Darlington, Aycliffe & Sedgfield
Advertiser wf
Newsquest Media Group
01325-381313

(Darlington) Northern Echo d
Newsquest Media Group
01325-381313
Hartlepool Mail d
Portsmouth & Sunderland Newspapers
01429-274441
Hartlepool Star wf
Portsmouth & Sunderland Newspapers
0191-417 0050
Peterlee Star wf
Portsmouth & Sunderland Newspapers
0191-417 0050
South Durham Herald wf
Trinity International Holdings
01642-245401
Teesdale Mercury w
Teesdale Mercury
01833-637140
Wear Valley Advertiser wf
Newsquest Media Group
01325-381313

ESSEX

(Basildon) Evening Echo d
Newsquest Media Group
01268-522792
Basildon Standard Recorder wf
Newsquest Media Group
01268-522792
Basildon Yellow Advertiser wf
United Provincial Newspapers
01268-522722
Braintree & Witham Times w
Newsquest Media Group
01206-761212
Braintree & Witham Yellow Ad wf
United Provincial Newspapers
01268-522722
Brentwood Gazette w
Northcliffe Newspapers Group
01277-219222
Brentwood Weekly News wf
Newsquest Media Group
01206-761212
Castlepoint Yellow Advertiser wf
United Provincial Newspapers
01268-522722
Castlepoint Recorder wf
Newsquest Media Group
01268-522792
Chelmsford Weekly News wf
Newsquest Media Group
01206-761212
Chelmsford Yellow Advertiser wf
United Provincial Newspapers
01268-522722
Clacton Coastal Express wf
Newsquest Media Group
01206-761212
Clacton & Frinton Gazette w
Newsquest Media Group
01206-761212

Colchester Evening Gazette d
Newsquest Media Group
01206-761212
Colchester Express wf
Newsquest Media Group
01206-761212
Colchester Yellow Adv wf
United Provincial Newspapers
01268-525091
Dunmow Broadcast wf
Eastern Counties Newspapers
01371-874537
Epping Forest Herald wf
Eastern Counties Newspapers
01708-766044
Epping Forest Independent wf
Newsquest Media Group
0181-531 4141
Epping Forest Recorder wf
Eastern Counties Newspapers
0181-478 4444
Epping, Ongar & District Gazette w
Newsquest
0181-531 4141
Epping Yellow Advertiser wf
United Provincial Newspapers
01268-522722
Essex Chronicle w
Northcliffe Newspapers Group
01245-262421
Essex County Standard w
Newsquest Media Group
01206-761212
Essex Weekly News wf
Newsquest Media Group
01206-761212
Frinton & Walton Gazette w
Newsquest
01206-761212
Grays Herald wf
Eastern Counties Newspapers
01708-766044
Halstead Gazette&Advertiser w
Newsquest Media Group
01206-761212
Harlow & Epping Herald wf
Eastern Counties Newspapers
01727-846866
Harlow Citizen wf
Newsquest Media Group
0181-531 4141
Harlow/Epping Star wf
Yattendon Investment Trust
01279-413401
Harwich Standard w
Newsquest Media Group
01206-761212
Loughton, Chigwell Gazette w
Newsquest
0181-531 4141

Maldon Standard w
Newsquest Media Group
01206-761212
Rayleigh Recorder wf
Newsquest Media Group
01268-522792
Rayleigh Times Group wf
Leigh Times Co
01702-77666
Redbridge Guardian w
Newsquest Media Group
0181-531 4141
Saffron Walden Observer wf
Yattendon Investment Trust
01279-757721
Saffron Walden Reporter wf
Eastern Counties Newspapers
01799-525100
Saffron Walden Weekly News wf
Yattendon Investment Trust
01223 358877
Southend on Sunday w
Leigh Times
01702-77666
Southend Standard Recorder wf
Newsquest Media Group
01268-522792
Southend Yellow Advertiser wf
United Provincial Newspapers
01268-522722
Thurrock Gazette wf
Newsquest Media Group
01268-522792
Thurrock & Lakeside Recorder wf
Eastern Counties Newspapers
01708-766044
Thurrock, Lakeside, Grays Post w
Independent Newspapers
0181-517 5577
Thurrock Yellow Advertiser wf
United Provincial Newspapers
01268-522722
Walden Local wf
Local Publications
01799-516161
Waltham Abbey Gazette w
Newsquest Media Group
0181-531 4141

GLOUCESTERSHIRE

Berkeley & Sharpness Gazette w
Southern Newspapers
01453-544000
Cheltenham & Gloucester Ind wf
Southern Newspapers
01242-519550
Cheltenham News wf
Northcliffe Newspapers
01242-526261
Chepstow & Caldicot Press w
Southern Newspapers
01453-544000

Cotswold Standard wf
Southern Newspapers
01285-642642
Dursley County Independent wf
Southern Newspapers
01453-544000
Forest of Dean Review wf
Tindle Newspapers
01594-841113
The Forester w
Forest of Dean Newspapers
01594-822126
Gloucester Independent wf
Southern Newspapers
01453-544000
Gloucester News wf
Northcliffe Newspapers Group
01452-424442
Gloucestershire Citizen d
Northcliffe Newspapers Group
01452-424442
Gloucestershire County Gazette w
Southern Newspapers
01453-544000
Gloucestershire Echo d
Northcliffe Newspapers Group
01242-526261
Stroud News & Journal w
Southern Newspapers
01453-762412
Tewkesbury Admag wf
Newsquest Media Group
01386-446544
Wilts & Gloucester Standard w
Southern Newspapers
01285-642642
Woton-under-Edge Gazette w
Southern Newspapers
01453-544000

HAMPSHIRE

Aldershot Courier series wf
Guardian Media Group
01252-28221
Aldershot Mail w
Guardian Media Group
01252-28221
Aldershot News series w
Guardian Media Group
01252-28221
Alton Gazette w
Tindle Newspapers
01420-84446
Alton Herald w
Farnham Castle Newspapers
01252-725224
Alton Times & Mail wf
Tindle Newspapers
01252-716444
Andover Advertiser w
Southern Newspapers
01264-323456

Andover Advertiser Midweek w
Southern Newspapers
01264-323456
Arlesford & District Times wf
Gazette Newspapers
01256-461131
Avon Advertiser (Hants/Dorset) w
Southern Newspapers
01722-337466
Basingstoke & N Hants Gaz. w
Southern Newspapers
01256-461131
Bordon Herald w
Farnham Castle Newspapers
01252-725224
Bordon Times & Mail wf
Tindle Newspapers
01252-716444
Eastleigh & S Hants News w
Hampshire Chronicle Group
01703-613000
Eastleigh Gazette Extra wf
Southern Newspapers
01256-461131
Fareham & Gosport Journal wf
Portsmouth & Sunderland Newspapers
01705-210105
Farnborough Courier wf
Aldershot News
01252-28221
Farnborough Mail w
Aldershot News
01252-28221
Farnborough News w
Aldershot News
01252-28221
Fleet & District Courier wf
Aldershot News
01252-28221
Fleet Mail w
Aldershot News
01252-28221
Fleet News w
Aldershot News
01252-28221
The Forest Journal w
Salisbury Journal Newspapers
01722-412525
Hampshire Chronicle w
Jacob & Johnston
01962-841772
Hart Courier Series wf
Guardian Media Group
01252-28221
Havant Journal wf
Portsmouth &Sunderland Newspapers
01705-210105
Liphook Times & Mail wf
Tindle Newspapers
01252-716444

Lymington Times w
Advertiser & Times
01425-613384
New Forest Post wf
Southern Newspapers
01590-671122
New Milton Advertiser w
Advertiser & Times
01425-613384
Petersfield Herald w
Farnham Castle Newspapers
01252-725224
Petersfield Mail wf
Tindle Newspapers
01252-716444
Petersfield & Bordon Post w
Portsmouth & Sunderland Newspapers
01730-264811
(Portsmouth) The News d
Portsmouth & Sunderland Newspapers
01705-664488
Portsmouth/Southsea Journal wf
Portsmouth & Sunderland Newspapers
01705-210105
Romsey Advertiser w
Portsmouth & Sunderland Newspapers
01794-513396
Solent Advertiser wf
Southern Newspapers
01329-280752
Southampton Advertiser wf
Southern Newspapers
01703-639211
Southern Daily Echo d
Southern Newspapers
01703-634134
Surrey & Hants Star wf
Star Newspapers (Camberley)
01252-316311
Winchester Gazette Extra wf
Southern Newspapers
01256-461131
Yately & District Courier wf
Aldershot News
01252-28221

HEREFORD & WORCS

Berrow's Worcester Journal wf
Newsquest Media Group
01905-748200
Bromsgrove/Droitwich Ad wf
Newsquest Media Group
01527-879211
B'grove/Droitwich Standard wf
Herald Observer Newspapers
01527-67714
Evesham Journal wf
Newsquest Media Group
01386-442555
Hereford & Leominster Jnl wf
Midland News Association
01432-355353

Hereford Admag wf
Adscene Group
01432-351544
Hereford Times w
Newsquest Media Group
01432-274413
Kidderminster Chronicle wf
Midland News Association
01562-829500
Kidderminster Shuttle wf
Newsquest Media Group
01562-823488
Kidderminster Why wf
Goodhead Publishing
01527-853625
Leominster Advertiser wf
Newsquest Media Group
01584-872183
Malvern Gazette w
Newsquest Media Group
01905-748200
Redditch & Bromsgrove Jnl wf
Journal Publishing
0121-693 3740
Redditch Advertiser wf
Newsquest Media Group
01384-63741
Redditch/Alcester Standard wf
Herald Observer Newspapers
01527 67714
Ross Gazette w
Ross Gazette
01989-768023
Stourport News wf
Newsquest Media Group
01299-822901
(Worcester) Evening News d
Newsquest Media Group
01905-748200
Worcester Why wf
Goodhead Publishing
01527-853625

HERTFORDSHIRE

Bishops Stortford Citizen wf
Newsquest Media Group
0181-531 4141
Bishops Stortford Herald wf
Eastern Counties Newspapers
01727-846866
Borehamwood & Radlett Adv wf
Eastern Counties Newspapers
01727-811555
Borehamwood Times wf
Newsquest Media Group
0181-203 0411
Cheshunt & Waltham Telegraph w
North London & Herts Newspapers
0181-367 2345
Harpenden Advertiser wf
Eastern Counties Newspapers
01727-811555

Hemel Hempstead Express wf
Johnston Press
01442-62311
Hemel Hempstead Gazette w
Johnston Press
01442-62311
Herts & Essex Observer w
Yattendon Investment Trust
01992-586401
Herts Mercury d
Yattendon Investment Trust
01992-586401
Herts Star wf
Yattendon Investment Trust
01992-586401
Herts Advertiser wf
Eastern Counties Newspapers
01727-811555
Hitchin Comet wf
Eastern Counties Newspapers
01462-422280
Hitchin, Letchworth Gazette w
Eastern Counties Newspapers
01462-423423
Hoddesdon Herald wf
Herald Newspaper Group
01727-846886
Lea Valley Star wf
Yattendon Investment Trust
01992-586401
Letchworth & Baldock Comet wf
Eastern Counties Newspapers
01462-422280
Letchworth & Baldock Gazette w
Eastern Counties Newspapers
01462-422280
North Herts Gazette w
Eastern Counties Newspapers
01462-422280
North London Review w
Review & Advertiser Newspaper Group
0181-953 9119
Potters Bar & Cuffley Press wf
Southnews
0181-367 2345
Potters Bar Times wf
Newsquest Media Group
0181-203 0411
Royston & Buntingford Crow w
Eastern Counties Newspapers
01799-525100
Royston Weekly News wf
Yattendon Investment Trust
01223-358877
St Albans/Harpenden Herald wf
Eastern Counties Newspapers
01727-846866
St Albans & Harpenden Obs wf
Newsquest Media Group
01727-840022
St Albans /Harpenden Review wf
Review Free Group Newspapers
01727-834411

Stevenage Comet wf
Eastern Counties Newspapers
01462-422280
Stevenage Gazette w
Eastern Counties Newspapers
01462-422280
Stevenage Leader wf
Eastern Counties Newspapers
01727-852444
Stevenage/Letchworth Herald wf
Eastern Counties Newspapers
01727-846866
Watford/Ricks'worth Review wf
Review Free Group Newspapers
01727-834411
Watford Free Observer wf
Newsquest Media Group
01923-242211
Welwyn & Hatfield Herald wf
Eastern Counties Newspapers
01727-846866
Welwyn & Hatfield Times w
Eastern Counties Newspapers
01727-811555
Welwyn Garden Review wf
Review Free Group Newspapers
01727-834411
West Herts & Watford Observer w
Newsquest Media Group
01923-242211

ISLE OF MAN
Isle of Man Courier wf
Johnston Press
01624-623451
Isle of Man Examiner w
Johnston Press
01624-623451
Manx Independent w
Johnston Press
01624-623451

ISLE OF WIGHT
Isle of Wight County Press w
Isle of Wight County Press
01983-526741

KENT
Ashford & Tenterden Adscene wf
Adscene Group
01227-767321
AshfordExtra wf
Kent Messenger
01233-623232
Canterbury Adscene wf
Adscene Group
01227-767321
Canterbury Extra wf
Kent Messenger
01227-768181

County Border News wf
Tindle Newspapers
01734-261669
Dartford/Swanley Informer wf
Local Publications
01322-220791
Dartford Leaderwf
Fletcher Newspapers
01474-354828
Dartford Times w
Fletcher Newspapers
01474-354828
Dover/Deal/S'dwich Adscene wf
Adscene Group
01227-767321
Dover Express w
Adscene Group
01227-767321
Dover Extra wf
Kent Messenger Group
01622-717880
East Kent Gazette w
Adscene Group
01227-767321
East Kent Mercury w
Kent Messenger
01233-623232
Edenbridge chronicle wf
Chronicle Newspapers
01732-865455
Faversham News w
Kent Messenger
01580-534545
Faversham Times w
Adscene Group
01795-475411
Folkestone & Hythe Adscene wf
Adscene Group
01227-767321
Folkestone & Dover Express w
Adscene Group
01227-767321
Folkestone Extra wf
Kent Messenger
01233-623232
Folkestone Herald w
Adscene Group
01323-850999
Gravesend & Dartford Extra wf
Kent Messenger
0171-404 6116
Gravesend Leader wf
Fletcher Newspapers
01474-564665
Gravesend Reporter w
Fletcher Newspapers
01474-354828
Herne Bay Gazette w
Kent Messenger
01227-372233

Herne Bay Times w
Adscene Group
01227-771515
Hythe Herald w
Adscene Kent Newspapers
01303-850999
Isle of Thanet Gazette w
Adscene Group
01843-221313
Kent & Sussex Courier w
Northcliffe Newspapers Group
01892-526262
Kent Messenger w
Kent Messenger
01622-717744
Kent Today d
Kent Messenger
01622-717880
Kentish Express w
Kent Messenger
01233-623232
Kentish Gazette w
Kent Messenger
01227-768181
Maidstone Adscene wf
Adscene Group
01227-76321
Maidstone Extra wf
Kent Messenger
01622-717744
Maidstone Weald Extra wf
Kent Messenger
01622-717744
Maidstone Star wf
Southern Newspapers
01622-678556
Medway & Disrict Adscene wf
Adscene Group
01227-767321
Medway Extra wf
Kent Messenger
01634-830600
Medway News w
Adscene Group
01634-841741
Medway Standard w
Adscene Group
01634-841741
Romney Marsh Herald w
Adscene Kent Newspapers
01303-850999
Sevenoaks Chronicle w
Northcliffe Newspapers Group
01732-451238
Sevenoaks Focus wf
Northcliffe Newspapers Group
01732-451238
Sevenoaks & Tonbridge Leader wf
Fletcher Newspapers
01474-564665

Sheerness Times Guardian w
Kent Messenger
01795-580300
Sheppey Gazette w
Adscene Group
01795-475411
Sittingbourne Extra WF
Kent Messenger
01795-580300
Thanet Adscene wf
Adscene Group
01227-767321
Thanet Extra wf
Kent Messenger
01843-593009
Thanet Times w
Adscene Group
01843-221313
Tonbridge&District Friday-Ad wf
Friday Ad Group
01732-363868
Tunbridge Wells Adscene wf
Adscene Group
01227-767321
Tunbridge Wells Extra wf
Kent Messenger
01892-544747
(Tunbridge Wells) News in Focus wf
Northcliffe Newspapers Group
01892-526262
Tunbridge Wells Friday-Ad wf
Friday Ad Group
01732-363868
Tunbridge Wells Leader wf
Fletcher Newspapers
01474-564665
Whitstable Gazette w
Kent Messenger Group
01622-717880
Whitstable Times w
Adscene Group
01227-771515

LANCASHIRE

Accrington Observer w
Guardian Media Group
01254-871444
Blackburn Citizen wf
Newsquest Media Group
01254-678678
Blackpool Citizen wf
Newsquest Media Group
01253-711921
(Blackpoo)l The Gazette d
United Provincial Newspapers
01253-839999
Burnley Citizen wf
Newsquest Media Group
01282-452131
Burnley Express & News w
United Provincial Newspapers
01282-426161

Chorley Citizen
Newsquest Media Group
01254-678678
Chorley Guardian w
United Provincial Newspapers
01257-269011
Clitheroe Advertiser & Times w
United Provincial Newspapers
01282-426161
Fleetwood Weekly News w
Tindle Newspapers
01253-772950
Fylde Extra wf
United Provincial Newspapers
01253-839999
Garstang Courier w
United Provincial Newspapers
01995-602494
The Garstang Guardian w
Lancaster & Morcambe Newspapers
01524-833111
Hyndburn Express wf
Guardian Media Group
01254-871444
Lancashire Evening Telegraph d
Newsquest Media Group
01254-67878
Lancashire Evening Post d
United Provincial Newspapers
01772-254841
Lancaster/Morcambe Citizen wf
Newsquest Media Group
01524-382121
Lancaster Guardian w
United Provincial Newspapers
01524-833111
Leyland Guardian
The Chorley Guardian
01257-264911
Longridge News w
United Provincial Newspapers
01772-783265
Lytham St Annes Express w
United Provincial Newspapers
01253-839999
The Morecambe Guardian w
Lancaster & Morcambe Newspapers
01524-833111
(Morecambe) The Visitor w
United Provincial Newspapers
01524-833111
Nelson Leader Series w
United Provincial Newspapers
01282-426161
Ormskirk Advertiser w
United Provincial Newspapers
01695-572501
Ormskirk Visiter wf
Trinity International Holdings
01704-536655

Preston Weekly Mail wf
United Provincial Newspapers
01772-201234
Preston Citizen wf
Newsquest Media Group
01772-824631
Rossendale Express wf
Guardian Media Group
01706-213311
Rossendale Free Press w
Guardian Media Group
01706-213311
Skelmersdale Advertiser w
Ormskirk Advertiser
01695-572501
Thornton Cleveleys News w
Tindle Newspapers
01253-772950

LEICESTERSHIRE

Ashby & Coalville Mail wf
Northcliffe Newspapers Group
0116-253 9539
Ashby Times w
Trident Midland Newspapers
01530-813101
Coalville/Ashby Echo wf
Echo Press
01509-232632
Coalville Extra w
Echo Press
01509-232632
Coalville Times w
Trident Midland Newspapers
01530-813101
Harborough Mail w
Adscene Group
01858-462626
Hinckley Herald & Journal wf
Midland Independent Newspapers
01455-891981
Hinckley Times w
Hinckley Times
01455-238383
Leicester Journal w
Journal Publishing Co
01332-369162
Leicester Mail wf
Northcliffe Newspapers Group
0116-253 9539
Leicester Mercury d
Northcliffe Newspapers Group
0116-251 2512
Long Eaton Advertiser w
Echo Press
0115-948 2000
Long Eaton Trader wf
Midland Independent Newspapers
0115-948 1200
Loughborough Echo w
Echo Press
01509-232632

Loughborough Echo Extra wf
Echo Press
01509-232632
Loughborough Herald & Post wf
Midland Independent Newspapers
0116-247 1000
Loughborough Mail wf
Northcliffe Newspapers Group
0116-253 9539
Market Harborough Herald wf
Midland Independent Newspapers
01604-614600
Melton Citizen wf
Johnston Press
01664-66666
Melton Times w
Adscene Group
01664-66666
N W Leicestershire Leader wf
Trident Midland Newspapers
01530-813101
Nu News w
Echo Press
01827-64222
Oadby & Wigston Mail wf
Northcliffe Newspapers Group
0116-253 3539
Rutland Times w
New Rutland Times
01572-757722
Shepshed Echo w
Echo Press
01509-232632

LINCOLNSHIRE

Alford Leader w
Mortons of Horncastle
01507-523456
Alford Standard w
Lincolnshire Standard Group
01205-311433
Boston Standard w
Adscene Group
01205-311433
Boston Target wf
Northcliffe Newspapers Group
01205-356262
Bourne Local w
Local Publications (Bourne)
01778-425876
Gainsborough Standard w
Adscene Group
01205-311433
Gainsborough Target wf
Northcliffe Newspapers Group
01427-810148
Gainsborough Trader News w
Adscene Group
01205-311433
Grantham & Melton Trader wf
Adscene Group
01909-483333

Grantham Citizen wf
Adscene Group
01476-562291
Grantham Journal w
Adscene Group
01476-562291
Horncastle News w
Mortons of Horncastle
01507-526868
Horncastle Standard series w
Adscene Group
01507-526868
Horncastle Target wf
Lincolnshire Publishing Co
01205-356262
Lincoln Chronicle w
Lincolnshire Standard Group
01205-311433
Lincolnshire Standard w
Lincolnshire Standard Group
01205-311433
Lincoln Target wf
Northcliffe Newspapers Group
01522-525252
Lincolnshire Evening Echo d
Northcliffe Newspapers Group
01522-525252
Lincolnshire Free Press w
Adscene Group
01775-725021
Louth Leader w
Mortons of Horncastle
01507-606656
Louth Standard w
Adscene Group
01205-311433
Louth Target wf
Northcliffe Newspapers Group
01472-359232
Mablethorpe & Sutton News w
Mortons of Horncastle
01507-523456
Mablethorpe & Sutton Standard s
Lincolnshire Standard Group
01205-311433
Market Rasen Mail w
Mortons of Horncastle
01652-844644
Rutland & Stamford Mercury w
Adscene Group
01780-62255
Scunthorpe Evening Tel. d
Northcliffe Newspapers Group
01724-843421
Scunthorpe Target wf
Northcliffe Newspapers Group
01724-871499
Scunthorpe Trader News wf
Adscene Group
01909-483333

Skegness News w
Mortons of Horncastle
01754-768000
Skegness Standard w
Adscene Group
01205-311433
Sleaford Herald & Express wf
Newark Advertiser
01636-643456
Sleaford Standard w
Adscene Group
01205-311433
Scunthorpe Trader News wf
Lincolnshire Standard Group
01205-311433
Skegness Target wf
Lincolnshire Standard Group
01205-311433
Spalding Guardian w
Adscene Group
01775-725021
Spilsby Standard w
Lincolnshire Standard Group
01205-311433
Spilsby Target wf
Lincolnshire Publishing Co
01205-356262
Stamford Herald wf
Midland Independent Newspapers
01775-713723
Stamford Citizen wf
Adscene Group
01780-62255
Woodhall Spa Target wf
Lincolnshire Publishing Co
01205-356262

NORTH LONDON
Barking & Dagenham Advertiser wf
United Provincial Newspapers
01268-522722
Barking & Dagenham Express wf
Independent Newspapers
0181-517 5577
Barking & Dagenham Post w
Independent Newspapers
0181-517 5577
Barking & Dagenham Recorder wf
South Essex Recorders
0181-478 4444
Barnet & Finchley Press wf
Southnews
0181-367 2345
Barnet Advertiser wf
United Provincial Newspapers
0181-449 5577
Barnet Borough Times wf
Newsquest Media Group
0181-203 0411
Brent & London Recorder wf
Tindle Newspapers
0181-568 1313

Brent Leader wf
Tindle Newspapers
0181-424 0044
Brentwood Recorder w
South Essex Recorders
01708-766044
Camden New Journal wf
New Journal Enterprises
0171-482 1960
Camden/St Pancras Chronicle w
Independent Newpapers
0181-340 6868
Central London Review & Adv
Review & Advertiser Group
0181-953 9119
Chelsea News w
Adscene Group
0181-741 1622
Chingford Guardian w
Newsquest Media Group
0181-531 4141
City of London Times w
City of London & Dockland Times
0171-606 0360
City Post w
Adscene Group
0181-741 1622
City of London Recorder w
Eastern Counties Newspapers
(Holdings)
0181-478 4444
City of Westminster Post wf
Adscene Group
0181-741 1622
Docklands Express wf
Independent Newspapers
0171-790 8822
Docklands Recorder w
South Essex Recorders
0181-472 1421
Ealing & Acton Gazette w
Southnews
0181-424 0044
Ealing & London Recorder wf
Tindle Newspapers
0181-568 1313
Ealing & Southall Informer wf
United Provincial Newspapers
01784-433773
Ealing Leader wf
Southnews
0181-424 0044
East London Advertiser w
Independent Newspapers
0171-790 8822
Edgware & Mill Hill Times wf
Newsquest Media Group
0181-203 0411
Enfield Advertiser wf
United Provincial Newspapers
0181-449 5577

Enfield Express wf
Southnews
0181-367 2345
Enfield Gazette series w
Southnews
0181-441 3003
Enfield Independent wf
Newsquest Media Group
0181-531 4141
Evening Standard d
Associated Newspapers
0171-938 6000
Finchley & Hendon Advertisers
United Provincial Newspapers
0181-449 5577
Fulham Chronicle w
Adscene Group
0181-741 1622
Greenford & Northolt Gazette w
Middlesex County Press
0181-579 3131
Hackney Echo wf
Newsquest Media Group
0171-790 8822
Hackney Gazette w
Independent Newspapers (UK)
0171-790 8822
Hammersmith Chronicle w
Adscene Group
0181-741 1622
Hammersmith/Fulham Post wf
Adscene Group
0181-741 1622
Hammersmith Guardian wf
Tindle Newspapers
0181-568 1313
Hammersmith/Fulham Times wf
Middlesex County Press
0171-381 6262
Hampstead & Highgate Express
Home Counties Newspaper Holdings
0171-433 0000
Harefield Gazette w
Middlesex County Press
0171-381 6262
Haringey Advertiser wf
United Provincial Newspapers
0181-449 5577
Haringey Independent wf
Newsquest Media Group
0181-531 4141
Haringey Weekly Herald wf
Independent Newspapers (UK)
0181-340 6868
Harrow Independent wf
Southnews
0181-424 0044
Harrow Informer wf
United Provincial Newspapers
01784-433773

Harrow Leader wf
Southnews
0181-424 4404
Harrow Observer w
Southnews
0181-424 4404
Harrow Recorder wf
Tindle Newspapers
0181-568 1313
Havering Herald wf
Eastern Counties Newspapers
01708-766044
Hayes & Harlington Gazette w
Middlesex County Press
0171-381 6262
Hendon & Finchley Times wf
Newsquest Media Group
0181-203 0411
Hornsey Journal w
Independent Newspapers (UK)
0181-340 6868
Hounslow Borough Chronicle w
Southnews
0181-424 0044
Hounslow/Chiswick Informer wf
United Provincial Newspapers
01784-433773
Hounslow Feltham Times w
Dimbleby & Sons
0181-940 6030
Hounslow & Isleworth Leader wf
Southnews
0181-424 0044
Hounslow Recorder wf
Tindle Newspapers
0181-568 1313
Ilford Herald wf
Eastern Counties Newspapers
01708-766044
Ilford Recorder w
Eastern Counties Newspapers
0181-478 4444
Ilford & Redbridge Post wf
Independent Newspapers
0181-517 5577
Ilford Yellow Advertiser
United Provincial Newspapers
01268-522722
Islington Chronicle wf
Independent Newspapers
0181-340 6868
Islington Gazette w
Independent Newspapers
0181-340 6868
Kensington & Chelsea Mail w
Middlesex County Press
0171-381 6262
Kensington & Chelsea Post wf
Adscene Group
0181-741 1622

Kensington & Chelsea Times wf
Adscene Group
0181-741 1622
Kensington News w
Adscene Group
0181-741 1622
Kilburn & Brent Advertiser w
Independent Newspapers
0181-450 5272
Kilburn Times w
Independent Newspapers
0181-568 1313
Leyton Guardian w
Newsquest Media Group
0181-531 4141
London Weekly Times wf
Southnews
0181-381 6886
London West End Extra w
New Journal Enterprises
0171-482 1960
Marylebone Mercury w
Adscene Group
0181-741 1622
Notting Hill & Bayswater Times w
Middlesex County Press
0171-381 6262
Paddington Mercury w
Adscene Group
0181-741 1622
Paddington Times w
Independent Newspapers
0181-568 1313
Putney Chronicle w
Adscene Group
0181-741 1622
Redbridge Guardian & West
 Essex Gazette w
Newsquest Media Group
0181-531 4141
Romford & Havering Post wf
Independent Newspapers
0181-517 5577
Romford Advertiser wf
United Provinicial Newspapers
01268-522722
Romford Recorder w
Home Counties Newspaper Holdings
01708-766044
Ruislip Informer wf
United Southern Publications
01784-433773
Ruislip Recorder wf
Tindle Newspapers
0181-568 1313
Southall Gazette w
Middlesex County Press
0171-381 6262
Stanmore Observer w
Middlesex County Press
0171-381 6262

Stratford & Newham Express wf
Independent Newspapers (UK)
0171-790 8822
Tottenham & Wood Green Journal w
Independent Newspapers
0181-340 6868
Uxbridge & Hillingdon Leader wf
Southnews
01859-233133
Uxbridge Gazette w
Southnews
01859-233133
Uxbridge Informer wf
United Provinicial Newspapers
01784-433773
Uxbridge & London Recorder wf
Independent Newspapers (UK)
0181-568 1313
Waltham Forest Guardian w
Newsquest Media Group
0181-531 4141
Waltham Forest Independent wf
Newsquest Media Group
0181-531 4141
Walthamstow Advertiser wf
United Provinicial Newspapers
01268-522722
Wembley & Brent Times w
Independent Newspapers (UK)
0181-568 1313
Wembley & Kenton Recorder wf
Tindle Newspapers
0181-568 1313
Wembley & Kingsbury Leader wf
Middlesex County Press
0171-381 6262
Westminster Mail w
Middlesex County Press
0171-381 6262
Westminster & Pimlico News
Adscene Group
0181-741 1622
Willesden & Brent Chronicle w
Independent Newspapers (UK)
0181-568 1313
Wood Green Herald wf
Independent Newspapers
0181-340 6868

SOUTH LONDON
Barnes, Mortlake Times w
Dimbleby & Sons
0181-940 6030
Bexley Borough Mercury wf
Trinity International Holdings
0181-692 1122
Bexley Leader wf
Fletcher Newspapers
01474-354828
Bexley News Shopper series wf
Newsquest Media Group
01689-836211

Bexleyheath Mercury wf
Newsquest Media Group
0181-692 1122
Bexleyheath/Welling Times w
Fletcher Newspapers
01474-354828
Biggin Hill News wf
Tindle Newspapers
01959-564766
Brentford, Chiswick Times
Dimbleby & Sons
0181-940 6030
Bromley, Beckenham Times w
Fletcher Newspapers
01474-354828
Bromley Borough News wf
Tindle Newspapers
01959-564766
Bromley Leader wf
Fletcher Newspapers
01474 354828
Bromley News Shopper wf
Newsquest Media Group
01689-836211
Chislehurst Times w
Kentish Times Newspapers
01474-363363
Croydon Advertiser series w
Southnews
0181-668 4111
Croydon Guardian wf
Newsquest Media Group
0181-644 4300
Croydon Post wf
Southnews
0181-668 4111
Eltham & Greenwich Times w
Kentish Times Newspapers
01474-363363
Erith & Crayford Times
Kentish Times Newspapers
01474-363363
Greenwich Borough Mercury wf
Trinity International Holdings
0181-692 1122
Kingston Guardian series wf
Newsquest Media Group
0181-644 4300
Kingston Informer wf
United Provincial Newspapers
01784-433773
Kingston, surbiton Times w
Dimbleby & Sons
0181-940 6030
Lewisham & Catford News wf
Trinity International Holdings
0181-769 4444
Lewisham Mercury wf
Newsquest Media Group
0181-692 1122

Lewisham News Shopper wf
Newsquest Media Group
01689-836211
Newham Recorder w
Eastern Counties Newspapers
(Holdings)
0181-478 4444
Newham Yellow Advertiser wf
United Provincial Newspapers
01268-522722
Orpington & Petts Wood Times
Kentish Times Newspapers
01474-363363
Putney & Wimbledon Times w
Dimbleby & Sons
0181-940 6030
Richmond Informer wf
United Provinicial Newspapers
01784-433773
Richmond/Twickenham Guardian wf
South London Guardian
0181-646 6336
Richmond/Twickenham Times w
Dimbleby & Sons
0181-940 6030
Sidcup & Bexley Mercury wf
Newsquest Media Group
0181-692 1122
Sidcup & Blackfen Times w
Kentish Times Newspapers
01474-363363
South London Press w
Trinity International Holdings
0181-769 4444
Southwark News w
Southwark News
0171-232 1639
Streatham Mercury wf
Trinity International Holdings
0181-769 4444
Streatham Guardian wf
Newsquest Media Group
0181-644 4300
Surrey Comet w
Newsquest Media Group
0181-644 4300
Sutton & Cheam Herald w
Trinity International Holdings
01737-732000
Sutton & Epsom Guardian wf
Newsquest Media Group
0181-644 2123
Teddington & Hampton Times
Dimbleby & Sons
0181-940 6030
Wandsworth/Putney Guard. wf
Newsquest Media Group
0181-644 2123
Wandsworth Borough News w
Dimbleby & Sons
0181-874 4226

Wimbledon Guardian wf
Newsquest Media Group
0181-644 4300
Woolwich/Charlton Mercury wf
Newsquest Media Group
0181-692 1122

GREATER MANCHESTER

(Ashton) The Advertiser wf
Guardian Media Group
0161-339 8200
Ashton-under-Lyne Reporter w
Regional Independent Media
0161-303 1910
Bolton Evening News d
Newsquest Media Group
01204-522345
Bolton Journal wf
Newsquest Media Group
01204-522345
Bury Journal/Messenger wf
Newsquest Media Group
0161-764 9421
Bury Times w
Newsquest Media Group
0161-764 9421
(Cheadle) District Advertiser wf
Guardian Media Group
0161-480 4491
Denton Reporter w
Regional Independent Media
0161-303 1910
Droylsden Reporter w
Regional Independent Media
0161-303 1910
East Manchester Reporter w
Regional Independent Media
0161-303 1910
Hale, Altrincham Courier w
Courier Group
01625-586140
Heywood Advertiser w
Guardian Media Group
01706-60626
High Peak Echo wf
Guardian Media Group
0161-339 8200
Horwich & Westhoughton Adv wf
The Advertiser
01204-696916
Leigh & Tyldesley Journal wf
Newsquest Media Group
01942-672241
Leigh Reporter/Golborne Star wf
Regional Independent Media
01942-603334
Manchester Evening News d
Guardian Media Group
0161-832 7200
Manchester Metro News wf
Guardian Media Group
0161-832 7000

Middleton Guardian w
Guardian Media Group
01706-354321
Middleton/Moston Express wf
Guardian Media Group
01706-354321
Mossley Reporter w
Regional Independent Media
0161-303 1910
North Cheshire Herald w
Ashton Weekly Newspapers
0161-303 1910
(Oldham) The Advertiser wf
Guardian Media Group
0161-339 8200
(Oldham) Evening Chronicle d
Hirst, Kidd & Rennie
0161-633 2121
(Oldham) Chronicle Weekend wf
Hirst, Kidd & Rennie
0161-633 2121
(Prestwich) The Advertiser wf
Guardian Media Group
0161-789 5015
Prestwich Guide w
Newsquest Media Group
0161-764 9421
Radcliffe Times w
Newsquest Media Group
0161-764 9421
Reddish Reporter wf
South Manchester Reporter
0161-446 2212
Rochdale/Heywood Express wf
Guardian Media Group
01706-354321
Rochdale Observer w
Guardian Media Group
01706-354321
Rochdale Recorder wf
Guardian Media Group
01706-354321
Sale & Altrincham Messenger wf
Newsquest Media Group
0161-908 3360
Sale & District Courier w
Courier Group
01625-586140
Salford City Reporter wf
Guardian Media Group
0161-789 5015
South Manchester Express wf
Guardian Media Group
0161-480 4491
South Manchester Reporter wf
Mortons of Horncastle
0161-446 2212
Stalybridge Reporter w
United Provinicial Newspapers
0161-303 1910
(Stockport) Express Advertiser w
Guardian Media Group
0161-480 4491

Stockport Times wf
Guardian Media Group
0161-480 4491
Stretford Messenger wf
Newsquest Media Group
0161-477 4600
West Manchester Advertiser wf
Guardian Media Group
0161-789 85015
West Manchester Echo wf
Guardian Media Group
0161-789 85015
Wigan Evening Post d
Regional Independent Media
01942-227233
Wigan Leader wf
Regional Independent Media
01942-227233
Wigan Observer w
Regional Independent Media
01942-228000
Wigan Reporter wf
Regional Independent Media
01942-228000

MERSEYSIDE

Anfield & Walton Star wf
Trinity International Holdings
0151-236 4422
Bebington News wf
Trinity International Holdings
0151-647 7111
Birkenhead News wf
Trinity International Holdings
0151-647 7111
Bootle Times wf
Trinity International Holdings
01704-536655
Crosby Herald w
Trinity International Holdings
01704-536655
Formby Times w
Trinity International Holdings
01704-536655
Heswall News wf
Trinity International Holdings
0151-647 7111
Hoylake/West Kirkby News wf
Trinity International Holdings
0151-647 7111
Huyton & Raby Star wf
Trinity International Holdings
0151-236 4422
(Liverpool) Daily Post d
Trinity International Holdings
0151-227 2000
Liverpool Echo d
Trinity International Holdings
0151-227 2000
Maghull Star wf
Trinity International Holdings
0151-236 4422

Neston News wf
Trinity International Holdings
0151-647 7111
Newton & Golborne Guardian w
Newsquest Media Group
01925-633033
Prescot Reporter wf
Regional Independent Media
01942-228000
Skelmersdale Champion wf
Champion Newspapers
01704-531302
South Liverpool Merseymart wf
Trinity International Holdings
0151-236 4422
Southport Champion wf
Champion Newspapers
01704-531302
(Southport) Midweek Visitor wf
Trinity International Holdings
01704-536655
Southport Visitor wf
Trinity International Holdings
01704-536655
St Helens Reporter wf
Regional Independent Media
01744-22285
St Helens Star wf
Newsquest Media Group
01744-611861
Wallasey News wf
Trinity International Holdings
0151-647 7111
West Derby Merseymart wf
Trinity International Holdings
0151-236 4422
Wirral Globe wf
Newsquest Media Group
0151-666 2222

NORFOLK

Dereham & Fakenham Times w
Eastern Counties Newspapers
01603-628311
Diss Express w
Johnston Press
01284-768911
Diss Mercury wf
Eastern Counties Newspapers
01603-628311
Great Yarmouth Advertiser wf
Anglia Advertiser
01493-601206
Great Yarmouth Mercury w
Eastern Counties Newspapers
01603-628311
Hunstanton,Citizen wf
Adscene Group
01533-761188
Lynn News w
Johnston Press
01533-761188

Norfolk Citizen wf
Johnston Press
01533-761188
North Norfolk News w
Eastern Counties Newspapers
01263-628311
Norwich Advertiser wf
Eastern Counties Newspapers
01603-740222
(Norwich) Eastern Daily Press d
Eastern Counties Newspapers
01603-628311
(Norwich) Evening News d
Eastern Counties Newspapers
01603-628311
Norwich Mercury wf
Eastern Counties Newspapers
01603-628311
Thetford & Brandon Times wf
Eastern Counties Newspapers
01603-628311
Thetford & Watton Times wf
Eastern Counties Newspapers
01603-628311
West Norfolk Mercury wf
Eastern Counties Newspapers
01603-628311
Wymondham Mercury wf
Eastern Counties Newspapers
01603-628311

NORTHAMPTONSHIRE

Brackley & Towcester Advertiser w
Central Counties Newspapers
01280-813434
Brackley & Towcester Post wf
Midland Independent Newspapers
01604-614600
Corby & Disrict Citizen wf
Johnston Press
01536-81111
Corby Herald & Post wf
Midland Independent Newspapers
01604-614600
Daventry Weekly Express w
Johnston Press
01327-703383
Kettering & Disrict Citizen wf
Johnston Press
01536-81111
Northamptonshire EveningTelegraph d
Johnston Press
01536-81111
Kettering Herald & Post wf
Midland Independent Newspapers
01604-614600
(Northampton) Chronicle & Echo d
Johnston Press
01604-231122
Northampton Mercury wf
01604-231122

Northants Herald & Post wf
Midland Independent Newspapers
01604-614600
Wellingborough Herald & Post wf
Midland Independent Newspapers
01604-614600
Wellingborough Citizen wf
Johnston Press
01536-81111

NORTHUMBERLAND

Berwick Advertiser w
Tweeddale Press Group
01289-306677
Berwick Gazette wf
Northeast Press
01289-308775
Hexham Courant w
CN Group
01434-602351
Morpeth Herald w
Portsmouth & Sunderland Newspapers
01670-519195
Morpeth Leader wf
Portsmouth & Sunderland Newspapers
01670-519195
News Post Leader w
Northeast Press
01670-517171
Northumberland Gazette w
Portsmouth & Sunderland Newspapers
01670-519195
Northumberland Herald wf
Trinity International Holdings
01670-517362

NOTTINGHAMSHIRE

Ashfield Chad wf
Johnston Press
01623-26262
Eastwood Advertiser w
Johnston Press
01773-713563
Hucknell & Bulwell Dispatch w
Johnston Press
0115-963 2128
Mansfield & Ashfield Obs. wf
Johnston Press
01623-655644
Mansfield Chad w
Johnston Press
01623-26262
Mansfield & Sutton Observer wf
North Notts Newspapers
01623-465555
Mansfield Weekly Post wf
Northcliffe Newspapers Group
0115-948 2000
Newark Advertiser series w
Newark Advertiser Co
01636-643456

Newark Horald & Express wf
Newark Advertiser Co
01636-643456
Newark Trader News wf
Adscene Group
01909-483333
Nottingham Evening Post d
Northcliffe Newspapers Group
0115-948 2000
Nottingham/Trent Valley Jnl wf
Journal Publishing Co
0115-948 4371
(Nottingam) Recorder wf
Nottingham Post Group
0115-948 2000
Nottingham Herald & Post wf
Midland Independent Newspapers
0115-948 1200
Nottingham Topper wf
Topper Newspapers
0115-950 6020
Nottngham Weekly Post wf
Northcliffe Newspapers Group
0115-948 2000
Retford & Worksop Times w
Northcliffe Newspapers Group
01777-702275
Retford & Bawtry Guardian wf
Johnston Press
01777-70242
Retford & Bawtry Trader wf
Adscene Group
01427-615800
(Worksop) Midweek Guardian wf
Johnston Press
01909-500500
Worksop Trader News wf
Adscene Group
01909-483333

OXFORDSHIRE

Abingdon Herald w
Oxford & County Newspapers
01865-244988
Banbury Cake wf
Bailey Group
01295-256111
Banbury Citizen wf
Johnston Press
01295-264321
Banbury Guardian w
Johnston Press
01295-264321
Bicester Advertiser w
Newsquest Media Group
01865-244988
Bicester Review wf
Johnston Press
01280-813434
Didcot Herald w
Oxford & County Newspapers
01865-244988

Henley Standard wf
Higgs and Co
01491-578676
Oxford Courier wf
Courier Newspapers (Oxford)
01235-553444
Oxford Guardian wf
Journal Pubishing Co
01926-451943
Oxford Journal wf
Courier Newspapers (Oxford)
01235-553444
Oxford Mail d
Newsquest Media Group
01865-244988
Oxford Star wf
Newsquest Media Group
01865-244988
Oxford Times w
Newsquest Media Group
01865-244988
South Oxfordshire Courier wf
Courier Newspapers (Oxford)
01235-553444
Wantage & Grove Herald w
Oxford & County Newspapers
01865-244988
Witney & W Oxon Gazette w
Newsquest Media Group
01865-244988

SHROPSHIRE

Bridgnorth Journal w
Midland News Association
01746-761411
Ludlow Advertiser w
Newsquest Media Group
01432-274413
Ludlow Journal wf
Midland News Association
01584-876311
Newport & Market Drayton Ad w
Midland News Association
01952-811500
Oswestry Advertiser w
North Wales Newspapers
01352-700022
Shrewsbury Admag wf
Adscene Group
01423-351544
Shrewsbury Chronicle w
Midland News Association
01743-363222
Shropshire Star d
Midland News Association
01952-242424
Telford Journal wf
Midland News Association
01952-242424
Whitchurch Herald w
Trinity International Holdings
01948-3971

BATH & NE SOMERSET

Bath Chronicle d
Newsquest Media Group
01225-444044
Bath & District Advertiser wf
Southern Newspapers
0117-923 1153
Bath & District Star series wf
Newsquest Media Group
01225-444044

SOMERSET

Bridgwater Mercury w
Southern Newspapers
01823-335361
Bridgwater/Burnham Times wf
Bristol United Press
01749-672430
Burnham & Highbridge News w
Southern Newspapers
01823-335361
Chard & Ilminster News w
Southern Newspapers
01823-335361
Cheddar Valley Gazette w
Newsquest Media Group
01793-528144
Mid-Somerset Gazette w
Bristol United Press
01749-672430
Norton Radstock Adv wf
Southern Newspapers
0117-923 1154
Sedgemoor Express & Star
Southern Newspapers
01823-335361
Shepton Mallet Journal w
Newsquest Media Group
01793-528144
Somerset & Avon Guardian w
Newsquest Media Group
01225-444044
Somerset & Dorset News wf
Bristol Evening Post
01935-74551
Somerset County Gazette w
Southern Newspapers
01823-335361
Somerset Standard w
Bristol United Press
01225-444044
Taunton Express & Star
Southern Newspapers
01823-335361
(Taunton) Midweek Gazette wf
Southern Newspapers
01823-335361
Wellington Weekly News w
Northcliffe Newspapers Group
01884-242500

West Somerset Free Press w
Tindle Newspapers
01984-632731
West Somerset Trader wf
Tindle Newspapers
01984-632731
Western Gazette w
Bristol Evening Post
01935-74551
Weston & Somerset Mercury w
Southern Newspapers
01934-414010
Weston & Worle News wf
Bristol Evening Post
01275-874248
Weston-Super-Mare Admag wf
Southern Newspapers
0117-923 1153
Yeovil Express & Star wf
Southern Newspapers
01823-335261

STAFFORDSHIRE

Biddulph Chroicle w
Heads (Congleton)
01260-273737
Blythe & Forsbrook Times w
Cheadle & Tean Times
01538-753162
Brownhills Advertiser w
SC Publishing
01992-721234
Burton Advertiser wf
Yattendon Investment Trust
01283-512345
Burton Daily Mail d
Yattendon Investment Trust
01283-512345
Burton Trader wf
Midland Independent Newspapers
01203-512000
Cannock Chase Chronicle wf
Midland News Association
01543-506311
Cannock Mercury wf
Adscene Group
01543-414414
Chase Post wf
Newsquest Media Group
01902-456776
Cheadle & Tean Times w
Cheadle & Tean Times
01538-399599
Cheadle & Post Times w
Hill Bros (Leek)
01538-750011
East Staffordshire Journal wf
Journal Publishing Co
01332-202532
Leek Post & Times w
Hill Bros (Leek)
01538-399599

Lichfield Chronicle wf
Midland News Association
01543-414455
Lichfield Mercury wf
Adscene Group
01543-414414
Lichfield Trader wf
Midland Independent Newspapers
01827-308000
North Staffs Advertiser wf
Northcliffe Newspapers Group
01782-271100
Rugeley Mercury w
Lichfield Mercury
01543-414414
Stafford Chronicle wf
Midland News Association
01785-54896
Stafford Post wf
Newsquest Media Group
01902-875800
Staffordshire Newsletter w
Yattendon Investment Trust
01785-257700
(Stoke) Evening Sentinel d
Northcliffe Newspaper Group
01782-289800
Tamworth Herald wf
Adscene Group Co
01827-60741
Tamworth/N Warks Times wf
Midland Independent Newspapers
01827-308000
Tamworth Post wf
Tamworth Herald
01827-848520
Tamworth Trader wf
Midland Independent Newspapers
01283-308000
Uttoxeter Advertiser w
Yattendon Investment Trust
01889-562050
Uttoxeter Echo w
Cheadle & Tean Times
01538-753162
Uttoxeter Post & Times w
Hill Bros (Leek)
01538-399599

SUFFOLK

Beccles & Bungay Journal w
Eastern Counties Newspaper Group
01603-628311
Bury Citizen wf
Johnston Press
01284-768911
Bury Free Press w
Johnston Press
01284-768911
Bury St Edmunds Mercury wf
Eastern Counties Newspapers Group
01284-755661

East Suffolk Mercury
Eastern Counties Newspapers
01473-230023
(Ipswich) E Anglian Daily Times d
Eastern Counties Newspapers
01473-230023
(Ipswich) Evening Star d
Eastern Counties Newspapers
01473-230023
Haverhill Echo w
Adscene Group
01440-703456
Haverhill Weekly News wf
Yattendon Investment Trust
01223-358877
Ipswich Advertiser wf
Anglia Advertiser
01473-611363
Lowestoft Journal w
Eastern Counties Newspapers
01603-628311
Mid Suffolk Advertiser wf
Anglia Advertiser
01473-611363
Newmarket Journal w
Johnston Press
01638-668441
Newmarket Weekly News wf
Yattendon Investment Trust
01223-358877
North Suffolk Mercury wf
Eastern Counties Newspapers
01473-230023
Stowmarket Mercury wf
Eastern Counties Newspapers
01473-230023
Sudbury Mercury wf
Eastern Counties Newspapers
01284-702588
Suffolk Advertiser wf
Anglia Advertiser
01473-611363
Suffolk Free Press w
Johnston Press
01787-75271
Waveney Advertiser wf
Anglia Advertiser
01493-601206
West Suffolk Mercury wf
Eastern Counties Newspapers Group
01284-702588

SURREY

Addlestone & Byfleet Review wf
Guardian Media Group
01483-769991
Ash Mail
Aldershot News
01252-28221
Banstead Herald
Surrey & South London Newspapers
01737-732000

Camberley & District Courier wf
Guardian Media Group
01252-28221
Camberley News w
Aldershot News
01252-28221
Caterham Mirror wf
Trinity International Holdings
01737-732000
Chobham & Windlesham News w
Surrey Advertiser
01483-755755
Cobham News & Mail w
Surrey Advertiser
01372-463553
County Border Times & Mail wf
Tindle Newspapers
01252-716444
Cranleigh Times wf
Guardian Media Group
01483-579244
Dorking Advertiser w
Trinity International Holdings
01737-732000
Epsom/Banstead Guardian wf
Newsquest Media Group
0181-644 4300
Epsom/Banstead Informer w
Southnews
0181-943 5171
Epsom & Banstead Extra wf
Trinity International Holdings
01737-732000
Epsom & Ewell Herald wf
Trinity International Holdings
01737-732000
Esher News & Mail series
Guardian Media Group
01483-571234
Farnham Herald w
Tindle Newspapers
01252-725224
Farnham Mail w
Aldershot News
01252-28221
Godalming Times wf
Guardian Media Group
01483-579244
Guildford Times wf
Guardian Media Group
01483-579244
(Haslemere) Messenger wf
PM Publications
01428-653999
Leatherhead Guardian wf
Newsquest Media Group
0181-644 4300
Leatherhead Advertiser w
Trinity International Holdings
01737-732000

Reigate & Banstead Ind. wf
Portsmouth & Sunderland Newspapers
01737-249372
Reigate & Redhill Life wf
Barrelfield Publishing
01737-218888
Staines & Egham News w
Southnews
01932-561111
Staines Informer wf
Southnews
01784-433773
Staines Leader wf
Southnews
01932-561111
Surrey & Hants News wf
Tindle Newspapers
01252-716444
Surrey Advertiser w
Guardian Media Group
01483-571234
Surrey Herald w
Southnews
01932-561111
Surrey Mirror w
Trinity International Holdings
01737-732000
Walton & Hersham News & Mail w
Surrey Advertiser
01372-463553
Walton & Weybridge Informer wf
Southnews
0181-943 5171
Walton & Weybridge Leader wf
Southnews
01932-561111
Woking Informer wf
Southnews
01784-433773
Woking News & Mail w
Guardian Media Group
01483-571234
Woking Review wf
Guardian Media Group
01483-769991

EAST SUSSEX

Bexhill Adnews wf
Johnston Press
01424-854242
Bexhill Observer w
Johnston Press
01424-854242
(Brighton) Evening Argus d
Newsquest Media Group
01273-544544
Brighton & Hove Leader wf
Newsquest Media Group
01273-544544
Brighton Friday-Ad wf
Friday-Ad Group
01825-766000

Eastbourne Advertiser wf
Johnston Press
01323-722091
Eastbourne Gazette w
Johnston Press
01323-722091
Eastbourne Herald w
Johnston Press
01323-722091
Hailsham Gazette w
Johnston Press
01323-722091
Hastings Observer w
Johnston Press
01424-854242
Hastings Friday-Ad wf
Friday-Ad Group
01825-766000
Hastings News wf
Johnston Press
01424-854242
Rye & Battle Observer w
Johnston Press
01424-854242
Seaford Friday-Ad wf
Friday-Ad Group
01825-766000
Seaford Gazette w
Johnston Press
01323-722091
South Coast Leader wf
Newsquest Media Group
01273-544544
Sussex Express & Herald w
Johnston Press
01273-480601
Uckfield Friday-Ad wf
Friday Ad Group
01825-766000

WEST SUSSEX

Bognor Regis Journal wf
Portsmouth & Sunderland Newspapers
01243-533660
Bognor Regis Observer wf
Portsmouth &Sunderland Newspapers
01243-533660
Burgess Hill Leader wf
Newsquest Media Group
01273-54454
Chichester Journal wf
Portsmouth & Sunderland Newspapers
01243-533660
Chichester Observer w
Portsmouth & Sunderland Newspapers
01243-533660
Crawley News
Trinity International Holdings
01293-534933
Crawley News Extra
Trinity International Holdings
01293-534933

Crawley Observer w
Johnston Press
01293-562929
Crawley Weekend Herald wf
Johnston Press
01293-562929
East Grinstead Courier w
Northcliffe Newspapers Group
01892-526262
East Grinstead Observer wf
Trinity International Holdings
01342-324333
Haywards Heath Friday-Ad wf
Friday-Ad Group
01825-766000
Haywards Heath Leader wf
Newsquest Media Group
01273-544544
Horley Life wf
Horley Publishing
01293-820494
Horsham Advertiser wf
Johnston Press
01403-253371
Lancing Herald w
TR Beckett
01903-230051
Littlehampton Guardian wf
Johnston Press
01903-209025
Littlehampton Gazette w
Johnston Press
01903-230051
Mid-Sussex Citizen/Times
Johnston Press
01444-452201
Shoreham Guardian wf
Johnston Press
01903-209025
Shoreham Herald w
Johnston Press
01903-230051
Steyning Herald w
TR Beckett
01903-230051
West Sussex County Times w
Johnston Press
01403-253371
West Sussex Gazette w
Portsmouth & Sunderland Newspapers
01903-882201
Worthing Advertiser wf
Johnston Press
01903-209025
Worthing Guardian wf
Johnston Press
01903-209025
Worthing Herald w
Johnston Press
01903-209025

TYNE & WEAR

Gateshead Post w
Trinity International
0191-232 7500
Houghton Star wf
Portsmouth & Sunderland Newspapers
0191-417 0050
(Newcastle) Evening Chronicle d
Trinity International Holdings
0191-232 7500
(Newcastle) The Journal d
Trinity International Holdings
0191-232 7500
Newcastle Herald & Post wf
Trinity International Holdings
0191-232 7500
(Newcastle) Sunday Sun w
Trinity International Holdings
0191-232 7500
News Guardian w
Northeast Press
0191-251 8484
North Tyneside Guardian wf
Portsmouth & Sunderland Newspapers
01670-519195
North Tyneside Herald & Post wf
Trinity International Holdings
01670-517362
Seaham Star wf
Portsmouth & Sunderland Newspapers
0191-417 0050
(S Shields) The Gazette d
Portsmouth & Sunderland Newspapers
0191-455 4661
South Tyne Star wf
Portsmouth & Sunderland Newspapers
0191-417 0050
S Tyneside Herald & Post wf
Trinity International
0191-427 1511
Sunderland Echo d
Portsmouth & Sunderland Newspapers
0191-534 3011
Sunderland Star wf
Portsmouth & Sunderland Newspapers
0191-417 0050
Washington Star wf
Portsmouth & Sunderland Newspapers
0191-417 0050

WARWICKSHIRE

Atherstone Herald w
Tamworth Herald Co
01827-848586
Bedworth Echo w
Midland Independent Newspapers
01203-312785
Coleshill Herald w
Tamworth Herald Co
01827-848586

Kenilworth Weekly News w
Johnston Press
01926-888222
Leamington Review wf
Johnston Press
01926-888222
Leamington Spa Courier w
Johnston Press
01926-888222
Leamington Spa Observer wf
Herald Observer Newspapers
01827-64222
(Nuneaton) Heartland Evening News d
Nuneaton & Disrict Newspapers
01203-353534
Nuneaton Tribune wf
Midland Independent Newspapers
01203-351111
Rugby Advertiser w
Adscene Group
01788-535363
Rugby Gazette wf
Journal Publishing
01926-450405
Rugby Observer wf
Herald Observer Newspapers
01827-64222
Rugby Review wf
Adscene Group
01788-546677
Stratford Gazette wf
Journal Publishing
01926-831338
Stratford-Upon-Avon Herald w
George Boyden & Son
01789-266261
Stratford Midweek wf
George Boyden & Son
01789-266261
Stratford Observer wf
Herald Observer Newspapers
01827-64222
Stratford Standard wf
Herald Observer Newspapers
01527-67714
Warwick Courier w
Central Counties Newspapers
01926-888222

WEST MIDLANDS

(Birmingham) Evening Mail d
Midland Independent Newspapers
0121-236 3366
Birmingham Metronews wf
Midland Independent Newspapers
0121-455 7877
Birmingham News wf
Midland Independent Newspapers
0121-626 6600
The Birmingham Post d
Midland Independent Newspapers
0121-236 3366

(Birmingham) Sunday Mercury w
Midland Independent Newspapers
0121-236 3366
Bloxwich Advertiser w
SC Pubishing
01922-721234
County Chronicle wf
Midland News Association
01902-313131
Coventry & Warks. Journal wf
Journal Publishing Co
01926-886388
Coventry Citizen wf
Midland Independent Newspapers
01203-633633
Coventry Evening Telegraph d
Midland Independent Newspapers
01203-633633
Dudley Chronicle wf
Midland News Association
01384-242424
Dudley News wf
Newsquest Media Group
01384-374321
The Express & Star d
Midland News Association
01902-313131
Falcon Lodge Observer w
SC Publishing
0121-355 6901
Great Barr Chronicle wf
Midland News Association
0121-553 7171
Great Barr Observer wf
Adscene Group
01827-64222
Halesowen Chronicle wf
Midland News Association
01384-242424
Halesowen News wf
Newsquest Media Group
01384-374321
Little Aston Observer w
SC Publishing
0121-355 6901
Sandwell Chronicle wf
Midland News Association
0121-553 7171
Solihull Journal wf
Journal Publishing Co
0121-693 5740
Solihull News wf
Midland Independent Newspapers
0121-626 6600
Solihull Times wf
Midland Independent Newspapers
0121-711 4777
Stourbridge Chronicle wf
Midland News Association
01384-370821

Stourbridge News wf
Newsquest Media Group
01384-374321
Sutton/Great Barr Obs wf
Adscene Group
01827-64222
Sutton Coldfield News wf
Midland Independent Newspapers
0121-626 6600
Sutton Coldfield Observer wf
Adscene Group
01827-64222
Sutton Coldfield Times wf
Journal Publishing Co
01827-64222
Vesey Observer w
SC Publishing
0121-355 6901
Walmley Observer
SC Publishing
0121-355 6901
Walsall Advertiser wf
SC Publishing
01827-64222
Walsall Chronicle wf
Midland News Association
01922-644644
Walsall Observer wf
Midland Independent Newspapers
0121-626 6600
News of Willenhall, Wednesbury wf
Midland Independent Newspapers
01902-870447
Wolverhampton Chronicle wf
Midland News Association
01902-313131

WILTSHIRE
Amesbury Journal w
Salisbury Journal Newspapers
01722-412525
Calne Gazette & Herald w
Newsquest Media Group
01793-528144
Chippenham Gazette & Herald w
Newsquest Media Group
01793-528144
Chippenham News w
Newsquest Media Group
01793-528144
Devizes Gazette & Herald w
Newsquest Media Group
01793-528144
Devizes News wf
Southern Newspapers
01380-729001
Devizes Star wf
Newsquest Media Group
01793-528144
Kennet Star wf
Newsquest Media Group
01793-528144

Marlborough Pewsey Gazette w
Newsquest Media Group
01793-528144
Marlborough Times w
Southern Newspapers
01285-642642
Melksham Indepndent News wf
Wiltshire Publications
01225-704761
North & West Wilts Star wf
Newsquest Media Group
01793 528144
Salisbury Journal w
Southern Newspapers
01722-412525
Salisbury Times w
Southern Newspapers
01722-412525
Salisbury Advertiser wf
Southern Newspapers
01722-337466
(Swindon) Evening Advertiser d
Newsquest Media Group
01793-528144
Swindon Messenger wf
Southern Newspapers
01793-511011
Swindon Star wf
Newsquest Media Group
01793-528144
Trowbridge/Melksham Adv wf
Eastern Counties Newspapers Group
01225-460556
Warminster Journal w
Coates & Parker
01985-213030
West Wiltshire Advertiser wf
Eastern Counties Newspapers
01225-760945
Westbury/Warminster Adv wf
Eastern Counties Newspapers Group
01225-460556
Wiltshire Gazette & Herald w
Newsquest Media Group
01793-528144
Wiltshire Star wf
Newsquest Media Group
01793-528144
Wiltshire Times w
Newsquest Media Group
01225-777292

EAST YORKSHIRE
Beverley Advertiser wf
Northcliffe Newspapers Group
01482-327111
Beverley Guardian wf
Johnston Press
01377-253213
Bridlington Free Press w
Johnston Press
01262-606606

Bridlington Leader wf
Johnston Press
01723-363636
Driffield Times w
Johnston Press
01377-43213
Goole HowdenThorne Courier wf
Johnston Press
01302-322144
Goole Times & Chronicle w
Chronicle Publications
01405-720110
Grimsby Evening Telegraph d
Northcliffe Newspapers Group
01472-359232
Grimsby Target wf
Northcliffe Newspapers Group
01472-359232
Haltemprice Advertiser wf
Northcliffe Newspapers Group
01482-327111
Holderness Advertiser wf
Northcliffe Newspapers Group
01482-327111
Holderness Gazette w
Holderness Newspapers
01964-612777
Hornsea Gazette w
Holderness Newspapers
01964-612777
Hull Advertiser series wf
Northcliffe Newspapers Group
01482-327111
Hull Daily Mail d
Northcliffe Newspapers Group
01428-327111
Wolds Weekly Trading Post wf
Johnston Press
01377-253213

NORTH YORKSHIRE
Cleveland Clarion wf
SR & VI Crane
01642-480397
Craven Herald & Pioneer w
Newsquest Media Group
01756-792577
Craven & Wharfedale Midweek wf
Newsquest Media Group
01274-729111
Easingwold Weekly News w
GH Smith
01347-821329
East Cleveland Herald & Post wf
Trinity International
01642-245401
Filey & Hunmanby Mercury w
Adscene Group
01723-363636
The Gazette & Herald
York & County Press
01904-653051

Harrogate Advertiser w
Regional Independent Media
01423-564321
Harrogate Herald wf
Regional Independent Media
01423-564321
Knaresborough Post
Regional Independent Media
01423-564321
(Middlesbrough) Evening Gazette d
Trinity International Holdings
01642-245401
Middlesbrough Herald & Post wf
Trinity International Holdings
01642-242222
North Yorkshire Advertiser wf
Newquest Media Group
01325-381313
North Yorkshire News wf
Regional Independent Media
01609-776451
North Yorkshire Star wf
Newsquest Media Group
01325-381313
Northallerton Times w
Regional Independent Media
01423-530033
Pateley Bridge Herald w
Regional Independent Media
01423-564321
Ripon Gazette w
Regional Independent Media
01423-564321
Ryedale Mercury w
Johnston Press
01723-363636
Ryedale Star wf
Newsquest Media Group
01904-653051
Scarborough Evening News d
Johnston Press
01723-363636
Scarborough) The Mercury w
Johnston Press
01723-363636
Selby Chronicle wf
Johnston Press
01924-357111
Selby Star wf
Newsquest Media Group
01904-653051
Selby Times w
Johnston Press
01924-357111
Stockton Herald & Post wf
Trinity International Holdings
01642-245401
Whitby Gazette w
Adscene Group
01947-602836

SOUTH YORKSHIRE

Axholme Herald w
Northcliffe Newspapers Group
01427-874417
Barnsley Chronicle w
Barnsley Chronicle
01226-734734
Barnsley Independent wf
Barnsley Chronicle
01226-734734
Barnsley Star d
Sheffield Newspapers
0114-276 7676
Dearne Valley Weekender wf
Garnett Dickinson Publishing
01709-571111
Dinnington Guardian wf
Johnston Press
01909-500500
Dinnington Trader News wf
Adscene Group
01909-565200
Doncaster Advertiser wf
Johnston Press
01302-366843
Doncaster Courier wf
Johnston Press
01302-322144
Doncaster Free Press w
Johnston Press
01302-322144
Doncaster Star d
Sheffield Newspapers
0114-276 7676
Epworth Bells Advertiser w
Adscene Group
01205-311433
Rotherham Advertiser w
Garnett Dickinson Publishing
01709-364721
Rotherham Record wf
Garnett Dickinson Publishing
01709-364721
Rotherham Star d
United News & Media
0114-276 7676
Sheffield Journal wf
Goodhead Publishing
0114-275 3377
Sheffield Mercury w
Sheffield Mercury Newspapers
0114-237 5995
Sheffield Telegraph w
Regional Independent Media
0114-275 4896
(Sheffield) The Star d
Regional Independent Media
0114-276 7676
Sheffield Trader wf
Barnsley Chronicle
0114-288 7206

Sheffield Weekly Gazette wf
Regional Independent Media
0114-275 1753
South Yorkshire Times w
Johnston Press
01924-375111

WEST YORKSHIRE

Aire Valley Target w
Newsquest Media Group
01274-729511
Batley News w
Regional Independent Media
01924-472121
Birstall News w
The Reporter
01924-468282
Bradford Star wf
Newsquest Media Group
01274-729511
(Bradford) Telegraph & Argus d
Newsquest Media Group
01274-729511
Brighouse Echo w
Johnston Press
01484-721911
Calderdale News wf
Johnston Press
01422-359932
Colne Valley Chronicle w
Express & Chronicle
01484-684011
Dewsbury Reporter w
Regional Independent Media
01924-468282
(Dewsbury) The Weekly Adv wf
Regional Independent Media
01924-468282
(Halifax) Evening Courier d
Johnston Press
01422-365711
Hebden Bridge Times w
Johnston Press
01422-365711
Hemsworth Express wf
Johnston Press
01924-375111
Holme Valley Express w
Express & Chronicle
01484-684011
Huddersfield Daily Examiner d
Trinity International Holdings
01484-430000
Huddersfield Express Chron w
Trinity International Holdings
01484-537444
Huddersfield Weekly News wf
Trinity International Holdings
01484-430000
Ilkley Gazette w
Newsquest Media Group
01532-388787

Keighley News w
Newsquest Media Group
01535-606611
Leeds Skyrack Express wf
Johnston Press
01924-375111
Leeds Weekly News wf
Regional Independent Media
0113-238 8507
Mirfield Reporter w
The Reporter
01924-468282
Morley Advertiser w
Johnston Press
01924-375111
Morley Observer w
Regional Independent Media
01924-468282
Normanton Advertiser wf
Normanton Advertiser
01924-892117
Ossett & Horury Observer wf
Johnston Press
01924-375111
Pontefract Express w
Johnston Press
01924-375111
Pontefract Weekend Times wf
Johnston Press
01924-375111
Pudsey Times wf
Regional Independent Media
01423-564321
Spenborough Guardian w
Regional Independent Media
01274-874635
Todmorden News w
Johnston Press
01706-815231
Wakefield Express w
Johnston Press
01924-357111
(Wakefield) Midweek Extra wf
Johnston Press
01924-357111
Weekend Times wf
Yorkshire Weekly Newspapers
01924-375111
Wetherby Advertiser wf
Four Counties Newspapers
01904-639136
Wetherby News w
Regional Independent Media
01423-564321
Wharfe Valley Times wf
Regional Independent Media
01423-564321
Wharfedale Observer w
Newsquest Media Group
01943-465555

YORK
York Advertiser wf
Adscene Group
01909-639136
York Star wf
Newsquest Media Group
01904-653051
Yorkshire Coast Leader wf
Adscene Group
01723-363636
Yorkshire Evening Post d
Regional Independent Media
0113-243 2701
Yorkshire Evening Press d
Newsquest Media Group
01904-653051
Yorkshire Gazette & Herald w
Newsquest Media Group
01904-653051
Yorkshire Post d
Regional Independent Media
0113-243 2701

WALES

BLAENAU GWENT
Gwent Gazette w
Trinity International Holdings
01222-583532
North Gwent Campaign wf
Regional Independent Media
01222-851100

COUNTY OF BRIDGEND
Bridgend Recorder wf
Recorder (Wales)
01656-669330
Bridgend & Ogwr Post wf
Trinity International Holdings
01222-583583
Glamorgan Gazette w
Trinity International Holdings
01222-583583

COUNTY OF CAERPHILLY
Blackwood & Risca News wf
01633-810000
Blackwood Campaign wf
01222-851100
Caerphilly Campaign wf
All three are Southern Newspapers
01222-851100

CARDIFF
Cardiff Post wf
Trinity International Holdings
01222-583583
(Cardiff) South Wales Echo d
Trinity International Holdings
01222-583532
(Cardiff) Western Mail d

Trinity International Holdings
01222-583583
Wales on Sunday
Trinity International Holdings
01222-223333

CARMARTHENSHIRE
Burry Port Star
Northcliffe Newspapers Group
01792-650841
Carmarthen Citizen wf
Northcliffe Newspapers Group
01267-221234
Carmarthen Journal w
Northcliffe Newspapers Group
01267-221234
Llanelli Star w
Northcliffe Newspapers Group
01554-774809
South Wales Guardian w
Regional Independent Media
01269-592074

CEREDIGION
Cambrian News w
Cambrian News
01970-611611
Cardigan Advertiser w
Southern Newspapers
01239-612513

COUNTY OF CONWY
Abergele Visitor w
Trinity International Holdings
01745-832230
Caernarfon Herald w
Trinity International Holdings
01286-671111
Lladudno Advertiser wf
Trinity International Holdings
01492-584321
(North Wales) The Pioneer wf
North Wales Newspapers
01352-700022
North Wales Weekly News w
Trinity International Holdings
01492-584321

DENBIGHSHIRE
Corwen Times w
County Press
01678-520262
Denbighshire Free Press w
North Wales Newspapers
01352-700022
Rhyl/Prestatyn Journal wf
North Wales Newspapers
01745-343515
Rhyl & Prestatyn Visitor wf
Trinity International Holdings
01745-344444

FLINTSHIRE
The Chroncile
Trinity International Holdings
01244-340151
Flintshire Herald & Post wf
01244-340151
Flintshire Leader wf
North Wales Newspapers
01352-700022

VALE OF GLAMORGAN
Barry& District News w
Southern Newspapers
01495-751133
Barry Gem wf
Tindle Newspapers
01446-774484
Cowbridge Gem wf
Tindle Newspapers
01446-774484
Glamorgan Gem wf
Tindle Newspapers
01446-774484
Llantwit Major Gem wf
Tindle Newspapers
01446-774484
Penarth Times w
Southern Newspapers
01222-707234
Vale Post wf
Trinity International Holdings
01222-583550

GWENT
Blackwood & Risca News wf
Southern Newspapers
01633-810000

GWYNEDD
Anglesey Chronicle wf
North Wales Newspapers
01248-352051
Bangor Mail wf
Trinity International Holdings
01286-671111
Y Cyfnod w
The County Press
01248-352051
Y Cymro w
North Wales Newspapers
01352-700022
Y Dydd
The County Press
01248-352051
Yr Herald w
Trinity International Holdings
01286-671111
Merioneth Express w
The County Press
01678-520262
North Wales Chronicle wf
North Wales Newspapers
01352-700022

ISLE OF ANGLESEY
Bangor & Caernarfon Chronicle wf
Trinity International Holdings
01248-352051
Holyhead Mail w
01286-671111

COUNTY OF MERTHYR
Merthyr Express w
01222-583532
Merthyr Campaign wf
Southern Newspapers
01222-851100
Merthyr Tydfil wf
Campaign Free Newspapers
01222-851100

MONMOUTHSHIRE
Abergavenny Chronicle w
Tindle Newspapers
01873-852187
Chepstow News wf
Southnews
01633-810000
Mon & Abergavenny News wf
Southnews
01633-810000
Monmouthshire Beacon w
Tindle Newspapers
01600-712142

NEATH/PORT TALOT
Neath & Port Talbot Guardian wf
Trinity International Holdings
01222-583583

COUNTY OF NEWPORT
South Wales Argus d
Southern Newspapers
01633-810000
Newport Free Press wf
Southern Newspapers
01453-751133
Newport News wf
Southnews
01633-810000

PEMBROKESHIRE
County Echo &St Davids Chronicle w
County Echo Newspapers
01348-874445
Fishguard County Echo w
Tindle Newspapers
01348-874445
Narberth & Whitland Obs w
Tindle Newspapers
01834-843262
Western Telegraph w
Southnews
01437-763133
Tenby Observer w
Tindle Newspapers
01834-84326

POWYS
Brecon & Radnor Express w
Powys Newspapers
01874-622932
Mid Wales Journal w
Midland News Association
01584-876311
(Welshpool) County Times w
North Wales Newspapers
01352-700022

RHONDDA CYNON TAFF
Cynon Valley Leader w
Trinity International Holdings
01222-583532
Pontypridd Campaign wf
Southern Newspapers
01222-851100
Pontypridd Observer w
Trinity International Holdings
01222-583532
Rhondda Campaign wf
Southnews
01222-851100
Rhondda Leader w
Trinity International Holdings
01222-583532

COUNTY OF SWANSEA
South Wales Evening Post d
Northcliffe Newspapers Group
01792-650841
Swansea Herald of Wales wf
Northcliffe Newspapers Group
01792-468833
Y Tyst w
John Penry Press
01792-652092

TORFAEN
Cwmbran & Pontypool News wf
Southnews
01633-810000
Cwmbran Free Press wf
Southern Newspapers
01495-751133
Pontypool & District Press w
Southern Newspapers
01495-751133

COUNTY OF WREXHAM
(Wrexham) Evening Leader d
North Wales Newspapers
01978-355151
Wrexham Leader wf
North Wales Newspapers
01978-355151

SCOTLAND

CITY OF ABERDEEN
Aberdeen & District Independent wf
Aberdeen & District Independent
01224-618300
(Aberdeen) Evening Express d
Northcliffe Newspaper Group
01224-690222
Aberdeen Herald & Post wf
Trinity International
01224-631872
(Aberdeen) Press & Journal d
Northcliffe Newspaper Group
01224-690222
Deeside Piper w
Angus County Press
01307-464899
Donside Piper & Herlad w
Angus County Press
01307-464899
Ellon & District Advertiser w
W Peters & Son
01888-56389
Ellon Times w
Eastern Counties Newspapers Group
01779-472017
Inverurie Advertiser w
W Peters & Son
01888-56389
Inverurie Herald w
Angus County Press
01307-464899

ABERDEENSHIRE
Banffshire Advertiser w
J & M Publishing
01542-832265
Banffshire Journal w
Scottish Provincial Press
01343-548777
Buchan Observer w
Eastern Counties Newspapers Group
01779-472017
Ellon Times w
Eastern Counties Newspaper Group
01779-472017
Fraserburgh Herald w
Eastern Counties Newspapers Group
01779-472017
Huntly Express w
J & M Publishing
01466-793622
Kincardineshire Observer w
Montrose Review Press
01561-377283
Mearns Leader w
Montrose Review Press
01569-762139
Turriff & District Advertiser w
W Peters & Son
01888-56389

ANGUS
Arbroath Herald w
The Herald Press
01241-872274
Brechin Advertiser w
Angus County Press
01307-464899
Forfar Dispatch w
Angus County Press
01307-464899
Kirriemuir Herald w
Angus County Press
01307-464899
Montrose/Brechin Review w
Montrose Review Press
01674-672605

ARGYLL & BUTE
The Buteman w
Bute Newspapers
01700-502931
Campbeltown Courier w
Oban Times
01586-554646
Dunoon Observer w
E & R Inglis
01369-703218
Helensburgh Advertiser w
Clyde & Forth Press
01436-673434
Oban Times w
Oban Times
01631-563058

AYRSHIRE EAST
Cumnock Chronicle w
Clyde & Forth Press
01294-464321
Kilmarnock Leader wf
Eastern Counties Newspapers
01292-611666
Kilmarnock Standard w
Trinity International Holdings
01294-78312

AYRSHIRE NORTH
Ardrossan/Saltcoats Herald w
Clyde & Forth Press
01294-464321
Ardrossan/Saltcoats Herald w
Clyde & Forth Press
01294-464321
Arran Banner w
Arran Banner Printing & Publishing
01770-302142
Clyde Weely News wf
Trinity International Holdings
01389-742299
Garnock Valley Herald w
Clyde & Forth Press
01383-728201
Irvine Herald w
01294-78312

Irvine Leader
Easter Counties Newspapers Group
01292-611666
Irvine Times
Clyde & Forth Press
01294-464321
Largs Weekly News w
Clyde & Forth Press
01294-464321
North Ayrshire Leader wf
Eastern Counties Newspapers Group
01292-611666
North Ayrshire World wf
Trinity International Holdings
0141-353 3366

AYRSHIRE SOUTH
Ayr Advertiser w
Clyde & Forth Press
01292-267631
Ayr Leader wf
Community Leader
01292-611666
Ayrshire Post w
Trinity International Holdings
01292-261111
Ayrshire World wf
Trinity International Holdings
01292-261111
Carrick Herald w
Clyde & Forth Press
01383-728201
Troon & Prestwick Times
Clyde & Forth Press
01383-728201

BORDERS
Berwickshire News w
Tweeddale Press Group
01289-306677
Berwick & Borders Gazette wf
Portsmouth & Sunderland Newspapers
01670-516066
Border Telegraph w
D & J Croal
01896-759395
Hawick News w
Hawick News
01450-372204
Peebles Times wf
Scottish County Press
0131-663 2404
Peeblesshire News w
D & J Croal
01896-58395
Selkirk Weekend Advertiser w
Portsmouth & Sunderland Newspapers
01670-516066
Southern Reporter w
The Tweeddale Press Group
01750-21581

DUMBARTON/C'BANK

Clydebank Post w
Clyde & Forth Press
0141-952 1345
Dumbarton Lennox Herald w
Scottish & Universal
0141-353 3366
Dumbarton Reporter w
Clyde & Forth Press
01436-673434

DUMFRIES & GALLOWAY

Annandale Herald w
Dumfriesshire Newspapers Group
01461-202078
Annandale Observer w
Dumfriesshire Newspapers Group
01461-202078
Carrick Gazette w
The Galloway Gazette
01465-712688
Dumfries Courier wf
Dumfriesshire Newspapers Group
01461-202078
Dumfries & Galloway Std w
Trinity International Holdings
01387-253123
Eskdale & Liddesdale Ad. w
Eskdale & Liddesdale Newspapers
013873-80066
Galloway Gazette w
Galloway Gazette
01671-402503
Galloway News w
Trinity International Holdings
01387-253123
Moffat News w
Dumfriesshire Newspapers Group
01461-202078
Stornoway Gazette w
Stornoway Gazette
01671-402503
Wigtown Free Press w
Wigtown Free Press
01776-702551

CITY OF DUNDEE

Broughty& Carnoustie Gazette w
The Herald Press
01241-872274
(Dundee) Courier & Advertiser d
DC Thomson
01382-223131
(Dundee) Evening Telegraph d
DC Thomson
01382-223131
(Dundee) The Sunday Post w
DC Thomson
01382-223131
(Dundee) Sporting Post w
DC Thomson
01382-223131

CITY OF EDINBURGH

Edinburgh Herald & Post wf
Barclay Bros/Ellerman
0131-228 5042
(Edinburgh) Evening News d
Barclay Bros/Ellerman
0131-225 2468
(E'burgh) Scotland on Sunday w
The Scotsman Publications
0131-225 2468
(Edinburgh) The Scotsman d
Barclay Bros/Ellerman
0131-225 2468
Lothian Times w
Scottish County Press
0131-663 2404

FALKIRK

Falkirk Advertiser wf
Johnston Press
01324 485028
Falkirk Herald w
Johnston Press
01324-624959

FIFE

Central Fife Times w
Dunfermline Press
01383-728201
Clyde Post wf
Clyde & Forth Press
01475-726511
Dunfermline Herald & Post wf
Barclay Bros/Ellerman
01383-621818
Dunfermline Press w
Dunfermline Press
01383-728201
East Fife Mail w
Johnston Press
01592-261451
Fife Advertiser wf
Johnston Press
01592-261451
Fife Free Press w
Johnston Press
01592-261451
Fife Heraldr w
Strachan & Livingston
01592-261451
Fife & Kinross Extra wf
Dunfermline Press
01383-728201
Fife Leader wf
01592-261451
Glenrothes Gazette w
01592-261451
Greenock Telegraph d
Clyde & Forth Press
01475-722205
St Andrews Citizen w
Johnston Press
01592-261451

CITY OF GLASGOW

Barrhead News w
Clyde & Forth Press
0141-889 8873
Bearsden Milngavie Courier w
Community Media
0141-427 7878
Cumbernauld Advertiser wf
Johnston Press
01236-725578
Cumbernauld News w
Johnston Press
01236-725578
East End Independent wf
East End Independent
0141-550 2220
East Kilbride News w
Trinity International Holdings
01355-266000
East Kilbride World wf
Trinity International Holdings
01698-283200
(Glasgow) Daily Record d
Scottish Daily Record and Sunday Mail
0141-248 7000
(Glasgow) Evening Times d
Caledonian Publishing
0141-552 6255
(Glasgow) The Herald d
Caledonian Publishing
0141-552 6533
Glasgow South Extra wf
Eastern Counties Newspapers
0141-427 0519
(Glasgow) Sunday Mail w
Mirror Group Newspapers
0141-248 7000
The Glaswegian wf
Mirror Group Newspapers
0141-242 3600
Kirkintilloch Herald w
Johnston Press
0141-775 0040
Milngavie & Bearsden Herald w
Johnston Press
0141-775 0040
Rutherglen Reformer w
Trinity International Holdings
0141-647 2271
Sunday Post
DC Thomspm w
01382-223131
Weekly News w
DC Thomspm w
01382-223131

HIGHLANDS

Caithness Courier w
Scottish Provincial Press
01955-602424
Fort William Extra wf
Oban Times
01397-703003

Highland News w
Scottish Provincial Press
01463-710999
Inverness Courier w
01463-233059
Inverness Herald wf
01463-710999
John O'Groats Journal w
01955-602424
Lochaber News w
Preceding four Scottish Provincial Press
01463-710999
Nairnshire Telegraph w
Nairnshire Telegraph
01667-453258
North Star w
01463-710999
Northern Times w
01408-633993
Ross-shire Herald wf
01463-710999
Ross-shire Journal w
01349-863436
Strathspey/Badenoch Herald w
Preceding five Scottish Provincial Press
01343-548777
West Highland Free Press w
West Highland Publishing
01471-822464

LANARKSHIRE NORTH
Airdrie & Coatbridge Advertiser w
Trinity International Holdings
01236-748048
Airdrie & Coatbridge World wf
Trinity International Holdings
01698-283200
Bellshill speaker w
D MacLeod
0141-775 0040
Carluke Gazette w
Johnston Press
01324-624959
Hamilton Advertiser w
Trinity International Holdings
01698-283200
Hamilton People wf
Eastern Counties Newspapers
01698-261321
Hamilton World wf
Trinity International Holdings
01698-283200
Lanarkshire People wf
Community Media
01698-261321
Lanarkshire World wf
Scottish & Universal
01698-283200
Motherwell People wf
Eastern Counties Newspapers
01698-261321

Motherwell Times w
Johnston Press
01698-264611
Wishaw Press w
Trinity International Holdings
01698-373111
Wishaw World wf
Trinity International Holdings
01698-283200

LANARKSHIRE SOUTH
Lanark Gazette w
Johnston Press
01324-624959

EAST LOTHIAN
East Lothian Courier w
D & J Croal
01620 822451
East Lothian News w
Scottish County Press
0131-663 2404
East Lothian Times wf
Scottish County Press
0131-663 2404
Musselburgh News w
Scottish County Press
0131-663 2404

WEST LOTHIAN
Linlithgow Gazette w
Johnston Press
01506-844592
Lothian Courier w
Trinity International Holdings
01506-633544
Lothian World wf
Trinity International Holdings
01506-633544
West Lothian Herald wf
Scotsman Publications
01506-634400

MIDLOTHIAN
Dalkeith Advertiser w
Scottish County Press
0131-633 2404
Midlothian Advertiser w
Scottish County Press
0131-663 4606

MORAY
Banffshire Herald w
J & M Publishing
01542-832265
Forres Gazette w
Scottish Provincial Press
01343-548777
Northern Scot w
Scottish Provincial Press
01343-548777

ORKNEY ISLANDS
The Orcadian w
The Orcadian
01856-873249

PERTHSHIRE & KINROSS
Blairgowrie Advertiser w
Trinity International Holdings
01738-636031
Perth Shopper wf
Trinity International Holdings
01738-626211
Perthshire Advertiser w
Trinity International Holdings
01738-626211
Strathearn Herald w
Trinity International Holdings
01738-626211

RENFREWSHIRE
Johnstone & Linwood Gazette w
Clyde & Forth Press
01383-728201
Paisley Daily Express d
Trinity International Holdings
0141-353 3366
Paisley People wf
Clyde & Forth Press
0141-887 7055
Paisley & Renfrewshire News wf
Eastern Counties Newspapers
0141-427 7878
Renfrew Gazette w
Clyde & Forth Press
0141-887 7055
Renfrewshire World wf
Trinity International Holdings
0141-887 7991

SHETLAND ISLANDS
Shetland Times w
Shetland Times
01595-693622

STIRLING
(Alloa) Wee County News w
Wee County Publishing
01259-724724
Stirling & Alloa Shopper wf
Trinity International Holdings
01786-451110
Stirling News wf
Dunfermline Press
01259-215111
Stirling Observer w
Trinity International Holdings
01786-451110
WESTERN ISLES
Stornoway Gazette w
The Galloway Gazette
01851-702687

N IRELAND

ANTRIM
Andersonstown News w
Andersonstown News
01232-619000
Ballymena Chronicle w
Observer Newspapers (NI)
01868-722557
Ballymena Guardian w
Northern Newspapers
01266-41221
Ballymena Times w
Morton Newspapers
01266-653300
Ballymoney Times w
Morton Newspapers
01762-326161
(Belfast) Irish News d
Irish News
01232-322226
(Belfast) News Letter d
Mirror Group Newspapers
01232-680000
Belfast Sunday Life w
01232-331133
Belfast Telegraph d
Preceding twoare Trinity Holdings
01232-321242
East Antrim Gazette w
Alpha Newspapers Group
01861-522639
East Belfast Herald & Post wf
Trinity International Holdings
01232-439993
East Belfast News wf
Mirror Group Newspapers
01232 680010
Larne Times w
Morton Newspapers
01574-272303
Lisburn Echo wf
Morton Newspapers
01846-601114
North Newtownabbey Herald wf
Trinity International Holdings
01232-439993
Portadown Times w
Morton Newspapers
01762-336111
Ulster Star w
Morton Newspapers
01846-679111

ARMAGH
Armagh Down Observer w
Observer Newspapers (NI)
01868-722557
Craigavon Echo wf
Morton Newspapers
01762-350041

Lurgan Examiner w
Observer Newspapers (NI)
01868-722557
Lurgan Mail w
Morton Newspapers
01762-327777
Portadown Times w
Morton Newspapers
01762-336111
Ulster Gazette w
Alpha Newspaper Group
01861-522639

DERRY
Coleraine Chronicle w
Northern Newspaper Group
01265-43344
Coleraine Constitution w
Northern Newspaper Group
01265-43344
Coleraine Leader w
Northern Newspaper Group
01265-43344
Coleraine Times w
Morton Newspapers
01265-55260
Derry Journal w
Mirror Group Newspapers
01504-265442
Derry People & Donegal News w
N W Ireland Printing & Publishing Co
01662-243444
(Londonderry) NW Echo wf
01504-268459
Londonderry Sentinel w
01504-267571
Mid-Ulster & S Derry Mail w
01648-762288
Mid-Ulster Echo wf
Preceding four Morton Newspapers
01648-761364
Mid-Ulster Observer w
Observer Newspapers (NI)
01868-722557
Northern Constitution w
Northern Newspaper Group
01265-43344

COUNTY DOWN
Armagh Down Observer w
Observer Newspapers (NI)
01868-722557
Banbridge Chronicle w
Banbridge Chronicle w
01820-662322
Banbridge Leader w
Morton Newspapers
01820-662745
County Down Spectator w
Spectator Newspapers
01247-270270

Down Recorder w
W Y Crichton & Co
01396-613711
Dromore Leader w
Morton Newspapers
01846-692217
Mourne Observer w
Mourne Observer
01396-722666
Newry Reporter w
Edward Hodgett
01693-67633
Newtownards Chronicle w
01247-813333
Newtownards Spectator w
Spectator Newspapers
01247-270270
North Down Herald & Post wf
Trinity International Holdings
01232-439993
The Outlook w
01820-630202

FERMANAGH
Fermanagh Herald w
North West of Ireland Printing County
01662-243444
Impartial Reporter w
William Trimble
01365-324422
Fermanagh News w
Observer Newspapers (NI)
01868-722557

TYRONE
(Dungannon) About Town wf
Dungannon Development Association
01868-725445
Dungannon News w
Alpha Newspaper Group
01868-722271
Dungannon Observer w
Observer Newspapers (NI)
01868-722557
Strabane Chronicle w
North West of Ireland Printing County
01662-243444
Strabane Weekly News w
Tyrone Constitution Group
01662-242721
Tyrone Constitution w
Tyrone Constitution Group
01662-242721
(Tyrone) The Democrat w
Observer Newspapers (NI)
01868-722557
Tyrone Times w
Morton Newspapers
01868-752801
Ulster Herald w
North West of Ireland Printing County
01662-243444

Ethnic press

Trevor Phillips

Trevor McDonald

The two black media Trevors - McDonald and Phillips - united to attack racism in the media. Trevor Phillips criticised an audience at the Royal Television Society for their inability to promote ethnic broadcasters to positions of power. "On the executive floors, where real decisions are made about scheduling, programme style and tone are taken, there are virtually no black faces. As usual there are no reliable numbers, but I would buy a magnum of champagne for the first person who can name more than six at head of department level or above. Talents like Samir Shah, Ben Robinson, Waheed Alli and Narinder Minhas all now work outside in the independent sector. For there to be fewer minority figures at the top of our major broadcasting institutions than there were ten years ago is a disgrace."

Phillips told of a white friend who returned from an unsuccessful deal with an American TV network. One of the US executives explained their failure to conclude a deal by saying "you looked old-fashioned. In N America no one would go into a negotiation like this with an all-white, all-male team.

McDonald, whom Phillips said "accounted for nearly 10 per cent of all peak-time appearances by a black person on ITV", agreed. "Historically," McDonald said, "there has always been an imbalance. But in the past there was not the number of people knocking at the door as there is now."

Reflecting on his popularity, McDonald said: "There is a complacency here. There is very much the feeling that everything is going to come right in the end if you let it alone. It will evolve. Look, there's always Trevor McDonald, they say. Sometimes I wonder if I have done a great disservice."

ETHNIC STATS

* The UK population is 55 million and the ethnic minority population is just over three million, or 5.5 per cent of the total. Indians are the largest group, nearly half of them having South Asian origin. The second largest group is black-Caribbean people of West Indian origin.

* Although five out of a hundred people in Britain are classified as ethnic, only one in a hundred is employed in the media.

* More than 90 per cent of ads have white actors in the lead role, with 5.3 per cent putting someone from an ethnic mionority at the centre of the action, according to the Glasgow University Media Group. The researchers watched 665 ads to arrive at their figure and one of them, Greg Philo, said: "The ethnic population as whole is only 5.5 per cent, so it's fairly representative." His colleague, Furzana Khan, pointed out that the most popular ad with a black in it showed an elderly man sitting in a tent. "The most frequently shown white main lead shows a man with responsibility having fun. The most frequentl non-white ad has a poor man doing nothing."

* Bobby Ayub Syed, who organises the Ethnic Minority Media Awards, says: "Black journalists only get so far and then they hit a glass ceiling. They go into PR and get paid a lot of money, or they go into TV. Britain has had an ethnic population since the fifties, yet I can't think of any black or Asian newspaper executives."

Ad-Diplomasi News
PO Box 138, London SW3 6BH
Fax 0171-266 1479　　Tel 0171-286 1372
Arabic, bi-monthly. Editor: Raymond Atallah

The African
25 Hester Road, London N18 2RF
Fax 0181-351 0516　　Tel 0181-350 0684
Bi-monthly. Editor: Zaya Yeebo

Akhbar-e-Watan
Chamber House, 306-308a Hoe Street, London E17 9PX
Fax 0181-925 0446　　Tel 0181-923 9222
E-mail: watan@wavenet.co,uk
Website: http://www.wavenet.co.uk/users/watan
Urdu. Editor: Taj Javaid

Al Ahram International
203-209 North Gower Street, London NW1 2NJ
Fax 0171-388 3130　　Tel 0171-388 1155
Arabic daily. Editor: Dr Amr Abdel El Sami

Al-Alaam
Banner House, 55-57 Banner Street, London EC1Y 8PX
Fax 0171-608 3581　　Tel 0171-608 3454
Arabic weekly. Editor: Sead Mahamed Shehabi

Al Arab
159 Acre Lane, London SW2 5UA
Fax 0171-326 1783　　Tel 0171-274 9381
Website: http://www.alarab.co.uk
Arabic daily. Editor: A S El Houni

Al Hayat
66 Hammersmith Road, London W14 8YT
Fax 0171-602 4963　　Tel 0171-602 9988
Website: http://www.alhayat.com
Arabic daily. Editor Jihad El Khazen

Al Muhajir
132 Mill Lane, London NW6 1NE
Fax 0171-813 6234　　Tel 0171 813 5553
Arabic fortnightly. Editor: M Assou

Amar Deep Hindi Weekly
2 Chepstow Road, London W7 2BG
Fax 0181-579 3180　　Tel 0181-840 3534
Weekly. Editor: J M Kaushal

Ananda Bazar Patrika
37 Lawns Court, The Avenue, Wembley Park, Middx HA9 9PN
Fax 0181-908 2625　　Tel 0181-904 2391
Bengali/English weekly. Editor: Aveek Sarkar; UK correspondent Shrabani Basu

Arab News
Arab Press House, 184 High Holborn, London WC1V 7AP
Fax 0171-405 7892　　Tel 0171-831 8181
E-mail: admin@arab.net
Editor: Mr Al-Omeir

Asharq Al Awsat
Arab Press House, 184 High Holborn, London WC1V 7AP
Fax 0171-831 2310　　Tel 0171-831 8181
E-mail: admin@arab.net
Arabic daily. Editor: Othman Al-Omeir

Asian Convenience Retailer
8-16 Coronet Street, London N1 6HD
Fax 0171-739 0358　　Tel 0171-729 5453
Fortnightly.

Asian Entertainment Guide
18 Molyneux Street, London W1H 5HU
Fax 0171-724 2971　　Tel 0171-723 6797
Weekly. Editor: Navtam Gusai

The Asian Express
212 Piccadilly, London W1V 9LD
Fax 0171-537 2141　　Tel 0171-439 8985
Fortnightly. Editor: Vallabh Kaviraj

Asian Hotel & Caterer
Garavi Gujarat House, 1 Silex Street, London SE1 0DW
Fax 0171-261 0055　　Tel 0171-928 1234
E-mail: garavi@gujarat.demon.co.uk
Monthly. Editor: Solanki Ramniklal

Asian Times
1st floor, 148 Cambridge Heath Road, `London E1 5QJ
Fax 0171-702 7937　　Tel 0171-702 8012
E-mail: name@eeye.demon.co.uk
Weekly. Editor: Sanjay Gohil

Asian Trader
1 Silex Street, London SE1 0DW
Fax 0171-261 0055　　Tel 0171-928 1234
English/Gujarati/Urdu. Fortnightly. Editor: R C Solanki

Awaz Asian Voice
10 Norfolk, Batley, West Yorkshire WF17 7RX
Fax 01924-470555　　Tel 01924-470555
E-mail: awaaz@pop3.poptel.org.uk
Monthly, English/Gujarati/Urdu. Editor: Ayub Bismillah

Awaze Quam
Unit 5B, Booth Street, Birmingham B66 2PF
Fax 0121-555 6899　　Tel 0121-555 5921
E-mail: 106004,1160@compuserve.com
Weekly. Editor: Raghbir Singh

Black Perspective
PO Box 246, London SE13 7DL
Fax 0181-692 6986　　Tel 0181-692 6986
E-mail editor@Blackper.demon.co.uk
Website: http://www.x-ms.com/blackper.htm
Bimonthly. Editor: Victor Amokeodo

Caribbean Times
148 Cambridge Heath Road, London E1 5QJ
Fax 0171-702 7937　　Tel 0171-702 8012
E-mail: name@eeye.demon.co.uk
Weekly.

Chinese Business Impact
16 Nicholas Street, Manchester M1 4EJ
Fax 0161-228 3739　　Tel 0161-228 0420
Chinese and English. Editors: Yan Shen/Juliet Zhou

Cineblitz
Dolphin Media House, Spring Villa Park, Spring Villa Road, Edgware HA8 7EB
Fax 0181-381 1177　　Tel 0181-381 1166
Monthly, Indian cinema news. Editor: Arvind Sikand

Cipher
184 Bridgewater Road, Alperton, Middlesex HA0 1AR
Fax 0181-795 0502   Tel 0181-903 6350
Bimonthly. Editor: Joan Smith
Cronica Latina
PO Box 1269, London SW9 9RN
Fax 0171-793 1743   Tel 0171-582 0943
Spanish monthly. Editor: Juan Toledo
Cypriots Review & Advertiser
Kinetic Business Centre, Theobald Street, Boreham
Wood, Herts WD6 4PJ
                          Tel 0181-953 9119
Weekly.
Daily Jang
1 Sanctuary Stre et, London SE1 1ED
Fax 0171-357 0158   Tel 0171-403 5833
English and Urdu daily. Editor: K Iman
Daily Millat
2 Baynes Close, Enfield, Middlesex EN1 4BN
Fax 0181-367 6941   Tel 0181-366 5082
E-mail: MUS77SMI@aol.com
Press correspondent: S Mustafa
Des Pardes
8 The Crescent, Southall, Middlesex UB1 1BE
Fax 0181-571 2604   Tel 0181-571 1127
Weekly, news concerning Indian people, in Punjabi.
Editor: G Virk
The East
FMS International, Crown House, North circular Road,
London NW10 7PN
Fax 0181-961 7410   Tel 0181-963 0510
Weekly. Editor: Shahid Khan
Eastern Eye
148 Cambridge Heath Road, London E1 5QJ
Fax 0171-702 7937   Tel 0171-702 8012
E-mail: eeye@demon.co.uk
Weekly news for the Asian community. Editor: Sanjay
Gohil
EU Japan Business News
Unit 10, 1 Benjamin Street, London EC1M 5QL
Fax 0171-251 1493   Tel 0171-251 1492
Japanese quarterly. Editor: Tomoo Oba
The Examiner
19 Angel Road, Harrow, Middlesex HA1 1JX
                          Tel 0181-520 8397
Irish news. Editor: Aidan Hennigan
The Filipino
5 Golders Garden, Golders Green, London NW11
9BP
Fax: 0181-458 1055   Tel 0181-731 7195
E-mail: philmedia@avnet.co.uk
Bimonthly. Editor: Mrs Bong Forouzan
Garavi Gujarat
1-2 Silex Street, London SE1 0DW
Fax 0171-261 0055   Tel 0171-928 1234
E-mail garavi@Gujaratdemon.co.uk
English/Gujarati. Bi-monthly. Editor: R C Solanki

The Gleaner
220-223 Elephant & Castle Shopping Centre, London
SE1 6TE
Fax 0171-277 1734   Tel 0171-277 1714
Website: http://www.jamaica-gleaner.com
Weekly Jamaican and Caribbean news. Editor: Collette
Hibbert
Greek Review
59 Stroud Green Road, London N4 3EG
Fax 0171-272 7274   Tel 0171-272 2722
Monthly news in English.
**Gujarat Samachar/Asian Voice/Asian
Business**
8-16 Coronet Street, London N1 6HD
Fax 0171-739 0358   Tel 0171-729 5453
Website: http://www.gujarat-samachor.com
Gujarati/English weekly.
Hurriyet
35 D'Arblay Street, London W1V 3FE
Fax 0171-287 3101   Tel 0171-734 1211
E-mail: zabaltd@.aol.com
Turkish daily. Editor: Faruk Zabci
Impact International
233 Seven Sisters Road, London N4 2BL
Fax 0171-272 8934   Tel 0171-263 1417
E-mail: impact@globalnet.co.uk
Monthly Muslim news. Editor: Ahmad Irfan
India-Home and Abroad
1 Park Close, London NW2 6RQ
Fax 0181-452 4182   Tel 0181-452 4182
Quarterly. Editor: K K Singh
India Link International
42 Farm Avenue, North Harrow, Middx HA2 7LR
Fax 0181-723 5250   Tel 0181-866 8421
Monthly. Editor: Krishan Ralleigh
India Monitor
1B Claverton Street, London SW1V 3AY
Fax 0171-630 8688   Tel 0171-630 8688
E-mail: 110213.227@compuserve.com
Website: http://www.ukindia.com
Editor: Rakesh Mathur
India Weekly
105 St John Street, London EC1M 4AS
Fax 0171-251 3289   Tel 0171-251 3290
E-mail: email@indiaweekly.co.uk
Website: http://www.indiaweekly.co.uk
Weekly. Editor: Premen Addy
Irish Independent
Vigilant House, 120 Wilton Road, London SW1V 1JZ
Fax 0171-808 7100   Tel 0171-353 4325
Editor: Bernard Purcell
Irish Post
464 Uxbridge Road, Hayes, Middx UB4 0SP
Fax 0181-561 3047   Tel 0181-561 0059
E-mail: irishpost@irishpost.co.uk
Website: http://www.irishpost.co.uk
Weekly. Editor: Nora Casey
Irish Times
76 Shoe Lane, London EC4A 3JB
Fax 0171-353 8670   Tel 0171-353 8970
Editor: Frank Millar

Irish World
934 North Circular Road, London NW2 7RJ
Fax 0181-208 1103   Tel 0181-453 7800
Weekly. Editor: Damien Gaffney

Janomot
Unit 2, 20B Spelman Street, London E1 5LQ
Fax 0171-247 0141   Tel 0171-377 6032
E-mail: janomot@easynet.co.uk
Bengali weekly. Editor: Nobab Euddin

Jewish Chronicle
25 Furnival Street, London EC4A 1JT
Fax 0171-405 9040   Tel 0171-415 1500
E-mail: jcadmin@jchron.co.uk
Website: http://www.jchron.co.uk
Editor: Ned Temko

Jewish Quarterly
PO Box 2078, London W1A 1JR
Fax 0171-629 5110   Tel 0171-629 5004
Culture and Jewish life. Editor: Matthew Reisz

Jewish Recorder
199 Pershore Road, Birmingham B5 7PF
Tel 0121-249 1997
Editor: Doctor S Abudarham

Jewish Tribune
95-97 Stamford Hill, London N16 5RE
Fax 0181-800 5000   Tel 0181-800 6688
Weekly. Editor: J Bentov

The Leader
2 Baynes Close, Enfield, Middlesex EN1 4BN
Fax 0181-367 6941   Tel 0181-366 5082
E-mail: MUS77SMI@aol.com
Editor: Syed Mustafa

London Irish Press
Unit 8, Concord Business Centre, London W3 0TR
Fax 0181-896 3654   Tel 0181-752 1202
Editor: Michael Hennessy

London Jewish News
28 St Albans Lane, London NW11 7QE
Fax 0181-731 8815   Tel 0181-731 8814
Bi-weekly. Editor: Ruth Getz

Mauritian International
PO Box 4100, London SW20 0XN
Fax 0181-947 1912   Tel 0181-947 1912
E-mail: jaclee@compuserve.com
Quarterly. Editor: Jacques K Lee

Mauritius News
583 Wandsworth Road, London SW8 8JD
Fax 0171-627 8939   Tel 0171-498 3066
E-mail: editor@mauritius-news.co.uk
Website: http://www.mauritius-news.co.uk
Monthly. Editor: Peter Chellen

Milap Weekly
Masbro Centre, 87 Masbro Road, London W14 0LR
Tel: 0171-385 8966
Urdu weekly. Editor: R Soni

The Muslim News
PO Box 380, Harrow, Middlesex HA2 6LL
Fax 0171-836 8870   Tel 0171-836 8988
E-mail: musnews@webstar.co.uk
Website: http://www.webstar.co.uk/~musnews
Monthly. Editor: Ahmad J Versi

The Nation
96c Ilford Lane, Ilford, Essex IG1 2LD
Fax 0181-478 6200   Tel 0181-478 3200
E-mail: msarwar@thenation.demon.co.uk
Website: http://www.thenation.demon.co.uk
English/Urdu. Editor Mr M Sarwar

Navin Weekly
Masbro Centre, 87 Masbro Rd, London W14 0LR
Tel: 0171-385 8966
Hindi weekly. Editor: Ramesh Kumar

New Horizon
144-146 King's Cross Road, London WC1X 9DH
Fax 0171-278 4797   Tel 0171-833 8275
E-mail icis@iibi.demon.co.uk
Monthly Muslim news, Islamic banking. Editor:
Ghazanfar Ali

New Impact
Anser House, Courtyard Offices, 3 High Street,
Marlow, Bucks SL7 1AX
Fax 01628-475570   Tel 01628-481581
Bi-monthly on "enterprise and diversity". Editor: Elaine
Sihera

New World
234 Holloway Road, London N7 8DA
Fax 0171-607 6706   Tel 0171-700 2673
Weekly news on international affairs. Editor: Dhiren
Basu

The News
Jang Publications, 1 Sanctuary Street, London SE1
1ED
Fax 0171-378 1653   Tel 0171-403 5833
Editor: Mr Shahid Ullah

Nigerian News
23 Aberdeen Court, Maida Vale, London W9 1AF
Fax 0171-266 4057   Tel 0171-266 4564
Fortnightly. Editor: Olubiyi Ayodeji

Noticias Latin America
59 St Martin's Lane, London WC2N 4JS
Fax 0171-928 9858   Tel 0171-928 0315
E-mail: noticias@dial.pipex.com
Monthly. Editor: Marcela Sariego

Notun Din
192-196 Hanbury Street, London E1 5HU
Fax 0171-247 2280   Tel 0171-247 6280
Editor: M Chowdhury

Pahayagan
49 Connaught Street, London W2 2BB
Tel 0171-402 6917
Filipino, bi-monthly.

Parikiaki
534A Holloway Road, London N7 6JP
Fax 0171-281 0127   Tel 0171-272 6777
Weekly. Editor: Kyriacos Tsioupras

Perdesan Monthly
478 Lady Margaret Rd, Southall, Middlesex UB1 2NW
Fax 0181-575 8659   Tel 0181-575 8694
Monthly. Editor: G K Bedi

The Polish Gazette
PO Box 1945, Edinburgh EH4 1AB
Tel 0131-343 2589
Business quarterly, in English. Editor: Maria Rayska

Pride Magazine
Hamilton House, 55 Battersea Bridge Road, London
SW11 3AX
Fax 0171-288 3130   Tel 0171-228 3110
Monthly for women of colour. Editor: Richard Liston

Probashi Samachar
20 Orchard Avenue, London N14 4ND
                             Tel 0181-886 4231
Bengali quarterly. Editor: S Mazumdar

Punjab Mail International
66 Dames Road, London E7 0DR
Fax 0181-522 0901   Tel 0181-519 5239
Monthly magazine written in Punjabi and English "to
promote culture and heritage".
Editor: Gurdip Singh Sandhu

Punjab Times International
24 Cottonbrook Road, Derby DE23 8YJ
Fax 01332 372833   Tel 01332 372851
E-mail: punjabtimes@aol.com
Weekly. Editor: Mr RF Purewal

The Punjabi Guardian
Soho News Building, 129 Soho Road, Handsworth,
Birmingham B21 9ST
Fax 0121-507 1065   Tel 0121-554 3995
Monthly. Editor: Inder Jit Singh Sangha

Q News International
Dexion House, 2-4 Empire Way, Wembley HA9 0XA
Fax 0181-903 0820   Tel 0181-903 0819
E-mail: qnews@aapi.co.uk
Target audience is second generation British Muslims-
Pakistanis, Bangladeshis, Afro-Caribbeans, Africans,
Malysians, Kurds and English Muslims. It has 4,500
subscribers and is available via the news trade.
Weekly. Editor: Fuad Nahdi

Ravi Asian News Weekly
Ravi House, Legrams Lane, Bradford BD7 1NS
Fax 01274-721227   Tel 01274-721227
Urdu weekly. Editor: Farida Sheikh

Rira Magazine
39-41 North Road,, London N7 9DP
Fax 0171-609 6716   Tel 0171-609 9010
Irish youth magazine. Editor: Sean Scally

RTE News
4 Millbank, London SW1P 3JA
Fax 0171-233 3383   Tel 0171-233 3384
Irish television magazine. Editor: Brian O'Connell

Sada Urdu Monthly
PO Box 639 CR9 2WN
Fax 0181-251 8689   Tel 0181-684 9429
Managing editor: Iqbal Mirza

Shang Ye Xian Feng
3 Richmond buildings, Dean Street, London W1V 5AE
Fax 0171-437 5002   Tel 0171-437 8001
E-mail: info@shangmagazine.com
Chinese bimonthly. Editor: Emile Bekheit

The Sikh Courier International
33 Wargrave Road, South Harrow, Middlesex HA2
8LL
Fax 0181-864 9228   Tel 0181-864 9228
Quarterly. Editors: A S Chatwal/S S Kapoor

The Sikh Messenger
43 Dorset Road, London SW19 3EZ
                             Tel 0181-540 4148
Quarterly. Editor: Indarjit Singh

Sing Tao (UK)
46 Dean Street, London W1V 5AP
Fax 0171-734 0828   Tel 0171-287 1525
E-mail: singtaoeu@yahoo.com
Website: http://www.singtaoeu.com
Chinese daily. Editor: S T Wan

Spice Lifestyle Magazine
420 Kingstanding Road, Birmingham B44 9SA
Fax 0121-350 9618   Tel 0121-350 9190
E-mail: enquiries@spice-magazine.demon.co.uk
Website: http://www.spice-magazine.demon.co.uk
Monthly. Editor: Parminder Singh

Surma
40 Wessex Street, London E2 0LB
Fax 0181-981 8829   Tel 0181-980 5544
E-mail: surma@netmatters.co.uk
Bengali weekly. Editor: Ahmed M Belal

Ta Nea
8-10 Stamford Hill, London N16 6XS
Fax 0181-806 0160   Tel 0181-806 0169
Fortnightly. Editor: Louis Vrakas

Teamwork
5 Westminster Bridge Road, London SE1 7XW
Fax 0171-928 0343   Tel 0171-928 7861
Bimonthly. Editor: Mr W Trant

Toplum Postasi
117 Green Lanes, London N16 DA
Fax 0171-354 0313   Tel 0171-354 4424
E-mail: toplum.postasi@btinternet.com
Turkish weekly. Editor: Artum Joksan

Touch Magazine
1st Floor, 51 Hoxton Square, London N1 6PB
Fax 0171-739 6504   Tel 0171 739 5727
Monthly. Editor: Vincent Jackson

La Voce Degli Italiani
20 Brixton Road, London SW9 6BU
Fax 0171-793 0385   Tel 0171-735 5164
E-mail ziliotto@dircon.co.uk
Fortnightly. Editor: Giandomenico Ziliotto

The Voice
370 Coldharbour Lane, London SW9 8PL
Fax 0171-274 8994   Tel 0171-737 7377
E-mail: veeteea@gn.apc.org
Weekly for Black British. Editor: Annie Stewart

Watan Weekend
Chamber Ho, 306-308a Hoe Street, London E17 9PX
Fax 0181-925 0446   Tel 0181-923 9222
E-mail: watan@wavenet.co.uk
Website: http://www.wavenet.co.uk/users/watan
Urdu. Editor: Taj Javaid

Weekly Des Pardes
8 The Crescent, Southall Middlesex UB1 1BE
Fax 0181-571 2604   Tel 0181-571 1127
Weekly, Punjabi. Editor: Mr Virk

Weekly Potrika
Wickham House, 10 Cleveland Way, London E1 4TR
Fax 0171-423 9122   Tel 0171-423 9270
Bengali, weekly. Editor: AS Chowdhury

Magazines

Estimates of the number of magazines vary according to definition. Taking all the tiddlers into account there are probably 10,000 titles, though the more conservative estimate is from British Rate and Data (Brad) which lists 7,933 titles that take advertising. Of these 5,261 are business and professional magazines and the remaining 2,672 are consumer mags, which the Periodical Publishers Association defines as "providing people with leisure time information and entertainment". While most consumer titles are paid for by their readers, many of the business magazines are financed by advertising to so-called "controlled circulation readerships" - magazine managements' euphemism for uncontrolled circulation via mailing lists.

In magazines, minnows can be beautiful and perhaps 1,000 people make a decent living writing newsletters for tiny niche trade markets prepared to pay hefty subscriptions for precisely targeted information - Car Wash Weekly, Funeral Service Insider, Migraine Treatment Alert and so on through a plethora of specialist financial titles. They're unknown outside their patches but, according to the UK Newsletter Association's best guesstimate, generate an unminnow-like £75 million annual turnover. Newsletters are, incidentally, a good place to begin a career because time spent on one gives detailed insights into all aspects publishing.

The main part of the magazine pool is inhabited by sharks, with a few large publishing houses owning the majority of titles - BBC Magazines, National Magazine Company, Condé Nast, DC Thomson, Emap, Reader's Digest, G&J of the UK and H Bauer. Reed-Elsevier was the largest until January 1998 when, in one of the biggest of management buyouts in British corporate life, it sold IPC Magazines for £860 million to a management team backed by Cinven venture capitalists. In the same month Reed announced its intention to merge with Wolters Kluwer in a £20 billion deal. Nigel Stapleton, Reed Elsevier's chairman, said: "In the context of content-ownership, big is beautiful. This will give us a better position to

Top selling magazines by circulation

1	AA Magazine	4,032,996
2	Sky TV Guide	3,513,241
3	What's on TV	1,694,278
4	Reader's Digest	1,493,912
5	Radio Times	1,406,152
6	Cable Guide1	258,538
7	The Somerfield Magazine	1,090,490
8	TV Times	863,281
9	Saga Magazine	679,880
10	Ford Magazine	811,892
11	Connections	748,926
12	Woman	731,764
13	Woman's Own	702,785
14	FHM	644,110
15	Woman's Weekly	638,306
16	Hello	574,686
17	Prima	540,727
18	Best	511,841
19	Top of the Pops	500,983
20	Chat	494,671
21	Sugar	485,944
22	Candis	469,860
23	Cosmopolitan	451,116
24	Good Housekeeping	450,183
25	Peoples Friend	449,595
26	Loaded	441,567
27	Smash Hits	434,525
28	Sainsbury's	422,718
29	Marie Claire	415,550
30	It's Bliss	400,799
31	My Weekly	376,148
32	Viz	356,005
33	The Economist	351,108
34	Now	348,109
35	Woman & Home	344,041
36	More!	343,150
37	BBC Good food	323,837
38	House Beautiful	305,087
39	BBC Gardeners' World	303,385
40	Company	284,092
41	Family Circle	280,295
42	The Big Issue	278,718
43	Essentials	272,885
44	New Woman	272,885
45	Yours	266,570
46	Loot	261,146

Source: ABC, June 1998

exploit new media. If we really want to get the attention of software providers like Microsoft and the delivery channels, then we must get bigger." The deal unravelled a couple of months later following Wolters' fears that American and European regulators would force it to sell off some of its interests. So Reed kept sole ownership of its business titles and grew bigger in April with the £988 million purchase of two American legal publishers, Matthew Bender and Company and Shepard's Company. The spending spree puts Reed level with Thomson Corp as the world's biggest legal publisher.

Over the past ten years the number of magazines published has increased by over a third. Total turnover is £1.7 billion and profit margins have increased from an average 6 per cent in 1991 to nearly 12 per cent for the last three years. The growth, which stimulated 180 launches in 1997, has been fuelled by increasing advertising expenditure and cover prices running ahead of inflation. High prices have led to a 1.1 per cent drop in sales during 1997, an example of simple economics which some publishers deny. But the evidence is there for them to see: IPC's young women's magazine 19 went up 10p a year since 1993 to £1.80 and its circulation has dropped from 214,000 to 167,000; Condé Nast has raised the price on the Face from £1.80 to £2.40 and watched sales drop from 78,100 to 60,300; Future's PC Answers rose from £2.95 to £4.99 and lost a third of its 27,000 sales.

Testosterone-titles, the new breed of men's mags which rely on only the mildest of porn, have gone against the trend. Magazines like FHM, Loaded and Esquire have prospered while the top women's mags - Cosmopolitan, Woman's Journal, Company, Options, She Woman and Woman's Own - have had a combined circulation falling from 3.4 million in 1987 to 2.1 million ten years later. In August FHM overtook Cosmopolitan when it sold over 500,000 copies with a single issue's copy sales generating £1.6 million and annual ad revenue headed for £6 million. There's a weight of theory as to why this should be so - perhaps it's just that modern blokes are more in need of the make-you-feel-better consumer formulae which magazines peddle so well.

MAGAZINE OWNERS

Academy Group
42 Leinster Gardens, London W2 3AN
Fax 0171-262 5093   Tel 0171-262 5097
Books and magazines.
Now owned by John Wiley.

Aceville Publications
97 High Street, Colchester, Essex CO1 1TH
Fax 01206-564214   Tel 01206-540621
E-mail: mail@maze.u-net.com
Trading/collectors magazines.

Academy Group
42 Leinster Gardens, London W2 3AN
Fax 0171-423 9540   Tel 0171-402 2141
Books and magazines.

Aceville Publications
97 High Street, Colchester, Essex CO1 1TH
Fax 01206-564214   Tel 01206-540621
E-mail: mail@maze.u-net.com
Trading/collectors magazines.

Addison Wesley Longman Group
Edinburgh Gate, Harlow, Essex CM20 2JE
Fax 01279-431059   Tel 01279-623623
A subsidiary of Pearson publishing journals and directories.

Affinity Publishing
2nd Floor, 1-5 Clerkenwell Road, London EC1M 5PA
Fax 0171-251 5490   Tel 0171-251 5489

Aim Publications
Silver House, 31-35 Beak Street, London W1R 3LD
Fax 0171-734 5383   Tel 0171-437 3493

Time spent reading magazines	
All paid for magazines	53.9 mins
Science & nature	73.3 mins
Gardening	73.1 mins
Boating	72.0 mins
Photography	70.8 mins
Retirement	69.4 mins
General interest, miscellaneous	68.5 mins
Motoring classics	67.0 mins
Music - dance	67.0 mins
Motorcycling	66.7 mins
Golf	65.8 mins
Current affairs & finance	60.1 mins
Women's interests - bridal	60.0 mins
Homes & decorations	58.7 mins
Motoring - performance	58.0 mins
Parenthood	58.0 mins
Motoring - other	57.9 mins
Women's general monthlies	57.6 mins
Men's & style	54.0 mins
Women's weeklies	53.7 mins

Source: IPA,ISBA,PPA

Angel Business Communications
361-373 City Road, London EC1V 1LR
Fax 0171-417 7500   Tel 0171-417 7400
E-mail: london@angelbcl.co.uk
Website: http://www.angelbc.co.uk

Apt Data Services
4th floor, 12 Sutton Row, London W1V 5FH
Fax 0171-439 1105   Tel 0171-208 4200

Asian Trade Publications
1 Silex Street, London SE1 0DW
Fax-0171-261 0055   Tel 0171-928 1234

Aspen Specialist Media
Christ Church, 35 Cosway Street, London NW1 5NJ
Fax 0171-706 4811   Tel 0171-262 2622

Attic Futura
17-18 Berners Street, London W1P 3DD
Fax 0171-323 1854   Tel 0171-664 6400
A youth, young women and entertainment publisher.

Auto Trader
1 Francis Grove, London SW19 4DT
Fax 0181-879 0110   Tel 0181-946 1155
E-mail: ak80@dial.pipex.com
Website: http://www.autotrader.co.uk
Publishes the 13 regional editions of Auto Trader.
Owned 50 per cent by the Guardian Media Group.

Avia Press Associates
75 Elm Tree Road, Locking, Weston-super-Mare,
BS24 8EL
Fax 01934-822400   Tel 01934-822524
E-mail: helicopter.international@compuserve.com
Publications about helicopters and other rotorcraft.

Axon Publishing
5th floor, 77-79 Farringdon Road, London EC1M 3JY
Fax 0171-242 1900   Tel 0171-242 0600
E-mail: axonpublish@compuserve.com

H Bauer Publishing
Shirley House, 25 Camden Road, London NW1 9LL
Fax 0171-284 3641   Tel 0171-284 0909

BBC Worldwide Publishing
Woodlands, 80 Wood Lane, London W12 0TT
Fax 0181-749 0538   Tel 0181-576 2000
Broadcasting House, Whiteladies Road, Bristol BS8
2LR
Fax 0117-9467075   Tel 0117-9738402
A division of BBC Worldwide Publishing.

BLA Group
Vinery Court, 50 Banner Street, London EC1Y 8QE
Fax 0171-577 9344   Tel 0171-577 9300
E-mail: bla@blagroup.co.uk

Blackwell Publishers
108 Cowley Road, Oxford, Oxfordshire OX4 1JF
Fax 01865-791347   Tel 01865-791100
Website: http://www.blackwellpublishers.co.uk
Publisher of humanities and social science journals and
learning materials.

Blackwell Science
Osney Mead, Oxford, Oxfordshire OX2 0EL
Fax 01865-721205   Tel 01865-206206
Website: http://www.blackwell-science.com
Specialists in technical, medical, scientific and
academic journals.

Blenheim Business Publications
See Miller Freeman

BMJ Publishing Group
BMA Ho, Tavistock Square, London WC1H 9JR
Fax 0171-383 6668   Tel 0171-387 4499
E-mail: 100336.3120@compuserve.com
Publisher of the British Medical Journal and 28 other
journals.

Brass Tacks Publishing
62-68 Rosebery Avenue, London EC1R 4RR
Fax 0171-833 8040   Tel 0171-833 5566

British European Associated Publishers
2nd Floor, Glenthorne House, Hammersmith Grove,
London W6 0LG
Fax 0181-741 7762   Tel 0181-846 9922
Website: http://www.beap.bogo.co.uk
A VNU subsidiary which publishes puzzle magazines.

Builder Group
Exchange Tower, 2 Harbour Exchange Square,
London E14 9GE
Fax 0171-560-4008   Tel 0171-560 4000
French-owned publisher of construction and security
magazines.

Caledonian Magazines
6th Floor, 195 Albion Street, Glasgow G1 1QQ
Fax 0141-302 7799   Tel 0141-302 7700
E-mail: info@calmags.so.uk
6 titles including The Scottish Farmer and The Great
Outdoors.

Top five magazine publishers

PUBLISHER	MARKET SHARE	OWNER	TOP TITLES
1 IPC Magazines	22%	Cinven & other investors -	Loaded, Country Life,
			Woman's Own, Marie Claire, NME
2 EMAP	13%	EMAP Group	FHM, Elle, New Woman,
			Smash Hits
3 BBC Magazines	6.5%	BBC	Radio Times, Top of the Pops,
			Gardener's World, Good Food
4 Bauker Sower	6%	Bauer	Bella, Take a Break, TV Quick
5 National Magazines	3%	Hearst Corporation	Good Housekeeping, Esquire,
			Cosmopolitan, Country Living

Cambridge University Press
The Edinburgh Building, Shaftesbury Road, Cambridge, Cambs CB2 2RU
Fax 01223-315052   Tel 01223-312393
E-mail: rsymons@cup.com.ac.uk
Website: http://www.cup.cam.ac.uk
Publisher of over 120 academic journals.

Carfax Publishing
PO Box 25, Abingdon, Oxfordshire OX14 3UE
Fax 01235-401550   Tel 01235-401000
E-mail: enquiries@carfax.co.uk
Website: http://www.catchword.co.uk
Publishes around 180 academic titles. One of the largest social science publishers.

Catholic Herald
Herald House, Lambs Passage Bunhill Row, London EC1Y 8TQ
Fax 0171-256 9728   Tel 0171-588 3101
E-mail: catholic@atlas.co.uk
Intellectual Catholic broadsheet.

Centennial Publishing
2nd Floor, 1-5 Clerkenwell Road, London EC1M 5PA
Fax 0171-251 5490   Tel 0171-251 0777

Centaur Communications
50 Poland Street, London W1V 4AX
Fax 0171-439 0110   Tel 0171-439 4222
Around 15 business titles.

Chapman and Hall
2-6 Boundary Row, London SE1 8HN
Fax 0171-522 9623   Tel 0171-865 0066
Website: http://www.chapmanhall.com
The subsidiary of the Thomson Corporation which publishes a range of specialist technical and scientific journals.

Combined Service Publications
PO Box 4, 273 Farnborough Road, Farnborough, Hampshire GU14 7LR
Fax 01252-517918   Tel 01252-515891
Military specialists, producing many British Army regimental journals.

Conde Nast Publications
Vogue House, Hanover Square, London W1R 0AD
Fax 0171-493 1345   Tel 0171-499 9080
The US-owned publisher of lifestyle magazines.

Consumers Association
2 Marylebone Road, London NW1 4DF
Fax 0171-830 6220   Tel 0171-830 6000
E-mail: which@which.net
Website:http://www.which.net
The campaigning body for consumers and a good place to start any consumer feature. David Chureetur is a star among pres oficers. The Association produces five magazines, including the flagship monthly Which?

Croner Publications
Croner House, London Road, Kingston-upon-Thames, Surrey KT2 6SR
Fax 0181-547 2637   Tel 0181-547 3333
E-mail: info@croner.co.uk
Website: http://www.croner.co.uk
Publishes reference guides on technical and business topics. Owned by the Dutch company Wolters Kluwer.

Cross-Border Publishing
111-113 Great Titchfield Street, London W1P 7FQ
Fax 0171-637 3594   Tel 0171-637 3579
Website: http://www.irmag.com

Dennis Publishing
19 Bolsover Street, London W1P 7HJ
Fax 0171-636 5668   Tel 0171-631 1433
Specialises in consumer and business to business magazines, also heavy metal, men's and one to one titles.

Director Publications
116 Pall Mall, London SW1Y 5ED
Fax 0171-766 8840   Tel 0171-766 8950

DMG Home Interest Magazines
Times House, Station Approach, Ruislip Middlesex HA4 8NB
01895-676027   Tel 01895-677677
Website: http://www.dmg.co.uk

Dog World
9 Tufton Street, Ashford, Kent TN23 1QN
Fax 01233-645669   Tel 01233-621877
E-mail: editorial@dogworld.co.uk

Economist Group
15 Regent Street, London SW1Y 4LR
Fax 0171-499 9767   Tel 0171-830 1000
Website: http://www.economist.com

Economist Newspaper
25 St James's Street, London SW1A 1HG
Fax 0171-930 3092   Tel 0171-830 7000
E-mail: letters@economist.com
Website: http://www.economist.com
Part of the Pearson Group.

Egmont Fleetway
25-31 Tavistock Place, London WC1H 9SU
Fax 0171-388 4154   Tel 0171-344 6400
A Danish-owned comic publisher with about 19 titles.

Elsevier Science Publishers
The Boulevard, Langford Lane, Kidlington, Oxon OX5 1GB
Fax 01865-843010   Tel 01865-843000
Website: http://www.elsevier.nl
Part of Reed Elsevier, Elsevier Science publishes over 400 scientific and technical journals for industry, science and academia.

European Magazines
2 Hatfields, London SE1 9PG
Fax 0171-261 5277   Tel 0171-261 5240
E-mail: marieclaire@ipc.co.uk
A subsidiary of IPC Magazines.

Emap

1 Lincoln Court, Lincoln Road, Peterborough, Cambs PE1 2RF
Fax 01733-562636   Tel 01733-568900
E-mail: janetj@plc.emap.co.uk
Website: http://www.emap.co.uk
Emap has three publishing divisions, two in the UK and one in France. It also has a radio division and a publications distribution arm.

Emap Business Communications

Meed House, 21 John Street, London WC1N 2BP
Fax 0171-831 3540   Tel 0171-470 6200
Over 100 titles are published in the UK and Europe by eleven subsidiaries.

Architecture	0171-505 6600
Fashion	0171-520 1500
Freight	0171-505 6600
Cars	01733-467000
Local Govt/Finance	0171-505 8000
Media/Marketing	0171-505 8000
Business/Commercial fishing/Middle East	
	0171-470 6200
Trade/Retail	0181-277 5000

Emap Consumer Magazines

Mappin House, 4 Winsley Street, London W1N 7AR
Fax 0171-312 8950   Tel 0171-436 1515
Nearly 100 consumer titles are published from seven centres:

Bikes/Cars	01733-237111
Computers/Games	0171-972 6700
Photography/Gardens/Pets/Rail	
	01733-898100
Retirement	01733-555123
Health/Parenting/Lifestyle/Women	
	0171-437 9011
Music/Entertainment/Men's lifestyle	
	0171-436 1515
Country pursuits/Sport	
	01733-264666

Faversham House Group

Faversham House, 232a Addington Road, Croydon, Surrey CR2 8LE
Fax 0181-651 7117   Tel 0181-651 7100
E-mail: fhg@dial.pipex.com

Financial Times Business

Maple House, 149 Tottenham Court Road, London W1P 9LL
Fax 0171-896 2099   Tel 0171-896 2000
It publishes numerous business newsletters, plus financial magazines. Its publishing centres are:

FTB Magazines	0171-463 3000
FTB Newsletters	0171-896 2222

Findlay Publications

Franks Hall, Franks Lane, Horton Kirby, Kent DA4 9LL
Fax 01322-289577   Tel 01322-222222

Frank Cass and Co

Newbury House, 890-900 Eastern Ave, Newbury Park, Ilford, Essex IG2 7HH
Fax 0181-599 0984   Tel 0181-599 8866
E-mail: info@frankcass.co,
Over 40 specialist academic journals and newsletters on a range of topics, including: Environmental Politics; Intelligence & National Security; Journal of Strategic Studies.

Future Publishing

Beauford Court, 30 Monmouth Street, Bath, BA1 2BW
Fax 01225-446019   Tel 01225-442244
A pioneer of the cover mount freebie computer disc and (with Classic CD) the sampler compact disc. Once owned by Pearson but in 1998 bought back by a consortium including the original owner.

G & J of the UK

197 March Wall, London E14 9SG
Fax 0171-519 5518   Tel 0171-519 5500
Publishes the two women's magazines Best and Prima, and the popular science title Focus.

GJ Palmer & Sons

St Mary's Works, Norwich, Norfolk NR3 3BH
Fax 01603-624483   Tel 01603-612914

G+B Magazines Unlimited

PO Box 90, Reading, Berks RG1 8JL
Fax 01189-568211   Tel 01189-560080
E-mail: info@gbhap.com
Website: http://www.gbhap.com
Publishes scientific and academic journals and newsletters.

Gramophone Publications

135 Greenford Road, Harrow, Middx HA1 3YD
Fax 0181-869 8400   Tel 0181-422 4562
E-mail: info@gramophone.co.uk
Publishes Gramophone and a series of specialist quarterly music titles.

Granta Publications

2-3 Hanover Yard, Noel Road, London N1 8BE
Fax 0171-704 0474   Tel 0171-704 9776
E-mail: editorial@grantamag.co.uk
Website: http://www.granta.com
Publishes Granta the magazine of new writing and Granta books.

Harcourt Brace

24-28 Oval Road, London NW1 7DX
Fax 0171-482 2293   Tel 0171-424 4200
Website: http://www.hbuk.co.uk

Haymarket Group

174 Hammersmith Road, London W6 7JP
Fax 0171-413 4504   Tel 0181-943 5000
Publishes 40 of the leading business, medical and consumer magazines, from offices at Lancaster Gate and Teddington (both on the same phone number).

Hello!

Wellington House, 69-71 Upper Ground, London SE1 9PQ
Fax 0171-667 8742   Tel 0171-667 8700

Hemming Group
32 Vauxhall Bridge Road, London SW1V 2SS
Fax 0171-233 5056   Tel 0171-973 6400
Henry Hemming Publishing
The Glasshouse, 49a Goldhawk Road, London W12 8QP
Fax 0181-743 0888   Tel 0181-743 8111
E-mail: info@hhpublishing.demon.co.uk
Contract publisher specialising in travel and technology.
Highbury House Communications
1-3 Highbury Station Road, London N1 1SE
Fax 0171-704 0758   Tel 0171-226 2222
E-mail: 106570.2027@compuserve.com
International publisher specialising in sport, leisure, finance, travel and business magazines.
HMSO
see The Stationery Office
Ian Allan
Riverdene, Molesey Road, Hersham, Surrey KT12 4RG
Fax 01932-266600   Tel 01932-266601
Publishes popular transport magazines books and videos.
IBC Business Publishing
57-61 Mortimer Street, Gilmore House, London W1N 8JX
Fax 0171-631 3214   Tel 0171-637 4383
Website: http://www.intbuscom.com
Specialises in financial technology and telecomms.
IDG Communications
99 Grays Inn Road, London WC1X 8UT
Fax 0171-414 0262   Tel 0171-831 9252
Website: http://www.macworld.co.uk
Publisher of computer titles.
Illustrated London News Group
20 Upper Ground, London SE1 9PF
Fax 0171-805 5911   Tel 0171-928 2111
IML Group
184 High Street, Tonbridge, Kent TN9 1BQ
Fax 01732-770049   Tel 01732-359990
E-mail: imlgroup@dial.pipex.com
12 technical and business titles.
Inside Communications
8th floor, Tubs Hill House, London Road, Sevenoaks, Kent TN13 1BL
Fax 01732-464454   Tel 01732-464154
IPC Magazines
King's Reach Tower, Stamford Street, London SE1 9LS
Fax 0171-261 6373   Tel.0171-261 5000
Website: http://www.ipc.co.uk
The consumer publishing division of Reed Elsevier is Britain's largest publisher of consumer and leisure magazines.
Jobson Publishing Corporation
Jobson House, Holbrooke Place, Hill Rise, Richmond, Surrey TW10 6UD
Fax 0181-332 6918   Tel 0181-332 6882
E-mail: sfarrer@jobson.co.uk
Publisher of optical magazines and special reports.

John Wiley & Sons
Baffins Lane, Chichester, Sussex PO19 1UD
Fax 01243-775878   Tel 01243-779777
E-mail: publicity@wiley.co.uk
Publishes 411 journals of all kinds.
Keesing (UK)
Keesing House, Stonecroft, 69 Station Road, Redhill, Surrey RH1 1DL
Fax 01737-767248   Tel 01737-769799
The Lady
39-40 Bedford Street, Londo WC2E 9ER
Fax 0171-836 4620   Tel 0171-379 4717
The Lancet
42 Bedford Square, London WC1B 3SL
Fax 0171-436 7570   Tel 0171-436 4981
E-mail: Clas.Advertising@ellsevier.co.uk
Website: http://www.thelancet.com
Law Society of England & Wales
113 Chancery Lane, London WC2A 1PL
Fax 0171-242 1309   Tel 0171-242 1222
Liberty Publishing
100 Brompton Road, London SW3 1ER
Fax: 0171-225 6725   Tel: 0171 225 6716
E-mail: adsales@punch.co.uk
Link House Magazines
Link House, Dingwall Avenue, Croydon CR9 2TA
Fax 0181-760 0973   Tel 0181-686 2599
LLP
Sheepen Place, Colchester, CO3 3LP
Fax 01206-772771   Tel 01206-772277
E-mail: subscriptions@llplimited.com
Website: http://www.llplimited.com
Publisher specialising in the provision of commercial, legal and financial information and data relatingt o shipping, maritime services, insurance, freighting and transport, commodities and energy.
Macmillan Magazines
Porters South, 4 Crinan Street, London N1 9XW
Fax 0171-843 4640   Tel 0171-833 4000
Website: http://www.macmillan.com
Publishes 13 titles, mainly health service and scientific.
Manor Publishing
Manor Ho, Edison Road, Eastbourne BN23 6PT
Fax 01323-509306   Tel 01323-507474
Trade mags and annual factbooks for the sports market.
Mark Allen Publishing
286a-288 Croxted Road, London SE24 9BY
Fax 0181-671 1722   Tel 0181-671 7521
E-mail: 100676.56@compuserve.com
Mainly medical titles.
Marvel Comics
Panini House, Coach and Horses Passage, The Pantiles, Tunbridge Wells, Kent TN2 5UJ
Fax 01892-545666   Tel 01892-500100
Maze Media
97 High Street, Colchester, Essex CO1 1TH
Fax 01206-564214   Tel 01206-540621
Hobby and leisure magazines.
Metal Bulletin
Park Terrace, Worcester Park, Surrey KT4 7HY

Fax 0181-337 8943   Tel 0171-827 9977
Miller Freeman
Miller Freeman House, 30 Calderwood Street, London
SE18 6QH
Fax 0181-854 7476   Tel 0181-885 7777
Website: http://www.mfplc.co.uk
A subsidiary of United News and Media, Miller
Freeman specialises in business, trade and professional
magazines. Divisions include: Miller Freeman Business
Information Services (annual directories), Miller
Freeman Publications and Miller Freeman
Entertainment.
Mining Journal
60 Worship Street, London EC2A 2HD
Fax 0171-216 6050   Tel 0171-216 6060
Website: http://www.mining-journal.com
AE Morgan
Stanley House, 9 West Street, Epsom KT18 7RL
Fax 01372-744493   Tel 01372-741411
E-mail: t.morgan@easynet.co.uk
Myatt McFarlane
Trident House, Heath Road, Hale, Altrincham,
Cheshire WA14 2UJ
Fax 0161-941 6897   Tel 0161-928 3480
National Geographic Society
16 The Pines, Broad Street, Guildford, Surrey GU3
3NX
Fax 01483-506331   Tel 01483-537111
National Magazine Company
National Magazine House, 72 Broadwick Street,
London W1V 2BP
Fax 0171-439 5179   Tel 0171-439 5000
Owned by the Hearst Corporation.
Needmarsh Publishing
71 Newcomen Street, London SE1 1YT
Fax 0171-378 6883   Tel 0171-403 0840
New Internationalist
55 Rectory Road, Oxford OX4 1BW
Fax 01865-793152   Tel 01865-728181
New Statesman
7th Floor, Victoria Station House, 191 Victoria Street,
London SW1E 5NE
Fax 0171-828 1881   Tel 0171-828 1232
E-mail: info@newstatesman.co.uk
Newhall Publications
Newhall Lane, Holylake, Wirral, Merseyside L47 4BQ
Fax 0151-632 5716   Tel 0151-632 3232
Website: http://www.candice.co.uk
Newsweek
18 Park Street London W1Y 4HH
Fax 0171-629 0050   Tel 0171-318 1600
E-mail: promotions@newsweek.co.uk
Website: http://www.newsweek-int.com
Nexus Media
Nexus House, Azalea Drive, Swanley, Kent BR8 8HU
Fax 01322 667633   Tel 01322 660070
    Nexus Special Interests   01442-66551
The Nexus group of companies publish magazines and
books, and organize events on a variety of subjects.
These include: industry, architecture, lifestyle, business,
education, horticulture, health, IT, hobbies, crafts and

puzzles.
Nursery World
Admiral House, 66-68 East Smithfield, London E1 9XY
Fax 0171-782 3131   Tel 0171-782 3120
Oxford University Press
Great Clarendon Street, Oxford OX2 6DP
Fax 01865-556646   Tel 01865-556767
E-mail: jnl.info@oup.co.uk
Publishes 170 academic journals.
Parliamentry Communications
10 Little College Street, London SW1P 3SH
Fax 0171-878 1585   Tel 0171-233 1388
E-mail: Hannah-
Merrick@PCL.MHS.compuserve.com>
Publishers of The House Magazine, covering
government policies and parliament.
Paul Raymond Publications
2 Archer Street, London W1V 8JJ
Fax 0171-734 5030   Tel 0171-292 8000
Britain's largest porn magazine publisher.
Perry-Motorpress
Russell Square House, 10-12 Russell Square, London
WC1B 5ED
Fax 0171-580 6676   Tel 0171-229 7799
E-mail: bustrav@compuserve.com
Personnel Publications
17 Britton Street, London EC1M 5NQ
Fax 0171-336 7637   Tel 0171-880 6200
Website: http://www.peoplemanagement.co.uk
Philip Allan Publishers
Market Place, Deddington, Oxon OX15 0SE
Fax: 01869 338803   Tel: 01869 338652
E-mail: philip_allan@compuserve.com
14 student-educational mags plus exam guides and
material for teachers.
Phillips Business Information
Forum Chambers, Stevenage SG1 1EL
Fax 01438-740154   Tel 01438-742424
E-mail: kbrody@phillipslid.co.uk
Website: http://www.phillips.com/phillipsuk
Publisher of business newsletters in telecoms, IT, cable,
satellite, broadcast and new media markets.
Police Review Publishing
Celcon House, 289-293 High Holborn, London WC1V
7HZ
Fax 0171-405 7167   Tel 0171-440 4700
E-mail: fabiana.angelini@policereview.co.uk
Website: http://www.policereview.com
Publishes three magazines, training books and course
material.
Premier Publishing
1 Oxendon Street, London SW1Y 4EE
Fax 0171-839 4491   Tel 0171-925 2544
Website: http://www.globalnews.com/premieronline
The Publishing Team
Exmouth House, 3-11 Pine St, London EC1R 0JH
Fax 0171-923-5401   Tel 0171-923 5400
E-mail: info@publishing-team.co.uk
Webste: http://www.publishing-team.co.uk
Publishes customer magazines and corporate
communications.

Quantum Publishing
Quantum House, 19 Scarbrook Rd, Croydon CR9 1LX
Fax 0181-565 4444   Tel 0181-565 4200
Formed in 1989. In 1997 Quantum bought 13 Emap titles including Press Gazette and Media Week.

Raven-Fox
Nestor House, Playhouse Yard, London EC4V 5EX
Fax 0171-779 8249   Tel 0171-779 8228
E-mail: ravenfox@compuserve.com

RCN Publishing
Nursing Standard House, 17-19 Peterborough Road, Harrow HA1 2AX
Fax 0181-423 4302   Tel 0181-423 1066
E-mail: nursingstandard@compuserve.com
Website: http://www.nursing-standard.co.uk
Publishes the weekly Nursing Standard and a wide range of journals for nurses with different specialities.

Reader's Digest Association
11 Westferry Circus, Canary Wharf, London E14 4HE
Fax 0171-715 8181   Tel 0171-629 8144
Website: http://www.readersdigest.co.uk

The Redan Company
Appleton House, 139 King Street, London W6 9JG
Fax 0181-563 1478   Tel 0181-563 1563

Redwood Publishing
12-26 Lexington Street, London W1R 4HQ
Fax 0171-312 2601   Tel 0171-312 2600
Website: http://www.redwood-publishing.com
Redwood is a contract publisher, with clients including: AA, Abbey National, BSkyB, Black & Decker, Boots, BT, Dulux, Early Learning Centre, English Heritage, Harvey Nichols, Homebase, Marks & Spencer, PSION, Safeway, Unisys, Volvo, Woolworths, Yellow Pages.

Reed Business Information
Quadrant House, The Quadrant, Sutton, Surrey SM2 5AS
Fax 0181-652 3960   Tel 0181-652 3500
E-mail: andrea@macpherson.rbi.co.uk
Website: http://www.reedbusiness.com
One of Britain's largest business publishers.

Reed Elsevier
25 Victoria Street, London SW1H 0EX
Fax 0171-227 5799   Tel 0171-222 8420
Website: http://www.reed-elsevier.com
In January 1993 Reed and the Dutch group Elsevier set up Reed Elsevier plc to create one of the world's biggest publishing companies employing over 25,000 people. The main UK magazine divisions (listed elsewhere in this section) are:
Butterworth-Heinemann
Elsevier Science Publishers
IPC Magazines
Reed Business Publishing

Register Information Services
2 Holford Yard, Cruikshank Street, London WC1X 9HF
Fax 0171-833 5630   Tel 0171-833 3883
E-mail: name@magbus.demon.co.uk
Subsidiary of Pearson Professional.

Rodale Press
7-10 Chandos Street, London W1M 0AD
Fax 0171-291 6080   Tel 0171-291 6000

Routledge
11 New Fetter Lane, London EC4P 4EE
Fax 0171-842 2298   Tel 0171-583 9855
Web: http://www.routledge.com/routledge.html

Saga Publishing
The Saga Building, Middleburg Square, Folkestone, Kent CT20 1AZ
Fax 01303-712699   Tel 01303-711523
Magazines for the over 50s.

Sage Publications
6 Bonhill Street, London EC2A 4PU
Fax 0171-374 8741   Tel 0171-374 0645
E-mail: market@sagepub.co.uk
Website: http://www.sagepub.co.uk/
Publishes around 65 academic/technical newsletters and journals.

Scholastic
Villiers House, Clarendon Avenue, Leamington Spa, Warwickshire CV32 5PR
Fax 01926-883331   Tel 01926-887799

TG Scott
Brettenham House, 10 Savoy Street, London WC2E 7HR
Fax 0171-379 7118   Tel 0171-240 2032

Shepherd Press
111 High Street, Burnham. Buckinghamshire SL1 7JZ
Fax 01628-664334   Tel 01628-604311
E-mail: publishing@shepherd.co.uk
Website: http://www shepherd.co.uk

The Spectator
56 Doughty Street, London WC1N 2LL
Fax 0171-242 0603   Tel 0171-405 1706

The Stage Newspaper
Stage House, 47 Bermondsey Street, London SE1 3XT
Fax 0171-403 1418   Tel 0171-403 1818
E-mail: info@thestage.co.uk
Website: http://www.thestage.co.uk

The Stationery Office
St Crispin's, Duke Street, Norwich NR3 1PD
Tel 01603-622211
Website: http://www.national-publishing.co.uk
To order material on credit card via phone, tel: 0171-873 9090.
HMSO was privatised in September 1996. A residual part of HMSO remains within the Cabinet Office putting legal material on the internet.
Website: http://www.hmso.gov.uk

Sterling Publishing Group
86 Edgware Road, London W2 2YW
Fax 0171-915 9643   Tel 0171-915 9600
120 technical and business journals and directories.

Style Publishing
109-110 Bolsover Street, London W1P 7HF
Fax 0171-436 9957   Tel 0171-436 9766
E-mail: Style.Publishing@btinternet.com
Publishers of hair and beauty consumer and trade titles.

Summerhouse Publishing
St Jaems' Yarn Mill, Whitefriars, Norwich NR3 1XU
Fax 01603-664410   Tel 01603-664242
Website: http://www.summerhouse-publishing.com

Sweet and Maxwell
100 Avenue Road, London NW3 3PF
Fax 0171-393 7010   Tel 0171-393 7000
E:mail: webmaster@smlawpub.co.uk
Website: http://www.smlawpub.co.uk
Legal publishing.

The Tablet Publishing Company
1 King St Cloisters, Clifton Walk. London W6 0QZ
Fax 0181-748 1550   Tel 0181-748 8484
Website: http://www.thetablet.co.uk

Taylor and Francis
1 Gunpowder Square, London EC4A 3DE
Fax 0171-583 0581   Tel 0171-583 0490
Over 100 scientific and technical newsletters and
journals.

DC Thomson and Co
2 Albert Square, Dundee, Tayside DD1 9QJ
Fax 01382-322214   Tel 01382-223131
Website: http://www.dcthomson.co.uk
Publishes 12 titles.

Thomson Corporation
180 Wardour Street, London W1A 4YG
Fax 0171-734 0561   Tel 0171-437 9787
Website: http://www.thomcorp.com
The magazine publishing subsidiary of the Thomson
Corporation of Canada. Its main UK subsidiaries are:
  Derwent Information
  Janes Information Group
  Primary Source Media
  Routledge
  Sweet and Maxwell
  Thomson Financial Services
  Westlaw

Time Life International
Brettenham House, Lancaster Place, London WC2E
7TL
Fax 0171-322 1005   Tel 0171-499 4080
Publishes Time magazine

Time Out
Universal House, 251 Tottenham Court Road, London
W1P 0AB
Fax 0171-813 6001   Tel 0171-813 3000
E-mail net@timeout.co.uk.**Times Supplements**
Admiral House, 66-68 East Smithfield, London E1 9XY
Fax 0171-782 3200   Tel 0171-782 3000
E-mail: mailbox@tesl,demon.co.uk
Website: http://www.tes.co.uk
A subsidiary of News International and publisher of the
Times Educational Supplement and the Times Higher
Educational Supplement.

Timothy Benn Publishing
39 Earlham Street, Covent Garden, London WC2H
9LD
Fax 0171-306 7101   Tel 0171-306 7000
E-mail: postmag@benn.co.uk
Trade titles and directories for insurance and
photography.

Tolley Publishing Co
2 Addiscombe Road, Croydon, Surrey CR9 5AF
Fax 0181-760 0588   Tel 0181-686 9141
E:mail: Stephanie_Hawthorne@tolley.co.uk
Website: http://www.tolley.co.uk
A business publishing subsidiary of Reed Elsveir.

TPD Publishing
Long Island Ho, 1-4 Warple Way, London W3 0RG
Fax 0181-600 9101   Tel 0181-600 9100
Website: http://www.tpd.co.uk
Producer of contract publications for technology
companies. Can publish in any country, in any
language, in print and online.

United News and Media
245 Blackfriars Road, London SE1 9UY
Fax 0171-921 5002   Tel 0171-921 5000
Website: http://www.unm.com
United News and Media (formerly United Newspapers)
has a total of about 120 magazines in Britain, and
roughly 150 abroad. Its main magazine subsidiaries are:
  Benn Business Publishing
  Miller Freeman

Unity Media Communications
Quebec Square, Westerham, Kent TN16 1TD
Fax 01959-564390   Tel 01959-565690
Publishers of ten business and professional titles from
Unity Business Press and three consumer motoring
titles from Unity Consumer division.

VNU Business Publications
32-34 Broadwick Street, London W1A 2HG
Fax 0171-316 9003   Tel 0171-316 9000
Website: http://www.vnu.co.uk

Voice Communications Group
370 Coldharbour Lane, London SW9 8PL
Fax 0171-274 8994   Tel 0171-737 7377
E-mail: veeteeay@gn apc.org

Which?
See Consumer Association

William Reed Publishing
Broadfield Park, Brighton Road, Crawley, W Sussex
RH11 9RT
Fax 01293-610322   Tel 01293-613400
Website:http://www.foodanddrink.co.uk

Yachting Press
196 Eastern Esplanade, Southend SS1 3AB
Fax 01702-588434   Tel 01702-582245
E-mail: YandY@compuserve.com

Ziff-Davis UK
International House, 1 St Katherine's Way, London
E19 UN
Fax 0171-403 0668   Tel 0171-378 6800
Website: http://www.zdnet.co.uk

Alternative magazines

The majority of magazines are about TV, sex or shopping. This section lists the other mags which, for want of a better title, are the alternative ones and whose ideology extends beyond boosting circulations in order to sell more advertising. "Why," Searchlight asked, "are you publicising fascist groups?. Some of their articles are clearly in breach of the Public Order Act (1986)." One reason for inclusion of mags like the Flag is balance. Another, and much better reason, is that journalists sometimes need to talk to these people.

LEFT AND ALTERNATIVES

Animal
PO Box 467, London E8 3QX
　　　　　　　Tel 0956-506946
E-mail: animal_magazine@hotmail.com
Providing "space for activists to debate new and better ideas in the revolutionary and libertarian tradition". Launched 1997 as an anarchist successor to Class War.

Big Issue, The
236-240 Pentonville Road, London N1 9JY
Fax 0171-526 3201　　　Tel 0171-526 3200
E-mail: london@bigissue.com
Website: http://www.bigissue.com
Top-selling magazine, campaigning for the homeless, sold by the homeless. Weekly. Editor: Becky Gardiner.

Black Flag
BM Hurricane, London WC1N 3XX.
Analysis of the revolutionary anarchist movement. 4pa.

CARF
BM Box 8784, London WC1N 3XX
　　　　　　　Tel 0171-837 1450
E-mail: info@carf.demon.co.uk
Website: http://www.carf.demon.co.uk
Voice of Campaign Against Racism and Fascism. 6pa.

Class War
PO Box 3241, Saltley, Birmingham B8 3DP
　　　　　　　Tel 0117-907 3667
E-mail: class_war@hotmail.com
Website: http://www.geocities.com/capitolhill.9482
The 13-year old revolutionary campaign paper was formally closed by the Class War Federation in mid-1997. Another version may appear. See: Animal.

Contemporary Review
14 Upper Mulgrave Rd, Cheam, Surrey SM2 7AZ
Fax 0181-241 7507　　　Tel 0181-643 4846
A liberal look at life. Founded 1866. Monthly.

Counter Culture
see Third Way

Earth First! Action Update
c/o Norfolk EF, the Greenhouse, 42-46 Bethel Street, Norwich NR2 1NR
E-mail: actionupdate@gn.apc.org
News and diary of the environmental direct action movement. Monthly.

Earth Matters
FoE, 26-28 Underwood St, London N1 7JQ
Fax 0171-490 0881　　　Tel 0171-490 1555
E-mail: andyn@foe.co.uk
Friends of the Earth news, background and updates. 4pa. Editor: Andy Neather; Deputy: Jean McNeil

Ecologist, The
Agriculture House, Bath Road, Sturminster, Dorset DT10 1DU
Fax 01258-473748　　　Tel 01258-473476
E-mail: ecologist@gn.apc.org
Website: http://www.gn.apc.org/ecologist
Journal with a wide academic perspective. 6pa. Editor: Edward Goldsmith, Zac Goldsmith.

Environmental Politics
Frank Cass, 900 Eastern Ave, Ilford IG2 7HH
Fax 0181-599 0984　　　Tel 0181-599 8866
E-mail: info@frankcass.com
Website: http://www.frankcass.com/juls/ep.htm
For an academic slant. 4pa.

Ethical Consumer
Unit 21, 41 Old Birley Street, Manchester M15 5RF
Fax 0161-226 6277　　　Tel 0161-226 2929
E-mail: ethicon@mcr1.poptel.org.uk
An alternative Which? 6pa.

Feminist Review
Routledge Journals, 11 New Fetter Lane, London EC4P 4EE
Fax 0171-842 2298　　　Tel 0171-583 9855
Website: www.routledge.com
Academic journal "contesting feminist orthodoxies". Published 3pa.

Festival Eye
BCM Box 2002, London WC1N 3XX.
　　　　　　　Tel 0171-794 1708
E-mail: festivaleye@stones.com
Website: http://www.festivaleye.com
Annual. News and forum for alternative festivals.

Fortnight
7 Lower Crescent, Belfast BT7 1NR
Fax 01232-232650　　　Tel 01232-232353
E-mail: mairtin@fortnite.dnet.co.uk
Northern Ireland news. Monthly.

Fuascailt (Liberation)
PO Box 6191, London NW5 !RA
Fax 0181-442 8778　　　Tel 0181-442 8778
Campaigning bi-monthly on Irish reunification.

Free Press
Campaign for Press and Broadcasting Freedom, 8 Cynthia St, London N1 9JF
Fax 0171-837 8868　　　Tel 0171-278 4430
Campaigning for a diverse and accountable media. 6pa.

Freedom
84b Whitechapel High St, London E1 7QX
Fax 0171-377 9526   Tel 0171-247 9249
Anarchist commentary on current affairs. Founded
1886 (longest-running anarchist paper in UK). 24pa.

Gay Scotland
17-23 Carlton Road, Edinburgh EH8 8DL
Fax 0131-557 2625   Tel 0131-556 3331
E-mail: Paul@gayscotland.co.uk
Monthly.

Gay Times
116-134 Bayham St, London NW1 0BA
Fax 0171-284 0329   Tel 0171-482 2576
E-mail: info@gaytimes.co.uk
Website: http://www.gaytimes.co.uk
Europe's biggest selling gay news and information
magazine. Monthly. Editor: David Smith.

Green Anarchist
BCM 1715, London WC1N 3XX
               Tel 0956-694922
Action-packed paper, often raided by the Special
Branch. Its three editors were sentenced to three years
in gaol in November 1997. 4pa.

Green Line
Catalyst Collective, PO Box 5, Lostwithiel, Cornwall,
PL22 0YT
               Tel 0870-7334970
E-mail: greenline@clara.net
Eco news: environment, roads, animal rights etc.
Monthly.

Green World
49 York Road, Aldershot, Hants GU11 3JQ
Fax 01252-330506   Tel 01252-330506
E-mail: green.world@gexpress.gn.apc.org
News, action and networks of the Green Party. 4pa.

HHH Video Mag
PO Box 888, 10 Martello St, London E8 3PE
Visuals from the anarcho video co-operative.

In Balance
50 Parkway, Welwyn Garden City, Hertfordshire AL8
6HH
Fax 01707 395550   Tel 01707-339007
E-mail: vbrown@pintail.u-net.com
Quarterly. Holistic health magazine with a source
directory of courses, clinics and therapists.

International Socialism
See: Socialist Worker

Irish Democrat
244 Grays Inn Rd, London WC1X 8JR
               Tel 0171-833 3022
Views of Irish politics. Founded 1939. 6pa.

Jewish Socialist
BM 3725, London WC1N 3XX
Debate, news and reviews. 4pa.

Labour Left Briefing
PO Box 2378, London E5 9QU
Fax 0181-985 6785   Tel 0181-985 6597
E-mail: llb@labournet.co.uk
Website: http://www.llb.labournet.org.uk/
Independent voice for socialist ideas in the labour
movement. 10pa.

Labour Research
78 Blackfriars Rd, London SE1 8HF
Fax 0171-928 0621   Tel 0171-928 3649
E-mail: lrd@geo2.poptel.org.uk
Website: http://www.lrd.org.uk/
Valuable data and research for the labour movement, by
the independent Labour Research Department. Formed
1917. Monthly.

LM
Informinc (LM) Ltd, Signet House, 49/51 Farringdon
Road, London EC1M 3JB
Fax 0171-278 9844   Tel 0171-278 9908
E-mail: lm@informinc.co.uk
Glossiest of the political organs. Formerly Living
Marxism, of the Revolutionary Communist Party.
Monthly. Editor: Mick Hume.

Lobster
214 Westbourne Ave, Hull HU5 3JB
                    Tel 01482-447558
E-mail: robin@lobster.karoo.co.uk
Digs into the clandestine activities of the state. 2pa.

Militant
see The Socialist.

Morning Star
1-3 Ardleigh Rd, London N1 4HS
Fax 0171-254 5950   Tel 0171-254 0033
E-mail: morsta@geo2.poptel.org.uk
The former Communist Party newspaper, founded
1930. Daily. Owned and published by People's Press
Printing Society, a co-operative. Editor: John Haylett.

Mother Earth
see Third Way

New Ground
SERA, 11 Goodwin St, London N4 3HQ
Fax 0171-263 7424   Tel 0171-263 7389
E-mail: SERAofice@aol.com
Website: http://www.netlink.co.uk/users2/sera
Magazine of SERA, the environment group affiliated to
the Labour Party. News, campaigns and features. 4pa.

New Humanist
Rationalist Press Association, 47 Theobalds Rd,
London WC1X 8SP
Fax 0171-430 1271   Tel 0171-430 1371
E-mail: jm.rpa@humanism.org.uk
Quarterly.news on life from a humanist point of view.

New Internationalist
55 Rectory Rd, Oxford OX4 1BW
Fax 01865-793152   Tel 01865-728181
E-mail: veroniques@newint.org
Reports on world poverty and inequalities. Monthly.

New Left Review
6 Meard St, London W1V 3HR
Fax 0171-734 0059   Tel 0171-734 8830
E-mail: newleftreview@compuserve.com
Academic thoughts and theories on politics. 6pa.

New Statesman
191 Victoria Street, London SW1E 5NE
Fax 0171-828 1881   Tel 0171-828 1232
E-mail: info@newstatesman.co.uk
The best-known leftish magazine. Founded 1913.
Weekly.

News Line
BCM Box 747, London WC1N 3XX
Fax 0171-620 1221   Tel 0171-928 3218
Daily newspaper of the Trotskyite Workers
Revolutionary Party (with TV and sport).

New Times
6 Cynthia St, London N1 9JF
Fax 0171-278 4425   Tel 0171-278 4451
E-mail: newtimes@pop3.poptel.org.uk
Newspaper of the Democratic Left, offspring of the
Communist Party. Fortnightly.

Organise!
84b Whitechapel High St, London E1 7QX.
Jounral of the Anarchist Communist Federation. 4pa.

Pagan Dawn
Pagan Fed. BM Box 7097, London WC1N 3XX.
                    Tel 01928-770909
E-mail: kate@pagmedia.demon.co.uk
Pre-Christian beliefs as practised today.

Peace News
5 Caledonian Road, London N1 9DX
Fax 0171-278 0444   Tel 0171-278 3344
E-mail: Peacenews@gn.apc.org
Website: http://www.gn.apc.org/peacenews
For non-violent revolution. 11 x pa.

Pink Paper, The
72 Holloway Rd, London N7 8NZ
Fax 0171-957 0046   Tel 0171-296 6210
E-mail: editor@pinkpaper.co.uk
Lesbian and gay news. Weekly. Editor: Tim Teeman.

Political Quarterly/Political Studies
Blackwell, 108 Cowley Road, Oxford OX4 1JF
Fax 01865-791347   Tel 01865-791100
Politics from many perspectives. 4pa. Also Politics(3pa).

Radical History Review
Cambridge University Press, Edinburgh Bldg,
Shaftesbury Rd, Cambridge CB2 2RU
Fax 01223-315052   Tel 01223-325757
Website: http://www.journals.cup.ac.uk
Academic study of the past from a non-sectarian
perspective. 3pa. CUP also publishes British Journal of
Political Science (4pa). Editor: Prof. Van Gosse.

Radical Philosophy
33 Court Road, Wolverhampton WV6 0JN
                    Tel 01902-742466
Website: http://www.ukc.ac.uk/CPRS/PHIL/RP
Journal of a socialist and feminist philosophy. 6pa.

Raven, The
84 b Whitechapel High Street, London E1 7QX
                    Tel 0171-247 9249
In-depth anarchist discussion and analysis. 4pa.

Red Kite
Brynmadog, Gwernogle, Carmarthen SA32 7RN
Fax 01267-202471   Tel 01267-202375
E-mail: redkite@democraticleft.org.uk
Independent radical magazine of Wales.

Red Pepper
1b Waterloo Road, London N19 5NJ
Fax 0171-263 9345   Tel 0171-281 7024
E-mail: redpepper@online.rednet.co.uk
Website: http://www.redpepper.org.uk
Non-partisan news mag of the British left. Monthly.

Resurgence
Ford House, Hartland, Bideford, Devon EX39 6EE
Fax 01237-441203   Tel 01237-441293
E-mail: ed@resurge.demon.co.uk
Website: http://www.gn.apc.org/resurgence
Aesthetic magazine on environmental and ecological
issues with a spiritual approach. 6pa. Editor: Satish
Kumar.

Rural Socialism
25 Townholm Crescent, London W7 2LY
Campaigning for a Labour Party "rural revival".
Occasional.

SchNews
Justice?, PO Box 2600, Brighton, East Sussex BN2
2DX.
Fax 01273-685913   Tel 01273-685913
Website: http://www.cbuzz.co.uk/SchNEWS/
The inside news story from the direct action alternative
frontline. Weekly.

Scottish Workers Republic
135 London Road, Glasgow G1 5BS
Fax 0141-552 7304   Tel 0141-357 3690
E-mail: donald@alba-pubn.demon.co.uk
Website: http://www.alba-pubn.demon.co.uk
Campaigning for an independent socialist Scotland.

Searchlight
37b New Cavendish Street, London W1M 8JR
Fax 0171-284 4410   Tel 0171-284 4040
E-mail: editor@s-light.demon.co.uk
Website: http://www.s-light.demon.co.uk
International in-depth news and research on the
extreme right. Monthly.

Socialism Today
See below (The Socialist)

Socialist, The
3-13 Hepscott Rd, London E9 5HB
Fax 0181-985 2932   Tel 0181-533 3311
E-mail: socialistparty.org.uk
Website: http://www.socialistparty.org.uk
The newspaper voice of the Socialist Party (known as
Militant Labour until early 1997; the paper was called
Militant). Weekly. The party also publishes the monthly
Socialism Today. See: Socialist Standard.

Socialist Affairs
Socialist International, Maritime House, Old Town,
Clapham, London SW4 0JW
Fax 0171-720 4448   Tel 0171-627 4449
E-mail: socint@gn.apc.org
Website: http://www.gn.apc.org/socint/
Debates of the international movement. 4pa.

Socialist Appeal
PO Box 226, London N1 7SQ
Fax 0171-251 1095   Tel 0171-251 1094
E-mail: socappeal@easynet.co.uk
Website:
http://easyweb.easynet,co.uk/-socappeal/IDOM.html
Marxist view of the labour movement. 12pa.Editor: Alan
Woods.

Socialist Standard
Socialist Party of Great Britain (aka Socialist Party), 52 Clapham High St, London SW4 7UN
Fax 0171-720 3665   Tel 0171-622 3811
E-mail: spgb@worldsocialism.org
Website: http://www.worldsocialism.org
A venerable Marxist monthly founded in 1904.

Socialist Worker
PO Box 82, London E3 3LH
Fax 0171-538 0140   Tel 0171-538 0828
E-mai: leters@socialstworker.co.uk
Website: http://www.swp.org.uk
Socialist Workers Party's newspaper. Weekly. SWP also publishes Socialist Review (monthly) and the more theoretical International Socialism journal(4pa).

Sorted
7 Rock Place, Brighton, East Sussex BN2 1PF
Fax 01273-620203   Tel 01273-683318
Website: http://www.nacro.org/sorted/welcome.htm
A free speech platform for wannabe journalists. Written by young people for young people on a variety of issues.

Soundings
Lawrence & Wishart, 99a Wallis Rd, London E9
Fax 0181-533 7369   Tel 0181-533 2506
E-mail: soundings@l-w-bks.demon.co.uk
Website: http://www.l.w.bks.co.uk
"A journal of culture and politics". 3pa. Editors: Stuart Hall, Doreen Massey, Michael Rustin.

Squall
PO Box 8959, London N19 5HW
Fax 0171-561 0800   Tel 0171-561 1204
E-mail: squall.co.uk
ebsite: http://www.squall.co.uk
Coverage of the frontiers of alternative politics and culture. 4pa.

The Spark Magazine
10-12 Picton Street, Bristol BS6 5QA
Fax 0117-914 3444   Tel 0117-914 3434
E-mail: john@spark.u-net.com.

Statewatch
PO Box 1516, London N16 0EW.
Fax 0181-880 1727   Tel 0181-802 1882
Monitor of the state and civil liberties in the UK and Europe. 6pa.

Taking Liberties
PO Box 446, Sheffield S1 1NY
Prison issues, from the Anarchist Black Cross.

Third Way
PO Box 1243, London SW7 3PB
Fax 0171-681 1191   Tel 0171-373 3432
E-mail: thirdway@dircon.co.uk
Website: http://www.users.dircon.co.uk/~thirdway
"Voice of the Radical Centre", seeking alternatives to capitalism and communism. 6pa. Also published: ecological newsletter Mother Earth (4pa) and Counter Culture (4pa).

Tribune
308 Grays Inn Rd, London WC1X 8DY
Fax 0171-833 0385   Tel 0171-278 0911
Website: http://www.tribpub.demon.co.uk
The "voice of the left". Launched 1937. Weekly.

Trouble and Strife
PO Box 8, Diss, Norfolk IP322 3XG
Feminist magazine. 2pa.

Undercurrents
16b Cherwell Street, Oxford OX4 1BG
Fax 01865-243562   Tel 01865-203663
E-mail: under@gn.apc.org
Website: http://www.undercurrents.org
An alternative video news magazine. Quarterly.

Voice, The
370 Coldharbour Lane, London SW9 8PL
Fax 0171-274 8994   Tel 0171-737 7377
General newspaper for Britain's black community, especially the young. Weekly.

RIGHT

Candour
Forest House, Liss Forest, Liss, Hants GU33 7DD
Tel 01730-892109
Defending national sovereignty from international monetary power. Founded 1953. Monthly.

Flag, The
PO Box 2269, London E6 3RF
Fax 0181-471 6872   Tel 0181-471 6872
News of the extreme right National Democrats. Monthly. Also publish Vanguard magazine (4pa).

Freedom Today
Freedom Association, 35 Westminster Bridge Rd, London SE1 7JB
Tel 0171-928 9925
E-mail: 100703.2174@compuserve.com
Website: www.pipe,edia.net/~freedom/freedty.htm
Exposure of official actions and attitudes which reduce choices and freedoms. 6pa.

Freemasonry Today
87 Guildhall Street, Bury St Edmunds, Suffolk IP33 1PU
E-mail: freemasonry.today@btinternet.com
Quarterly launched in July 1997. Ed: Tobias Churton.

Masonic Square
Coomblands House, Coomblands Lane, Addlestone, Surrey KT15 1HY
Fax 01932-821258   Tel 01932-820552
Forum for the freemasons.

Right Now
BCM Right, London WC1N 3XX
Fax 0181-692 7099   Tel 0181-692 7099
E-mail: rightnow@compuserve.com
Rght-of-centre conservative comment. 4pa.

Salisbury Review
33 Canonbury Park South, London N1 2JW
Fax 0171-354 0383   Tel 0171-226 7791
E-mail: Salisbury-Review@easynet.co.uk
http://www.easyweb.easynet.co.uk/tilder.salisburyreview
Dry conservative thought, comment and analysis. 4pa.

Spectator, The
56 Doughty St, London WC1N 2LL
Fax 0171-242 0603   Tel 0171-405 1706
E-mail: editor@spectator.demon.co.uk
Best-known and most popular vehicle of centre-right news and reviews. Founded 1828. Weekly.

Magazine listings

Oxbridge Communications, Inc.

Maximise Your Subscription Potential on the World Wide Web...Join the Mediafinder Community

- ▶ MediaFinder attracts a global readership of over 2,000 to its site every day.
- ▶ Consumers regularly use our database to request subscriptions.
- ▶ Media buyers use our database to request media packs.
- ▶ Direct marketers use our database to research and rent US subscriber mailing lists.
- ▶ MediaFinder provides a cost-effective method of acquiring new subscribers, particularly from the North American market.

───── The Mediafinder Options ─────

Enhanced Listings Make your title stand out in our community of 95,000 print media and mail order catalogs! This package includes the title in bold, a picture of the publication cover and a brief description. The introductory special is £50.00 per title, per year, for this option.

Enhanced Listings & Keywords If you want your publication to come out "on top of the list" when a visitor to the site is searching a specific sector/subject, this is the option for you. You buy certain keywords which best sum up your title and the site's search engine will seek out your publication when the visitor enters one or more of these keywords. This package also includes all the features of the Enhanced Listing option. The introductory special is £650.00 per title for the first year of this option, which covers two keywords plus an Enhanced Listing.

Subscriptions On-line We can sell subscriptions for each of your titles as part of your web listing. All we charge is a 10% commission on each paid subscription generated by **MediaFinder**. Our service is very flexible: we can simply capture details and forward them on to you, or capture details and verify credit card information before forwarding them to you.

Marketing Extras Ltd.

43 St. James' Drive, LONDON SW17 7RN

Tel: 44 (0)181 767 9960 • ***Fax:*** 44 (0)181 767 9969

Marketing Extras are the exclusive European agents for Oxbridge Communications and are here to look after the needs of their UK and European customers.

Brand Strategy 0171-439 4222
Bride & Groom Magazine
0171-437 0796
Brides & Setting Up Home
0171-499 9080
British Archaeology 01904-671417
British Baker 0181-565 4200
British Birds 01767-640025
British Dental Journal
0171-387 4499
British Horse 0171-261 5000
British Jeweller 0171-520 1500
British Journal of Community
Nursing/Health Care
Management/Hospital Medicine/
Midwifery/Nursing/Optometry
0181-671 7521
British Journal of Photography
0171-306 7000
British Medical Journal
0171-387 4499
British Nationalist (BNP)
0181-316 4721
British Printer 01732-364422
British Rate & Data (BRAD)
0171-505 8000
Broadcast 0171-505 8000
Building 0171-560 4000
Building Design 0181-855 7777
Bunty 01382-223131
Burlington Magazine
0171-388 8157
Bus Fayre 01274-881640
Business Equipment Digest
01732-359990
Business and Technology
0171-631 1433
BusinessAfrica/Asia/China/Europe/
Latin America/Middle East/Russia
0171-830 1000
Business Equipment Digest
01732-359990
Business Franchise 0181-742 2828
Business Traveller 0171-229 7799
Business Travel World
0171-505 6600
Butterfly Conservation
01206-322342
Buy a Boat 01243-533394
Buying Cameras 01733-898100
The Buzz 01232 331694

C

Cabinet Maker 01732-364422
Cab Driver 0171-493 5267
Cable & Satellite Europe
0171-896 2700
Cable Television Engineering
0191-281 7094
CadCam 0171-388 2430
Cage & Aviary Birds 0171-261 5000
Cake Decorating 01225-442244

Camcorder User 0171-331 1000
Campaign 0181-943 5000
The Campaigner 0181-846 9777
Camping & Caravanning
01203-694995
Canal & Riverboat 01372-741411
Candis 0151-632 3232
Canoeist 01235-847270
Car 0171-312 8902
Car & Accessory Trader
0181-943 5000
Car Boot Calendar 0118-940 2165
Car Mechanics 01959 541444
Car Russia 0171-216 6200
Caravan Club Magazine
01342-326944
Caravan Life 01778-391000
Caravan Magazine 0181-686 2599
Caribbean Times 0171-702 8012
Carribean Travel News Europe
0181-855 7777
Caribbean World 0171-581 9009
Cars & Car Conversions
0181-686 2599
CarSport 01232 783200
The Cartoonist 0171-353 2828
Car World 01733-237111
Cash & Carry Management
0181-688 2696
Cat 0181-943 5000
The Cat 01403-221900
Cat World 01273-462000
Catalyst 01869-338652
Caterer & Hotelkeeper
0181-652 3500
Catering Update 0181-652 3500
Catholic Herald 0171-588 3101
Cats 0161-236 0577
Caves & Caving 01278-691539
C B Radio Active 01705-613800
Celebrations in Cross Stitch
01225-442244
Centrepoint 0181-539 3876
Chat 0171-261 5000
Checkout 0181-652 3500
Checkout Fresh 0181-652 3243
Chemical Engineer 01788-578214
Chemist & Druggist 0181-855 7777
Chemistry in Britain 01223-420066
Chemistry Review 01869-338652
Chess 0171-388 2404
Chic 0171-308 5090
China Economic Review
0171-834 7676
China In Focus 01253-894582
Choice 01733-555123
Christian Socialist 0171-833 0666
Church Times 01603-612914
City Life 0161-839 1416
Civil Engineer International
0171-505 6600

Classic & Sportscar 0181-943 5000
Classic Bike/Motor Cycle
01733-237111
Classic Boat 0181-686 2599
Classic Car Weekly 01733-237111
Classic CD 01225-442244
Classic Stitches 01382-223131
Club Mirror 0181-681 2099
Coach & Bus Week 01733-467000
Coach Tours & Excursions
01733-467000
Coarse Angling 0171-261 5000
Coat of Arms 0118-932 0210
Colour 0171-312 2600
Comagazine 01895-444055
Combat 0121-344 3737
Combat & Survival 01484-435011
Commercial Motor 0181-652 3500
Commercial Vehicle Manager
01733-467000
Common Cause 0171-281 4101
Communications Africa
0171-834 7676
Communications International
0171-505 8000
Communications Law
0181-686 9141
Community Care 0181-652 3500
Community Nurse 0171-843 3600
Community Pharmacy
0171-334 7333
Community Transport Magazine
0161-351 1475
Commuter World 01628-664334
Company 0171-439 5000
Computer Arts 01225-442244
Computer & Video Games
0171-972 6700
Computer Buyer/Shopper
0171-631 1433
Computer Weekly 0181-652 3500
Computing 0171-316 9000
Conde Nast Traveller
0171 499 9080
Conference and Incentive Travel
0181-943 5000
Construction News 0171-505 6600
Containerisation International
0171-505 3550
Contemporary Visual Arts
0171-823 8373
Contract Journal 0181-652 3500
Control & Instrumentation
0181-855 7777
Control Systems 01732-359990
Convenience Store 01293-613400
Cornish Banner 01726-843501
Corporate Money 0171-439 4222
Coroporate Networks
0181-652 3500
Cosmopolitan 0171-439 5000

Counter Culture 0171-373 3432
Country Homes & Interiors
0171-261 5000
Country Life 0171-261 5000
Country Living 0171-439 5000
Country Music International
0181-686 2599
Country Music People
0181-692 1106
Country Sports 01206-263234
Country Walking 01733-264666
The Countryman 0181-686 2599
Countryside 01242-521381
CPRE Voice 0171-976 6433
Crafts 0171-278 7700
Craftsman Magazine
01377-255213
Creative Review 0171-439 4222
Creative Technology 0181-742 2885
Cricketer International
0181-699 1796
Crops 0181-652 3500
Cross Stitch 01225-442244
Cross Stitch Collection
01225-442244
Cross Stitcher 01225-442244
Crossbow 0171-727 9845
CTN 0181-565 4200
CU Amiga 0171-972 6700
Cult Times 0181-875 1520
Cult TV 01225-442244
Current Archaeology
0171-435 7517
Custom Car 0181-658 3531
Cuts 0171-437 0801
Cycle Sport 0171-261 5000
Cycle Touring & Campaigning
01483-417217
Cycling Plus 01225-442244
Cycling Weekly 0171-261 5000
Cymru 01222-231944
D
D & A Magazine 0171-312 2600
Dairy Farmer 01473-241122
Dalton's Weekly 01202-445000
Dance & Dancers 0171-813 1049
Dancing Times 0171-250 3006
Dandy 01382-223131
Darts World 0181-650 6580
Database Management
0181-855 7777
Day by Day 0181-856 6249
Dealer Principal 01733-467000
Defence Helicopter 01628-604311
Defence Industry Digest
0171-242 2548
Defence Upgrades 0181-700 3700
Defence Weekly 0181-700 3700
The Dentist 01483-304944
Design Engineering 0181-855 7777

Design Products & Applications
01732-359990
Design Week 0171-439 4222
Diesel Car 01225-442244
Digital Photo FX 01733-898100
Diplomat 0171-405 4874
Direct Mail 0181-855 7777
The Director 0171-730 6060
Disability Now 0171-636 5020
Disability Times 0171-233 7970
Disco International (DI)
01322-660070
Disney & Me 0171-344 6400
Diver Magazine 0181-943 4288
DIY Week 01732-364422
DJ 01322-660070
Do It Yourself 01322-660070
Docklands Recorder
0181-472 1421
The Doctor 0181-652 3500
Doctor Who Magazine
01892-500100
Dog World 01233-621877
Dogs Today 01276-858880
Dorset Life 01929-551264
Drapers Record 0171-520 1500
Druglink 0171-928 1211
E
Earth Matters 0171-490 1555
Early Music Today 0171-333 1744
Eastern Eye 0171-702 8012
The Ecologist 01258-473476
Economic Review 01869-338652
Economic Trends 0171-873 0011
The Economist 0171-830 7000
Edge 01225 442244
Electrical Products 01732-359990
Electrical Review 0181-652 3113
Electrical Times 0181-652 3500
Electronic Engineering
0181-855 7777
Electronic Manufacture & Test
01732-359990
Electronic Product Design
01732-359990
Electronic Product Review
01322-277788
Electronic Showcase
01732-359990
Electronics 01702-554155
Electronics & Wireless World
0181-652 3500
Electronics Times 0181-855 7777
Electronics Weekly 0181-652 3500
Electronics World 0181-652 3500
Elle 0171-437 9011
Elle Decoration 0171-437 9011
Elvis Monthly 0116 2537271
Empire 0171-436 1515
Employee Benefits 0171-439 4222

Employer's Law 0181-652 4669
Enchanted Lands 0181-653 1563
Energy Management
0181-277 5000
The Engineer 0181-855 7777
Engineering 01564-771772
English Churchman 01227-781282
English Review 01869-338652
Environmental Health News
0171-928 6006
ES Magazine (free) 0171-938 6000
Esquire 0171-439 5000
Essentials 0171-261 5000
Essential Playstation
01225-442244
Essex Countryside 01799-544 2000
Estate Agency News
01253-722142
Estates Gazette 0181-652 3000
Ethical Consumer 0161-226 2929
Euroguy 0181-348 9963
European Chemical News
0181-652 3153
European Pig and Poultry Fair
0181-855 7777
European Plastics News
0181 277 5000
European Sign Magazine
03465-737777
Eva 0171-261 5000
Eventing 0171-261 5000
Events In Scotland 0131-332 2433
Exchange & Mart 01202-445000
Exe 0171-439 4222
Executive Woman 0181-420 1210
Expert Systems & Applications
01732-359990
Export Management
0171-463 3000
Eyecontact Magazine
01444-445566
Eyestyle Magazine 01444-445566
F
The Face 0171-837 7270
Fairplay International Shipping
0181-660 2811
Family Circle 0171-261 5000
Family Tree Magazine
01487-814050
Farmers Guardian 01772-203800
Farmers Weekly 0181-652 3500
Farming News 0181-855 7777
Fast Car 01689-874025
Fast Ford 01452-307181
FHM - For Him Magazine
0171-247 5447
The Field 0171-261 5000
Fiesta 01376-510555
Film Review 0181-875 1520
Financial Adviser 0171-896 2525

Financial Director	0171-316 9000
Financial Pulse	0181-855 7777
Fire Prevention	0181-236 9690
First	0171-439 1188
Fish Farming International	0171-470 6200
Fishing News International	0171-470 6200
The Flag (Nat Dem)	0181-471 6872
Fleet Car	01733-467000
Fleet Dealer	01733-467000
Fleet News	01733-467000
Flight International	0181-652 3500
Flying Angel News	0171-248 5202
Flying Saucer Review	01923-779018
Focus	0171-519 5500
Focus on Africa	0171-257 2792
Folk Roots	0181-340 9651
Food Manufacture	0181-855 7777
Food Manufacture Ingredients & Machine Survey	0181-555 7777
Food Processing	01732-359990
Food Service Management	0181-652 8389
Food Worker	01707-260150
Football Monthly	0181-868 5801
For a Change	0171-828 6591
Fore!	01733-264666
Foreign Report	0181-700 3700
Forestry and British Timber	01732-364422
Forestry News	01732-364422
Fortnight	01232-232353
Fortune	0171-499 4080
Forum	0171-308 5090
Four Four Two	0181-943 5000
Franchise Magazine	01603-620301
Free Church Chronicle	01782-614407
Free Press	0171-278 4430
Freedom	0171-247 9249
Freelance Informer	0181-652 3500
Freemasonry Today	0171-486 3852
The Friend	0171-387 7549
Frontiers	01225-442244
Fun to Learn	0181-563 1563
Furnishing	01895-677677
Future Music	01225-442244
Future Net	01225-442244
FW	0171-520 1500

G

Gamesmaster	01225-442244
Garavi Gujarat	0171-928 1234
The Garden/Garden Answers	01733-898100
Garden Trade News	01733-898100
Gardeners World (BBC)	0181-576 2000
Gatelodge	0181-803 0255

Gatwick News	01293-775000
Gay Times	0171-482 2576
Genealogists Magazine	0171-251 8799
General Practitioner	0181-943 5000
Geographical Magazine	0171-938 4011
Geography Review	01869-338652
Geoscientist	01225-445046
Geriatric Medicine	01732-464154
Girl About Town	0171-872 0033
Girl Talk	0181-576 2000
Global Transport	0171-385 7766
GMTV Magazine	0171-261 5000
Goal	0171-261 5000
Going Wild In London	0171-261-0447
Golf Industry News	0171-436 1515
Golf Monthly	0171-261 5000
Golf Weekly	01733-264666
Golf World	017733-264666
Good Food (BBC)	0181-576 2000
Good Housekeeping	0171-439 5000
Good Vibrations	01733-370777
Good Woodworking	01225-442244
The Gospel Magazine	01462-811204
GP	0181-943 5000
GQ	0171-499 9080
GQ Active	0171-499 9080
Gramophone	0181-422 4562
Grand Prix Review	0181-943 5000
Granta	0171-704 9776
Grassroots Campaigner	01422-843785
The Great Outdoors	0141-302 7700
Greek Review	0171-272 2722
Green Futures	01223-568017
Greenscene	0161-928 0793
Greybike	01565-652424
The Grocer	01293-613400
Ground Engineering	0171-505 6600
The Guardian Weekly	0171-713 4400
Guiding	0171-834 6242
Guitarist	01225-442244
Guitar Techniques	01225-442244

H

Hair	0171-261 5000
Hairdressers' Journal	0181-652 3500
Ham Radio Today	01442-66551
Hansard	0171-873 0011
Harpers & Queen	0171-439 5000
Hazards Magazine	0114-276 5695
Headlight	0181-660 2811
Headlines	01442-233656
Health & Beauty Salon	0181-652 3500

Health & Fitness	01322-660070
Health Insurance	0171-505 6600
Health & Safety at Work	0181-686 9141
Health Club Management	01462-431385
Health Service Journal	0171-843 3600
Healthy Eating	01608-811266
Heavy Horse World	01243-811364
Helicopter International	01934-822524
Helicopter World	01628-664334
Hello!	0171-334 7404
Here's Health	0171-437 9011
Heritage Scotland	0131-226 5922
Heritage Today	0171-973 3000
Hi-Fi Choice	0171-631 1433
Hi-Fi World	0171-289 3533
High Life	0171-925 2544
Hindsight	01869-338652
Hip Hop Connection	01225-442244
History Today	0171-534 8000
History Workshop Journal	01865-556767
HN	0171-312 2600
Homebase Living	0171-312 2600
Home & Country	0171-371 9300
Home & Family	0171-222 5533
Home Entertainment	0171-631 1433
Homes & Antiques (BBC)	0181-576 2000
Home Furnishings	01732-364422
Homes & Gardens	0171-261 5000
Homes & Ideas	0171-261 5000
Homestyle	0171-928 5869
Horoscope	0171-396 8000
Horse	0171-261 5000
Horse Exchange	0171-261 5000
Horse & Hound	0171-261 5000
Horse Magazine	0171-261 5000
Horse & Pony	01733-264666
Horticulture Week	0181-943 5000
Hospital Doctor	0181-652 3500
Hospital Equipment & Supplies	01322-277788
Hot Shoe International	01622-687031
Hotel	01323-507474
Hotel & Restaurant Magazine	0181-681 2099
The House	0171-878 1500
House & Garden	0171-499 9080
House Beautiful	0171-439 5000
Housewares	01732-364422
Housing	0171-837 8727
Housing Today	0171-843 2275

I

I-D Magazine	0171-813 6060
IBM Computer Today	0181-652 3500
Ideal Home	0171-261 5000
The Idler	0171-239 9575
Illustrated London News	0171-805 5555
Image	01379-640908
The Image	0171-495 7070
Improve Your Course Fishing	01733-264666
Improve Your Sea Angling	01733-264666
In Balance	01707-339007
In-Store Marketing	0171-439 4222
Independent Retail News	0181-652 8754
Index on Censorship	0171-278 2313
India Weekly	0171-251 3290
Individual Homes	0171-439 4222
Industrial Exchange & Mart	01202-445000
Inflight	01628-664334
Inside Cosmetics	0181-855 7777
Inside Eye	0171-439 4222
Inside Guides	0171-312 2600
Inside Soap	0171636 5095
Inspirations	0171-836 0519
Insurance Age	0171-505 6600
In Touch	0181-343 2576
Intelligence & National Security	0181-599 8866
Intelligence Review	0181-700 3700
InterMedia	0171-388 0671
International	0171-463 3000
International Broadcasting	0171-505 8000
International Defense Review	0181-700 3700
International Express	0171-928 8000
International Food Ingredients	0181-855 7777
International Food Manufacture	0181-855 7777
International Freighting Weekly	0171 505 6600
International Money Marketing	0171-439 4222
International Police Review	0171-440 4700
International Press Directory	0171-833 5888
International Risk Management	0171-505 6600
International Socialism	0171-538 5821
Internet	0171-388 2430

Internet Magazine	01733-898100
Internet Works	01225-442244
Interzone Science Fiction	01273-504710
Investment Fund Index (CD Rom)	0171-439 4222
Investors Chronicle	0171-405 6969
Irish Post	0181-561 0059
Irish World	0181-453 7800
IT	0171-485 0340
IT-Mag	0171-491 3737

J

Jane's Defence Weekly	0181-700 3700
Jane's Intelligence Review	0181-700 3700
Janomot Bengali Newsweekly	0171-377 6032
Japan Forum	01264-343062
Jazz Journal International	0171-608 1348
Jewish Chronicle	0171-415 1500
Jewish Quarterly	0171-629 5004
Jewish Telegraph	0161-740 9321
Jewish Tribune	0181-800 6688
The Job (The Met)	0171-230 1212
The Journal	0171-505 6600
The Journalist	0171-278 7916
Journal of Wound Care	0171-505 6600
Just 17	0171-437 9011

K

Kerrang!	0171-436 1515
King-Size Arrows/Crosswords	01737-769799
Kitchens, Bedrooms & Bathrooms	01895-677677
Knave	01376-510555
Kriss Kross	0181-846 9922

L

Labour Left Briefing	0181-985 6597
Labour Market Trends	0171-873 9090
Labour Research	0171-928 3649
The Lady	0171-379 4717
The Lancet	0171-436 4981
Land Rover Owner International	01733-237111
The Landworker	0171-828 7788
Law Society's Gazette	0171-242 1222
The Lawyer	0171-439 4222
Leather	01732-364422
Legal Action	0171-833 2931
Legal Business	0171-396 9292
Leisure Management	01462-431385
Leisure Manager	01491-874800
Leisure Opportunities Magazine	01462-431385

Leisure Week	0171-439 4222
Library Association Record	0171-636 7543
Lifeguard	01789-773994
Lifewatch	0171-722 3333
Linedancer	01704-501235
Line Up	01323-491739
The List	0131-558 1191
Literary Review	0171-437 9392
The Little Ship	0171-236 7729
Live & Kicking	0181-576 2000
Living	0171-261 5000
Lloyd's List International	01206-772277
Loaded	0171-261 5000
Lobster	01482-447558
Local Government Chronicle	0171-505 8000
Local Government News	0181-680 4200
Local Government Tenders	0171-505 8000
Local History Magazine	0115-9706473
Logic Special	01737-769799
Logisitic Europe	0181-943 5000
London Cyclist	0171-928 7220
London Gazette	0171-394 4580
London Magazine	0171-925 2544
London Portrait	0171-261 5000
London Review of Books	0171-209 1141
Looks	0171-437 9011
Loot	0171-625 0266

M

M magazine	0171-439 5000
M & S Magazine	0171-312 2600
Mac Format	01225-442244
The Mac/MacUser	0171-631 1433
Machine Knitting News	01225-442244
MacWorld	0171-831 9252
Madam	0131-662 4445
Mag	0181-731 9666
Magazine	0171-278 7603
Magazine News	0171-404 4166
Mailout	01484-469009
Majesty	0171-436 4006
Making Music	01322-660070
Management Today	0181-943 5000
Manchester United Magazine	0161-872 1661
Manufacturing Chemist	0181-855 7777
Marie Claire	0171-261 5000
Marie Claire Health & Beauty	0171-261 5000
Marine Conservation	01989-566017
Marketing	0181-943 5000

Marketing Direct	0181-943 5000
Marketing Events	0181-943 5000
Marketing Week	0171-439 4222
Master Builder	0171-242 7583
Match	01733-264666
Materials Recycling Week	
	0181-277 5540
Maxim	0171-631 1433
Max Power	01733-237111
Mayfair	0171-734 9191
MBUK Specials	01225-442244
M & E Design	0181-652 3115
Meat Trades Journal	
	0181-277 5000
Medeconomics	0181-943 5000
Media & Marketing Europe	
	0171-505 8000
Media, Culture & Society	
	0171-374 0645
Media International	0181-652 3500
Media Week	0171-505 8000
Medical Imprint	0181-943 5000
Melody Maker	0171-261 5000
Men Only	0171-734 9191
Men's Wear	0171-520 1500
Mensa Quest	0171-616 8480
Metal Bulletin	0171-827 9977
Metal Hammer	0171-631 1433
Metalworking Production	
	0181-855 7777
Methodist Recorder	0171-251 8414
Micro Computer Mart	
	0121-233 8712
MicroScope	0171-631 1433
Microwave Engineering Europe	
	0181 855 7777
Middle East Economic Digest	
	0171-470 6200
Middle East Electricity	
	0181-652 3500
Middle East International	
	0171-373 5228
Midweek Magazine	0171-636 3666
Milap Weekly	0171-385 8966
Mims Magazine	0171-413 4330
Mims UK	0181-943 5000
Mind Body & Spirit	0181-801 0569
Mind Your Own Business	
	0181-771 3614
Miniature Wargames	
	01202-512355
Mining Journal/Magazine	
	0171-216 6060
MiniWorld	0181-686 2599
Minx	0171-437 9011
Missles And Rockets	
	0181-700 3700
The Mix	01225-442244
Mixmag	0171-436 1515
Mizz	0171-261 5000

Model Rail	01733-898100
Model Railway Journal	
	01235-816478
Modern History Review	
	01869-338652
Modern Railways	01892-514116
Mojo	0171-436 1515
Mondex Magazine	0181-740 1740
Money Management	
	0171-896 2525
Money Marketing	0171-439 4222
Money Marketing Focus Surveys	
	0171-439 4222
Money Observer	0171-713 4188
Moneywise	0171-629 8144
More!	0171-437 9011
Mother & Baby	0171-437 9011
Motor Cycle News	01733-237111
Motor Industry Management	
	01992-511521
Motor Ship	0181-652 3500
Motor Sport	0181-943 5000
Motor Trader	0181-652 3500
Motor Transport	0181-652 3500
Motorboat & Yachting	
	0171-261 5333
Motorcaravan Monthly	
	01778-393313
Motoring News	0181-943 5000
Mountain Bike Rider	0171-261 5000
Mountain Biker International	
	0181-686 2599
Mountain Bike UK	01225-442244
Movie Idols	0181-875 1520
Movie International	0181-574 2222
Moving Pictures International	
	0171-520 5200
MS London Magazine	
	0171-636 3322
Municipal Journal	0171-973 6400
Musclemag International	
	0121-327 7525
Museums Journal	0171-250 1834
Music Magazine	01733 370777
The Musical Times	0171-482 5697
Music Week	0171-620 3636
Muzik	0171-261 5000
My Weekly	01382-23131
N	
N64	01225-442244
National Trust Magazine	
	0171-222 9251
National Geographic	
	0171-365 0916
Natural World	0171-306 0304
Nature	0171-833 4000
Navy International	0181-700 3700
Navy News	01705-826040
Needlecraft	01225-442244
Needlework	01225-442244

Neon	0171-436 1515
.net	01225 442244
Network Reseller	0171-631 1433
Network Week	0171-208 5061
Netwrok World	0171-3882430
New African	0171-713 7711
New Christian Herald	
	01903-821082
New Civil Engineer	0171-505 6600
New Ground	0171-263 7424
New Humanist	0171-430 1371
New Internationalist	01865-728181
New Law Journal	0171-400 2500
New Left Review	0171-734 8830
New MediaAge	0171-439 4222
New MediaFinance	0171-439 4222
New Moon	0181-731 8031
New Musical Express	
	0171-261 5000
New Scientist	0171-261 5000
New Statesman	0171-828 1232
New Times	0171-278 4451
New Woman	0171-437 9011
Newsweek International	
	0171-629 8361
Nine to Five	0171-436 3331
Nineteen	0171-261 6390
Nintendo Magazine	0171-972 6700
NME	0171-261 5000
Noddy	0181-576 2000
No Limits World	01225-442244
Northamptonshire Image	
	01604-231122
Notes From The Borderline	
	0956-694922
Now	0171-261 7366
Nursery Choice	0171-713 7000
Nursery World	0171-278 7441
Nursing Standard	0181-423 1066
Nursing Times	0171-843 3600
O	
Observer Life (free)	0171-278 2332
Occupational Health	
	0181-652 3500
Off-Licence News	01293-613400
Office Equipment News	
	01322-277788
The Official Playstation Magazine	
	01225-442244
Offshore Engineer	0171-505 6600
Offshore Financial Review	
	0171-463 3000
OK!	0171-308 5090
Old Glory	01780-763063
The Oldie	0171-734 2225
Omnia	0171-925 2544
On Target	01787-376374
One Shots	0171-631 1433
Opera	0171-359 1037
Opera Now	0171-333 1740

Optician	0181-652 3198
Options	0171-261 5000
Oral History	01206-873055
Orbit	0181-780 2266
Organic Gardening	01984-623998
Our Baby	0171-261 5000
Our Dogs	0161-236 2660
Outscoring	01732-359990

P

Pacemaker Update	0181-943 5000
The Pacific Review	01264-343062
Packaging News	0181-565 4200
Packaging Week	01732-364422
Panel Building	01732-359990
Parents	0171-437 9011
Parentwioo	01903-821082
Parikiaki	0171-272 6///
Parkers Car Price Guide	
	0181-579 1082
Parliamentary Magazine	
	0171-878 1500
Parliamentary Monitor	
	0171-878 1500
PASS	0181-652 3500
PATA Travel News Europe	
	0181-855 7777
PC Answers/Format/Plus	
	01225-442244
PC Dealer/Week	0171-316 9000
PC Direct/Magazine	0171-378 6800
PC Gamer	01225-442244
PC Guide	01225-442244
PC Pro	0171-917 3870
PC Review	01225 442244
PCS Magazine	0171-924 2727
PC Zone	0171-631 1433
Peace News	0171-278 3344
Pensions Week	0171-463 3000
Pensions Management	
	0171-896 2525
Pensions World	0181-686 9141
Penthouse	0171-308 5090
People's Friend	01382-223131
Perfect Home	01895-677677
Performance Bike/Car	
	01733-237111
Performance Chemicals	
International	0181-652 8126
Period Living	0171-437 9011
Personal Computer World	
	0171-316 9000
Personnel Today	0181-652 3500
Pet Product Marketing	
	01733-898100
Petroleum Economist	
	0171-831 5588
The PFI Report	0171-439 4222
Pharmacy Today	0171-334 7333
Pharmaceutical Journal	
	0171-735 9141

Photo Answers	01733-898100
Photo Technique	0171-261 5000
The Photographer	01920-464011
Physics Review	01869-338652
Physics World	0117-929 7481
The Picture Business	
	0181-855 9201
Pig Farming	0181-855 7777
Pig Meet	0181-855 7777
Pingu	0181-576 2000
Plain Truth	0181-953 1633
Planet	01970-611255
Planet News	0171-221 8137
Planned Savings	0171-505 6600
Planning	0171-413 4454
Plant Managers Journal	
	0181-652 3500
Plastics & Rubber Weekly	
	0181-277 5000
Playdays	0181-576 2000
Playstation Plus	0171-972 6000
Playstation Power	01225-442244
Pocket Arrows/Crosswords/	
Wordsearch	01737-769799
Pocket Kidz!	01737-769799
Police	0181-399 2224
Police Review	0171-393 7600
Policing Today	0181-700 3700
Politics Review	01869-338652
Popular Crafts	01442-66551
Popular Patchwork	01442-66551
Postgraduate Doctor	
	01243-576444
Pot Black	0171-607 8585
Poultry World	0181-652 3500
PR Week	0171-943 5000
Practical Boat Owner	
	0171-261 5000
Practical Caravan	0181-943 5000
Practical Classics	01733-237111
Everyday Practical Electronics	
	01202-881749
Practical Fishkeeping	
	01733-898100
Practical Gardening	01733-898100
Practical Householder	
	01322 660070
Practical Parenting	0171-261 5000
Practical Photography	
	01733-898100
Practical Wireless	01202-659910
Practical Woodworking	
	01442-66551
Practice Nurse	0181-652 3123
The Practitioner	0181-855 7777
Precision Marketing	0171-439 4222
Prediction	0181-686 2599
Pregenancy & Birth	0171-437 9011
Premiere	0171-972 6700

Premises & Facilities Management	
	01732-359990
Pre Press World	01732-364422
Press Gazette	0181-565 4448
Pride	0171-228 3110
Prima	0171-519 5500
Prima - Baby	0171-519 5500
Prima- Christmas Traditions	
	0171 519 5500
Prima - Your Home	0171-519 5500
Prime Time Puzzles	01737-769799
Print Week	0181-943 5000
Printing World	01732-364422
Private Eye	0171-437 4017
Probation Bulletin	01332-621112
Process Engineering	
	0181-855 7777
Processing	01732-359990
Processing Control Products	
	01732-359990
Production Journal	01442-233656
Production Solutions	
	0171-505 8000
Professional Engineering	
	01284-763277
Professional Nurse	0171-843 3600
Professional Printer	01892-538118
Promotions and Incentives	
	0181-943 5000
Property Finance Development	
	01787-378607
Property Week	0171-560 4000
Prospect	0171-255 1281
Psion User	0171-312 2600
Psychic News	01279-817050
The Psychologist	0116-254 9568
Psychology Review	01869-338652
Public Administration	
	01865-791100
Public Service & Local Govt	
	01959-565690
Public Treasurer	0171-505 8000
Publican	0181-681 2099
Publishing News	0171-404 0304
Pulse	0181-855 7777
Punch	0171-225 6716
Punjab Times	01332-372851
Puzzle Compendium	
	0181-846 9922
Puzzle Corner	01737-769799
Puzzle Corner Special	
	01737-769799
Puzzle Kids	01737-769799
Puzzle Monthly	01442-66551
Puzzle Mix Special	01737-769799
Puzzle World	01442-66551
Puzzler Collection/Puzzler	
	0181-846 9922

Q

Q	0171-436 1515
Quick and Easy Cross Stitch	01225-442244
Quiz Crosswords Special	01737-769799
Quizkids	01737-769799
Quizkids Special	01737-769799

R

Race and Class	0171-837 0041
Racing & Football Outlook	01635-578080
Radio Communication	01707-659015
Radio Control Models	01442-66551
Radio Magazine	01536-418558
Radio Modeller	01442-66551
Radio Times	0181-576 2000
Rail	01733-898100
Railway Gazette International	0181-652 3500
Railway Magazine	0171-261 5000
Railway World	01932-873105
Rambling Today	01480-496130
The Raven	0171-247 9249
Readers Digest	0171-629 8144
Record Collector	0181-579 1082
Record Mirror	0171-620 3636
Red	0171-437 9011
Redline	01225-442244
Red Pepper	0171-281 7024
Regiment	01442-66551
Resident Abroad	0171-405 6969
Resurgence	01237-441293
Retail Jeweller	0171-520 1500
Retail Newsagent	0171-689 0600
Retail Week	0181-277 5000
Review of Social Economy	01264-343062
The Review - Worldwide Insurance	0171-505 6600
Revolution	0181-943 5000
Revs	01733-237111
Rhythm	01225-442244
RIBA Journal	0171-560 4000
Ride	01733-237111
Right Start	0171-403 0840
The Round Organ	01202-889669
Rugby News	0171-323 1944
Rugby World	0171-261 5000
Runners World	0171-291 6000
RUSI Journal	0171-930 5854

S

Safeway Magazine	0171-312 2600
Saga Magazine	01303-711527
Sailing Today	01225-442244
Sainsbury's: The Magazine	0171-633 0266
Sales Manager	01733-467000

Salisbury Review	0171-226 7791
Satellite Times	0113-258 5008
Satellite Trader	0171-896 2700
Sayidaty	0171-831 8181
Scene	01702-435328
SchNews Magazine	01273-685913
Scots Law Times	0131-225 4879
Scots Magazine	01382-223131
Scottish Farmer	0141-302 7700
Scottish Field	0131-551 2942
Scottish Memories	0141-204 3104
Scouting	0171-584 7030
Screen Digest	0171-482 5842
Screen International	0171-505 8000
Sea Angler	01733-264666
Searchlight	0171-284 4040
Seatrade Review	01206-545121
Security Management Today	01689-874025
Sega Saturn	0171-972 6700
Select	0171-436 1515
Sen- Shop Equipment & Shop Fitting News	0181-277 5000
SFX	01225 442244
She	0171-439 5000
Shivers	0181-875 1520
Shoot!	0171-261 5000
Shooting & Conservation	01244-573000
Shooting Times	0171-261 5000
Shopping Centre	01293-613400
Short Wave Magazine	01202-659910
Shropshire Magazine	01743-362175
Sight & Sound	0171-255 1444
The Sign	01603-615995
The Singer	0171-333 1733
Skin Deep	01565-652424
Sky	0171-436 1515
SkyTVGuide	0171-312 2600
Slimming	0171-437 9011
Smallholder	01453-544000
Smash Hits	0171-436 1515
Soccer Stars	0171-261 5000
Social Housing	0171-700 4199
Socialism Today	0181-533 3311
Socialist Affairs	0171-627 4449
Socialist Standard	0171-622 3811
Socialist Worker	0171-538 0828
Sociology Review	01869-338652
Solicitors Journal	0171-242 2548
Sorted?	01273-683318
Special Schools in Britain	0171-439 4222
The Spectator	0171-405 1706
Spectrum	0171-833 5566
Sport First	0171-878 1507
Sported!	01733 264666
Sporting Gun	0171-261 5000

Sports Industry	0171-498 0177
Sports Management	01462-431385
Sports Marketing	0171-439 4222
Spot	0181 576 2000
Spotlight	0171-437 7631
Squall Magazine	0171-561 1204
Stage, Screen & Radio	0171-437 8506
The Stage & Television Today	0171-403 1818
Starburst	0181-875 1520
Stars & Cars	0181-943 5000
Statewatch	0181-802 1882
Steam Railway	01733-898100
Steam World	01753-898100
Stillwater Trout Angler	0171-261 5000
Storyland	0181-653 1563
Straight No Chaser	0171-613 1594
The Strad	0181-863 2020
Street Machine	01733-237111
Streetwise	01737-769799
Streewise Special	01737-769799
Structural Engineer	0171-235 4535
Stuff	0171-631 1433
Subcon	0181-855 7777
Sunday Express Magazine (free)	0171-922 7297
Sunday Mirror Magazine (free)	0171-293 3000
Sunday Times Magazine (free)	0171-782 4000
SuperMarketing	0181-652 3500
Surrey County Magazine	01622-687031
The Surveyor	0171-973 6400
Swarovski Magazine	0171-312 2600
Sweet FA	0171-284 0417

T

T3	01225-442244
The Tablet	0181-748 8484
Talking Business	0171-312 2600
Take a Break/Crossword/ Look/Puzzle	0171-284 0909
Tatler	0171-499 9080
Taxation	0181-686 9141
Technical Review Middle East	0171-834 7676
Teeny Weeny Families	01737-769799
Telegraph Magazine (free)	0171-538 5000
Teletubbies	0181-576 2000
Television (Reed)	0181-652 3500
Television (Royal TV Soc)	0171-430 1000
Television Business Internat	0171-896 2700

Television Buyer	0171-505 8000	Tunnels and Tunnelling		What's On TV	0171-261 5000
Televisual	0171-439 4222		0181-855 7777	When Saturday Comes	
That's Life!	0171-462 4700	Turf Management	0181-943 5000		0171-251 8595
Therapy Weekly	0171-843 3600	Twinkle	01382 223131	Which Motorcaravan	
Third Text	0171-372 0826	**U**			01778-391000
Third Way	0171-373 3432	UFO Times	01924-444049	Which?	0171-830 6000
The Thomas Cook Magazine		UK press gazette	0181-565 4200	Wide World	01869-338652
	0171-312 2600	Ulster Nation	0171-373 3432	Wild London	0171-261 0447
Timber For Architects		Uncut	0171-261 5000	Wildfowl and Wetlands	
	01732-364422	Under Five Contact	0171-833 0991		01453 890333
Timber Trades Journal		Union Review	0181-462 7755	The Wire	0171-439 6422
	01732-364422	The Universe	0161-236 8856	Wisden Cricket Monthly	
Time Life International		Unmanned Vehicles	01628-664334		01483-570358
	0171-499 4080	Update	0181-652 3500	Woman	0171-261 5000
Time Out	0171-813 6060	Used Car Dealer	01733-467000	Woman & Home	0171-261 5000
Times Education Supplements		Utility Europe	0181-652 3500	Woman Alive	01903-821082
	0171 782 3000	**V**		Woman's Journal	0171-261 5000
Times Literary Supplement		Vanguard (Nat Dems)		Woman's Own	0171-261 5000
	0171-782 3000		0181-471 6872	Woman's Realm	0171-201 5000
Titbits	0171-351 4995	Vanity Fair	0171-499 9080	Woman's Weekly	0171-261 5000
Today's Golfer	01733-264666	The Var	0171-631 1433	Women & Golf	0171 261 5000
Today's Runner	01733-264666	Vegetarian Good Food (BBC)		Women in General Practice	
Top Of The Pops	0181-576 2000		0171-576 2000		0171-843 3600
Top Gear	0181-576 2000	Veterinary Times	01733-325522	Wood Based Panels International	
Top Sante	0171-437 9011	Vintage Motor Cycle	01283-540557		01732-364422
Top Sante Health & Beauty		Viz	0171-470 2400	Woodworker	01442-266551
	0171-938 3033	Vogue	0171-499 9080	Woodworking News	
Total Bike	01225-442244	The Voice	0171-737 7377		01474-536535
Total Film	01225-442244	Volvo Magazine	0171-312600	Word Search	0181-846 9922
Total Football	01225-442244	Vox	0171-261 5000	Workers' Health	0114-276 5695
Total Guitar	01225-442244	**W**		Working Women	0181-947 3131
Total Sport	0171-436 1515	Wanderlust	01753-620426	Works Management	
Townswoman	01603-616005	The War Cry	0171-236 5222		01689-850156
Toybox	0181-576 2000	Water & Environment		World of Interiors	0171-499 9080
Toy Soldier & Model Figures			0118-972 3532	World Paper	01732-364422
	01403-711511	Water	0171-240 2032	World Soccer	0171-261 5000
Toy Trader	01993-775545	Water Gardener	01233-621877	The World Today	0171-957 5700
Trade It	01202-445000	Waterways	01283-790447	World's Fair	0161-624 3687
Trade Marks Journal		Wedding & Home	0171-261 5000	Working Together	01522-544400
	01633-811448	The Week	0171-229 0006	Writers News	01667-454441
Traditional Homes	0171-437 9011	Weekly Law Digest	01243-783637	Writers Newsletter	0171-723 8074
Trail	01733-264666	Weekly News	01382-223131	Writing Magazine	01667-454441
Training	0181-652 3500	Whatever	0181-959 8720	**X**	
Transit	01733-467000	What Bike?	01733-237111	XL for Men	0171-436 1515
Transport Retort	0171-388 8386	What Camera?	0171-261 5000	Xpose	0181-875 1520
Travel Trade Gazette		What Car?	0181-943 5000	**Y**	
	0181-855 7777	What Hi-Fi?	0181-943 5000	Yachting Monthly	0171-261 5000
Treasure Hunting	01376-521900	What Investment?	0171-638 1916	Yachting World	0171-261 5000
Trees	01342-712536	What Mortgage?	0171-638 1916	You Magazine (free)	0171-938 6000
Trees are News	01342-712536	What PC & Software?		Your Cat/Dog	01733-898100
Tribune	0171-278 0911		0171-316 9000	Your Garden	01202 680586
Trout Fisherman	01733-264666	What Plant?	0171-505 6600	Your Greatest Guide to Calories	
Trout & Salmon	01733-264666	What Satellite?	0171-331 1000		0171-437 9011
Truck	0181-652 3500	What to Buy for Business		Your Horse	01733-264666
Truck & Driver	0181-652 3500		0181-652 3500	Your Mortgage?	0171-833 5566
TV & Satellite Week	0171-261 5000	What Video?	0171-331 1000	Yours	01733-555123
TV Hits	0171-636 5095	What's New in Building/Design		**Z**	
TV Quick	0171-284 0909	/Electronics/Electronics Europe/		Zest	0171-439 5000
TV Times	0171-261 5000	Farming/Industry/Interiors/		Zipper	0171-482 2576
TV World	0171-505 8000	Process & Control	0181-855 7777		

Book publishing

Last year's introduction to this section concluded "book publishing has settled down after the merger mania of the early nineties". Wrong again. As this book was going to press last August, Pearson sold its Churchill Livingstone publishing division to Harcourt General for £57 million. Shortly afterwards Reed Professional sold its Reed Consumer Books to Random House for £17.5 million. These deals were dwarfed in March when Bertelsmann bought Random for £840 million to create a publishing behemoth with 10 per cent of the North American market and an early large presence in the UK. Then, in May 1998, Pearson came back into the market with the $3.6 billion purchase of the educational publisher Simon and Schuster. This, explained the Pearson chief executive Marjorie Scardino, revealed the strategy of concentrating on core businesses "to meet, in print and electronically, the growing demand of students of all ages and in all parts of the world for stimulating and education programmes".

The concentration of ownership - and the subsequent elimination of independent publishers - continued converting what was once a slightly dozy and gentlemanly trade into multi-national large scale specialisations. Meanwhile rumours persist that Rupert

Top publishing imprints

	'96/97 sales	%increase		'96/97 sales	%increase
1 Reed Professional	£1,062m	13.3%	**33 Thames & Hudson**	£19.4m	5.2%
2 Harper Collins	£565m	-17.1%	**34 Tolley Pubishing**	£17.7m	4.7%
3 Addison Wesley	£554.3m	-54.4%	**35 David & Charles**	£16.8m	2.6%
4 Reed Scientific	£553m	3.9%	**36 IOP Publishing**	£16.3m	7.6%
5 Penguin	£380.2m	3%	**37 Kingfisher^**	£14.5m	-6%
6 Macmillan	£293.6m	8.46%	**38 Bloomsbury**	£13.7m	20.1%
7 OUP	£278.2m	10.6%	**39 Usborne**	£13.3m	-25%
8 FT Professional*	£193.2m	7.5%	**40 Collins & Brown**	£12.3m	47.2%
9 Dorling Kindersley	£180m	3.2%	**41 Whitaker**	£11m	5.7%
10 Blackwell Science	£96.7m	3.9%	**42 Chadwyck-Healey**	£9.7m	8.4%
11 Random House (est)	£93m	13.4%	**43 Wayland**	£9.3m	63%
12 Hodder Headline	£92.8m	4.6%	**44 Phaidon Press**	£8.8m	
13 Quarto	£80.6m	21.3%	**45 Gieves**	£8.8m	-3.3%
14 Transworld	£65.4m	17%	**46 Kogan Page**	£7.4m	8.4%
15 Parragon Book Service	£52.2m	15.6%	**47 Guinness**	£7m	-4.4%
16 Wiley Europe	£51.4m	10.7%	**48 Lion Publishing**	£6.4m	-6.4%
17 Harcourt Brace	£44.8m	3.8%	**49 New Holland**	£4.7m	14.6%
18 Croner Publications	£41.1m	10%	**50 Piatkus**	£4.5m	0%
19 Little Brown	£34.6m	8.1%	**51 Batsford**	£4.4m	-2.7%
20 Orion	£31.7m	17.9%	**52 Cadogan**	£4.4m	141.9%
21 Walker Books	£29.3m	30.1%	**53 Sutton Publishing**	£4.1m	30.9%
22 Grolier	£29.1m	6%	**54 Fourth Estate**	£3.8m	72.6%
23 Taylor & Francis	£28.6m		**55 Andre Deutsch**	£3.3m	
24 Haynes	£27.4m	-0.2%	**56 Constable**	£3m	14.6%
25 Scholastic	£27.4m	19.1%	**57 John Murray**	£2.9m	23.10%
26 Cassell	£24.4m	5.30%	**58 Michael O'Mara**	£2.8m	-26.7%
27 Blackwell Publishers	£23.7m	6.40%	**59 Portland Press**	£2.7m	8.4%
28 Thomas Nelson	£21.8m	-5.9%	**60 Aurum Press**	£1.9m	12.9%
29 Stanley Thornes	£20.6m	8.4%	**61 Cavendish Publishing**	£1.8m	13.7%
30 Harlequin Mills & Boon	£20.3m	-1.7%	**62 Quartet Books**	£0.5m	-6.6%
31 BPP (Pubishers)	£20.1m	14.7%	*formerly Pearson Professional. ^formerly Larousse		
32 Simon & Schuster	£19.7m	15.9%	Source: The Bookseller.		

Murdoch has lost interest in book publishing and is looking for a buyer for Harper Collins.

More than 100,000 books are published a year in a cut-throat business where marketing strategies seem more important than what's actually in the books. At the top of the business, people do very nicely indeed but the pay is low. Faber's Joanna Mackle says good interviewees for a fiction editor's post she had advertised were on £20,000 a year, a figure she thought would be doubled by equivalent talent elsewhere in the media. "We haven't paid people enough," admits the Penguin boss Michael Lynton. "We haven't set enough store by recruitment of fresh blood."

Publishing conglomerates

Transworld/Hodder Headline

9.5% UK book turnover

Owned by Bertelsmann AG

Main imprints: Edward Arnold, Headline Review, Delta, Liaison, Hodder and Stoughton, New English Library/Sceptre, Hodder Christian, Anchor, Bantam, Clack Swan, Doubleday, Corgi, Partridge Press

Harper Collins

9% UK book turnover

Owned by News Corporation

Main imprints: Collins, Flamingo, Harper Collins, Marshall Pickering, Times Books, Voyager

Penguin

8.5% UK book turnover

Owned by Pearson

Main imprints: Allen Lane/The Penguin Press, Hamish Hamilton, Michael Joseph, Pelham Books, Penguin, Puffin, Signet, Viking, Frederick Warne

Macmillan

4% UK book turnover

Owned by Holtzbrink AG

Main imprints: Macmillan Children's, Macmillan Educational, Macmillan General, Pan, Papermac, Picador, Sidgwick & Jackson, Macmillan Press

MAJOR BOOK PUBLISHERS

Addison Wesley Longman Group
Edinburgh Gate, Harlow, Essex CM20 2JE
Fax 01279-431059   Tel 01279-623623
E-mail: awi.co.uk
Website: http://www.awi.co.uk
Subsidiary of Pearson. Journals and directories.

Aurum Press
25 Bedford Avenue, London WC1B 3AT
Fax 0171-580 2469   Tel 0171-637 3225
E-mail: aurum@ibm.net

Batsford
583 Fulham Road, London SW6 5BY
Fax 0171-471 1101   Tel 0171-471 1100
E-mail: info @batsford.com
Website: http://www.batsford.com
Batsford specialises in chess, bridge, crafts, gardening, fashion and design and has recently acquired a business and finance list. Its three best sellers in 1997 were: TV Film & Video Guide - David Quinlan; Complete Guide to Creative Embroidery - Beaney & Littlejohn; Kasparov v Deeper Blue - Daniel King.

Birchin International
10 Throgmorton Avenue, London EC2N 2DL
Fax 0171-628 4113   Tel 0171-628 4112
E-mail: birchin@birchin.co.uk
Website: http://www.birchin.com

A & C Black
35 Bedford Row, London WC1R 4JH
Fax 0171-831 8478   Tel 0171-242 0946
E-mail: enquiries @acblack.co.uk

Blackwell Publishers
108 Cowley Road, Oxford OX4 1JF
Fax 01865-791347   Tel 01865-791100

Blackwell Science
Osney Mead, Oxford OX2 0EL
Fax 01865-721205   Tel 01865-206206
Website: http://www.blackwell-science.com

Bloomsbury
38 Soho Square, London W1V 5DF
Fax 0171-434 0151   Tel 0171-494 2111
Website: http://www.bloomsbury.com
1997 best-sellers: Snow Falling on Cedars - David Guterson; Emotional Intelligence - Daniel Goleman; Fugitive Pieces - Anne Michaels.

BPP (Publishing)
142-144 Uxbridge Road, London W12 8AW
Fax 0181-740 1184   Tel 0181-740 2211
E-mail: sales@bpp-pub.co.uk
Website: http://www.bpp.co.uk

Cadogan Books
3rd Floor, 27-29 Berwick Street, London W1V 3RF
Fax 0171-734 1733   Tel 0171-287 6555
Travel guides, chess and Everyman's Library.

Cavendish Publishing
The Glass House, Wharton Street, London WC1X 9PX
Fax 0171-278 8080   Tel 0171-278 8000
E-mail: info@cavendishpublishing.com
Specialises in legal and medico-legal books.

Cassell
125 Strand, London WC2R 0BB
Fax 0171-240 7261   Tel 0171-420 5555
E-mail: AnneGodfre@aol.com
Website: http://www.cassell.co.uk
1997 best sellers: High Fidelity - Nick Hornby; Mrs
Beetons Cookery & Household Management (non-
fiction); Refelective Teaching in Primary School -
Pollard (academic); Jerome Biblical Commentary -
Raymond Brown (religion).

Chadwyck-Healey
The Quorum, Barnwell Road, Cambridge CB5 8SW
Fax 01223-215513   Tel 01223-215512
E-mail: mail@chadwych.co.uk

Collins & Brown
London House, Parkgate Road, London SW11 4NQ
Fax 0171-924 7725   Tel 0171-924 2575

Constable & Co
162 Fulham Palace Road, London W6 9ER
Fax 0181-748 7562   Tel 0181-741 3663
E-mail: hbconstab@aol.com
Website: http://www.constable-publishers.co.uk
1997 best-sellers - Origins: Our Place in Hubble's
Universe - Gribbin & Goodwin; Hubble's Universe -
Goodwin; Celtic Art - George Bain.

Croner Publications
London Road, Kingston upon Thames, KT2 6SR
Fax 0181-547 2637   Tel 0181-547 3333
E-mail: info@croner.co.uk
Website: http://www.croner.co.uk

David & Charles
Brunel House, Newton Abbot, Devon TQ12 4PU
Fax 01626-334998   Tel 01626-61121

Andre Deutsch
106 Great Russell Street, London WC1B 3LJ
Fax 0171-631 3253   Tel 0171-580 2746

Dorling Kindersley
9 Henrietta Street, London WC2E 8PS
Fax 0171-836 7570   Tel 0171-836 5411
E-mail: comments@dkonline.com
Website: http://www.dk.com

Faber & Faber
3 Queen Square, London WC1N 3AU
Fax 0171-465 0034   Tel 0171-465 0045

Financial Times Business
149 Tottenham Court Road, London W1P 9LL
Fax 0171-896 2099   Tel 0171-896 2000

Fourth Estate
6 Salem Road, London W2 4BU
Fax 0171-792 3176   Tel 0171-727 8993
E-mail: general@4thestate.co.uk
1997 best-sellers: The Diving Bell and the Butterfly - J-D
Bauby; Longitude -Dava Sobel; Fermat's Last Theorem -
Simon Singh.

Gieves & Hawkes
21-22 The Hard, Portsmouth PO1 3DY
Fax 01705-817236   Tel 01705-826648

Grolier
21 Morgan Way, Bowthorpe, Norwich NR5 NHH
Fax 01603-740401   Tel 01603-740740

Guinness Publishing
33 London Road, Middlesex EN2 6DJ
Fax 0181-367 5912   Tel 0171-891 4567

Harcourt Brace & Co
24-28 Oval Road, London NW1 7DX
Fax 0171-482 2293   Tel 0171-424 4200
Website: http://www.hbuk.co.uk

Harlequin Mills & Boon
18-24 Paradise Road, Richmond, Surrey TW9 1SR
Fax 0181-288 2899   Tel 0181-948 0444

HarperCollins Publishers
77-85 Fulham Palace Road, London W6 8JB
Fax 0181-307 4440   Tel 0181-741 7070
E-mail: name.surname@harpercollins.co.uk

Haynes
Sparkford, Yeovil, Somerset BA22 7JJ
Fax 01963-440023   Tel 01963-440635

Hodder Headline
338 Euston Road, London NW1 3BH
Fax 0171-873 6024   Tel 0171-873 6000

IOP Publishing
Dirac House, Temple Back, Bristol BS1 6BE
Fax 0117-929 4318   Tel 0117-929 7481
E-mail: margaret.ogorman@ioppublishing.co.uk
Website: http://www.iop.org
1997 best-sellers: In Search of Lost Time - York; Eureka!
- Blin-Stoyle; States of Matter, States of Mind - Barton.

John Murray
50 Albemarle Street, London W1X 4BD
Fax 0171-499 1792   Tel 0171-493 4361
E-mail: Johnmurray@dial.pipex.com
1997 best-sellers: For the Island I Sing - George Mackay
Brown; South from the Limpopo - Dervla Murphy; Old
Chestnuts and Other Favourites - John R Murray.

Kingfisher Publications
283-288 High Holborn, London WC1V 7HZ
Fax 0171-242 4979   Tel 0171-903 9999

Kogan Page
120 Pentonville Road, London N1 9JN
Fax 0171-837 6348   Tel 0171-278 0433
E-mail: kpinfo@kogan-page.co.uk
Website: http://www.kogan-page.co.uk

Lion Publishing
Peter's Way, Sandy Lane West, Oxford OX4 5HG
Fax 01865-747568   Tel 01865-747550

Little Brown
Brettenham Ho., LancasterPlace, London WC2E 7EN
Fax 0171-911 8100   Tel 0171-911 8000
Hardback and large format paperbacks, its imprints are
Abacus, Orbit, Virago and Warner. 1997 best-sellers:
Unnatural Exposure - Patricia Cornwell; Autobiography
- Kevin Keegan; The Last Governor - J Dimbleby.

Macmillan Publishers
25 Eccleston Pace, London SW1W 9NF
Fax 0171-881 8001   Tel 0171-881 8000

New Holland
24 Nutford Place, London W1H 6DQ
Fax 0171-258 1293   Tel 0171-724 7773
E-mail: vobis@nhpub.u-net.com

Michael O'Mara Books
9 Lion Yard, Tremadoc Road, London SW4 7NQ
Fax 0171-627 8953   Tel 0171-720 8643
General non-fiction - royalty, history and humour.

Orion
5 Upper St Martin's Lane, London WC2H 9EA
Fax 0171-240 4822   Tel 0171-240 3444

OUP (Oxford University Press)
Great Clarendon Street, Oxford OX2 6DP
Fax 01865-556646   Tel 01865 556767
Website: http://www.oup.co.uk

Parragon Book Service
4 Mulberry Close, London NW3
                          Tel 0171-431 5480

Pearson Professional
see Financial Times Business

Penguin Books
Bath Road, Harmondsworth, Middx UB7 0DA
Fax 0181-899 4099   Tel 0181-899 4000

Phaidon Press
Regent's Wharf, All Saints Street, London N1 9PA
Fax 0171-843 1010   Tel 0171-843 1000
E-mail: sales@phaidon.com
Leading publishers of books on art, architecture, design,
photography, decorative arts and music. Their three
best sellers in 1997 were: The Art Book; The
Photography Book; The Story of Art - E H Gombrich.

Piatkus
5 Windmill Street, London W1P 1HF
Fax 0171-436 7137   Tel 0171-631 0710
E-mail: info@piatkus.co.uk

Plexus Publishing
55a Clapham Common Southside
clapham, London SW4 9BX
Fax 0171-622 2441   Tel 0171-622 2440
E-mail: plexus@plexusuk.demon.co.uk

Portland Press
59 Portland Place London W1N 3AJ
Fax 0171-323 1136   Tel 0171-580 5530
E-mail: sales@portlandpress.co.uk
Website: http://www.portlandpress.co.uk
Publishes books and journals for academic and general
readership. Their three best sellers for 1997 were: Poo,
You and the Potoroo's Loo - David Bellamy; Brainbox -
Rose and Lichtenfels; Metabolic Regulation: A Human
Perspective - Keith Frayn.

Quartet Books
27 Goodge Street, London W1P 2LD
Fax 0171-637 1866   Tel 0171-636 3992
E-mail: quartetbooks@easynet.co.uk

Quarto
The Old Brewery, 6 Blundell Street, London N7 9BH
Fax 0171-700 4191   Tel 0171-700 6700

Random House
20 Vauxhall Bridge Road, London SW1V 2SA
Fax 0171-932 0761   Tel 0171-840 8400

Reed Books
81 Fulham Road, London SW3 6RB
Fax 0171-225 9424   Tel 0171-581 9393

Reed Elsevier
25 Victoria Street, London SW1H 0EX
Fax 0171-227 5799   Tel 0171-222 8420
Website: http://www.reed-elsevier.com

Reed Educational & Professional Publishing
Halley Court, Jordan Hill, Oxford OX2 8EJ
Fax 01865-314641   Tel 01865-314097
Includes the former Reed Scientific & Medical.

Salamander Books
8 Blenheim Court, Brewery Road, London N7 9NT
Fax 0171-700 3572   Tel 0171-700 7799

Scholastic
Commonwealth House, 1-19 New Oxford Street,
London WC1A 1NU
Fax 0171-421 9001   Tel 0171-421 9000

Simon & Schuster
West Garden Place, Kendal Street, London W2 2AQ
Fax 0171-402 0639   Tel 0171-316 1900

Stanley Thornes
Edinburgh House, Wellington Street, Cheltenham
GL50 1YW
Fax 01242-221914   Tel 01242-228888
Website: http://www.thornes.co.uk

Sutton Publishing
Phoenix Mill, Thrupp, Stroud, Gloucestershire GL5 2BU
Fax 01453-731117   Tel 01453-731114
General and academic high quality illustrated books.

Taylor & Francis
1 Gunpowder Square, London EC4A 3DE
Fax 0171-583 0581   Tel 0171-583 0490
E-mail: first name.surname@tandf.co.uk
Website: http://www.tandf.co.uk

Thames & Hudson
30-34 Bloomsbury Street, London WC1B 3QP
Fax 0171-636 4799   Tel 0171-636 5488
Website: http://www.thameshudson.co.uk

Thomas Nelson & Sons
Nelson House, Mayfield Road, Walton-on-Thames,
Surrey KT12 5PL
Fax 01932-246109   Tel 01932-252211
E-mail: nelinfo@nelson.co.uk
Website: http://www.nelson.co.uk
Educational publishing company.

Tolley Publishing
2 Addiscombe Road, Croydon, Surrey CR9 5AF
Fax 0181-686 3155   Tel 0181-686 9141
E-mail: services@tolley.co.uk
Website: http://www.tolley.co.uk

Transworld Publishers
61-63 Uxbridge Road, London W5 5SA
Fax 0181-579 5479   Tel 0181-579 2652
E-mail: info@transworld-publishers.co.uk
Publishes general trade fiction and non-fiction, plus
children's books, and the Expert list of gardening books.

Usborne
83-85 Saffron Hill, London EC1N 8RT
Fax 0171-430 1562   Tel 0171-430 2800

Walker Books
87 Vauxhall Walk, London SE11 5HJ
Fax 0171-587 1123   Tel 0171-793 0909
Children. 1997 best-sellers: Where's Wally? The
Wonder Book; Guess How Much I Love You; We're
Going on a Bear Hunt.

Wayland Publishers
61-61a Western Road, Hove, East Sussex BN3 1JD
Fax 01273-329314   Tel 01273-722561
Children's information books.

Whitaker
12 Dyott Street, London WC1A 1DF
Fax 0171-836 2909   Tel 0171-420 6000

Wiley Europe
Baffins Lane, Chichester, West Sussex PO19 1UD
Fax 01243-775878   Tel 01243-779777
E-mail: europe@wiley.co.uk

OTHER PUBLISHERS

A
AA Publishing	01256-20123
Addison Wesley Longman	01279-623623
Allen Lane	0171-416 3121
Allison & Busby	0171-636 2942
Andre Deutsch	0171-580 2746
Anness Publishing	0171-401 2077
Arrow Books	0171-840 8400
Athlone Press	0181-458 0888
Aurum Press	0171-637 3225

B
Bantam	0181-579 2652
Batsford	0171-471 1100
Baylin Publications	0118-941 4468
BBC Books	0181-576 3017
Bedford Square Press	0171-713 6161
Billboard	0171-323 6686
A&C Black	0171-242 0946
Blackwell	01865-791100
Blandford Press	0171-420 5555
Bloodaxe Books	01434-684855
Bloomsbury	0171-494 2111
Bodley Head	0171-840 8400
Bowker-Saur	01342-330100
Boxtree	0171-881 8000
British Film Institute	0171-255 1444
Broadcast Books	0181-769 3483
Butterworth	0171-400 2500
Butterworth-Heinemann	01865-310366

C
Cambridge University Press	01223-312393
Carcanet Press	0171-734 7338
Cassell	0171-420 5555
Cavendish Publishing	0171-278 8000
CBD Research	0181-650 7745
Chambers	0171-903 9889
Chapman & Hall	0171-865 0066
Chatto & Windus	0171-840 8400
Collins & Brown	0171-924 2575
Conran Octopus	0171-240 6961
Constable	0181-741 3663
Corgi	0181-579 2652
Coronet	0171-873 6000

D
Darton, Longman & Todd	0181-875 0155
David & Charles	01626-61121
Demos	0171-353 4479
JM Dent & Sons	0171-240 3444
Dorling Kindersley	0171-836 5411
Doubleday	0181-579 2652
Dragonflair Publishing	01694-722504

E
Ebury Press	0171-840 8400
Egmont Fleetway	0171-344 6400
Element Books	01747-851339

Emap Media	0171-837 1212
Euromonitor	0171-251 8024

F
Faber & Faber	0171-465 0045
Flicks Books	01225 760756
Focal Press	01865-311366
Fontana	0181-741 7070
Fourth Estate	0171-727 8993
Frank Cass	0181-599 8866
Frederick Warne	0171-416 3000
FT Management	0171-379 7383

G
Gaia Books	0171-323 4010
George Philip	0171-581 9393
GMP Publishers	01366-328101
Guinness Publishing	0181-891 4567

H
Hamish Hamilton	0171-416 3000
Hamlyn	0171-581 9393
Harcourt Brace	0171-267 4466
HarperCollins	0181-741 7070
Harrap	0131-557 4571
Heinemann	0171-840 8400
HMSO Books	0171-873 0011
Hodder Headline	0171-873 6000
Hollis Directories	0181-977 7711
How To Books	01865-793806
Hutchinson Books	0171-840 8400

I
Interactive Media Publications	0171-837 3345

J
Jarrold	01603-763300
John Libbey & Co	0181-947 2777
John Wiley & Sons	01243-779777
Jonathan Cape	0171-840 8400
Journeyman Press	0181-348 2724

K
Kingfisher	0171-903 9999
Kogan Page	0171-278 0433

L
Ladybird Books	01509-268021
Larousse	0171-903 9999
Lawrence & Wishart	0181-533 2506
Longman Group	0171-623693
Lutterworth Press	01223-350865

M
Macdonald Young Books	01273-722561
McGraw-Hill	01628-623432
Macmillan Publisher	0171-881 8000
Mandarin	0171-840 8400
Mansell Publishing	0171-420 5555
Marion Boyars	0181-788 9522
Marshall Cavendish	0171-734 6710
Methuen	0171-840 8400
Michael Joseph	0171-416 3000
Miller Freeman	01732-362666
Mills & Boon	0181-948 0444
Mitchell Beazley	0171-840 8400

N
Network Books	0181-576 3017
New English Library	0171-876 6000
Nicholas Brealey	0171-713 7455
NTC Publications	01491-574671

O
Octopus Publishing	0171-557 7700
Osprey	0171-225 9365
OUP	01280-823388
OUP	01865-556767

P
Paladin Books	0181-741 7070
Pan Books	0171-373 4997
Pandora Press	0181-741 7070
Parragon Books	0117-973 0522
PDQ Publishing	01865-820387
Penguin Books	0171-416 3000
Pergamon Press	01865-310111
Piatkus Books	0171-631 0710
Picador	0171-373 6070
Philips	0171-225 9826
Pitkin Guides	01264 334303
Pluto Press	0181-348 2724
Polity Press	01223-324315
Puffin	0171-416 3000

Q
Quartet Books	0171-636 3992

R
Random House	0171-840 8400
Readers Digest	0171-629 8144
Reed Information Services	01342-335832
Reed Books	0171-581 9393
Routledge	0171-583 9855
Rushmere	01502-574515

S
Salamander Books	0171-700 7799
Secker & Warburg	0171-840 8400
Shire Publications	01844-344301
Sidgwick & Jackson	0171-373 6070
Simon & Schuster	0171-316 9100
Sweet & Maxwell	0171-538 8686

T
Thames & Hudson	0171-636 5488
Thames Publishing	0181-969 3579
Thomas Nelson & Sons	01264-342832
Tolley Publishing	0181-686 9141
Transworld Publishers	0181-579 2652

U
Usborne Publishing	0171-430 2800

V
Verso	0171-437 3546
Victor Gollancz	0171-420 5555
Viking	0171-416 3000
Virago Press	0171-383 5150
Virgin Publishing	0171-386 3300

W
Ward Lock	0171-420 5555
Weidenfeld & Nicolson	0171-240 3444
J Whitaker & Sons	0171-420 6000
William Heinemann	0171-840 8400
Windrush Press	01608-652012
Womens Press	0171-251 3007

Z
Zed Books	0171-837 4014

Best selling media books sold in Waterstone's Charing X between Sep'97- June'98

1 Media Guide 1998 Paul Fisher & Steve Peak , Fourth Estate, £12

2 BFI Film & Television Handbook BFI, £17.99

3 The Knowledge '98 Miller Freeman

4 Media Student's Book Gill Branston, Routledge £14.99

5 Power Without Responsibility James Curran, Routledge £12.99

6 Introduction to Communication Studies John Fiske, Routledge £14.99

7 Manufacturing Consent Noam Chomsky, Vintage £8.99

8 Key Concepts in Communication & Cultural Studies Tim O'Sullivan,   Routledge £10.99

9 Writing Feature Articles Brendan Hennessy, Focal Press £18.99

10 Media: An Introduction ed. Briggs, Longman £16.99

11 The Global Media Edward Herman, Cassell £14.99

12 Broadcast Journalism Andrew Boyd, Focal Press £18.99

13 Amusing Ourselves to Death Neil Postman, Methuen £6.99

14 Universal Journalist David Randall, Pluto £12.99

15 Media Control Noam Chomsky, Seven Stories Press £3.50

16 Studying the Media Tim O'Sullivan, Arnold £15.99

17 Understanding Media Marshal McLuhan, Routledge £10.99

18 Mass Communication Theory Denis McQuail, Sage £14.99

19 Bourdieu on Television Pierre Bourdieu, Pluto £9.99

20 Introductory History of British Broadcasting Andrew Crisell, Routledge £12.99

21 Newspaper Power J Tunstall, Oxford University Press £13.99

22 Dictionary of Communication and Media Studies James Watson, Arnold £12.99

23 Medium is the Message Marshal McLuhan, Penguin £6.99

24 Mass Media & Power in Modern Britain Eldridge, Oxford University Press £8.99

25 Television Culture John Fiske, Routledge £12.99

26 Mass Media & Society J Curran, Arnold £15.99

27 English for Journalists Wynford Hicks, Routledge £7.99

28 Modern Newspaper Practice FW Hodgson, Focal Press £15.99

29 Newspapers Handbook Richard Keeble, Routledge £14.99

30 Media Semiotics Bignell, Manchester University Press £11.99

31 Media & Cultural Regulation Kenneth Thompson, Sage £13.99

32 How to Become a Freelance Journalist Christine Hall, How To Books £8.99

33 Media Virus Douglas Rushkoff, Titan USA, £8.95

34 Media Culture & Environment Anderson, UCL Press, £12.95

35 Understanding News John Hartley, Routledge, £10.99

36 Tabloid Television J Langer, Routledge, £14.99

37 Inside Prime Time Todd Gitlin, Routledge, £14.99

38 Live Direct and Biased Brent MacGregor, Arnold, £13.99

39 News and Journalism in the UK Brian McNair, Routledge, £13.99

40 Advertising as Communication Gillian Dyer, Routledge, £10.99

41 Media Studies Marris, Blackwell, £16.95

42 Television Handbook Patricia Holland, Routledge, £13.99

43 News Revolution MD Alleyne, Macmillan, £12.99

44 Desperately Seeking the Audience Ian Ang, Routledge, £11.99

45 Ill Effects: Media Violence Debate Martin Baker, £12.99

46 Media Ethics Matthew Kiernan, Routledge, £12.99

47 Investigating Mass Media Paul Trowler, Harper Collins, £10.99

48 How to Watch TV News Neil Postman, US import, £8.99

49 War and Peace in the Global Vision Marshal McLuhan, Hardwire, Penguin, £6.99

50 Audience Analysis Denis McQuail, Sage, £13.99

Waterstone's: Thank you Rosy Lyne for a fine list which is the better for making the Media Guide a number one best seller. This, she says is not a fix, and the least we can do is to repeat her blurb. "We have a fantastic selection of media titles, from core student texts to popular best-sellers, to American imports. We have knowledgeable staff who can recommend and answer any query. Hmmm!!"

Press awards 1998

Guardian/NUS Student Media Awards
NUS Nelson Mandela House, 461 Holloway Road
London N7
The awards are one of the best established routes for
journalists, editors and photographers to a successful
career in media. The awards are launched in February
and the winners announced in November.The
categories are: Newspaper of the year; Magazine of the
year; Reporter of the year; Feature writer of the year;
Photographer of the year; Publication design of the
year; Website of the year; Impact award.

NEWSPAPER AWARDS

British Press Awards
Press Gazette,19 Scarbrook Road, Croydon CR9 1LX
Fax 0181-565 4395   Tel 0181-565 4200
1999 awards: 4 March (provisional), entry deadline
early December 1998 (provisional).
Newspaper of the year: Daily Mail
Reporter of the year: Bill Deedes, Daily Telegraph
Team reporting award: Guardian, Aitken investigation
Feature writer of the year: Nick Davies, Guardian
Financial journalist of the year: Ben Laurance, Observer
Foreign reporter: Anton Antonowicz, Mirror
Specialist reporter: Christine Doyle, Daily Telegraph
Business journalist: Neil Bennett, Sunday Telegraph
Columnist of the year: Ruth Picardie, Observer
Interviewer of the year: Lesley White, Sunday Times
Scoop of the year: James Whitaker, Di and Dodi, Mirror
Young journalist of the year: Libby Brooks, Guardian
Sports feature writer: Michael Parkinson, Telegraph
Photographer of the year: Mike Moore, Mirror
Sports photographer: David Ashdown, Independent
Cartoonist of the year: Matt Pritchett, Daily Telegraph
Critic of the year: Alexander Walker, Evening Standard
Sports reporter of the year: Harry Harris, Mirror
On-line/news service award: PA News Centre
Subbing/design team: Mail on Sunday

Press Gazette Regional Press Awards
Press Gazette,19 Scarbrook Road, Croydon CR9 1LX
Fax 0181-565 4395   Tel 0181-565 4391
E-mail: emmaj@qpp.co.uk
1999 awards: 2 July (provisional), deadline mid April
Newspaper of the year: Western Morning News
Weekly newspaper of the year: South London Press
Free newspaper of the year: Manchester Metro News
Daily/Sunday paper of the year:
Evening newspaper of the year (sales over 40,000):
Birmingham Evening Mail
Evening newspaper of the year (sales under 40,000):
Evening Star, Ipswich
Reporter of the year: Andrew Edwards, Liverpool Echo
Photographer: Toby Melville, Bristol Evening Post &Press
Columnist: Richard Williamson, Sunday Mercury
Feature writer: Anthony Clavane, East Anglian Times

What the Papers Say
Granada Television, Manchester M60 9EA
Fax 0161-953 0291   Tel 0161-832 7211
E-mail: paul.tyrell@granadatv.careof.uk
Journalist of the year: John Sweeney
Columnist of the year: John Diamond, Times
Broadcasting writer of the year: David Aaronovitch,
Independent on Sunday
Gerald Barry award: Ruth Picardie, Observer
Scoop of the year: Nate Thayer, Far Eastern Econmic
Review, trial of Pol Pot
Political commentator of the year: Boris Johnson, Daily
Telegraph
Royal reporter of the year: Richard Kay, Daily Mail
Newspaper of the year: the Guardian

MAGAZINE AWARDS

Magazines '98 Awards: PPA
Periodical Publishers Association, Queens House, 28
Kingsway, London WC2B 6JR
Fax 0171-404 4167   Tel 0171-404 4166
Consumer magazine of the year: New Woman, Emap
Elan
Business magazine of the year: The Grocer, William
Reed Publishing
International magazine of the year (consumer): Sugar,
Attic Futura
International magazine of the year (business): Nature,
Macmillan Magaznes
Customer magazine of the year: Colour Magazine,
Redwood Publishing
Consumer specialist magazine of the year: Top of the
Pops, BBC Worldwide
Editor of the year (consumer): Ed Needham, FHM
Editor of the year (business): Stuart Rock, Real Business
News designer of the year (consumer): Tony Chambers,
GQ
Designer of the year (business): Dara Allegranza,
Business & Technology
Specialist writer of the year (consumer): James May, Car
Columnist of the year (business): Martin Pawley, the
Architects' Journal
Writer of the year (consumer): Byron Rogers, Saga
Magazine
Writer of the year (business): Alastair McLellan, New
Civil Engineer
**Publisher of the year (for companies with less than 25
employees):** Becca Watson, Inspirations for Your Home
Publisher of the year (consumer): Gillian Laskier, Top of
the Pops, Toybox, BBC Family Life, Teletubbies
Publisher of the year (business): Tim Weler, Investment
Week
Editorial campaign of the year: Amateur Gardening,
IPC Magazines

The picture that earned John Reardon a Nikon award

PHOTOGRAPHY AWARDS

Nikon
380 Richmond Road, Kingston, Surrey KT2 5PR
Fax 0181-541 4584   Tel 0181-541 4440
PHOTOGRAPHERS OF THE YEAR
Press: Ian Waldie, Reuters
Regional: Ian Rutherford, the Scotsman
Royals: John Stillwell, Press Association
Sports: Toby Melville, Bristol Evening Post & Press
Arts/entertainment: Roger Bamber, freelance (The Guardian)
Fashion: Sheridan Morley, freelance (Independent on Sunday)
News: Sion Touhig, freelance (Sygma)
Features: John Reardon, freelance
Photo essay: Gideon Mendel, freelance (Network Photographers)
Electronic imaging: Ray Little, freelance

British Picture Editors' Awards
Gold Stag Public Relations, Victoria House, Consort Way, Horley, Surrey RH6 7AF
Fax 01293 821399   Tel 01293 822055
Photographer of the year: Stuart Conway, Herald, Glasgow, Daily Record, freelance
Regional photographer of the year: Stuart Conway, Herald, Glasgow, Daily Record, freelance
Art & entertainment photographer of the year: Ian Torrance, Daily Record
Sport photographer of the year: Toby Melville, Bristol Evening Post & Press
Royal photographer of the year: Mike Moore, Mirror

Features photographer of the year: Mike Moore, Mirror
Business and industry photographer of the year: Brendan Corr, Financial Times
News photographer of the year: Mathew Polak, freelance, Sygma
Young photographer award: Stuart Conway, Herald, Glasgow, Daily Record, freelance
National award for best B&W picture: Jason Bell, freelance
Regional award for best b&w picture: Pauline Nield, freelance
Best use of B&W photography: Yorkshire Post
Newspaper of the year: The Independent
Regional newspaper of the year: Yorkshire Post
Newspaper magazine of the year: Guardian Weekend
Regional newspaper magazine of the year: The Scotsman Weekend

Observer David Hodge Award
The Observer, 119 Farringdon Road, London EC1R 3ER
Set up in 1986 in memory of David Hodge, a photographer who died aged 30 of injuries sustained during the Brixton riots. The award is given to photographers under 30. First prize is £3,000 and an expenses paid assignment for the Observer. Plus Best Student caegory (prize £1,500) and runners up. Winners include Jonathan Olley (Network Photographers), Stephen Dupont, Craig Stennett, Jez Coulson (Insight Photographers)
1998 winner: Zoe Sinclair

Press agencies

The top international news agencies are: Associated Press (AP), Reuters and United Press International (UPI). The main agency which gathers news inside the UK is the Press Association (PA) which is owned by the regional newspaper publishers.

Advance Features
Stubbs Wood Cottage, Hammerwood, East Grinstead, West Sussex RH19 3QE
Fax 01342-850480   Tel 01342-850480
Provides cartoons, crosswords and puzzles for newspapers, magazines and TV.

Agence France Presse
78 Fleet Street, London EC4Y 1HY
Fax 0171-353 8359   Tel 0171-353 7461
E-mail: london.bureau@ldn.afp.com
London office of the international global French news agency. Supplies international news and picture services to the UK media, and collects British material for the foreign media.

AllScot News & Features Agency
PO Box 6, Haddington, East Lothian EH41 3NQ
Fax 01620-825079   Tel 01620-822578
E-mail 101324.2142@compuserve.com
Provides social, religious, political, economic, industrial. business, environmental, news and sports services across Scotland for UK and overseas media outlets.

Andes Press Agency
26 Padbury Court, London E2 7EH
Fax 0171-739 3159   Tel 0171-613 5417
                         Tel.0171-739 3159
E-mail: photos@andespress.demon.co.uk
Covers global social, religious, political, economic and environmental, especially in Latin America.

Anglia Press Agency
91 Hythe Hill, Colchester, Essex CO1 2NU
Fax 01206-797962   Tel 01206-797961
Covers: Essex, Suffolk and Norfolk, news and pictures.

Anglo-Danish Press Agency
Grosvenor Works, Mount Pleasant Hill, London E5 9NE
Fax 0181-806 3236   Tel 0181-806 3232

ANSA
12-13 Essex Street, London WC2R 3AA
Fax 0171-240 5518   Tel 0171-240 5514
Website: http://www.ansa.it
The leading Italian news agency.

Associated Press (AP)
12 Norwich Street, London EC4A 1BP
Fax 0171-353 8118   Tel 0171-353 1515
UK office of the giant American agency, co-operatively owned by US media companies. Supplies international news and picture services to the UK media, and collects British material for American and other clients. Also runs the AP-Dow Jones.

Australian Associated Press
12 Norwich Street, London EC4A 1EJ
Fax 0171-583 3563   Tel 0171-353 0153
Australia's only domestic news agency. Reports on events in Britain and Europe of interest to Australia and the South Pacific.

Bellis News Agency
Seabreezes, 14b Kenelm Road, Rhos-on-Sea, Colwyn Bay LL28 4ED
Fax 01492-544925   Tel 01492-549503
E-mail: bellis@aol.com
News reporters for most of north Wales .

Bloomberg Business News
Citygate House, 39-45 Finsbury Square, London EC2A 1PQ
Fax 0171-392 6000   Tel 0171-330 7500
Website: http://www.bloomberg.com\uk
Business and financial service.

Bournemouth News & Picture Service
14 Lorne Park Road, Bournemouth BH1 1JN
Fax 01202-553875   Tel 01202-558833
Covers: Hants, Dorset, Wilts. News, features and photos.

Bristol & West News Agency
80 Combe Avenue, Portishead, North Somerset BS20 6JT
                         Tel 01275-842053
Specialises in sports coverage of the region.

Britannia Press Features
1 Pettits Close, Romford, Essex RM1 4EB
Fax 01708-761833   Tel 01708-761186
Provides wide range of features Travel isa speciality.

Cambrian News Agency
PO Box 30, Methyr Tydfil, CF 48
Fax 01685-375190   Tel 01685-382070
Covers: South Wales.

Canadian Press
12 Norwich Street, London EC4A 1EJ
Fax 0171-583 4238   Tel 0171-353 6355
The leading Canadian news agency.

Cassidy & Leigh (Southern News Service)
Exchange House, Hindhead, Surrey GU26 6AA
Fax 01428-606351   Tel 01428-607330
E-mail: southernnews@compuserve.com
News and pictures: Surrey, Sussex, Hants and Kent.

Caters News Agency
Queens Gate Suite 19, 121 Suffolk Street, Queensway, Birmingham B1 1LX
Fax 0121-616 2200   Tel 0121-616 1100
Covers: West Midlands.

Cavendish Press
17 Whitworth Street, Manchester M1 5WG
Fax 0161-237 5353   Tel 0161-237 1066
                         ISDN 0161-236 1370
Covers: North west England. News, features, pictures.

Central News Network
30a Newmarket Street, Falkirk, FK1 1JQ
Fax 01324-630515   Tel.01324-630505

Central Office of Information (COI)
Hercules Road, London SE1 7DU
Fax 0171-928 5037   Tel 0171-928 2345
Website: http://www.coi.gov.uk/coi
The government press and publicity agency.
COI South East
Hercules Road, London SE1 7DU
Fax 0171-928 6974   Tel 0171-261 8795
COI Eastern
Three Crowns House, 72-80 Hills Road, Cambridge CB2 1LL
Fax 01223-316121   Tel 01223-311867
COI Merseyside
Cunard Buildings, Pier Head, Liverpool L3 7QB
Fax 0151-224 6470   Tel 0151-224 6412
COI West Midlands
Five Ways Tower, 4th floor, Islington Row, Middleway, Edgbaston, Birmingham B15 1SL
Fax 0121-626 2041   Tel 0121-626 2023
COI East Midlands
Belgrave Centre, Talbot Street, Nottingham NG1 5GG
Fax 0115-971 2791   Tel 0115-971 2780
COI North East
Wellbar House, Gallowgate, Newcastle-upon-Tyne NE1 4TB
Fax 0191-261 8571   Tel 0191-202 3600
COI North West
Piccadilly Plaza, Manchester M1 4BD
Fax 0161-236 9443   Tel 0161-952 4513
COI Plymouth
Phoenix House, Notte Street, Plymouth PL1 2EW
Fax 01752-227647   Tel 01752-635053
COI South West
The Pithay, Bristol BS1 2NF
Fax 0117-945 6975   Tel 0117-945 6969
COI Yorkshire & Humberside
City House, New Station Street, Leeds, LS1 4JG
Fax 0113-283 6586   Tel 0113-283 6591
Central Press Features
Temple Way, Bristol BS99 7HD
Fax 0117-934 3575   Tel 0117-934 3000
E-mail mail@central-press.co.uk.
Website: http://www.cpost.co.uk
Features syndication worldwide. Specialists in TV listings, crosswords, puzzles and motoring.
Central Press Lobby
Press Gallery, House of Commons, London SW1A 0AA
Fax 0171-799 1026   Tel 0171-219 3673
Specialists in Parliamentary reporting for regional press and TV.
Chapman & Page
Denegate House, Amber Hill, Boston,Lincs PE20 3RL
Tel 01205-290477
Syndications agency supplying regular weekly columns and crosswords plus editorial to support ad features.
Chester News Service
Linen Hall House, Stanley Street, Chester CH1 2LR
Fax 01244-326075   Tel 01244-345562
Covers: Chester, including local courts, sport and features

Chester Press Bureaux
Riverside Ho, River Lane, Saltney, Chester CH4 8RQ
Fax 01244-678749   Tel 01244-678575
Provides press agency, PR and contract publishing services.
Cotswold & Swindon News Service
101 Bath Road, Swindon, Wilts SN1 4AX
Fax 01793-485462   Tel 01793-485461
Specialist cover of magistates' and crown courts. Also research, business profiles and features. Media training courses provided.
Coventry News Service
1st Floor, 3 Queen Victoria Road, Coventry CV1 3JS
Fax 01203-634906   Tel 01203-633777
Website: http://www.advent-communications.co.uk
JW Crabtree & Son
Cheapside Chambers, 43 Cheapside, Bradford, West Yorkshire BD1 4HP
Fax 01274-732937   Tel 01274-732937
Covers: Bradford area for sport and news.
Dee News Service
12 Chester Street, Mold, Clwyd CH7 1EG
Fax 01352-759009   Tel 01352-754016
Covers: NE Wales area, Mold Crown Court, Mold, Hawarden, Flint magistrates.
Derek Bellis
See Bellis News Agency
Deutsche Presse Agentur
30 Old Queen Street, London SW1H 9HP
Fax 0171-233 3534   Tel 0171-233 2888
E-mail: 100726,2370@compuserve.com
German national news agency, owned by the German media.
Devon News Agency
4 Clifton Road, Exeter, Devon EX1 2BR
Fax 01392-435248   Tel 01392-276338
Covers: Devon and Cornwall.
Dow Jones Newswires
10 Fleet Place, Limeburner Lane, London EC4M 7RB
Fax 0171-832 9102   Tel 0171-832 9105
E-mail: helen.donnellan@cor.dowjones.com
Website: http://www.downjones.com
UK office of global real-time newswire service owned by Dow Jones & Co, publishers of the Wall Street Journal. Supplies international news that affects all global financial markets. Produced in co-operation with the Associated Press.
Dragon News & Picture Agency
21 Walter Road, Swansea, SA1 5NQ
Fax 01792-475264   Tel 01792-464800
Covers: South and west Wales.
Dundee Press Agency
10 Victoria Road, Dundee DD1 1JN
Fax 01382-907790   Tel 01382-907700
Covering east and central Scotland.

EDIT UK
24 Northfield Way, Aycliffe Park, Newton Aycliffe,
Co.Durham DL5 6EJ
Fax 01325-308082   Tel 01325-308081

Elliott News Service
1 Fisher Lane, Bingham, Nottingham NG13 8BQ
Fax 01949-836583   Tel 01949-836566

Essex News Service
121 High Street, Witham, Essex CM8 1BE
Fax 01376-521222   Tel 01376-521222

Ewan MacNaughton Associates
6 Alexandra Road, Tonbridge, Kent TN9 2AA
Fax 01732-771160   Tel 01732-771116
E-mail: EMA@dial.pipex.com
Syndication agents for the Telegraph newspaper group.

Extel Financial
13-17 Epworth Street, London EC2A 4DL
Fax 0171-251 2725   Tel 0171-251 3333
Website: http://www.info.ft.com
Extel is one of the biggest agencies, supplying financial
information and business news around the world.

Features International
Tolland, Lydeard St Lawrence, Taunton, Somerset TA4
3PS
Fax 01984-623901   Tel 01984-623014
Syndicates internationally newspaper and magazine
features.

Ferrari Press Agency
1A Hurst Road, Sidcup, Kent DA15 9AE
Fax: 0181-302 6611   Tel 0181-302 6622
For pictures telephone 01634-373 572
Covers: South east London and Kent.

First Features Syndicate
39 High Street, Battle, East Sussex.
Fax 01424-870877   Tel 01424-870877
E-mail: first.features@dial.pipex.com
Supplies all types of feature material to press and radio .

Fleet News Agency
Fleet House, 68a Stanfield Road, Bournemouth,
Dorset BH9 2NR
                Tel 01202-515151
Covers: Bournemouth, Dorset and surrounding area.

Fleetline News Service
1a Bedford Road, London N2 9DB
Fax 0181-444 2313   Tel 0181-444 9183
Covers: London and Home Counties.

Fourth Estate Press Agency
12 North Campbell Avenue, Milngavie, Glasgow G62
7AA
                Tel 0141-956 1540
Covers: Glasgow and west of Scotland.

Fowlers Press Agency
11 Village Way, London SE21 7AN
Fax 0171-236 8136   Tel 0171-248 6858
E-mail: smeddum@lotinternet.com
Nationwide bankruptcy and liquidation service.

Frank Ryan News Service
Cargenriggs, Islesteps, Dumfries DG2 8ES
Fax 01387-251121   Tel 01387-253700
Covers: South west Scotland- news, features, PR,
photography.

Freemans Press Agency
Raleigh Mill, Lower Raleigh Road, Barnstaple, Devon
EX31 4JQ
Fax 01271-344922   Tel 01271-324000
Covers: News features, PR and pix all SW England.

Front Page News Agency
1st Floor, 67 High Street, Bidford-on-Avon,
Warwickshire B50 4BQ
Fax 01789-490286   Tel 01789-778590
Covers: True life features in the UK.

Gemini News Service
9 White Lion Street, London N1 9PD
Fax 0171-837 5118   Tel 0171-833 4141
E-mail gemini@gn.apc.org
Website: http://www.oneworld.org/gemini
International news and features.

Gloucester & County News Service
26 Westgate Street, Gloucester GL1 2NG
Fax 01452-300581   Tel 01452-522270

Great North News & Features
Woody Glen, How Mill, Carlisle, Cumbria CA4 9JY
Fax 01228-70381   Tel 01228-70381
E-mail: gnorthnews@aol.com
News from the northern Lake District to southern
Scotland.

Great Scot International
Camerons, Midton Road, Howwood PA9 1AG
Fax 01505-702333   Tel 01505-705656
E-mail: great.scot@glasgow.almac.co.uk
Newspaper, magazine, TV, radio, book design and
research. They have Scottish experts and international
medicine specialists. Close to Glasgow Airport,

Guardian/Observer News Services
119 Farringdon Road, London EC1R 3ER
Fax 0171-837 1192   Tel 0171-278 2332
International syndication services of news and features
from the Guardian and Observer. Most national daily
and Sunday newspapers have similar syndication
operations; contact via their main switchboards.
See also London News Service and Solo Syndication,
below, and Ewan MacNaughton, above.

Hayter's Sports Agency
146-148 Clerkenwell Road, London EC1R 5DP
Fax 0171-837 2420   Tel 0171-837 7171
Website: http://www.hayters.co.uk
Specialises in sports features and statistics.

Hebridean Press Service
1 Maritime Buildings, Stornaway, Isle of Lewis HS1 2XU
Fax 01851-704270   Tel 01851-702737/706060
Covers: Western Isles.

Hill's Welsh Press
58 Lower Cathedral Road, Cardiff CF1 8LT
Fax 01222-224947   Tel 01222-227606
A news and photographic agency specialising in news,
sport, features, PR. Mac facilities.

Hopkinson News & Feature Service
12 Hallfield Road, Bradford BD1 3RQ
Fax 01274-725565   Tel 01274-725565
Yorkshire and Humberside.

Hull News & Pictures
Room 115, Hull Microfirms Centre, 266-290
Wincolmlee, Hull HU2 0PZ
Fax 01482-210267   Tel 01482-210267
E-mail: hull@hullnews.karoo.co.uk
East Yorkshire and north Linclonshire.

INS News Group
211a London Road, Reading, Berks RG1 3NU
Fax 01118-935 1232   Tel 0118-935 1234
E-mail: rkerr.icd@dial.pipex.com

Inter-Continental Features
48 Southerton Road, London W6 0PH
Fax 0181-741 3819   Tel 0181-748 9722
Agents for Universal Press Syndicate and Tribune
Media Services. Syndicated cartoons, features, KRT,
news and graphics and photos on line.

Ireland News
Apartment 67, 100 Parnoll Street, Dublin 1
                    Tel 00353-1-8788813
News and features across Ireland.

Islamic Republic News Agency
3rd Floor, 390 High Road, Wembley, Middlesex HA9
6AS
Fax 0181-900 0705   Tel 0181-903 1630
E-mail: PAYAM@Irna.co.uk

Jarrolds Press Agency
68 High Street, Ipswich, Suffolk IP1 3QJ
Fax 01473-218447   Tel 01473-219193
Covers: Suffolk and surrounding area and football
coverage.

Jenkins Group
186 High Street, Rochester, Kent ME1 1EY
Fax 01634-830930   Tel 01634-830888
E-mail: thechrismurphy@msn.co
Covers Kent for news features.

Jiji Press
76 Shoe Lane, London EC4A 3JB
Fax 0171-583 8353   Tel 0171-936 2847
Japanese news agency.

John Connor Press Associates
57a High Street, Lewes, East Sussex BN7 1XE
Fax 01273-486852   Tel 01273-486851
E-mail: connors@pavilion.co.uk
Covers: Sussex.

Kett's News Service
53 Christchurch Road, Norwich, Norfolk, NR2 3NE
Fax 01603-508055   Tel 01603-508055
Covers news and features in Norfolk and Suffolk.

Knight Ridder Financial Europe
KR House, 78 Fleet Street, London EC4Y 1HY
Fax 0171-583 0519   Tel 0171-842 4000
Website: http://www.bridge.com

Kuwait News Agency
150 Southampton Row, London WC1B 5AL.
Fax 0171-278 6232   Tel 0171-278 5445

Kyodo News
Suites 119-130, NW Wing, Bush House, Aldwych,
London WC2B 4PJ
Fax 0171-438 4512   Tel 0171-438 4501
Japanese news agency that covers UK and Scandinavia.

Lakeland Press Agency
Birch Garth, Beemire, Birthwaite Road, Windermere,
Cumbria LA23 1DW
Fax 015394-45128   Tel 015394-45127
Covers: Lake District.

Leicester News Service
Belmont House, Salisbury Road, Leicester LE1 7QR
Fax 0116-255 6565   Tel 0116-255 5055
Covers: Leicestershire

London At Large
36 Aybrook Street, London W1M 3JL
Fax 0171-224 4452   Tel 0171-224 4464
E-mail: londonatlarge@dial.pipex.com
A forward planning press agency specialsing in arts and
entertainment.

M & Y News Agency
65a Osborne Road, Southsea, Hants PO5 3LS
Fax 01705-291709   Tel 01705-820311
Covers: Hants, West Sussex, IoW, Dorset. Specialists in
sport, particularly soccer and cricket.

Masons News Service
Unit 9, Chesterton Mill, French's Road, Cambridge
CB4 3NP
Fax 01223-361508   Tel 01223-366996
E-mail: on51@dial.pipex.com
News, photographs and TV packages from eastern
England for national and international news outlets.

Mercury Press Agency
7th floor, The Cotton Exchange, Old Hall Street,
Liverpool L3 9LQ
Fax 0151-236 2180   Tel 0151-236 6707
E-mail: mercury@livpool.u-net.com
Covers: north west of England and north Wales, with
news, features and pictures.

MAPA
Second Star on the Right, Land of Green Ginger, Hull
HU1 2EA
Fax 01482-589926   Tel 01482-589900
E-mail: Group@MAPA.demon.co.uk
Formerly Mike Ackroyd Press Agency. Covers Hull area
sport. Produces local publications.

Midlands Associated Media
Bradford Court, Bradford Street, Birmingham, B12
0NS
Fax 0121-608 1141   Tel 0121-608 1166
News, pictures and features from West Midlands,
Warwickshire, Staffordshire, Worcestershire.

National Association of Press Agencies
See Press Support Organisations

National News Press Agency
109 Clifton Street, London EC2A 4LD
Fax 0171-684 3030   Tel 0171-684 3000
E-mail: national.news@dial.pipex.com
Website: national.pictures-library.com
Court and general news and features in London and the
south east. Also works in partnership with BB TV to
produce short news pieces for home and foreign use.

New Zealand Press Association
12 Norwich Street, London EC4A 1EJ
Fax 0171-583 3563   Tel 0171-353 7040
E-mail: aapnzpa@compuserve.com
The co-operatively owned national news agency.

Newsflash Scotland
Unit 22K, Thistle Industrial Estate, Kerse Road, Stirling FK7 7RW
Fax 01786-446145   Tel 01786-448497/446210
E-mail: rcf78@dial.pipex.com
3 Grosvenor Street, Edinburgh EH12 5ED
Fax 0131-225 9009   Tel 0131-226 5858
A news, features and picture agency.

News Team International
8th floor, Albany House, Hurst Street, Birmingham B5 4BD
Fax 0121-666 6370   Tel 0121-346 5511
Website: http://www.newsteam.co.uk
News, pictures and features from the West Midlands and Manchester areas. Syndicates for Midland Independent Newspapers, Manchester Evening News and other papers.

North Scot Press Agency
18 Adelphi, Aberdeen AB11 5BL
Fax 01224-212163   Tel 01224-212141
Covers; Grampian

North Wales Press Agency
157 High Street, Prestatyn, Denbighshire LL19 9AY
Fax 01745-855534   Tel 01745-852262

North West News & Sports Agency
148 Meols Parade, Meols, Merseyside L47 6AN
Fax 0151-632 5484   Tel 0151-632 5261
Covers: Wirral and Merseyside.

Northants Press Agency
28 Hunter Street, Northampton, Northants NN1 3QD
Fax 01604-638008   Tel 01604-638811
E-mail: crispin@northamptonpress.demon.co.uk
Covers: Northamptonshire, north Beds and north Bucks for news, features and pictures.

Northern Ireland Information Service
Parliament Buildings, Stormont, Belfast BT4 3ST
Fax 01232-528473   Tel 01232-520700
http://www.nio.gov.uk
Government information service.

Nottingham News Service
8 Musters Road, West Bridgford, Nottingham NG3 7PL
Fax 0115-982 2568   Tel 0115-982 1697

Novosti
See Russian Information Service

Orbit News Service
1 Froghall Lane, Warrington, Cheshire WA2 7JJ
                      Tel 01925-631592
News and picture service in Cheshire and South Manchester.

Page One Press Agency
11 West Avenue,West Bridgford, Nottingham NG2 7NL
Fax 0115-981 3133   Tel 0115-981 8880
E-mail: news@pageone-pa.co.uk
Website: http://www.pageone-pa.co.uk
Features, news, photos and TV coverage of the east Midlands.

Parliamentary & EU News Service
19 Douglas Street, London SW1P 4PA
Fax 0171-821 9352   Tel 0171-233 8283
News on major developments in Parliament and the EU.

PA News - London
PA News Centre, 292 Vauxhall Bridge Road, London SW1V 1AE
Fax 0171-963 7192   Tel 0171-963 7000/7146
Pictures: 0171-963 7155
Teletext: 0171-963 7222
Marketing: 0171-963 7511
Website: http://www.pa.press.net
PA News is the national news agency of the UK and the Republic of Ireland. Operating 24 hours a day, 365 days a year, it is the UK's leading supplier of news and sports editorial, photographs, weather and listings to the print, broadcast and electronic media. It transmits an average of 1,500 stories and 100 pictures every day. The PA News library contains over 14 million cuttings and the PA News Photo library more than 5 million pictures. PA News - along with PA Sport, PA Listings and PA New Media - is part of the Press Association group. Other subsidiary companies are Tellex Monitors (all types of media monitoring) and Two Ten Communications (media information and press release distribution).

PA News - Leeds
PA NewsCentre, Central Park, New Lane, Leeds LS11 5DZ
Fax 0113-244 0758   Tel 0113-234 4411

PA REGIONAL OFFICES
PA Belfast
Queen's Buildings, 10 Royal Avenue, Belfast, BT1 1DB
Fax 01232-439246   Tel 01232-245008

PA Birmingham
1st Floor, Charles House, 148/149 Great Charles Street, Birmingham B3 3HT
Fax 0121-212 3350   Tel 0121-212 3225

PA Bristol
3rd Floor, 64 Queens Road, Clifton, Bristol BS81RE
Fax 0117-925 2055   Tel 0117-925 1744

PA Cardiff
11 Brynawelon Road, Cardiff CF2 6QR3
Fax 01222 764213   Tel 01222 764211

PA Dublin
41 Silchester Road, Glenageary, Dublin
Fax 00 353 128 00936   Tel 00 353 128 00936

PA East Anglia
3 Edieham Cottages, Angle Lane, Shepreth, Royston SG8 6QJ
Fax 01763 262638   Tel 01763 262638

PA Edinburgh
16/18 Chapel Lane, Leith Edinburgh EH6 6SG
Fax 0131-554 3140   Tel 0131-554 3140

PA Exeter
143 Sweetbriar Lane, Exeter Devon EX1 3AP
Fax 01392 431166   Tel 01392 431166

PA Glasgow
8th Floor, 96 Warroch Street, Glasgow G3 8DB
Fax 0141-221 0283   Tel 0141-221 8521

PA Liverpool
93 Princes Garden, Highfield Street, Liverpool L3 6LH
Fax 0151-236 6270   Tel 0151-236 6270

PA Loughborough
11 St Mary's Close, Loughborough, Leics LE11 5DB
Fax 01509 238911   Tel 01509 238911

PA Manchester
5th Floor, 33 Piccadilly, Manchester M1 1LQ
Fax 0161-228 7331   Tel 0161-228 7717

PA Newcastle
16 Shearwater, Souter POint, Whitburn, Sunderland, Tyne-and-Wear SR6 7SF
Fax 0191-529 5022   Tel 0191-529 5012

PA Southampton
11 Wembley Way, Fair Oak, Hampshire SO5 7JN
Fax 01703 692015   Tel 01703 692015

PA Thames Valley
12a Wades Lane, Teddington, Middlesex TW11 8HF
Fax 0181-977 7025   Tel 0181-977 7025

Press Agency (Gatwick)
Europe House, Station Road, Horley, Surrey RH6 9HL
Fax 01293-820517   Tel 01293-822713
Covers: Gatwick Airport and surrounding area.

Raymonds Press Agency
Gower Street, Derby DE1 1SD
Fax 01332-386036   Tel 01332-340404
E-mail: ako@raymonds.demon.co.uk
Covers: Central and east Midlands. One of the largest regional agencies. Provides news, sport, photo and feature coverage.

Reuters
85 Fleet Street, London EC4P 4AJ
Fax 0171-542 4970   Tel 0171-250 1122
Website: http://www.reuters.com
The Reuters Television network of more than 70 bureaux around the world provides broadcasters with a fast, reliable news service. The Reuters Television World News Service (WNS) delivers news feeds, news flashes, live coverage and in-depth features via satellite to more than 200 broadcasters plus their networks and affiliates in 85 countries 24 hours a day. Reuters is an independent public company, founded in 1851.

Russian Information Agency - Novosti
3 Rosary Gardens, London SW7 4NW
Fax 0171-244 7875   Tel 0171-370 1873/3002
E-mail: ria@nòvosti.demon.co.uk
Russian news and information service. Soviet/Russian photo library.

Samuels News & Photo Service
71 Stafford Road, Uttoxeter, Staffs ST14 8DW
Fax 01889-567181   Tel 01889-566996

Saudi Press Agency
18 Cavendish Square, London W1M 0AQ
Fax 0171-495 5074   Tel 0171-495 0418/9

Scarborough News/Ridings Press Agency
77 Westborough, Scarborough, North Yorks YO11 1TP
Fax 01723-865054   Tel 01723-365535

Scase News Service
Congham, Kings Lynn, Norfolk PE32 1DR
Fax 01485-600672   Tel 01485-600650
Covers: East Anglia and specialises in news, royal news and features.

Scottish Office Information Directorate
St Andrews House, Edinburgh EH1 1DG
Fax 0131-244 1721   Tel 0131-244 2709
Website: http://www.scotland-gov.uk
Government information service.

Scottish News Agency
99 Ferry Road, Edinburgh EH6 4ET
Fax 0131-478 7327   Tel 0131 478 7711
News and sports pictures.

Scottish News & Sport
74 York Street, Glasgow G2 8JY
Fax 0141-221 3595   Tel 0141-221 3602
E-mail: scotnews@btinternet.com
Showbusiness and sport, PR, words and photos.

Seven Day Press
193 Bath Street, Glasgow G2 4HU
Fax 0141-248 1099   Tel 0141-572 0060
E-mail: a@sevendaypress.aol.com
Covers: Scotland.

Shrewsbury Press Service
1a Victorian Arcade, Hills Lane, Shrewsbury, Salop SY1 1PS
Fax 01743-247701   Tel 01743-352710
Covers: Shropshire.

Sirius Media Services
Green Farm, Harleston, Stowmarket, Suffolk IP14 3HW
Fax 01449-736894   Tel 01449-736889
E-mail: grnfarm@globalnet.co.uk
Provides a range of editorial features, including crosswords and horoscopes.

Smith Davis Press
8 Westport Road, Burslem, Stoke-on-Trent, Staffs ST6 4AW
Fax 01782-812428   Tel 01782-812311
E-mail: smith-davis@smith-davis.co.uk
Provides press agency, PR and contract pubishing services.

Solent News & Photo Agency
21 Castle Way, Southampton SO14 2BW
Fax 01703-232983   Tel 01703-223217
Covers: Hants, IoW, Wilts and Dorset.

Solo
49 Kensington High Street, London W8 5ED
Fax 0171-938 3165   Tel 0171-376 2166
Features and news from Associated Newspapers, The European, News Limited of Australia. Also archive library of three million photos including 12,000 Spanish images.

Somerset News Service
43-44 High Street, Taunton, Somerset TA1 3PW
Fax 01823-332862   Tel 01823-331789
-Covers: Somerset. News and photo coverage for national and regional TV, radio and newspapers.

South Bedfordshire News Agency
134 Marsh Road, Luton, Beds LU3 2NL
Fax 01582-493486   Tel 01582-572222
Covers: Herts, Beds and Bucks.

South Coast Press Agency
22 St Peters Road, Bournemouth, Dorset BH1 2LE
Fax 01202-297904   Tel 01202-290199
Covers: Dorset and surrounding counties.

South West News Service
24-30 Hotwell Road, Clifton, Bristol BS8 4UD
Fax 0117-922 6744   Tel 0117-927 6661
E-mail: swnews@hotmail.com
Covers: West Country and South Wales.

Space Press
Bridge House, Blackden Lane, Goostrey, Cheshire
CW4 8PZ
Fax 01477-535756   Tel 01477-534440/533403
E-mail: post2001@aol.com.uk
Covers: Cheshire & surrounding counties, news,
features, photos.

Spanish News Agency (EFE)
5 Cavendish Square, London W1M 0DP
Fax 0171-436 3562   Tel 0171-636 5226
http://www.efe.londrespagenciaefe.demon.co.uk
The news agency for Spain and Latin America.

Steve Hill Agency
12 Steep Hill, Lincoln LN2 1LT
Fax 01522 569571   Tel 01522 569595
Covers: Lincolnshire & surrounding counties, news,
features, photos.

Stewart Bonney News Agency
17 St Peter's Wharf, 26 Pudding Chare, Newcastle-
on-Tyne NE1 1UE
Fax 0191-275 2609   Tel 0191-275 2600
E-mail: powdene@compuserve.com
St Peter's Wharf, Newcastle-upon-Tyne NE6 1TZ
Covers: North east England.

Strand News Service
226 The Strand, London WC2R 1BA
Fax 0171-936 2689   Tel 0171-353 1300
General coverage.

Tartan Tec News Agency
See Great Scot International

Tass/Itar
12-20, Second Floor, Morley House, 320 Regent
Street, London W1R 5AB
Fax 0171-580 5547   Tel 0171-580 5543
London office of the Russian news agency.

Teespress Agencies
15 Baker Street, Middlesbrough, Teeside TS1 2LF
Fax 01642-880744   Tel 01642-880733
Covers: Teesside, North Yorkshire, South Durham.

Tim Wood Agency
11 Village Way, Dulwich, London SE21 7AN
Fax 0171-236 8136   Tel 0171-248 6858
Covers: London courts, including Old Bailey.

Torbay News Agency
45 Lymington Road, Torquay, Devon TQ1 4BG
Fax. 01803-214557   Tel 01803-214555
Covers: Torbay and south Devon.

UK News
St George Street, Leicester LE1 9FQ
Fax 0116-251 2151   Tel 0116-253 0022
Founded in 1993 by Northcliffe Newspapers and
Westminster Press. It provides national and
international news, sport. and pictures to 33 regional
papers. UK News has reciprocal arangements with
subscriber newspapers, giving it access to the work of
hundreds of journalists. It also has a team of lobby
journalists based at the House of Commons.

United Press International (UPI)
2 Greenwich View, Millharbour, ondon E14 9NN
Fax 0171-538 1051   Tel 0171-333 1690
Covers: Middle East, business, sport, features, news and
political events.

UNS Newswire
210 Old Street, London EC1V 9UN
Fax 0171-490 1255   Tel 0171-490 8111
Website: http://www.twoten.press.net
Transmits news and feature stories direct onto
journalists' screens in 180 newsrooms around the UK.

Wales News Service
Womanby Street, Cardiff CF1 2UD
Fax 01222-664181   Tel 01222-666366
Covers: Wales and the West.

Warwickshire News & Picture Agency
41 Lansdowne Crescent, Leamington Spa,
Warwickshire CV32 4PR
Fax 01926-424760   Tel 01926-424181
Covers: Warwickshire and West Midlands.
Specialists in features, investigations and a range of
photographic services.

Watson's Press Agency
103 Adelaide Street, Blackpool, Lancs FY1 4LU
Fax 01253-623996   Tel 01253-623996
Covers: Lancashire and South Cumbria.The agency
specialises in local news, sport and feature work.

Welsh Office - Information Division
Cathays Park, Cardiff CF1 3NQ
Fax 01222-825508   Tel 01222-825449
E-mail: webmaster@wales.gov.uk
Website: http://www.wales.gov.uk
Government communications agency.

Wessex News & Features Agency
Neates Yard, 108 High Street, Hungerford, Berkshire
RG17 0NB
Fax 01488-686900   Tel 01488-686810
E-mail: news@britishnews.co.uk
         features@britishnews.co.uk
Website: http://www.britishnews.co.uk
News, features and photos covering England and
Scotland.

West Riding News & Sports Service
Field House, Welington Road, Dewsbury, West
Yorkshire WF1 3IH
Fax 01924-437564   Tel 01924-437555
Covers: West Yorkshire.

White & Reed
10 Castle Street, Reading, Berkshire RG1 7RD
Fax 0118-939 1753   Tel 0118-957 6628
Covers: Thames Valley.
Supplies news and feature pictures. Also covers public
relations and photography.

Xinhua News Agency of China
8 Swiss Terrace, Belsize Road, London NW6 4RR
Fax 0171-722 8512   Tel 0171-586 8437
E-mail: xinhua@easynet.co.uk
Covers: foreign and domestic affairs.

Yaffa Newspaper Service
Suite 305-7, 29 Gt Pulteney Street, London W1R 3DD
Fax 0171-439 7318   Tel 0171-437 5133
UK representatives of US syndication King Features.

Press cuttings agencies

The Newspaper Licensing Agency gathers copyright revenue from organisations that do large scale photocopying of newspaper articles. Charities and schools are exempted.

The NLA was launched in January 1996 by a number of national newspapers and in October 1997 News International joined other newspaper publishers as a member of the Newspaper Licensing Agreement. "NI's participation means that companies and other organisations will be able to buy a single licence covering all national newspapers," said Guy MacNaughton, the NLA managing director.

The NLA represents the publications listed below and has granted photocopying licences to the agencies opposite:

Newspaper Licensing Agency
Lonsdale Gate, Lonsdale Gardens, Tonbridge, Kent TN1 1NL
Fax 01892-525275   Tel 01892-525274
Licensing   Tel 01892-525273
E-mail: copy@nla.co.uk
Website: http://www.nla.co.uk
National newspapers: Daily Mail, Mail on Sunday, Evening Standard, Express, Express on Sunday, Daily Star, Financial Times, Mirror, People, Daily Telegraph, Sunday Telegraph, Independent, Io S, Guardian, The Observer, Times, Sunday Times, Sun, NoW
Other publications: The European, Press & Journal (Aberdeen), International Herald Tribune, The Scotsman, Scotland on Sunday, Daily Record, Sunday Mail, The Sunday Mercury (Birmingham), The Birmingham Post, Birmingham Evening Mail, The Coventry Evening Telegraph, Grimsby Evening Telegraph, The Sentinel (Stoke), Hull Daily Mail, Leicester Mercury, Western Morning News, South Wales Evening Post, Nottingham Evening Post, Derby Evening Telegraph, Scunthorpe Evening Telegraph, Yorkshire Post, Yorkshire Evening Post, The Star (Sheffield, Barnsley, Doncaster, Rotherham editions)

A-Line
86 Hilton Drive, Aberdeen AB24 4NL
Fax 01224 276010   Tel 01224 484661
E-mail: Shewell@wintermute.co.uk
CIS Information Services
73 Farringdon Road, London EC1M 3JB
Clipability
Chapel Allerton Centre, Harrogate Road, Leeds LS7 4NY
Fax 0113-268 7981   Tel 0113-269 3290
E-mail: pressclip@aol.com

CXT Media Monitoring
CXT House, One Tanner Street, London SE1 3UB
Fax 0171-378 8633   Tel 0171-378 8139
E-mail: 100741.217@compuserve.com
Energy Data Services
19-23 Ironmonger Row, London EC1V 3QN
Fax 0171-336 8877   Tel 0171-336 8899
Entertainment Press Cuttings Agency
Unit 11.g.2, The Leathermarket, Weston Street, London SE1 3ER
House of Cuttings
2 Glentrammon Road, Orpington, Kent BR6 6DE
Fax 01689-810050   Tel 01689-817000
E-mail: info@hocl.com
Website: http://www.hocl.com
McCallum Media Monitor
Tower House, 10 Possil Road, Glasgow G4 9SY
Market Movements
Tey House, Market Hill, Royston, Hertfordshire SG8 9JN
Fax 01763-245151   Tel 01763-248828
Media Shadowfax Europe
10 Barley Mow Passage, London W4 4PH
Fax 0181-994 9888   Tel 0181-994 6477
NewsIndex
55 Farringdon Road, London EC1 3JB
Precise Press Cuttings
19-23 Ironmonger Row, London EC1V 3QN
Fax 0171-250 3506   Tel 0171-250 3505
Press Cutting Partnership
5 Hillgate Street, London W8 7SP
Press Data Bureau
76-78 Rose Street, North Lane, Edinburgh EH2 3DX
Fax 0131-225 4503   Tel 0131-225 4988
Press Express
53-56 Great Sutton Street, London EC1V 0DE
Fax 0171-251 1412   Tel 0171-689 0123
PressScan
5 New Street, Edinburgh EH8 5EH
Fax 0131-557 8737   Tel 0131-557 9010
Press Select
18-20 Farringdon Lane, London EC1R 3AU
Fax 0171-336 6537   Tel 0171-336 6453
The Prominent Information Company
Bear Wharf, 27 Bankside, London SE1 9DP
Fax 0171-203 0101   Tel 0171-203 3500
Smith Willis Communications
The Bond, Fazeley Street, Birmingham B5 5SE
Fax 0121-608 0073   Tel 0121-608 0777
Strata Matrix
25 North Parade, Aberystwyth, Ceredigion SY23 2JN
Fax 01970-612774   Tel 01970-625552
E-mail: strata.aber@btinternet.com
Tellex Monitors
210 Old Street, London EC1V 9UN
Fax 0171-490 8595   Tel 0171-490 1447
E-mail: sales@tellex.press.net
Website: http://www.tellex.press.net

Picture agencies and libraries

James Eisen had just finished his postgraduate journalism exams at Harlow College and was out celebrating in the West End when he recognised the person who'd just brushed past him.

"I rubbed my booze 'n' fags-affected eyes to make sure I was seeing clearly," Eisen wrote. "It was him. I froze. I stood staring at him as he slowly shuffled into a doner kebab takeaway. Looking at Paul Gascoigne, I didn't see England's so-called ace midfielder, or allegedly the finest British footballer since George Best. I saw lucre. Dough. Dosh."

Eisen, unlike most others who have had inebriated visions of wealth, immediately did something about it. He rushed to an all-night shop, bought a cheap Kodak camera, took the snaps and sold them to the Mirror. The two journalistic morals from Eisner's tale are: 1) it pays to be quick witted and; 2) the most basic technology can still deliver the goods.

But in the main, digital cameras predominate and Digital Photography, a new how-to-do-it book by Alastair Fuad-Luke, includes a history of a new tool of the journalistic trade. "The London Evening Standard's photographer Ken Towner was first past the post capturing the winner of the 1989 Derby, Quest for Fame, using a Canon RC-760," says Fuad-Luke. "The image was sent by modem connected to a standard telephone line and was printed in the paper just 45 minutes later. In the early nineties the Guardian's Eamonn McCabe used a Sony ProMavica and Canon RC-760 to capture the London Marathon. McCabe, a sports photographer and current photo editor of the Guardian and the Observer newspapers, found the lack of rapid sequential shots a limitation, but nonetheless produced good reportage works.

Fuad-Luke continues: "Digital photography was not just used for straight reportage. Mike Laye's picture of the cricketer Mark Ramprakash was given the electronic treatment in the Daily

James Eisen, the student journalist who was quick-thinking enough to grab a shot of Gazza eating a kebab

Telegraph's Saturday magazine in late 1991. Ramprakash was montaged into an old cigarette card style background. Celebrating and lampooning those in the limelight was facilitated at the touch of a mouse and comping digital images with graphic elements has become everyday fare in today's newspapers. In the Guardian and Observer alone, digital composites from Steve Caplin, Graham Rawl and Roger Tooth provide a stream of visual satire. While many regarded this technology as ideal for late breaking news, the general consensus was that portable still digital cameras weren't quite up to the mark as regards print quality. While press photographers wrestled with the new technology, backroom people were getting carried away with retouching using image manipulation software. Digitally retouched photos have appeared in UK national newspapers from 1990 onwards. Broadsheets took the high moral ground, as photo editors from the tabloids revelled in the ease with which they could clone heads to bodies. The debate continues and even broadsheets are not exempt from succumbing to the digital excesses. The Guardian published a photograph of the Chancellor of the Exchequer, Gordon Brown, in the 1997 budget. While all the other papers had him flanked by aides, mysteriously the Guardian was the only newspaper to have captured Brown alone with the red Budget box."

Though the future is digital, the demise of Fast News Photos shows that a loudly trumpeted adherence to new tech is not necessarily good enough as a main selling point. Fast News, which billed itself as the only digital photo agency in the UK, closed in March 1998 with its owner, Chris Blishen, saying he needed more investment. Blishen blamed newspapers and magazines rather than photographers who, he said, are prepared to spend just under £10,000 for the latest high specification cameras. However, Blishen believes there is still some time to go before the press as a whole invests in enough kit to buy significant numbers of pictures via the Internet.

KEY CONTACTS

British Association of Picture Libraries and Agencies (BAPLA)
18 Vine Hill, London EC1R 5DX
Fax 0171-713 1211   Tel: 0171-713 1780
E-mail: bapla@bapla.demon.co.uk
Website: http://www.bapla.org.uk
BAPLA is the trade association representing 350 picture libraries and agencies (500,00,00 images). It provides a fast and comprehensive referral service for image research. Publishes the industry magazine Light Box, and an annual directory. As well as work in copyright, BAPLA assesses many industry issues including copyright clearance, ethics, pricing, marketing and technology.

Council of Photographic News Agencies
Oak Trees, Burrows Lane, Gomshall, Guildford, Surrey GU5 9QF
Fax 01483-203378   Tel 01483-203378
Represents the UK's six largest press agencies/photo libraries.

Picture Research Association
455 Finchley Road London NW3 6HN
Fax 0171-431 9887   Tel 0171-431 9886
E-mail: pra@pictures.demon.co.uk
Professional body for all those involved in the research, management and supply of visual material to all forms of the media. It promotes professional standards and provides a forum for the exchange of information. Gives advice to members, organises meetings, quarterly magazine, monthly newsletter and Freelance Register.

Picture Researchers Handbook
by Hilary & Mary Evans; Pira International
Fax 01372-377526   Tel 01372-802000
The standard reference book to picture sources

PICTURE AGENCIES

Ace Photo Agency
Satellite House, 2 Salisbury Road, Wimbledon, London SW19 4EZ
Fax 0181-944 9940   Tel 0181-944 9944
E-mail: info@acestock.com
Website: http://www.acestock.com
A wide-ranging colour photo library with material on many subjects.

Action Images
Image House, Station Road, London N17 9LR
Fax 0181-808 6167   Tel 0181-885 3000
E-mail: actionimages@cityscape.co.uk
Website: http://www.actionimages.com
Sports picture library covering all major events.

Action Plus
54 Tanner Street, London SE1 3PH
Tel 0171-403 1558
130 professional and amateur sports worldwide.

Adams Picture Library
156 New Cavendish Street, London W1M 7FJ
Fax 0171-436 7131   Tel 0171-636 1468
General library with the work of more than 400 photographers.

The Advertising Archives
45 Lyndale Avenue, London NW2 2QB
Fax 0171-794 6584   Tel 0171-435 6540
Collection of US and British press ads and magazine covers. Official UK agents for Saturday Evening Post artwork including Norman Rockwell cover illustrations.

Aerofilms
Gate Studios, Station Road, Borehamwood, Herts WD6 1EJ
Fax 0181-207 5433   Tel 0181-207 0666
E-mail: aerofilms@simmonsmap.com
Aerial photography with library, 1.75 million images, dating back to 1919.

AKG London
10 Plato Place, 72-74 St Dionis Road, London SW6 4TU
Fax 0171-610 6125   Tel 0171-610 6103
Website: http://www.akg-london.co.uk
London representative of the large Berlin picture library AKG and the Erich Lessing Archive of Fine Art and Culture, Vienna. Specialists in arts and history.

Alan Jones Photos
10 Pelwood Road, Camber, E Sussex TN31 7RU
                          Tel 01797-225448
Covers: Sussex and Kent. Has ISDN facilities.

Allsport (UK)
3 Greenlea Park, London SW19 2JD
Fax 0181-648 5240   Tel 0181-685 1010
E-mail: lmartin@allsport.co.uk
Website: http://www.allsportuk.allsport.co.uk
The world's largest specialist sports library, represented in 27 countries. Has over six million images, dating from 1880.

Alpha Photographic Press Agency
63 Gee Street, London EC1V 3RS
Fax 0171-250 1149   Tel 0171-608 2796
International photo feature agency and picture library specialising in celebrities.

Andes Press Agency
26 Padbury Court, London E2 7EH
Fax 0171-739 3159   Tel 0171-613 5417
E-mail: photos@andespress.demon.co.uk
Covers social, religious, political, economic and environmental issues around the world, especially in Latin America.

Aquarius Picture Library
PO Box 5, Hastings, East Sussex TN34 1HR
Fax 01424-717704   Tel 01424-721196
Over 1 million film stills, current and archival, dating back to silent days. Also TV, vintage pop, some opera and ballet.

Archive Films
17 Conway Street, London W1P 6EE
Fax 0171-391 9111   Tel 0171-312 0300E-mail: ipurdie@theimagebank.com
Website:http://www.imagebank.co.uk
Historical library with more than 20 million photos, drawings and engravings, representing nearly every subject from the beginning of civilization to the present.

Archive Photos
See Image Bank

Ardea London
35 Brodrick Road, London SW17 7DX
Fax 0181-672 8787   Tel 0181-672 2067
E-mail: ardea@globalnet.co.uk
Wildlife, pets and the environment, worldwide.

Assignments Photographers
189-191 Reepham Road, Norwich, NR6 5NZ
Fax 01603-789175   Tel 01603-789234
E-mail: assignments@paston.co.uk
Website:
 http://www.netlink.co.uk/users/lightbox/assign
Covers eastern region in news, features, sport, commercial and PR photography.

Associated Sports Photography/Headline
21 Green Walk, Leicester LE3 6SE
Fax 0116-231 1123   Tel 0116-232 0310
E-mail: KCW80@dial.pipex.com
National and international coverage. Has ISDN facilities.

Autograph
Zetland House, 5/25 Scrutton Street, London EC2A 4LP
Fax 0171-729 9400   Tel 0171-739 1777
E-mail: mark@auto.demon.co.uk
Website: http://www.autograph-abp.co.uk

Barnaby's Picture Library
19 Rathbone Street, London W1P 1AF
Fax 0171-637 4317   Tel 0171-636 6128
E-mail: barnabyspicturelibrary@ukbusiness.com
Website:
http://www.ukbusiness.com/barnabyspicturelibrary/
A library of over 4 million colour transparencies, b/w prints. The coverage is worldwide and historic.

Barnardo's Film & Photographic Archive
Tanners Lane, Barkingside, Essex IG6 1QG
Fax 0181-550 0429   Tel 0181-550 8822
500,000 photos dating from 1871, film from 1905, covering the work of the UK's largest children's charity.

Barratts Photopress
63 Gee Street, London EC1V 3RS
Fax 0171-250 1149   Tel 0171-278 1223/336 0632
E-mail: alphapress@compuserve.com
Has ISDN facilities.

BBC News Stills
Room 4225, The Spur, TV Centre, Wood Lane, London W12 7RJ
Fax 0181-576 7020   Tel 0181-576 0690
E-mail: picture-desk@bbc.co.uk
A wide range of stills from the BBC News and Current Affairs collection.

BBC Photograph Library
Room B116, TV Centre, Wood Lane, London W12 7RJ
Fax 0181-746 0353   Tel 0181-225 7193
Programme stills, mainly comedy, drama and light entertainment dating back to 1924,

Beken Maritime Services
16 Birmingham Road, Cowes, Isle of Wight PO31 7BH
Fax 01983-291059   Tel 01983-297311
Marine photographers and stock library, built around the Beken family's photos. Images from 1888 to the present.

The Bridgeman Art Library
17-19 Garway Road, London W2 4PH
Fax 0171-792 8509   Tel 0171-727 4065
E-mail: info@bridgeman.co.uk
Website: http://www.bridgeman.co.uk
A specialist source of the world's finest paintings, drawings, manuscripts, sculpture, antiques and antiquities; offering large format colour transparencies and a picture research service.

British Film Institute (Stills, Posters & Designs)
21 Stephen Street, London W1P 2LN
Fax 0171-323 9260   Tel 0171-255 1444
E-mail: info@bfi.org.uk
Website: http://www.bfi.org.uk
Holds 7 million pictures recording the history of cinema-tography and includes, film, TV and portraits.

British Library Reproductions
British Library, 96 Euston Road, London NW1 2DB
Fax 0171-412 7771   Tel 0171-412 7614
E-mail: bl-repro@bl.uk
Website: http://portico.bl.uk/repro/
12 million books and 5 million other items can be photographed to order. A 'browsable' picture library service is now available.

Bruce Coleman Collection
16 Chiltern Business Village, Arundel Road, Uxbridge, Middlesex UB8 2SN
Fax 01895-272357   Tel 01895-257094
E-mail: info@brucecoleman.co.uk
Website: http://www.brucecoleman.co.uk
Transparencies on natural history and travel.

Bulletin International Video Library
5-8 Hardwick Street, London EC1R4RB
Fax 0171-278 6349   Tel 0171-278 6070
E-mail: rabia.bapu@bulletin-intl.com
Recent stock footage of industry, commerce, medicine, leisure, locations; mainly UK, Europe and Asia.

Caledonian Newspapers Picture Library
195 Albion Street, Glasgow G1 1QP
Fax 0141-553 2642   Tel 0141 553 3209
E-mail: watson@cims.co.uk
6 million news photos from 1900 onwards, many of Scotland.

Calyx Multimedia
41 Churchward Avenue, Swindon SN2 1NJ
Fax: 01793-513640   Tel 01793-520131
E-mail: calyx@compuserve.com
Covers: Wiltshire + M4 corridor. Picture stories, features, public relations.

Camera Press
21 Queen Elizabeth Street, London SE1 2PD
Fax 0171-278 5126   Tel 0171-378 1300
Website: http://www.campress.co.uk
Long-established general picture library of over ten million items, covering more than a century of news. Famous photographers include Karsh, Lichfield, Snowdon and Beaton. Has ISDN facilities.

Capital Pictures
54a Clerkenwell Road, London EC1M 5PS
Fax 0171-253 1414   Tel 0171-253 1122
Specialises in pictures of famous people. ISDN facilities.

Centrepix
Unit 215, The Custard Factory, Gibb Street, Digbeth, Birmingham B9 4AA
Fax 0121-608 6777   Tel 0121-608 6777/6888
Has ISDN facilities.

Cephas Picture Library
Hurst House, 157 Walton Road, East Molesey, Surrey KT8 0DX
Fax 0181-224 8095   Tel 0181-979 8647
E-mail: mickrock@cephas.co.uk
Website: http://www.cephas.co.uk
Wine and vineyards of the world, spirits, beers and ciders, 85,000+ images. Also large food and drink archive - free 116 page catalogue.

Christian Aid Photo Library
PO Box 100, London SE1 7RT
Fax 0171-620 0719   Tel 0171-523 2235
E-mail: caid@gn.apc.org
Website: http://www.oneworld.org/christian_aid
Social pictures on community programmes in Africa, Asia and Latin America.

Collections
13 Woodberry Crescent, London N10 1PJ
Fax 0181-883 9215   Tel 0181-883 0083
E-mail: collections@btinternet.com
Website: http://www.com/tildercollections/
The life and landscape of the British Isles. Also child development from pregnancy to adulthood.

Colorific!
Innovation Centre, 225 Marsh Wall, London E14 9FX
Fax 0171-538 3555   Tel 0171-515 3000
E-mail: colorifi@visualgroup.com
Large colour photo library, covering wide range of current topics.

Colorsport
44 St Peters Street, London N1 8JT
Fax 0171-226 4328   Tel 0171-359 2714
E-mail: ofice@colorsport@demon.co.uk
Extensive library of sport photos, including football and cricket history. All other sports date from late 1960s to the present. Has ISDN facilities.

Comstock
28 Chelsea Wharf, 15 Lots Road, London SW10 0QQ
Fax 0171-352 8414   Tel 0171-359 4448
E-mail: info@comstock.co.uk
Website: http://www.comstock.com
World renowned general library. Specialist suppliers to advertising and design industries. Free catalogues and CD-Roms. Digital and transparencies available.

David Hoffman Photo Library
21 Norman Grove, London E3 5EG
Fax 0181-980 2041 Tel 0181-981 5041
E-mail: lib@hoffmanphotos.demon.co.uk
Social issues. Policing, drugs, youth, race, homelessness, housing, environmental demos, waste disposal, energy, industry and pollution. Wide range of images mainly UK and Europe, also USA, Venezuela and Thailand.

David King Collection
90 St Pauls Road, London N1 2QP
Fax 0171-354 8264 Tel 0171-226 0149
Photos, posters and ephemera covering political/cultural history of Russia, USSR, China, Spanish civil war. Communist leaders. Gulag. Collection of Stalinist falsifications. 250,000 images.

Dobson Photo Agency
13 Falconers Road, Scarborough, N Yorks YO11 2SN
Fax 01723-363661 Tel 01723-363661
E-mail: camerhire@aol.com
Covers: Yorkshire coast. Press and PR photographers, broadcast video and 40 year picture library

David Williams Picture Library
50 Burlington Avenue, Glasgow G12 0LH
Fax 0141-337 3031 Tel 0141-339 7823
Specialist Collections of Scotland and Iceland. Smaller collections of Faroe Islands, France and Western USA. Commissions undertaken, catalogue.

Ecoscene
The Oasts, Headley Lane, Passfield, Liphook, Hants GU30 7RX
Fax 01428-751057 Tel 01428-751056
E-mail ecoscene@photosource.co.uk
Website: http://www.
photosource.co.uk/photosource/ecoscene.htm
80,000 images on the environment, natural history, industry, energy, agriculture, conservation and recycling.

Empics Sports Photo Agency
26 Musters Road, West Bridgford, Nottingham NG2 7PL
Fax 0115-840 4445 Tel 0115-840 4444
E-mail info@empics.co.uk
Website: http://www.empics.co.uk
International sports photo agency covering major sports events. ISDN facilities. On-line picture archive.

Environmental Investigation Agency Photo Library
15 Bowling Green Lane, London EC1R 0BD
Fax 0171-490 0436 Tel 0171-490 7040
E-mail: eiauk@gn.apc.org
Website: http://www.pair.com/eia/
Library following the charity's campaigns. Most pictures cover endangered subjects (wild birds, rhinos, whales, tigers, elephants, forests and wildlife trade).

Environmental Images
Finsbury Business Centre, 40 Bowling Green Lane, London EC1R 0NE
Fax 0171-713 6348 Tel 0171-713 6347
E-mail: environmentalimages@compuserve.com
Specialises in environmental issues. Agriculture, conservation, demonstrations, planning etc.

Farmers Weekly Picture Library
Quadrant House, The Quadrant, Sutton, Surrey SM2 5AS
Fax 0181-652 4005 Tel 0181-652 4914
E-mail: farmers.library@rbi.co.uk
Website: http://www.fwi.co.uk
Britain's biggest agricultural picture library holding 250,000 images of all aspects of farming and country life. Has ISDN facilities.

ffotograff
10 Kyveilog Street, Cardiff CF1 9JA
Fax 01222-229326 Tel 01222-236879
E-mail ffotograff@easynet.co.uk
Website: http://www.
cf.ac.uk/ccin/main/buscomm/ffotogra/ffoto1.html
Photolibrary, specialising in travel, exploration and the arts and covering the Middle, Far East, and Wales. Has ISDN facilities.

Forest Life Picture Library
Forestry Commission, 231 Corstorphine Road, Edinburgh EH12 7AT
Fax 0131-314 6285 Tel 0131-314 6411
E-mail: n.campbell.forestry.gov.uk
Official image bank of the Forestry Commission. It has comprehensive coverage of tree species, forests, woodland landscapes, timber production and a collection of wildlife and recreation images.

Format Photographers
19 Arlington Way, London EC1R 1UY
Fax 0171-833 0381 Tel 0171-833 0292
E-mail: format@formatphotogs.demon.co.uk
Social documentary library and agency. Includes: education, health, disability, religion and women. UK and abroad. Archive from 70's. Colour and b/w.

Francis Frith Collection
Old Rectory, Bimport, Shaftesbury, Dorset SP7 8AT
Fax 01747-855065 Tel 01747-855669
E-mail: sales@francisfrith.com
Website: http://www.francisfrith.com
4,000 British towns and villages taken between 1860 and 1970. Has ISDN facilities.

Frank Spooner Pictures
B7 Hatton Square, 16-16a Baldwins Gardens, London EC1N 7US
Fax 0171-632 5828 Tel 0171-62 5800
Large general photo library representing Gamma (Paris), Liaison (NY) for current international material and Roger Viollet for historic. Has ISDN facilities.

Gaze International
4c Hazlitt Road, London W14 0JY
Fax 0171-610 4762 Tel 0171-602 1162
E-mail: info@gaze.co.uk
Website: http://www.gaze.co.uk
Picture library covers all aspects of gay, lesbian and transgender life and culture for editorial, reportage, features, ad campaigns and health promotions.

GeoScience Features Picture Library
6 Orchard Drive, Wye, Kent TN25 5AU
Fax 01233-812707 Tel 01233-812707
E-mail: gsf@geoscience.demon.co.uk
All aspects of earth sciences and natural history worldwide. Over 330,000 pictures.

George Outram Picture Library
See Caledonian Newspapers Picture Library
Greater London Record Office
See London Metropolitan Archives
Greenpeace Communications
See Environmental Picture Library
Greenpeace UK
Canonbury Villas, London N1 2PN
Fax 0171-865 8200   Tel 0171-865 8294
Email angela.glienicke@uk.greenpeace.org
Website: www.greenpeace.org
Holds approximately 60,000 photos of campaigns and
environmental issues.
Greg Evans International Photo Library
6 Station Parade, Sunningdale, Ascot, Berks SL5 0EP
Fax 0171-637 1439   Tel 0171-636 8238
E-mail: greg@geipl.demon.co.uk
Website: http://www.geipl.demon.co.uk
Comprehensive colour photo library.
Guardian/Observer Photo Service
119 Farringdon Road, London EC1R 3ER
Fax 0171-837 1192   Tel 0171-713 4423
International syndication service for all Guardian
pictures and for the pre-1989 Observer archive library.
Has ISDN facilities.
Hulton-Getty
101 Bayham Street, London NW1 0AG
Fax 0171-544 3334   Tel 0171-544 3333
E-mail: info@getty-images.com
Website: http://www.getty-images.com
The Hulton Getty Picture Collection is part of Getty
Images. It is one of the world's greatest picture libraries,
covering nearly all topics and periods. The overall
archive holds more than 50 special collections,
including Picture Post, Keystone, Fox, Central Press and
the world's oldest news collection.
Hutchison Picture Library
118b Holland Park Avenue, London W11 4UA
Fax 0171-792 0259   Tel 0171-229 2743
Half a million worldwide documentary colour
transparencies. Subjects include: agriculture, energy,
environments, families, festivals, industry, landscape,
religion, transport and weather.
ICCE Photo Library
1 Sceftbeara House, Shebbear, Beaworthy, Devon
EX21 5RU
Fax 01409 281302   Tel 01409 281302
Website: http://www.icce.demon.co.uk
International Centre for Conservation Education
photolibrary specialising in wildlife, habitats,
conservation and environmental issues worldwide:
including acid rain, agriculture, erosion, pollution etc.
Illustrated London News Picture Library
20 Upper Ground, London SE1 9PF
Fax 0171-805 5905   Tel 0171-805 5585
News images from 1842 onwards. Covers all aspects of
history.

The Image Bank
17 Conway Street, London W1P 6EE
Fax 0171-391 9111   Tel 0171-312 0300
Source for contemporary and archive photography,
illustration and film footage. Purchased Archive Photos
in 1998. Free catalogue.
Image Bank, Manchester
4 Jordan Street, Manchester M15 4PY
Fax 0161-236 8723   Tel 0161-236 9226
Image Bank, Scotland
14 Alva Street, Edinburgh EH2 4QG
Fax 0131-225 1660   Tel 0131-225 1770
Image Bank, Ireland
11 Upper Mount Street, Dubin 2
Fax 3531-676 0873   Tel 3531-676 0872
E-mail: ukmarketing@theimagebank.com
Website: http://www.imagebank.co.uk

Images of Africa Photobank
11 The Windings, Lichfield, Staffs WS13 7EX
Fax 01543-417154   Tel 01543-262898
Wide range of subjects covering 14 African countries
from Egypt to South Africa. Excellent on wildlife,
habitat, national parks, tourism and traditional peoples.
Impact Photos
26-27 Great Sutton Street, London EC1V 0DX
Fax 0171-608 0114   Tel 0171-251 5091
Worldwide images covering all subjects.
Imperial War Museum
Photograph Archive, All Saints Annex, Austral Street,
London SE11 4SJ
Fax 0171-416 5355   Tel 0171-416 5333
E-mail: photos@iwm.org.uk
National archive of more than five million photos
dealing with 20th century warfare, especially the two
world wars.
In-Focus
Sitwell Centre, Scarborough, N Yorks YO12 5EX
Fax 01723-503749   Tel 01723 501904
E-mail: in-focus.co.uk
Web: http://www.in-focus.co.uk
Sport, politics, royals and celebrities.
Insight Photographers
10 Lambs Conduit Passage, London WC1R 4RH
Fax 0171-419 7777   Tel 0171-419 0171
E-mail: marcjackson@insight-visual.com
Photos covering a wide range of political and social
issues, including urban deprivation, pollution, ethnic
tensions and nationalism. Has ISDN facilities.
Insport International
Home Farm Cottage, Church Lane, Church Langton,
Market Harborough LE16 7SX
Fax 01858-545492   Tel 01858-545492
E-mail: INSPORT@compuserve.com
Photolibrary and service covering sporting events.
ITN Archive
200 Grays Inn Road, London WC1X 8XZ
Fax 0171-430 4453   Tel 0171-430 4480
E-mail: archive.sales@itn.co.uk
http://www.frith.7sohosquare.com/itn/frame1.htm
News events from 1955 to the present day and feature
material from every continent.

ITV Sport Archive
London Television Centre, Upper Ground, London SE1 9LT
Fax 0171-827 7634   Tel 0171-261 3064
E-mail: kahns@itsarc.demon.co.uk
Holds the majority of sports coverage on ITV since the late '60s.

Janine Wiedel Photolibrary
8 South Croxted Road, London SE21 8BB
Fax 0181-761 1502   Tel 0181-761 1502
The photojournalist's coverage of contemporary society.

John Frost Historical Newspaper Service
8 Monks Avenue, New Barnet , Herts EN5 1DB
Fax 0181-440 3159   Tel 0181-440 3159
Over 65,000 British and overseas newspapers, and 100,000 cuttings, relating to outstanding events from 1640 to the present.

Julian Cotton Photo Library
55 Upper Montagu Street, London W1H 1FQ
Fax 0171-724 7555   Tel 0171-723 5800
Aerial photography covering Britain, New York, Provence and natural abstracts. Also 100,000 pictures ranging from life style, landscapes to animals and food.

Katz Pictures
Zetland House, 5-25 Scrutton Street, London EC2A 4LP
Fax 0171-377 5558   Tel 0171377 5888
E-mail: katzpictures@katzpictures.com
International photo agency and library covering many topics, including personalities, news and current affairs.

Kevin Fitzpatrick Photography
40 Woodville Drive, Sale, Cheshire M33 6NF
Fax 0161-962 9441   Tel 0161-969 2709
Covering the northwest from south Manchester. News, features, library and wire facilities.

Kobal Collection
184 Drummond Street, London NW1 3HP
Fax 0171-383 0044   Tel 0171-383 0011
Collection of 1 million movie images including portraits and scene stills in colour and b&w, from 1895 to the present.

London Metropolitan Archives
40 Northampton Road, London EC1R 0HB
Fax 0171-833 9136   Tel 0171-332 3820
E-mail: ima@ms.corpotlondon.gov.uk
Half a million photos covering the history and topography of the London area. Run by the Corporation of London.

MacQuitty International Collection
7 Elm Lodge, Stevenage Road, London SW6 6NZ
Fax 0171-384 1781   Tel 0171-385 6031
Library of 250,000 photos on social life and culture in over seventy countries dating back to the 1920s. Also some archive film.

Magnum Photos
5 Old Street, London EC1V 9HL
Fax 0171-608 0020   Tel 0171-490 1771
E-mail: magnum@magnumphotos.co.uk
Website: http://www.magnumphotos.co.uk
International agency and library for leading photojournalists. Over one million photos cover all aspects of C20 life from the 1936 Spanish Civil War onwards.

Mary Evans Picture Library
59 Tranquil Vale, London SE3 0BS
Fax 0181-852 7211   Tel 0181-318 0034
E-mail: lib@mepl.co.uk
Comprehensive historical archive of prints, engravings, photographs and ephemera. Free brochure.

Max Jones Archive
14 Manor Way, Bognor Regis, Sussex PO22 6LA
                              Tel 01243-584670
Jazz photographs (1920-1980) and memorbilia, plus blues, R&B, psychedelic and underground.

McKenzie Heritage Picture Archive
90 Ardgowan Road, London SE6 1UU.
Fax 0181-697 0147   Tel 0181-697 0147
E-mail: MkHeritage@aol.com
Black African, Afro Caribbean & Asian people in Britain and abroad.

Military Picture Library
28a Station Road, Aldershot, Hants GU11 1HT
Fax 01252 350546   Tel 01252-350547
E-mail: pictures@mpl1.demon.co.uk
Website: http://www.mpl1.demon.co.uk

Mirror Syndication International
1 Canada Square, Canary Wharf, London E14 5AP
Fax 0171-293 2712   Tel 0171-266 1133
E-mail: desk@mirrorpix-com
Website: http://www.mirpix.com
Picture agents for Mirror Group Newspapers . It includes the Picture Goer archive. Has ISDN facilities.

Monitor Syndication
17 Old Street, Clerkenwell, London EC1V 9HL
Fax 0171-250 0966   Tel 0171-253 7071
Picture agency/large library specialising in personalities from 1959. Also personality file 1870-1930, music hall, theatre; file on Lotus cars and personalities from 1964.

Motoring Picture Library
John Montagu Building, Beaulieu, Brockenhurst, Hampshire SO42 7ZN
Fax 01590-612655   Tel 01590-612345
E-mail: motorpiclibrary@compuserve.com

Museum of London Picture Library
London Wall, London EC2Y 5HN
Fax 0171-600 1058   Tel 0171-600 3699
E-mail mus@museum-london.org.uk
Website: http://www.museum-london.org.uk
London views, daily life and events since prehistoric times illustrated through paintings, prints, drawings, historic photographs, artefacts etc.

National Maritime Museum
Romney Road, Greenwich, London SE10 9NF
Fax 0181-312 6722   Tel 0181-312 6631
Website: http://www.nmm.ac.uk
Photos and other visual material covering all maritime topics as well as the Greenwich sites.

National Monuments Record
National Monuments Record Centre, Kemble Drive, Swindon, Wilts SN2 2GZ
Fax 01793-414606   Tel 01793-414600
E-mail info@rchme.gov.uk
Website: http://www.rchme.gov.uk
The national collection of aerial photos, pictures of historic buildings, and archaeological sites.

National Museum of Photography
See: Science Museum
National Railway Museum
Leeman Road, York, North Yorks YO26 4XJ
Fax 01904-611112   Tel 01904-686216
E-mail: e.bartholemew@nmsi.ac.uk
Extensive library of railway and transport photos.
National Remote Sensing Centre
Arthur Street, Barwell, Leicestershire LE9 8GZ
Fax 01455-841785   Tel 01455-849227
E-mail: data-services@nrsc.co.uk
Website: http://www.nrsc.co.uk
UK's largest archive of satellite and vertical colour aerial
photography at varying scales.
Neil Setchfield Travel
23 Crofters Court, Croft Street, Surrey Quays, London
SE8 5DW
Fax 0171-394 9246   Tel 0171-394 9246
E-mail: SETCHFIELD@compuserve.com
Photographs of the major cities of the world, including
a comprehensive collection of images of London.
Network Photographers
3-4 Kirby Street, London EC1N 8TS
Fax 0171-831 4468   Tel 0171-831 3633
E-mail: netphoto@compuserve.com
Group of dedicated photojournalists, with extensive
news collection. Represents Rapho (Paris) and
Bilderberg (Hamburg). Has a library which includes
social documentary, travel and feature stories.
Newsflash Scotland
See Press Agencies
Novosti Photo Library
3 Rosary Gardens, London SW7 4NW
Fax 0171-244 7875   Tel 0171-370 3002
E-mail: photos@novosti.demon.co.uk
Russian photo agency with archive and current
material.
Nunn Syndication Library
13b Limehouse Cut, 46 Morris Road, London E14
6NT
Fax 0171-537 2661   Tel 0171-537 2660
Specialise in the British royal family.
Olympic Television Archive Bureau
Axis Centre, Burlington Lane, London W4 2TH
Fax 0181-233 5354   Tel 0181-233 5353
Archive library of Olympic sporting history.
PA News Photo Library
PA NewsCentre, 292 Vauxhall Bridge Road, London
SW1V 1AE
Fax 0171-963 7192   Tel 0171-963 7000
E-mail: photo-sales@pa.press.net
Over five million news sport and entertainment
pictures from the 1890s to the present day.
Pacemaker Press International
787 Lisburn Road, Belfast, N Ireland BT9 7EX
Fax 01232-682111   Tel 01232-663191
All Ireland, covering news, sport, politics, current
affairs and PR.

Panos Pictures
1 Chapel High St, Borough High St, London SE1 1HH
Fax 0171-357 0094   Tel 0171-234 0010
E-mail: pics@panos.co.uk
Documentary library specialising in Third World and
Eastern European photography.
Parachute Pictures
1 Navarino Grove, London Fields, London E8 1AJ
Fax 0171-249 2751   Tel 0171-275 7066
Specialist Third World photo library, with coverage of
narcotics, human rights, children at risk, development
issues and 'World' music.
Pearson Television Stills Library
Teddington Studios, Broom Road, Teddington,
Middlesex TW11 9NT
Fax 0181-614 2250   Tel 0181-781 2789
E-mail: stillslibrary@pearsontv.com
Website: http://www.pearsontvarchive.com
Stills library dates back to the mid-fifties and includes
all Thames, Grundy, ACI, Alomo and All American
programmes with total of 1.5 million stills.
Photofusion
17A Electric Lane, London SW9 8LA
Fax 0171-738 5509   Tel 0171 738 5774
E-mail: library@photofusion.org
Website: http://www.photofusion.org
All aspects of contemporary life in Britain, particularly
social issues. Photographers available for commission.
Photonews Scotland
36 Washington Street, Glasgow G3 8AZ
Fax 0141-248 2470   Tel 0141-248 4888
One of Scotland's leading picture, news and feature
agencies. Has ISDN facilities.
Picture House Photography
West Leam, Station Road, Baildon, W Yorks BD17 6HS
Fax 01274-531058   Tel 01274-531058
Pictor International
Lymehouse Studios, 30-31 Lyme Street, London
NW1 0EE
Fax 0171-267 1396   Tel 0171-482 0478
E-mail: info@london.pictor.co.uk
Website: http://www.pictor.co.uk
A prominent library, over 30 years old, with 3 million
photos on a variety of topics, especially travel, business
and industry. Has ISDN facilities.
Popperfoto
The Old Mill, Overstone Farm, Overstone,
Northampton NN6 0AB
Fax 01604-670635   Tel 01604-670670
E-mail: Popperfoto@msn.com
One of Britain's leading picture libraries, home to over
13 million images covering 150 years of photographic
history. Major collections include photos from Reuters,
HG Ponting, AFP and Bob Thomas Sports
Photography.
Powerstock
9 Coborn Road, London E3 2DA
Fax 0181-983 3846   Tel 0181-983 4222
E-mail: info@powerstock.com
Web: http://www.powerstock.com/powerstock/
The International Stock Exchange collection.

The Press Features Syndicate
9 Paradise Close, Eastbourne, Sussex BN20 8BT
Tel 01323-728760
International photo-feature agency and picture library.

Professional Sport International
8 Apollo Studios, Charlton Kings Mews, London NW5 2SA
Fax 0171-482 2441   Tel 0171-482 2311
E-mail: pictures@prosport.co.uk
Website: http://www.prosport.co.uk
International sports library covering sporting events. Has ISDN facilities.

Public Record Office Image Library
Ruskin Avenue, Kew, Surrey TW9 4DU
Fax 0181-392 5266   Tel 0181-392 5225
E-mail: image-library@pro.gov.uk
Website: http://www.pro.gov.uk/imagelibrary/
Source for historical, social and political images from the national archive. Free CD-Rom available.

RAF Museum
Grahame Park Way, Hendon, London NW9 5LL
Fax 0181-200 1751   Tel 0181-205 2266
E-mail: onfo@rafmuseum.org.uk
Website: http://www.rafmuseum.org.uk
Archive of the history of military aviation. Written requests only.

Retrograph Nostalgia Archive
164 Kensington Park Road, London W11 2ER
Fax 0171-229 3395   Tel 0171-727 9378
E-mail: Pix@Retrograph.com
Website: http://www.Retrograph.com
Specialist picture library/design source of worldwide nostalgia.Posters, labels, magazine advertising (1860-1960). RetroTravel has worldwide travel/tourism images (1900-1960).

Reaction Photographic
3 Berkley Grove, London NW1 8XY
Fax 0171-586 4500   Tel 0171-586 2370

Reuters
See Popperfoto.

Rex Features
18 Vine Hill, London EC1R 5DX
Fax 0171-837 4812   Tel 0171-278 7294
E-mail: mselby@rexfeatures.com
Large international picture agency and photo library, strong on news. Represents the work of over 1,500 photographers. Several million images covering news, personalities and features. Also handles some newspaper and magazine syndication.

Robert Harding Picture Library
58-9 Great Marlborough St, London W1V 1DD
Fax 0171-631 1070   Tel 0171-287 5414
E-mail: info@robertharding.com
Over 2 million photos on all topics. ISDN facilities.

Royal Geographical Society Picture Library
1 Kensington Gore, London SW7 2AR
Fax 0171-591 3061   Tel 0171-591 3060
E-mail: pictures@rgs.org
Archive specialising in geographical and explorational activity from 1830 to the present day (including moving footage). For commercial and academic use.

Royal Photographic Society
Octagon Gallleries, Milsom Street, Bath BA1 1DN
Fax 01225-448688   Tel 01225-462841
E-mail: info@rps.org
Website: http://www.rps.org
Founded in 1853 for the advancement and promotion of the art and science of photography. Arranges many exhibitions, lectures, seminars and workshops. The RPS runs its own gallery, museum and archives. Publishes monthly Photographic Journal and bi-monthly Journal of Photographic Science.

RSPCA Photolibrary
Causeway, Horsham, West Sussex RH12 1HG
Fax 01403-241048   Tel 01403-223150
E-mail: photolibrary@rspca.org.uk
Animal welfare, wildlife and natural history.

SOA Photo Agency
87 York Street, London W1H 1DU
Fax 0171-258 0188   Tel 0171-258 0202
E-mail: sabine.soa@btinternet.com
Website: http://www.btinternet.com/~sabine.soa
Specialising in funny photos, avant garde images and imagery from and about Germany.

Sally and Richard Greenhill
357a Liverpool Road, London N1 1NL
Fax 0171-607 7151   Tel 0171-607 8549
E-mail: library@shadow.org.uk
Website: http://www.shadow.org.uk/photoLibrary
Large library of social documentary photos. UK and China.

Science and Society Picture Library
Exhibition Road, London SW7 2DD
Fax 0171-938 9751   Tel 0171-938 9750
E-mail: piclib@nmsi.ac.uk
Website: http://www.nmsi.ac.uk/piclib
Pictures from the collections of three major museums: the Science Museum, York's National Railway Museum and Bradford's National Museum of Photography, Film and Television. The latter's stock includes important collections (Frith, Fox Talbot, Sutcliffe, Herschel, Daily Herald Archive, etc).

Scottish Highland Photo Library
Croft Roy, Crammond Brae Tain, Ross-shire, Scotland IV19 1JG
Fax 01862-892298   Tel 01862-892298
E-mail: shpl@call.co.uk
Images of all aspects of the Highlands and Islands of Scotland.

SIN
Unit 4, 2 Somerset Road, London N17 9EJ
Fax 0181-808 1821   Tel 0181-808 8660
E-mail: 101457.1516@compuserve.com
Website: http://www.sin-photo.co.uk
Rock and pop, and youth culture.

Skyscan Photolibrary
Oak House, Toddington, Cheltenham, Glos GL54 5BY
Fax 01242-621343   Tel 01242-621357
E-mail: info@skyscan.co.uk
Website: http://www.skyscan.co.uk
Collection of 'balloon's-eye' views of Britain, now extended to cover aircraft, international air to ground photography, aerial sports, in fact anything aerial.

Sport & General Press Agency
63 Gee Street, London EC1V 3RS
Fax 0171-250 1149   Tel 0171-336 0632
E-mail: alphapress@compuserve.com
One of Britain's oldest press photo libraries,
specialising in sport, also general news stock. Allied to
London News Service.

Sporting Pictures (UK)
7A Lambs Conduit Passage, London WC1R 4RG
Fax 0171-831 7991   Tel 0171-405 4500
E-mail: photos@sportingpictures.demon.co.uk
International library of over 3 million pictures

Sportsphoto
20 Clifton Street, Scarborough, North Yorks YO12
7SR
Fax 01723-500117   Tel 01723-367264
E-mail: stewart@sportsphoto.co.uk
Website: http://www.sportsphoto.co.uk
Established agency covering sport, entertainment,
politicians and royals at national and international level.

Stewart Ferguson Photography
11 Moredun Vale Grove, Edinburgh EH17 7QZ
Fax 0131-664 6614   Tel 0131-664 6614
Press and features covering all Scotland.

Still Moving Picture Co
67a Logie Green Road, Edinburgh EH7 4HF
Fax 0131-557 9699   Tel 0131-557 9697
E-mail: stillmovingpictures@compuserve.com
Website: http://
ourworld.compuserve.com/homepage/stillmoving
250,000 images of Scotland including Scottish Tourist
Board's collection. Free CD rom browser.

Still Pictures Whole Earth Photo Library
199 Shooters Hill Road, London SE3 8UL
Fax 0181-858 2049   Tel 0181-858 8307
E-mail: stillpictures@stillpic.demon.co.uk
A leading source on environment, the Third World and
nature.

Sygma
Cairo Studios, 4 Nile Street, London N1ZZ
Fax 0171-608 3757   Tel 0171-608 3690
London office of the large French photographic agency,
specialising in news, showbusiness, history and
personalities. Has ISDN facilities.

Syndicated Features
PO Box 33, Edenbridge, Kent TN8 5PB
Fax 01342-850244   Tel 01342-850313
E-mail: syn@dial.pipex.com
Website: http://www.topham.co.uk/features
A weekly general and showbiz features service available
by post or internet.

Thames Television Library
See Pearson Television Stills Library

Tony Stone Images
101 Bayham Street, London NW1 0AG
Fax 0171-544 3334   Tel: 0171-544 3333
Website: http://www.getty-images.com
One of the leading contemporary stock photography
businesses. The company has around 900
photographers constantly updating the collection. The
subjects range from families to wildlife, finance to
science. Part of Getty Images.

Topham Picturepoint
PO Box 33, Edenbridge, Kent TN8 5PB
Fax 01342-850244   Tel 01342-850313
E-mail: pictures@topham.demon.co.uk
Website: http://www.topham.co.uk
General agency and library, with over seven million
pictures. Includes United Press International's
collection from between 1932-70.

Travel Ink Photo & Feature Library
The Old Coach House, 14 High Street, Goring-on-
Thames, Berkshire RG8 9AR
Fax 01491-875558   Tel 01491-873011
E-mail: info@travel-ink.co.uk
Website: http://www.travel-ink.co.uk
All aspects of travel images and information.
Worldwide coverage. From classic picture postcard
material to cultures, lifestyles and realism.

Tropix
156 Meols Parade, Meols, Merseyside L47 6AN
Fax 0151-632 1698   Tel 0151-632 1698
E-mail: tropixphoto@postmaster.co.uk
Website: http://www.merseyworld.com/tropix/
Specialists in developing nations and in environment
topics worldwide.

United Northern Photographers
2-4 Lower Green, Baildon, Bradford BD17 7NE
Fax 01274 598756   Tel 01274 412222
E-mail: hamlet@unp.co.uk
Website: http://www.unp.co.uk
Editorial reportage and documentary mainly for
nationals and magazines.

Universal Pictorial Press & Agency
29-31 Saffron Hill, London EC1N 8FH
Fax 0171-421 6006   Tel 0171-421 6000
Archive for British and international personalities from
1944 to the present. Digital archive with ISDN facilities.

Waterways Photo Library
39 Manor Court Road, London W7 3EJ
Fax 0181-567 0605   Tel 0181-840 1659
Britain's inland waterways.

Wellcome Centre for Medical Science
210 Euston Road, London NW1 2BE
Fax 0171-611 8577   Tel 0171-611 8588
E-mail: photolib@wellcome.ac.uk
Website: http://www.wellcome.ac.uk
Over 150,000 images covering the history of medicine
and human culture, from ancient times to the present.

Wessex Photos
108 High Street, Hungerford, Berkshire RG17 0NB
Fax 01488-686900   Tel 01488-686810
E-mail: pictures@britishnews.co.uk
Website: http://www.britishnews.co.uk
Photos for newspapers, magazines and PR.

Windrush Photos
99 Noahs Ark, Kemsing, Kent TN15 6PD
Fax 01732-763285   Tel 01732-763486
Extensive coverage of British wildlife.

Woodfall Wild Images
17 Bull Lane, Denbigh, Denbighshire LL16 3SN
Fax 01745-814581   Tel 01745-815903
Landscape, environment, conservation, agriculture and
wildlife collection with worldwide coverage.

Publications about the press

MAGAZINES

The Author
84 Drayton Gardens, London SW10 9SB
Fax: 0171-373 5768   Tel 0171-373 6642
E-mail: authorsoc@writers.org.uk
Website: http://www.writers.org.uk/society
Publisher: Society of Authors
Quarterly news magazine. £7 non-members.

The Bookseller
12 Dyott Street, London WC1A 1DF
Fax 0171-420 6013   Tel 0171-420 6000
Publisher: Bookseller Publications
E-mail: letters.to.editor@bookseller.co.uk
Website: http://www.theBookseller.com
The trade paper of the book industry. It publishes two
annual guides -Spring Books and Autumn Books - with
details of forthcoming titles. £2.50. Editor: Louis Baum.

Books in the Media
15-Up, East Street, Chesham, Bucks HP5 1HQ
Fax 01494-784850   Tel 01494-792269
E-mail: 100615.1643@compuserve.com
Publisher: Bookwatch
Weekly newsletter keeping bookshops and libraries
informed of books appearing in the media. £112 non-
members, £102 members. Editor: Claire MacRae.

British Journalism Review
Faculty of Humanities, University of Luton, 75 Castle
Street, Luton Beds LU1 3AJ
Fax 01582-743298   Tel 01582-743297
Publisher: John Libbey Media
Scholarly quarterly for discussion of media topics.

British Printer
Sovereign Way, Tonbridge, Kent TN9 1RW
Fax 01732-377362   Tel 01732-364422
E-mail: ulp@luton.ac.uk
Website: http://www.dotprint.com
Publisher: Miller Freeman
Monthly news and features from the printing industry.

Comagazine
Tavistock Road, West Drayton, Middx UB7 7QE
Fax 01895-433602   Tel 01895-433600
Publisher: Comag
Alternate monthly review of the magazine industry.

Communications Law
2 Addiscombe Road, Croydon, Surrey CR9 5AF
Fax 0181-686 3155   Tel 0181-686 9141
E-mail: Rajni_Boswell@tolley.co.uk
Publisher: Tolley Publishing
6 issues a year. Journal of computer, media and
telecommunications law.

Financial Times Newsletters
149 Tottenham Court Road, London W1P 9LL
Fax 0171-896 2748   Tel 0171-896 2222
Publisher: FT Telecom & Media Publishing
Newsletters: Asia-Pacific Telecoms Analyst; Business
Computing Brief; Music & Copyright; New Media
Markets; Screen Finance; and Telecom Markets.

Folio
64-65 North Road, Bristol BS6 5AQ
Fax 0117-942 0369   Tel 0117-942 8491
E-mail: editor@venue.co.uk
Website: http://www.venue.co.uk
Publisher: Venue Publishing
Magazine for magazine managers.

Free Press
8 Cynthia Street, London N1 9JF
Fax 0181-837 8868   Tel 0171-278 4430
E-mail: CPBF@architechs.com
Website: http://www.architechs.com/CPBF
Publisher: CPBF
Members news magazine, with analysis of monopoly
media ownership and control, and other issues. 6x pa.

Freelance Market News
7 Dale Street, Manchester M1 1JB
Fax 0161-228 3533   Tel 0161-228 2362
E-mail: writersbureau@zen.co.uk
Website: http://www.zen.co.uk
Monthly newsletter with details of markets for the work
of freelance writers.

Freelance News
7 Wharf Lane, Old Stratford, Milton Keynes MK19 6AD
Fax 01908-267078   Tel 01908-262560
E-mail: fln@northern-light.co.uk
Publisher: Northern Light
Magazine of the freelance division of the Chartered
Institute of Journalists.Only available to CIOJ members.

Headlines
2 Avebury Court, Mark Road, Hemel Hempstead,
Herts HP2 7TA
Fax 01442-219641   Tel 01442-233656
E-mail: gc@cullumassoc.co.uk
Website: http://www.newstech.co.uk
The Newspaper Society's news magazine with much
data on the regional press. 6x pa.

Index on Censorship
33 Islington High Street, London N1 9LH
Fax 0171-278 1878   Tel 0171-278 2313
E-mail: contact@indexoncensorship.org
Website: http://www.indexoncensorship.org
International magazine for free speech, with interviews,
reportage and debates on the important issues of the
day. Paperback format. 6x pa.

The Journalist
314 Grays Inn Road, London WC1X 8DP
Fax 0171-837 8143   Tel 0171-278 7916
E-mail: thejournalist@mcr1.poptel.org.uk
Publisher: National Union of Journalists
For NUJ members. 6x pa.

Journalist's Handbook
2/1 Galt House, 31 Bank Street, Irvine KA12 0LL
Fax 01294-311322   Tel 01294-311322
E-mail: jh@carrickmedia.demon.co.uk
Publisher: Carrick Media
Quarterly journal with articles and a contacts list.
Editor: Fiona MacDonald.

The Magazine Business Weekly Report
2 Holford Yard, London WC1X 9HD
Fax 0171-833 5632   Tel 0171-833 5888
E-mail: caroline.watt@registergroup.com
Publisher: Register Information Services
Weekly faxed newsletter.

Magazine News
Queens House, 28 Kingsway, London WC2B 6JR
Fax 0171-404 4167   Tel 0171-404 4166
Publisher: Periodical Publishers Association
Mainly for advertisers and agencies. 5x pa.

Media Law Review
200 Aldersgate Street, London EC1A 4JJ
Fax 0171-600 5555   Tel 0171-600 1000
E-mail: jeremy.ison@cliffordchance.com
Website: http://www.cliffordchance.com
Editor: Jeremy Ison. Newsletter from law firm Clifford
Chance and the PPA. 3x pa free.

Media Lawyer
3 Broom Close, Broughton in Furness, Cumbria LA20
6JG
Fax 01229-716621   Tel 01229-716622
A newsletter for media lawyers, trainers, journalists and
all concerned with media law. Bi-monthly. £30 pa.

Media Week
Quantum House, 19 Scarbrook Road, Croydon,
Surrey CR9 1LX
Fax 0181-565 4394   Tel 0181-565 4200
E-mail: mweeked@qpp.co.uk
News on the buying and selling of advertising.

Multi Media
Winchester Walk, London SE1 9AG
Fax 0171-403 3735   Tel 0171-357 6161
E-mail: multimedia@saintjp.com
The magazine for interactive business
communications. 12x pa.

New Media Age
50 Poland Street, London W1V 4AX
Fax 0171-970 4899   Tel 0171-970 4000
E-mail: mikeb@centaur.co.uk
Website: http://www.nma.co.uk
Weekly subscription news title for the new media
industry.

New Media Investor
50 Poland Street, London W1V 4AX
Fax 0171-970 4899   Tel 0171-287 9800
E-mail: feliciaj@centaur.co.uk
Website: http://www.nma.co.uk

PrePress News
111 Upper Richmond Road, London SW15 2TJ
Fax 0181-788 2302   Tel 0181-780 7800
E-mail: prepressnews@forme.com
Website: http://www.forme.com
Publisher: Forme Communications
News. reviews and features relating to print production.

Press Gazette
19 Scarbrook Road, Croydon, Surrey CR9 1LX
Fax 0181-565 4395   Tel 0181-565 4200
Publisher: Quantum Publishing
The old UK Press Gazette. A weekly paper for all
journalists with a concentration on newspapers and
magazines, plus coverage of television and radio.

Print Week
174 Hammersmith Road, London W6 7JP
Fax 0171-413 4455   Tel 0171-413 4397
Publisher: Haymarket
Originally Litho Week and still a weekly print magazine,
covering all sectors of the industry. Editor: Jo Francis.

Printing Industries
11 Bedford Row, London WC1R 4DX
Fax 0171-405 7784   Tel 0171-242 6904
E-mail: info@bpif.org.uk
Website: http://www.bpif.org.uk
Publisher: British Printing Industries Federation
The printers management journal (also known as Pi),
published 10x pa.

Printing World
Sovereign Way, Tonbridge, Kent TN9 1RW
Fax 01732-377552   Tel 01732-364422
E-mail: printing.world@unmf.com
Website: http://www.dotprint.com
Publisher: Miller Freeman Publishers
Large circulation weekly covering all aspects of the
printing industry and its personalities.

Private Eye
6 Carlisle Street, London W1V 5RG
Fax 0171-437 0705   Tel 0171-437 4017
E-mail: strobes@cix.compulink.co.uk
Website: http://www.compulink.co.uk/.private-eye/
Publisher: Pressdram
An in-house fortnightly for journalists. It is one of the
few mags which does not depend on ads to survive.

Production Journal
Mark Road, Hemel Hempstead, Herts HP2 7TA
Fax 01442-219641   Tel 01442-233656
E-mail: gc@cullumassoc.co.uk
Website: http://www.newstech.co.uk
Pubished for the industry since 1958, reviewing
newspaper and new media technology. 11x pa.

Professional Printer
8 Lonsdale Gardens, Tunbridge Wells, Kent TN1 1NU
Fax 01892-518028   Tel 01892-538118
E-mail: iop@globalprint.com
Website: http://www.globalprint.com/uk/iop
Publisher: Institute of Printing
Journal of news and articles. Published 6x pa.

Publishing
Forme Communications, Carlton Plaza, 111 Upper
Richmond Road, London W15 2TJ
Fax 0181-788 2302   Tel 0181-780 7800
Publisher: Forme Communications
Management monthly on issues affecting the
newspaper, book and catalogue market.

Publishing News
43 Museum Street, London WC1A 1LY
Fax 0171-242 0762   Tel 0171-404 0304
E-mail: pub.news@dial.pipex.com
The weekly newspaper of the book trade.

Retail Newsagent
11 Angel Gate, City Road, London EC1V 2PT
Fax 0171-689 0500   Tel 0171-689 0600
E-mail: rn@newtrade.demon.co.uk
Publisher: Newtrade Publishing
Weekly newspaper, founded 1888.

WHATEVER THE MEDIA, WHEREVER IT IS...

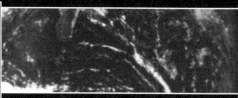

- **Over 44,000 listings** ● **Three Volumes** ●
- **The whole World** ●

Benn's Media is the essential reference source to media in the UK, Europe and throughout the world. It will provide you with comprehensive and accurate information on the press, television, radio and other media related organisations.

The UK Volume:
● 16,000 entries

The European Volume:
● 11,500 entries

The World Volume:
● 17,000 entries

● Advertising and editorial contact details including:

✔ e-mail numbers
✔ advertising rates
✔ readership data
✔ frequency and circulation data

● **Benn's Media Guide** is the *complete* guide to national, regional and international newspapers, consumer and business periodicals, reference publications and broadcasting.

... BENN'S MEDIA
HAS IT COVERED.

If you would like to purchase a copy of *Benn's Media* or would like some additional information please phone: 01732 377591, or fax, 01732 367301.
Alternatively, write to us at: Miller Freeman Information Services, Miller Freeman UK Ltd, Riverbank House, Angel Lane, Tonbridge, Kent, TN9 1SE. Internet: http:\\www.mfplc.co.uk/mfinfo E-mail:bennsmedia@unmf.com

DPA

un Miller Freeman
A United News & Media publication

European Association
of Directory Publishers

Secrets
Suite 102, 16 Baldwins Gardens, London EC1N 7RJ
Fax 0171-831 7461   Tel 0171-831 7477
E-mail: admin@cfoi.demon.co.uk
Website: http://www.cfoi.org.uk
Publisher: Campaign for Freedom of Information
A newspaper which monitors unnecessary official
secrecy and its effects on the public and the media.
Spokesman
20 Cardigan Road, London E3 5HU
Fax 0181-981 3779   Tel 0181-981 3779
Quarterly report on the process of projecting policy
through media, financed by subscription only.
The Week
5-11 Westbourne Grove, London W2 4UA
Fax 0171-229 0049   Tel 0171-229 0006
Weekly. £1.50. A digest of British and foreign press.
Writers News
PO Box 4, Nairn IV12 4HU
Fax 01667-454401   Tel 01667-454441
Subscription monthly for all writers and would-be
writers. also publishes quarterly Writing Magazine.
Writers' Newsletter
430 Edgware Road, London W2 1EH
Fax 0171-706 2413   Tel 0171-723 8074
E-mail: postie@wggb.demon.co.uk
Website: http://www.writers.org.uk/guild
Publisher: Writers' Guild of Great Britain
News from the writers' trade union. 6x pa.

PRESS YEARBOOKS

Benn's Media
Riverbank HoUse, Angel Lane, Tonbridge, Kent TN9
1SE
Fax 01732-367301   Tel 01732-362666
Publisher: Miller Freeman Information Services
Contact: Sarah Creech
Three vols UK, Europe and the rest of the world.£297,
two vols £266, single vols £133. Benn's has the most
comprehensive listings amongst the general directories.
The UK volume lists 17,000 organisations, publications
and broadcasting stations. Est. 1846.
The Circulation Report
2 Holford Yard, Cruickshank Street, London WC1X
9HD
Fax 0171-833 5632   Tel 0171-833 5888
E-mail: alan.macfarlane@registergroup.com
Publisher: Register Information Services.
Contact: Alan Maacfarlane
£95, bi-annual. Also available on disc. Circulation and
vital statistics on all 450 ABC and independently
audited newstrade magazines.
**Directory of Book Publishers, Distributors &
Wholesalers**
272 Vauxhall Bridge Road, London SW1V 1BA
Fax 0171-834 8812   Tel 0171-834 5477
E-mail: 100437.2261@compuserve.com
Publisher: Booksellers Association.
Editor: Sydney Davies
£47.50. Ordering guide/reference for the book trade.

Directory of Publishing
Wellington House, 125 Strand, London WC2R 0BB
Fax 0171-240 8531   Tel 0171-420 5555
E-mail: cassellacad@msn.com
Publisher: Cassell & the Publishers Association
Editor: Verona Higgs
£60. The definitive guide to the book publishing
business, with all main publishers, organisations and
agencies detailedin the UK and the Commonwealth.
Freelance Directory
Acorn House, 134 Grays Inn Road, London WC1X
8DP
Fax 0171-278 1812   Tel.0171-278 7916
E-mail: nuj@mcr1.poptel.org.uk
Publisher: National Union of Journalists
Editor: Dawn Macklew
£30, inc p&p, Biennial directory of 1,500 freelance
reporters, photographers, broadcasters, editors, subs,
cartoonists and illustrators.
Freelance Photographer's Market Handbook
BFP Books, Focus House, 497 Green Lanes, London
N13 4BP
Fax 0181-886 5174   Tel 0181-882 3315
Publisher: Bureau of Freelance Photographers
Editors: John Tracy, Stewart Gibson
£10.95. How to find markets for photographs, mainly
with magazines.
IPO Directory
PO Box 30, Weatherby, West Yorkshire LS23 7YA
Fax 01937-541083   Tel 0171-261 8527
Publisher: Central Office of Information
£13. The official directory of the information and press
officers in government departments and public
corporations. Bi-annual.
Institute of Printing Handbook
8A Lonsdale Gardens, Tunbridge Wells, Kent TN1
1NU
Fax 01892-518028   Tel 01892-538118
E-mail: iop@globalprint.com
Institute of Printing
Contact: David Freeland
Contains technical articles relevant to the printing and
related industries with a complete listing of all the
names and addresses of members of IOP. £100 or free
to members.
MDB Magazine Directory
Fax 0171-833 5632   Tel 0171-833 5888
E-mail: alan.mcfarlane@registergroup.com
The Magazine Business
Contact: Alan Macfarlane
£17.50 Biannual ad-oriented directory of magazines for
sale in British newsagents. Its stablemate is the annual
International Press Directory, £15, listing publications
available for export. Also published is the bi-annual
Circulation Report, £60 each.
Media Disc
9-10 Great Sutton Street, London EC1V 0BX
Fax 0171-253 4762   Tel 0171-251 9000
E-mail: mediadisc@mediainfo.co.uk
Editor: Nick Elliot
Dial up media info on 15,000 titles and contacts. Label
and check list service. Subs £190/month.

The Media Guide
Fourth Estate, for The Guardian
Tel 0171-727-8993
Media Pocket Book
Farm Road, Henley on Thames, Oxon RG9 1EJ
Fax 01491-571188   Tel 01491 411000
E-mail: info@ntc.co.uk
Publisher: NTC Publications
Editor: Sarah Hudson
£24. Statistical data across the media.
Multimedia & CD Rom Directory
6-14 Underwood Street, London N1 7JQ
Fax 0171-324 2312   Tel 0171-324 2345
E-mail: gbuecker@waterlow.com
Publisher: Waterlow New Media Information
Contact: Gesche Beucker
CD Rom annual subscription £229, Vol 1 The
Marketplace £149, Vol 2 The Titles £149. Lists 15,000
companies that are active in multimedia industry
worldwide with contact details, description of company,
newsletters, mags and events targetted at multi-media
professionals. Vol 2 lists 28,000 commercially available
DVD and CD Rom titles as well as publishers.
Newspaper Yearbook
35-37 Brent Street, London NW4 2EF
Fax 0181-203 6424   Tel 0181-203 6525
Regent Publishing
Editor: Sheila Golding
A £9.95 + £1 p&p. Overview first published in 1997
Pims Media Directories
Mildmay Avenue, London N1 4RS
Fax 0171-354 7053   Tel 0171-226 1000
E-mail: press@pims.co.uk
Publisher: Pims International
Editor: Andy Saunders
Pims produces a range of detailed, loose-leaf guides to
editorial media contacts, all regularly updated, aimed
mainly at the public relations sector. Titles include: UK
Media Directory (£365 pa), A-Z Towns Directory (£250)
USA Directory (£215), European Directory(£205).
Printing Trades Directory
Riverbank House, Tonbridge,Kent TN9 1SE
Fax 01732-367301   Tel 01732-362666
E-mail: scrouch@unmf.com
Publisher: Miller Freeman
Contact:Sandy Crouch
£107. Listing more than 7,200 print related companies
(printers, manufacturers and suppliers).
Publishers Handbook
Grosvenor Press   Tel 0171-278 7772
£49.95.
Commercial services available for publishers.
Small Press Yearbook
Small Press Group, BM Bozo, London WC1N 3XX
£7.95.
Guide to the many small presses in the UK.
Studies in Newspaper & Periodical History
3 Henrietta Street, London WC2E 8LU
Fax 0171-379 0609   Tel 0171-240 0856
Publisher: Eurospan.
Scholarly look at press history. Formerly published as
the Journal of Newspaper and Periodical History.

Two-Ten Media Directories
Communications House, 210 Old Street, London
EC1V 9UN
Fax 0171-490 1255   Tel 0171-490 8111
E-mail: info@twoten.press.net
Publisher: Two-Ten Communications
Contact: Chris Jackson
UK Media - 6 issues pa - £268.00
UK Media Town by Town - 2 issues pa - £158.00
European Media - 2 issues pa - £459.00
UK Press Directory
32 South Road, Saffron Walden, Essex CB11 3DN
Fax 01799-502665   Tel 01799 502665
E-mail: showell@ukmd.demon.co.uk
Publisher: UK Media Directories
Contact: Simon Howell
£145 for UK, £85 for Republic of Ireland. Financial
profiles and maps of the 125 leading newspaper
publishers in the UK and the 40 in the Republic of
Ireland.
Ulrich's International Periodicals Directory
Maypole House, Maypole Road, East Grinstead, West
Sussex RH19 1HU
Fax 01342-330191   Tel 01342-330100
E-mail: info@bowker.com
Publisher: Bowker-Saur
A five volume £385 American guide to the world's
periodicals, detailing approx 200,000 titles.
Willings Press Guide
Harlequin House, 7 High Street, Teddington,
Middlesex, TW11 8EL
Fax 0181-943 5141   Tel 0181-943 3138
E-mail: willings@hollis-pr.demon.co.uk
Website: http://www.hollis-pr.co.uk
Contact: Nesta Hollis
Publisher: Hollis Directories
Two vols £189. Alphabetical list detailing over 26,000
news-papers and periodicals worldwide. The leading
title in its field.
World Magazine Trends
PO Box 69, Henley-on-Thames, Oxon RG9 1GB
Fax 01491-571188   Tel 01491-411000
E-mail: tobyhoward@ntc.co.uk
Publisher: NTC Publications
Contact: Toby Howard
£75.95. Industry data on 44 countries.
Writers' & Artists' Yearbook
35 Bdford Row, London WCR
Fax 0171-404 7706   Tel 0171-242 0946
Publisher: A & C Black
Contact: Christine Robinson
£11.99.A long-established handbook, mainly for writers
and authors.
Writer's Handbook
25 Eccleston Place, London SW1 W9NF
Fax 0171-881 8001   Tel 0171-881 8000
Publisher: Macmillan
Contact: Claire Robinson
£12.99. A directory for all writers covering publishers,
publications, broadcasting, agents, services, prizes, etc.

Press support organisations

MAIN TRADE UNIONS

British Association of Journalists
600 members
Chartered Institute of Journalists
1,500 members
Graphical, Paper and Media Union
200,000 members
National Union of Journalists
29,000 members
Society of Authors
6,000 members

MAIN TRADE ASSOCIATIONS

Newspaper Publishers Association
National papers
Newspaper Society
Local papers
Periodical Publishers Association
Magazines
Scottish Daily Newspaper Society
Scottish dailies and Sundays
Scottish Newspapers Publishers' Association
Scottish regional and local papers

ABC
See Audit Bureau of Circulations
Amalgamated Engineering & Electrical Union (AEEU)
Hayes Court, West Common Road, Bromley, Kent BR2 7AU
Fax 0181-315 8234   Tel 0181-462 7755
E-mail: h.jefferies@headoffice.aeeu.org.uk
Website: http://www.aeeu.org.uk
Formed from the merger of the Amalgamated Engineering Union the Electrical, Electronic, Telecommunications and Plumbing Union. It has members in newspaper production and broadcasting and publishes quarterly newspaper Contact.
Amnesty International Journalists' Network
99-119 Rosebery Avenue, London EC1R 4RE
Fax 0171-833 1510   Tel 0171-814 6200
E-mail: journos@amnesty.org.uk
Website: http://www.amnesty.org.uk
Campaigns on behalf of media workers who have been imprisoned, tortured or threatened with death. Holds meetings and publishes a quarterly newsletter.
Article 19, the International Centre Against Censorship
33 Islington High Street, London NN1 9LH
Fax 0171-713 1356   Tel 0171-278 9292
E-mail: article19@gn.apc.org
Website: http://www.gn.apc.org/article19
International human rights organisation campaigning

for the right to freedom of expression and information. Promotes improved legal standards for freedom of expression and defends victims of censorship. Publishes regular newsletter and a range of country and theme reports, with emphasis on media freedom.
Association of American Correspondents in London
AP, 12 Norwich Street, London EC4A 1BP
Fax 0171-936 2229   Tel 0171-353 1515
The association represents a broad spectrum of 200 American journalists. It was founded in 1919. and holds regular lunches.
Association of British Editors
49 Frederick Road, Birmingham B15 1HN
Fax 0121-454 6187   Tel 0121-455 7949
E-mail: info@broadv.u-net.uk
An organisation for editors and senior editorial executives. It publishes the quarterly British Editor. Chairman, Peter Preston.
Association of British Science Writers
23 Savile Row, London W1X 2NB
Fax 0171-973 3051   Tel 0171-439 1205
E-mail: absw@absw.demon.co.uk
Its aim is to improve standards of science journalism. The association organises meetings with scientists and policy makers, and arranges visits. It publishes a monthly newsletter The Science Reporter.
Association of European Journalists
7a St Albans Grove, London W8 5PN
Fax 0171-937 0025   Tel 0171-376 9998
A pan-European group of individual journalists. Its aim is to increase knowledge of Europe and to defend the freedom of the media.
Association of Golf Writers
c/o M Garrod   Tel 01707-654112
Association of Illustrators
1st Floor, 32-8 Saffron Hill, London EC1N 8FH
Fax 0171-831 6277   Tel 0171-831 7377
E-mail: a-o-illustrators.demon.co.uk
Website: http://www.aoi.co.uk
Professional association promoting British illustration and supporting illustrators through membership services. Also campaigns and lobbies. Publishes guides and monthly newsletter.
Association of Little Presses
25 St Benedict's Close, Church Lane, London SW17 9NX
E-mail: asslp@geocities.com
Website:
http://www.geocities.com/Athens/Oracle/7911
Represents 200 members producing books and magazines on all topics, especially poetry. Publishes newsletter, magazine, Poetry and LittlePress Information bulletins and annual catalogue; organises bookfairs. Does NOT publish any creative writing.

Association of Newspaper & Magazine Wholesalers

Celcon House, 6th Floor, 289-293 High Holborn, London WC1V 7HZ
Fax 0171-405 1128   Tel 0171-242 3458
E-mail: enquiries@anmw.co.uk

Association of Photographers

9-10 Domingo Street, London EC1Y 0TA
Fax 0171-253 3007   Tel 0171-608 1441
E-mail: aop@dircon.co.uk
Website: http://www.aphoto.co.uk
Trade association for professional fashion, advertising, design and editorial photographers. Publishes monthly magazine Image. Holds annual awards and runs own gallery at address above.

Association of Publishing Agencies (APA)

Queen's House, 55-56 Lincoln's Inn Fields, London WC2A 3LJ
Fax 0171-379 5661   Tel 0171-379 6268
E-mail: sarah@apa.xo.uk
Website: http://www.apa.co.uk
Trade body for customer magazine industry, providing research, training, events and marketing support. It aims to promote awareness of customer magazines as a marketing medium and to act as a central source.of information. Affiliated to the PPA.

Association of UK Media Librarians

PO Box 14254, London SE1 9WL
                    Tel 0171-813 6105
Website: http://www.aukml.org.uk
A network of information professionals keeping pace with technological developments. Publishes quarterly journal Deadline.

Audit Bureau of Circulations (ABC)

Black Prince Yard, 207-209 High Street, Berkhamsted, Herts HP4 1AD
Fax 01442-877407   Tel 01442-870800
E-mail abcpost@abc.org.uk
Website: http://www.abc.org.uk
Regulatory body for the publishing industry, providing certified circulation data for newspapers and magazines. Also runs Verified Free Distribution, checking distribution claims of publishers of free newspapers. Figures are available via the Internet:

Authors' Licensing & Collecting Society

Marlborough Court, 14-18 Holborn, London EC1 2LE
Fax 0171-395 0660   Tel 0171-395 0600
E-mail alcs@alcs.co.uk
Website: http://www.alcs.co.uk
Collects and distributes royalties to writers (books, television, radio and film) and campaigns for collective rights schemes.

Birmingham Press Club

Grand Hotel,Colmore Row, Birmingham B3 2DA
The world's oldest press club founded in Birmingham in 1865 has nearly 500 members. Visiting press welcome.

Book Trust

Book House, 45 East Hill, London SW18 2QZ
Fax 0181-516 2978   Tel 0181-516 2977
E-mail: booktrust@dial.pipex.com
Website:
http://www.dialspace.dial.pipex.com/booktrust/
The Trust organises and promotes literary prizes, including the Booker Prize, runs Children's Book Week and a Book Information Service. Publishes author profiles plus guides to book selection.

Book Trust Scotland

Scottish Book Centre, 137 Dundee Street, Edinburgh EH11 1BG
Fax 0131-228 4293   Tel 0131-229 3663
E-mail: scottish book.trust.scotland@dial.pipex.com
Website: http://www.webpost.net/bts
Publishes directories of authors, literary guides, poetry posters, resources for schools and parents. Organises readership campaigns, operates a Book Information Service and adminsters the Fidler and Stakis literary prizes and the Writers in Scotland scheme.

British Association of Communicators in Business

42 Borough High Street, London SE1 1XW
Fax 0171-378 7140   Tel 0171-378 7139
E-mail: bacb@globalnet.uk
Webste: http://www.bacb.org.uk
Formerly the BAIE, the association is for editors of in-house journals. It publishes Crucible 10x pa, the quarterly magazine Communicators in Business and the Editors' Handbook. It runs training programmes and organises an annual convention and awards.

British Association of Journalists

88 Fleet Street, London EC4Y 1PJ
Fax 0171-353 2310   Tel 0171-353 3003
A small non-TUC trade union set up as a rival to the National Union of Journalists in 1992 by some Mirror Group journalists and the former NUJ general secretary Steve Turner. It has over 600 members.

British Association of Picture Libraries and Agencies (BAPLA)

18 Vine Hill, London EC1R 5DX
Fax 0171-713 1211   Tel 0171-713 1780
E-mail: bapla@bapla.demon.co.uk
Webste: http://www.bapla.org.uk
BAPLA is the trade association that represents 350 libraries. BAPLA provides a referral service for image research. Publishes the industry magazine 'Light Box' and annual directory. As well as valuable work in copyright, BAPLA assesses many industry issues for both picture users and libraries, including copyright clearance, ethics, pricing, marketing and technology.

British Copyright Council

29 Berners Street, London W1P 4AA
Fax 0171-306 4069   Tel 0181-306 4069
Liaison committee for the organisations representing owners of copyright in literary, musical and artistic works. Not an advice service, but will try to answer written queries. Publishes two guides to the law.

British Guild of Travel Writers
7 Roman Road, London W4 1NA
Tel 0181-995 0460
Association of writers, authors, broadcasters and
photographers specialising in travel. Publishes monthly
internal newsletter, Globetrotter, and annual yearbook
with details of 170 members.

British Inst. of Professional Photography
Fox Talbot House, Amwell End, Ware, Herts SG12
9HN
Fax 01920-487056   Tel 01920-464011
E-mail: bipp@compuserve.com
Website: http://www.bipp.com
Founded in 1901, this is the leading professional
organisation for photographers. It publishes the
respected monthly magazine The Photographer, and
the annual Directory of Professional Photography (with
details of the 4,000 members).

British Printing Industries Federation
11 Bedford Row, London WC1R 4DX
Fax 0171-405 7784   Tel 0171-242 6904
E-mail: info@bpif.org.uk
Website: http://www.bpif.org.uk
The BPIF is the business support organisation for
employers in the printing, packaging and graphic
communications industry. Based in London and with
six regional business centres around the country, the
BPIF represents more than 3000 member companies.
Publishes: Printing Industries (monthly), surveys,
Directions (quarterly economic digest) and books.

British Society of Magazine Editors
c/o Gill Branston & Associates, 137 Hale Lane
Edgware Middx HA8 9QP
Fax 0181-959 2137   Tel 0181-906 4664
E-mail: bsme@cix.compulink.co.uk
Professional association for magazine editors and
senior editorial staff. The Society organises annual
editorial awards and industry forums.

Bureau of Freelance Photographers
497 Green Lanes, London N13 4BP
Fax 0181-886 5174   Tel 0181-882 3315
Gives advice and market information to freelance
photographers supplying publishing markets
(magazines, newspapers, books, picture agencies, etc).
Publishes monthly Market Newsletter and annual
Freelance Photographers Market Handbook. Annual
membership £40.

Campaign for Freedom of Information
Suite 102, 16 Baldwin Gardens, London EC1N 7RJ
Fax 0171-831 7461   Tel 0171-831 7477
E-mail: admin@cfoi.demon.co.uk
Website: http://www.cfoi.org.uk
The campaign is pressing for a Freedom of Information
Act which would create a general right of access to
official records subject to exemptions protecting
information whose disclosure would cause real harm to
essential interests such as defence, law enforcement
and privacy. Campaigns for a public interest defence
under the Official Secrets Act. It also seeks disclosure
in the private sector on issues of public interest. It
occasionally publishes the newspaper Secrets, plus
briefings and other publications.

Campaign for Press and Broadcasting Freedom
8 Cynthia Street, London N1 9JF
Fax 0171-837 8868   Tel 0171-278 4430
E-mail: cpbf@architechs.com
Website: http://www.architechs.com/cpbf
Campaigns for a democratic, diverse and accountable
media, accessible to all. The CPBF opposes monopoly
ownership of the press and seeks a Freedom of
Information Act. It organises events and publishes 6x
pa journal Free Press, occasional pamphlets and the
Media Catalogue of mail order books, videos and
postcards. The wall chart Britain's Media shows the
ways British media companies are connected.

Cartoon Art Trust
New Ho, 67-68 Hatton Garden, London EC1N 8JY
Fax 0171-404 3896   Tel 0171-405 4717
E-mail: SKp@escape.u-net.co.uk
Website:
http://www.atreides.demon.co.uk/world.html
Aims to preserve and promote the art of cartooning.
Runs an appeal to establish a national museum of
cartoon art and is building up a library of cartoon
material. Publishes quarterly newsletter and exhibition
catalogues. They run the Cartoon Art Trust Awards
which are given in November every year.

Cartoonists' Club of Great Britain
46 Strawberry Vale, Twickenham, Middlesex TW1 4SE
Fax 0181-891 5946   Tel 0181-892 3621
E-mail: terryc@axiom.co.uk
The Club is a social one for professional cartoonists. It
meets on the first Tuesday of every month at The
Cartoonist pub, Shoe Lane, London EC4, publishes the
monthly magazine Jester and holds regular exhibitions.

Central Criminal Court Journalists' Association
Press Room, Old Bailey, London EC4N 7EH
Fax 0171-248 0133   Tel 0171-248 3277
Represents media interests in court coverage.

Chartered Institute of Journalists
2 Dock Offices, Surrey Quays Road, London SE16
2XU
Fax 0171-232 2302   Tel 0171-252 1187
E-mail: cioj@dircon.co.uk
Certificated independent trade union concerned with
preserving standards and protecting the pay and
conditions of its members. It publishes The Journal.

Chartered Society of Designers
1st Floor, 32-38 Saffron Hill, London EC1N 8FH
Fax 0171-831 6277   Tel 0171-831 9777
E-mail: csd@csd.org.uk
Website: http://www.designweb.co.uk/csd
Main professional body for designers in all fields,
setting and maintaining standards. Organises events,
seminars and awards and publishes a newsletter.

Childrens Express London Bureau
Exmouth House, 3-11 Pine Street, London, EC1R 0JH
Fax 0171-278 7722   Tel 0171-833 2577
A charitable organisation which gives children aged
between 8 -18 years the opportunity to learn journalism
skills, such as reporting and interviewing. Part news
agency and part youth club.

Commonwealth Journalists Association
17 Nottingham Street, London W1M 3RD
Fax 0171-486 3822   Tel 0171-486 3844
Fosters interest in Commonwealth affairs, undertakes
training of journalists in Commonwealth countries and
defends journalists' rights where these are threatened.
Publishes newsletter 3x pa and holds international
conferences every 3 years.

Commonwealth Press Union
17 Fleet Street, London EC4Y 1AA
Fax 0171-583 6868   Tel 0171-583 7733
E-mail: cpu@compressu.demon.co.uk
Website: http://www.compressu.co.uk
Association of Commonwealth newspapers, news
agencies and periodicals, upholding the ideals and
values of the Commonwealth. Activities include press
freedom monitoring and extensive training
programmes throughout the Commonwealth,
fellowhsips , biennial conferences. Publishes CPU
News, bi-monthly.

Copyright Licensing Agency
90 Tottenham Court Road, London W1P 0LP
Fax 0171-436 3986   Tel 0171-436 5931
E-mail cla@cla.co.uk
Website: http://www.cla.co.uk
Non-profit company looking after the interests of
copyright owners in copying from periodicals and
books. Collects copying fees and pays them to authors
(via Authors Licensing and Collecting Society, 0171-255
2034) and publishers (via Publishers Licensing Society,
0171-829 8486).

Council of Photographic News Agencies
Oak Trees, Burrows Lane, Gomshall, Shere, Surrey
GU5 9QF
Fax 01483-203378   Tel 01483-203378
Represents the UK's six largest press agencies/photo
libraries.

Cricket Writers Club
2 Bobble Court, Little Rissington, Glos GL54 2ND
                         Tel 01451-810435
Represents most cricket writers in newspapers,
magazines, TV and radio. It celebrated its 50th
anniversary in 1996.

Crime Reporters Association
John Weeks, 15/17 Langley Road, Surbiton, Surrey
KT6 6LP
Fax 0181-390 2249   Tel 0181-399 2224
Represents crime reporters in their dealings with the
Home Office and police organisations.

Critics' Circle
c/o Stage Newspaper, 47 Bermondsey Street,
London SE1 3XT
Fax 0171-357 9287   Tel 0171-403 1818x106
Organisation of professional critics in theatre, film,
music, dance and visual arts.

Defence, Press & Broadcasting Advisory Committee
Room 2235, Main Building, Ministry of Defence,
London SW1A 2HB
Fax 0171-218 5857   Tel 0171-218 2206
Website: http://www.btinternet.com/~d.a.notices
Aka the D-Notice Committee. The Defence, Press and
Broadcasting Advisory Committee oversees the
voluntary code which operates between the media and
those government departments with responsibilities for
national security. The vehicle for this is the DA Notice
system, where "advisory notices" are issued to the
media at editor level describing sensitive areas. The
notices were published openly for the first time in July
1993. Editors are invited to consult the committee
secretary - currently Rear Admiral David Pulvertaft -
where there may be doubt. Committee founded 1912.

Directory & Database Publishers Assoc.
93a Blenheim Crescent, London W11 2EQ
                         Tel 0171-221 9089
The DPA was established in 1970 for directory and
database publishers.

Edinburgh Book Festival
137 Dundee Street, Edinburgh EH11 1BG
Fax 0131-228 4333   Tel 0131-228 5444
E-mail: admin@edbookfest.co.uk
Website: http://www.go-edinburgh.co.uk
Organises the annual festival, described by the
Guardian as Europe's happiest and largest. 14-30
August 1999.

Edinburgh Press Club
19 Rutland Street, Edinburgh EH1 2AE
No fax.   Tel 0131-229 2800
Social club for the media in the Edinburgh area.

EETPU
See Amalgamated and Electrical Union

Electronic Media Round Table
26 Rosebery Avenue, London EC1R 4SX
Fax 0171-837 8901   Tel 0171-837 3345
E-mail eps@epsltd.demon.co.uk
Independent and informal grouping of publishers,
hardware and software manufacturers, developers,
integrators, distributors, retailers and other companies
and individuals interested in promoting closer working
relationships for all forms of electronic publishing
activity.

European Society for News Design
28 Holden Road, London N12 8HT
Fax 0181-992 6964   Tel 0181-445 1262
For anyone - not just designers - interested in design in
newspapers and magazines, looking at all aspects of the
subject.

Federation of Entertainment Unions
1 Highfield, Twyford, Hants SO21 1QR
Fax 01962-713288   Tel 01962-713134
E-mail: harris@interalpha.co.uk
Collective body of trade unions, representing the
interests of 140,000 members in the broadcasting and
entertainment industries. The unions are: BECTU,
Equity, Musicians Union, NUJ, Writers Guild and the
AEEU. It provides liaison, lobbying and co-ordination
services on issues of common concern.

Financial Journalists' Group
c/o The Association of British Insurers
51 Gresham Street, London, EC2V 7HQ
Fax 0171-696 8996   Tel 0171-216 7411
E-mail: financialjournalistsgroup@compuserve.com
Aims to improve the quality of financial journalism by
holding group briefings to reporters to help expand
their knowledge on a variety of financial topics. Contact
- Suzanne Moore

Fleet Street Motoring Group
Elmleigh, Old Perry Street, Chislehurst, Kent BR7 6PP
Fax 0181-300 5694   Tel 0181-300 2140
Association of motoring correspondents.

Football Writers Association
6 Chase Lane, Barkingside, Ilford, Essex IG6 1BH
    Tel 0181-554 2455
Represents members' interests and liaises with football
bodies to improve working conditions at football
grounds.Since 1948 selects the Footballer of the Year.

Foreign Press Association in London
11 Carlton House Terrace, London SW1Y 5AJ
Fax 0171-925 0469   Tel 0171-930 0445
Founded 1888. Helps London-based foreign
correspondents in their professional work, providing
extensive facilities and assistance at its headquarters.
Arranges briefings and social events. Publishes
newsletter and members list.

Freedom Forum European Centre
Stanhope House Stanhope Place, London W2 2HH
Fax 0171-262 4631   Tel 0171-262 5003
E-mail: freedomforumeurop@compuserve.com
Website: http://www.freedomforum.org
Provides a forum for debate about the media. Holds
discussions and talks on topical media isues and
photojournalism exhibitions. Has a news library.

Government Relations Unit (Media Division)
3 Goodwins Court, London WC2N 4LL
Fax 0171-379 6095   Tel 0171-240 7172
Aspecialist source of advice and assistance to the media
about how best to identify, approach and influence key
decision-makers in Westminster, Whitehall and
Brussels. The unit offers guidance on Parliamentary
procedure, amending legislation and contesting
European regulations.

Graphical, Paper and Media Union
Keys House, 63-67 Bromham Road, Bedford MK40
2AG.
Fax 01234-270580   Tel 01234-351521
E-mail gpmu@geo2.poptel.org.uk
Website: http://www.gpmu.org.uk
GPMU is the trade union for the printing, paper and
allied trades industry. Membership covers managerial,
administrative, clerical and production workers in
printing, publishing, papermaking, advertising and
information tchnology. Represents, and negotiates on
behalf of, its 200,000 members in advertising
agencies, art studios, newspapers, general print,
publishing, ink and papermaking and numerous
specialist industries. Provides legal and educational
services, pubishes GPMU Journal free to members ten
times a year.

Guild of Editors
Bloomsbury House, 74-77 Great Russell Street,
London WC1B 3DA
Fax 0171-631 5119   Tel 0171-636 7014
Professional association for local newspaper editors,
editorial directors and training editors. It provides a
medium for collective consultation and representation
on matters of editorial concern and interest. Publishes
quarterly Guild Journal. Lobbies in defence of press
freedom.

Guild of Food Writers
48 Crabtree Lane, London SW6 6LW
Fax 0171-610 0299   Tel 0171-610 1180
E-mail: ckthomas@compuserve.com
Professional association of food broadcasters and
writers. Established in 1984 it has over 300 members.

Independent Publishers Guild
25 Cambridge Road, Hampton, Middlesex TW12 2JI
Fax 0181-979 6393   Tel 0181-979 0250

INK
170 Portobello Road, London W11 2EB
    Tel 0171-221 8137
The trade association for alternative periodicals.

Institute of Journalists
See Chartered Institute of Journalists

Institute of Printing
8A Lonsdale Gardens, Tunbridge Wells, Kent TN1
1NU
Fax 01892-518028   Tel 01892-538118
E-mail: IOP@Globalprint.com
Website: http://www.globalprint.com/uk/iop
The professional body for the printing industry. Holds
lectures, debates, seminars, conferences and local
branch activities. Publishes journal Professional Printer,
Guide to Educational Courses in the Printing Industry,
Career Guide, Handbook and list of members.

**International Association of Women Sports
Photographers**
Wayside, White Lodge Lane, Baslow, via Bakewell,
Derbyshire DE45 1RQ
Fax 01246-582227   Tel 01246-582376
Aims to attract more women into the profession, help
beginners and raise standards. Produces videos, books,
posters, calendars and exhibitions.

**International Federation of the Periodical
Press (FIPP)**
Queens House, 55/56 Lincoln's Inn Fields, London
WC2A 3LJ
Fax 0171-404 4170   Tel 0171-404 4169
E-mail: info@fipp.com
Website: http://www.fipp.com
FIPP works through national associations to establish
and promote worldwide the optimum conditions for
developing periodical publishing. It fosters formal and
informal alliances between publishers to exploit
successful publishing ideas, marketing initiatives and
technological opportunities. Publishes quarterly
Magazine World, holds biennial FIPP World Congress.

JICNARS
See National Readership Surveys

JICREG
Bloomsbury House, 74-77 Great Russell Street, London WC1B 3DA
Fax 0171-631 5119   Tel 0171-636 7014
E-mail: ns@newspapersoc.org.uk
Website: http://www/newspapersoc.org.uk
The statistics gathering part of the Newspaper Society, JICREG updates its database of local newspapers twice a year.

Library Association
7 Ridgmount Street, London WC1E 7AE
Fax 0171-436 7218   Tel 0171-636 7543
E-mail info@la-hq.org.uk
Website: http://www.la-hq.org.uk
Professional body for librarians which awards chartership status, sets standards and lobbies government. It works for freedom of access to information and against censorship and library cuts. Publishes monthly magazine Library Association Record.

London International Research Exchange Media Group
BM LIRE, London WC1N 3XX
Fax 0171-267 8003   Tel 0171-267 8003
E-mail: media@easynet.co.uk
Website: http://www.easynet.co.uk/LIRE/home.htm
An independent, international, voluntary media group set up to research media issues. Organises media conferences, publishes reports and a quarterly newsletter Eyewitness.

London Press Club
c/o Freedom Forum, European Centre, Stanhope House, Stanhope Place, London W2 2HH
Fax 0171-363 4631   Tel 0171-402 2566
E-mail: lpressclub@aol.com
Club for journalists and media in general which makes three annual awards: Scoop of the Year; Edgar Wallace Trophy for outstanding writing; Freedom Award to the journalist or organisaiton doing the most for fredom of the press. Also runs seminars and lectures.

Media Research Group
36 Howard Street, London W1A 1AT
Fax 0171-915 2165   Tel 0171-580 6690
Website: http://www.mccann.co.uk
Provides forum for debating issues relating to media planning and research. Holds bi-annual conference.

Media Resource Service
Novartis Foundation, 41 Portland Place, London W1N 4BN
Fax 0171-637 2127   Tel 0171-580 0100/631 1634
E-mail mrs@novartisfound.org.uk
Web: http://www.novartisfound.demon.co.uk/
This service gives journalists free and independent access to experts in medicine, science and technology. It is run by the the Ciba Foundation. A twice yearly newsletter contains news of the MRS and the world of science communication.

Media Society
56 Roseneath Road, London SW11 6AQ
Fax 0171-223 5631   Tel 0171-223 5631
Forum for discussing issues pertinent to the media. Membership includes editors, journalists, pr, media lawyers, MPs and academics. Also submits evidence to appropriate select committees, commissions and enquiries.

Medical Journalists' Association
2 St Georges Road, Kingston-upon-Thames, Surrey KT2 6DN
Fax 0181-255 4964   Tel 0181-549 1019
The MJA aims to improve understanding between health and medical journalists and the health and medical professions. The Association organises awards and social events and publishes directory of members and newsletter.

National Artists Association
Spitalfields, 21 Steward Street, London E1 6AJ
Fax 0171-426 0282   Tel 0171-426 0911
E-mail: naa@gn.apc.org
It represents visual artists on UK national and European bodies. Produces quarterly bulletin.

National Association of Press Agencies
41 Lansdowne Crescent, Leamington Spa, Warwickshire CV32 4PR
Fax 01926-424760   Tel 01926-424181
Trade association for news and photographic agenies. A free handbook is available.

National Federation of Retail Newsagents
Yeoman House, Sekforde Street, London EC1R 0HD
Fax 0171-250 0927   Tel 0171-253 4225
Represents the interests of 28,500 independent retail newsagents in the UK and Ireland. It publishes the weekly journal Retail Newsagent and has 16 regional offices

National Readership Surveys
11-15 Betterton Street, London WC2H 9BP
Fax 0171-240 4399   Tel 0171-379 0344
E-mail: nrs.co.uk
Website: http://www.nrs.co.uk
The NRS measures newspaper and magazine readership in the UK. NRS are funded by the IPA, NPAC and the PPA.

National Small Press Centre
BM Bozo, London WC1N 3XX
                    Tel 01234-211606
A self-funding independent organisation for self-publishers. It organises exhibitions, courses and workshops; runs a consultancy service, has a reference library and a collecion of samples. Their annual fair is held at the Royal Festival Hall.

National Union of Journalists
Acorn House, 314-320 Grays Inn Road, London
WC1X 8DP
Fax 0171-837 8143   Tel 0171-278 7916
E-mail: nuj@mcr1.poptel.org.uk
Website: http://www.nuj.org.uk
The leading trade union representing all editorial
sectors of the media, including photographers and
freelancers. Membership totals 29,000, including
1,800 student journalists. It provides many services for
members, including legal. Campaigns for journalists'
rights and freedom of information, and against
censorship. Publishes: the prominent and widely read
bi-monthly magazine The Journalist; bi-monthly
bulletin Freelance, with news for freelancers; Freelance
Directory; Freelance Fees Guide; Careers in Journalism
guide booklet; comprehensive annual report; the NUJ
Code of Conduct; and much other material. Holds
conferences, seminars and training sessions.
General secretary: John Foster
Deputy general secretary: John Fray
Assistant secretary (Ireland): Eoin Ronayne
Regional organiser (Ireland): Seamus Docley
National organiser: Jeremy Dear
Freelance organiser: Bernie Corbett
Legal officer: Sally Gilbert
Editor: Tim Gopsill
National organiser (magazines, PR): Linda Rogers

Newspaper Library (British Library)
Colindale Avenue, London NW9 5HE
Fax 0171-412 7379   Tel 0171-412 7353
E-mail newspaper@bl.uk
Website: http://www.bl.uk/collections/newspaper
The national collection of local, regional and national
UK newspapers, plus a large overseas holding. Has
photocopying, photographic and microfilm services.
Open Monday-Saturday, 10am-5pm, admission free but
only to persons over 18. Allow plenty of time when
visiting, and take proof of identity. Publishes a series of
Newsplan Reports, and a newsletter (2x pa)

Newspaper Press Fund
35 Wathen Road, Dorking, Surrey RH4 1JY
Fax 01306-876104   Tel 01306-887511
A charity set up in 1864 to assist member journalists
and their dependants in need. It runs residential homes
for retired journalists and dependants. Life
membership is £50.

Newspaper Publishers Association
34 Southwark Bridge Road, London SE1 9EU
Fax 0171-928 2067   Tel 0171-207 2200
Trade association for the eight publishers of national
newspapers. It promotes good relations with the
advertising industry and opposes government restraints
on the press.

Newspaper Society
Bloomsbury House, 74-77 Great Russell Street,
London WC1B 3DA
Fax 0171-631 5119   Tel 0171-636 7014
E-mail: ns@newspapersoc.org.uk
Website: http://www/newspapers
Trade association for publishers of the local press in
England, Wales and Northern Ireland. Founded in

1836, the society is the oldest publishers' association. Its
secretariat and committees cover a wide range of
activities, from advertisement control advice to lobbying
in Brussels and Whitehall on legislation. Publishes
newspapers Production Journal (monthly) and
Headlines (6x pa). Runs a series of conferences,
seminars and exhibitions throughout the year.

Newspapers in Education
Manchester Evening News
164 Deansgate, Manchester M60 2RD
Fax 0161-839 0968   Tel 0161-832 7200
Website: http://www.manchesteronline.co.uk
NIE provides resources for teachers to help pupils
become competent and confident writers and readers.

Paper Federation of Great Britain
Papermakers House, Rivenhall Road, Westlea,
Swindon, Wilts SN5 7BD
Fax 01793-886182   Tel 01793-886086
E-mail: fedn@paper.org.uk
Website: http://www.paper.org.uk
The employers federation for all sectors of the paper
industry. Runs the Pulp and Paper Information Centre,
supplying data to the media.

Paper Industry Technical Association
5 Frechville Court, Bury, Lancashire BL9 0UF
Fax 0161-764 5353   Tel 0161-764 5858
E-mail: pita@wam.co.uk
For people interested in the technology of the paper
industry. Publishes: Paper Technology.

Parliamentary Press Gallery/Lobby Journalists
House of Commons, London SW1A 0AA
    Tel 0171-219 4700

PEN
7 Dilke Street, London SW3 4JE
Fax 0171-351 0220   Tel 0171-352 6303
English centre of the International association for
published writers, with over 130 centres in 100
countries. Fights for freedom of expression and against
censorship, and helps imprisoned writers worldwide.
Makes annual awards, holds regular meetings and
publishes newsletter. Hires out cassettes of meetings.
PEN stands for Poets, Playwrights, Editors, Essayists
and Novelists.

Periodical Publishers Association
1 Kingsway, London WC2B 6XF
Fax 0171-836 4543   Tel 0171-565 7474
E-mail: info1@ppa.co.uk
Website: http://www.ppa.co.uk
The trade association for magazine publishers,
representing nearly 200 companies generating 80 per
cent of the industry's revenue. Lobbies on behalf of
members, and organises conferences, seminars and
awards. Produces many publications, including the
journal Magazine News, annual Magazine Handbook
with key data on the industry, and industry overviews.
The PPA provides secretariats for the Association of
Publishing Agencies (customer magazines), the
International Federation of the Periodical Press (FIPP)
UK Newsletter Publishers' Association and the British
Society of Magazine Editors (BSME). Also runs the
Periodicals Training Council - see below.

Periodicals Training Council
See Training section

Picture Research Association
455 Finchley Road London NW3 6HN
Fax 0171-431 9887   Tel 0171-431 9886
E-mail: pra@pictures.demon.co.uk
Website: http://www.pictures.demon.co.uk
Professional body for those involved in visual material for the media. Gives advice to members, organises meetings, quarterly magazine, monthly newsletter and Freelance Register.

Pira International
Randalls Road, Leatherhead, Surrey KT22 7RU
Fax 01372-802244   Tel 01372-802000
E-mail marionc@pira.co.uk
Website: http://www.pira.co.uk
A Research & Technology Organisation for the packaging, paper, printing, publishing and new media industries worldwide. It provides research, consultancy, information services and comprehensive training events for these industries. It is also one of the UK's largest business to business publishers. The Publishing & New Media Group offers Internet based research, strategic business and management consultancy and marketing services.

Press Complaints Commission
See How to Complain

Press Standards Board of Finance
Merchants House Buildings, 30 George Square, Glasgow G2 1EG
Fax 0141-248 2362   Tel 0141-221 3957
Co-ordinates and finances self-regulation in the newspaper and magazine publishing industry.

PressWise
25 Easton Business Centre, Felix Road, Bristol BS5 0HE
Fax 0117-941 5848   Tel 0117-941 5889
E-mail: pw@presswise.org.uk
Non-profit making organisation promoting high standards of journalism and aiming to empower those ordinary people who become victims of unfair media intrusion and inaccurate or irresponsible reporting. Also provides media training and briefings on current media policy issues. Appointed to a European forum on the Information Society.

Publishers Association
1 Kingsway, London WC2B 6XF
Fax 0171-836 4543   Tel 0171-565 7474
E-mail: mail@publishers.org.uk
Website: http://www.publishers.org.uk
Trade association for UK book publishers, offering a wide range of services, and producing many of its own publications.

Publishers Licensing Society
See Copyright Licensing Agency

Publishers Publicity Circle
48 Crabtree Lane, London SW6 6LW
Fax 0171-385 3708   Tel 0171-385 3708
E-mail: ppc-@lineone.net
Provides a forum for book publicists to meet and share information. Monthly meetings with members of the media. Publishes directory and monthly newsletter.

St Bride Printing Library
St Bride Institute, Bride Lane, Fleet Street, London EC4Y 8EE
Fax 0171-583 7073   Tel 0171-353 4660
A unique public reference library covering all aspects of printing, with an extensive historical collection including artefacts, archive material, photographs and patents. The collection is strong on newspaper history and is housed in atmospheric surroundings just off Fleet Street. Hours: 9.30am-5.30pm, Monday-Friday.

Scottish Daily Newspaper Society
48 Palmerston Place, Edinburgh EH12 5DE
Fax 0131-220 4344   Tel 0131-220 4353
Trade association for Scottish newspaper publishers.

Scottish Newspaper Publishers Association
48 Palmerston Place, Edinburgh EH12 5DE
Fax 0131-220 4344   Tel 0131-220 4353
Trade association for the Scottish weekly press.

Scottish Print Employers Federation
48 Palmerston Place, Edinburgh EH12 5DE
Fax 0131-220 4344   Tel 0131-220 4353
The employers' organisation and trade association for the Scottish printing industry.

Scottish Publishers Association
Scottish Book Centre, 137 Dundee Street, Edinburgh EH11 1BG
Fax 0131-228 3220   Tel 0131-228 6866
E-mail: enquiries@scottishbooks.org
Trade association working for 68 Scottish publishers. Publishes Directory of Publishing in Scotland (annually) and new books lists. Provides training, advice, marketing and promotion services to members.

Society of Authors
84 Drayton Gardens, London SW10 9SB
Fax 0171-373 5768   Tel 0171-373 6642
E-mail: authorsoc@writers.org.uk
Website: http://www.writers.org.uk/society/html
An independent trade union, which was founded in 1884, to promote the interests of authors and to defend their rights. The Society gives a personal service to writers, with wide range of facilities including advice on contracts. It arranges conferences, meetings and social events. The Society publishes a quarterly journal, The Author, plus numerous guides and has over 6,000 members.

Society of Freelance Editors and Proofreaders
Mermaid House, 1 Mermaid Court, London SE1 1HR
        Tel 0171-403 5141
Professional body representing editors, especially freelances, and working to improve editorial standards by providing training, information and advice. Publishes newsletter, directory, conference proceedings and other publications.

Society of Indexers
Mermaid House, Mermaid Court, London SE1 1HR
Fax 0171-357 0903   Tel 0171-403 4947
E-mail: admin@socind.demon.co.uk
Promotes indexing, the quality of indexing and the profession of indexers. Publishes quarterly newsletter, twice-yearly journal The Indexer, and ad hoc papers. Provides open learning course.

Society of Typographic Designers
Chapelfield Cottage, Randwick, Stroud, Gloucester
GL6 6HS
Fax 01453-759311   Tel 01453-759311
Promotes high standards of typographic design.

Society of Women Writers & Journalists
110 Whitehall Road, Chingford, London E4 6DW
                                    Tel 0181-529 0886
Founded 1894. Encourages literary achievement and
the upholding of professional standards. Organises
competitions, social events and monthly meetings.
Publishes magazine The Woman Journalist 3x pa.

Sports Writers Association of Gt Britain
c/o English Sports Council, 16 Upper Woburn Place,
London WC1H 0QP
Fax 0171-383 0273   Tel 0171-273 1555
Founded 1948 for sports journalists. Now has over 500
members. Organises meetings and social events.
Makes awards for the Sportsman, Sportswoman and
Sports Team of the Year. Organises the British Sports
Journalism Awards and Sports Photographer of the
Year Awards in conjunction with the English Sports
Council. It appoints the Olympic press attache for the
British media.

Talking Newspaper Association
National Recording Centre, Heathfield, East Sussex
TN21 8DB
Fax 01435-865422   Tel 01435-866102
E-mail: 101761.167@compuserve.com
A registered charity that provides 200 national
newspapers and magazines on audio cassette,
computer disk and E-mail for blind, visually impaired
and disabled people. There are over 530 local groups,
providing two million tapes of over 900 newspapers
and magazines for 200,000 visually impared people.
TNEL is the commercial trading arm of the charity.

Teenage Magazine Arbitration Panel
c/o PPA Queen House, 28 Kingsway, London WC2B
6JR
                                    Tel 0171-405 0819
Website: http://www.ppa.co.uk
The TMAP was formed in 1996 as part of a self-
regulatory system to consider complaints about the
editorial content of a sexual nature in magazines which
have more than 25 per cent of readers who are young
women under the age of 15.

UK Newsletter Association
Queens House, 55/56 Lincoln's Inn Fields, London
WC2A 3LJ
Fax 0171-404 4167   Tel 0171-404 4166
E-mail: ukna@ppa.co.uk
UKNA is the organisation of newsletter publishers in
the UK.

Women in Publishing
Information Officer, Publishers Association, 1
Kingsway, Floor 3, London WC2B 6XF
Website: http://www.cyberiacafe.net/wip/
Provides support and encouragement for women
working in publishing and related fields through
training courses and monthly meetings . Publishes
monthly newsletter, surveys and Women in Publishing
Directory.

Women Writers Network
c/o 23 Prospect Road, London NW2 2JU
Helps women writers further their professional
development by providing a forum for exchanging
information and giving support. Holds monthly
meetings, and publishes monthly newsletter and
annual directory of members.

**Worshipful Company of Stationers &
    Newspaper Makers**
Stationers' Hall, Ave Maria Lane, London EC4M 7DD
Fax 0171-489 1975   Tel 0171-248 2934
E-mail: clerk@stationers.demon.co.uk
City livery company for stationers, printers newspaper
makers, publishers, booksellers, paper makers and
packagers.

Writers Guild of Great Britain
430 Edgware Road, London W2 1EH
Fax 0171-706 2413   Tel 0171-723 8074
E-mail: postie@wggb.demon.co.uk
Website: http://www.writers.org.uk/guild
Trade union representing professional writers in film,
TV, radio, theatre and books. Has scored many
successes in improving terms and conditions. Holds
regular meetings and publishes bi-monthly Writers'
Newsletter.

Yachting Journalists' Association
3 Friars Lane, Maldon, Essex CM9 6AG
Fax 01621-852212   Tel 01621-855943
Promotes yachting - sail and power - in all its forms,
and furthers the interests of its members. Open to
writers, broadcasters, photographers and illustrators.
Publishes annual directory of members, with media
advice for event organisers. Organises awards:
Yachtsman of the Year, Young Sailor of the Year and
Global Achievement all sponsored by BT.

Young Newspaper Executives' Association
Newspaper Society, 74 Great Russell Street, London
WC1B 3DA
Fax 0171-631 5119   Tel 0171-636 7014
E-mail: ns@newspapersoc.org.uk
Website: http://www.newspapersoc.org.uk
Focal point for newspaper managers aged under 40.
Formerly the Young Newspapermen's Association.

The BBC

BRAINS AND BEAUTY

4 AUGUST 1997: John Simpson, the BBC foreign editor, said broadcasters need to combine good looks and good knowledge. "Viewers want bimboys and bimbettes. Who wants to see Martyn Lewis?" Simpson asked, immediately answering his question by say that he didn't. He continued: "Appearance is less important than knowledge, although TV has always been a beauty contest. You don't want some muttering don doing these things."

SALMON LEAP

1 SEPTEMBER: Peter Salmon (above) was appointed BBC1's new controller. A Beeb returnee, he worked there before stints at C4, then as director of programmes at Granada. "The challenge of leading BBC1 forward into the 21st century is an unmissable opportunity," he said. No mark for sound bites to the man in charge of a £650 million programme budget.

U-TURN ON NEWS REVAMP

15 SEPTEMBER: All BBC TV and radio news will be run by five editors with present programme editors downgraded to associate editors. All 700 BBC journalists went into uproar mode with Jeremy Paxman saying: "It's like turning news into a sausage factory. Can you imagine a world in which none of our newspapers had editors?" Within a week it turned out nothing was to change when BBC chairman Sir Christopher Bland stamped out this outbreak of managerialism. "We need more time to consider elements of the changes, to explain them further, and to make absolutely certain they will enhance and not detract from the quality, programme identity and editorial value of BBC News," he waffled reassuringly.

IMPERFECT COMPETITION

24 SEPTEMBER: The Perfect Day video, the four minute promo where 29 singers endorse the BBC by singing a line from Lou Reed's classic song, faced criticism from commercial rivals. Such cross-corporate puffery is not fair, they said, pointing out that the going rate to show the ad at 5pm on a Saturday would be £124,000 on ITV and £50,837 on Channel 4.

ONLY FOUR TIMES AN HOUR

4 OCTOBER: The Fix, a football drama, was broadcast with four F-words, seven fewer than in the original version. The cuts were ordered by BBC execs and thus set a definitive de facto standard. "The film has become a victim of the nervousness at the heart of the BBC," said Kennith Trodd, the film's producer.

BALLOONING HYPE

4 OCTOBER: First showing, between programmes, of the BBC1's red and yellow balloon. Filmed rising above Canary Wharf, the Forth Bridge, Cardiff City Hall and elsewhere over green and pleasant landscapes, the balloon replaced an inter-programme globe and is part a £5 million image revamp. Alan Yentob, the BBC's director of television, justified the expenditure saying: "The rapid increase in competition and the pace of change now means BBC1 needs an identity which is flexible and etc etc etc etc"

DAVID BURKE
JEAN LOTUS

Read this book,
switch off and
have more fun

GET A LIFE!

GET A LIFE!

"Every single day you are spending four hours staring at a piece of furniture. That is half the time you are not sleeping or working. All the things you wanted to be in your life - a lover, an adventurer, a parent, a friend - when are you going to do all that?"

So says White Dot, the society dedicated to getting rid of tellies. Its book - Get A Life! published by Bloomsbury at £12.99 - begins with a demolition of the most common myths about TV:

* TV gives you experience
* TV relaxes you
* Life without TV is boring
* TV is just another medium
* TV is educational
* TV gives parents peace
* TV is a friend to the housebound
* TV binds the nation together
* TV makes people aware of what's going on
* Giving up TV is extreme

The people at White Dot use the language of the snake oil salesman and YOU the reader are given more than YOUR share of exclamation marks. But their sales pitch is strong. Listen!

"All you have to do is turn the TV off! It's that simple. You are going to be amazed at what happens next. Give up TV and you are doubling your free time! It's a whole extra ten years of your life to be the person you tell everybody your are. For more details about the book - and White Dot's annual Turn Off TV Week, contact:
E-Mail: whitedot@mistral.co.uk

ONWARD TO THE MILLENNIUM

13 OCTOBER: The start of a week long nostalgia-fest commemorating the BBC's 75th birthday.

ADS ON THE BEEB

1 NOVEMBER: UKTV goes live as the first BBC-backed network to carry advertising. The four channels are: UK Arena (music and arts); UK Gold (repeats); UK Horizons (factual series and natural history); UK Style (life-style stuff). This joint venture between the BBC's Worldwide division and Flextech relies on the latter putting up the £150 million launch budget and paying the BBC for programmes used. Dependence on ad revenue means the BBC doesn't attach its name directly to UKTV promo material spelling out just how easy it is to receive: "Select the tuning function and tune into frequency 10.8175 GHz. Then select the polarity function and set to V."

CARTOON CRITICISM

4 NOVEMBER: Two thirds of children's TV is cartoons: the BBC and ITV were censured by the Broadcasting Standards Commission for allowing children's factual and drama series to become "an endangered species". The report said that despite increasing numbers of channels, there had been no increase in diversity. In 1981 cartoons comprised 9 per cent of BBC1's children's programming and 35 per cent in 1996. (In December stories from Japan suggested cartoons are bad for physical as well as mental health when high frequency flashing from the eyes of Pikachu the Pocket Monster triggered epilepsy-like convulsions from hundreds of children.)

POLITICAL CRITICISM

6 NOVEMBER: Oliver Tickner is a 12 year old who watched Pirates and objected to a character say an old people's home had been closed by a

Conservative council. His Dad Michael, Conservative leader of Bromley Council, took the objections to the BBC Complaints Unit which said: "Political remarks like that are quite out of place in a children's programme. We hold our hands up to this one. They have us bang to rights."

SENSITIVE SAUDIS

6 NOVEMBER 1997: A Panorama programme was pulled for fear it would upset Saudi Arabia. It alleged the two British nurses, Deborah Parry and Lucille McLauchlan, had been framed for murdering a fellow nurse. The Foreign Office, anxious to avoid the diplomatic unpleasantness that followed the Death of a Princess documentary in 1980, applied pressure. A BBC source said: "Diplomats like to stress the BBC is seen in Riyadh as the voice of the British establishment so if we criticise the Saudi judicial system, it could backfire on the nurses."

24 HOUR NEWS

9 NOVEMBER: BBC News 24, the £30 million a year rolling news service, went live on Remembrance Day amidst fears that its whizzy Electronic News Production System would not be able to take the strain. "We are pushing the technology as far as we can," said Tony Hall, chief exec of BBC News. News junkies can receive it via cable or on BBC1 overnight. It competes with CNN and Sky News. At the beginning of the week BBC News Online went online.

COOK REPORT

13 NOVEMBER: Roger Cook, 54, retired from his brand of in-your-face investigative consumer journalism saying he had been assaulted more than 20 times and had had guns aimed at him four times. "There is not one part of his body that hasn't been injured," Cook's agent said.

QUEEN'S RATINGS

25 DECEMBER: The Queen's speech reversed a downward trend in viewers, having been watched by 8.2 million on the BBC and 3.8 million on ITV.

PARTY POLITICALS

13 JANUARY: The BBC and ITC jointly suggested party political broadcasts should be dropped except during elections. William Hague described the proposals as "sensible". Peter Mandelson, then minister without portfolio, thought the exact opposite and said: "Millions and millions of British citizens look at these broadcasts and listen to what politicians have to say throughout the year. Now that is their democratic right."

TV NEWS NEWS

31 JANUARY: BBC2 started Saturday morning broadcasting of news shows with an hour long programme culled from the BBC's new 24 hour cable channel News 24. A week before, BBC News was delighted to learn that audience ratings for its regional evening news programmes had overtaken ITV's for the first time in a decade.

GUVNORS

21 FEBRUARY: The culture secretary Chris Smith (right) said he aimed to recruit more young people and women to the BBC board of governors. In spurning the great and good, he wants the guvnors to start acting tough. "There are no formal mechanisms for the governors to make the BBC accountable to the public," Smith said. "There is not enough sense that these are people who are there to uphold the public interest."

DISCOVERY JOINT VENTURE

19 MARCH: The BBC took its largest single step toward commercialism with a £340 million deal with Discovery Channel to launch its own American cable channel and set up pay-for channels elsewhere. BBC America began broadcasting on 29 March with predictions it would reach 25 million US homes within a couple of years. Meanwhile BBC executives talked up a 400 million household global market.

GOOD

MORNING
TELEVISION

For over 25 million viewers*

*Average monthly reach Jan-Jun 1998. Source: BARB

NATIONAL LOTTERY ROW

28 MARCH 1998: The Big Ticket Show - a 50-minute advert for Camelot as well as a television programme - started on BBC1 after pressure on the BBC forced it to withdraw the BBC logo from some new scratchcards. Gerald Kaufman, Labour chairman of the culture select committee, said: "The BBC is promoting the sale of a commercial product and, more than that, is paying to make the programme which does it. It has not stretched the limits of its charter, it has completely broken them." The BBC says the scratchcard is not a BBC competition and so the rules don't apply. "This is of utmost concern," said the shadow culture secretary Francis Maude. "Can you imagine what Lord Reith would think of this? His eyeballs would be swivelling in his head." The BBC's role as a gambling impresario took a further knock when the first scratchcard draw included an invalid number and had to be gone through again after the shabby show had finished.

STAFF UNREST

30 MARCH: Unions representing the 7,000 employees of BBC Resources threatened to strike. They wanted the abandonment of further BBC commercialisation plans to make production crews compete in the private sector. On the same day the Directors' and Producers Rights Society demanded a fairer share of repeat fees. Alan Parker, the film director, said: "As new technologies allow our film and television work to be shown in more ways around the world, we are crazy not to insist on benefitting from the considerable and continued exploitation of our work." See entry for 4 June opposite.

NEWS 24 SCRUTINISED BY EU

5 APRIL: Bitter complaints made by BSkyB executives ended up with a European Commission investigation into claims that the BBC's News 24 presents unfair competition to Sky News. A BBC spokesman said: "It is really a matter for government. However, the BBC is confident that the complaint will be turned down."

BIRT TO GO EARLY

9 APRIL: The BBC director general John Birt (pictured above) decided he would stand down in March 2000, a few months before his present contract expires. In the absence of any deputy since Bob Phillis had left to join the Guardian at the end of 1997, speculation about the succession looked across a wide field. Candidates for Sir John's replacement are:

Who will be the new John Birt?

Michael Jackson Channel 4 chief executive
Tony Hall BBC News chief executive
Patricia Hodgson BBC's digital strategist
Greg Dyke Pearson Television chief executive
John McCormick BBC Scotland controller
David Elstein Channel 5 chief executive
Matthew Bannister BBC director of radio
Mark Byford BBC director of regional b'casting
Rupert Gavin BBC Worldwide chief executive

Likely lads for BBC DG: Elstein (left) and Jackson

TECHNICIANS' STRIKE

4 JUNE: Live TV and radio all but dropped off the airwaves when unions representing the 7,000 employees of BBC Resources went on a one day strike. The BECTU members were unhappy at BBC plans to make production crews compete in the private sector. See 30 March.

CULTURE SECRETARY'S CRITICISMS

20 MAY: Chris Smith, the culture secretary, accused a meeting attended by BBC managers of down-playing serious programmes and promoting commercial interest at the expense of public service duties. Smith expressed anger at having to defend the scratchcard Lottery fiasco and he was worried that programmes like Panorama, Question Time and Omnibus have moved away from peak time to allow time for sit coms and quiz shows.

FIRST DIGITISED TELLY

10 JUNE: The BBC mainstream digital television with widescreen soccer transmitted to a handful of sites including Heathrow's terminal 2. Patricia Hodgson, director of policy, predicted that by 2007 between a half and two-thirds of British homes will have gone digital.

"BIG, BORING AND COMPLACENT"

6 JULY: A Sun leader, which made no mention of any links between itself and BSkyB, said the government should "cut off the supply of the tax-payers' money" to the BBC. "BBC TV and radio should be told to broadcast adverts to pay for their programmes - and their bureaucracy. At least we might then get the programmes people want. Instead of the claptrap that the public school and Oxbridge BBC types think they should make as 'public service'."

"PUBLIC SERVICE OBLIGATION"

9 JULY: The BBC's Public Service Obligation and Commercial Activities - a report prepared by the ITV - was submitted to the culture secretary Chris Smith. Richard Eyre, chief executive of ITV Network Centre had already reacted angrily to reports that the BBC plans to spend £1 billion on digital TV and radio over the next five years. Eyre denied the report was intended to nobble his rivals and said: "We're trying to say that the licence-funded BBC is an extraordinarily beneficial institution [and] this report is written under an umbrella of admiration for its importance. But we're concerned that some of the activities of the BBC may make it more difficult to preserve that foundation stone. It's important they don't succumb to market pressures. The last thing we are suggesting is that the BBC shouldn't be a broadcaster of attractive programmes ... it needs to be doing something for everyman. But, unless it moves away from the sector occupied by the commercial stations, how can it argue in defence of its current funding?"

THE MARKET AND PUBLIC SERVICE

15 JULY: Sir Christopher Bland, chairman of the BBC, used publication of the BBC's Annual Report to reaffirm a dual approach taking in both public service and commercial values. "Our audiences must always be at the centre of the BBC's thinking," Sir Christopher said. "Everything we do must be designed to provide high quality, distinctive programmes and services which offer something of value to everybody. Our growing commercial activities have the same end - to support public service broadcasting by maximising the benefit for the licence payer."

£100+ LICENCE FEE

16 JULY: Coincident with publication of the BBC's Annual Report, another report emerged that BBC management was seeking an above inflation increase to the annual licence fee. This would break the £100 a year barrier and reverse a Conservative regime which kept increase below inflation. In 1997 the director general, Sir John Birt, had a 9 per cent pay rise to £397,000.

NEW COMPLAINTS SYSTEM

28 JULY: the BBC announced a revised classification of complaints "to better reflect concerns of viewers and listeners". The changes are: the category of "unfair treatment of the complainant" is bolstered by "infringement of the complainant's privacy" and "harm to individuals/organisations featured in programmes"; the category of bias is split into "party political bias" and "other bias"; categories of "sensitivity and portrayal" bring together complaints about the treatment of particular groups which have sat awkwardly in the categories of "racism" and "poor taste"; "bad example"; "standards of interviewing/ presentation"; and "commercial concerns".

Independent TV

MONEY = VIEWERS

14 AUGUST 1997: Merrill Lynch confirmed the obvious when it recommended ITV boost its programming budgets in order to recapture viewers. Its research showed the following:

ITV & C4 budgets and audiences

ITV '96/'97 **budget increase 3%** to £602m
C4 '96/'97 **budget increase 16%** to £310m
ITV '96/'97 **audience decrease 34.4%** to 31.6%
C4 '96/'97 **audience increase 10.6%** to 10.7%

More bad news for ITV was the ending of the C4 funding formula whereby C3 companies used to get a share of C4 profits and the rise of satellite, cable and C5.

INSANITARY TELLY

ITV accused the ITC of attempting to "sanitise" TV following ITC suggestions that programmes should be "suitable for family viewing" until 10pm. The concern was that it would mean adult programmes couldn't be shown until 10.30pm - after the increasingly tabloid News at Ten.

ITV WANTS TIME

21 AUGUST: ITV chiefs publicly asked for more time to consider the ITC's proposals on licence renewals and privately criticised the dense prose of the ITC's document on licence renewal. Instead of basing payments on a cash bid figure, the ITC suggested that 75 per cent of license fees should be linked to ad revenue.

BLACK AND WHITE TV ADS

25 AUGUST: More than 90 per cent of ads have white actors in the lead role, with 5.3 per cent putting someone from an ethnic minority at the centre of the action, according to the Glasgow University Media Group. The researchers watched 665 ads to arrive at their figure and one of them, Greg Philo, said: "The total UK ethnic population is only 5.5 per cent, so it's fairly representative." His colleague, Furzana Khan, said the most popular television advertisement with a black in it showed an elderly man sat in a tent. "The most frequently shown white main lead shows a man with responsibility having fun. The most frequently shown non-white ad has a poor man doing nothing."

BETTER THAN AMERICA ...

13 SEPTEMBER: Sir Robin Biggam (pictured above), the chairman of the ITC, said: "The quality of American television, even to a casual observer, is way, way behind what it is here in Britain. Regulation in the US focuses on communication systems rather than the viewer. We see the ITC as representing the interests of the viewer. The viewer is probably oblivious to the technology that delivers the programmes." In October he warned Channel 3 licensees that regional programming commitments were non-negotiable and that negotiations for licence renewal, due to start in 1998, would be tough. "We are talking about licence renewal, not licence renegotiation," Sir Robin said.

Are you going to Edinburgh, or don't you want to stay in Television?

The Edinburgh TV Festival is the one that no-one in the business can afford to miss. Every year it sets the agenda. With big name Masterclasses. Policy debates. Programme sessions. Everything you need to know about the latest technology and market information. Daily screenings of the latest TV ideas from around the world. The traditional MacTaggart lecture. And a very lively, non-traditional TV Festival fringe. Don't miss it. Everyone who's anyone in Television (and wants to stay that way) will be there. Dates: 27th to 30st August 1999. Tel: 0171-379 4519. Fax: 0171-836 0702. E-mail: geitf@festival.demon.co.uk

The **Guardian** Edinburgh International Television Festival
The most important 4 days on television.

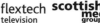

the perfect party

THROWING A PARTY?

We spent years looking for the best party organisers, finally the ultimate company Capital VIP provided the answer.

Don't even think about throwing a party until you've consulted Justin Etzin and his team at Capital VIP. From the moment you call them you just know that you've come to the right people. Capital VIP is London's leading party organiser, with a list of private clients reading like the pages of Who's Who.

Even fashion gurus like *Gucci, Louis Vuitton, MTV* and *Harrods* are turning to Capital VIP in recognition of its outstanding ability to organise the ultimate party. Capital VIP provides every ingredient for the perfect party, including catering, marquees and entertainment. They are particularly noted for their stunning interiors, imaginative theming and attention to detail. Rumour has it that the head Honcho of Gucci said that the recent party that Capital VIP organised to launch their diamond G watch was a total success, but all for the wrong reasons. Why? Because all his guests were heard to be commenting on the wonderful food, and not the extravagant watch displays!

Capital VIP is renowned for organising spectacular events. Two recent film premiere parties organised by Capital VIP were held at the famous Café de Paris. Justin Etzin explains that choosing the right venue is paramount to the success of a party.

Capital VIP has earned its title as "The Ultimate Party Organiser". I'll let you into a little secret - when you call Capital VIP (0171) 495 7070 - would you believe that they send you their company brochure hand-delivered by a black-tie messenger? With attention to detail like this, it's no wonder that everyone is turning to Capital VIP to have their party organised.

CAPITAL VIP

C4 FAVOURS HOME GROWN

21 SEPTEMBER 1997: Michael Jackson, the new C4 boss, pledged more "home grown productions" in favour of imported American series like Friends, Frasier and Cybill. He said the changes would take a couple of years.

AD STRIKE

OCTOBER: The majority of actors boycotted work on TV ads, following moves to cut their repeat fees by two thirds. Advertising execs scuttled round looking for old ads to repeat and for drama students to stand in for highly paid stars who can earn £100,000 for a morning's work. Equity, the actor's union, lifted the ban four months later.

C4 FILM BOSS QUITS

27 OCTOBER: David Aukin, the Channel 4 film chief responsible for Four Weddings and a Funeral and Trainspotting, resigned to take up a job in Hollywood.

CARTOON CRITICISM

4 NOVEMBER: Two thirds of children's TV is cartoons: the BBC and ITV were censured by the Broadcasting Standards Commission for allowing children's factual and drama series to become "an endangered species". The report said that despite increasing numbers of channels, there had been no increase in diversity. In 1981 cartoons comprised 9 per cent of ITV's children's programming and 40 per cent in 1996.

C4 GOES TO LAW

8 JANUARY: Vanni Treves, a lawyer whose clients include Richard Branson and John Paul Getty II, succeeded Sir Michael Bishop as C4 chairman.

NEW LOOK ITV

13 JANUARY: Richard Eyre, ITV's new chief executive, pledged that a revised programme strategy would reverse audience decline and regain a 2 per cent share over the next two years. ITV saw its future in upmarket and younger audiences during peak time and housewives during the day. A translation of this market-speak is better sit-coms, better news and more expensive sport. First to go were Network First documentaries.

C4 REVIEW DELAYS

21 JANUARY: Delays to the ITC's new remit for Channel 4 came from pressure for more multi cultural broadcasts and ITV companies complaining of the channel's audience-grabbing populism.

C3 LICENCE FEE CUTS

28 JANUARY: A lobbying campaign by ITV owners resulted in the ITC promising to reduce licence fees from £420 million a year to as low as £150 million. Negotiations were already starting for the 15 Channel 23 franchises to renew their licences in 2001.

ITC CODE OF PRACTICE

1 FEBRUARY: The ITC revised Programme Code came into force with the following new provisions:
* more viewer information "to assist parents make appropriate viewing choices"
* "the graphic depiction of sexual violence is justifiable only very exceptionally"
* examples of what defines public interest
* guidance on "fairness toward innocent parties" in TV reconstructions
* guidance on CCTV footage where people didn't know they were being filmed
* new guidance on "reuse of sensitive material"
* a five second labelling of video news releases
* modified constraints for on-screen smoking
* clarification on payment to criminals
* defining promo rules for spin-off mags

WORLD IN ACTION DEFEAT

3 MARCH: Granada's World in Action current affairs programme lost a £1.2 million court action brought by Marks and Spencer. M&S denied allegations it had sold goods marked "Made in the UK" knowing them to have been produced by children employed for 10p an hour. A Granada source said: "The pressure is to get away from stories that make people feel uncomfortable. In will come consumery items. We are run by accountants now."

RETREADS

24 MARCH 1998: ITV said it would resurrect the Wombles and remake the seventies daytime TV classic Crown Court with a programme called Accused. C3 is following similarly bold BBC programming which has seen revivals of University Challenge and the Generation Game.

ITN SELLS HQ

15 APRIL: Independent Television News sold its Gray's Inn Road offices for £80 million. ITN is likely to continue there as a tenant and the building will continue appearing on News at Ten and lunchtime bulletins.

C3 HITS OUT AT SKY

27 APRIL: The ITV companies announced their refusal to allow BSkyB to digitally broadcast Channel 3 services or their own ITV2 digital channel. An ITV exec said: "We all need to limit the increase in digital satellite television, not encourage it."

LICENCE RENEWAL

MAY: The majority of ITV franchise holders started working on licence bids, all hoping to share an ITC rebate which may be worth up to £100 million a year.

ITC ANNUAL REVIEW

5 MAY: The ITC end of term report on its franchise holders said Channel 3 companies should provide better Saturday night programmes and boost international news coverage. More criticism was reserved for Channel 4 which was accused of "losing some of its innovative drive". For a precis of ITC station-by-station comments, see C3 and C4 listing sections.

BORING ITV

5 MAY: The ITC said it was time Channel 3 companies stopped relying on an old warhorse of Saturday schedule which leans too heavily on the likes of Blind Date, Catchphrase, Family Fortunes and Stars in the Eyes. "They have to try and bring some freshness to the evening's viewing," said Sarah Thane, the ITC director of programmes.

GONG I: LORD BIG BREAKFAST

14 JUNE: Waheed Ali, boss of Planet 24 production company and the man behind Channel 4's Big Breakfast, was made the Lords' youngest life peer. Alli, who is a friend of the culture secretary Chris Smith, co-owns Planet 24 with Sir Bob Geldof.

GONG II: PROFESSOR ELSTEIN

JUNE: In another handout of gongs, Oxford University appointed David Elstein as the News International Visiting Professorship in Broadcast Media. The Channel 5 chief executive said he would use the Murdoch funded bursary to give lectures and seminars on "the changing perception of the role of television in post-war society." Elstein has personal experience of changing perception. In 1991, before taking up his role as BSkyB head of programming, he'd given a James McTaggart memorial lecture about his perception of Sky TV as a threat to quality broadcasting.

AD RESTRICTION EASED

22 JUNE: The ITC modified controls on broadcasting sanitary towel advertising and announced that from 1 August they can be shown before the 9pm watershed. They remain banned during children's programmes.

ITV RECORD

1 JULY: A record ITV audience of 26 million viewers watched the England vs Argentina penalty shoot-out. England lost both the World Cup matches assigned to Channel 3.

ITV GOES FOR MIDDLE CLASSES

21 JULY: David Liddiment, the ITV's director of programmes, talked demographics when he announced his autumn schedule. "ITV must move away from its ageing, working-class image," Liddiment said. "By 2003, half the country will be ABC1 viewers. The label applies to almost the majority of Britain now. We are projecting to an audience a bit younger, a bit more upmarket but without sacrificing our broad appeal." So out go gameshows and in comes more drama and factual programming - plus the first new logo in a decade.

New TV

CLOUDY DIGITAL DAWN

4 AUGUST 1997: Only 12% of households will have digital receiving equipment by 2000, according to analysts at Goldman Sachs. On 7 August Cable plans for digital TV suffered a dual setback with Telewest's announcement its was delaying launch plans beyond Christmas and halving investment to £250 million and rumours that BSkyB and British Telecom were considering postponing launch plans for its British Interactive Broadcasting consortium. Telewest also announced plans to cut its 5,500 workforce by a quarter.

SKY AND GRAVITY

15 AUGUST: The soon-to-depart BSkyB boss Sam Chisholm, whose 1996 salary was £3.8 million, was blamed for wiping £600 million from Sky's market valuation when he said BSkyB would be "defying the laws of gravity" if its profits continued growing at the same rates. He blamed digital satellite investment costs. The same day David Mellor's football task force promised to investigate Sky's sports' pricing.

HOLLICK VS SKY

10 SEPTEMBER: Lord Hollick, who is a part-time adviser to the Department of Trade as well as United News and Media chief executive, said BSkyB should pay a tax similar to the licence fees levied via the Independent Television Commission on Channel 3 companies. In another attack on BSkyB, he also said the telecomms regulator Oftel should play a fuller role in "policing" digital broadcasting.

C&W CHASING CUSTOMERS

15 SEPTEMBER: Cable and Wireless Communications began a £50 million marketing campaign to woo and retain phone and TV customers. C&WC - whose cable operation is the result of merger with Mercury, Bell Cablemedia and Videotron - loses 28 per cent of its cable TV customers within a year of their signing up and is in a race against new digital channels.

MAN U DEAL

24 SEPTEMBER: Manchester United football club signed a deal with Granada and BSkyB to start a footie-only digital TV channel. A spokesman for the venture said the channel won't show the big matches - only old games, reserve games, testimonials, friendlies and interviews with Ryan Giggs being bashful.

DIGITAL DOUBTS

25 SEPTEMBER: Euro rules banning restrictive practices threatened to delay launch of the British Digital Broadcasting digital TV service. Though the British government licensed Granada and Carlton to go ahead with BDB, Brussels wants to examine the £70 million programme supply deal whereby BSkyB (which had been barred as a BDB shareholder) would predominate. The European Commission was responding to complaints made by Digital Television Network, the group which lost the bidding fight with BDB.

TRAD MEDIA ONLINE

OCTOBER: The BBC and ITV announced plans for web sites. The BBC promised a £10 million investment on a range of online services aimed at young people who understood the Internet was "a third force in broadcasting". ITV awarded a web site deal to a consortium formed by its news service ITN and the magazine publisher IPC. Log into: itv.co.uk or (more one for journalists and advertisers) itv.org.uk.

WIRED FOR EVERYTHING

8 OCTOBER: A technique for sending Internet data down electricity cables at a megabit per second (30 times the speed of most modems) was announced by Norweb Communications. This potential for a ubiquitous network via the national grid is good news for consumers and the privatised electricity companies, bad news for BT because the new system could handle phone calls as well as Internet and television signals.

CABLE FILM DEAL

17 OCTOBER 1997: Telewest, General Cable, Diamond Cable and NTL secured cable TV rights for Warner Bros and Columbia Tristar films so that their customers can watch movies direct rather than going via BSkyB. "BSkyB won't enjoy the dominance it has had to date," said one journalist. "It will see a decline in its exclusivity."

WARNING TO BSKYB

21 OCTOBER: The Oftel chief executive Don Cruickshank told the European Cable Communications conference that BSkyB should not be allowed to use its control of sports events and films to dominate the emerging digital TV market. The telecomms regulator, whose brief includes scrutinising access to digital TV markets, said: "It is essential to a competitive market that a dominant operator should not be able to leverage market power from premium to basic programmes." Sir Robin Biggam, head of ITC and thus the man responsible for programme content, disagreed saying that digital TV operators should buy film and sports rights rather than rely on regulation.

NET APATHY

21 OCTOBER: A Mori survey revealed that regular Internet usage has inched up from 9 to 11 per cent of the population.

BBC NEWS

2 NOVEMBER: BBC News Online went online with a staff of 30 journalists and access to the BBC news-gathering operation.

OFFLINE

10 NOVEMBER: Judge Hiller Zobel's pronouncement on the Louise Woodward appeal was to be the Internet's big day. 1500 hours GMT was the big moment when a decision made in Massachusetts should have been flashed instantly round the world. Then a power-cut disabled the file server and so news of a murder conviction reduced to manslaughter was distributed in the conventional way. The story stayed bang on script with a newspaper bidding war for Woodward's version of events.

NEW BSKYB BOSS

12 NOVEMBER: Mark Booth, a 41 year old American, was announced as Sam Chisholm's replacement as BSkyB's chief executive.

ITC INTO NET-WATCHING

14 DECEMBER: In anticipation of high quality video via the net, the Independent Television Commission signalled interest in online regulation by establishing links with the Internet Watch Foundation. The IWF comprises information providers committed to self-regulation.

BDB LICENCE

19 DECEMBER: British Direct Broadcasting, the new TV consortium owned by Carlton and Granada, got its licence from the ITC. The major changes to the draft licence were that programme supply contracts should last no more than five years and a bar on British Direct Broadcasting directors joining the BSkyB board.

EURO BLOCK ON MAGIC BOXES

15 JANUARY: British Interactive Broadcasting plans to introduce a box accessing digital TV and the Internet were threatened by European Commission objections. An EU official expressed concerns that British Interactive Broadcasting's major shareholders - British Telecom and BSkyB - would have too dominant positions in the emerging market.

SKY BIDS FOR C4 NEWS

23 January: BSkyB put in a bid to produce Channel 4 News. Independent Television News, which holds the current contract, wants to renew a deal that expires in June 1999. Channel 5 News, which occupies the same 7pm slot, was attracting younger viewers. ITN learned it had retained the contract in March.

WEATHER BLOW

25 JANUARY: The Weather Channel closed, a victim of a sluggish market for cable television and the perfectly decent weather forecasting already being broadcast on the main terrestrial channels.

ITC FINE

30 JANUARY: The Kurdish satellite channel Med TV was fined £90,000 for "serious breaches of the ITC programme code ... on due impartiality". Med TV had: broadcast a "40-minute programme [which] consisted entirely of a political rally organised by the Workers' Party of Kurdistan (£50,000); for asserting a US government list of terrorist organisations "was intended to 'cover up the USA's own terrorist activities'" (£25,000); and for "describing members of the Kurdish Democratic Party as 'treacherous and murderous'".

BSKYB'S DIGITAL DELAY

12 FEBRUARY: BSkyB put back the June launch date of digital TV services until autumn 1998. "We will be rather quiet about digital until that time," promised Mark Booth, Sky's new chief exec.

NO BT TV

12 FEBRUARY: British Telecom revealed plans to become an Internet broadcasting market leader and ended its previous plans to distribute mass market TV. "It is unlikely we'll be squirting TV channels down our wires," said the chairman Sir Peter Bonfield.

NET SCEPTICISM

24 FEBRUARY: The trouble with surfing for information is that users can end up scanning the words of a "serial murderer in a secure mental establishment". So said media researchers at Salomon Smith Barney in a report that also scorned publishing futurologist's chatter about the majority of people soon going straight to the Net for their information. The investment bank says electronic publishing's greatest effect has been in financial publishing while paperbacks, consumer mags and newspapers have remained largely unaffected.

DIGITAL TV RECEIVERS

8 MARCH: BDB, the Granada and Carlton digital TV enterprise, said it had appointed six manufacturers to make plug and play digital receivers for around £200 by Christmas 1998. These will bring digital quality to existing terrestrial broadcasts and compete with similar BSkyB boxes promised to give access to up to 200 channels. But by May a the new BDB boss Stephen Grabiner declared: "I am confident there will be no set-top box war because it is in nobody's interest to have one."

GOOD CABLE NEWS

9 MARCH: The ITC announced: "One in ten of all UK households now take their television service through broadband cable. As of 1 January 1998, 2,374,000 homes were connected to cable TV. 1997 was a record breaking year for the broadband cable industry. Cable operators built their networks past and marketed services to 2.3 million new homes. Cable is available to 10,694,000 UK homes, nearly a third of which are taking a cable service of some kind from their local operator. Cable operators were also installing phone lines at a rate of 3,189 per day and now serve more than three million homes."

INTERNET TV

18 MARCH: British Telecom and American software united in a deal to pioneer Internet-based TV and to see whether viewers want the net through their TV and how much they might pay. Two manufacturers of set-top technology, Pace and Philips, pledged involvement in the trials. Days later the telecoms regulator Don Cruickshank said the government should tear up broadcasting laws regulating what people watch. In an attack on the existence of the ITC the Oftel boss said: "The new world in which a flood of data and images will flow over networks spanning national and regulatory boundaries is already with us. Consumers browse content from thousands of different sources whenever they like."

TELEWEST: BIGGEST IN CABLE

29 MARCH: Telewest announced a £666 million share and cash deal to buy General Cable, thus trumping a £545 million bid from NTL. Telewest was also planning to pay some £200 million to control Cable London. The consolidation promised Telewest-owned cable would pass over six million homes, more than CWC Communications.

NO TO BUNDLING

2 APRIL 1998: The ITC ruled that bundling - jargon for satellite and cable companies compelling their subscribers to buy lots of channels they don't particularly want in order to access the ones they do want - is anti-competitive. Cable operators argue that this will reduce choice and maybe force smaller channels out of business. As of the ruling, BSkyB's subscribers have to pay a monthly £11.99 for 30 channels before they can buy mainstream sport or films. The ITC chairman Sir Robin Biggam said he would be "very disappointed" if lower priced starter options were not available by Christmas. Live TV, home of the News Bunny, squealed loudest and Kelvin MacKenzie said the ITC ruling "if not reversed, will leave us with no choice but to close the station".

D-DAY

8 APRIL: Broadcasting chiefs urged European governments to decide on their deadlines for compelling the conversion from analogue to digital services. Techno-enthusiasts gathered at the European Audiovisual conference in Birmingham said that Euro-interests would be undermined if America and Japan take a digital lead and implement their designated Digital-Days in 2006. Politicians are wary of forcing consumers into replacement equipment which, for British television sets alone, will cost an estimated £10 billion.

LABOUR PR MAN GOES TO SKY

19 APRIL: Tim Allan, deputy to the prime minister's press secretary Alastair Campbell, confirmed he was moving to become director of corporate communications at BSkyB. The 28 year old's skills will reportedly be earning him more than £100,000 a year. A media analyst commented: "Allan sold Labour to the middle class. Now he's got to sell the same people BSkyB."

C&W's NET GAIN

28 MAY: Cable & Wireless' intention to be a leading Internet company was underlined by a $625 million purchase of MCI's service providing technology.

SKY SOCCER SETBACK

29 MAY: The 20 clubs which form the FA Premier League rejected BSkyB's pay-to-view proposals. The effect of BSkyB's plan would have compelled fans to pay up to £10 a game. Sky wants to use pay-per-view as part of its digital television launch but the clubs feared it would give TV executives too much influence on match schedules. Combined turnover for football's top clubs increased 32 per cent to £455 million, thanks to a 123 per cent increase in TV income. Vic Wakeling, the BSkyB sport boss, said: "There are many details to be discussed and Sky shares the Premier League's wish to get it right for all football fans."

SKY FILM COUP

4 JUNE: The BBC's long-serving film critic Barry Norman took a £350,000 a year job at Sky. He had been frustrated that the BBC was transmitting his show at late and irregular hours. Elisabeth Murdoch, Sky's general manager of broadcasting, was cock-a-hoop and said: "Barry Norman is the face and voice of film in the UK, and is held in the highest regard both within the film industry and by film fans everywhere."

FIRST DIGITISED TELLY

10 JUNE: The BBC mainstream digital television with widescreen soccer transmitted to a handful of sites including Heathrow's terminal 2. Patricia Hodgson, director of policy, predicted that by 2007 between a half and two-thirds of British homes will have gone digital. A fortnight later began its own pilot digital broadcasts.

GRANADA TO SELL SKY HOLDING

10 JUNE: Reports emerged of Granada Group's intention to sells its 10.8 per cent share of BSkyB. The value of its stake would be over £800 million.

CABLE CONSOLIDATION

16 JUNE: NTL spent £720 million to take over ComTel and Diamond Cable. The deal brought its total of cable subscribers to 5.2 million, a fraction behind its two rivals at C&W and Telewest.

Radio

NOT SO ONE-DERFUL

8 AUGUST 1997: Radio 1's weekly audience fell to under ten million listeners for the first time since it began broadcasting, according to Rajar figures. "Sophie McLauglin, head of the BBC's radio strategy, put a the obligatory spin on the news, saying: "Radio 1 is still the biggest radio station in Europe. Forty per cent of 15 to 24 year olds tune in each week, and that's not a sign of a station in crisis. BBC Radio and the commercial sector continue to vie for market share in a contracting market."

BREAKFAST POP

3 OCTOBER: The launch of Chris Evans' Virgin breakfast show coincided with Zoe Ball taking over Radio 1's breakfast slot. Evans was pencilled in for a ten week DJ-ing stint. He had other proprietorial ideas on his mind and by the New Year Evans had an even more valuable contract as one of the owners of Virgin Radio.

MAIL GOES DOWN UNDER

10 OCTOBER: The Daily Mail - which owns 19 per cent of GWR, 27 per cent of Essex Radio and 39 per cent of Radio Trust - went global with the £40 million cash purchase of 25 Australian radio stations.

ME FIRST SPAT

20 OCTOBER: Newspaper journalists told a Radio Academy conference that they get the scoops. Georgina Henry, Guardian deputy editor, said: "BBC radio is more diary and event-driven than newspapers are." Stuart Kuttner, managing editor of the News of the World, said: " The flow of news stories is largely in one direction - from us to you." James Naughtie, formerly of the Guardian but now Today, responded: "Interviews are what we do best ... newspapers feed ravenously off the scraps from the table. Phil Harding, the BBC's controller of editorial policy, said radio had to be more accurate and that "newspapers are used to fly kites and if the kites doesn't fly, the stories are dropped."

40 TODAY

9 OCTOBER: The fortieth birthday of Today. Radio 4's morning current affairs programme is the leading news source for the great and good. "If the Trident commander could not pick up Today, that would be that," said Professor Peter Hennessy on Royal Navy procedure to determine whether Britain has survived a nuclear strike.

Brian Redhead (above) and James Naughtie, Guardian ex-staffers who made it big on Today

"BBC SLOWLY DYING ..."

NOVEMBER 1997: "The BBC is slowly dying." So said Hugh Sykes, a BBC radio reporter for over 20 years, when he bit the feeding hand in the staff magazine Ariel. "It is hard writing this," he wrote. "I have always kept these thoughts within these walls. I wonder if our listeners realise quite what a struggle is going on behind the scenes; quite how undervalued by the BBC itself its cherished medium is? There are terrible tensions in our offices now. As reporters, we work almost entirely on our own ... people who rely on Radio 4 for sober news every day should know that we are all flying on a wing and prayer."

THOUGHTS FOR THE DAY

8 NOVEMBER: "Too political," was what the BBC chairman Sir Christopher Bland thought of Radio 4's Thought for the Day. "I don't accept it has become political, let alone too political," was the Bishop of Bath and Wells' thought. "The world of politics is all about caring," thought Canon Eric James. Ann Atkins had huffy thoughts about Anglican homosexuals; a thousand letter writers and phone callers thought otherwise.

RA THOUGHTS

11 NOVEMBER: Having rethought its thoughts on Amnesty International's political aims, the Radio Authority decided to allow Amnesty to advertise. And the RA backed up its thoughts on Heartbeat AM and City Beat FM by imposing £1,000 fines on the Northern Irish stations for breaching terms of their licences.

RADIO 3 REVAMP

27 NOVEMBER: Radio 3's bid to see off competition from Classic FM comprised simpler schedules, more accessible peak time programming and the return of Joan Bakewell, Richard Baker and Peter Hobday. "Only in Britain could the introduction of three middle-class radio presenters with a combined age of 196 and scarcely a trace of a regional accent between them bring allegations that the network was plunging into populist mire," Peter Barnard wrote in The Times.

DIGITAL RADIO LICENCES

3 DECEMBER: The Radio Authority - having already guaranteed places for Classic FM, Virgin and Talk Radio - announced an intention to issue the remaining six or seven national digital radio licences by September 1998.

CHRIS EVANS BUYS VIRGIN RADIO

8 DECEMBER: After long consideration of a bid by Capital Radio, Richard Branson sold Virgin Radio to Chris Evans' Ginger Productions for £85 million. Financiers at Apax Partners arranged a deal where Evans put up £2 million of his own money. Evans, whose assets are estimated at over £50 million, crowed: "I stay on air which seems to be a popular decision with the listeners. I get to be in control, which seems to be a popular decision with the staff."

DIGITAL DRIVE-TIME

14 DECEMBER: Of over 3,000 motoring enthusiasts asked at the London Motor Show, 83 per cent said they wanted digital radio.

DIGITAL LICENCE FEES

5 JANUARY: The Radio Authority announced its latest fee structure: from £50,000 for a national multiplex with a £10,000 annual fee to £1,000 for a local multiplex pitched at up to 450,000 adults.

RADIO GETS MUCH WORSE

15 JANUARY: International Radio Journalism, a book by Tim Crook, noted "a steady decline in the training, pay and conditions of radio journalists since 1987". Crook quoted a radio news editor's comments on today's harsher regimes: "Twenty years ago you could write satirical messages about the managing director on the notice board and he would chuckle. Now you would be sacked on the spot."

7 x 8 = 54

21 JANUARY: Eleanor Oldroyd, the Radio 5 Live presenter, interviewed the education minister Stephen Byers about the government's numeracy drive. "What," she asked the man who is so critical of shoddy teaching, "are seven times eight?" See above for his answer.

SERIAL SUICIDE

25 FEBRUARY: John Archer died in a tractor accident in what was dubbed a "serial killing". In fact the death blow was dealt by a radio actor's desire to transfer his good looks to television. Sam Barriscale, 23, had been with the Archers man and boy, having made his first invisible appearance in 1988.

RADIO 1 CHANGES

25 FEBRUARY: Matthew Bannister, the Radio 1 controller who found fame in his falling out with Chris Evans, quit his post to concentrate on his role as director of BBC radio. Since he took the Radio 1 job in 1994, the station has lost four million listeners. Bannister's deputy, Andy Parfitt, took over.

MELODY RADIO

26 FEBRUARY: Emap bought Melody Radio from Lord Hanson for £25 million.

LAISSEZ FAIRE RADIO

28 FEBRUARY: The Commercial Radio Companies Association went before the Commons media select committee and made a predictable call for the privatisation of Radios 1 and 2. The CRCA also called for local licences to be awarded to the highest bidder (as national licences are already), for the 15 per cent ownership ceiling to be raised to 20 per cent and for less stringent regulations.

ISLAND RADIO

10 MARCH: Tindle Newspapers diversified from local papers when it bought Island Radio in Guernsey from Stewart and Radio Investments.

DIGITAL RADIO

24 MARCH: The Radio Authority advertised the first and only national digital licence. The multiplex, to be granted for 12 years from autumn 1998, will be able to carry up to eight channels with near CD-quality sound.

PARLIAMENTARY COVERAGE

2 APRIL: The BBC main board backed its management proposal to put the bulk of parliamentary broadcasts onto long wave. Sir Christopher Bland, BBC chairman, wrote to Betty Boothroyd, speaker of the House of Commons assuring her that Today would continue to carry highlights.

DIGI-BIDS

23 APRIL: Digital Media Broadcast joined Chris Evans' Digital One in placing a bid for the sole national digital radio licence available from the Radio Authority. DMD is backed by German radio manufacturers plus Intelfax data services company and Castle Transmission International, the transmission business formerly owned by the BBC.

CAPITAL BUYS XFM

1 MAY: London's indie rock station went to Capital Radio for £15.9 million. Xfm main owner, Chris Parry, stood to make £4 million from a station which only began broadcasting on FM in summer 1997.

NATIONAL DIGITAL LICENCE

23 JUNE: The closing date for a national digital multiplex licence and only Digital One had put itself in the running. Digital One is 57 per cent owned by GWR, 33 per cent by NTL Digital Radio and 10 per cent by Talk Radio.

RADIO SLUMBER

25 JUNE: Phil Holmes, a DJ for Sun FM in Sunderland, was sacked for sleeping whilst in the line of duty. "One minute I was sitting there reading my advert list," Homes explained. "The next I had my boss in the studio shouting at me to wake up."

BYE BYE BROADCASTING HOUSE

26 JUNE: Today did its final Broadcasting House transmission before going bi-media and sharing new offices with TV news at Shepherd's Bush.

MILLENNIAL KENYON

6 JULY: Nicholas Kenyon announced his departure as Radio 3 controller. He will continue directing the Proms and coordinate the BBC's millennium programming to the end of 2000.

Television: introduction

Until 1998 British television split into three categories:

1) **the public sector BBC**, which is paid for by an annual licence fee that raised £1.9 billion in 1997 and is broadcast nationally (with regional variations) on BBC 1 and BBC 2 (pages 174-179);

2) **the commercial sector ITV**, which is funded by advertisements to the tune of £2.6 billion a year and is broadcast regionally on 16 Channel 3 stations and nationally on Channel 4 (S4C in Wales) and Channel 5 (pages 182-193);

3) **satellite and cable**, which is funded by £285 million worth of ad sales and £1.25 billion in subscription and is broadcast nationally (pages 218-230).

From now on, digital is a fourth category, though the fuss here is primarily technological in that the addition to the nation's happiness will not be about the programmes we watch but how they arrive on our screens. Its big money backers - the BBC included - concentrate on enhanced picture quality and present digital TV as a great opportunity. It is more an inevitability, given that digital transmission is technically more efficient and that the government is therefore committed over the long term to selling off the analogue spectrum to companies running mobile telephones and private networks. The drawbacks have nothing directly to do with technology other than that digital transmission will enable the continuing proliferation of channels. This in turn will spread programme budgets so thinly that there's a danger there will be little worth watching. In this sense more could equal less and the digital consumer's choice (if that's what it is) lies between digital terrestrial, digital satellite or digital cable. More details are on pages 194-195.

A recent Independent Television Commission survey revealed that despite all the hyped up newness, viewing habits are only changing slowly. There has been little shift in our channel hopping habits and, as for the last few years, nearly one in ten people watches telly every day of an average week. The average amount watched remains at 26 hours a week with 59 per cent of those surveyed watching between two and five hours per day. The cable and satellite

---

Share of total television audience

BBC 41.7%

ITV (C3) 32.4%

Channel 4   10.4%

Cable   5.9%

Sky   5.3%

Channel 5   3.2%

A graphic representation of popularity comes when typographic point size stands for 1% of audience share. Channel 5 - for those who don't have microscopic vision (or who can't receive it) - got a 3.2% share of viewers.

In 1997 the figures were as follows: BBC 43.9%, ITV 33.1%, Channel 4 10.7%, Cable 8%, Sky 4.3%

subscribers continue watching slightly more of their televisions than terrestrial-only viewers - who still form a majority of the TV-watching public.

According to the ITC, the majority of people think programme standards have remained the same. Those who do notice a decline complain about the number of repeats and just under two-thirds of the ITC's sample did not report having seen anything offensive on their TVs. Among all viewers, the main cause of offence continues to be bad language (32 per cent), violence (25 per cent) and sex and nudity (20 per cent). The ITC also reported a widespread resentment about having to subscribe to watch major sporting events.

The BBC dominates British television with a 41.7 per cent share of audiences. The ITC puts a different spin on the figures saying that "ITV remains the favoured channel if viewers could have only one of those currently available" which is fair enough if you disaggregate BBC1 and BBC2 viewing figures. Do that and the per channel BSkyB market share, which remains the same as the year before, looks even tinier; and that would be silly because its multi-channel approach has given it an income a third larger than Granada, its closest independent TV competitor. Channel 5 charted a rise to its current modest eminence as cable TV charted a tiny fall.

There is a general and complacent view that British telly is the best in the world. Certainly better than America, with the ITC chairman Sir Robin Biggam remarking: "The quality of American television, even to a casual observer, is way, way behind what it is here. Regulation in the US focuses on communication systems rather than the viewer. The viewer is probably oblivious to the technology that delivers the programmes." Others would point to the BBC's advertising-free centrality to national life or they could use a Royal Television Society survey showing that home grown, mass appeal television is winning out against the imported stuff. The RTS survey of the top 100 individual programmes of 1997 shows that only three were made abroad - Mrs Doubtfire, the X-Files and The Mask.

Share of total audience

CHANNEL	'96-97	'97-98
BBC 1	32.2%	30.4%
BBC 2	11.7%	11.3%
Channel 4	10.3%	10%
Sky	4.3%	5.3%
Central	5.4%	4.8%
Granada	4.0%	3.9%
Yorkshire	3.4%	3.4%
Channel 5	2.8%	3.2%
Carlton	3.2%	2..9%
Meridian	2.6%	2..5%
HTV	2.6%	2..4%
Scottish	2.2%	2..1%
LWT	2.1%	2..0%
Anglia	2.1%	1.9%
GMTV	1.8%	1.7%
Tyne Tees	1.7%	1.7%
Ulster	1.1%	1.0%
Westcountry	0.9%	0.9%
Cartoon Network	0.7%	0.8%
Nickelodeon	0.5%	0.7%
Grampian	0.7%	0.6%
UK Gold	0.6%	0.6%
Border	0.6%	0.5%
Living	0.3%	0.4%
S4C Wales	0.4%	0.4%
Bravo	0.2%	0.3%
Discovery	0.2%	0.3%
Disney Channel	0.3%	0.3%
Eurosport	0.3%	0.3%
MTV	0.2%	0.3%
Challenge TV		0.2%
Granada Plus	0.1%	0.2%
VH-1	0.2%	0.2%
The Box	0.1%	0.1%
Channel Television	0.1%	0.1%
CNN		0.1%
Discovery Home & Leisure		0.1%
Fox Kids Network	0.1%	0.1%
Live TV		0.1%
Network 2	0.1%	0.1%
Paramount Channel	0.1%	0.1%
QVC	0.1%	0.1%
RTE 1	0.1%	0.1%
Sci-Fi Channel	0.1%	0.1%
TCC	0.2%	0.1%
TNT	0.1%	0.1%
ZEE TV (Indian)	0.1%	0.1%

Source: ITC

'97-'98 programme budgets

CHANNEL	£ MILLION
BBC 1	£652.5m
ITV	£620m
BBC 2	£346.8m
Channel 4	£320m
Channel 5	£110m

Source: Royal Television Society

Viewing figures

ITV DOWNS

The Bill	-16%
Inspector Morse	-7%
Emmerdale	-5%
Coronation Street	-4%

BBC UPS

Keeping Up Appearances	+47%
Only Fools and Horses	+27%
Animal Hospital	+12%
East Enders	+2%

figures from October 1997

The Brit-ain't-so-good brigade look to the overall buying pattern and the Office for National Statistics figures showing the TV industry recorded a net deficit of £282 million for 1996 compared with a £155 million deficit a year earlier. "We think our programmes are the best in the world and we're a great exporter," says Jane Lighting, who runs the company handling global distribution of the Australian soap Heartbreak High. "But compared with the Americans we're not even on the scale." And inevitably the Americans deal in the biggest bucks, with NBC paying the producers of ER £7.9 million per episode. Nice for the stars who earn between £61,500 and £92,000 per show and reasonable business for NBC which charges up to £606,000 for 30 seconds of advertising.

A ratcheting up of costs in bad news for consumers everywhere. The prime British example is that armchair fans of mainstream sporting events must now pay far more than they ever did in a more regulated market. A report on British television commissioned by the Institute for Public Policy Research concluded that deregulation has damaged the industry. Its

Top 20 programmes of 1997

TITLE	AUDIENCE	DATE	CHANNEL
Funeral of Diana, Princess of Wales	19.29m	Sep 6	BBC1
Heartbeat	18.35m	Nov 16	Yorkshire
Touch of Frost	18.22m	Feb 16	Yorkshire
EastEnders (Thurs)	18.06m	Jan 2	BBC1
Coronation Street (Mon)	18.03m	Nov 17	Granada
Coronation Street (Wed)	17.72m	Nov 12	Granada
EastEnders (Tue)	17.65m	Jan 7	BBC1
Coronation Street (Fri)	17.50m	Nov 7	Granada
Coronation Street (Sun)	17.45m	Nov 9	Granada
EastEnders (Mon)	16.89m	Feb 3	BBC1
Casualty	16.42m	Feb 22	BBC1
Men Behaving Badly	16.34m	Dec 25	BBC1
One Foot in the Grave	15.76m	Dec 25	BBC1
News & Weather (22.10)	15.46m	Dec 25	BBC1
Before They Were Famous	15.34m	Mar 31	BBC1
It'll Be Alright on the Night 8	14.89m	Jan 4	LWT
Procession to Westminster (Diana)	14.78m	Sep 6	BBC1
Emmerdale (Thur)	14.23m	Feb 20	Yorkshire
The Bill (Fri)	14.15m	Jan 17	ITV
London's Burning	14.10m	Feb 2	LWT

Source: Royal Television Society

authors wrote: "In television, employment levels have tumbled and permanent jobs have been replaced in large numbers by contract and freelance labour. These changes have not lifted productivity or the quality of work performed. Nor is it the case that employers have universally welcomed the changed environment in which they now operate. Half of the ITV employers suggested the introduction of flexible working patterns had resulted in increased working hours. The BBC reported that average weekly working hours had increased for production, resources, post-production staff and journalists. Our study indicates that the regulatory shocks to TV, administered by the Conservative government in the late eighties, have had adverse consequences."

Other studies blame the output produced by the television industry's hard workers for just about every ill. Even the family meal is under threat, according to research commissioned by the pharmaceutical firm Roche. Almost half of those surveyed said they balanced dinner on their laps while watching television and only 45 per cent said they chatted round the dinner table.

Thus John - Sir John - Birt can be seen as corrupter of a nation's dining habits as well as the man who has ensured the BBC's survival by mixing the values of commercial managerialism with a public service ethos. He aims to make the BBC "the world's leading content provider". Meanwhile Rupert Murdoch says it is time the power of the BBC was curbed. In a clash of the regulated vs the deregulated Birt used his platform at the April 1998 European Audiovisual Conference to warn of how new technology could create a "knowledge underclass".

The following day Murdoch, making his first public speech in the Britain for five years, took to the same platform where he sneered at Birt's "elitism". He went on to say that it was time to end "the culture of cronyism and protectionism" and presented himself as the victim of a ruthless BBC cartel which was working flat out to do down News Corporation's global media role as "a small part of an ever-widening rainbow". Ever widening rainbow? There's a phrase. Anyway, a precis of their two speeches is on the following pages.

A record British TV audience of over 30 million watched Princess Diana's funeral on 6 September 1997

Regulation v deregulation/Birt v Murdoch

*"*The consumer will be increasingly asked to pay directly for what they see. The cost of watching a screen will rise enormously. We will see the emergence of the information rich, and the information poor. We risk a knowledge underclass. Public policy in the digital age should ensure that public service broadcasting remains universally available. At the heart of the public broadcasting tradition is universality - reaching out to every household in the land - the poor and the prosperous - offering enriching experience and information which extends understanding. Public service broadcasters seek not only to delight, but to give individuals the knowledge they need to live fuller, more satisfying lives.

The ubiquitous soft drink world of jeans, trainers and baseball cap will advance inexorably. We cannot halt the advance with barriers or quotas. Nor should we. One of the glories of the modern world is being exposed to the best of other cultures. There is no more effective way of doing that than by encouraging a flourishing public service sector in each EU country.

In the space of 12 months or so the BBC will have introduced three new publicly funded channels, focused on news, learning and on enhancing our existing services. The BBC will offer greater convenience to licence payers with the BBC's News 24 channel offering news as it breaks; and the BBC News Online offering instant access, via the internet, to the world's most powerful force in news gathering. BBC News Online offers the opportunity to tap into the rich reservoirs of expertise available from BBC World Service and from other of the BBC's specialised journalists, and to brief yourself on a wide range of current matters. A wonderful research tool.

Public broadcasters have a critical role to play in raising consciousness about these matters, and - through our educational services - enabling individuals to acquire the necessary skills. The BBC will play its part in the UK. But unless everyone - and most especially the government - puts their shoulders to the wheel and tries to advance toward a digital society, we shall simply take too long to achieve lift-off. *"*

SIR JOHN BIRT
BBC DIRECTOR GENERAL

"We have a vision in this country of a publicly-funded broadcaster, a regulated commercial sector, and a lightly regulated cable and satellite sector which has mushroomed, and we at the BBC have done nothing to resist it. That is a balanced approach. The question is: 'Do you want to have a public service broadcaster providing a range of services?' There is generally the view that yes, you do."

" I read Mr Birt's shaky claims that the poor are in danger of being cut off from information in the new media age. With the burgeoning of free radio, television and the Internet this has to be wrong. But if unhealthy concentration does exist today, it exists not in the private sector, but with state broadcasting.

In the UK no-one challenges the power of the BBC, nor other countries' own state broadcasters. Even worse, the European Broadcasting Union represents a concentration of buying power that would not be permitted in any other industry. This cartel has for many years used its extraordinary buying power to acquire exclusive sporting rights. The European Court of Justice refused to endorse the commission's decision to exempt public-service broadcasters from cartel restrictions; it is now up to the authorities to put a stop to their practices. Over the last 30 years, state and long-established private broadcasters, have fought diversity in broadcasting at every step. What saddens me is that they continue to receive all the privileges. The first bite of UK satellite was given to BSB, an establishment coalition; the first bite of the next revolution, digital terrestrial TV has once again gone to the main UK terrestrial operators.

The BBC and the ITV companies have automatically received access; and all three commercial multiplexes have gone to the two main commercial players. The BBC is the biggest media owner in the UK. With its £2 billion annual guaranteed income and vast commercial freedom, there's absolutely no chance of its being driven out of business by satellite broadcasters or anybody else. Commentators tout the achievements of public-service broadcasters - the drama, the culture - as astonishing. But if you give 75 years of access to every home in the land and guarantee billions of pounds every year, it would be truly astonishing if they didn't achieve a level of excellence.

Nor should this blind us to the competitive distortions that result when a dominant state broadcaster is allowed to overstep its bounds. For instance, in 1989 Sky created Europe's first 24 hour news channel, Sky News. Nine years and millions of pounds later, the service had established itself as the third force in UK television news broadcasting. But now the BBC has introduced a 24-hour news channel and is allowed to give it away free to cable companies, putting not only Sky News in jeopardy, but other future commercial news channels. *"*

RUPERT MURDOCH
NEWS CORP CHAIRMAN

"The BBC is the biggest media owner in the UK. With its £2 billion annual guaranteed income and vast commercial freedom, there's absolutely no chance of it being driven out of business by satellite broadcasters or anybody else. If you give someone 75 years of access to every home in the land and guarantee them billions every year, it would be astonishing if they didn't achieve a level of excellence."

BBC TV

The BBC, being the biggest single part of the British media, generates the most media based stories. Many of these centre on the two strands of John Birt's managerial regime, namely the internal reorganisation and the move toward commercialism.

The reorganisation has been a matter of abiding interest to BBC insiders ever since Producer Choice meant programme makers could use outside contractors. From Spring 1997, the BBC reorganised itself into bi-media divisions - BBC Broadcast, BBC News, BBC Production, BBC Resources and BBC Worldwide - which make no distinction between TV and radio. Viewing figures have held up better than many expected and the changes have, by and large, gained acceptance. True, drama producers come over all of a faint at the mention of their director-general and the news staff saw off a scheme to amalgamate TV and radio news.

The BBC's new commercialism shows itself in a number of ways. On its two main channels there are dubious ventures like the Perfect Day video, a four minute promo endorsing the BBC and using time which its commercial rivals point out would have cost millions. Dodgier still is the BBC's tireless efforts on behalf of Lottery entrepreneurs. In March, a new Lottery wheeze which televised invitations to punt on Camelot scratch cards had Gerald Kaufman, Labour chairman of the culture select committee, observe: "The BBC is promoting the sale of a commercial product, and more than that is paying to make the programme which does it. It has not stretched the limits of its charter, it has completely broken them."

In May, the culture secretary Chris Smith accused a meeting of BBC managers of downplaying serious programmes and promoting commercial interests at the expense of public service duties. He was reportedly angry at having to defend the scratch-card fiasco and worried that programmes like Panorama, Question

THE 75 YEAR OLD AUNTIE WHO GOES HUSTLING

UKTV/FLEXTECH

On 1 November UKTV, a joint venture between the BBC and Flextech, went live as the first BBC-backed network to carry advertising. The four channels are: UK Arena (music and arts); UK Gold (repeats); UK Horizons (factual series and natural history); UK Style (life-style stuff). This joint venture between the BBC's Worldwide division and Flextech relies on the latter putting up the £150 million launch budget and paying the BBC for programmes used. Dependence on ad revenue means the BBC doesn't attach its name directly to UKTV promo material.

BBC NEWS 24

A rolling news service went live in November 1997 at a cost of some £30 million a year. "We are pushing the technology as far as we can," said Tony Hall, chief exec of BBC News. A marker for digital TV, news junkies can receive it via cable or on BBC1 overnight. It competes with CNN and Sky News and is central to the director-general's vision of the BBC as "the world's leading content provider".

ICL

The Internet service beeb@the bbc was launched simultaneously with BBC News 24. It is a tie in with ICL which gives the BBC access to external funding and the computer company's technical and marketing know-how. The service offers sports results and online versions of the Radio Times and Top Gear. It is an extension of BBC Online, a public service website on www.bbc.co.uk which claimed 18 million page views in March 1998. In canvassing licence payers' views on investing in such things the BBC chairman Sir Christopher Bland wrote: "The Internet is becoming the

Time and Omnibus have moved from peak time to accommodate sit-coms and quiz shows.

The direct business manifestation of BBC commercialism is seen in a number of relationships with commercial partners, in particular the cable and satellite company Flextech, the Washington based TV channel Discovery, and the computer company ICL.

Early in 1998 John Birt visited the Microsoft headquarters in Seattle. He came home thrilled. "It was like the Gold Rush, - without the mud," Birt said. "Everyone I met shared a sense of awed enthusiasm about the infinite possibilities of the digital age. I had a long session with Bill Gates, and spent a whole day with his people. As an organisation, we recognised the truth that the technology we have been working in for 75 years, analogue, was giving way to a new technology, digital, which is changing in the most extraordinary way." In July the BBC linked up with Microsoft to work on "enhanced TV" technology. It will impose VDU style icons onto TV screens to give viewers a way into digitised archives containing details on the programme they are watching.

The BBC is now into its 76th analogue year as a cartel of radio manufacturers licensed by the government. It became a public body in 1927 when it was granted a Royal Charter to "provide broadcasting services as public services". When the whole notion of public service was attacked head on during the eighties it seemed as if the BBC might be entirely opened up to market forces. Free market ideologues calculated a £7 billion asset value and anticipated a privatisation to match the sell-offs of the other public utilities. The more inscrutable ideology of New Labour prompted Chris Smith, the culture secretary, to instruct BBC directors that they should calculate the BBC's worth as a brand. Meanwhile it has been business as usual ever since the last government renewed theBBC's Royal Charter for ten years until 2006. Thus BBC1 is still "the channel of wide appeal" and BBC2 "the channel of innovation and flexibility". BBC ratings have held up against the competition. It showed half the top 20 most popular programmes for 1997 and is the place people go to for big events: it had 19.29 million viewers for the Diana funeral, whereas ITV got 11.71 million.

AFTER PUNTERS ....

third broadcasting medium ... It enables our viewers and listeners to speak directly to the BBC."

DISCOVERY CHANNEL

In March 1998 the BBC took its largest single step toward commercialism with a £340 million deal with Discovery Channel to launch its own American cable channel and set up pay-for channels elsewhere. BBC America began broadcasting on 29 March with predictions it would reach 25 million US homes within a couple of years. Meanwhile BBC execs talked up a 400 million household global market.

PUBLISHING

There is nothing new about the BBC seeking to turn a profit, for it has been publishing the Radio Times for decades. In 1997 the BBC earned £118 million from its magazines.

... AND THE LICENCE FEE

While commercial ventures provided the BBC with £75 million extra cash flow in 1997-98, the 22 million licence fee payers created a revenue of £2.1 billion. Immediately before Christmas 1997 the culture secretary Chris Smith rubber-stamped an inflation plus (6.6 per cent) increase of the BBC annual licence to £97.50. Six months later the BBC management started lobbying for further inflation plus increases.

There are many opponents to the licence fee. Comedy writers Maurice Gran and Laurence Marks, for example,say:"We're of the generation that once took it as an article of faith that the BBC licence fee must be preserved. We now feel the fee has outlived its usefulness and should be scrapped. The BBC believes it must maintain market share to justify the licence fee. This forces the BBC to shadow ITV's programming, as it moves remorselessly towards the safe, the repetitive and the cloned."

BBC structure

The BBC is split into five directorates:

BBC MAIN OFFICES

BBC Corporate HQ & BBC Broadcast
Broadcasting House, Portland Place, London W1A 1AA
Fax 0171-637 1630   Tel 0171-580 4468
The hub of the BBC and the HQ for BBC Broadcast, including Regional Broadcasting.
BBC News and BBC Production
Television Centre, Wood Lane, London W12 7RJ
Fax 0181-749 7520   Tel 0181-743 8000
The HQ for BBC News and BBC Production, with the main television productionfacilities.
BBC Worldwide Television Publishing & Learning
Woodlands, 80 Wood Lane, London W12 0TT
Tel 0181-743 5588
Headquarters of BBC commercial activities.
BBC World Service
Bush House, PO Box 76, London WC2B 4PH
Tel 0171-240 3456
BBC White City
201 Wood Lane, London W12 7TS
Tel 0181-752 5252
New offices of several departments, including educational broadcasting, some current affairs production, personnel, finance and resources.
BBC Written Archives
Caversham Park Reading, Berks RG4 8TZ
Tel 01734-472742

BBC PRESS OFFICES

The main BBC press office is at Television Centre. Its opening hours are 8.30am to midnight on weekdays, and 10am to 11pm at the weekend. For specific enquiries, use Publicity numbers after the addresses on the following three pages.

Main press office   0181-576 1865
International press office 0171-257 2941

BBC TOP MANAGEMENT

Day-to-day decisions are taken by the Board of Management. The governors lay down broad policy guidelines, recruit senior staff, and are responsible for maintaining programme standards.

Appointments are for five years. The governors' responsibility for programmes is shared in Wales, Scotland and Northern Ireland with National Broadcasting Councils. The councils control the policy and content of broadcasting. The BBC also has a General Advisory Council, regional advisory councils in England, and local radio advisory councils.

BBC Board of Governors
Chairman: Sir Christopher Bland (to 31.3.01)
Vice-chairwoman: Baroness Young of Old Scone
National governor for Scotland: The Rev Norman Drummond (31.9.99)
National governor for Northern Ireland: Sir Kenneth Bloomfield KCB (31.7.99)
National governor for Wales: Roger Spencer Jones (31.12.01)
Other governors
Bill Jordan (31.7.98)
Dame Pauline Neville-Jones DCMG (31.12.01)
Mrs Margaret Spurr (31.7.98)
Mrs Janet Cohen (28.2.99)
Sir David Scholey (31.10.00)
Adrian White (31.10.00)
Richard Eyre (31.10.00)
BBC Executive Committee
Director general: John Birt
Chief executive, BBC Broadcast: Will Wyatt
Chief executive, BBC Production: Ronald Neil
Chief executive, BBC News: Tony Hall
Chief executive, BBC Resources: Rod Lynch
Managing director, World Service: Sam Younger
Chief executive, BBC Worldwide: Rupert Gavin
Director of personnel: Margaret Salmon
Director of finance: John Smith
Director of policy and planning: Patricia Hodgson CBE
Director of corporate affairs: Colin Browne
Board of Management
This comprises members of the executive committee, together with BBC Broadcast
Director of television: Alan Yentob
Director of radio: Matthew Bannister
Director of regional broadcasting: Mark Byford
Director of Education: Jane Drabble
BBC Production, Director of production: Jana Bennett

BBC directorates

BBC BROADCAST

BBC Broadcast HQ
Broadcasting House, London W1A 1AA
Fax: 0171-637 1630   Tel: 0171-580 4468
Chief executive, broadcast: Will Wyatt
Director, finance and business affairs: Tony Dignum
Head of financial control: Carolyn Foxall
Head of business affairs: Rowan Veevers/Judith Bennett
Director, marketing and communications: Sue Farr
Head of television press & publicity: Vanda Rumney
Director, broadcasting and presentation: Pam Masters
Senior technical advisor: David King
Controller, personnel: Kate Smith
Broadcast secretary: Angie Stephenson

BBC Television
Almost 14,000 hours of television programmes are broadcast per year on its two current channels BBC1 and BBC2. The great majority of programmes are commissioned from BBC Production, but BBC Broadcast has a statutory obligation to ensure that 25 per cent of its network television programmes are made by independent producers and, further, that a significant proportion are made in the regions outside London.

BBC Regional Broadcasting
About a third of network television and radio programmes are made outside London and the south east.

BBC Network Radio
In total BBC Radio broadcasts 33,000 hours of programming a year on Radios 1, 2, 3 and 4 (Radio 5 Live is part of the News Directorate).

BBC Education
BBC Education works across all media and provides "learning for life for everyone from early childhood to retirement". In the classroom, schools programmes cover

Over 2,000 hours of education and training programmes for schools and adults, on radio and television, are broadcast each year, with related books, videos or audio cassettes, and a developing range of digital services.

BBC Television
Television Centre, Wood Lane, London W12 7RJ
Fax 0171-749 7520   Tel 0181-743 8000

General publicity:	0181-225 6042
Drama publicity:	0181-576 1861
Entertainment publicity:	0181-576 7786
Sports publicity:	0181-576 1871
Factual programmes:	0181-752 6414
Music and Arts publicity:	0181-576 7714
Children's publicity:	0181-576 1860
Feature Films publicity:	0181-576 1868
Purchased programmes:	0181-576 1539
Religious publicity:	0161-244 4890

Director of television: Alan Yentob
Deputy director of television: David Docherty
Controller, BBC1: Peter Salmon
Controller, BBC2: Mark Thompson
Controller, television sport: Jonathan Martin
Controller, programme acquisition: Alan Howden
Head of purchased programmes: Sophie Turner Laing
Senior vice president, programme acquisition, USA: Rebecca Segal
Head of business and legal affairs: Simon Taylor
Head of independent commissioning (with responsibility for factual programming): Jane Root
Head of independent commissioning, entertainment: Bill Hilary
Head of independent commissioning, drama: Tessa Ross
Head of children's commissioning: Roy Thompson
Head of daytime commissioning: Jane Lush
Head of programming, BBC Choice: Katharine Everett
Controller, online & interactive: Edward Briffa

BBC Network Radio
Broadcasting House, Portland Place, London W1A 1AA

General publicity:	0171-765 2265
Radio 1 publicity:	0171-765 4575
Radio 2 publicity:	0171-765 5712
Radio 3 publicity:	0171-765 2722
Radio 4 publicity:	0171-765 5337
Radio 5 publicity:	0171-765 2139

Director of radio: Matthew Bannister (also controller, Radio 1)
Deputy controller, Radio 1: Andy Parfitt
Controller, Radio 2: Jim Moir
Controller, Radio 3: Nicholas Kenyon
Controller, Radio 4: James Boyle
Managing Editor, DAB: Glyn Jones

BBC Regional: general

Central: BBC White City (London HQ)
Broadcasting House, Portland Place, London W1A 1AA

Tel 0181-752 5252

Regional HQ Press office Tel 0171-765 2797

Director of regional broadcasting: Mark Byford
Deputy director, RB: Michael Stevenson
Financial controller: Peter White
Controller, English regions: Nigel Chapman
Head of press and publicity, regional broadcasting: Tim Brassell
Head of press and public affairs, English regions: Jerry Johns
Secretary, regional broadcasting: Moyra Tourlamain

BBC Scotland
Broadcasting House, Queen Margaret Drive, Glasgow G12 8DG

Tel 0141-338 2000

Controller, Scotland: John McCormick
Head of broadcasting: Ken MacQuarrie
Head of production: Colin Cameron
Head of drama: Barbara McKissack
Head of news and current affairs: Ken Cargill

BBC Wales
Broadcasting House, Llantrisant Road, Llandaff, Cardiff CF5 2YQ

Tel 01222-572888

Controller, Wales: Geraint Talfan Davies
Head of broadcast (Welsh): Gwynn Pritchard
Head of broadcast (English): Dai Smith
Head of production: John Geraint
Head of drama: Pedr James
Head of strategy and channel development: Keith Jones

BBC Northern Ireland
Broadcasting House, Ormeau Avenue, Belfast BT2 8HQ

Tel 01232-338000

Controller, Northern Ireland: Pat Loughrey
Head of broadcasting: Anna Carragher
Head of production: Paul Evans
Head of drama: Robert Cooper

BBC Regional: TV

The BBC divides Britain into six regions, three in England (Midlands/East, South and North) and Wales, Scotland and Northern Ireland. The HQ is in London. Below are regional HQs and TV centres; local radio stations are later on in the book.

BBC White City (London HQ)
201 Wood Lane, London W12 7TS

Tel 0181-752 5252

MIDLANDS & EAST

Birmingham (Regional HQ)
BBC, Pebble Mill, Birmingham B5 7QQ
Fax 0121-432 8634   Tel 0121-414 8888
Daily news programme: Midlands Today

Nottingham
York House, Mansfield Rd, Nottingham NG1 3JB
Fax 0115-955 0501   Tel 0115-955 0500
Daily news programme: East Midlands Today

Norwich
St Catherine's Close, All Saint's Green, Norwich, Norfolk NR13ND
Fax 01603-667865   Tel 01603-619331
Daily news programme: Look East

SOUTH

Bristol (Regional HQ)
Broadcasting House, Whiteladies Road, Bristol BS8 2LR

Tel 0117-973 2211

Daily news programme: News West

Elstree
Clarendon Road, Borehamwood, Herts WD6 1JF
Fax 0181-228 8092   Tel 0181-953 6100
Daily news programme: Newsroom South East

Southampton
Broadcasting House, Havelock Road, Southampton, Hants SO14 7PU
Fax 01703-339931   Tel 01703-226201
Daily news progamme: South Today

Plymouth
Broadcasting House, Seymour Road, Mannamead, Plymouth, Devon PL3 5BD
Fax 01752-234595   el 01752-229201
Daily news programme: Spotlight

NORTH

Manchester (Regional HQ)
New Broadcasting House, PO Box 27, Oxford Road, Manchester M60 1SJ
Fax 0161-236 1005 Tel 0161-200 2020
Daily news programme: North West Tonight

Leeds
Broadcasting Centre, Woodhouse Lane, Leeds, LS2 9PN
Fax 0113-243 9387 Tel 0113-244 1188
Daily news programe: Look North

Newcastle
Broadcasting Centre, Barrack Road, Newcastle-upon-Tyne NE99 2NE
Fax 0191-221 0112 Tel 0191-232 1313
Daily news programme: Look North.

SCOTLAND

Glasgow (National HQ)
Broadcasting House, Queen Margaret Drive, Glasgow G12 8DG
Fax 0141-334 0614 Tel 0141-338 2000
Daily news programme: Reporting Scotland

WALES

Cardiff (National HQ)
Broadcasting House, Llantrisant Road, Llandaff, Cardiff CF5 2YQ
Fax 01222-555960 Tel 01222-572888
Daily news programme: Wales Today

NORTHERN IRELAND

Belfast (National HQ)
Broadcasting House, Ormeau Avenue, Belfast BT2 8HQ
Fax 01232-338800 Tel 01232-338000
Daily news programme: Newsline 6.30

BBC Broadcast Strategy and Channel Management
Broadcasting House. Portland Place, London W1A 1AA
Fax 0171-765 5709 Tel 0171-565 1569
Director of strategy and channel management: Robin Foster
Controller, strategy and broadcasting analysis: Jane Scott
Head of channel management: Vaughan Williams
Head of strategic projects: Ian Hunter
Head of commissions and development BBC1: Don Cameron
Head of commissions and development BBC2: Jill Pack
Head of scheduling BBC1: Adam MacDonald
Scheduler BBC2: Matthew Tombs
Head of marketing & strategy, radio: Sophie McLaughlin
Head of strategy and broadcast analysis, television: Jeremy Olivier
Head of strategy and broadcast analysis, regional broadcasting: Peter Davies
Head of strategy, education: Mark Collinson
Head of performance analysis: Robin McCron

BBC Education
BBC White City, 201 Wood Lane, London W12 7TS
Fax 0181-752 4398 Tel 0181-752 5252
Press office Tel 0181-752 5152
Director of education: Jane Drabble
Head of commissioning, adults: Fiona Chesterton
Head of commissioning, schools and colleges: Frank Flynn
Head of strategy: Mark Collinson
Head of finance: Darryl Young
Head of policy: tba
Head of marketing: Dafna Israeli
Head of commissioning, OU: Paul Gerhardt
Head of learning channels and digital media: Jonathan Drori
Head of learning support: Steve Pollock
Personnel manager: Sue Hillman

BBC NEWS

BBC News is the biggest newsgathering operation in the world. It is a bi-media organisation with journalists reporting for BBC World Service radio and BBC World television as well as the BBC's UK radio and television outlets. BBC News has bureaux in 50 countries and 250 correspondents around the world - the largest network of foreign correspondents of any international broadcaster, and employs some 2,000 journalists in total.

There are four specialist units: foreign affairs; economics and business; politics; and social affairs. News crews are trained in health and safety, including battlefield first-aid, and are taught to minimise personal risk. They are equipped with flak jackets, helmets, medication and, when necessary, armoured vehicles and nuclear, biological and chemical warfare suits. They are trained in satellite and terrestrial broadcasting technology, so that film and audio reports can be transmitted back to the UK quickly and efficiently.

BBC News
Television Centre, Wood Lane, London W12 7RJ
Tel 0181-743 8000
Press office Tel 0181-576 7645
Chief executive, news: Tony Hall
Deputy to chief executive: Richard Ayre
Controller, finance: Peter Phillips
Controller, personnel: Lesley Hopkins
Controller media and public relations: Michele Grant
Controller, programme policy: Peter Bell
Head of newsgathering: Richard Sambrook
Head of business programmes: Helen Boaden
Deputy head: Ray Gowdridge
Head of news programmes: Richard Clemmow
Deputy head: Steve Mitchell
Executive editor bulletins: Malcolm Balen
Executive editor TV daily current affairs: Jon Barton
Executive editor radio daily current affairs: Anne Koch
Executive editor core news: John Morrison
Head of weekly programmes: tba
Head of political programmes: Mark Damazer
Deputy head: Alexandra Henderson
Editor, continuous news services: Jenny Abramsky
Controller, Radio 5 Live: Mike Lewis
Controller, television news channels: Tim Orchard
Managing editor, news 24: Margaret Budy
Head of production, continuous news: Michele Romaine

BBC PRODUCTION

The creation of BBC Production brought together 4,000 staff based in London, Bristol, Birmingham and Manchester. They make network programmes for BBC Television, BBC Radio and the BBC World Service, with an annual budget of £600 million. BBC Production is the largest single programme maker in Europe. There are 20 bi-media programme departments based in London and the English regions including BBC Sport, the Natural History Unit, Music, Drama, Features, Religion, Education and Children's, to Entertainment, Consumer/Leisure, Science, Documentaries/History and the Arts.

BBC Production
Television Centre, Wood Lane, London W12 7RJ
Tel 0181-743 8000
Press office Tel 0181-225 7892
Chief Executive, Production: Ronald Neil
Director of productions: Jana Bennett
Controller, production: Paula Higson
Controller, multimedia development: Caroline Millington
Controller, finance: Anne Bulford
Controller, personnel: Sandra Horne
Controller, drama production: Colin Adams
Head of drama series: Mal Young
Head of films and single drama: David Thompson
Senior executive, production BBC1 films & serials: Jane Tranter
Executive producer, Birmingham TV drama: Richard Longridge
Head of radio drama: Kate Rowland
Head of entertainment: Paul Jackson
Head of comedy: Geoffrey Perkins
Head of comedy entertainment: Jon Plowman
Head of factual entertainment: Tony Moss
Head of light entertainment: Mike Leggo
Head of sport: Bob Shennan
Head of science: Glenwyn Benson
Head of history unit: Keith Scholey
Head of features, Bristol: Jeremy Gibson
Head of network production, Birmingham: Rod Natkiel
Head of religion: Ernie Rea
Head of arts: Kim Evans
Head of entertainment features, Manchester: Wayne Garvie
Head of children's: Lorraine Hegessey
Head of education production: Marilyn Wheatcroft
Head of music entertainment: Trevor Dann
Head of documentaries and history: Paul Hamann
Head of classical music: Roger Wright
Head of commercial and business affairs: Chris Pye
Head of features and events: Anne Morrison

BBC RESOURCES

BBC Resources comprises the BBC's radio and television production plus support services. In the summer of 1998 the directorate was split into two new entities - BBC Resources, operating as a wholly owned subsiduary of the BBC, and Production Services.

BBC Resources has always had spare capacity due to the cyclical nature of the industry. As demand for BBC Production declined, demand from non-BBC customers grew to an extent which raised competition and use of public money issues.

Needing to continue to develop its external work to preserve the craft base, the BBC incorporated the relevant trading business units into a limited company - with transparent separate accounts. From 1 August 1998 the following were transferred to BBC Resources: Location Resources; Television Studio Production Resources; Post Production and Graphic Design; Resources Wales, Scotland and Northern Ireland; and the non-news operation in the English regions.

Operating from London and 20 other bases nationwide, BBC Resources supplies the entire range of broadcast facilities. These are available to programme-makers and the corporate world alike. Its external businesses including location resources for ITV's Formula 1 motor racing coverage and the recent launch of Ford's touring car team in Television Centre's largest studio. For details of all services across the UK, BBC Resources can be contacted on 0645 883883 .

BBC Resources Directorate
201 Wood Lane, London W12 7TS
                Tel 0181-752 5252
Press office Tel 0181-752 4047
Chief Executive: Rod Lynch
Company Secretary/Legal Adviser: Rikki Nath
Chief Operating Offier: Michael Lumley (acting)
Director of Sales & Marketing: Paula Carter
Head of Strategy: Olivier Garrigue
Controller, production services: John Lightfoot (acting)

BBC WORLDWIDE

BBC Worldwide was formed in May 1994 to coordinate the BBC's international and commercial activities. It encompasses cable and satellite channels and international programme distribution and publishing.

A joint venture with Flextech led to the the launch of three channels - UK Horizons, UK Arena and UK Style - and the relaunch of UK Gold, all under the banner of UKTV. A further joint venture with Discovery was signed in March. This deal has resulted in the launch of the BBC America plus two global joint venture channels, Animal Planet and People & Arts. BBC Worldwide's other channel interests are in BBC World, the BBC's 24 hour international news and information channel, available in more than 52 milliion homes in 187 countries and territories, and BBC Prime, an entertainment channel for Europe, which has nearly six million subscribers. BBC Worldwide is also a 20 per cent shareholder in UK TV, an entertainment subscription channel in Australia, along with Pearson and Foxtel.

BBC Worldwide is the UK's third largest consumer magazine publisher with 23 titles. During 1997/98 circualtions rose 15 per cent and four titles were launched - Teletubbies, BBC Family Life, BBC Good Homes and BBC Tomorrow's World.

BBC Worldwide
Woodlands, 80 Wood Lane, London W12 OTT
Fax 0181-749 0538   Tel 0181-576 2000
Press office   Tel 0181-576 2339
Website: http://www.bbcworldwide.com
Chief executive: Rupert Gavin
Managing director, UK region & deputy chief executive: Peter Teague
Managing director EMIA: Mark Young
Acting director of finance: David King
Director, rights agency: Mike Phillips
Director, new media: Jeremy Mayhew
Managing director, BBC World: Patrick Cross
Director, human resources: Bob McCall
Director, global brand development: Jeff Taylor
Director of strategy: Carolyn Fairbairn
Director of communications: Janie Ironside Wood
President and chief executive officer of BBC Worldwide Americas: Peter Phippen
Chief operating officer of JVP: Candace Carlisle

Independent TV/ITC

The Independent Television Commission's job is to limit the independence of independent broadcasters. It is a statutory corporation which derives it power from the 1990 and 1996 Broadcasting Acts, and its wide-ranging remit is to "ensure fair and effective competition in the provision of television programme services".

The ITC is thus responsible for licensing non-BBC television services in Britain, including the 16 Channel 3 companies, Channels 4 and 5, the 85 "licensable programme services" on cable and the 170 "satellite programme services". During the past year it has it has awarded digital terrestrial to BDB and Digital 3 & 4, and the new terrestrial local Restricted Service Licences which are covered later on in the book.

A major effect of the 1996 Broadcasting Act was the power given to the ITC to apply a public interest test to acquisitions and mergers. It was first applied to the first incarnation of BDB, and an ITC ruling granted the digital licence only on condition Sky was decoupled from the original consortium. During the latter half of 1997 it kept its fangs drawn in deciding that two commercial marriages - Grampian's merger with the Scottish Media Group and United News and Media's take-over of HTV - did not operate against the public interest.

When licensees fail to comply with these and other conditions set out in the Broadcasting Act and in individual licences, the ITC imposes penalties ranging from warnings and the requirement to broadcast an apology, to fines and the shortening or revocation of a licence.

The ITC maintains an excellent broadcasting library and archive at its head office and generally brings together information from the disparate sector it scrutinises. The following paragraphs are from its annual report: "Total revenue for the commercial television sector in the UK in 1997 amounted to £4,733 million, an increase of 14 per cent when compared with 1996. Advertising remains the principal source of revenue, accounting for almost 56 per cent of the total. Although there was a 9 per cent increase in advertising revenue to £2,648 million, its share declined from 58 per cent in 1996. The satellite and cable programme service licensees experienced the biggest increase in advertising revenue, with a 50 per cent jump, and consequently their aggregate market share increased from 8 per cent to 11 per cent.

"Just under half the income for commercial television as a whole was devoted to the production, commissioning and acquisition of programmes. The proportions are 53 per cent for Channel 3 and 58 per cent for Channel 4, with the percentage for BSkyB being somewhat lower at 45 per cent.

"The number employed on a permanent, contract or freelance basis increased in 1997 to 12,800. (People employed in related businesses such as airtime sales houses and some Channel 3 programme production companies are excluded.) Forty-four per cent of the total worked in programme areas. There were increases in the number employed by Channel 3 licensees (32 staff), and there was an increase of 375 staff, principally in subscriber management, at BSkyB."

Independent TV money I: Total revenue, £4.7 billion		
CHANNEL	1996	1997
Channel 3	54%	48%
Cable & satellite	31%	36%
Channel 4	13%	12%
Other	2%	4%

Total include sponsorship, subscription, sale of goods, programme sales and other income

Independent TV money II: Advertising revenue, £2.6 billion		
CHANNEL	1996	1997
Channel 3	72%	66%
Channel 4	20%	20%
Cable & satellite	8%	11%
Channel 5	-	3%

Ad revenue grew from £2.4 billion in '96 to £2.6 billion in '97

The ITC is a regulator as well as a licensor and there are five categories of Channel 3 programmes for which the ITC sets minimum requirements.

1) **News:** three programmes each weekday with 20 minutes at lunchtime, 15 minutes early evening and half an hour in peak times. This requirement is met by ITN.
2) **Current affairs:** an average of one and a half hours a week.
3) **Children:** ten hours weekly average
4) **Religion:** two hours weekly average
5) **Regious programmes:** minimum amounts vary from one region to another.

'97-'98 programme budgets

CHANNEL	£ MILLION
BBC 1	£652.5m
ITV	£620m
BBC 2	£346.8m
Channel 4	£320m
Channel 5	£110m

Source: Royal Television Society

The big five independents

BSKB
BSkyBhas the highest income of all independent TV companies
GRANADA
Granada is the second largest independent TV company, with an income two thirds of BSkyB, owns **Granada TV, LWT** and has shares in **BDB, Yorkshire TV** and **BSkyB**
CARLTON
Carlton has half BSkyB's income. It owns **Carlton TV, Central TV** and **Westcountry Television** and has shares in **BDB** and **GMTV**
MAI
MAI owns **Anglia TV** and **Meridian TV** and has shares in **Yorkshire TV, HTV** and **C5**
CHANNEL 4
Channel 4 is two fifths the size of BSkyB

ITC Head Office
33 Foley Street, London W1P 7LB
Fax 0171-306 7800   Tel 0171-255 3000
E-mail: ITC_general@compuserve.com
Website: http://www.itc.co.uk
Chief executive: Peter Rogers
Director of programmes& cable: Sarah Thane
Director of advertising and sponsorship: Frank Willis
Director of regions & public affairs: Paul Smee
Director of engineering: Gary Tonge
Director of administration: Michael Redley
Secretary to the Commission: Michael Redley

ITC board of members
Chairman: Sir Robin Biggam
Chairman of the Fairey Group, non-executive dirctor of British Aerospace, British Energy and Redland.
Deputy chairman: Earl of Dalkeith
Director of Buccleuch Estates.
Alastair Balls
Chief exec of Tyne & Wear Development Corporation.
Dr John Beynon
Member of the British Library Advisory Council.
Sir Michael Checkland,
Non-executive director of Nynex Cablecoms,a trustee of Reuters, and former director general of the BBC
Jude Goffe,
Venture capitalist and non-executive director of Moorfields Eye Hospital
Eleri Wynne Jones,
Member for Wales, and a lecturer in psychotherapy.
Dr Maria Moloney,
Member for Northern Ireland, and member of the Industrial Development Board for Northern Ireland.
John Ranelagh,
Producer and media consultant and former secretary to the board of Channel 4.
Dr Michael Shea
Member for Scotland. Writer and broadcaster and visiting professor of personal and corporate communications at the University of Strathclyde.

ITC National and regional offices:

Northern Ireland	01232-248733
Scotland	0141-226 4436
Wales	01222-384541
East of England	01603-623533
Midlands - Birmingham	0121-693 0662
Midlands - Nottingham	0115-952 7333
North East England	0114-276 9091
North of England	0191-261 0148
North West England	0161-834 2707
S of England, Winchester	01962-883950
S of England, Plymouth	01752-663031
West of England	01222-384541

ITC Engineering/Research/Finance:
Kings Worthy Court, Kings Worthy, W i n c h e s t e r, Hants SO23 7QA
Fax 01962-886141   Tel 01962-848600

Channel 3 companies

Channel 3 (aka ITV) consists of 15 regional licensees and the GMTV national breakfast station. They divide the UK into 14 regions, all but one of which has a single Channel 3 company monopolising regional broadcasting rights. The exception is London, where there is a split between Carlton on weekdays and LWT at weekends. Channel 3's record 26 million England v Argentina audience in July 1998 notwithstanding, the audience share continues falling. Taken as a whole, Channel 3 can still claim to be the nation's most popular broadcaster but only by a whisker with its 1997 viewing figure only a fraction ahead of BBC1. Competition from Channel 5, cable and satellite has meant Channel 3's share of a growing TV advertising has fallen and that its 1997 ad receipts of £1.7 billion did not rise from 1996. The good news for the ITV owners is that a successful lobbying campaign has resulted in the ITC promising to reduce licence fees from current levels of £420 million a year to as low as £150 million. This will happen from 2003 and negotiations for these licence renewals have already begun.

Current legislation prevents any one company from serving more than 15 per cent of the audience or the merging of the two London stations. However those rules could be relaxed in the face of a commercial logic which says the current ITV structure is too cumbersome to compete, and speculation continues that there may be legislative changes to allow just one or two ITV companies.

For the present, the stations must concentrate on improving programmes to maintain their share of audiences and advertising. The consistent regulator's complaint on scheduling has been about caution and predictability. It says factual programming has leaned too heavily on sensationalising crime and that international issues have had minimal coverage. The ITC, anxious to give praise where it is due, says: "Amongst welcome developments the volume of documentaries, arts and children's drama increased in response to concerns expressed in 1996. One of the key successes of 1997 was the increased coverage of ITV Sport following the acquisition of rights to motor racing, soccer and rugby."

The cost of programmes in 1997 was £822 million, a single percentage increase on 1996. The majority of this budget - £551 million - was accounted for by the Network Centre. ITV Network Centre is wholly owned by the ITV companies and it commissions and schedules programmes shown across the network. In January 1998 Richard Eyre, ITV's new chief executive, pledged that a revised programme strategy would reverse audience decline and regain a 2 per cent share over the next two years.

Channel 3 news is produced at ITV Network Centre's HQ in Gray's Inn Road, by Independent Television News. It has a weekly output of some 30 hours, including News at Ten and Early Evening News. ITN also supplies Channel 4 and Channel 5 news. ITN took over operating control of Euronews in November 1997. Euronews is a pan-European broadcaster which transmits TV news in six languages to 43 countries for 20 hours a day.

ITV Network Centre
200 Grays Inn Road, London WC1X 8HF
Fax 0171-843 8158   Tel 0171-843 8000
Council of ITV Association chairman: Leslie Hill
Chief executive: Richard Eyre
Children's programmes: Nigel Pickard
Drama: Nick Elliot
Entertainment: Claudia Rosencrantz
Documentary/factual: Grant Mansfield
Head of sport production: Brian Barwick
News/current affairs, religion: Steve Anderson

ITN
200 Grays Inn Road, London WC1X 8XZ
Fax 0171-430 4016 (news)
                                Tel 0171-833 3000
Press office   Tel 0171-430 4700
Website: http://www.itn.co.uk
ITN's UK television programmes have a total weekly output of 29 hours including News at Ten, Early Evening News, C4 News and Channel 5 News.

Euronews
60 Chemin des Moules, BP 161, 69131 Lyon, France
Fax: 0033 4 72 18 93 71 Tel: 0033 4 72 18 80 00
Website: www.euronews.net

Anglia Television

Anglia House, Norwich, Norfolk NR1 3JG
Fax 01603-631032   Tel 01603-615151
E-mail: angliatv@angliatv.co.uk
Website: http://www.anglia.tv.co.uk
London office: 48 Leicester Square, WC2H 7FB
Fax 0171-493 7677   Tel 0171-389 8555
Regional newsrooms:

Norwich	01603-619261
Cambridge	01223-467076
Chelmsford	01245-357676
Ipswich	01473-226157
Luton	01582-29666
Milton Keynes	01908-691660
Northampton	01604-624343
Peterborough	01733-269440

Covers: East of England.
Owner: United News and Media
Regional news programme: Anglia News East/West.
1993-2002 licence fee: £17.8 million pa.

ITC 1997 Performance Review: "Anglia Television improved the regional identity of its service in 1997, strengthening its relationship with the east of England audience. It addressed criticisms in the ITC's 1996 review, reducing both co-productions and repeats, and creating new series, which enhanced the coverage of arts activities in the region. Some initiatives, including the staging of the national awards for regional theatre in Norwich and regional business awards in Cambridge, added diversity to the schedule. A half-hour news programme was added to late Friday evening. The amount of regional programmes commissioned from independent producers fell from 34 per cent of qualifying programmes in 1996 to 25 per cent in 1997."

Chairman: David McCall.
Managing director: Graham Creelman
Director of programmes and production:
    Malcolm Allsop
Controller news: Guy Adams
Press and regional affairs: Martin Morrall

Border Television

The Television Centre, Carlisle, Cumbria CA1 3NT
Fax 01228-541384   Tel 01228-525101
Website: http://www.border-tv.com
Newsroom: 01228-829229
Covers: Scottish borders, Lake District and the Isle of Man. Also has local radio involvement.
Owner: Border Television; largest shareholder Cumbrian Newspapers Group (18 per cent).
Regional news programme: Look Around, Border News.
1993-2002 licence fee: £52,000 pa.

ITC 1997 Performance Review: "1997 was a milestone year for Border Television. Scottish devolution provided the greatest impetus for reassessment in the 38 year history of the company and its unique cross-broder service. Against this background, Border had a strong year in programme terms, marked in particular by its first venture into regional drama. There were also particular successes in factual and arts series, while the weekday evening news magazine sustained its high standards and continued to enjoy the highest ratings of any regional news magazine. The company supplied a second religious series to the network. The ITC feels that more regional programmes should be shown in peak, especially given the quality of material produced. Border deserves special credit for the drama 'Writing on the Edge' which gave budding local writers the opportunity to display their talent."

Chairman: James Graham
Chief executive: Paul Corley
Managing director: Peter Brownlow
Controller of programmes: Neil Robinson
Head of news: Ian Proniewicz

CARLTON COMMUNICATIONS

Carlton Communication's prime asset is Carlton Television which is made up of three licensees - Carlton Broadcasting, Central Broadasting and Westcountry. Carlton Broadcasting is responsible for the ITV regional licence for London weekdays and the South East, Central Broadcasting for the Midlands and Westcountry for ITV in the south West of England.

Carlton Productions produces network and regional programmes for both Carlton and Central Broadcasting and for other national and international markets. Carlton Sales sells airtime and sporsorship for all three broadcasters.

Carlton Television also operates two facilities operations - Carlton Studios in Nottingham supplying studios and related services and Carlton 021, the largest commercial operator of outside broadcast services in Europe.

Carlton Communications
25 Knightsbridge, London SW1X 7RZ
Fax 0171-663 6300   Tel 0171-663 6363
Chairman: Michael Green
Managing director: June de Moller
Finance director: Bernard Cragg
Director for broadcasting: Nigel Walmsley

Carlton Television

101 St Martins Lane, London WC2N 4AZ
Fax 0171-240 4171   Tel 0171-240 4000
E-mail: dutyoffice@carltontv.co.uk
Website: http://www.carltontv.co.uk
ITC 1997 Performance Review: "Carlton's new early evening schedule contained a diverse range of regional material but, at a fiercely competitive part of the day, found ratings success a little more elusive. Regional news and social action programmes were strengths, and programmes of all types combined high production values with a good regional focus. The minimum licence figures in all regional programme categories were exceeded, by first-run material in most cases. Carlton again provided high quality programmes, especially drama and children's TV."
Covers: London area, from 0600 Monday to 1715 Friday
Owner: Carlton Communications (100 per cent).
Chairman: Nigel Walmsley
Chief executive: Clive Jones
Director of programmes: Steve Hewlett
Chief executive, Carlton sales: Martin Bowley
Finance director: Mike Green
Controller business affairs: Martin Baker
Controller of regional & public affairs: Hardeep Kalsi
Legal affairs: Don Christopher

Carlton Productions
35-38 Portman Square, London W1H 0NU
Fax 0171-486 1132   Tel 0171 486 6688
Carlton Studios, Lenton Lane, Notts NG7 2NA
Fax 0115-964 5552   Tel 0115-986 3322
Website: http://www.carltontv.co.uk
Carlton Productions makes regional and network programmes for Carlton Broadcasting and Central Broadcasting.
Director of programmes: Andy Allan
Director of drama and co-production: Jonathan Powell
Entertainment and comedy: John Bishop
Factual programmes: Steve Clark
Children's programmes: Michael Forte
Network affairs: Claire Lummis
Finance director: Martin McCausland
Community programmes unit: Peter Lowe
Commissioning & network business affairs: Tom Betts
Production executive, Carlton Films: William Turner

Broadcasting
London Television Centre, Upper Ground, London SE1 9LT
Fax 0171-827-7500   Tel 0171-620 1620
Central House, Broad Street, Birmingham B1 2JP
Fax 0121-643 4897   Tel 0121-643 9898
Controller of broadcasting: Coleena Reid
Finance director: Ian Hughes
Promotions: Jim Stokoe
Acquisitions: George McGhee
Presentation, Carlton Broadcasting: Wendy Chapman
Presentation, Central Broadcasting: David Burge

Carlton Broadcasting
101 St Martins Lane, London WC2N 4AZ
Fax 0171-240 4171   Tel 0171-240 4000
Chairman: Nigel Walmsley
Managing Director: Colin Stanbridge

Carlton Studios
Lenton Lane, Nottingham NG7 2NA
Fax 0115-9645552   Tel 0115-9863322
A facilites operation providing studios and related services.
Managing director: Ian Squires
Director of operations: Paul Flanaghan
Production controller: John Revill

Carlton 021
12-13, Gravelly Hill Industrial Estate, Gravelly Hill, Birmingham B24 8HZ
Fax 0121-327 7021   Tel 0121-327 2021
Carlton's outside broadcasting service.
Managing director: Ed Everest
Business manager: Mike McGowan
Head of operations: Rob Hollier
Chief engineer: John Fisher

Central Broadcasting

Central Court, Gas Street, Birmingham B1 2JT
Fax 0121-634 4414   Tel 0121-643 9898
                      Press office 01159-863322
Website: http://www.carltontv.co.uk
London Television Centre, Upper Ground, London SE1 9LT
Fax 0171-827-7500   Tel 0171-620 1620

Carlton Studios
Lenton Lane, Nottingham NG7 2NA
Fax 0115-964 5552   Tel 0115-986 3322
Unit 9, Windrush Court, Abingdon Business Park, Abingdon OX14 1SA
Fax 01235-524024   Tel 01235-554123
Covers: English Midlands
Owner: Carlton Communications
Regional news programme: Central News East/ South/ West.
1993-2002 licence fee: £2,000 pa.

ITC 1997 Performance Review: "Central delivered a popular and high quality schedule of regional and network programmes. Midlands interests and characteristics were well reflected in a good range of regional and sub-regional programmes, including a high quality news service. Proposals outlined in 1996 for changes to social action programming were successfully implemented and a licence variation, to replace regional drama with additional factual, sport and news material, provided further enhancements. Construction of a new studio centre in Birmingham was completed and opened as planned. Technical problems resulting from the changeover to digital systems presented a challenge to the company but caused limited disruption to viewers. Central continued to make a substantial contribution to the network schedule. However, there is still scope to produce more arts/entertainment material to reflect the particular interests of young black viewers."

Chairman: Nigel Walmsley
Managing director: Ian Squires
Finance director: Ian Hughes
News and operations: Laurie Upshon
Presentation & planning: David Burge
Promotions: Mike Villiers-Stuart
Regional programmes: Mike Blair
Regional affairs: Kevin Johnson
Technical director: Mike Snalam

Channel Television

Television Centre, La Pouquelaye, St Helier, Jersey, Channel Islands JE1 3ZD
Fax 01534-816817   Tel 01534-816816
E-mail: newsroom@channeltv.co.uk
Website: http://www.channeltelevision.co.uk
Regional newsrooms:
  Guernsey   01481-41877
  Jersey   01534-816688
Covers: Channel Islands
Owner: Channel Islands Communications (TV), whose largest shareholders are Lapwing Investments (28 per cent) and 3i Capital Jersey (8.42 per cent).
Regional news programme: Channel Report
1993-2002 licence fee: £1,000 pa.

ITC 1997 Performance Review: "Channel Television underwent major changes in 1997 both on and off-screen. The weekday news programme Channel Report was revamped and a new studio opened in Guernsey. A new management structure was created. There was also the death of presenter Paul Brown. In spite of the general upheaval, Channel provided a service, which was well appreciated by viewers, including comprehensive coverage of local elections and the Island Games. A second drama series for teenagers was supplied to the network."

Deputy Chairman: Julian Mounter
Chief executive: John Henwood
Managing director, licensee: Michael Lucas
Head of programmes: Karen Rankine
Head of resources & transmission: Tim Ringsdore
Head of sales: Gordon de Ste Croix
Financial director: Charles Day

GMTV

London Television Centre, Upper Ground, London SE1 9TT
Fax 0171-827 7009   Tel 0171-827 7000
GMTV took over the ITV network breakfast-time service from TV-am in January 1993. Weekday programmes cover news, topical interviews, live reports, entertainment and lifestyle. Children's programming is provided at the weekend. The Sunday Programme from 0700 to 0800 deals with the week's political issues.
Covers: National, breakfast time from 0600-0925 daily.
Owners: Walt Disney (25 per cent), the Granada Group (20 per cent), Scottish TV (20 per cent), Carlton Communications (20 per cent), Guardian Media Group (15 per cent).
1993-2002 licence fee: £34.61 million pa.
News programme: News Hour.

ITC 1997 Performance Review: "GMTV performed very well in a year when breakfast-time television became ever more competitive. Audiences for cable and satellite television, and in particular children's programmes on other terrestrial networks, increased. There was some decline in the company's financial position, and programme-making resources were not all that GMTV would have wished. Against this competitive background, the company's performance was creditable, holding its leading share of audiences, and providing a programme service of high overall quality Two breaches of the Programme Code were recorded, but there were no problems with programme sponsorship of the kind found in previous years. It was disappointing that the commitment given by GMTV to improving the quality of information programming for children seemed to have come to a halt in 1997."

Commercial director: Simon Davey
Managing director: Christopher Stoddart
Sales and marketing: Clive Crouch
Finance co-ordinator: Rhian Jones
Director of programmes: Peter McHugh
Editor: Gerard Melling
Mananging editor, GMTV: John Scammell
Managing editor, Reuters: Henry Clark
Press and publicity: Sue Brealey
Personnel: Rhian Jones

Grampian Television

Queen's Cross, Aberdeen, Grampian AB15 4XJ
Fax 01224-846800   Tel 01224-846560
Personnel: Tel 01224-846846
E-mail: gtv@grampaintv.co.uk
Other production studios:
Seaforth House, 54 Seaforth Road, Stornoway HS1 2SD
Fax 01851-706406   Tel 01851-704433
Regional newsrooms:
    Inverness   01463-242624
Covers: North Scotland
Owner: Grampian Television, whose largest shareholders are Edinburgh Fund Managers (9.5 per cent), Abtrust Fund Managers (8.08 per cent), D Thomson & Co (5.57 per cent) and Aberforth Partners (5.90 per cent). 1997 pre-tax profits: £11.82 million.
Regional news programme: North Tonight.
1993-2002 licence fee: £720,000 pa.index-linked

ITC 1997 Performance Review: "A number of staff changes at management and executive board level happened early in 1997, at a time when the possibility of a merger with Scottish Media Group was becoming more than just idle gossip. The rumours became fact towards the end of the year. The immediate result of the merger was a further reorganisation of the staffing structure. Despite the unsettling effect of these changes, Grampians's performance over the year was confident and included impressive factual programmes, some of which won awards. Gaelic output was also generally strong. 'The National Television Awards' was again the only network contribution, although a range of proposals were put forward. The 9.00pm news bulletin was dropped and that at 10.30pm reduced from 2 minutes to 1 minute. However a news bulletin was introduced at around 11.30pm."

Chairman: Calum Macleod
Controller: Alastair Gracie
Deputy chairman and chief executive: Donald Waters
Director of prgrammes: George Mitchell
Head of Gaelic: Robert Kenyon
Chief engineer: John Robertson
Head of broadcasting services: Derrick Thomson
Head of PR: Michael McLintock
Property and administration: Saddiq Ahmed
Personnel: Elizabeth Gray
Deputy company secretary: Brian Hay
Operations manager (Stornoway): Murdo Maclennan

Granada Television

The Granada Group has four businesses in restaurants, hotels, rental and media.

Granada Media Group controls Granada Television, LWT, Yorkshire and Tyne Tees. Granada TV is the ITV's biggest programme supplier.

Granada Television
Quay Street, Manchester M60 9EA
Fax 0161-827 2029   Tel 0161-832 7211
London office:
TV Centre, Upper Ground, London SE1 9LT
Fax 0171-261 3307(press)
                            Tel 0171-620 1620
Website: http://www.granadatv.co.uk
Regional newsrooms:
　Blackburn   01254-690099
　Chester   01244-313966
　Lancaster   01524-60688
　Liverpool   0151-709 9393
　Manchester   0161-832 7211
Covers: North-west England.
Owner: Granada Group
Regional news programme: Granada Tonight.
1993-2002 licence fee: £9 million pa.

ITC 1997 Performance Review: "Granada responded positively to criticism in the 1996 review by comfortably exceeding the minimum regional requirement with new material which was of more relevance to the North West and contained some welcome new ideas. A strong regional service was complemented by continued excellence on the network, with Granada providing high quality programmes across a wide range of programme strands. The effort put into developing new comedy formats was particularly welcome. However, the way in which Granada handled some programme complaints, including those about changes to 'Coronation Street', was unsatisfactory and its complaints procedure was amended following ITC guidance."

Chairman: Charles Allen
Chief executive: Steve Morrison
MD, Granada TV: Brenda Smith
Joint MDs, Granada Productions: Jules Burns, Andrea Wonfor
Commercial and media development director: Kate Stross
Director of programmes: Simon Shaps
Sales director: Mick Desmond
Controller of comedy: Andy Harries
Controller of entertainment: Duncan Grey
Head of factual programmes: Charles Tremayne
Controller of drama: Simon Lewis
Head of regional programmes: Sue Woodward
Director of personnel: Philippa Hird
Director of public affairs: Chris Hopson

HTV

HTV (Cymru) Wales, Television Centre, Culverhouse Cross, Cardiff CF5 6XJ
Fax 01222-597183   Tel 01222-590590
Website: http://www.htv.co.uk

West
TV Centre, Bath Road, Bristol, BS4 3HG
Fax 0117-972 2400   Tel 01179-972 2722
E-mail: htv@htv.co.uk
Website: http://www.htv.co.uk
Regional newsrooms:
　Cardiff   01222-590754
　Carmarthen   01267-236806
　Colwyn Bay   01492-534555
　Newtown   01686-623381
　Taunton   01823-270293
Covers: Wales and Bristol, Gloucestershire, Somerset and Wiltshire.
Regional news programme: Wales Tonight, the West Tonight.
1993-2002 licence fee: £20.53 million pa.

ITC 1997 Performance Review: "1997 was dominated by the restructuring of HTV following the take-over by United News & Media at the end of July. Several senior members of staff left. However, HTV Wales and HTV West retained separate management structures within the United group and programme making areas saw few job losses. The programme services were diverse and overall of high quality. Most weaknesses identified in the two previous ITC reviews were addressed satisfactorily. In Wales, documentary and feature programming and weekend news output improved, although repeat levels in certain strands were still a concern. In the West a major development was the opening in April of the new digital Regional Broadcast Centre in Bristol, bringing significant improvements in news. For the second year running, the supply to the network, principally of drama and children's programmes, increased significantly."

HTV
Managing director: Malcolm Wall

HTV Wales
Chairman: Gerald Davies
Managing director: Menna Richards
Light entertainment: Emlyn Penny Jones
Programme planning: Sian Thomas
Press and PR: Mansel Jones

HTV West
Chairman: Louis Sherwood
Managing director: Jeremy Payne
Press and PR: Richard Lister

London Weekend Television (LWT)

London Television Centre, Upper Ground, London SE1 9LT
Fax 0171-261 1290   Tel 0171-620 1620
Newsroom (LNN)   Tel 0171-827 7700
Website: http://www.lwt.co.uk
Covers: London area, from 1715 Friday until 0600 Monday.
Owner: Granada Group, whose largest shareholder is SG Warburg. LWT splits into LWT Productions, LNN, the London News Network (a joint news gathering and production venture between LWT and Carlton TV), and The London Studios which has production facilities for hire to independent producers and the corporate sector.
Regional news programme: London Today, provided by LNN.
1993-2002 licence fee: £7.59 million pa.

ITC 1997 Performance Review: "LWT made some changes to its regional programming in 1997, modifying the style and content of its main current affairs programme and - in response to viewers' declared preferences - introducing new lifestyle programmes. Overall the regional service was attractive and varied. However, the arrival of network Formula One coverage on ITV reduced the availability of valuable regional slots at Sunday lunchtime. LWT was again a major supplier of programmes to the network, particularly in drama, entertainment and arts. With some notable exceptions, however, much of the material continued to rely on familiar faces and approaches."

Chairman: Charles Allen
Chief executive: Steve Morrison
Managing director: Eileen Gallagher
Director of programmes: Simon Shaps
Chairman of LNN: Clive Jones
Managing director of The London Studios: Harry Urquhart
Public affairs: Chris Hopson
Controller of entertainment: Nigel Lythgoe
Controller of drama: Sally Head
Controller of arts: Melvyn Bragg
Controller of factual: James Allen

Meridian Broadcasting

Television Centre, Northam, Southampton SO14 0PZ
Fax 01703-335050   Tel 01703-222555
Website: http://www.meridian.tv.co.uk
London office: Ludgate House, 245 Blackfriars Road, London SE1 9UY
Fax 0171-579 4435   Tel 0171-579 4400
Regional centres:
    New Hythe, Kent   01622-882244
    Newbury, Berks   01635-522322
Covers: South and south-east England
Owner: United News & Media (76 per cent), Carlton Communications (20 per cent). Meridian took over its region from TVS in January 1993.
1993-2002 licence fee: £36.52 million pa.

ITC 1997 Performance Review: "The regional service provided by Meridian improved in several areas in 1997, including current affairs and arts. Criticisms in the 1996 review relating to shortfalls against licence requirements in certain strands were addressed and there was a welcome increase in new material overall. The ITC remained concerned about the particular regional relevance of certain programmes and the quality of regional entertainment programmes. However, the licensee deserves credit for trying out new ideas and for the wide range and general high quality of material provided. Meridian again slightly increased its supply of programmes to the network in 1997 and rightly won widespread praise for commissioning the uncompromising documentary, 'No Child of Mine', shown in February. The ITC's Viewer Consultative Council felt that the poor quality of the on-screen advice offered on the series 'Home Truths' undermined the effectiveness of the series."

Chief executive: Roger Laughton
Managing director: Mary McAnally
Director of public affairs: Simon Albury
Director of finance: Tim Ricketts
Director of broadcasting: Richard Platt
Director of news, sport and current affairs: Jim Raven
Personnel: Peter Ashwood
Press & PR: John Morrell

Scottish Television

Cowcaddens, Glasgow G2 3PR
Fax 0141-300 3030   Tel 0141-300 3000
Website: http://www.stv.co.uk
London: 20 Lincoln's Inn Field, London WC2A 3ED
Fax 0171-446 7010   Tel 0171-446 7000
Scottish Television continues to achieve the highest
audience share of all broadcasters in Central Scotland at
35.5 per cent, remaining above the ITV national average
and with a lead over its nearest challenger, BBC1.
Covers: Central Scotland and south-west Highlands.
Owner: Flextech (5.95 per cent), Flextech Investments
(13.90 per cent), Scottish Daily Record/Sunday Mail
(19.81 per cent), Chase Nominees (5.38 per cent), FMR
Corp (4.94%).
Regional news programme: Scotland Today.
1993-2002 licence fee: £2,000 pa.

ITC 1997 Performance Review: "Scottish Television
maintained the high quality of its regional
programming in 1997 and increased the amounts of
current affairs and documentaries. In a momentous
year for Scotland, political coverage was particularly
comprehensive. A new multicultural series was also a
welcome initiative. Gaelic programmes met the
minimum requirements and included high quality
material. Some well-received documentary
programmes were added to Scottish Television's
established nework strands, drama, entertainment and
children's, although the amount of programmes
supplied to the network continued to fall. The ITC was
concerned at the company's decision to drop Scottish
Parliamentary Question Time; the decision went
against the spirit of Scottish Television's core
programming proposals."

Chairman: Gus MacDonald
Managing director: Andrew Flanagan
Director of finance: Gary Hughes
Managing director of broadcasting: Donald Emslie
Head of public affairs: Bob Tomlinson
Head of news: Mark Smith
Head of sport: Ian Crawford
Head of current affairs: Alan Smart
Personnel: Gerry Stevenson

Tyne Tees Television

City Road, Newcastle-upon-Tyne NE1 2AL
Fax 0191-261 2302   Tel 0191-261 0181
E-mail: tttv.regional.affairs@gmg.co.uk
Covers: North East England and North Yorkshire.
Owner: Granada Media Group since 1997
Regional news programmes: North East Tonight.
1993-2002 licence fee: £17 million pa.

ITC 1997 Performance Review: "Significant
developments took place at Tyne Tees both on and off-
screen in 1997. The arrival of a new managing director
and the departure of the director of programmes were
followed by a period of considerable uncertainty
surrounding the merger between Yorkshire Tyne Tees
Televison Holdings and Granada Media Group. A new
management structure and further changes in senior
staff were announced at the end of the year. In the
circumstances Tyne Tees performed well in programme
terms. The introduction of a regional drama series was
a creditable attempt to add diversity to the schedule,
although it met with limited success in audience
ratings. News coverage was generally strong. However,
the ITC is looking for better quality in certain aspects of
the regional service and in particular more innovation
in political and religious programmes. There were
some notable successes but new ideas are needed for
network drama and entertainment in particular."

Chairman: Charles Allan
Managing director: Margaret Fay
Director of broadcasting: Graeme Thompson
Managing editor - news: Graham Marples
Editor, current affairs & features: Jane Bolesworth
Head of young people's programmes: Lesley Oakden
Head of network features: Malcolm Wright
Head of sport: Roger Tames
Regional affairs executive: Norma Hope
Personnel manager: Lynda Wadge

UTV (Ulster Television)

Havelock House, Ormeau Road, Belfast BT7 1EB
Fax 01232-246695 Tel 01232-328122
E-mail: info@utv.live.com
Website: http://www.utvlive.com
Covers: Northern Ireland.
Owner: Ulster Television. No single holdingover 6%
Regional news programme: UTV Live at Six.
1993-2002 licence fee: £1.03 million pa.

ITC 1997 Review: "Against a background of major
political developments UTV maintained a high
standard of programming, particularly in news. A range
of other quality regional material included a series
exploring north/south differences and a new
entertainment series for older teenagers. The company
improved the range of its offers to the ITV network but
was unsuccessful in securing any commissions. The
ITC is now satisfied that sufficient resources are being
allocated to this by UTV. "

Chairman: John McGuckian
Managing director: Desmond Smyth
General manager: John McCann
Controller of programming: Alan Bremner
Programme services manager: Brenden Hehir
Operatioons manager: Robert McCourt
Corporate affairs: Michael Mc Cann
Personnel: Mariead Regan

Westcountry Television

Langage Science Park, Plymouth PL7 5BQ
Fax 01752-333444 Tel 01752-333333
E-mail: info@westcountry.co.uk
Covers: Cornwall, Devon, west Dorset, south Somerset
Owner: Carlton Communications
Regional news programme: Westcountry Live.
1993-2002 licence fee: £7.82 million pa.

ITC 1997 Review: "1997 was the first year in which
Westcountry operated, not as a free-standing company,
but as part of Carlton Communications. Any doubts
that this development might inhibit or dilute the strong
regional appeal of Westcountry's output proved
unfounded. The parent company was supportive but
operationally hands off. Against a number of standards
by which viewers rate the quality of the regional
television service, Westcountry performed in most
respects above the national average. News reporting was
professional and comprehensive, and factual
programmes were high quality. Westcountry's regional
entertainment was generally effective even if humour
was occasionally at the margins of acceptability."

Chairman: Sir John Banham
Chief executive: Stephen Redfarn
Director of programmes: Jane McCloskey
Controller, operations & engineering: Mark Chaplin
Controller of news: Brad Higgins
Controller of public affairs: Mark Clare

Yorkshire Television

Kirkstall Road, Leeds, West Yorks LS3 1JS
Fax 0113-244 5107 Tel 0113-243 8283
Covers: Yorkshire, Humberside, Derbyshire, Notts, Lincs.
Owner: Granada Plc .
Regional news programme: Calendar.
1993-2002 licence fee: £37.7 million pa.

ITC 1997 Performance Review: "Viewers to Yorkshire
Television were offered a more self-assured programme
service than the previous year. Various strands were
included in a nightly magazine, which began hesitantly
in 1996 but developed a more distinct style in 1997 and
tried ideas which were encouragingly ambitious. A new
approach was taken to current affairs and the strengths
of the regional news service were apparent for example
through the large numbers of stories covered on a day-
to-day basis and the resources employed to report major
developments. The sub-regional news services also
maintained the high standard of previous years but the
licensee did not meet the requirement for other sub-
regional programming. This needs to be addressed in
1998. Yorkshire was a major supplier of network
programmes in popular drama, children's and current
affairs strands."

Chairman: Charles Allen
Managing director: Richard Gregory
Documentaries and current affairs: Chris Bryer
Entertainment: David Reynolds
Drama: Keith Richardson
News: Clare Morrow
Director of group corporate affairs: Chris Hopson
Director of programmes: John Whiston

Channel 4

Channel 4 is a minority station by design and is a deliberate compromise between public sector and commercial television. It was set up in 1981 as a general public information service of "information, education and entertainment".

Michael Jackson took over from Michael Grade as the channel's third chief executive in July 1997. John Willis, Grade's trusted director of programmes, left his departure sweetened with a reported £600,000 pay off. Jackson then altered the hierarchy to accommodate more directors of programmes, many poached from the BBC, Jackson's former employer. Their job, according to Jackson's statement in the annual report is: "to extend and improve Channel 4."

The task of extension and improvement became somewhat easier once Michael Grade's dream came true and the government lifted the levy Channel 4 had been compelled to pay to its much richer rivals on Channel 3. Since 1993 this arrangement, the price for a safety net installed when Channel 4 went on air in November 1982, had leached away some £346.5 million. Small wonder that the ITV stations then started complaining of Channel 4's drift away from its original minority brief and into commercialism. In February the ITC responded by imposing stricter public service requirements covering disability, education, multi-culturalism, training, regional and film output. In April 1997 Jackson launched the Film Four subsidiary. By then he had stamped his personality on the station with a revamp of Channel 4 News. He brought Jim Gray from BBC2's Newsnight and took more control of the bulletins from ITN. "Now Channel 4 runs its news, not ITN," Jackson declared.

The Welsh fourth channel frequencies are used by S4C or Sianel Pedwar Cymru (Channel Four Wales). It began in 1982 alongside Channel Four and broadcasts about 30 hours of Welsh language programmes. The BBC supplies 10 hours of them with the remainder coming from HTV and independent producers. S4C has been directly funded by the Treasury since 1993.

Channel 4
124 Horseferry Road, London SW1P 2TX
Fax 0171-306 8366   Tel 0171-396 4444
E-mail Channel4.co.uk
Website: http://www.channel4.com
Chairman: Vanni Treves
Deputy chairman: Bert Hardy
Chief executive: Michael Jackson
Managing director: David Scott
Director & general manager: Frank McGettigan
Director of strategy & development: David Brook
Director of Advertising & marketing: Andy Barnes
Director of business affairs: Janet Walker
Head of programmes: Stuart Cosgrove
Head of corporate affairs: Sue Robertson
Corporation secretary: Andrew Yeates
Head of film: Paul Webster
Head of drama & animation: Gub Neal
Commissioning editor, sport: Mike Miller
Commissioning editor, schools: Paul Ashton
Commissioning editor, youth: Andi Peters
Commissioning editor, arts: Janey Walker
Commissioning editor, documentaries: Peter Dale
Independent film & video: Robin Gutch
Commissioning editor, multicultural: Yasmin Anwar
Religion & features: Peter Grimsdale
Science, business & talks: Sara Ramsden
Head of factual & features: Steve Hewlett
Head of news and current affairs: David Lloyd
Head of entertainment: Kevin Lygo
Commissioning editor of current affairs: Dorothy Byrne
Entertainment: Caroline Leddy, Graham Smith
Commissioning editor, animation: Claire Kitson
Commissioning editor, education: Liz Warner
S4C (Sianel Pedwar Cymru)
Parc Busnes ty Glas, Llanishen, Cardiff CF4 5DU
Fax 01222-751457   Tel 01222-741458
E-mail: s4c@s4c.co.uk
Website: http://www.s4c.co.uk
Chairman: Elan Closs Stephens
Chief executive: Huw Jones
Director of production: Huw Eirug
Press and PR: David Meredith

Four facts
* It backed Four Weddings and a Funeral but decided not to back The Full Monty
* Don't Forget Your Toothbrush is its most financially successful programme
* C4's highest weekly audience share of 13 per cent was in August 1995
* The Daily Mail doesn't like C4. Nor did the 1,959 people who complained about The Last Temptation of Christ in 1995

Channel 5

"It's not just football and films," Channel 5's chief executive David Elstein protested. "The steady growth of viewing since the beginning of 1998 has occurred with all types of programmes. Original documentaries such as Family Confidential have regularly been watched by up to 1.5 million viewers. Themed weekends have also been successful," he said and then grasped at statistical straws. "The Titanic special brought 5 its best ever Sunday share of viewing (5.1 per cent), with 5's peak-time share of viewing that day exceeding Channel 4's and almost equalling BBC2's."

Licensed pessimists still say Channel 5 exists because advertisers had demanded an alternative to the Channel 3 monopoly during the mid-eighties and that it was still about choice for advertisers rather than viewers. It is a choice only exercised by the 70 per cent of households which can receive it, and of those only 55 per cent get a top quality picture. Elstein admits that "aerial reception is a bigger issue than anyone had expected. It has made life much harder."

The C5 finances for prgramme making place it somewhere between cable channels and the conventional terrestrial channels, with its £110 million programming budget dwarfed by the £600 million available to ITV's networked programme makers. In March it promised the ITC that it would invest more in peak time programmes in return for being allowed to show more repeats.

Paul Longhurst, the media director of Ammitari Puris Lintas, remained unimpressed. "The channel just doesn't have the investment in programming you'd expect from the UK's fifth terrestrial channel. The positive things it has achieved are at the margins. It is a tiny channel and it shouldn't be. This is not a big dynamic channel changing the broadcasting landscape."

Dawn Airey, the Channel 5 programme director, hit back in fine style when she said: "I wonder how many of these media buyers actually sit down and watch television. It is interesting they all cite Jack Docherty as the only thing they watch. That's probably because it's the only thing they come home to at 11 o'clock in the evening."

Channel 5 is reaching its revenue targets, having gone £3 million over the projected £80 million that was in the launch plan's first nine months. As with Channel 4 - the last terrestrial station to be launched - early audience figures were below target, in C5's case 5 per cent. During its first year, viewing has gone up and in April 1998 it claimed a 4 per cent share of total TV viewing.

Five facts

* 20 million viewers tune in each week
* C5's top rated broadcast, the Poland vs England game on 31 May 1997, attracted 4.,5 million viewers
* Others value C5's management staff: David Berg, the head of acquisitions, was acquired by ITV; the marketing director David Brook was poached by C4; and Dawn Airey was offered a job by News Corp
* It has a £110 million annual programme budget
* It went £3 million over the projected £80 million revenue in the launch plan's first nine months

Channel 5 Broadcasting

22 Longacre, London WC2E 9LY
Fax 0171-550 5554   Tel 0171-550 5555
Value of ITC bid: £22,002,000
Shareholders: United News & Media, CLT ufa, Pearson Television, Warburg Pincus

Chief executive: David Elstein
Director of finance: Damien Harte
Director of legal & business affairs: Colin Campbell
Director of sales: Nick Milligan
Director of marketing & communication: Jim Hytner
Director of programmes: Dawn Airey
Controller, news, current affairs/documentaries: Tim Gardam
Controller, drama: Corinne Hollingworth
Controller, arts and features : Michael Atwell
Controller, entertainment: Alan Nixon
Controller, sport: Robert Charles
Controller, children's: Nick Wilson
Head of regional productions & special events: Adam Perry
Head of programme planning: Ashley Hill
Head of acquisitions: Jeff Ford

Digital television

Digital transmission translates pictures and sound as a string of binary digits - or bits or ones and noughts - to give better pictures and sound, the possibility of wide-screen viewing and the capacity for more channels. Initially there will be 36 digital channels but, once satellites begin transmitting up to a theoretical limit, there will be potential for hundreds of channels.

Beyond choice of channels and higher quality pictures, the advantage of digital transmission is in efficiency gains over existing analogue techniques which use airwaves that might better be used for all manner of communications. All these things together mean that in the long run every television broadcast will be transmitted digitally.

Digital TV

Multiplex A	Probably S4C in Wales, Gaelic programmes in Scotland
Multiplex B	On Digital Multiplex: Granada Plus, Sky Movies, Carlton Select, BBC Horizon, Sky Sports
Multiplex C	On Digital Multiplex: BBC Style/ Showcase, Sky 1, the Movie Channel, Carlton Films, Granada Good Life
Multiplex D	On Digital Multiplex: Carlton Entertainment, Public Eye (including Sky News), Granada TV Shopping, Granada Sports Club, BBC One-TV
BBC Multiplex	BBC 1 & 2, 24 hour news, BBC Choice, BBC Inform
C3/C4 Multiplex	Digital 3 and 4. Channel 3, Channel 4, Teletext, ITV 2, C4 Film Club

NB: Multiplexing combines the signals of several broadcasters into a single stream on a single-frequency channel. The signals are received and decoded by digital receivers within set-top boxes. This means there is no longer a direct one-to-one relationship between a television service and a frequency.

The bad news is that behind-the-screens technology will cost consumers up to £11 billion in receiving equipment and alterations to video recorders. The other worry is that in opening up a quantity of new channels, programme budgets will be spread so thinly that the quality of what is on our screens will deteriorate.

The change in the way we get at our programmes has already shifted the power balances within TV. The biggest political shift lies in the way the BBC's enthusiasm for all things digital has taken it into an explicitly commercial arena, notably in its deal with Flextech. BBC Worldwide has struck two deals with Flextech: the more important is for the UKTV digital TV venture where Flextech looks after distribution, airtime, off-air marketing and some management chores while BBC Broadcast retains editorial control; the other part of the deal allows Flextech to broadcast old BBC programmes via cable and satellite on UK Gold.

UKTV will be financed by subscription and advertising. Meanwhile the BBC's old analogue output - plus BBC Learning, BBC Choice (repeats) and BBC News 24 (the rolling news channel) - will be available free to view for those with set-top decoders. It will be broadcast on what the Independent Television Commission calls the BBC Multiplex or Multiplex A.

Each multiplex provides six channels and. On Digital (which was known as BDB until July 1998) the other big player, has an ITC licence to occupy mutiplexes B, C and D. Jointly owned by Carlton and Granada, BDB will offer the following: Select (more repeats); Granada Plus (yet more repeats); and Granada Breeze. These are already available, albeit in lower broadcast quality, to satellite and cable subscribers. The new BDB channels will be: Film (classics); Public Eye (crime); Entertainment (quizzes and lifestyle); Granada Shopping and Granada Sports Club.

Channels 3 and 4 share the remaining multiplex and the ITV Network is working on a free-to-air service while Channel 4 is likely to run a subscription channel concentrating on movies. Meanwhile hovering in he wings are companies like CNN, NBC, Disney, Zee TV and TNT, all anxious to capitalise on their cable or satellite investments.

Sky, which the ITC barred from direct investment in BDB, has a large share in the decoders and is investing in the next generation of digital satellite transmission channels. These should be available by Christmas 1998. Around ten of the digital satellite channels will be taken up by British Interactive Broadcasting, an Internet oriented company owned by BSkyB, British Telecom, Matsushita, and Midland Bank. Where satellite has a capacity for up to 200 channels, cable has the potential to carry 500. Cable and Wireless Communications is the first of the cable companies to have announced a digital cable service, another consumer choice for the 18 per cent of people who are passed by CWC cabling.

Most will go for the terrestrial option via rooftop aerials connected to a £250-ish set-top decoding box plus a smart card for subscription services. All will become clear in a blitz of advertising which began in June 1998 when BBC Digital bought full page ads in the national press. It contained these phrases: "Over the next few months digital broadcasting will become a reality ... you will have more news, more sport, more drama, more comedy. You'll be able to receive digital television via an ordinary TV aerial, cable or satellite. For each of these, you'll need the relevant digital decoder boxes which will plug into your TV. In time, decoder boxes will be integrated into TVs too. If you want digital cable, you'll also need a cable connection and if you want digital satellite, you'll need a new dish. Just think, in a few years' time, digital broadcasting will be as much a part of your life as telephones, electricity and the motor car are. But don't worry, there's bound to be something else for sceptics to be sceptical about."

Digital terrestrial/satellite/cable

Digital terrestrial
Channels: up to 36
Cost: programmes free from most existing terrestrial broadcasters but some subscription - set top box will cost something over £200
Suppliers: BBC, ITV, On Digital/BDB

Digital satellite
Channels: 150+
Cost: Subscription plus a new dish
Supplier: BSkyB

Digital cable
Channels: 100-400
Cost: Probably the same as for existing cable
Supplier: CWC ... and its rival will follow.

New jargon: NVOD or New Video on Demand or the new TV world where there's a movie starting every ten minutes.

DIGITAL TV CONTACTS

BBC Digital TV
Digital Consultation, BBC Broadcasting House, London WC1A 1AA
Tel: 0990 118833
Website: www.bbc.co.uk/digital

On Digital (British Digital Broadcasting)
346 Queenstown Road, London SW8 4NE
Fax 0171-819 8100   Tel 0171-819 8000

British Interactive Broadcasting
47-53 Canon Street, London EC4M 5SQ
Fax 0171-489 7772   Tel 0171-489 7770

Cable and Wireless Communications
Tel 0500 941 940

Digital 3 and 4 Ltd
124 Horseferry Road, London SW1P 2TX
Fax 0171-306 8076   Tel 0171-396 4444

Flextech Television
160 Great Portland Street, London W1N 5TB
Fax 0171-299 6000   Tel 0171-299 5000

Local TV: Restricted Service Licences

The Broadcasting Act 1996 provides for local terrestrial television through Restricted Services Licences' (RSLs). These new licences are available in two forms: the RSL E covers a maximum 56 day festival or sporting event while the RSL L is a renewable two year licence for city or location based broadcasting.

The Independent Television Commission invited applications for RSL L licences in June 1997 and by the closing date on 30 September 1997 had received 31 proposals. By the end of the year preliminary awards had been made to ten applicants, the first of which go on air in Autumn 1998.

Applicants for the TV RSL L licences cover commercial, community-based and minority organisations which have formed the Local Independent Television Network. Some services will use low powered transmitters to reach particular minority communities in the midst of larger urban areas (Slough) or cover the general population of smaller, isolated cities (Perth). Other channels propose using larger transmitters to cover bigger cities (Aberdeen and Oxford).

The new public service network will begin broadcasting on spare analogue frequencies. In most areas viewers will not require new aerials to obtain good reception. All the initial applicants opted to supply free-to-air programming and many will carry shopping channels and educational programmes to sustain their local programme commitments.

In June 1998 Channel 6 Broadcasting in Scotland was the first of the new services to be awarded an RSL L licence and will offer a mix of local and network services. With four licences granted (Edinburgh, Aberdeen, Stirling and Perth) and others in the pipeline (including Dundee, Glasgow and Inverness) Channel 6 is currently the largest local public service broadcaster. Also in Scotland, Lanarkshire

Dave Rushton, chairman of Channel 6

Television is establishing a service to reach south Lanarkshire covering households in Motherwell, Hamilton and East Kilbride.

In Northern Ireland, TVC9 has been established by Derry Media Access offering a mixture of community and commercial services; in Leicester, Midland Broadcasting Corporation (MATV) will respond to the interests of the Asian community. On the Isle of Wight, TV12 plans to reach most of the north of the island via several relays and offer programming aimed at both local viewers and summer visitors; in Oxford, the Oxford Channel will carry news, arts and community programmes and offer public service programming; in Slough, the Panjabi Centre will run Panjabi TV to provide community programming.

A further 39 applications for RSL Ls were received by the ITC for its second call for applications at the end of April 1998 deadline, bringing the total number of local services expecting to be on air by the end of 1999 at between 20 and 30. While fresh calls for applications for the two year licence are made at six monthly intervals, applications for the event based 56 day licence can be made at any time.

LOCAL TV STATIONS

Below are local TV services due for launch by the end of 1998 or early 1999

Channel 6 Broadcasting
PO Box 606, Edinburgh EH7 4YH
Fax 0131-557 8608   Tel 0131-557 8610
Covers: Licences for Edinburgh, Aberdeen, Perth and Stirling with provisional offers of licences for Dundee, Glasgow and Inverness.
Owner: Channel 6 Broadcasting Ltd
Programme plan: Local public service broadcaster offering music and arts videos, local and network programming, home shopping, education and community programming and local news and information on video and teletext.
Chairman: Dave Rushton
Managing director: David Treadway
Director of Programmes: TBA
Sales and marketing: TBA
Finance director: Michael Dixon

Oxford Channel
Fax 01865-433885   Tel 01865-433775
E-mail: oxfordchannel@compuserve.com
Owner: Oxford Broadcasting Ltd
Programme plan: Local public service programming. Sport, news, arts and community. 18 hours per day.
Chairman: Frank Harding
Managing directors: Deborah Cackler/Thomas Harding
Non-executive director: Mike Hollingsworth

MATV
Midland Broadcasting Corporation, 233 Belgrave Gate, MPK House, Leicester LE1 3HT
Fax 0116-253 8900   Tel 0116-253 2288
E-mail: mbc.matv@technocom.com
Owner: V Popat, H Popat, S M Majithia
Chairman: Ashwin Mistry
Managing director: Vinod Popat
Sales and marketing: Paul Kalwa
Finance director: Hitesh Popat
Programme controller: Nilesh Thanki

Panjabi TV
174 Kensington Park Road, London W11 2ER
Fax 0171-792 2820   Tel 0171-792 2820
Covers: Slough area
Owner: The Panjabi Centre
Chairman: A K Khera
Managing director: J P S Kundi
Sales and marketing: R S Mangat
Finance director: B S Heera

TV12
The Medina Centre, Fairlee Road, Newport, Isle of Wight PO30 2DX
Fax 01983 521660   Tel 01983 524745
Website: www.tv12.demon.co.uk
Covers: Isle of Wight and Solent region
Programme plan: Plans to broadcast 24 hours a day. In addition to an overnight local graphics service, TV12 will broadcast digital quality local programmes between 4pm and 11pm. TV12 will have programmes aimed at tourist and will carry a very local weather forecast.
Chairman: Graham Benson
Managing director: Paul Meade
Director of programmes: Paul Topping
Sales and marketing: Steve Lloyd
Finance director: Adam Humphreys

TVC9
9 Crawford Square, Londonderry BT48
Fax: 01504 265357   Tel: 01504 370019
E-mail: paulboyle@btinternet.com.
Covers: Greater Londonderry
Owner: Derry Media Access, Honeybee Enterprises, Highland Radio
Programme plan: Local in-house production 30 per cent; acquisitions/independents 50 per cent; community access programming 10 per cent; trainee productions 10 per cent. Plus Interactive teletext, video jukebox and home shopping
Chairman: Robert Gavin
Managing director/director of programmes: Paul Boyle
Sales and marketing: Loughry Associates
Finance director: John Ward

Independent TV producers

The 900 members of Pact - the Producers Alliance for Cinema and TV - have an annual turnover of over £1 billion. In 1996 Channel 4 made programme payments of £217 million to 714 different companies.

The concentration of wealth has been dependent on two factors: first, Channel 4 setting up as a TV publisher in 1982 to establish a working precedent which proved TV stations could rely on independent producers; second is the subsequent legislation compelling UK terrestrial broadcasters to commission at least a quarter of their schedules from outside their organisations.

In 1997 their total of first run hours is shown in the chart at the start of the listings. The Independent Television Commission encourages the independents and highlighted some discouraging news in its latest annual report. According to the ITC "non-regional independent productions overall declined from an average 35 per cent in 1996 to 28 per cent in 1997". While no ITV company fell below the stipulated 25 per cent quota, the ITC gathered assurances that "the decline would be reversed in 1998".

Pact notes that domestic broadcasters are becoming less willing to provide all the funding for particular broadcasts. Its members have thus turned to international co-production deals and forged partnerships with programme distributors which are acting as co-financiers with the independent producers. It is also bullish about opportunities in cable and satellite and digital TV.

Pact
45 Mortimer Street, London W1N 7TD
Fax 0171-331 6700   Tel 0171-331 6000
E-mail: enquiries@pact.co.uk
Website: http://www.pact.co.uk

First run hours

CHANNEL	HOURS
BBC 1	729 hours
BBC 2	871 hours
Channel 3	1,284 hours
Channel 4	2,369 hours
Channel 5	960 hours

Source: Pact

123 Productions	0171-263 4199
2.4 Media	01562-822099
25 May Productions	01276-855418
3BM Television	0171-439 2664
3Di TV Software	0113-274 4933
400 Company	0181-746 1400

A

A19 Film & Video	0191-565 5709
A38 Films	01822 833955
Aardman Animation	0117-984 8485
Abbey Films	01865-725015
About Face Media	01232-894555
Absolutely Productions	0171-930 3113
ABTV	0171-351 7070
Acacia Productions	0181-341 9392
Achievement Concepts	01584-890893
Action Cuts	34 68 150702

Action Time (North)	0161-236 8999
Addictive Television	0181-960 2233
Adventure Pictures	0171-613 2233
Afro Wisdom Films	0171-490 8386
After Image	0171-737 7300
Age Film and Video	01763 852128
Agenda Television	01792-510610
Agran Barton TV	0171-351 7070
Aimimage Productions	0171-916 3734
Alan Torjussen	01222 624669
Alchemy	0171-2879964
Alcibiades	0181-9688873
Alfalfa Entertainments	0171-284 3275
Alhambra Films	01505 874111
Alive Productions	0171-384 2243
Allison & Humphreys	0171-570 6000
Amirani Films	0171-328 7057
Amy International	01295-760256
Anchor Marine	01548 561511
Animation Partnership	0171-636 3300
Animation Works	0181-883 3402
Annalogue	0181-743 3630
Annex(Films)	0171-734 4471
Antelope Productions	0171-209 0099
Antidote	01225-722262
Antonine Films	0141-420 3410

Apex TV	01223-872900
Aphrodisia Films	0191-281 7289
API Television	0171-839 4646
Approaching Fish	0181-960 6616
Apt Film & TV	0171-284 1695
Arcadia Films	0171-235 5935
Arcadian Productions	0113-222 8385
Ardent Productions	0171-636 5010
Argo Productions	0171-485 9189
Aries Productions	01372-457724
Arion Media	0231-376301
Ark Productions	0181-788 8762
Armac Films	0141-337 2322
Armadillo Films	0171-439 0400
Arrowhead Productions	0171-376 8222
Arts Council Films	0171-973 6443
ASD Films	0171-437 3898
Assembly Film & TV	0181-600 2311
At It Productions	0181-636 0151
Atlantic Productions	0181-742 0500
Atlas Adventures	0117 970 6756
Attic Productions	01423-504386
Atticus TV	0181-876 0406
Aurora Productions	0117-924 3320
Available Light	0117-929 1311
Avalon TV	0171-434 3888
Avie Littler Assoc	9171-794 2742
Avonbridge Film	0131-478 4439

B

B&T Productions   0181-525 7812
Bachaks Productions
                   0171-624 8455
Back 2 Back TV   0171-431 0202
Bailey Partnership 01727-861449
Baker Tilly   0171-413 5100
Bamboo Film & TV   0171-916 9353
Bandung   0171-482 5045
Bangaw Cyf   01222-590225
Banshee   0181-482 7252
Bard Entertainments
                   0171-253 0353
Bare Faced Productions
                   0171-258 1823
Barraclough Carey 0181-741 4777
Barraclough Carey North
                   0161-827 2073
Barrass Company   0181-749 3527
Basilisk Communications
                   0171-580 7222
Bazal   0171-462 9000
Bazal Midlands, Scotland, West
                   0121-605 5445
Beach, The   0171-437 6957
Beambright   01483-39343
Beckmann Productions
                   01624-816585
Bedford Productions
                   0171-436 7766
Bell TV Assoc   01206-240192
Bench-Mark Productions
                   01753-771955
Bentley Productions 01753-656594
Berwick Universal Pictures
                   0171-923 1998
Berwin Leighton   0171-623 3144
Besom Productions 01504-370303
Beyond International
                   0171-636 9611
BFI Production   0171-636 5587
Big H Productions 0181-657 2272
Big Bear Films   0171-736 9707
Big Ed's   0131-667 9982
Big Eye Film Productions
                   0161-228 2457
Big Issue Film Unit 0171-418 0425
Big Red Heart Productions
                   01222-342900
Big Table Film Co, The
                   0171-287 7622
Big Talk Productions
                   0171-255 1131
Big Wide World   0114-249 2206
Bigger Picture Company
                   0181-758 8566
BigWig Productions 01462-768306
Bitcom International 01483-574545
Black and Blond   0171-734 1166

Black Audio Film Collective
                   0171-267 0846
Black Bear Productions
                   0131-447 7448
Black Coral Productiions
                   0181-880 4860
Black Hill Productions
                   01981-240161
Blackbird Productions
                   0171-352 4882
Black Coral   0181-880 4860
Black Star Films   01232-463636
Blackstone Pictures 0181-563 2223
Blackwatch Productions
                   0141-341 0033
Blakeway Productions
                   0181-748 3113
Blast! Films   0171-267 4260
Blenheim TV Films 01491-614288
Blow By Blow Productions
                   01522-754901
Blue Chaos Productions
                   0171-636 2262
Blue Heaven Productions
                   0171-404 4222
Blueprint Productions
                   0171-287 6623
Blue Water Films   0171-609 1362
Blueboy TV   0121-233 9944
Bob Godfrey Films 0171-278 5711
Boot   01225-852268
Bounds Away   01892-521373
Boxclever Productions
                   0171-619 0606
Bramble Production 01569-731980
Branded Entertainment
                   0171-437 4736
Brass Monkey Company, The
                   0171-229 8893
Break Future   0181-444 3303
Breakout Productions
                   01235-835226
Brechin Productions
                   0181-876 2046
Brenda Rowe Productions
                   0117-973 0390
Brian Waddell Productions
                   01232-427646
Brighter Pictures 0171-738 4048
Britt Allcroft Group, The
                   01703-331661
British Car Films 0171-281 2859
Britt Allcroft Company
                   01703-331661
Broad Productions 01505-842840
Broadsword TV   01603-762211
Bronco Films   0141-334 4971
Bronson Knight   0171-403 1900
Brook Lapping Productions
                   0171-428 3100

Brookside Productions
                   0151-722 9122
Buena Vista   0181-222 1000
Buffalo Pictures   0171-439 0401
Bumper Films   01934-418961
Buxton Raven   0171-296 0012

C

Cactus Television 0171-465 6232
Cadiz Films   0181-977 7752
Cafe Productions   0171-460 4700
Caledonia, Sterne & Wyld
                   0141-353 3153
Callister Commuications
                   01846-673717
Cambrensis   01222-257075
Cambridge Film & TV
                   01638-743313
Cambridge Video   01223-553416
Capital Group Studios
                   0181-874 0131
Capron Productions 0181-871 5107
Carlton UK   0171-486 6688
Carlyle TV   0171-439 8967
Carnival Films   0181-968 1818
Carol Gould   0171-266 1953
Carpe Diem Productions
                   0131-557 0960
Carte Blanche TV Productions
                   0171-580 5432
Case TV   0171-296 0010
Castellar Films   0171-625 1162
Cat's Eye   0171-722 9065
Catalist Films   0141-942 5621
Catalyst TV   0171-603 7030
Catherine Bailey   0171-483 2681
CBTV   01434-602867
Celador Productions
                   0171-240 8101
Celtic Films   0171-637 7651
Celtic Productions 01222-752532
Central Reservation 0141-337 3537
Century Films   0171-722 7241
Chain Production   0171-229 4277
Chameleon Television
                   0113-244 4486
Channel X   0171-387 3874
Chapman Films   0171-287 5416
Chapter One   0171-580 8636
Chariot Productions 0191-265 2275
Charisma Films   0171-603 1164
Charlotte Metcalf Productions
                   0171-371 2389
Chatsworth   0171-734 4302
Cheeky Ideas   01923-859692
Cheerful Scout   0171-287 0076
Cheerleader Productions
                   0171 437 6177
Cheriton Enterprises
                   01963-350113

Children's Film/TV Foundation
0181-953 0844
Children's Film Unit   0181-785 0350
Childsplay Productions
0171-328 1429
Chistera Productions
01232-615573
Christmas TV & Film Co
0171-733 0110
Christopher Swann Assocs
0181-749 9056
Christopher Sykes Production
0181-748 8748
Christopher Young Films
0141-339 1112
Chrysalis Sport   0171-284 2288
Chrysalis Television 0171-465 6353
Chrysalis Visual Entertainment
0171-465 6208
Cicada Films   0171-266 4646
Cin & Beannie   0181-675 7739
Cine Electra   0171-287 1123
Cine Europe   0181-743 6792
Cinecam Productions
01954-211924
Cinecontact   0171-323 1690
Cinecosse   01358-722150
Cinema Verity   0181-741 1515
Cinesite(Europe)   0171-973 4000
Cinnabar Films   0181-348 0918
Clarioncall Film & TV 01943-607553
Clark Television Production
0171-388 7700
Class Productions 01462-742914
Classic Productions 0171-730 6265
Clear Definition   0171-636 0366
Clearwater Films   0171-794 9563
Coleridge Video   01752-761138
Comedy Unit, The   0141 353 1500
Common Features 0191-477 5532
Company Pictures 0171-734 8114
Compulsive Viewing 0171-836 8330
Connections Communications
0181-741 1767
Contrast Films   0181-472 5001
Convergence Productions
0181-993 3666
Cool Crew Company
0141-300 3063
Cormorant Productions
0131-657 3393
Cosgrove Hall Films 0161-882 2500
Cotton City Pictures 0161-877 5579
Cottonwood Films 0171-385 4323
Couch Potato TV   0171-413 8006
Counterpoint Films 0171-700 4933
Countrywide Films 01703-230286
Courtyard Productions
01732-700324

Covent Garden Pioneer
01753-789661
Cowboy Films   0171-287 3808
Creation Company, The
0171-586 7012
Creation Video   0800 731945
Creative Alliance   0171-637 2927
Creative Law   01732-460592
Crew Cut Productions
01738-630815
Crewed Up   0161-228 2700
Cronk Dromgoole   0181-749 0253
Crucial Films   0171-229 8899
Cruickshank Cazenove
0171-735 2933
Crux Productions   01730-894720
Crystal Media   0131-558 8766
CS Productiions   0171-733 3507
CST Productions   0117-909 0909
CSV Media (Midlands)
0121-643 9886
CTVC   0181-950 4426
Cultural Partnerships
0171-254 8217
Cunliffe & Franklyn 01243-532531
Curtis & Freud   0171-221 9434
Cutting Edge   0181-780 1476
Cyclops Vision   0171-385 5119

D
Dakota Films   0171-287 4329
Dan Films   0171-916 4771
Dancelines Productions
0171-352 6261
Dancing Fleas   0171-713 1330
Danny Boon   01273-270300
Dark Horse Productions
01874-665435
Darlow Smithson Productions
0171-428 7027
Dave Knowles Films 01703-842190
Davenhall   01565-653369
David Hickman   0171-436 1862
David Wickes Productions
0171-225 1382
Davros Productions 0181-467 9125
Dawkins Associates 01622-741900
Day-Lewis Productions
01278-671334
Daylight Productions
0171-254 5604
Deco Films & TV   01736 871334
Decoupage Films   01287-633038
Deep Water   0410-095581
· Deepwater Productions
01865-450343
Demaine Associates
0171-376 1739
Denham Productions
01752-345444

Dennis Woolf Productions
0161-442 8175
Desmond Wilcox   0181-743 7431
Diamond Time   0171-433 3355
Dibb Directions   0181-748 1579
Diplomat Films   0161-929 1603
Direct TV   01865-437878
Disckit   0181-964 2077
Disruptive Element Films
0114-268 1350
Distant Horizon   0171-813 3134
Diva Pictures   0181-567 6655
Diverse Production 0171-603 4567
DLT Entertainment 0171-631 1184
DNA   0171-485 4411
Domaine   0171-437 3084
Domino Films   0171-582 0393
Double Band Films 01232-243331
Double E Productions
0181-993 2394
Double Exposure   0171-490 2499
Double Take   0181-788 5743
Double-Band Films 01232-243331
DPTV   01436-820084
Dragonhorse Productions
0181-549 7149
Drama House   0171-388 9140
Dramatic Productions
0118-975 0754
Dreug Productions 0141-644 4327
Driftwood Films   0181-332 6365
Duchess Productions
0171-436 8230

E
Eagle & Eagle   0181-995 1884
Eagle Dancer Productions
0171-379 8485
Eagles Productions 0141-639 4217
East Wind Films   01603-664727
ECM Productions   0171-727 5721
Ecosse Films   0171-371 0290
Eden Productions   0171-435 3242
Edinburgh Film   01968-672131
Edinburgh Film Workshop
0131-557 5242
Educational & TV Films
0171-226 2298
Educational Broadcasting
0171-765 5023
EFS TV Production 0181-950 8394
Eight Syndicate   0181-883 9929
Electric Sky   01273-384208
Element Productions
0117-973 8799
Elephant Productions
01932-562611
Elgin Productions   0171-727 9174
Elm Road Entertainment
0117-923 2324

Elmgate Productions
01932-562611
Elstree Production Co
01932-572680
Emme Productions 0171-602 2595
Endboard Productions
0121-429 9779
English & Pockett 0171-287 1155
Enigma Productions
0171-287 6565
Enterchoice 0171-373 6796
Entertainment Film Production
0171-439 1606
Eo teilifis 353 91 83500
Eolas 01851-705638
Eon Productions 0171-493 7953
EPA International 0171-267 9198
Epicflow Films 0171-328 8768
Epik TV 0117-927 6712
Erik Knudsen Films 01706-813742
Essential Pictures 0181-969 7017
Esta's TV Company 0181-741 2843
Euphoria Films 0171-226 4224
EuroArt Media 0171-221 4162
Euroarts-Primetime 0171-935 9000
Evans Woolfe 0181-892 1670
Excalibur Productions
01422-843871
Excelsior Group Productions
01737-812673
Eye Eye 0171-485 6924
Eye to Eye TV 0171-498 5335

F
Fabulous Fruits 0131-229 5370
Face Films International
0181-898 6328
Faction Films 0171-608 0654
Fair Game Films 0171-286 8602
Fairline 0141-331 0077
Fairwater Films 01222-578488
Farnham Film 01252-710313
Farthings Productions
0181-974 8060
Fat Chance Productions
0117-972 2725
Feature Films 01202-736666
Felgate Media 0171-624 1525
Feline Films 01225-461138
Festival Film & TV 0181-297 9999
Field Illeray 01360-770805
Fierce Bird Films 0181-767 8397
Figment Films 0171-287 3209
Film Bakery 0181-449 1128
Film Company, The 0171-586 3686
Film Education 0171-976 2291
Film Form Productions
0171-794 6967
Film & General Productions
0171-221 1141

Film Video Multimedia
01708-640860
FilmFair Animation 0181-960 6415
Filmit 0171-738 4175
FilmNOVA 0191-402 0017
Films Of Record 0171-286 0333
Filmworks 0181-741 5631
Final Draft Films 0171-386 7010
Fine Art Productions 0171-321 0011
Finetake Productions
0171-359 5786
Firestone Productions
0585-197207
First Avenue Films 01663-733684
First Choice Productions
0171-485 5000
First Circle Films 0171-221 3737
First City Features 0171-437 3344
First Film Company 0171-439 1640
First Freedom Productions
0171-916 9355
First Growth 0171-434 3655
First Light 01273-327344
First Light Productions
0141-226 2255
First Take 0171-328 8765
Firstmile 0171-376 3547
Flashback Communication
0141-554 6868
Flashback Television
0171-490 8996
Flicker Films 0171-289 7964
Flying Brick Films 0171-249 7440
Flying Dutchman Co, The
0171-223 9067
Flying Fox Films 01232-244811
Focus Films 0171-435 9004
Focus International TV
0171-284 3422
Focus Productions 0117-930 0889
Folio Productions 0171-437 6177
Footage Productions
01232-237326
Footprint Films 01202-396105
Footstep Productions
0171-836 9990
Formation Films 0181-723 2371
Forward Films/Altogether Now
0181-888 2533
Foundation TV 01622-684692
Foundry Productions
0171-793 9976
Fountain TV 0181-900 1188
Fragile Films 0171-287 6200
Fred Wolf Films 353 1 478 3199
Freeform Productions
0181-986 3425
Freelance Film Partners
0171-328 8202
Freeway Films 0131-225 3200

Fremantle Productions
0171-284 0880
Fresh Air Productions
0161-491 0700
Fresh Film & TV 0131-557 8770
Friday Productions 0171-730 0608
Front Page Films 0171-329 6866
Frontier Films 353 1 497 7077
Frontrunner Films 0171-436 5373
Fugitive Group 0171-637 3300
Fuji International 0171-734 9964
Fulcrum Productions
0171-253 0353
Full On Films 01273-623697
Fulmar West TV & Film
01222-227700

G
GM Productions 0141-357 5066
Gabriel Productions 01225-311194
Gabriela Productions
0181-993 3158
Gael Media 091-592 888
Gainsborough Productions
01753-651700
Garfield Kennedy Co
0141-353 0456
Gauvain Productions
01508 532682
Gavin Weightman 0171-704 2452
Geestor Productions
0181-985 7726
Geofilms 01235-537400
Getzels/Gordon 01865-512556
Gimlet Productions 0171-350 2878
Ginger TV 0171-577 7100
Giro Rosso 01865-308 397
Glasgow Film Office 0141-287 0424
Glass Pictures 0171-609 3360
Global Arts 0171-428 0323
Global Productions 0117-946 6110
Global Sports Productions
0171-610 6444
GM Partnership, The
0161-929 8339
GMTV 0171-827 7000
GNU Productions 0171-267 3399
Goldcrest Films & TV
0171-437 8696
Golden Eagles Production
0141-331 0525
Golden Square Pictures
0171-446 0080
Goldhawk Media 01494-729777
Goldwyn Associates
0181-876 3700
Gordon Getzels 01865-512556
Gosh That's Big Entertainment
0141-353 0456
Grade Company, The
0171-409 1925

Granada Film Productions
0161-827 2090
Granite Film & TV   0171-354 3232
Grant Naylor Productions
01932-572175
Grant Thornton   0131-229 9181
Gaphite Film & TV   0181-994 6617
Grasshopper Productions
0171-229 1181
Green House Productions
0181-679 9049
Green Inc Productions
01232-573000
Green Man   0171-413 8081
Green Umbrella   0117-973 1729
Greenpark Productions
01566-782178
Greenpoint Films   0171-437 6492
Greg Angel (Film & TV)
01734-794607
Gruber Brothers   0171-436 3413
Gwynhelek Productions
01736-762132

H

Haffy Rice Productions
0171-434 0022
Halcyon Films   0171-352 0209
Half Way Production House
0181-673 7926
Halo Productions   0171-379 7398
Hamilton TV   01298-79424
Hammer Film Productions
0181-207 4011
Hammersley Productions
0171-439 1449
Hand Pict Independent
0131-558 1543
HandMade Films   0171-434 3132
Hanrahan TV Productions
01789-450182
Harbottle & Lewis   0171-629 7633
Harcourt Films   0171-267 0882
Hart Ryan Productions
0171-403 6363
Hartswood Films   0181-607 8736
HarumScarum Films
01225-329400
Harvest Entertainment
01222-590590
Hasan Shah Films   0171-722 2419
Hat Trick Productions
0171-434 2451
Hawkshead   0171-462 9555
Hayes Bolton   0171-209 2244
HD Thames   01753-657100
Headflicks   0171-494 2329
Headlightvision   0171-287 1953
Healthcare Productions
0171-267 8757

Heart of England Productions
01789-298100
Heavy Entertainment
0181-960 9001
Helen Langridge Associates
0171-299 1000
Hewland International
0171-308 9955
Hexagon Productions
0171-437 1552
Hexagram Film & TV 0181-579 0076
Hibbert Ralph Entertainment
0171-494 3011
Highflyer Productions
01653-658599
Hightimes Prods   0171-482 5202
Hindi Picture   0181-245 2534
Hit Entertainment 0171-224 1717
Hobson's Production Co
0181-742 7118
Holdings Ecosse   0131-557 2678
Hollyoaks Productions
0151-722 9122
Hollywood Reporter, The
0171-331 1964
Holmes Associates 0171-813 4333
Hop Productions   0171-498 4497
Hot Property Films 0171-323 9466
Hot Shot Films   01232-245495
Hourglass Productions
0181-540 8786
HTV International 01222-590299
Hummingbird Films 0117-923 8887
Hungry Eye & Worrell Film
0171-439 4343
Hungry Horse Pictures
0171-734 7979
Hunter Productions 0141-334 5018
Hutchins Film Co   0171-636 2104
Hyphen Films   0171-734 0632

I

Iambic Productions 0117-923 7222
IBT   0171-482 2847
Icon Films   0117-924 8535
Ideal World Productions
0141-353 3222
IKG Productions   0171-384 3381
Illuminations TV   0171-226 0266
Illustra TV   0171-437 9611
Images First   0181-579 6848
Imagicians   0171-287 5211
Imagination   0171-323 3300
Imago Productions 01603-615151
INCA   0181-255 6255
Independent Image 0171-292 4300
Independent Production Co
0171-245 1288
Indica Films   0171-287 4228
Indigo Television 0171-486 4443
Initial   0171-462 9999

INP   0171-229 1265
Inside Broadcast   0171-240 5567
Insight Films   0171-252 5328
Insight Productions 01647-432686
Interesting Television
01926-844044
Intermedia   0115-955 6909
International Broadcast Trust
0171-482 2847
International Films 01732-874784
Intrepid Films   0171-435 9590
Intrinsica Films   0171-923 7070
Invideo Productions 0131-557 2151
Invincible Films   0181-237 1150
InVision Productions
0171-371 2123
IPCA   0117-922 1342
IPH   0171-207 2965
Ipso Facto Films   0191-230 2585
IPTV   0131-659 6566
Isis Productions   0181-748 3042

J

Jacaranda Productions
0181-741 9088
Jane Balfour Films 0171-267 5392
Jane Walmsley Productions
0171-290 2676
January Films   0141-339 5504
Jay Film & Video   0191-201 2131
Jeremy Isaacs Productions
0171-240 9920
Jim Henson Productions
0171-428 4000
Jo and Co   0181-878 5455
Jo Lustig   01223-461001
Jo Manuel Productions
0181-930 0777
John Adams TV   01453-885700
John Gau Productions
0181-788 8811
John Lawrence Enterprises
0171-482 7138
John Peel Productions
01697-371703
Jon Blair Film Co 0171-839 3444
JT Fleming   0181-207 2041
Judy Counihan   0171-734 9870
Julian Seddon   0171-831 3033
Juniper   0171-722 7111
Just Television   0171-404 6744

K

Kai Productions   0181-673 4550
Karma Productions 01455-202278
Kayfay Productions 0171-485 9352
Kazan River Productions
01603-872336
Kelso Films   0181-746 1566
Kennedy Mellor   0171-483 3241
Keo Films   0171-490 3580

Kestrel Film Company	0181-788 6244
Keystone (Ealing)	0181-992 9993
Kilroy Television	0181-943 3555
Kilroy Television (Midlands)	0121-693 5515
Kinetic Film	0171-610 6619
King Rollo Films	01404-45218
Kingfisher TV Productions	0115-964 5226
Kingsfire Services	0171-584 1664
KPA TV	0121-248 3900
Kudos Productions	0171-580 8686

L

L&M Productions Ireland	353 1 670 9389
La Plante Productions	0171-734 6767
Lambent Productions	0171-609 3881
Lambeth Video	0171-737 5903
Landmark Productions	01962-734227
Landseer Film & TV	0171-485 7333
Langham Productions	0181-743 7431
Large Door	0171-978 9500
Lark International	0181-742 0919
Last Ditch TV	01986-892549
Lateral Productions	0171-372 7566
Lauderdale Productions	0181-780 0072
Laurel Productions	0171-267 9399
Lauriston Film & TV Production	0171-485 6302
Lawless Films	0171-494 1025
Lawson Productions	04-046 9497
Leading Ladies Film Co	0171-229 5529
Learning Media	0181-332 9984
Leda Serene	0181-969 7094
Lee-Wright Productions	01494 883078
Left Handed Pictures	0171-735 2933
Legend Productions	0181-940 8285
Leila Films	0181-291 6339
Leisure Time Midlands	01564-742520
Leisure Time Productions	0171-837 8777
Leman Productions	0131-447 1082
Lexington Films	0171-434 1262
Liba Productions	0181-904 8136
Libra Films	0171-385 8899
Lichen Films	0131-667 4110
Lifesize Pictures	0114-249 2211

Lifetime Group	0171-577 7500
Light Industry Pictures	0151-707 0071
Lighthouse Films	01406-351173
Lightyears Films	0191-233 2550
Lilyville Productions	0171-371 5940
Limelight	0171-255 3939
Limited Company Limited	0171-439 4277
Lindley Stone	0171-379 8664
Line TV	0171-792 8480
Link Entertainment	0181-996 4800
Liion TV	0181-987 6300
Lionhead Productions	0181-749 6071
Lionsgate Productions	0181-288 7400
Little Bird Co	0171-434 1131
Little Dancer Films	0181-653 9343
Living Tape Productions	0171-439 6301
Lluniau Lliw Cyf	01222-255630
Loaded Productions	0141-337 3025
Lodestar Productions	0171-287 3302
Lomond TV	0141-420 3132
London Film & Video Dev.	0171-383 7755
London Post	0171-439 9080
London Weekend TV	0171-620 1620
Longbow Productions	01822-610210
Longeye	0171-624 5444
Look Lively TV	01703-695550
Loose Arrangement Film & TV	0181-994 3396
Loose Moose	0171-287 3821
Loud Mouse Productions	0171-371 9429
Loud Productions	0171-359 0275
Louise Panton Productions	0171-284 2870
Lucas Media	07000 782468
Lucida Productions	0181-699 5070
Lucinda Broadbent	0141-332 2042
Lucky Dog	0181-983 6775
Lucky World Productions	0171-499 0321
Lunchtime Productions	0181-959 3545
Lusia Films	0171436 3050
Luther Pendragon	0171-353 1500

M

MacHeath Productions	01952-201212
Macmillan Media	01232-683800
Magic Lantern Productions	0181-769 6116
Mair Golden Moments	0181-743 7152
Makar Productions	0131-443 1482
Malachite Productions	01790-763538
Malavan Media	0171-794 5509
Mallory Films	01396-828632
Malone Gill Productions	0171-287 3970
Man Alive Group	0181-743 7431
March Hare Productions	01884-820877
Mark 4 Film & TV	01932-227675
Mark Forstater Productions	0171-624 1123
Mark Patterson & Associates	01895-673610
Marriott Harrison	0171-209 2000
Mars Productions	0171-243 2750
Martin Gates Productions	0171-580 8440
Martin Pope Productions	0171-734 6911
MASC Productions	0181-769 2286
Matinee Films	0181-800 1171
Maverick Enterprises	0181-459 3858
Maverick Television	0121-771 1812
Maya Vision	0171-836 1113
Mayfair Entertainment	0171-304 7911
MBC Midlands	0121-233 9944
MBC North	0161-827 2073
MC Video Productions	01392-434118
McConnell Film Assoc	0141-337 1414
McDougall Craig	0171-240 7272
McGuffin Films	0181-672 7089
McKenna & Co	0171-606 9000
MCM Entertainment	0171-385 3858
Melrose Film Productions	0171-627 8404
Memoir Film Productions	0191-265 2215
Mental Health Media	0171-700 8131
Mentorn Barraclough Carey	0171-287 4545
Mentorn Films	0171-734 7067
Mentorn Midlands	0121-233 9944
Merchant Ivory Productions	0171-437 1200
Merlin Films	0191-414 7995

Mersey Television   0151-722 9122
Mersham Productions
                     01233-503636
Metamedia Productions
                     0171-287 6690
Michael Cole Productions
                     0181-994 4821
Michael Howes Productions
                     0171-928 7851
Michael Hurll Television
                     0171-287 4314
Michael Weigall Productions
                     0171-229 5725
Michael White   0171-734 7707
Michaelides & Bednash
                     0171-468 1168
Middlemarch Films   0171-371 4596
Midlantic Films Inc UK
                     0171-240 9823
Migrant Media   0171-254 9701
Mike Mansfield TV   0171-494 3061
Millar Movies   0171-370 1830
Mills Video Company
                     0151-709 9822
Mintai   01222-489813
Mirror Image Productions
                     0976-794418
Mirus Production   0181-740 5505
Mission, the   0171-287 4455
MJW Productions   0171-713 0400
ML International Pictures
                     0171-460 6465
MNE TV   0141-353 3135
Mogul TV   01344-622140
Molehill Productions 01703-615688
Molitor Productions 0171-491 3985
Momentum Video   0171-729 3536
Monogram Productions
                     0171-734 9873
Moonbase Alpha Productions
                     0171-491 9817
Moondance Films & TV
                     0171-323 6458
Mosaic Films   01594-530708
Mosaic Pictures   0171-437 6514
Mostly Movies   0181-788 6120
Move On Up   01381-600777
Moving Image Development
                     0151-708 9858
Moving Still Productions
                     353 1 670 9275
Multi Media Arts   0151-476 6050
Multi-Story Productions
                     01483-416336
Music Box   0171-478 7300
Music Mall   0171-534 1444
Music House (International)
                     0171-434 9678
Music on Earth   0181-998 5675

N
National Film & TV School
                     01494-671234
Nautilus Films   0181-444 4334
NCTV   01224-492020
Nebraska Productions
                     0181-444 5317
Nelvana Enterprises 0171-287 2770
Network Five TV   01902-640014
Never Summer Productions
                     07071-222171
New Era TV   0171-927 8817
New Media TV   01904-621331
New Street Productions
                     0121-248 2425
NFH   0171-584 7561
Nicholas Claxton Productions
                     0181-956 2261
Nick Patten Productions
                     0121-693 7117
Noble Films   0171-448 1000
Nobles Gate   0181-994 8161
Noel Gay Motion Picture Co
                     0181-600 5200
Noel Gay Television 0171-412 0400
Normal Films   0171-388 2360
North South Productions
                     0171-388 0351
Northern Exposure TV Co
                     0161-839 9394
Northlight Productions
                     01224-646460
Northridge Entertainment
                     0181-455 7125
Nova Inc Fim & TV   0151-474 9176
Nova Productions   01302-833422
NVC Arts   0171-388 3833

O
OR Media   0171-838 9690
Objective Productions
                     0181-348 5899
Octagon Pictures   0171-721 7571
October Films   0171-916 7198
Oil Factory   0171-837 0007
Old Street Films   01865-722357
One Lung Productions
                     0171-490 4433
Open Eye Productions
                     0171-287 4177
Open Media   0171-229 5416
Open Mike Productions
                     0171-434 4004
Open Mind   0171-437 0624
Optomen TV   0171-967 1234
Opus TV   01222 223456
Orbit Media   0171-221 5548
Oriana Production   0181-964 8221
Origami Films   01572-747692
Orlando TV Productions
                     01608-683218

Orpheus Productions
                     0181-892 3172
Otmoor Productions
                     01865-331445
Outrider International
                     0171-723 6021
Oxford Scientific Films
                     01993-881881
Oxford Television Company
                     0171-483 3637
Oxymoron Films   0171-437 5905
Oyster Productions 0181-960 0108
P
Palace Gate Productions
                     0171-584 3025
Paladin Pictures   0181-740 1811
Palindrome Productions
                     0181-262 7484
Palm Tree Productions
                     0141-552 3774
Panache Pictures   0181-809 7465
Parallax Pictures   0171-836 1478
Parisio Productions 0171-250 3630
Partners in Production
                     0171-490 5042
Partridge Films   0117-972 3777
Passion Pictures   0171-323 9933
Pathe Productions   0171-323 5151
Pathway Productions
                     0131-447 3531
Paul Berriff Productions
                     01482-641158
Paul Trijbits Productions
                     0171-439 4343
Pauline Muirhead Productions
                     0131-447 2219
Pavilion International
                     0171-636 9421
PDP   01465-871215
Peakviewing Productions
                     01452 863217
Pearl Catlin Associates
                     01483-567932
Pelicula Films   0141-945 3333
Pendragon Productions
                     0171-353 1500
Peninsula Films   0181-964 2304
Pentagon Communications
                     01482-226298
Penumbra Productions
                     0171-328 4550
Performance Films 01494-670505
Perx Productions   0113-274 2379
Peter Batty Productions
                     0181-942 6304
Peter Sasdy Productions
                     0181-783 1147
PGTV   0181-993 9613

Phoenix TV Productions
0171-386 5810
Photoplay Productions
0171-722 2500
Picasso Pictures   0171-437 9888
Pictorial Heroes   0141-554 5643
Picture Factory   0181-347 9233
Picture House Productions
0117-973 8859
Picture Palace Films 0171-586 8763
Picture This Independent Film
0117-972 1002
Pierrot Productions 0181-244 9161
Pilgrim Films   0191-230 3930
Pillarbox Productions
0171-700 0505
Pilot Film & TV Productions
0181-960 2771
Pineapple Productions
0171-323 3939
Pioneer Film & TV Productions
01753-651700
Piotrowska Films   0181-748 4518
Piranha Productions
0171-607 3355
Pirate Productions   0171-403 2007
Pizazz Pictures   0171-434 3581
Planet 24   0171-345 2424
Platform Films & Video
0171-278 8394
Platinum Film & TV   0171-916 9091
PMA   0181-893 3743
PM Murphy Productions
01273-564796
Pola Jones Film   0171-439 1165
Polite Company   0181-567 0437
Polkadot Productions
0171-831 4002
Pomegranate Pictures
0171-935 3400
Poorhouse Productions
0171-439 2637
Popular Films   0171-419 0722
Portman Entertainment
0171-468 3440
Portobello Pictures 0171-379 5566
Poseidon Productions
0171-734 4441
Post Raphaelite Productions
01189-50552
Pozzitive   0171-734 3258
Praxis Films   01472-398547
Premiere Productions
0171-255 1650
Presentable Productions
01222-55729
PrimaVista Productions
0171-274 6689
Primetime Television 0171-935 9000

Princess Productions
0171-565 6565
Principal Film Company
0171-494 4348
Principal Media Group
0171-928 9882
Producers Films   0171-636 4226
Projector Productions
0171-434 1110
Promenade Film Productions
0171-813 0208
Prominent Features 0171-284 0242
Propeller Productions
01222-377128
Prospect Cymru Wales
01222-551177
Prospect Pictures   0171-636 1234
Pueblo Productions 0181-969 2134
Pulse Productions 0171-794 1514
Puppetoon Productions
0171-636 2000
Q
Quadrant Broadcast
01222-237333
Quadrillion   01628-487522
Quality Time Television
01672-540281
Quanta   01666 826366
Quicksilver Films   0171-603 8339
Quintessence Films 01626-770750
R
Ragdoll Productions
01789-262772
Rapid Eye Movies   0171-613 0010
Rapido TV   0171-229 9854
Raw Charm   01222-641511

Raw Nerve Productions
01504-260562
Ray Fitzwalter Associates
0161-832 3337
RDF Television   0171-887 7500
RD Productions   0181-780 3819
Real Films   0181-348 6171
Real Life Productions
0113-234 7271
Real Radio & Television
01453-843101
Real World Pictures 0171-978 1178
Really Animated Productions
01625-612459
Rebecca Television 0171-923 7166
Recorded Picture Co
0171-636 2251
Red Door Productions
0171-637 3220
Red Galaxy Pictures 0171-622 2230
Red Green and Blue Company
0181-746 0616

Red Letter Productions
01442 833126
Red Rooster Film   0171-379 7727
Redcar Productions 01442-60694
Redlight Productions
0141-337 3269
Redwave Films   0171-436 2225
Reel Life Television 0171-713 1585
Reg Grundy Productions
0171-691 6000
Regent Productions 0181-789 5350
Reiner Moritz Associates
0171-439 2637
Remote Films   0171-738 2727
Renegade Films   0171-637 0957
Replay   0181-672 0606
Resource Base   01703-236806
Reuters Television   0181-965 7733
Revere Entertainment
0171-304 0047
Revolution Films   0171-242 0372
Richmond Films & TV
0171-734 9313
Richmond Light Horse
0171-937 9315
Ricochet Films   0171-251 6966
Ritefilms   01303-252335
Riverfront Pictures 0171-481 2939
Roadshow Productions
0171-584 0542
Roberts & Wykeham Films
0171-602 4897
Rocket Pictures   0181-741 9090
Rodney Read   0181-891 2875
Roger Bolton Productions
0171-209 2244
Rose Bay Film Productions
0181-600 5200
Rosetta Pictures   0171-493 1022
Rosso Productions 01843-823992
Rough Sea Productions
0191-259 1184
Rugby Vision Cyffro 01222 666800
S
SATV   0131-558 8148
Safe and Sound Productions
01789-450182
Saffron Productions 01440-785200
St Elmo Films   0181-749 0583
Sally Head Productions
0181-607 8730
Salsa Rock Productions
01932 856102
Salt Island Productions
0171-894 9900
Samba Films   0181-674 3649
Samuelson Productions
0171-236 5532
Sandercock Films   0181-874 3457
Sands Films   0171-231 2209

Sankofa Film & Video
0171-485 0848
Sarah Radclyffe Productions
0171-437 3128
Satel Doc　0171-437 5250
Saunders & French Productions
0171-344 1010
Scala Productions　0171-734 7060
Science Pictures　01462-421110
Scimitar Films　0171-603 7272
Scope Picture Productions
0141-332 7720
Scorer Associates　0117-946 6838
Scottish Screen　0141-337 2526
Screen First　01825-712034
Screen Partners　0171-247 3444
Screen Resource　01865-744451
Screen Ventures　0171-580 7448
Screenhouse Productions
0113-242 4900
Secret Garden　01993-831904
September Films　0171-494 1884
Serendipity Picture Company
0117-929 0417
Seventh Art Productions
01273-777678
Seventh House Films
01603-749068
Severn Pictures　01886-884745
SFTV　0181-780 0678
Shaker Films　0181-968 4278
Sharp Image Productions
0171-234 0092
Sharpshooter Films 0181-940 9938
Shattered Images　0181-946 9865
Shipleys　0171-312 0000
Shooting Star　0171-409 1925
Shorna Productions 0115-956 5070
Showplay　0171-371 3234
Sigma Films　0141-339 1241
Signals　01206-560255
Siguy Films　0171-543 1700
Sindibad Films　0171-823 7488
Siriol mm　0121-488400
Skreba　0171-437 6492
Skreba-Creon Films 0171-437 6492
Skyline Productions 0131-557 4580
Skyscraper Films　0171-625 6465
Smith & Watson Productions
01803-863033
Snap Productions　0181-346 9310
Soho Group　0171-437 0831
SOI Film & TV　0171-267 4373
Solid Productions　0171-267 9479
Songbird Film Productions
0171-249 1477
Soul Purpose Productions
0181-960 7987
South Productions 0181-297 2195
Spafax　0171-706 4488

Speakeasy Productions
01738-828524
Specific Films　0171-580 7476
Spelthorne Productions
0181-979 6215
SPI 1980　0171-435 1007
Spider Pictures　0171 287 6707
Spire Films　01865-371979
Spirit Films　0171-734 6642
Spitting Image Productions
0171-251 2626
Splash Productions 0171-730 9641
Spoken Image (Broadcast)
0161-236 7522
St Pancras Films　0171-385 2094
Stagescreen Productions
0171-497 2510
Stampede　0171-278 6878
Stand & Deliver Productions
0171-465 6249
Stark Productions　0181-748 2517
Stirling Film　01232-333848
Stone City Films　0171-240 8789
Stone House Pictures
01932-571044
Stories　0171-813 3323
Storyline　0191-232 2050
Straight Forward Productions
01232-426298
Straight TV　0161-834 7162
Stawberry Productions
0181-994 4494
Strawberry Vale Film & TV
0171-494 1399
Studio Arts TV　0191-261 2023
Studio Z　01622-684545
Suffolk Films　01986-875875
Sundog Media　01752 265562
Sunstone Films　0171-485 2884
Supervision　0181-251 9500
SVC Screen Entertainment
0171-460 6060
Swanlind Communication
0121-616 1701
Sweaterheads Productions
0141-204 2864
Swingbridge Video　0191-232 3762
T
Table Top Productions
0181-742 0507
Taft TV Associates　0171-223 0906
Takeaway Media　0171-722 5539
Talent Television　0171-434 1677
Talisman Films　0171-603 7474
Talkback　0171-323 9777
Tall Man Films　0171-439 8113
Tall Order Productions
0121-766 5911
Tall Stories　0171-607 1705
Tandem Television　0171-465 6365

Tapecraft Productions
01986-782266
Tapson Steel Films　0171-287 7244
Taylored Productions
0141-334 1462
TC TV　01962-714359
Team Pictures　0181-981 3770
Telemagination　0171-828 5331
Television Company, The
0171-837 0789
Television Sport & Leisure
0171-820 0700
Television Junction　0121-248 4466
Teliesyn　01222-667556
Tell-A-Vision TV　0131-556 3743
Tempest Films　0181-340 0877
Tern Television Productions
01224-211123
Terra Firma Film Productions
0171-820 1580
Testimony Films　0117-925 8589
Theodore Goddard 0171-606 8855
Thin Man Films　0171-734 7372
Third Eye Productions
0181-969 8211
This Guy's Films　0171-284 0108
Thomas Gray Productions
01865 284236
Thura Film　0181-735 0828
Tiger Aspect　0171-434 0672
Tiger Lily Films　0171-287 1716
Tigervision　0171-383 2267
Tilt Films　0171-503 3699
Tin Fish Films　0181-874 0342
TKO Communications
01273-550088
TNTV　0171-483 3526
Toledo　0171-485 4411
Tomboy Films　0171-436 3324
Tonic Pictures　0171-229 2512
Topaz Productions 0181-749 2619
Topical TV　01703-712233
Total Communications
01983-752326
Touch Productions 0171-287 5520
Touchdown Films　0171-917 2871
Track 29　0141-424 1124
Trans World International
0181-233 5400
Transatlantic Films 0181-735 0505
Transmedia Productions
0171-287 3680
Tricorn Associates 0181-995 3898
Triple Echo Productions
01503-272428
True Corner Productions
0151-281 0741
True TV and Film　0141-554 1196
True Visions Productions
0181-742 7852

Try Again 01225-862705
Tucker Partnership 01245-260307
Tullstar Productions 01786-825587
Tumble Hill Productions
01222-594044
Turn On Television 0171-720 8353
Turning Point Productions
01753-630666
Tu-Tone Productions
0171-221 2213
TV Cartoons 0171-388 2222
TV Choice 0171-379 0873
TV 6 0181-789 3883
TV 6 Scotland 0131-319 2333
TV21 0171-287 4545
TVF 0171-837 3000
Twentieth Century Fox
0171-437 7766
Twenty Twenty Television
0171-284 2020
Two Four Productions
01752-345424
Two Sides TV 0171-439 9882
Ty Gwyn Films 01286-881235
Tyburn Productions 01753-651700

U
UBA 0171-371 0160
Uden Associates 0171-351 1255
Umbrella Entertainment
0171-267 8834
Umbrella Television Productions
0141-429 1750
Unhooked Prods 0181-208 0947
Unicorn Organisation
0171-229 5131
Union Pictures 0171-287 5110
United Broadcasting
0171-389 8654
United Television Artists
0171-287 2727
Up 'N' Under 01222 255630
Uptown Film and TV 0171-833 1153

V
Vanguard Productions
·0171-582368
Ventura Productions
01564-794320
Vera Productions 0171-436 6116
Victoria Real 01273-774469
Video Arts 0171-637 7288
Video Assignments 0181-343 2513
Video Visuals 0171-384 2243
Videotel Productions
0171-439 6301
Visage Productions 0171-487 2641
Visible Ink TV 01494-791806
Visionworks 01232-241241
Vis Television Services
0116-233 5599
Viz 01383-412811

Volcanika 0171-5806486
Volcano Films 0171-424 0146
Vortex TV 0171-485 5326
Voyager Productions
01301 703336
Voyager Television 01865-407474

W
Wall to Wall Television
0171-485 7424
Waller Film Co 0181-675 0947
Walnut Partnership 0113-245 6913
Wark, Clements & Co
0141-429 1750
Warner Brothers 0171-465 4830
Warner Sisters Film 0181-960 3550
Watchmaker Productions
0171-465 6000
Watchword 0181-741 9112
Watermark Productions
0181746 1634
Watershed TV 0117-973 3833
Wayward Films 0171-587 1007
West Heath Productions
01730-816062
West Highland Animation
01877-384671
Westbourne Films 0171-221 1998
Westerley Productions
01752-830522
Westway Film Production
01504 308383
Whistling Gypsy 0181-892 4477
Whitby Davison Productions
0181-579 3811
Whitehorse Films 0171-586 8940
White Magic 07000 784707
Whole Films 0171-402 3323
Wide Eye Pictures 0171-636 1918
Wild & Fresh Liverpool
0151-288 8000
Wild & Fresh Productions
0171-609 6465
Wildcard Film and Television
01752 262968
Wild Dream Films 01222-666311
Wild Films 0181-672 2489
Wildcat Films 01434 381772
Wildflower Productions
0171-234 0330
Winchester Entertainment
0171-434 4374
Windfall Films 0171-637 2666
Wink Productions 0171-599 8955
Wobbly Picture Productions
0181-746 3126
Women Now Films 0181-830 5156
Women's Ind. Cinema House
0151-707 0539
Wonderworks Productions
01973-634161

Woodfilm Productions
0171-243 8600
Word-Pictures 01494-481629
Workhouse TV 01962-626400
Working Title Films 0171-307 3000
World of Wonder 0171-737 2222
World Productions 0171-734 3536
World Television 0117-930 4099
World Wide Pictures
0171-434 1121
Worldmark Productions
0171 792 9800
WoW Productions 0181-830 5978
Wright Ideas 01628 484 780

X
XYTV 0113-237 1199
Xanadu Productions •
0181-985 0035

Y
Year 200 Productions
01253-395403
YI Productions 0191-281 2256
Yorkshire Film Co 0113-244 1224
Yorkshire International
0113-222 8360
Yorkshire-Tyne Tees TV
0113-243 8283

Z
Zanzibar Film Productions
01425-472892
ZCZ Films 0171-284 0521
Zebra Film Productions
0117-970 6026
Zenith North 0191-261 0077
Zenith Productions 0171-224 2440
Zephir Films 0171-431 1534
Zephyr Films 0171-221 8318
Zin Zan Productions 01734-503816
ZKK 0171-482 5885
Zoo Gang 0181-789 9277
Zooid Pictures 0171-281 2407
Zoom Production Co
0171-434 3895

Broadcast agencies

FILM LIBRARIES

A19 Film and Video
21 Foyle Street, Sunderland, SR1 1LE
Fax 0191-565 6288   Tel 0191-565 5709
Documentary makers, focussing on the north-east.

Archive Film Agency
21 Lidgett Park Avenue, Leeds LS8 1EU
Fax 0113-266 2454   Tel 0113-266 2454
E-mail: 100657.1661@compuserve.com
Website: http://www.archivefilms.com
Specialists in early newsreel, documentary, fiction. With
a current stock shot library covering the world.

Archive Films
17 Conway Street, London W1P6EE
Fax 0171-391 9123   Tel 0171-391 9129
E-mail: dcass@theimagebank.com
Website: http://www.imagebank.co.uk
14,000 hours of historical entertainment footage
including silent films, feature films, newsreels and
documentaries.

BBC Worldwide Television Library Sales
Woodlands, 80 Wood Lane, London W12 0TT
Fax 0181-576 2939   Tel 0181-576 2861
E-mail: ukls@bbcfootage.com
The BBC has Britain's largest library of film and
videotape, with over 400 million feet of film.

Beulah
66 Rochester Way, Crowborough, Sussex TN6 2DU
Fax 01892-652413   Tel 01892-652413
E-mail: iainlogan@enterprise.net
Website: http://homepages.enterprose.net/beulah
Films and stills library of transport and social history
subjects.

British Film Institute
21 Stephen Street, London W1P 2LN
Fax 0171-580 5830   Tel 0171-255 1444
E-mail: helpdesk@bfi.org.uk
Website: http://www.bfi.org.uk
300,000 titles. BFI Films also handles sales from the 7
million images in the Stills, Posters and Designs
collection.

British Movietone News
North Orbital Road, Denham, Middlesex UB9 5HQ
Fax 01895-834893   Tel 01895-833071
1929-79 newsreel, including the Look at Life collection.

British Pathe
4th Floor, 60 Charlotte Street, London W1P 2AX
Fax 0171-436 3232   Tel 0171-323 0407
E-mail: pathe@enterprise.net
50m feet of historical film footage from 1895 to 1970.

British Universities Film and Video Council
See Researcher's Guide to British Film and TV
Collections, page 308

Central Office of Information Footage File
4th Floor, 184-192 Drummond Street, London NW1
3HP
Fax 0171-383 2333   Tel 0171-383 2292
E-mail: filmimages@compuserve.com
40,000 Crown Copyright titles from the government's
News and Information archives spanning over 75 years
of British industrial, political, social and sporting
history.

Channel 4 Clip Library
Channel 4 International, 124 Horseferry Road, London
SW1P 2TX
Fax 0171-306 8363   Tel 0171-306 8490
E-mail: cowstin@channel4.co.uk
Website: http://www.chanel4.com

East Anglian Film Archive
University of East Anglia, Norwich NR4 7TJ
Fax 01603-458553   Tel 01603-592664
E-mail: eafa@uea.ac.uk
Web: http://www.
lib.uea.ac.uk/libinfo/archives/eafawelc/eafawelc.htm
Non-profit archive of film showing life and work in East
Anglia from 1896 to the present.

Educational & Television Films
247a Upper Street, London N1 1RU
Fax 0171-226 8016   Tel 0171-226 2298
Soviet Union, Eastern Europe, China, Vietnam and
Cuba.

Energy Film Library
101 Bayham Street, London NW1 0AG
Fax 0181-574 3400   Tel 0181-574 3410
E-mail: energy@getty-images.com
Website: http://www.digital-energy.com
Stock film library. Short production quality 35mm
footage.

Environmental Investigation Agency
15 Bowling Green Lane, London EC1R 0BD
Fax 0171-490 0436   Tel 0171-490 7040
E-mail: eiauk@gn.apc.org
Website: http://www.pair.com/eia/
Video archive devoted to illegal trade in wild life.

Film Archive Management & Entertainment
see Beulah

Film Images
See Central Office of Information Footage File

Film Research
177-183 Regent Street, London W1R 8LA
Fax 0171-734 8017   Tel 0171-734 1525
E-mail: frps@aol.com.
Provides a research service for footage for all media
purposes.

GMTV Library Sales
The London Television Centre, Upper Ground, London
SE1 9TT
Fax 0171-827 7043   Tel 0171-827 7363
E-mail: librarysales@gmtv.co.uk
UK and worldwide news, showbiz, fashion and feature
items and stockshots from October 1992 to the present
day.

Huntley Film Archives
78 Mildmay Park, London N1 4PR
Fax 0171-241 4929   Tel 0171-923 0990
E-mail: films@huntleyarchives.com
Website: http://www.huntleyarchives.com
Adverts, animation, art, dance, education, fashion,
features, food, geography, history, industry, media,
medicine, music, nature, personalities, places, royalty,
science, social history, sport, stills, transport, war.

The Image Bank Film
17 Conway Street, London W1P 6EE
Fax 0171-391 9111   Tel 0171-312 0300
E-mail: ukmarketing@theimagebank.com
Website: http://www.imagebank.co.uk
The largest source of film imagery in the world with
thousands of hours of footage available including
lifestyle, sports, business, industry, archive and many
more. 70 offices worldwide.

Imperial War Museum Film and Video Archive
Lambeth Road, London SE1 6HZ
Fax 0171-416 5299   Tel 0171-416 5291
E-mail: film@iwm.org.uk
Holds material covering all aspects of conflict from the
Boer War to Bosnia. Totals 120 million feet of film and
6,000 hours of videotape.

Index Stock Shots
12 Charlotte Mews, London W1P 1LN
Fax 0171-436 8737   Tel 0171-631 0134
E-mail: index@msn.com
Stock footage on 35mm film and tape, including
extremes of nature and world climate, time-lapse and
aerial photograhy, cities, aircraft and wildlife.

IVN Entetainment
Centre 500, 500 Chiswick Road, London W4 5RG
Fax 0181-956 2339   Tel 0181-956 2454
E-mail: ivnentuk@aol.com
World-wide destinations, travel, adventure, natural
history, and nature footage. Includes Reader's Digest
and Lonely Planet footage. Free loan of BITC VHS.

ITN Archive
200 Grays Inn Road, London WC1X 8XZ
Fax 0171-430 4453   Tel 0171-430 4480
E-mail: archive.sales@itn.co.uk
Contains 70,000 hours and 14 million feet of news and
feature footage covering every news event from 1955 to
the present day.

ITV
The ITV companies have libraries of material:
Anglia	01603-615151
Central	0121-643 9898
Channel Four	0171-396 4444
Granada	0161-827 2207
HTV	01222-590590
LWT	0171-620 1620
Meridian	01703-222555
Scottish	0141-300 3000
Ulster	01232-328122
Yorkshire - Tyne Tees	0113-243 8283

London Stockshots Library
London News Network, London TV Centre, Upper
Ground, London SE1 9LT
Fax 0171-827 7579   Tel 0171-827 7784
E-mail: lnn-tv.co.uk
Website: http://www.lnn-tv.co.uk
LNN library of London region coverage during the
nineties.

North West Film Archive
The Manchester Metropolitan University, Minshull
House, 47-49 Chorlton Street, Manchester M1 3EU
Fax 0161-247 3098   Tel 0161-247 3097
E-mail: n.w.filmarchive@mmu.ac.uk
Website:
http://www.mmu.ac.uk/services/library/west.htm
Documentary collection about life in the North West
region dating from 1896 to the present. Contact
Rachael Holdsworth for access enquiries.

Nova Productions
11a Winholme, Armthorpe, Doncaster DN3 3AF
                        Tel 01302-833422
Production company with a social documentary archive
of shopping, transport and ways of life. Also runs the
Doncaster Film & Video Archive.

Oxford Scientific Films
Lower Road, Long Hanborough, Oxon OX8 8LL
Fax 01993-882808   Tel 01993-881881
E-mail: enquiries@osf.uk.com
Natural history films, commercials, non-broadcast film
and extensive stills and footage resources.

Pearson Television International Archive
1 Stephen Street, London W1P 1PJ
E-mail: archive@pearsontv.com
Website: http://www.pearsontvarchive.com
Footage library dates back to mid-fifties and includes
Thames, Grundy, ACI, Alomo and All American
productions with total of 15,000 hours of programming.

PolyGram Film and Television Library
Oxford House, Oxford Street, London W1N 0HQ
Fax 0171-307 7501   Tel 0171-307 7500
The ATV/ITV libraries from 1955-1981.

Reuters Television
40 Cumberland Avenue, London NW10 7EH
Fax 0171-542 8568   Tel 0171-542 6444/6733
The world's largest TV news archive, with more than
26,000 hours of material.

Ronald Grant Archive
The Master's House, The Old Lambeth Workhouse, 2
Dugord Way, off Renfrew Road, London SE11 4TH
Fax 0171-840 2299   Tel 0171-840 2200
E-mail: martin@cinemamuseum.org uk
Images of cinema and film from 1896 to the present
day.

RSPB Film Library
The Lodge, Sandy, Beds SG19 2DL
Fax 01767-692365   Tel 01767-680551
E-mail: birds@rspb.demon.co.uk
Natural history footage (not just birds).

Scottish Film & Television Archive
74 Victoria Crescent Road, Glasgow G12 9JN
Fax 0141-302 1713   Tel 0141-302 1742
Covers Scottish social, cultural and industrial history.

Sky News Library Sales
Grant Way, Isleworth TW7 5QD
Fax 0171-705 3201   Tel 0171-705 2872/3132
E-mail: libsales@sky2.bskyb.com
Website: http://www.sky.co.uk/news/
Sky News and current affairs footage since 1989. Held
on Beta SP. Available 24 hours a day.

Sports Video Library
TWI, Axis Centre, Burlington Lane, London W4 2TH
Fax 0181-233 5301   Tel 0181-233 5500
E-mail: rcostantinou@imgworld.com
Video library of TWI, the world's largest independent
producer of sports programming.

Wales Film & Television Archive
Unit 1, Science Park, Cefn Llan, Aberystwyth SY23 3AH
Fax 01970-626008   Tel 01970-626007
E-amil: sgrin@sgrinwales.demon.co.uk
Website: http://www.sgrinwales.demon.co.uk
Moving images of all aspects of Welsh society, work and
culture, spanning the 20th century.

Wessex Film & Sound Archive
Sussex Street, Winchester, Hants.SO23 8TH
Fax 01962-878681   Tel 01962-847742
E-mail: sadedm@hants.gov.uk
Covers Hants, IoW, Dorset, Wilts and Berks.

RADIO AND TV NEWS

ABC News Intercontinental
8 Carburton Street, London W1P 8JD
Fax 0171-631 5084   Tel 0171-637 9222
London office of the American news network.

Bloomberg LP
Citygate House, 39-45 Finsbury Square, London
EC2A 1PQ
Fax 0171-392 6000   Tel 0171-330 7500
Website: www.bloomberg.com
Financial information for City desks and direct to the
money markets.

CBS News
68 Knightsbridge, London SW1X 7LL
Fax 0171-581 4431   Tel 0171-581 4801
London office of the American news network.

CNN International
19-22 Rathbone Place, London W1P 1DF
Fax 0171-637 6738   Tel 0171-637 6700
Website: http://www.cnn.com
Cable News Network International, a wholly owned
subsidiary of Time Warner Inc., is the world's only
global network. Distributing 24-hour news via 15
satellites CNN and CNNI are seen by 200 million
households in more than 210 countries. and territories
world-wide, and have 36 international bureaux and
nearly 700 affiliated TV stations around the world.
Nearly 90 per cent of CNNI's programming is
generated specifically for the network and during 1998
a number of new programmes and regional-specific
broadcasting will be introduced.

FT Business News
50 Lisson Street, London NW1 5DF
Fax 0171-723 6132   Tel 0171-402 1011
Business and personal finance news for commercial
radio stations from Unique Broadcsting, FT and ABC
Radio.

IRN - Independent Radio News
200 Gray's Inn Road, London WC1X 8X2
Fax 0171-430 4092   Tel 0171-430 4090
News desk   Tel 0171-430 4814
E mail: news@irn.co.uk
Website: wttp://www.irn.co.uk
IRN is Britain's main radio news agency, supplying
bulletins and services to over 90 per cent of the
commercial radio stations. The news is provided to IRN
by ITN, using the resources of ITN at its headquarters
in 200 Grays Inn Road. IRN is effectively a
commissioning agency acting on behalf of its
customers. Its owners are the main radio groups.

ITN
200 Grays Inn Road, London WC1X 8XZ
Fax 0171-833 3000   Tel 0171-833 3000
Press office   Tel 0171-430 4700
Website: http://www.itn.co.uk
ITN produces the daily news programmes for three competing British TV channels: ITV, Channel 4 and Channel 5. Other output includes radio news bulletins, documentaries, educational programmes, Internet websites and archive clips. ITN is also responsible for Euronews, a news channel in six languages which is seen in 43 countries. Founded in 1955 as the news department of ITV, ITN is now an independent commercial public service broadcaster owner by a consortium comprising Carlton Communications, the Granada Group, Daily Mail & General Trust, United News & Media and Reuters.

London News Network
London Television Centre, Upper Ground, London SE1 9LT
Fax 0171-827 7710   Tel 0171-827 7700
Website: http://www.lnn-tv.co.uk
Jointly set up and run by the London ITV companies Carlton and LWT to provide their local news. Began in January 1992. Also supplies news to breakfast ITV station GMTV.

NBC News Worldwide
8 Bedford Avenue, London WC1B 3AP
Fax 0171-636 2628   Tel 0171-637 8655
E-mail: nhaw@nbc.com
London office of the American network.

Parliamentary Channel
160 Great Portland Street, London W1N 5TB
Fax 0171-299 5300   Tel 0171-299 5000
E-mail: viewer_tpc@flextech.co.uk
Website: http://www.parlchan.co.uk/
Provides unedited live coverage of daily proceedings in the House of Commons and recorded coverage of the Lords, Parliamentary committees, business statements, the European Union and Question Time. Run as a non-profit organisation, the channel was created by the British Cable Industry.

Reuters Television
85 Fleet Street, London EC4P 4AJ
Fax 0171-542 7574   Tel 0171-250 1122
E-mail: rtv@reuters.com
Reuters Television (RTV) supplies video news material via satellite 24 hours a day to more than 200 broadcasters, plus their networks and affiliates, in 90 countries.

TV News London
Premiere House, 10 Greycoat Place, London SW1P 1SB
Fax 0171-222 0832   Tel 0171-222 0807
E-mail: roz@tvnews.ftech.co.uk
London news agency supplying stories about events in the capital to regional broadcasting companies. Started in 1992.

Unique Entertainment News
50 Lisson Street, London NW1 5DF
Fax 0171-724 5373   Tel 0171-453 1650
E-mail: katy.topping@unique.co.uk
Entertainment news for commercial radio. .

WRN (World Radio Network)
Wyvil Court, 10 Wyvil Road, London SW8 2TG
Fax 0171-896 900/   Tel 0171-890 9000
E-mail: online@wrn.org
Website: http://www.wrn.org
WRN operates a 24 hour-a-day network with news, current affairs and feature programmes from 28 of the world's public service broadcasters. WRN has three language streams: English, German and Mulit-lingual, for listeners across Europe, Africa, the Middle East, Asia, the Pacific and North America. WRN's European English-language stream is available live via the Internet and is also transmitted on DAB in both London and Warsaw.

Worldwide Television News (WTN)
Interchange, 32 Oval Road, Camden Lock, London NW1 7DZ
Fax 0171-413 8302   Tel 0171-410 5200
E-mail: wtnlib@abc.com
WTN provides a 24-hour satellite service from camera crews in 90 cities to more than a thousand broadcasters. WTN also has one of the most comprehensive film and video archives.
Owned by ITN, ABC (USA) and Nine Network (Australia). WTN HQ is in London, with bureaux in 55 other cities.

Broadcast awards 1998

BAFTA Performance Awards (TV Section)

British Academy of Film and Television Arts, 195 Piccadilly, London W1V 0LN
Fax 0171- 734 1792   Tel 0171-734 0022
Best single drama: No Child of Mine, ITV
Best drama series: Jonathan Creek, BBC1
Best drama serial: Holding On, BBC2
Best factual series: The Nazis, BBC2
Best light entertainment: The Fast Show, BBC2
Best comedy: I'm Alan Partridge, BBC2
Best news/current affairs: Valentina's Story, Panorama, BBC1
Best sports event: Rugby Union, Sky
Best actress: Daniela Nardini, This Life, BBC2
Best actor: Simon Russell-Beale, A Dance to the Music of Time, Channel 4
Best light entertainment performance: Paul Whitehouse, The Fast Show, BBC2
Best comedy performance: Steve Coogan, I'm Alan Partridge, BBC2
Best arts programme: Gilbert & Gorge, South Bank Show, ITV
Best documentary: The Grave, True Stories, Channel 4
Best original music: Tom Jones, by John Parker, BBC1
Outstanding creative achievement: Ted Childs
Personal contribution to factual television: David Dimbleby
Dennis Potter award: Kay Mellor
Special award: Roger Cook

The Indies

Single Market Events, 23-24 George Street, Richmond, Surrey TW9 1HY
Fax 0181-332 0495   Tel 0181-948 5522
The Indie: This Life, World Productions, BBC2
Hat Trick Pioneer: Talkback Productions
Drama: This Life, World Productions, BBC2
Light entertainment: Alan Partridge, Talkback, BBC2
Music and arts: The Fake Van Goghs, Third Eye, C4
Factual: Changing Rooms, Bazal Productions, BBC2
News: Mother Russia's Children, October Films, C4
Documentary: One Night Stand, Blast! Films, C4
Animation: Crapston Villas, Spitting Image, C4
Sport: Tour de France, Venner Television, C4
Cable and satellite: Dream Team, Hewland, Sky1
Archive award: Royals and Reptiles, Blakeway, C4
Children: Teletubbies, Ragdoll Productions, BBC1/2

Voice of the Listener and Viewer Awards

101 King's Drive, Gravesend, Kent DA12 5BQ
                    Tel 01474-352835
Best television contributor: Jeremy Paxman
Best radio contributor: Sue MacGregor
Best radio programme: I'm Sorry I Haven't a Clue
Best television programme: Channel 4 News

Royal Television Society Awards

Holborn Hall, 100 Grays Inn Road, London WC1X 8AL
Fax 0171-430 0924   Tel 0171-430 1000
Journalist of the year: Dennis Murray, BBC Belfast
Young journalist of the year: Glenn Campbell, London News Network
Daily news magazine: BBC Midlands Today
Regional current affairs: Meridian Focus, Murky Waters
News (home): Bloody Sunday, ITN for Channel 4 News
News (international): News at Ten, Plight of Romania's Children, Paul Davies
Current affairs (home): Dispatches, Secrets of the Gaul, Anglia TV for Channel 4
Current affairs (international): Correspondent, Getting Away with Murder, BBC & Panorama, Valentina's Story
News event: death and funeral of the Princess of Wales, Sky News, BBC and ITN
News technician of the year: Alan Thompson, ITN News on ITV
Interview of the year: Jeremy Paxman interviews Michael Howard on BBC
Production award: Channel 5 News, ITN News on Channel 5
Judges award: Peter Snow
Sports coverage: British Grand Prix 1997, MACH 1 for ITV
Sports news: Round the World Yacht Race, ITN for ITV, Michael Nicholson
Sports documentary: Equinox-Losing it, Union Pictures for Channel 4
Regional sports news: Kevin Keegan's Resignation, BBC North East
Regional sports documentary: 24 hours: Losers Limited, Central Broadcasting for Carlton
Sports presenter: Jim Rosenthal (MACH 1/ISN for ITV)
Sports commentator: Ewen Murray and Bruce Critchley (Sky Sports)
Judges award: Brian Moore

Industrial Journalism Awards

The Industrial Society, 48 Bryanston Square, London W1H 7LN
Fax 0171-479 2222   Tel 0171-262 2401
Industrial Journalist of the Year (national): Simon Caulkin, Observer
Industrial Journalist of the Year (regional): Richard Hazlewood, Evening Chronicle (Newcastle)
Industrial Journalist of the Year (broadcast): Lesley Curwen, BBC (Radio Five Live)
Scoop of the Year: Alan Jones, PA News (BA/T&G;GE railway passengers as guards)

Broadcasting Press Guild Awards

Tiverton, The Ridge, Woking, Surrey GU22 7EQ
Fax 01483-764895   Tel 01483-764895
Best single drama: Breaking the Code, The Drama House for BBC1
Best drama series: Holding On, BBC2
Best documentary series: The Nazis-A Warning From History, BBC2
Best single documentary: Cutting Edge: The Dinner Party, Granada for C4
Best entertainment: I'm Alan Partridge, Talkback Productions for BBC2
Best actor: Simon Russell Beale, A Dance to the Music of Time, C4
Best actress: Helen Baxendale, Cold Feet, An Unsuitable Job for a Woman
Best performer: Jeremy Paxman, University Challenge, Newsnight, election night, 1997
Writer's award: David Renwick, One Foot in the Grave, Jonathan Creek
Radio programme of the year: I'm Sorry I Haven't a Clue, Radio 4
Radio broadcaster: Susan Sharpe, Midweek Choice, Radio 3
Outstanding contribution award: Michael Wearing, Head of drama serials, BBC TV

Broadcast Production Awards

33-39 Bowling Green Lane, London EC1R 0DA
Fax 0171-505 8050   Tel 0171-505 8014
E-mail: bcast@media,emap.co.uk
Cable or satellite programme: Ibiza Uncovered, LWT Productions
Children's programme: Throways, Zenith North for BBC
Drama: Hillsborough, Granada for ITV
Documentary programme: Witness: Tottenham Ayatollah, RDF Television for C 4
Comedy: Harry Hill, Avalon TV for C4
Light entertainment: Election Night Armstice, BBC production for BBC2
Sports programme: Monday Night Football, BSkyB for Sky Sports
Popular factual programme: Driving School, BBC features for BBC1
New programme: Brass Eye, Talkback Productions for Channel 4
Independent production co.: Talkback Productions
Post production house: Molinare
Studio facilities: The London Studios

Sony Radio Awards

Sony, The Heights, Brooklands, Weybridge, Surrey KT13 0XN
Tel 01932 816000
UK station of the year: BBC Radio 5 Live
Talk or news broadcaster: Anna Raeburn, Talk Radio
News gold award: The Death of the Princess of Wales, BBC Radio 4 and BBC RAdio 5 Live
Sony gold award: Chris Evans, Virgin Radio
Event gold award: The Funeral of the Princess of Wales,BBC Network, regions and local radio
Daytime talk or news gold award: The Nicky Campbell Show, BBC Radio 5 Live
DJ award: Jo Whiley, Radio 1
Breakfast music award: Steve Jackson, Morning Glory, Kiss FM
Breakfast talk award: Breakfast Programme, BBC Radio 5 Live
Daytime music: Mark Radcliffe Show, BBC Radio 1
Drivetime music: The John Dunn Show, BBC Radio 2
Comedy gold award: Blue Jam, Chris Morris, BBC Radio 1
Sport gold award: Wimbledon and the British Lions Test, John Inverdale, BBC Radio 5 Live
Late night talk: Up All Night, Rhod Sharp, BBC Radio 5 Live

Ethnic Minority Media Awards

Hearsay Communications, 67-69 Whitfield Street, London W1P 5RL
Fax 0171-636 1255   Tel 0171-468 3527
Best written feature: Maya Jaggi, Guardian Weekend
Best graphic design: Everton Wright, Creative Hands Design
Best female media newcomer: Okailey Dua, Pride Magazine
Best male media newcomer: Mark Dwayne, 11 Time Publishing
Best marketing campaign: Shami Ahmed, Joe Bloggs
Best advertising campaign: Ian Wright, One to One
Best PR campaign: Simon Woolley, Operation Black Vote
Best music presenter, radio: Angie Greaves, BBC GLR Radio
Best music production: Nitin Sawhney, Outcaste Records
Best TV production: Behroze Gandhi, Flight Hindi Pictures
Best print journalist: Anjana Ahuja, Times Newspaper
Beat audio journalist: Henry Bonsu, freelance radio journalist
Best visual journalist: Martin Bashir, BBC, Panorama
Ethnic minority charity: Neville Clare, Sickle Cell
Politician/public figure: Paul Boateng MP
Business personality: Shami Ahmed, MD Joe Bloggs
Media professional/personality: George Alagiah, BBC News Correspondence

Teletext

Teletext is written copy broadcast on TV sets. One way and another the main television companies each operate a teletext service, offering constantly updated bulletins on news, sport, travel, weather and entertainment. The BBC and Channels 3, 4 and 5 provide subtitling for people with hearing difficulties. About a half of all households have teletext decoders and the weekly audience is over 20 million.

The main teletext services are: Ceefax on BBC; Teletext Ltd on ITV; Simple Active on Channel 4; Data Broadcasting International (DBI) which uses spare capacity within the Channel 3 signal to provide commercial services; and Sky Text from BSkyB.

Ceefax is an in-house BBC operation. Its editorial extends beyond text related to BBC TV programming and has recently expanded with a local news, sport, weather, travel and TV listings for each of the BBC's 13 regions. Teletext Ltd is a profitable ITC-licensed consortium which is 75 per cent owned by the Daily Mail and General Trust. By the end of 1997 it was transmitting 272 main pages of non-regional information and 72 pages of regional information.

Simple Active has an ITV licence to use spare capacity within the Channel 4 signal to transmit "data packages for provision to a range of professional and consumer markets, with sub-licensing of some capacity to other users". Simple Active shares a senior management with DBI, which has another ITC licence "to use spare capacity within the Channel 3 signal and provide commercial services, operated by sub-licensees, to subscription and to closed user groups".

Sky Text has been available on Sky channels since 1992 and, according to Sky's 1997 annual report, is "now accessed by 1.4 million people every day".

Ceefax (BBC teletext)
Room 7013, BBC Television Centre, Wood Lane, London W12 7RJ
Fax 0181-749 6734   Tel 0181-576 1801
E-mail: ceefax@bbc.co.uk
Editor: Peter Clifton

Data Broadcasting International
Allen House, Station Road, Egham, Surrey TW20 9NT
Fax: 01784 438732   Tel: 01784 471515
Website: http://www.databroadcasting.co.uk
Commercial additional service Channel 3 teletext
Chairman: Peter Mason
Managing director: Justin Cadbury

SimpleActive
Allen House, Station Road, Egham, Surrey TW20 9NT
Fax: 01784 477722   Tel: 01784 477721
Additional commercial service Channel 4 teletext
Chairman: Peter Mason
Deputy chairman: Justin Cadbury

Sky Text
Welby House, 96-97 Wilton Road, London SW1 1DW
                              Tel: 0171-599 8900
Main contact: David Klein

Teletext (ITV teletext)
101 Farm Lane, Fulham, London SW6 1QJ
Fax 0171-386 5002   Tel 0171-386 5000
E-mail: dutyed@teletext.co.uk
Website: http://www.teletext.co.uk
Editorial director: Graham Lovelace

The Internet

Listed throughout this guide to the media are many websites which may well herald an information revolution, the death of distance, the most important cultural invention since printing, the media to make print redundant etc etc. The Internet could be all these things and more but all further expressions of astonishment or scepticism will be set aside. Instead, in both the interests of byte sized information and cross-corporate puffery, this section sticks with three of the Guardian's Internet projects:

1) Guardian Unlimited, a network of specialist websites constituting the online interpretation of the Guardian and Observer;

2) The Guardian Guide to the Internet by Jim McLellan is a Guardian book, as is;

3) The Cyberpix Guide by Alastair Fuad-Luke

GUARDIAN UNLIMITED

Guardian Unlimited
http://www.guardian.co.uk

Six sites were launched in summer 1998 covering football (re-launch), cricket (re-launch), news, politics, film and work. RecruitNet, a re-engineered version of the jobs database, and three smaller, existing sites for Pass Notes, Notes and Queries and the crossword will also be integrated into the network.

Subjects covered by the network will be areas of core Guardian strength or ones where the Guardian sees a clear commercial opportunity. The sites will cover subjects in greater depth (and frequency) than our print titles. They will, in general, use all relevant material from the Guardian and Observer, but will supplement this with a web-only material commissioned or produced by the Guardian's New Media Department, or obtained from content partners and suppliers.

In many cases the Guardian will partner with other content owners to ensure that we have the resources to dominate a particular niche. These partnerships will range from 50-50 joint ventures like the cricket site to more limited collaboration, such as the TeamTalk news service on the football site. Sites provisionally planned for launch by 2000 include education, media, travel, money, relationships, books, students, food, home/lifestyle and property.

GUARDIAN INTERNET GUIDE

The Guardian Guide to the Internet,
by Jim McLellan, Fourth Estate

Here are Jim McLellan's essential clicks from his new book. .

NEWS
BBC News Online
http://news.bbc.co.uk
A part of the BBC's s impressive online operation and an excellent regular news site.
Electronic Frontier Foundation
www.eff.org
A good site to catch up on current debates and news concering online issues, from censorship and privacy to intellectual property
McSpotlight
www.mcspotlight.org
Site set up during the McLibel trial still arguing the case against McDonalds and multinationals in general.
The Onion
www.theonion.com
Satirical spoof news, much ripped off but rarely bettered.
Press Association
www.pa.press.net
The Press Association's huge and hugely impressive news site.

FILM
Ain't It Cool News
www.aint-it-cool-news.com
Reviews from punters who catch the advanced screenings of big Hollywood films.
Internet Movie Database
http://uk.imdb.com
For those who want more than film gossip.

TECHNOLOGY
Carl Freedman
www.freedonia.com/~carl
A home page maintained by the net celeb who co-founded the webzine Suck. Check his online art projects and parodies and read his diary.
Cybergeography Research
www.cybergeography.org
The place to go if you want to know what a map of the net might look like.
NASA
www.nasa.gov
A vast site covering Nasa's multiple projects, past present and future.
Tasty Bits from the Technology Front
www.tbtf.com
News culled from a variety of online sources is an alternative to news sites like news.com and wired.com.

WEBZINES
Salon
www.salonmagazine.com
The most dependable of the attempts to bring a New Yorker style intelligent general interest mag to the net.
Urban 75
www.urban75.com
All strands of alternative culture and featuring the infamous Slap a Spice game, in which you can interactively take it out on the remaining Spice Girls.
Need To Know
www.ntk.net
Geek news and culture.

SHOPPING
Amazon
www.amazon.com
The best online bookshop.

TRAVEL
A2Btravel
www.a2btravel.com
Emap's UK-slanted travel resource with everything from booking hotels to the latest cheap flights.
Railtrack
www.railtrack.co.uk
Access the train information in a fraction of the time it takes to call the telephone timetable

ART
Irational
www.irational.org
A site maintained by techno-artist/provocateur Heath Bunting with links to his various online art escapades.

SPORT
Football.guardian
http://football.guardian.co.uk
There's plenty of football sites out there - this one has the results and stats fans need, quality writing and a few interactive extras to add some spice.

PICTURES ON THE WEB

The Cyberpix Guide
by Alastair Fuad-Luke, Guardian Books

Picture research is the main journalistic area served by the web. Alastair Fuad-Luke's top sites and his comments on them:

The Barbie Chronicles
http://www.erols.com/browndk/index.html
Barbie lives. In fact she appears in some of the world's most famous paintings in this art history portfolio . A delightful mix of the surreal, and ridiculous, which succeeds in providing Barbie with a soul.
Black Star
http://www.blackstar.com/
This North American agency, founded in 1935, represents a network of 350 photographers. It was one of the first news photo agencies to establish a Web presence.
Center for Creative Photography
http://www.ccp.arizona.edu/ccp.html
70,000 photographs, comprising 150 collections from some of the great American and Mexican photographers of the nineteenth and twentieth centuries.
Color Matters
http://www.lava.net/~colorcom/
This site has the answers to everything you want to ask about colour and the brave new digital world.
Corbis
http://www.corbis.com/
This c library of 700,000 images is the largest digital database of images in the world. Owned by Microsoft's boss Bill Gates, Corbis is an act of alturism for its owner and simultaneously endorses the new media business ethos by confirming that content is king.
Corel Photo CD-ROM Catalogue
http://www.commerce.corel.com/catalog.html
The home page opens with an A-Z listing of hundreds of themed CD-ROMs, offering quality stock and archive photography, each CD-ROM comprising 100 high resolution royalty free images.
first VIEW
http://www.FirstView.com/home.html
The listing of Collections On-Line is a who's who of the fashion world.
Focal Point f8
http://www.f8.com/
A meeting place, forum and auction house for, photojournalists.
Galeria Realidad Imaginara
http://www.internet.com.mx/fotoseptiembre/
Ten of Mexico's leading photographers, including the surrealist specialist Pedro Meyer, present a selection of their work in this Spanish language virtual gallery.
Hurrell, Unseen
http://www.oscars.org/
An archive of George Hurrell's Hollywood glamour, stars and starlets from the 1920s to 1940s.

Index Stock Photography
http://www.indexstock.com/
Professionals are offered access to over 100,000 images online once they have registered and downloaded the free TeleFocus Image Browser.

Infolink
http://www.infolink.co.uk/
Contact directory for the creative media community.

Kodak
http://www.kodak.com/
The sheer size of this site, loaded with digital technology, demonstrates Kodak will still be a dominant force in photography in the next millenium.

The Library of Congress
http://lcweb.loc.gov/rr/print
There are 13.6 million images about American people.

Lycos Pictures and Sounds
http://www.lycos.com/lycosmedia.html
Search for photos, art, designs, videos, music and other sounds. Simply specify Pictures or Sounds, and enter your search query. Keep the queries simple and usually you'll be rewarded with a few direct hits.

National Museum of Photography, Film & TV
http://www.nmsi.ac.uk/nmpft/

Photo District News
http://www.pdn-pix.com/
One of the best pro photo e-zines on the information highway, Photo District News sets the standards for web design in the photo publishing arena.

Photo Electronic Imaging Magazine
http://www.peimag.com
Definitely one for the image manipulation boys and girls, who will find lots of interest here, whether they've just started or are hard-bitten Wacom fiends.

Photo Exhibitions and Archives
http://www.algonet.se/~bengtha/photo/exhibits.html
A list of over 700 hotlinks to photography on the Web, and an ideal starting point for a first time Web surfer.

PhotoDisc
http://www.Photodisc.com/
A leading purveyor of royalty free digital stock photography with over 50,000 images.

Polaroid
http://www.polaroid.com/homepage.html
A clean corporate site, which hasn't forgotten it's photographers who keep the brand name alive.

Publishers Depot - PNI
http://www.publishersdepot.com/
Perhaps the second largest digital image database in cyberspace after Corbis.

Schwarz Illustrated
http://www.michaelschwarz.com/index.html
Michael A Schwartz is a freelance American photojournalist who exhibits his quality wares and provides a long list of hotlinks to some of the best photography resources on the Web, albeit a little US centric.

Silicon Graphics Image Gallery
http://www.sgi.com/Fun/free/gallery.html
There are some beautiful examples of digital images, high quality graphics and 3D images, created on Silicon Graphics workstations.

SITO - Artchives
http://www.sito.org/artchives/
Grab a fix of West coast digital imagination for an eclectic mixture of 47 subject categories including abstracts, bodyart, collage, fantasy, installation, morph, photomanip, photorealism, pixel, raytrace, and xerograph.

Smithsonian Photos Online
http://photo2.si.edu/
The Smithsonian houses an unparalleled record of the history of America spanning 150 years.

Sygma
http://www.rever.fr/SYGMA/Default.html
Over 100 photo stories, each containing one to 20 pictures. A clickable world map locates the individual offices and contact details of the Sygma empire.

Time Life Photo Sight
http://pathfinder.com/@@LMxmTQUAjHx3rOXn/photo/sighthome.html
Drawing on its 20 million photographs from its pedigree stable of Time, Life, Fortune, Sports Illustrated and the People magazine and newspaper titles, Time Warner shows you the true colours of the star-spangled banner. Glory, glory, hallelulljah. Slick and corporate, and beautifully American.

Tony Stone Images
http://www.tonystone.com/
A leading supplier of stock photography, its site has smart animated icons, and a rich graphic design.

Toy Camera Photographers Unite!
http://www.concom/~winters/toy_home.htm
All you wanted to know but never dared to ask about..toy cameras, is here. This delightful potpouri of facts, dry humour and eye-catching images should have everyone hooked.

UC Berkeley Digital Library Project
http://elib.cs.berkeley.edu
Over 53,000 images from the State Department of Water Resources; Brother Alfred Brousseau's (1908-1988) photo collection of California wildflowers and landscapes; and Corel Stock photos (27,000 of the image database).

Virtual Image Archive
http://imagiware.com/via/
An extensive list of photography, multimedia and computer links.

Webseek
http://www.itnm.co.umbia.edu/webseek/
A content-based image and video search and catalogue tool for the Web to browse a database of over 660,000 records.

Yahoo
http://www.yahoo.com/
This is the mother of all Internet search engines, when it comes to locating photography Web sites. A search for 'photography' reveals 80 sub-sub categories related to photography and 2,873 site matches.

Yell
http://www.yell.co.uk/
Yell, the Internet Yellow Pages for the UK, generated 112 hits for the search query 'photography'.

Satellite television

Sky dominates satellite TV and is well justified in billing itself as "the leading provider of programming to the UK multi-channel sector" and to market itself as offering "the freedom to watch what you want, when you want". At a price though.

A price, evidently, which many feel is worth paying, for Sky, which is 40 per cent owned by Rupert Murdoch's News International, is one of the 20 biggest companies in the UK. Murdoch's biggest gamble is well in profit and in nine years has expanded from a five to a 40 channel network. It has 6.37 million subscribers (many attracted by twice-weekly live Premier League football) in the UK and Ireland. Of these subscribers, around 3.5 million tune in via satellite and the remainder through cable. The cheapest dishes cost under £50.

Sky channels

WHOLLY OWNED	JOINTLY OWNED
Sky 1	Nickelodeon
Sky News	QVC
Sky Travel	Paramount Comedy
Sky Soap	Granada Plus
Sky Sports 1	Granada Men & Motors
Sky Sports 2	Granada Good Life
Sky Sports 3	History Channel
Computer Channel	National Geographic
Movie Channel	Sky Scottish
Sky Movies	Playboy TV
Sky Movies Gold	

Source: BSkyB.

Sky scepticism

On the basis of 1996, the BBC prepared the price per hour of viewing and listening comparing the licence fee and other media:

BBC, viewing only	4.8p/hour
Satellite channels	18p/hour

The BBC spends £648.4 million annually on BBC1 alone

A fifth of homes have a satellite dish, nearly all homes receive terrestrial TV

Total viewing figures, as of Spring 1997, were:

BBC	43.9%
ITV	33.1%
Channel 4	10.7%
Cable	8%
Sky	4.3%

The Simpsons, Sky's most popular non-sporting programme, attracts less than 750,000 viewers. An old Avengers on C4 will attract over a million viewers and the BBC's Eastenders can get over 10 million.

A CIA MediaLab survey of attitudes to satellite and cable revealed a hotbed of apathy among the British public, even among subscribers who pay to view:

Satellite/cable gives ...	subscribers	all
... best films on TV	38%	21%
... best sports	46%	25%
... best news	25%	13%
... best kids' progs.	24%	11%
... value for money	25%	10%
... important part of life	6%	2%

Sky boosterism

BSkyB is the world's most successful satellite pay television operator.

In 1990 Sky Movies broke new ground by becoming the first encrypted DTH satellite channel on UK television. In 1997, BSkyB's three dedicated movie channels screened over 2,300 movies and an average of more than one UK television premiere a day.

BSkyB has quadrupled the amount of sport on British television: the launch of Sky Sports 3 took BSkyB's live coverage to over 14,000 hours a year.

BSkyB's commitment to live sport has made it the UK's biggest user of outside broadcast facilities.

During the first five years of BSkyB's exclusively live coverage of Premier League football, attendances at matches rose by 30%.

Programming is claimed as BSkyB's biggest area of investment, accounting for 64% of all expenditure.

Sky's "affluent family biased audience matches most advertisers' needs". Thus the UK's top 50 advertisers use Sky.

Compared with the average Briton, a Sky viewer is 20% more likely to be employed full time, 75% more likely to own a mobile phone and 30% more likely to own a computer.

Source: Sky: The Facts and the 1997 Annual Report

BSkyB bills itself as the "world's most successful satellite pay-television operator". Its 1997 turnover was £1,270 million and pre-tax profits were £314 million.

In 1997 subscriber numbers rose by 2.5 million newcomers. However there were a large number of disconnections and Sky's cash generators - the two Screen and three Sport channels - only accumulated 900,000 viewers.

BSkyB has moved into direct competition with the BBC as a digital TV broadcaster. It is also a 32.5 per cent shareholder in British Interactive Broadcasting, the consortium which will supply interactive services. In a separate agreement, BSkyB will supply On Digital - formerly British Digital Broadcasting (a joint venture between Carlton and Granda) - with programming for its digital terrestrial TV service.

BSkyB

6 Centaurs Business Park, Grant Way, Isleworth, Middlesex TW7 5QD
Fax 0171-705 3030   Tel 0171-705 3000
Website http://www.sky.co.uk
This site is one of the most popular in the UK with three million hits a week. It has pages on sport, world news, a TV guide and a Sky shop. Also available is Sky Text and Sky Intertext.

Chairman: Jerome P Sydoux
Company secretary: Dave Gormley
Chief executive and managing director: Mark Booth
Managing director of Sky Ventures: James Ackerman
Director of corporate communications: Tim Allan
Head of legal and business affairs: Deanna Bates
Director of distribution: Jon Florsheim
Director of public affairs: Ray Gallagher
Group head of personnel: Cynthia Guthrie
Chief financial officer: Martin Stewart
General manager, broadcasting: Elisabeth Murdoch
Head of Sky news: Nick Pollard
Director of sales: Peter Shea
Director of movies & pay per view: Bruce Steinburg
Head of sport: Vic Wakeling
Director of engineering and services: Geoff Walters
Director of digital & business development: Ian West

FLEXTECH

Flextech's channels account for a quarter of Britain's satellite and cable viewing so, as the other main pay TV provider, it too is listed in this section.

Flextech
160 Great Portland Street, London W1N 5TB
Fax 0171-299 6000   Tel 0171-299 5000
Chief executive: Roger Luard
Head of PR: Nicola Howson

Flextech's interests

CHANNEL	% HOLDING	PROGRAMME TYPE
Bravo	100%	Films - horror, humour
Trouble	100%	Teenage soap, drama
TCC	100%	Cartoons, drama
Challenge TV	100%	Interactive games
UK Living	100%	Women
Maidstone Studios	100%	Production facilities
Action Studios	93%	Adventure park
HSN Direct	62%	Home shopping
Playboy	51%	Soft porn
UK Gold/BBC	50%	Old BBC/Thames footage
Sell a Vision	50%	Home shopping
Discovery Channel	48%	"Home and leisurre"
Kindernet	31%	Dutch children
EBN	30%	Business news
GMTV	20%	Channel 3 franchise
STV	20%	Channel 3 franchise
Parliamentary Channel	15%	Westminster coverage
Sega		Interactive video games

The Flextech majority shareholder is Tele-Communications International Inc. Other shareholders include Cox Comunications, Pearson, US West and BBC Worldwide.

The Observer
PHOTO ARCHIVE

ON CD-ROM

This album, the first of a series, is designed to make some of the classic photographs in the archive easily accessible. This is achieved by using a sophisticated search engine, developed by Hulton Getty Picture Collection and System Simulation Ltd, which enables images to be retrieved from the database by factual and conceptual search queries. Thus it is possible to search by specifying a named individual, a date and/or a subject, or by diverse themes such as mood, action and location.

Images are stored at resolutions up to 800 x 600 pixels (SVGA resolution) suitable for using for proofing and layout purposes. High resolution images can be ordered from the Observer Photo Archive.

It contains 2,500 classic photographs covering a momentous period in British Life, 1949 to 1989. They fall into the following categories:

UK Personalities
International
 Personalities
UK Events 1949 to 1989
International Events
 1949 to 1989
War
Arts and Entertainment
Sport – UK and
International
UK Social Documentation
 (Lifestyles, leisure, recreation, health, culture, transport)
UK Topography
International Topography
Odd and Quirky
Photography as Art

SYSTEM REQUIREMENTS
IBM PC
Windows 3.1, 3.11; Windows 95; Windows NT; CD-ROM drive (x2 upwards, better with x8 upwards); 8Mb RAM minimum; 4Mb minimum hard disk space; 32K colour or greater video adaptor; Monitor display minimum 800 x 600 pixels; Mouse and keyboard.
Apple Macintosh
System 7.5 upwards; Power PC processor; CD-ROM drive (x2 upwards, better with x8 upwards); 8Mb RAM minimum, 16Mb recommended; 'Thousands of colours' video mode; Monitor display minimum 800 x 600 pixels; Mouse and keyboard.

album **1**

The CD costs £39.00 plus VAT and is available from: The Observer Photo Archive
119 Farringdon Road, London EC1R 3ER   Telephone 0171 713 4423   Fax: 0171 837 1192

SATELLITE CHANNELS

3+
Scandinavian entertainment
01895-433327

A

Ace TV
Entertainment
0181-947 8841
Adult Channel
Porn
0181-581 7000
AMC
Asian music
0116-233 5599
African Channel
African programming
10 Cleveland Way, London E1
Ag Vision*
Livestock info
01295-250501
Animal Planet
0171-462 3600
Apna TV
Asian entertainment and radio
0171-359 6464
Ark 2
Christian programming
0117-972 27777
Asianet
Asian programming
0181-930 0930

B

Babylon Blue
Porn
0171-287 6623
Bloomberg Info TV
Financial news and info
0171-330 7500
Bravo
Classic films
0171-813 7000

C

CNBC*
Business programming
0181-600 6600
CNE*
News from China, Hong Kong & Taiwan
0171-610 3880
CNN International*
International news
0171-637 6700
Carlton Food Network*
Cookery & lifestyle
0171-432 9000
Carlton Select
Entertainment
0171-432 9000
Cartoon Network*
0171-478 1000

Catholic Television Trust
Catholic programming
017217-52625
Challenge TV
Interactive
01622-69111
Chand Televsion
Asian programming
01384-291854
Channel One
Infotainment
0171-209 1234
Chinese Channel*
News & entertainment
0171-636 6818
Christian Channel Europe*
Christian programming
01622-850085
Christian Communication Net
Christian programming
01232-853997
Computer Channel
Education & entertainment
0171-705 3000
Cultural Television
Documentaries
01268-775362

D

Discovery Channel*
Documentaries
0171-462 3600
Disney Channel*
Family entertainment
0171-605 1300
Dragon
Chinese family entertainment
0161-236 3557

E

EBN*
European business news
0171-653 9300
EDTV
Arabic service from Dubai
01403-217727
European Family Christian Net
01442-219525
European Network Broadcasting
Christian programming
0171-287 4908
Event Online
Sporting events

F

Fantasy Channel*
Porn
0171-712 0800
Fox Kids Network
Children's programming
0171-705 3000

G

GSTV
Asian programming
0171-404 5014
Goodlife TV
Porn
0171-287 6623
Granada Good Life*
0171-578 4002
Granada Men + Motors*
0171-578 4002
Granada Talk TV*
0171-578 4002

H

HBO
Entertainment for Poland
0171-972 7310
Het Weer Kanaal
Dutch weather channel
0171-927 8429
History Channel*
Historical documentaries
0171-705 3000
Home Order Television
Shopping channel
0171-631 4048
Home Shopping Network
0171-705 6800

I

Indus Television
Multiracial entertainment
0171-722 2922
Intershop
Home shopping
0181-891 2202

J

Japansat*
Entertainment
0171-607 7677
Jones Computer Networks*
Computer programming
0171-209 1234

K

Kanal 5
Entertainment for Sweden
0171-972 7310

L

Landscape Channel*
Classical music
01424-830688
Live TV*
Live local network
0171-293 3900

RICARDO-HALL BROADCAST

Ricardo-Hall Broadcast is a fully integrated film and broadcast
consultancy providing specialist PR advice as well as programme
sponsorship, film financing,and product placements within films, show
research, show/programme formats, event management, monitoring,
VTR and production through our subsidiary production company SKI TV.

RICARDO-HALL CARNEGIE PR

We approach each client's brief with a fresh set of eyes, building a team
appropriate to the campaign, as opposed to allocating each client a
predetermined media solution.

PRACTICE AREAS INCLUDE

Arts - Beauty, Cosmetics & Personal Grooming - Broadcast
Crisis Management - Evaluation, Tracking & Media Research
Event Management & Corporate Hospitality - Fashion - Film & Video
Hotels - Media - Music - Product Placement - Property - Publishing
Showbiz - Sport & Leisure - Travel & Tourism - Youth Matters

RICARDO-HALL COMMUNICATIONS GROUP

Deanery House, 7 Deanery Street, London W1Y 5LH
Telephone: 0171 495 7002, Fax: 0171 495 7003

SATELLITE CHANNELS

M

MED TV*
Kurdish, Turkish entertainment
0171-494 2523

MTV Europe*
Music video channel
0171-284 7777

Mediashop TV
0171-722 0242

Middle East Broadcasting*
Arabic entertainment
0171-501 1111

Minaj Broadcast International
Afro-centric entertainment
0171-491 2393

Movie Channel*
Subscription film channel
0171-705 3000

Muslim TV Ahmadiyya*
Programming from Ahmadiyya Muslims
0181-870 8517

N

NBC Europe*
News and entertainment
0181-600 6100

Namaste*
Asian programming
0181-507 8292

Nickelodeon*
Children's programming
0171-462 1000

Nickelodeon Scandinavia
Scandinavian children's programming
0171-462 1000

Novashop One/Two
Home shopping
0171-465 1234

P

Paramount Channel*
Entertainment
0171-462 1000

Parliamentary Channel*
Parliament and political coverage
0171-813 5000

Penthouse Channel
Porn
0181-581 7000

Performance*
The performing arts
0171-209 1234

Playboy TV*
Porn
0171-287 2223

Pro Sieben
Entertainment in German
0171-631 4048

Q

Q24
Home shopping
0171-465 1234

QVC Deutschland
German language home shopping
0171-705 5600

QVC Shopping Channel
0171-705 5600

Quantum Home Shopping
0171-465 1234

R

Racenet
0181-568 3511

Racing Channel
0171-696 8704

Rainbow Television
Gay entertainment
0171-328 1566

Regal Shop
Home shopping
0171-434 0567

S

Sat 1
Entertainment
0171-972 7310

STEP-UP*
Educational & business
01752-233635

Satellite Information Services*
Racing information
0171-696 8704

Sci-Fi Channel Europe*
Sci-Fi programming
0171-805 6100

Sell-a-Vision Shopping*
0171-465 1234

Setanta Sport*
Sports service for pubs
0171-930 8926

Showtime*
Films for the Middle East
0171-478 6800

Sima TV
Entertainment in Farsi
0181-959 3611

Sportswire
0171-705 3200

Supershop*
0171-465 1243

T

TCC/TCC Nordic*
Children's programming
0171-813 7000

TESUG TV*
Satellite industry info
01222-361004

Thaiwave
Thai language service

(continued)

0181-974 1942
TLC*
Educational
0171-462 3600

TNT Classic Movies
0171-478 1000

TV Land*
Middle Eastern entertainment
0171-478 6800

TV Shop
0171-722 0242

TV3 Denmark*
Entertainment for Denmark
01895-433327

TV3 Norway*
Entertainment for Norway
01895-433433

TV3 Sweden*
Entertainment for Sweden
01895-433327

Travel Channel*
0171-636 5401

Travel Industry Channel
Training programmes
01273-728809

U

UK Channel
General entertainment
0171-307 1300

UK Gold*
0171-306 6100

UK Living*
Daytime magazine
0171-306 6100

V

VH1*
Music
0171-284 7777

VT4*
Entertainment for Benelux
0171-584 9761

Vedic TV
Entertainment
0171-370 2255

Visual Arts
General entertainment
0171-307 1300

W

Weather Channel
0171-209 1234

What's in Store
0171-465 1234

World Health Network
01734-816666

X

X1
German language programming
0171-452 6213

Z

Zee TV*
Asian programming

Cable television

One in ten UK households now takes its television via broadband cable. 1997 was a record breaking construction year for the cable companies which built their networks past 2.3 million new homes. Their services are available to 11 million UK homes, nearly a third of which are taking a cable service of some kind. "There is a roll here," says Bob Frost, head of the Cable Communications Association. "There is a momentum." But there is still a long way before the cable companies get a return on the £8 billion already spent digging up the streets. Or, indeed, the additional £4 billion they must spend to complete the wiring of Britain.

Cable carries between 30 and 65 TV channels, including terrestrial and satellite channels, plus videos and telecomms. To date those prepared to pay directly for their television have chosen Sky, but this pattern is changing and the word now is that cable is reaching for the sky and is also ready to exploit any uncertainty about digital television. Meanwhile cable phone connections are proving more popular than TV connections, with the cable operators claiming a 10 to 25 per cent saving on British Telecom prices

The Telewest finance director Charles Burdick recognises the story of cable has two separate strands. He says: "I think we do provide effective competition to BT, and our hit rate of three out of 10 homes converting to cable telephones exceeds our wildest dreams. In cable TV we have been less successful, largely because of Sky's vice-like grip on pricing its programming to us has stopped us offering attractive packages."

Cable operator companies may or may not act as broadcasters. ITC licences are required for systems to serve more than 1,000 homes and are awarded exclusively to single areas.

Top cable operators

CABLE OPERATOR	HOMES CONNECTED	HOMES PASSED
CWC	780,206	3,850,308
Telewest	620,534	2,794,836
Comcast	306,903	1,157,898
NTL	344,893	944,419
Comtel	164,773	908,097
General Cable	113,196	666,818
Diamond	91,169	458,871

source: ITC June 1998

Cable & satellite channels

CHANNEL	AUDIENCE
Sky 1	2,506,299
Channel Guide	2,410,784
UK Gold	2.384,944
Live TV	2,206,708
Eurosport	2,206,149
QVC	2,193,239
Living	2,162,176
VH1	2,135,275
BBC News 24	2,128,711
Discovery	2,047,370
TNT/Cartoon Network	2,039,063
Nickelodeon	2,016,588
Bravo	2,001,800
Discovery Home & Leisure	2,000,561
Parliamentary Channel	1,994,766
MTV	1,975,677
Sci-Fi Channel	1,927,087
Granada Men/Motors	1,912,612
Travel Channel	1,912,121
Granada Plus	1,912,111
The Box	1,906,933
CNN	1,900,050
Performance	1,855,278
Sky News	1,810,354
TCC	1,776,029
Paramount	1,730,500
Challenge TV	1,618,771
Carlton Select	1,543,378
History Channel	1,300,365
Granada Goodlife	1,215,234
Carlton Food	1,186,182

Source: ITC June 1998.

The state of cable

Number of franchises	132
Homes passed	11,037,814
Homes connected (TV &/or phone)	3,644,536
Homes connected (TV)	2,469,754

Source: ITC June 1998.

CABLE OPERATORS I ...

...or Franchised Cable Systems...

ITC licences for cable operators fall into two groups. Franchised Cable Systems is the first. The first part of this list is the Multiple Systems Operators (MSOs). They have exclusive rights for the licensee to provide multi-channel TV over a large scale purpose-built cable system for 15 years. The licence also allows for phone services to be supplied. The second group is: Unfranchised Cable Systems.

Atlantic Telecom Group (Atlantic)
303 King Street, Aberdeen AB24 5AP
Fax 01224-644601   Tel 01224-646644
E-mail: atlantic@atlantic-telecom.co.uk
Website: http://www.atlantic.telecom.co.uk
Franchises: Aberdeen
Subsidiaries: Aberdeen Cable Services, Atlantic Telecommunications, Atlantic Logical
British Telecommuications (BT)
87/89 Baker Street, London W1M 2LV
                              Tel 0171-487 1270
Subsidiaries: BT New Towns Cable TV, Westminster Cable Company.
Cable & Telecoms (C&T)
PO Box 319, Whipsnade, Dunstable LU6 2LT
                              Tel 01582-873006
Franchises: Carlisle, Shrewsbury, Bridgnorth, south Staffordshire, Chichester & Bognor Regis.
Subsidiaries: Cumbria Cable & Telecoms, South Cumbria Cable & Telecoms, Ayrshire Cable & Telecoms, Northumberland Cable & Telecoms.
Owner: US Cable Corporation
Cable & Wireless Communications (CWC)
Red Lion House, 26 Red Lion Square, London WC1R 4HQ
Fax 0171-528 2181   Tel 0171-528 2000
Website: http://www.cwcom.co.uk
Franchises: East Lancashire, Bolton, Totton & Hythe, Chichester, Bognor Regis, Folkestone, Dartford, Dover, Eastbourne, Hastings, Brighton, Hove, Shoreham, Worthing, Bournemouth, Poole, Christchurch, Portsmouth, Winchester, Southampton, Eastleigh, Chilterns, North Surrey, Derby, North Yorkshire & S Co Durham, Bury, Rochdale, Oldham, Wearside, Stoke-on-Trent, Macclesfield, Leeds, the Wirral, North East Cheshire, Newcastle-under-Lyme, Stockport, Manchester, Norwich, Great Yarmouth, Whittlesey, March, Wisbech, Harrow, Thamesmead, Epping Forest, South Hertfordshire, London Boroughs of: Bromley, Waltham Forest, Wandsworth, `Lambeth, Southwark, Newham, Tower Hamlets, Kensington, Chelsea, Hammersmith, Fulham, Ealing, Havering, Greater London East

Comcast Europe (Comcast)
Network House, Bradfield Close, Woking GU22 7RE
                              Tel 01483-880800
Franchises: Managing partner in several London franchises plus Bury St Edmunds, Stowmarket, Sudbury, Braintree, Ipswich, Colchester, Clacton, Cambridge, Stanstead, Harlow, Birmingham, Teeside, Darlington, London Boroughs of Camden, Haringey, Enfield, Hackney, Islington,
Subsidiaries: Anglia Cable, Birmingham Cable, Cable London, Cambridge Cable, East Coast Cable. Southern East Anglia Cable.
Owner: Comcast, USA.
ComTel (Vision Networks)
Wharfedale Road, Winnersh, Wokingham RG41 5TZ
                              Tel 0118-954 4000
Website: http://www.comtel.co.uk
Franchises: Tamworth, North Warwickshire, Meriden, Stafford, N.E. Northamptonshire, Coventry, Northampton, Rugby, Daventry, Nuneaton, Stratford, West Hertfordshire, Thames Valley, Swindon, Andover, Oxford, Stafford, Salisbury, Romsey.
Subsidiaries: Andover Cablevision, Stafford Comms, Wessex Cable, Oxford Cable, Jersey Cable.
The Convergence Group (Convergence)
Martlet Heights, Burgess Hill, West Sussex RH15 9NJ
Fax 01444-250550   Tel 01444-250555
Franchises: East Grinstead, Haywards Heath, mid Sussex, Yeovil
Owner: Convergence Group
Diamond Cable Communications (Diamond)
Daleside Road, Nottingham NG2 3GG
Fax 0115-912 2211   Tel 0115-912 2240
Website: http://www.diamond.co.uk
Franchises: Nottingham, Newark, Mansfield, Grantham, Melton Mowbray, Cleethorpes, Grimsby, Lincoln, Leicester, Loughborough, Burton-on-Trent, Ashby-de-la-Zouch, Coalville, Uttoxeter, Hinckley, Bosworth, Ravenshead, Bassetlaw, Lincs&Humberside, Chesterfield, Bolsover, NE Derbyshire, Vale of Belvoir,
Owner: European Cable Partners (66.5%), Macdonld Family Trust (14.8%), Creative Artists Agency (6.6%), Investor Investments (6.6%).
Eurobell
Lloyds Court, Manor Royal, Crawley RH10 2PT
Fax 01293-400440   Tel 01293-400444
Franchises: Gatwick, Crawley, Horley, Tunbridge Wells, Sevenoaks, Tonbridge, Exeter, Plymouth, Torbay, Totnes, Newton Abbot.
Subsidiaries: Eurobell (South West), Eurobell (Sussex), Eurobell (West Kent).
Owner: Detecon
General Cable (General)
37 Old Queen Street, London SW1H 9JA
Fax 0171-393 2800   Tel 0171-393 2828
Website: http://www.generalcable.co.uk
Franchises: Windsor, Hillingdon & Hounslow, Birmingham, Bradford, Sheffield, Doncaster, Rotherham, Wakefield, Barnsley, Halifax, Brighouse.
Subsidiaries: Cable Corporation, Yorkshire Cable.
Owner: Public Holdings 60%, Compagnie Generale des Eaux, France 40%.

THE UK's

LEADING

AVALON
MANAGEMENT GROUP LTD.
Tel: 0171 434 3888

AVALON
PROMOTIONS LIMITED
Tel: 0171 734 9988

ERTAINMENT

GROUP

-AVALON-

PUBLICITY

Tel: 0171 734 6677

-AVALON-

TELEVISION LIMITED

Tel: 0171 432 3252

NTL CableTel
CableTel House, 1 Lakeside Road, Farnborough
Hampshire GU14 6XP
Fax 01252-402100   Tel 01252 402000
E-mail: davis1@cabletel.co.uk
Website: http://www.cabletel.co.uk
Franchises: Glasgow, Paisley, Renfrew, Beasden, Milngavie, Inverclyde, South Glamorgan, Mid Glamorgan, Gwent, Glyncorrwg, Newport, Pontypool, Guildford, Woking, Camberley, Aldershot, Farnham, Fleet, south Bedford, Hertfordshire, Hampshire, Huddersfield, Northern Ireland.
Subsidiaries: CableTel Herts & Beds/Glasgow/Kirklees/Northern Ireland/South Wales/Surrey.
Owner: NTL Inc USA
The third largest franchise holder.

Telewest Communications (Telewest)
Genesis Business Park, Albert Drive, Woking, Surrey GU21 5RW
Fax 01483-750901   Tel 01483-750900
Website: http://www.telewest.co.uk
Franchises: One of the two largest operators in UK, with franchises in north Kent, south Essex, Merton, Sutton, Kingston, Richmond, Croydon, Newcastle, Gateshead, Tyneside, the Black Country, Telford, Liverpool, Southport, Blackpool and Fylde, St Helens, Knowsley, central Lancashire,Wigan, Falkirk, Livingston, Edinburgh, Lothian, Fife, Dundee, Perth, Motherwell, Dumbarton, Falkirk, Cumbernauld, Glenrothes, Kirkcaldy, Taunton, Bridgewater, Bristol, Bath and area, Cheltenham, Gloucester, Worcester.
Subsidiaries: Telewest Communications: (London South), (Midlands), (North East), (North West), (Scotland), (South East), (South West), Cable Corporation.
Owners: Principal shareholders are TeleCommunications Inc and US West Inc (29.8 per cent each), Cox Comms (10 per cent), SBC Comms (10 per cent. Remainder is public.

Other franchisees
Franchised cable systems whose parent company is not immediately apparent from their name as being one of the above Multiple Systems Operators (MSOs).

Aberdeen Cable Services
303 King Street, Aberdeen AB24 5AP
Fax 01224-644601   Tel 01224-646644
Franchises: Aberdeen and area.
Owner: Atlantic Telecom

Anglia Cable
Owner: Comcast

Birmingham Cable
Owner: Comcast

The Cable Corporation
Owner: General Cable

Cable London
Owner: Comcast

Cambridge Cable
Owner: Comcast

East Coast Cable
Owner: Comcast

Southern East Anglia Cable
Owner: Comcast

Yorkshire Cable Communications
Owner: General Cable

CABLE OPERATORS II ...

...or Unfranchised Cable Systems...
These cable operators have a restricted channel capacity predating the current franchising arrangement. They don't have exclusive rights, are subject to shorter term licences and liable to be superseded by a franchised system.

Hull Cablevision
Atlanric Telecom Group, 303 King Street, Aberdeen, AB24 5AP
                        Tel 01224-646644
Kingston upon Hull

John Sulwyn Evans
1 West End, Dolrhedlin, Tanygrisiav, Blaenau Ffestiniog, Gwynedd LL41 3SR
Blaenau Ffestiniog

John Jones
97 Rhosemean Street, Llandeilo, Dyfed, Llandeilo

Metro Cable TV
Unit 12, 23 Park Royal Road, London NW10 7JH
Fax 0181-961 6771   Tel 0181-961 6776
Eastbourne, Hastings, Leicester, Lewes, Northampton, Rochdale.

Metro South Wales
Bridge Terrace, Gwent MP1 5FE
                        Tel 01495-247595
Abergavenny, Afan Valley, Ammanford, Blaenavon, Brecon, Cwm, Ebbw Vale, Haverford West, Merthyr, Milford Haven, Newbridge, Pembroke Dock, Pontypridd, Rhonda, Rhymney, Tredegar.

Salford Cable Television
Black Horse House, Bentalls, Basildon, Essex SS14 3BX
Fax 01268-450455   Tel 01268-450450
Salford, Sunnyside Court.

Tawd Valley Cable
82 Sandy Lane, Skelmersdale, Lancashire WN8 8LQ
                        Tel 01695-51000
Skelmersdale.
Owners: O'Shea Systems

A Thomson Relay
1 Park Lane, Beith, Ayrshire KA15 2FG
Fax 01505-503030   Tel 01505 503441
Beith, Kilbirnie

CABLE CHANNELS

*= services in operation

A

ATM
0161-627 1207
Adam and Eve Channel
0171-240 4404
Africa TV
0181-395 4014
Afro-Caribbean Channel
0181-802 4576
Airport Television*
01753-580233
Andover Now*
01264 401402
Arcade Avon
01484-612290
Arcade Costwolds
01452-535353
Arcade Scotland
0131-539 0002
Arcade South East
01268-471000
Arcade London South
0181-760 0222
BET International*
0181-960 3338

B

BVTV*
0181-301 0250
Black Music Television
0181-740 5505
The Box*
0171-376 2000
Bradford Festival News
01274-727488
Bradford Festival TV
01274-884863
British Greek Channel
0181-807 6035

C

CLTV*
0171-911 0555
CSV Media
01274-736413
Cable Daily*
01203-231099
Cable Video Store
0181-964 1141
Cable 10*
01639 8999999
Cable 17*
01384-867889
Cambridge Interactive TV
01223-567200
The Channel Guide*
01902-469238
Channel Seven*
01384-838483
Channel 17*
0181-760 0222

Channel 10
01224-649444
Clyde Cablevision
0141-564 0000
Colt TV*
01203-505345
Community Channel
0113-293 2000

D

Diamond Cable 7*
0116-233 4100
Discovery Channel
0171-482 4824
Dubai
0171-935 6699

E

East
0181-573 4000
Edinburgh Television
0131-557 8610
Education & Training Channel*
0191-515 2070
Education Channel*
01254-55144
Epping Forest Community Channel
0171-363 2000

F

The Food Channel
01562-882633

H

Havering Community Channel*
0171-363 2000
Hellenic Television*
0171-292 7037
History Channel
0171-705 3652
Home Video Channel
0181-581 7000

I

Ice TV*
01743-810810
Interactive Channel
0181-244 1234
Interactive London News
0171-827 7700
Interactive Multimedia Services*
0171-492 2935

L

LTT-Turkish Language TV
0181-502 9360
Leicester Community Channel
0116-233400

M

Metrovision*
0171-935 6699
Mind Extension University*
0171-209 1234
Movie Channel
0171-705 3000
Multi-Screen Channel, Avon*
01454-612290

Multi-Screen Channel, Costwolds*
01459-535353
Multi-Screen Channel, NE*
0191-420 2000
Multi-Screen Channel, SE*
01268-471000
Multi-Screen Channel, Scotland*
0131-539 0002

N

Network 021*
0121-628 1234
Nynex Community Television
01273-413021
Nynex Community Television
0161-946 0388

P

PTV
0181-455 0413
Performance*
0171-209 1234
Preview Channel
0113-230 5105

R

Redbridge Community Channel*
0171-363 2000
Royal Opera House Channel*
0171-240 1200

S

Sheffield Local Cable
0114-281 2661
Silverstone TV*
0171-487 2641
Skelmersdale Local Channel*
01695-51000
Swindon Local
01793-615601

T

Telewest Channel*
01772-90288
TellyWest*
01454-612290
Tower Hamlets*
0171-363 2000

V

Videonet Interactive TV
01707-362500
Videotron Channel*
0181-244 1234
Vision Channel*
01793-511244

W

Waltham Forest
0171-363 2000
West Herts TV
01442-369111
Williams Worldwide Television
0171-734 7010

Y

YCTV-Youth Cable Television
0181-964 4646

CABLE AREAS

A

Aberdeen area:
Aberdeen Cable (Devanha)
01224-649444
Andover:
Andover Cablevision (IVS)
01264-334607
Avon:
United Artists (TeleWest)
01454-612290

B

Bedfordshire: south, Luton:
Cablevision Beds (CableTel)
01582-401044
Birmingham, Solihull:
Birmingham Cable (Comcast)
0121-628 1234
Bolton:
Cable and Wireless
0161-946 0388
Bradford:
Yorkshire Cable
01274-828282
Brighton, Hove, Worthing,
Shoreham:
Cable and Wireless
01273-880000
Burton-upon-Trent, Swadlincote,
Ashby-de-la-Zouch
LCL Cable
0116-233 4100

C

Cambridge, Ely, Newmarket,
Huntingdon:
Cambridge Cable (Comcast)
01223-567200
Coventry:
Coventry Cable (Devanha)
01203-505345

D

Derby:
Cable and Wireless
01332-200002
Dundee, Perth area:
United Artists (TeleWest)
01382-322220

E

Edinburgh:
United Artists (TeleWest)
0131-539 0002

G

Gatwick, Crawley:
Eurobell
01293-400444
Glasgow area:
CableTel
0141-221 7040
Guildford, W Surrey, E Hants:
CableTel
01483-254000

H

Hampshire: east, Portsmouth,
Gosport:
Cable and Wireless
01705-266555
Harlow, Bishops Stortford, Stansted:
Anglia Cable (Comcast)
01279-867000
Hertfordshire: south:
Jones Cable
01923-464000
Hertfordshire: west:
Telecential
01442-230444
Hinckley, Bosworth
LCL Cable
0116-233 4100

L

Lancashire: central/south,
Merseyside:
Cable North West (SBC)
01772-832888
Lancashire: east:
Cable and Wireless
0161-946 0388
Leeds:
Jones Cable
0113-293 2000
Leicester, Loughborough:
LCL Cable
0116-233 4100
Lichfield, Burntwood, Rugeley
LCL Cable
0116-233 4100
London:
    Barking, Bexley, Dagenham,
    Havering, Newham, Tower
    Hamlets:
Cable and Wireless
0171-363 2000
    Barnet, Brent, Ealing, Fulham,
    Greenwich,
    Harrow, Hammersmith,
    Kensington, Lambeth, Lewisham,
    Southwark, Thamesmead,
    Wandsworth:
Cable and Wireless
0181-244 1234
    Bromley:
Cable and Wireless
0181-446 9966
    Camden, Enfield, Hackney,
    Haringey, Islington:
Cable London (Comcast/TeleWest)
0171-911 0911
    Croydon, Kingston, Merton,
    Richmond, Sutton:
United Artists (TeleWest)
0181-760 0222
    Hillingdon, Hounslow:
Middx Cable (Gen Cable)
01753-810810

(untitled)

Westminster:
Westminster Cable (BT)
0171-935 4400

M

Motherwell, Hamilton, East Kilbride:
United Artists (TeleWest)
01698-322332

N

Northampton:
Telecential
01604-643619
Northern Ireland
CableTel Northern Ireland
01483-254000
Norwich:
Norwich Cable (Cable and Wireless)
01603-787892
Nottingham, Grimsby, Lincoln,
Mansfield:
Diamond Cable
0115-952 2240

P

Peterborough:
Cable and Wireless
01733-371717

S

Southampton, Eastleigh:
Cable and Wireless
01703-315000
Surrey: north, north east:
Cable and Wireless
01372-360844
Swansea, Neath, Port Talbot:
CableTel
01222-456644
Swindon:
Swindon Cable (Telecential)
01793-480483

T

Tamworth, north Warwicks and
Meriden
Tamworth Cable (LCL)
0116-233 4100
Thames Valley, Basingstoke,
Wycombe:
Telecential
01734-756868
Tyneside:
United Artists (TeleWest)
0191-420 2000

W

Windsor, Slough, Maidenhead,
Heathrow:
Windsor TV (Gen Cable)
01753-810810
Wolverhampton, Walsall, Dudley,
Telford:
Cable Midlands (SBC)
01384-838483

DIGITAL
PHOTOGRAPHY
HOW TO CAPTURE, MANIPULATE AND OUTPUT IMAGES

*A companion title to the Media Guide
obtainable from good booksellers
or call 01483 268888*

A **Guardian Book**

PUBLISHED BY FOURTH ESTATE AT £15.99

Radio: Introduction & BBC

British radio is divided between the licence-funded BBC and a growing number of profit making companies. The latter are overseen by the Radio Authority, the statutory equivalent of the Independent Television Commission. Radio companies operate under licence to the Radio Authority which was set up by the 1990 Broadcasting Act. Where the BBC once had a monopoly, the UK now has some 240 radio services, nearly 200 of them provided by commercial broadcasting. The average listener can receive 15 radio stations, six from the BBC and nine from commercial radio. In London, listeners can hear 24 services of which six are BBC. Yet more choice will come as digital radio spawns more stations, starting in 1999.

The BBC runs five national networks and 38 local radio stations serving England and the Channel Islands, and national regional radio services in Scotland, Wales and Northern Ireland including Welsh and Gaelic language stations.

In August 1997 Radio 1's weekly audience fell under 10 million for the first time. Hardly a surprise, given that a chunk of the audience had been bound to leave the station when Chris Evans left earlier that year. Sophie McLauglin, head of the BBC's radio strategy took control of damage limitation and said: "Radio 1 is still the biggest radio station in Europe. Forty per cent of 15 to 24 year olds tune in each week, and that's not a sign of a station in crisis. BBC Radio and

Listening figures

	WEEKLY REACH	AVERAGE HOURS PER LISTENER	SHARE OF LISTENING
ALL RADIO	40.29m	20.7	100%
ALL BBC	26.61m	14.7	46.8%
BBC Radio 1	9.36m	8.4	9.5%
BBC Radio 2	8.79m	12	12.6%
BBC Radio 3	2.54m	4	1.2%
BBC Radio 4	8.25m	10.4	10.3%
BBC Radio 5 Live	5.22m	5.9	3.7%
BBC Local/regional	8.59	9.3	9.6%
ALL COMMERCIAL	28.65m	14.9	51.5%
All national commercial	11.83m	7.2	10.2%
Atlantic 252	2.97m	4.9	1.7%
Classic FM	5.05m	6.1	3.7%
Talk Radio	2.38m	6	1.8%
Virgin Radio	3.36	7.4	3%
All local commercial	23.84m	14.3	40.8%

Source: Rajar, April-June 1998

Radio bands

		MHz88-90.2	90.2-92.4	92.4-94.6	94.9 London	95.1	95.8	97.3	97.6-99.8
FM		Radio 2	Radio 3	Radio 4	GLR	GMR	CapitalFM	London News	Radio 1
		Light music	Classical	Talk	Pop/talk	All talk	Pop	News	Pop/rock

		194m	206m	1332/1413	1341	247m	261m	275/285	290m
		1548kHz	1458kH	1305kHz	873kHz	1215kH	1152kHz	1089/1053kHz	1035kHz
AM		Capital Gold	Sunrise	Premier	Radio Ulster	Virgin	LBC	Talk Radio	Country
		Oldies/sport	Asian	Christian	General	Pop/rock	Talk/news	Talk/news	C&W

the commercial sector continue to vie for market share in a contracting market." Meanwhile Radio 2 motors on and increased its share of listeners from 12.6 in the first three months of 1997 to 13.2 per cent a year later.

In November 1997 Radio 3 attempted to deal with Classic FM with simpler schedules, more accessible peak time programming and the return of Joan Bakewell, Richard Baker and Peter Hobday. Result: a rumbling among the great and good. "Only in Britain could the introduction of three middle-class radio presenters with a combined age of 196 and scarcely a trace of a regional accent between them bring allegations that the network was plunging into populist mire," Peter Barnard wrote in the Times.

In April 1998 James Boyle, the Radio 4 controller, risked the ire of middle Britain when he introduced his long-anticipated revamp of schedules. "We will be unstintingly Reithian in our values," Boyle promised, "but we are not going to be po-faced."

The 9 am weekday slot changed as follows: Monday and Wednesday, Melvyn Bragg (at least until his ennoblement) and Libby Purves had less time and fewer guests; Tuesday, Michael Buerk's The Choice; Thursday, Jonathan Dimbleby's The Candidate; Friday, five minutes more time - but still only one guest - on Sue Lawley's Desert Island Discs.

The consensus within the BBC is that its overall radio market share will eventually drop from the current 47 per cent to settle at 30 per cent. The BBC has kept a global presence with the World Service and leads the field in digital radio, a reach for the future which has had it running an experimental digital radio service covering 60 per cent of the country since September 1995.

All change on Radio 4

IN

Today	extended to 3 hours
The Exchange	phone-in with Robin Lustig
Front Row	arts programme with Mark Lawson
The Beaton Generation	satirical show
Late Tackle	sport chat with Martin Bashir
Home Truths	with John Peel

OUT

Yesterday in Parliament	to long wave
The Afternoon Shift	
Kaleidoscope	
Week Ending	
Sport on 4	
Breakaway	

100 London			102.2			
102.-Manchester	100.7 Midlands	100-101.9	100.4	105.4	105.8 London/SE	106.2 London
KissFM	Heart	Classic FM	JazzFM	Melody	Virgin	Heart
Dance	Adult pop	Classical	Jazz/blues	Light music	Pop/rock	Adult pop

330/433m			417/1500m (lw)		463m	
909/693kHz	882kHz	810kHz	720/198kHz	648kHz	
Radio 5 Live	Radio Wales	Radio Scotland	Radio 4	World Service	
News/sport	General	General	Talk/general	General	

BBC NATIONAL RADIO

Administratively, Radio 1, 2, 3 and 4 belong the BBC's Broadcast directorate while Radio 5 comes under the BBC News directorate.

BBC Radio HQ
Broadcasting House, Portland Place, London W1A 1AA
Publicity office: 0171-765 4990
Director of radio: Matthew Bannister
Managing Editor, digital radio: Glyn Jones

Radio 1
Broadcasting House, Portland Place, London W1A 1AA
Publicity office: 0171-765 4575
Controller, Radio 1: Andy Parfitt
Managing editor: Ian Parkinson

Radio 2
Broadcasting House, Portland Place, London W1A 1AA
Publicity office: 0171-765 4330
Controller, Radio 2: Jim Moir
Managing editor: Lesley Douglas

Radio 3
Broadcasting House, Portland Place, London W1A 1AA
Publicity office: 0171-765 2722
Controller, Radio 3: Nicholas Kenyon
Managing editor: Brian Barfield

Radio 4
Broadcasting House, Portland Place, London W1A 1AA
Publicity office: 0171-765 5337
Controller, Radio 4: James Boyle
Managing editor: tba

Radio 5 Live
Television Centre, Wood Lane, London W12 7RJ
Publicity office: tba
Controller, Radio 5 Live: Roger Mosey
Controller, radio sports rights and deputy controller, Radio 5 Live: Mike Lewis

BBC LOCAL RADIO: SOUTH

BBC Radio Bristol
PO Box 194, Bristol BS99 7QT
                        Tel 0117-974 1111
BBC Radio Cornwall
Phoenix Wharf, Truro, Cornwall TR1 1UA
                        Tel 01872-275421
BBC Radio Devon
Broadcasting House, Seymour Road, Mannamead, Plymouth PL3 5BD
Fax 01752-234599   Tel 01752-260323
BBC Radio Gloucestershire
London Road, Gloucester GL1 1SW
                        Tel 01452-308585
BBC GLR 94.9 (London)
PO Box 94.9, 35c Marylebone High Street, London W1A 4LG
Tel 0171-224 2424
BBC Radio Guernsey
Commerce House, Les Banques, St Peter Port, Guernsey GY1 2HS
                        Tel 01481-728977
BBC Radio Jersey
18 Parade Road, St Helier, Jersey JE2 3PL
                        Tel 01534-870000
BBC Radio Kent
Sun Pier, Chatham, Kent ME4 4EZ
                        Tel 01634-830505
BBC Radio Solent
Havelock Road, Southampton SO1 7PW
                        Tel 01703-631311
BBC Somerset Sound
14-15 Paul Street, Taunton TA1 3PF
Tel 01823-252437
Southern Counties Radio (Sussex & Surrey)
Broadcasting House, Guildford GU2 5AP
                        Tel 01483-306306
BBC Thames Valley (Oxon & Berkshire)
PO Box 952, Oxford OX2 7YL
PO Box 954, Slough SL1 1BA
PO Box 1044, Reading RG30 1PL
                        Tel 01645-311444
Wiltshire Sound
Broadcasting House, Prospect Place, Swindon, Wilts SN1 3RW
                        Tel 01793-513626

BBC RADIO: MIDLAND/EAST

BBC Asian Network
Epic House, Charles Street, Leicester LE1 3SH
                        Tel 0116-251 6688
Pebble Mill Road, Birmingham B5 7SD
Tel 0121-414 8000
BBC Radio Cambridgeshire
Broadcasting House, 104 Hills Road, Cambridge CB2 1LD
                        Tel 01223-259696
BBC Radio Derby
56 St Helens Street, Derby DE1 3HY
                        Tel 01332-361111

BBC Radio Essex
PO Box 765, Chelmsford, Essex CM2 9XB
Tel 01245-262393
BBC Hereford & Worcester
Hylton Road, Worcester WR2 5WW
Tel 01905-748485
43 Broad Steet, Hereford HR4 9HH
Tel 01432-355252
BBC Radio Leicester
Epic House, Charles Street, Leicester LE1 3SH
Tel 0116-251 6688
BBC Radio Lincolnshire
PO Box 219, Newport, Lincoln LN1 3XY
Tel 01522-511411
BBC Radio Norfolk
Norfolk Tower, Surrey Street, Norwich NR1 3PA
Tel 01603-617411
BBC Radio Northampton
PO Box 1107, Abington Street, Northampton NN1 2BH
Tel 01604-239100
BBC Radio Nottingham
York House, Mansfield Road, Nottingham NG1 3JB
Tel 0115-955 0500
BBC Radio Shropshire
PO Box 397, Shrewsbury, Shropshire SY1 3TT
Tel 01743-248484
BBC Radio Stoke
Cheapside, Hanley, Stoke-on-Trent, Staffs ST1 1JJ
Tel 01782-208080
BBC Radio Suffolk
St Matthews Street, Ipswich, Suffolk IP1 3EP
Tel 01473-250000
BBC Three Counties Radio (Beds, Herts & Bucks)
PO Box 3CR, Hastings Street, Luton LU1 5XL
Tel 01582-441000
BBC Radio WM (West Midlands)
PO Box 206, Birmingham B5 7QQ
Tel 0121-414 8484

BBC LOCAL RADIO: NORTH

BBC Radio Cleveland
PO Box 95FM, Broadcasting House, Newport Road, Middlesbrough, Cleveland TS1 5DG
Tel 01642-225211
BBC Radio Cumbria
Annetwell Street, Carlisle, Cumbria CA3 8BB
Tel 01228-592444
BBC GMR Talk (Manchester)
Oxford Road, Manchester M60 1SJ
Tel 0161-200 2000
BBC Radio Humberside
9 Chapel Street, Hull, N Humberside HU1 3NU
Tel 01482-323232
BBC Radio Lancashire
20-26 Darwen Street, Blackburn, Lancs BB2 2EA
Tel 01254-262411
BBC Radio Leeds
Broadcasting House, Woodhouse Lane, Leeds, West Yorks LS2 9PN
Tel 0113-244 2131

BBC Radio Merseyside
55 Paradise Street, Liverpool L1 3BP
Tel 0151-708 5500
BBC Radio Newcastle
Barrack Road, Newcastle-upon-Tyne NE99 1RN
Tel 0191-232 4141
BBC Radio Sheffield
60 Westbourne Road, Sheffield S10 2QU
Tel 0114-268 6185
BBC Radio York
20 Bootham Row, York YO3 7BR
Tel 01904-641351

WALES, SCOTLAND & NI

BBC Radio Wales
Cardiff CF5 2YQ
Tel 01222-572888
BBC Radio Cymru
Broadcasting House, Llantrisant Road, Llandaff, Cardiff CF5 2YQ
Tel 01222-572888
BBC Radio Scotland
Broadcasting House, Queen Margaret Drive, Glasgow G12 8DG
Fax 0141-334 0614   Tel 0141-338 2000
BBC Radio Nan Gaidheal
7 Culduthel Road, Inverness IV2 4AD
Tel 01463-720720
BBC Radio Ulster
Broadcasting House, Ormeau Avenue, Belfast BT2 8HQ
Tel 01232-338000
BBC Radio Foyle
8 Northland Road, Londonderry, Northern Ireland BT48 7NE
Tel 01504-262244

INTERNATIONAL RADIO

BBC World Service - HQ
Bush House, The Strand, London WC2B 4PH.
Publicity Office   0171-557 2941
Managing director: Sam Younger
Deputy managing director: Caroline Thomson
Director, news and programme commissioning: Bob Jobbins
Director, World Service regions: Andrew Taussig
Controller, resources and technology: Chris Gill
Controller, personnel: Lesley Granger
Finance and commercial director: Andrew Hind

BBC Monitoring
Caversham Park, Reading, Berks RG4 8TZ
Fax 01734 463823   Tel 01734 469289
BBC Monitoring reports on foreign broadcasts to the BBC and the government. This information is also sold to the press, businesses, academic staff and public bodies.
Director: Andrew Hills

Independent radio

Local independent radio has been available since the first commercial services set up in London during the mid-seventies. The numbers increased after 1986 when stations were allowed to transmit different programming on AM and FM frequencies and by the 1990 Broadcasting Act there were some 130 stations. The Act allowed for three national licenses and these, plus a lighter regulatory touch lightened further by the 1996 Broadcasting Act, have ensured ad-funded radio to claim half the audience and ever increasing amounts of advertising revenue.

The Radio Authority was established by the 1990 Broadcasting Act to take responsibility for the regulation and licensing of independent radio. In its February 1998 evidence to the House of Commons Culture, Media and Sport Committee inquiry into audio-visual communications, the RA said: "The Authority has currently issued 205 Independent Local Radio licences, three Independent National Licences [Classic FM, Virgin and Talk Radio], and is currently awarding local licences at the rate of about two a month. The Authority also has 18 cable radio licensees as well as licensing one additional service for data which operates within a sub-carrier of the INR FM frequency allocation. In addition, the Radio Authority issues between 300 and 350 Restricted Service

ULTRA-LOCAL RADIO

In June 1998 the Radio Authority issued its 2,000th Restricted Service Licence for Radio Avalon to broadcast news, reviews, interviews and welfare information to Glastonbury Festival.

Two-thirds of RSLs have been used to cover such events festivals with the remaining third for trial services which gain support and test the market before companies apply for an eight year broadcasting licence.

Thirty Asian RSLs were licensed in 1997, many in areas like Glasgow which do not have their own independent ethnic local radio stations. Experiments with local digital radio saw 30 digital RSLs issued covering multiplexes in London (2), Birmingham, Glasgow and Edinburgh.

licenses each year either as trial services or for the coverage of special events."

The biggest amount of independent radio news and noise has come from Chris Evans. Having left Radio 1 in January 1997, he resumed a career as breakfast DJ when he joined Virgin Radio the following October. By Christmas Richard Branson had sold Virgin Radio to Chris Evans' Ginger Productions for £85 million. Financiers at Apax Partners arranged a deal where Evans put up £2 million of his own money. It must be nice for him to be to simultaneously be a plutocrat and to play Jack the lad. Evans will have to keep on delivering the audiences to repay his investors' faith and he'll only do that by sticking to playlists determined by the charts and other market research.

There's not much scope for a DJ's individual taste, as David Thomas pointed out in the Telegraph. "The great strength of British pop over the past three decades has been its eclecticism. Whereas American radio has been trapped in strict formats for more than 20 years, British kids have grown up listening to a near-random mix of music served by DJs who spoke to the entire country. Radio 1 could be as bland as Simon Bates, as inspirational as John Peel, or as globe-trottingly obscure as Andy Kershaw, but children who grew up to be musicians had their imaginations fertilised by an astonishing range of influences ... Virgin listeners will seldom be surprised by what they hear ... Our pop stars set trends around the world and generate enormous export earnings. But they won't stay ahead of the pack listening to Virgin Radio."

Radio Authority
Holbrook House, 14 Great Queen St, Holborn, London WC2 5DG.
Fax 0171-405 7064   Tel 0171-430 2724
Chairman: Sir Peter Gibbings
Deputy chairman: Michael Moriarty
Chief executive: Tony Stoller
Head of development and deputy chief exec: David Vick
Head of finance: Neil Romain
Head of programming and advertising: David Lloyd
Head of engineering: Mark Thomas
Press officer: Tracey Mullins
Head of legal services: Eve Saloman

The big news on radio.

200 Stations – 23 million listeners.

Source Rajar Quarter 1/1998

NATIONAL FRANCHISES

Until 1992 the only national radio channels belonged to the BBC. The Broadcasting Act changed all that and gave the Radio Authority power to issue licenses for three new Independent National Radio (INR) networks. Only INR1 could be on an FM frequency and the other two had to be on AM. The Act also said that INR1 should concentrate "wholly or mainly, in the broadcasting of music which ... is not pop music" and that the first AM service could offer any programming that did not duplicate INR1. INR3 would have to be primarily speech-based. Hence the arrivals of Classic FM, Virgin 1215 and, in February 1995, Talk Radio UK.

Classic FM - INR1
24-28 Oval Rd, London NW1 7DQ
Fax 0171-713 2630   Tel 0171-284 3000
E-mail: enquiries@classicfm.co.uk
Starting date: 7.9.92
Dial: 100-102 FM

Talk Radio UK - INR3
76 Oxford Street, London W1N 0TR
Fax 0171-636 1053   Tel 0171-636 1089
Parent company: CLT UFEA
Starting date: 14.2.95
Dial: 1053/1089/1107 kHz AM

Virgin 1215 - INR2
1 Golden Square, London W1R 4DJ.
Fax 0171-434 1197   Tel 0171-434 1215
E-mail: virgin@vradio.co.uk
Parent company: Ginger Productions
Starting date: 30.4.93
Dial: Nationally: 1215 and 1197 - 1260 AM/MW;
London: 105.8 FM

Atlantic 252
Mornington House, Trim, County Meath
Fax 00353 4636688   Tel 00353 4636655
Atlantic 252 broadcasts from Southern Ireland without a British government licence, but is effectively a national station due to a 10 per cent national audience share garnered from two-thirds of the UK, north and west of a line from the Wash to Dorset.
Parent company: CLT UFEA
Starting date: 1.9.89
Dial: 252 kHz LW

MAIN OWNERS

Capital Radio
30 Leicester Square, London WC2H 7LA
Fax 0171-766 6100   Tel 0171-766 6000
Website: http://www.capitalradio.co.uk
Subsidiaries: Capital Radio London, Ocean Radio Group, Southern Sound Group, Invicta Radio, BRMB Radio, Red Dragon Radio, Fox Radio.
Stations: BRMB-FM, Capital FM, Capital Gold,Invicta FM, OceanFM, PowerFM, S Coast Radio, Southern FM.

Emap On Air
97 Tottenham Court Road, London W1P 9HF
Fax 0171-504 6001   Tel 0171-504 6000
Shares: Owns over 50% of Radio City (Sound of Merseyside), 19% of East Anglian Radio and 10% of Essex Radio.
Stations: broadcast on 17 FM and AM frequencies and cover London, Wales, Liverpool, Manchester, Preston, Leeds, Sheffield, Hull, Newcastle Upon Tyne and Stockton on Tees, Hallam FM, Great North, Great Yorkshire, Metro FM, The Pulse, TFM, Viking FM.

GWR Group
PO Box 2345, Swindon, Wiltshire SN5 7HF
Fax 01793-440302   Tel 01793-440300
Subsids: Mid-Anglia Radio .Chiltern Radio Network
Stations: Beacon, Brunel Classic Gold, CN FM, Gem-AM, GWR FM, Hereward, Leicester Sound, Mercia FM/Classic Gold, Ram FM, 1332, Trent FM/Gem AM, 2CR FM/Classic Gold, 2Ten FM/Classic Gold, WABC, B97/Classic Gold, Broadland 102/Amber Radio, Chiltern FM/Classic Gold, FM 103-Horizon, Northants 96, Q103 FM, SGR Colchester/Amber Radio, 102.4 Severn Sound, Radio Wyvern.

Independent Radio Group
The Lodge,Orrell Road, Orrell Wigan WN5 8HJ
Fax 01942-777657   Tel 01942-777666
Stations: Mercury FM, Fame 1521, Scot FM, Lite 1458,AM, 96.3 QFM, 102.4 Wish FM, Wire FM 102.7

Scottish Radio Holdings
Clydebank Business Park, Glasgow G81 2RX
Fax 0141-565 2322   Tel 0141-565 2202
Stations: Clyde 1 FM, Clyde 2, Downtown FM, Cool FM, Forth FM/AM, Westsound FM/ AM, Tay FM, Northsound 1/2, Radio Tay, Borders 69%, Carlisle 40%, Moray Firth 97%.

Sunrise Radio Group
Sunrise Road, Southall, Middlesex UB2 4AU
Fax 0181-813 9800   Tel 0181-574 6666
Stations: Sunrise, Sunrise East Midlands, Sunrise FM.

LOCAL RADIO STATIONS

2CR FM
5 Southcote Road, Bournemouth, Dorset BH1 3LR
Fax 01202-259259   Tel 01202-255244
Website: http://www.2crfm.co.uk
Parent company: GWR Group
Starting date: 15.9.80
Area: Dorset, west Hampshire
Dial: 102.3 MHz (2CR FM) 828 kHz (Classic Gold)

2-Ten FM
PO Box 2020, Reading, Berks RG31 7FG
Fax 0118-928 8433   Tel 0118-945 4400
E-mail: musicmix@2tenfm.musicradio.com
Website: http://www.2-TENFM.co.uk
Parent company: GWR Group
Starting date: 8.3.76
Area: Reading, Basingstoke, Andover
Dial: 97.0 & 102.9 FM, 103.4 FM

A1 FM
11 Woodland Road, Darlington DL3 7BJ
Fax 01325-255551   Tel 01325-255552
E-mail: admin@alpharadio.demon.co.uk
Area: Darlington and Newton Aycliffe.
Dial: 103.2 FM

96.3 Aire FM
51 Burley Road, Leeds, West Yorkshire LS3 1LR
Fax 0113-283 5501   Tel 0113-283 5500
Website: http://www.airefm.co.uk
Parent company: Emap
Starting date: 1.9.81
Area: Leeds
Dial: 96.3 MHz

96.7 FM
PO Box 77, 18 Blackfriars Street, King's Lynn, Norfolk PE30 1NN
Fax 01553-766453   Tel 01553-772777
E-mail: klfmradio.co.uk
Area: west Norfolk

Amber Classic Gold
PO Box 4000, Norwich NR3 1DB
Fax 01603-666353   Tel 01603-630621
Parent company: GWR Group
Starting date: 24.9.95
Area: Great Yarmouth & Norwich
Dial: 1152 KHz

Amber Radio (Suffolk)
Radio House, Alpha Business Park, White House Road, Ipswich, Suffolk IP1 5LT
Fax 01473-741200   Tel 01473-461000
Parent company: GWR Group
Starting date: 24.9.95
Area: Bury St Edmunds, Ipswich
Dial: 1152,1170 AM

Asian Sound
Globe House, Southall Street, Manchester M3 1LG
Fax 0161-288 9000   Tel 0161-288 1000
E-mail: asiansound@aol.com
Area: East Lancashire

B97
55 Goldington Road, Bedford MK40 3LT
Fax 01234-218580   Tel 01234-272400
Parent company: GWR Group
Starting date: 1.3.82
Area: Bedford & Bedfordshire
Dial: 96.9 FM

The Bay
PO Box 969, George's Quay, Lancaster LA1 3LD
Fax 01524-848787   Tel 01524-848747
E-mail: thebay.co.uk
Starting date: 1.3.93
Policy: classic hits, local news, community information
Area: North Lancashire & south Cumbria.
Dial: 96.9, 102.3 & 103.2 FM

The Beach
PO Box 103.4 Lowestoft, Suffolk
Fax 07000 001036   Tel 07000 001035
E-mail: 103.4@thebeach.co.uk
Website: http://www.thebeach.co.uk
Parent company: Tindle Newspapers
Starting date: 29.9.96
Area: Great Yarmouth & Lowestoft
Dial: 103.4 MHz

Beacon FM/WABC Classic Gold
267 Tettenhall Road, Wolverhampton, West Midlands WV6 0DQ
Fax 01902-838266   Tel 01902-838383
E-mail: timlawrence@beaconfm.musicradio.com
Parent company: GWR Group
Starting date: 12.4.76; Shrewsbury & Telford 14.7.87
Area: Wolverhampton & Black Country, Shrewsbury & Telford
Dial: 97.2 & 103.1 MHz

The Breeze
Clifftown Road, Southend-on-Sea, Essex SS1 1SX
Fax 01702-345224   Tel 01702-333711
E-mail: studios@breeze.co.uk
Website: http://www.breeze.co.uk
Parent company: Essex Radio/DMG Radio
Starting date: 16.7.89
Dial: 1431 kHz (Southend), 1359 kHz (Chelmsford)

96.4 FM BRMB
Aston Road North, Birmingham B6 4BZ
Fax 0121-359 1117   Tel 0121-359 4481
Parent company: Capital Radio
Starting date: 19.2.74
Area: Birmingham.
Dial: 96.4 FM

Broadland
47 Colegate, Norwich, Norfolk NR3 1DB
Fax 01603-666252   Tel 01603-630621
E-mail: sales@broadland102.co.uk
Website: http://www.broadland102.co.uk
Parent company: GWR Group
Starting date: 1.10.84
Area: Norwich and Great Yarmouth.
Dial: 102.4 MHz, 1152kHz

Brunel Classic Gold
PO Box 2000, Bristol BS99 7SN
Fax: 0117-984 3202   Tel 0117-984 3200
E-mail: reception@gwrfm.musicradio.com
Parent company: GWR Group
Starting date: 25.11.88
Dial: 1260 kHz (Bristol), 936 kHz (west Wilts), 1161 kHz (Swindon)

Capital FM/Capital Gold
30 Leicester Square, London WC2H 7LA
Fax 0171-766 6100   Tel 0171-766 6000
Parent company: Capital Radio
Starting date: 16.10.73 (Capital FM), 28.11.88 (Capital Gold)
Area: London.
Dial: 95.8 MHz (Capital FM), 1548 kHz (Capital Gold)

Capital Gold, Birmingham
Radio House, Aston House, Aston Road North, Birmingham B6 4BZ
Fax 0121-359 1117   Tel 0121-359 4481
Area: Birmingham
Dial: 1152 AM

Central FM
201-203 High Street, Falkirk FK1 1OU
Fax 01324-611168   Tel 01324-611164
Starting date: 4.6.90
Area: Stirling an Falkirk.
Dial: 103.1 MHz

Century Radio
Century Ho, PO Box 100, Gateshead NE8 2YX
Fax 0191-477 1771   Tel 0191-477 6666
Parent company: Border Media
Policy: Speech, easy listening and country music.
Starting date: 1.9.94
Area: North East
Dial: 100.7, 101.8 & 96.2 MHz

Ceredigion
Yr Hen Ysgol Gymraeg, Ffordd Alexandra, Aberystwyth, Dyfed SY23 1LF
Fax 01970-627206   Tel 01970-627999
Bilingual community station
Starting date: 14.12.92
Area: Ceredigion.
Dial: 103.3 & 96.6 MHz, 97.4FM

CFM
PO Box 964, Carlisle, Cumbria CA1 3NG
Fax 01228-818444   Tel 01228-818964
Starting date: 14.4.93
Area: Carlisle.
Dial: 96.4 Penrith, 102.2 Whitehaven, 103.4 Workington

Channel 103 FM
6 Tunnel Street, St Helier, Jersey, Channel Islands JE2 4LU
Fax 01534-887799   Tel 01534-888103
E-mail: radio@103fm.itl.net
Website: http://www.103fm.itl.net
Starting date: 25.10.92
Area: Jersey.
Dial: 103.7 MHz

Channel Travel Radio
PO Box 2000, Folkestone, Kent CT18 8XY
Fax 01303-283874   Tel 10303-283873
Starting date: 20.4.95
Area: along the M20 towards the Kent Channel ports

Chiltern FM/ClassicGold 792 & 828
Chiltern Road, Dunstable, Beds LU6 1HQ
Fax 01582-676241   Tel 01582-676200
Parent company: GWR Group
Starting date: 15.10.81 (Chiltern FM); 15.7.90 (Classic Gold)
Area: Bedford, Luton.
Dial: 97.6 MHz Chiltern FM, 792 & 828 kHz Classic Gold

Choice FM
16 Trinity Gardens, London SW9 8DP
Fax 0171-738 6619   Tel 0171-738 7969
E-mail: onair@choice1022.co.uk
Website: http://www.choice1022.co.uk
Starting date: 31.3.90
Area: Brixton.
Dial: 96.9 MHz

Choice FM - Birmingham
95 Broad Street, Birmingham B15 1AU
Fax 0121-616 1011   Tel 0121-616 1000
Starting date: 1.1.95
Area: Birmingham.
Dial: 102.2 MHz

CityBeat 96.7
Lamont Buildings, 46 Stranmills Embankment, Belfast BT9 5DF
Fax 01232-200023   Tel 01232-205967
Starting date: 6.9.90
Area: Belfast
Dial: 96.7 MHz

Classic Gold 828
5 Southcote Road, Bournemouth, BH1 3LR
Fax 01202-255244   Tel 01202-259259
Website; www.classicgold828.co.uk
Parent company: GWR Group
Area: Dorset, west Hampshire

Classic Gold 1332
PO Box 2020, Queensgate, Peterborough PE1 1LL
Fax 01733-281445   Tel 01733-460460
E-mail: tima@musicradio.com
Parent company: GWR Group
Starting date: 14.4.92
Area: Peterborough.
Dial: 1332 kHz

Classic Gold 1359
Hertford Place, Coventry CV1 3TT
Fax 01203-868202   Tel 01203-868200
Parent company: GWR Group
Area: Coventry

Classic Gold 1431
PO Box 2020, Reading, Berks RG31 7FG
Fax 0118-925 4456   Tel 0118-945 4400
E-mail: musicmix@twotenfm.musicradio.com
Parent company: GWR Group
Starting date: 8.3.76
Area: Reading.
Dial: 1431 kHz

smiles ahead...

* One adult in every three in Sussex tunes in every week...
and * Southern FM reaches 52% of all 15 to 44 year olds
across the county...

So...if you want to talk to Sussex
...talk to Southern FM!

Telephone: 01273 430111
Fax: 01273 430098
e-mail:info@southernradio.co.uk

* Source: Rajar Qtr 2 '98

Clyde 1/Clyde 2
Clydebank Business Park, Glasgow G81 2RX
Fax 0141-565 2265   Tel 0141-306 2200
E-mail: clydenews@srh.co.uk
Parent company: Scottish Radio Holdings
Starting date: 31.12.73
Dial: Clyde 1, 102.5 MHz (Glasgow), 97.0 MHz (Vale of Leven), 103.3 MHz (Firth of Clyde). Clyde 2, 1152 kHz

Cool FM
PO Box 974, Belfast BT1 1RT
Fax 01247-814974   Tel 01247-817181
E-mail: music@coolfm.co.uk
Website: http://www.coolfm.co.uk
Starting date: 7.2.90
Area: Belfast.   **Dial:** 97.4 MHz

Country 1035
Hurlingham Business Park, London SW6 3DU
Fax 0171-546 1030   Tel 0171-546 1010
Country music
Starting date: 1.9.94
Area: Greater London. **Dial:** 1035 kHz

County Sound Radio 1476AM
Dolphin House, North Street, Guildford GU1 4AA
Fax 01483-531612   Tel 01483-300964
E-mail: eagle@countysound.co.uk
Website: http://www.cableol.net/ukrd/
Parent company: UKRD Group
Starting date: 4.9.95
Area: W Surrey and NE Hampshire
Dial: 1476 KHz

CTFM
16 Lower Bridge Street, Canterbury, Kent CT1 2HQ
Fax 01277-785106   Tel 01277-789106
Starting date: 21.9.97
Area: Canterbury, Whitstable, Herne Bay

Delta Radio
65 Weyhill, Haslemere, Surrey GU27 1HN
Fax 01428-658971   Tel 01428-651971
E-mail: 100722.721@compuserve.com
Website: http://www.cableol.net/ukrd/
Parent company: UKRD Group
Starting date: 9.5.96
Area: Haslemere
Dial: 97.1 MHz

Downtown Radio
Newtownards, Co Down, Northern Ireland BT23 4ES
Fax 01247-818913   Tel 01247-815555
E-mail: programmes@downtown.co.uk
Website: http://www.downtown.co.uk
Parent company: MaxAM
Starting date: 16.3.76
Dial: 1026 kHz (Belfast), 102.4 MHz (Londonderry), 96.4 MHz (Limavady), 96.6 MHz (Enniskillen)

Dune FM
The Power Station, Victoria Way, Southport PR8 1RR
Fax 01704-502540   Tel 01704-502500
E-mail: dunefm@aol.com
Website: http://www.dunefm.co.uk
Starting date: 12.10. 97
Area: Sefton and west Lancashire
Dial: 107.9 fm

96.4 The Eagle
Dolphin House, North Street, Guildford GU1 4AA
Fax 01483-531612   Tel 01483-300964
E-mail: eagle@countysound.co.uk
Website: http://www.cableol.net/ukrd/
Parent company: UKRD Group
Starting date: 4.1.96
Area: W Surrey and NE Hampshire
Dial: 96.4 MHz

eleven SEVENTY AM
PO Box 1170, High Wycombe, Bucks HP13 6YT
Fax 01494 447272   Tel 01494 446611
E-mail: elevenseventy@pipex.dial
Starting date: 31.12.93
Area: High Wycombe.
Dial: 1170 kHz

Essex FM
Clifftown Road, Southend, Essex SS1 1SX
Fax 01702-345224   Tel 01702-333711
E-mail: studios@essexfm.co.uk
Website: http://www.essexfm.co.uk
Parent company: Essex Radio, a subsidiary of DMG Radio
Starting date: 12.9.81
Dial: 96.3 MHz (Southend), 102.6 MHz (Chelmsford)

Fame 1521
Radio Mercury, The Stanley Centre, Kelvin Way, Crawley, W Sussex RH10 2SE
Fax 01293-565663   Tel 01293-519161
Parent company: Independent Radio Group
Starting date: 4.5.92
Area: Reigate & Crawley

FM 102 The Bear
Guard House Studios, Banbury Road, Stratford upon Avon, Warwicks CV37 7HX
Fax 01789-263102   Tel 01789-262636
Starting date: 24.5.96
Area: Stratford upon Avon

FM 103 Horizon
Broadcast Centre, Crownhill, 14 Vincent Avenue, Milton Keynes, Bucks MK8 0AB
Fax 01908-564893   Tel 01908-269111
E-mail: morning crew@fm103.musicradio.com
Area: Milton Keynes

Forth FM/Forth AM
Forth House, Forth Street, Edinburgh EH1 3LF
Fax 0131-558 3277   Tel 0131-556 9255
Parent company: Scottish Radio Holdings
Starting date: 22.1.75
Area: Edinburgh, Lothian & Fife
Dial: 97.3/97.6 Hz Forth FM, 1548 kHz Forth AM

Fox FM
Brush House, Pony Road, Oxford OX4 2XR
Fax 01865-871036   Tel 01865-871000
E-mail: fox@foxfm.co.uk
Starting date: 15.9.89
Area: Oxford, Banbury.
Dial: 102.6 & 97.4 MHz

Galaxy 101
Millennium House, 26 Baldwin Street, Bristol BS1 1SE
Fax 0117-901 4555   Tel 0117-901 0101
E-mail: FirstinitialSurname@Galaxy101.co.uk
Parent company: Chrysalis Group
Starting date: 4.9.94
Area: South Wales and the West
Dial: 101 MHz & 97.2 MHz

Galaxy 102
PO Box 102, Manchester M60 1GJ
Fax 0161-228 1020   Tel 0161-228 0102
Parent company: FazeFM
Starting date: 16.10.94
Area: Greater Manchester.
Dial: 102 MHz

Galaxy 105
Joseph's Well, West Gate, Leeds LS3 1AB
Fax 0113-213 1055   Tel 0113-213 0105
Parent company: Chrysalis Group
Starting date: 14.2.97
Area: Yorkshire
Dial: 105 MHz

Gem-AM
29-31 Castle Gate, Nottingham NG1 7AP
Fax 0115-912 9333   Tel 0115-952 7000
E-mail: direct@gemam.musicradio.com
Parent company: GWR Group
Starting date: 4.10.88
Area: Nottingham and Derby.
Dial: 999 & 945 kHz

Gemini AM/Gemini FM
Hawthorn House, Exeter Business Park, Exeter,
Devon EX1 3QS
Fax: 01392-444433   Tel 01392-444444
Starting date: 1.1.95
Area: Exeter, east Devon and Torbay.
Dial: 666/954 kHz, 96.4/97.0/103 Mhz

GWR FM
PO Box 2000, Bristol, Avon BS99 7SN
Fax 0117-984 3202   Tel 0117-984 3200
E-mail: reception@gwrfm.musicradio.com
Parent company: GWR Group
Starting date: 27.10.81 (Bristol), 22.5.87 (Bath)
Dial: 96.3 MHz (Bristol), 103.0 MHz (Bath)

GWR-FM Wiltshire
PO Box 2000, Swindon SN4 7EX
Fax 01793-440302   Tel 01793-440300
Parent company: GWR Group
Starting date: 12.10.82
Dial: 97.2 MHz (Swindon), 102.2 MHz (west Wilts),
96.5 MHz (Marlborough)

Hallam FM
900 Herries Road, Sheffield S6 1RH
Fax 0114-285 3159   Tel 0114-285 3333
E-mail: programmes@hallamfm.co.uk
Website: http://www.fmradio.demon.co.uk
Parent company: EMAP
Starting date: 1.10.74
Dial: 97.4 MHz (Sheffield), 102.9 MHz (Barnsley),
103.4 MHz (Doncaster)

100.7 Heart FM
1 The Square, 111 Broad Street, Birmingham B15 1AS
Fax 0121-696 1007   Tel 0121-626 1007
E-mail: addressee@heartfm.co.uk
Parent company: Chrysalis
Policy: Soft adult contemporary music
Starting date: 7.9.94
Area: West midlands, Warwickshire
Dial: 100.7 MHz

Heart 106.2 FM
PO Box 1062, Chrysalis Building, Bramley Road,
London W10 6WR
Fax 0171-470 1095   Tel 0171-468 1062
E-mail: kpalmer@heart1062.co.uk
Parent company: Chrysalis Group
Starting date: summer 1995
Area: Greater London. Dial: 106.2 MHz

Heartland FM
Lower Oakfield, Pitlochry, Perthshire PH16 5DS
Fax 01796-474007   Tel 01796-474040
Some Gaelic and mixed language output.
Starting date: 21.3.92
Area: Pitlochry and Aberfldy.
Dial: 97.5 MHz

102.7 Hereward FM
PO Box 225, Queensgate, Peterborough,
Cambridgeshire PE1 1XJ
Fax 01796-281444   Tel 01733-460460
Parent company: GWR Group
Starting date: 20.7.80
Area: Peterborough
Dial: 102.7 MHz
Area: Milton Keynes.
Dial: 103.3 FM, Classic Gold 1332 AM

Invicta FM/Capital Gold
Radio House, John Wilson Business Park, Whitstable,
Kent CT5 3QX
Fax 01227-771558   Tel 01227-772004
E-mail: info@cis.compuserve.com
Parent company: Capital Radio
Starting date: Invicta FM: 1.10.84, Capital Gold 27.3.89
Dial: Invicta FM 103.1 MHz (Maidstone & Medway),
102.8 MHz (Canterbury, 95.9 MHz (Thanet), 97.0
MHz (Dover), 96.1 MHz (Ashford). Capital Gold 1242
kHz (west Kent), 603 kHz (east Kent)

Island FM
12 Westerbrook, St Sampsons, Guernsey GY2 4QQ
Fax 01481-496768   Tel 01481-42000
E-mail: uikki@islandfm.guernsey.net
Starting date: 15.10.92
Dial: 104.7 MHz (Guernsey), 93.7 MHz (Alderney)

Isle of Wight Radio
Dodnor Park, Newport, Isle of Wight PO30 5XE
Fax 01983-822109   Tel 01983-822557
E-mail: admin@iwradio.co.uk
Website: http://www.iwradio.co.uk
Starting date: 15.4.90
Area: Isle of Wight
Dial: 107 & 102 MHz

Jazz FM
The World Trade Centre, Exchange Quay, Manchester M5 3EJ
Fax 0161-877 1005   Tel 0161-877 1004
Website: http://www.jazzfm.com
Parent company: Golden Rose Communications
Starting date: 1.9.94
Area: North west
Dial: 100.4 MHz

Jazz FM 102.2
26 Castlereagh Street, London W1H 6DJ
Fax 0171-723 9742   Tel 0171-706 4100
Parent company: Golden Rose Communications.
Starting date: 4.3.90
Area: Greater London.   Dial: 102.2 MHz

KCBC
PO Box 1584, Kettering, Northants NN16 8PU
Fax 01536-517390   Tel 01536-412413
E-mail: 107.4@kcbc.co.uk
Parent company: TLRC
Starting date: 6.4.90
Area: Kettering, Corby.
Dial: 1548 kHz

Key 103
Castle Quay, Castlefield, Manchester M15 4PR
Fax 0161-288 5001   Tel 0161-288 5000
Website: http://www.key103fm.com
Parent company: Emap Radio
Starting date: 3.9.88
Area: Manchester
Dial: 103MHz

KFM
1 East Street, Tonbridge, Kent TN9 1AR
Fax 01732-369201   Tel 01732-369200
E-mail: kfm@cis.compuserve.com
Website: http://www.kfm.co.uk
Starting date: 8.7.95
Area: Tonbridge, Tunbridge Wells and Sevenoaks
Dial: 96.2 Hz (south), 101.6 MHz (north)

Kiss 100 FM
80 Holloway Road, London N7 8JG
Fax 0171-700 3979   Tel 0171-700 6100
Website: http://www.musiclinks.com/grahamgold
Parent company: Emap
Starting date: 1.990
Area: Greater London.
Dial: 100 MHz

Kix 96
St Mark's Church Annex, Bird Street, Stoney Stanton Road, Coventry CV1 4FH
E-mail: klfmradio.co.uk
Fax: 01203-551744   Tel 01203-525656
Website: http://www.indiscrete/kix96
Starting date: 28.8.90
Area: Coventry. Dial: 96.2 MHz

KL-FM
18 Blackfriars Street, Kings Lynn, Norfolk PE30 1NN
Fax 01553-766453   Tel 01553-772777
Parent company: Dawe Media
Starting date: 1.7.92
Area: Kings Lynn. Dial: 96.7 MHz

Lantern FM
The Lighthouse, 17 Market Place, Bideford, Devon EX39 2DR
Fax 01237-423333   Tel 01237-424444
Starting date: 19.10.92
Area: North Devon.
Dial: 96.2 MHz

LBC 1152am
200 Gray's Inn Road, London WC1X 8XZ
Fax 0171-312 8565   Tel 0171-973 1152
Website: http://www.lbc.co.uk
Britain's first commercal station, LBC had its 25th anniversary on October 8 1998. Relaunched in its current format in July 1996, the station provides 24 hour news and comment for London with phone-ins.
Parent company: London News Radio
Starting date: July 1996
Area: Greater London
Dial: 1152 am

Leicester Sound
Granville House, Granville Road, Leicester LE1 7RW
Fax 0116-256 1303   Tel 0116-256 1300
E-mail: admin@leicesterfm@musicradio.com
Parent company: GWR Group
Starting date: 7.9.84
Area: Leicester.
Dial: 105.4 MHz

Liberty
Trevor House, 100 Brompton Road, London SW3 1ER
Fax 0171-893 8965   Tel 0171-893 8966
E-mail: liberty963@aol.com
Parent company: Liberty Publishing
Starting date: 3.7.95
Area: Greater London
Dial: 963 kHz

Lincs FM
Witham Park, Waterside South, Lincoln LN5 7JN
Fax 01522-549911   Tel 01522-549900
E-mail: lincsfm@msn.com
Starting date: 1.3.92
Area: Lincolnshire

1458 Lite AM
Quay West, Trafford Park Manchester M17 1FL
Fax 0161-872 0206   Tel 0161-872 1458
Website: http://www.crazyprices.com/liteam/
Starting date: 20.6.94
Area: Greater Manchester. Dial: 1458 kHz

Lochbroom FM
Mill Street Industrial Estate, Ullapool, West Ross IV26 2UN
Fax 01854-613131   Tel 01854-613131
Starting date: 97
Area: West Ross
Dial: 102.2 MHz

London Greek Radio
Florentia Village, Vale Road, London N4 1TD
Fax 0181-800 8005   Tel 0181-800 8001
E-mail: lgrhgc@globalnet.co.uk
Music, news and info for Greek speaking listeners
Starting date: 13.11.89
Area: Haringey. Dial: 103.3 MHz

London Turkish Radio
185b High Road, Wood Green London N22 6BA
Fax 0181-881 5151   Tel 0181-881 0606
Music for the Turkish community
Starting date: summer 1995
Area: north London, Haringey.
Dial: 1584 kHz

Magic AM
900 Herries Road, Sheffield S6 1RH
Fax 0114-285 3159   Tel 0114-285 2121
E-mail: programmes@fmradio.demon.co.uk
Website:http://www.fmradio.demon.co.uk
Parent company: EMAP
Starting date: 12.2.97
Dial: 990 kHz, 1305 kHz, 1548 kHz

Magic 828
PO Box 2000, 51 Burley Road, Leeds LS3 1LR
Fax 0113 283 5501   Tel 0113 283 5500
E-mail: MAGIC 828@firstnet.co.uk
Website: http://www.magic 828.co.uk
Parent company: Emap
Starting date: 17.7.90
Area: Leeds, west Yorkshire
Dial: 828 kHz

Magic 1152
Newcastle-upon-Tyne NE99 1BB
Fax 0191-488 0933   Tel 0191-420 3040
Parent company: Emap Radio
Starting date: 8.4.89
Area: Tyne & Wear, Teesside.
Dial: 1152AM

Magic 1161
Commercial Road, Hull HU1 2SG
Fax 01482-587067   Tel 01482-325141
E-mail: programme@hallamfm.co.uk
Parent company: Emap Radio
Starting date: 13.9.93
Dial: 1161 kHz

Magic 1548
8-10 Stanley Street, Liverpool L1 6AF
Fax 0151-471 0330   Tel 0151-227 5100
Parent company: Emap
Starting date: 21.10.74
Area: Merseyside
Dial: 1548 kHz

Radio Maldwyn
Studios, The Park, Newtown, Powys SY16 2NZ
Fax 01686-623666   Tel 01686-623555
E-mail: radio.maldwyn@ukonline.co.uk
Starting date: 1 .7.93
Area: Montgomeryshire.
Dial: 756 kHz

Manx Radio
PO Box 1368, Broadcasting House, Douglas, Isle of Man IM99 1SW
Fax 01624-682604   Tel 01624-661066
E-mail: postbox@manxradio.com
Starting date: 5.6.64
Area: Isle of Man.

Marcher Coast FM
The Studios, 41 Conway Road, Colwyn Bay, Conway
Fax 01492-535248   Tel 01492-533733
Area: North Wales

Marcher Gold
The Studios, Mold Road, Wrexham, Conway LL11 4AF
Fax 01978-759701   Tel 01978-752202
E-mail: mfm.radio@ukonline.co.uk
Starting date: 5.9.83
Area: Wrexham, Chester, Deeside and Wirral.
Dial: 1260 kHz

Medway FM
Berkeley House, 186 High Street, Rochester ME1 1EY
Fax 01634-841122   Tel 01634-841111
Website: http://www.medwayfm.com
Starting date: 1.9.97
Area: Medway towns
Dial: 107.9MHz, 100.4MHz

Mellow 1557
Media Centre, 2 St Johns Wynd, Culver Square, Colchester CO1 1WQ
Fax 01206-764672   Tel 01206-764466
E-mail: mellow@enterprise.co.uk
Starting date: 7.10.90
Area: Tendring
Dial: 1557 kHz

Melody FM
180 Brompton Road, London SW3 1HF
Fax 0171-581 7000   Tel 0171-581 1054
Website: http://www.melody.co.uk
Starting date: 9.7.90
Area: Greater London.
Dial: 105.4 MHz

Mercia FM/Classic Gold 1359
Hertford Place, Coventry, W Midlands CV1 3TT
Fax 01203-868203   Tel 01203-86820
E-mail: merviafm@radio.com
Parent company: GWR
Starting date: 7.3.94 (Mercia Classic Gold), 23.5.80 (Mercia FM)
Area: Coventry, Warwickshire.
Dial: 1359 kHz Mercia Classic Gold, 97.0 & 102.9 Hz Mercia FM

Mercury FM/Fame 1521
The Stanley Centre, Kelvin Way, Crawley, West Sussex RH10 2SE
Fax 01293-565663   Tel 01293-519161
Parent company: Independent Radio
Starting date: 20.10.84 (Mercury FM East), 4.5.92 (GRP. Fame 1521)
Area: Reigate, Crawley
Dial: 102.7 MHz (Mercury FM) 1521 kHz (Fame 1521)

Metro FM
Long Rigg Road, Swalwell, Newcastle-upon-Tyne NE99 1BB
Fax 0191-488 9222   Tel 0191-420 0971
Parent company: Emap Radio
Starting date: 15.4.74
Areas: Tyne & Wear
Dial: 97.1 MHz (Tyne & Wear)
103.0 MHz (Tyne Valley)

MFM
The Studios, Mold Road, Wrexham LL11 4AF
Fax 01978-759701   Tel 01978-752202
E-mail: mfm.radio@ukonline.co.uk
Starting date: 31.8.89
Area: Wrexham, Chester, Deeside and Wirral
Dial: 97.1 & 103.4 MHz

Millenium Radio
Harrow Manor Way, Thamesmead, London SE2 9XH
Fax 0181-312 1930   Tel 0181-311 3112
mfm@greenwichuk.com
Starting date: 18.3.90
Area: Thamesmead
Dial: 106.8 MHz

Minster FM
PO Box 123, Dunnington, York YO1 5ZX
Fax 01904-488811   Tel 01904-488888
E-mail: minsterfm@demon.co.uk
Starting date: 4.7.92
Area: York.
Dial: 104.7 MHz

Mix 96
Friars Square Studios, 11 Bourbon Street, Aylesbury,
Bucks HP20 2PZ
Fax 01296-398988   Tel 01296-399396
E-mail: mix@mix96.demon.co.uk
Website: http://www.mix96.demon.co.uk
Starting date: 15.4.94
Area: Aylesbury Vale, Thame, Tring, Leighton Buzzard
Dial: 96.2 MHz

Moray Firth
PO Box 271, Inverness, IV3 6SF
Fax 01463-243224   Tel 01463-224433
E-mail: moray.firth.radio@mfr.uk.com
Starting date: 23.2.82
Area: Inverness
Dial: 97.4 & 96.6 MHz, 1107 kHz

Neptune Radio 96.4 & 106.8FM
PO Box 1068, Dover CT16 1GB
Fax 01304-212717   Tel 01304-202505
Starting date: 29.9.97
Area: Dover & Folkestone
Dial: 106.8 MHz Dover, 96.4 MHz Folkestone

Nevis Radio
Inverlochy, Fort William PH33 6LU
Fax 01397 701007   Tel 01397-700007
E-mail: nevisradio@lochaber.co.uk
Starting date: 1.8.94
Area: Fort William
Dial: 96.6 & 102.3 MHz

News Direct 97.3FM
200 Grays Inn Road, London WC1 8XZ
Fax 0171-312 8470   Tel 0171-333 0033
Website: http://www.newsdirect973.co.uk
Providing a 24-hour rolling news and information
service for London with news, traffic, weather, sport,
entertainment, city and headlines every 20 minutes..
Parent company: London News Radio
Starting date: December 1996
Area: Greater London
Dial: 97.3FM

Northants 96/Classic Gold 1557
19-21 St Edmunds Road, Northampton NN1 5DY
Fax 01604-795601   Tel 01604-795600
E-mail: reception@northants96.musicradio.com
Parent company: GWR Group
Starting date: 1.10.86
Area: Northampton
Dial: 96.6 MHz, 1557 AM

NorthSound One/Two
45 Kings Gate, Aberdeen, Grampian AB15 4EL
Fax 01224-637289   Tel 01224-337000
E-mail: northsound@srh.co.uk
Parent company: Scottish Radio Holdings
Starting date: 27.7.81
Area: Aberdeen. Dial: 96.9, 97.6, 103 MHz (One),1035
kHz (Two)

Oasis FM
9 Christopher Place, Shopping Centre, St Albans,
Herts AL3 5DQ
Fax 01727-834456   Tel 01727-831966
Parent company: Essex Radio
Starting date: 22.10.94
Area: St Albans & Watford
Dial: 96.6 FM

Oban FM
McLeod units, Lochavullin Estate, Oban, Argyll
Fax 01631-570057   Tel 01631-570057
Starting date: 1.7.96
Area: Oban

Ocean FM
Radio House, Whittle Avenue, Segensworth West,
Fareham PO15 5SH
Fax 01489-589453   Tel 01489-589911
E-mail: info@oceanradio.co.uk
Parent company: Capital Radio
Starting date: 12.10.86
Area: Portsmouth, Soton and Worcester.
Dial: 96.7, 97.5 MHz

Orchard FM
Haygrove House, Taunton, Somerset TA3 7BT
Fax 01823-321044   Tel 01823-338448
Website: http://www.orchardfm.co.uk
Starting date: 26.11.89
Area: Yeovil and Taunton.
Dial: 96.5, 97.1, 102.6 MHz

Oxygen 107.9
Suite 41, Westgate Centre, Oxford OX1 1PD
Fax 01865-726161   Tel 01865-724442
E-mail: mail@oxygen.demon.co.uk
Website: http://www.oxygen.demon.co.uk
Parent company: The Local Radio Company (49%),
Oxford Student Radio (51%)
Starting date: 14.2.97
Area: Oxford   Dial: 107.9 MHz

Piccadilly 1152/Key 103
Castle Quay, Castlefield, Manchester M15 4PR
Fax 0161-228 5051   Tel 0161-288 5000
Website: http://www.key103fm.com
Parent company: Emap
Starting date: 2.4.74 (1152), 3.9.88 (Key 103)
Area: Manchester
Dial: 1152 kHz, 103 MHz (Key 103)

Pirate FM 102
Carn Brae Studios, Wilson Way, Redruth, Cornwall
TR15 3XX
Fax 01209 314345   Tel 01209-314400
E-mail: piratefm102.co.uk
Starting date: 3.4.92
Area: Cornwall, W Devon, Isles of Scilly
Dial: 102.2 MHz (east Cornwall, west Devon), 102.8
(west Cornwall, Isle of Scilly)

Plymouth Sound AM/FM
Earls Acre, Plymouth, Devon PL3 4HX
Fax 01752-670730   Tel 01752-227272
Web: http://www.users.zetnet.co.uk/psound/
Starting date: 19.5.75
Area: Plymouth
Dial: 1152 kHz (AM), 97.0, 96.6 MHz (FM)

Power FM
Radio House, Whittle Avenue, Segensworth,
Fareham, Hampshire PO15 5PA
Fax 01489-589453   Tel 01489-589911
E-mail: info@powerfm.co.uk
Parent company: Capital Radio
Starting date: 4.12.88
Area: Portsmouth, Southampton and Winchester
Dial: 103.2 MHz

Premier Radio
Glen House, Stag Place, London SW1E 5AG
Fax 0171-233 6706   Tel 0171-233 6705
E-mail: premier@premier.org.uk
News and lifestyle issues reflecting beliefs of the
Christian faith.
Starting date: 10.6.95
Area: Greater London
Dial: 1305, 1332 & 1413 kHz

The Pulse (FM) Classic Gold (AM)
Forster Square, Bradford, W Yorkshire BD1 5NE
Fax 01274-203130   Tel 01274-203040
E-mail: general@pulse.co.uk
Parent company: The Radio Partnership
Starting date: 31.8.91
Area: Bradford, Halifax, Huddersfield
Dial: 97.5 FM Bradford, 102.5 FM Huddersfield &
Halifax, 1278 AM Bradford, 1530 AM Huddersfield &
Halifax

96 3 QFM
26 Lady Lane, Paisley, Strathclyde PA1 2LG
Fax 0141-887 0963   Tel 0141-887 9630
E-mail: requests@qfmclassichits.co.uk
Starting date: 1.9.92
Area: Paisley. Dial: 96.3 MHz

Q102.9 FM
Old Waterside Station, Duke Street, Waterside,
Londonderry BT47 6DH
Fax 01504-311177   Tel 01504-344449
E-mail: q102@iol.ie,
Website: http://www.q102-fm.com
Starting date: 21.10.93
Area: Londonderry
Dial: 102.9 MHz

Q103 FM
PO Box 103, Vision Park, Chivers Way, Histon,
Cambridge CB4 4WW
Fax 01223-235161   Tel 01223-235255
E-mail: reception@Q103.musicradio.com
Parent company: GWR Group
Area: Cambridge, Newmarket

Quay West Radio
The Harbour Studios, Watchet, Somerset
Fax 01643-702600   Tel 01643-704646
Area: west Somerset and Exmoor
Dial: 102.4 FM

Radio Borders
Tweedside Park, Galashiels, Borders TD1 3TD
Fax 01896-759494   Tel 01896-759444
Parent company: Scottish Radio Holdings
Starting date: 22.1.90
Area: Scottish Borders.
Dial: 96.8, 97.5, 103.1 & 103.4 MHz

Radio City 96.7/Magic 1548
8-10 Stanley Street, Liverpool L1 6AF
Fax 0151-471 0333   Tel 0151-227 5100
Parent company: Emap
Starting date: 21.10.74
Area: Merseyside.
Dial: 96.7 MHz

Radio 1521/Heartbeat 1521 AM
Carn Business Park, Craigavon, co Armagh BT63 5RH
Fax 01762-391896   Tel 01762-330033
Starting date: 8.4.96 & 5.11.97

Radio XL 1296 AM
KMS House, Bradford St, Birmingham B12 0JD
Fax 0121-753 3111   Tel 0121-753 5353
For the Asian community in the West Midlands
Starting date: 30.5.95
Area: Birmingham Dial: 1296 kHz

Ram FM
The Market Place, Derby DE1 3AA
Fax 01332 292229   Tel 01332 292945
E-mail: reception@ramfm.musicradio.com
Parent company: GWR Group
Starting date: 3.3.87
Dial: 102.8 MHz

Red Dragon FM
Radio House, West Canal Wharf, Cardiff CF1 5XL
Fax 01222-384014   Tel 01222-384041
E-mail: mail@rdfm.co.uk
Parent company: Emap
Starting date: 11.4.80 (Cardiff), 13.6.83 (Newport)
Area: south east Wales
Dial: 103.2 MHz (Cardiff), 97.4 (MHz (Newport)

Red Rose Gold/Red Rose Rock FM
St Pauls Square, Preston, Lancashire PR1 1XS
Fax 01772-201917   Tel 01772-556301
Website: http://www.redrose.demon.co.uk
Parent company: Emap
Starting date: 1.6.90
Area: Blackpool, Preston Dial: 999kHz (Gold),
97.4 Hz (Rock FM)

RTL Country
PO Box 1035 London SW6 3QQ
Fax 0171-546 1030   Tel 0171-546 1010
Starting date: 1.9.94
Area: Greater London
Dial: 1035 kHz

Sabras Sound
63 Melton Road, Leicester LE4 6PN
Fax 0116-266 7776   Tel 0116-261 0666
24 hour music, news and info service to Asian communities.
Starting date: 7.9.95
Area: Leicester, Nottingham, Derby and the east Midlands
Dial: 1260 kHz

Scot FM
Number 1 Shed, Albert Quay, Leith EH6 7DN
Fax 0131-554 2266   Tel 0131-554 6677
Starting date: 16.9.94
Policy: Speech and adult contemporary music
Area: Central Scotland
Dial: 100.3 & 101.1 MHz

Severn Sound/Severn Sound SuperGold
Broadcast Centre, Southgate Street, Gloucester GL1 2DQ
Fax 01452-529446   Tel 01452-423791
Parent company: Chiltern Radio Network
Starting date: 23.10.80
Area: Gloucester and Cheltenham
Dial: 102.4 & 103 MHz (Severn Sound), 774 kHz (SuperGold)

SGR FM Bury
Radio House, Alpha Business Park, Whitehouse Road, Ipswich, Suffolk IP1 5LT
Fax 01473-741200   Tel 01284-702622
Parent company: GWR
Starting date: 6.11.82
Area: Bury St Edmunds
Dial: 96.4 MHz, 1251 kHz

SGR Colchester
9 Whitewell Road, Colchester CO2 7DE
Fax 01206-561199   Tel 01206-575859
E-mail: prog.col@sgrfm.co.uk
Parent company: East Anglian Radio
Starting date: 17.10.83
Area: Colchester **Dial:** 96.1 MHz

SGR FM Ipswich
Radio House, Alpha Business Park, Whitehouse Road, Ipswich, Suffolk IP1 5LT
Fax 01473-741200   Tel 01473-461000
E-mail: chris@sgrfm.co.uk
Parent company: GWR
Starting date: 28.10.75
Area: Ipswich
Dial: 97.1 MHz

SIBC
Market Street, Lerwick, Shetland ZE1 0JN
Fax 01595-695696   Tel 01595-695299
Website: http://www.sibc.co.uk
Starting date: 19.10.91
Area: Shetland Islands
Dial: 96.2 MHz

Signal 104.9/96.4
Regent House, Heaton Lane, Stockport, Greater Manchester SK4 1BX
Fax 0161-474 1806   Tel 0161-480 5445
E-mail: signal@signal1049.com
Parent company: The Radio Partnership
Starting date: 17.2.90
Area: south Manchester & Cheshire
Dial: 104.9 - south Manchester, 96.4 Cheshire

Signal Gold/Signal One
Studio 257, Stoke Road, Stoke-on-Trent, ST4 2SR
Fax 01782-747777   Tel 01782-747047
E-mail: name@signalradio.com
Parent company: Signal Radio
Starting date: 14.9.92 (Gold), 5.9.83 (One)
Area: Cheshire, Staffordshire
Dial: 1170 kHz (Gold), 102.6 & 96.9 MHz (One)

South Coast Radio/Ports
Radio Ho, Franklin Road, Portslade BN41 2SS
Fax 01273-430098   Tel 01273-430111
E-mail: info@southernradio.co.uk
Parent company: Capital Radio
Starting date: 29.8.83 (Brighton), 10.3.91 (Portsmouth & Southampton)
Area: Brighton, Southampton, Portsmouth
Dial: 1323 kHz (Brighton), 1170, 1557 kHz (Portsmouth, Southampton)

South West Sound
Campbell House, Bankend Road, Dumfries DG1 4TH
Fax 01387-265629   Tel 01387-250999
Parent company: West Sound Radio
Starting date: 21.5.90
Area: Dumfries and Galloway
Dial: 97.2 MHz

Southern FM
Radio Ho, Franklin Road, Portslade BN41 2SS
Fax 01273-430098   Tel 01273-430111
E-mail: info@southernradio.co.uk
Parent company: Capital Radio
Starting date: 12.2.88
Area: Brighton, Newhaven, Eastbourne and Hastings
Dial: 103.5 MHz (Brighton), 96.9 MHz (Newhaven), 102.4 MHz (Eastbourne), 102.0 MHz (Hastings)

Spectrum Radio
204-206 Queens Town Road, London SW8 3NR
Fax 0171-627 4433   Tel 0171-627 3409
E-mail: Spectrum@spectrum558am.co.uk
Music, news and information for ethnic communities
Starting date: 25.6.90
Area: London
Dial: 558 kHz

Spire FM
City Hall Studios, Malthouse Lane, Salisbury, Wiltshire SP2 7QQ
Fax 01722-416688   Tel 01722-416644
E-mail: spirefm.co.uk
Starting date: 20.9.92
Area: Salisbury
Dial: 102.0 MHz

Spirit FM
Dukes Court, Bognor Road, Chichester, West Sussex
PO19 2FX
Fax 01243-786464   Tel 01243-773600
Starting date: 21.4.96
Area: Chichester & Bognor Regis
Dial: 96.6 MHz & 102.3 MHz

Star FM
Observatory Shopping Centre, Slough, Berks SL1
1LH
Fax 01753-512277   Tel 01753-551066
Website: http://www.starfm.co.uk
Starting date: 21.5.93
Area: Windsor, Slough, Maidenhead
Dial: 106.6 MHz

97.2 Stray FM
PO Box 972, Station Parade, Harrogate HG1 5YF
Fax 01423-522922   Tel 01423-522972
E-mail: YourRadio@97.2strayfm.co.uk
Starting date: 4.7.94
Area: Harrogate
Dial: 97.2 FM

Sun FM
PO Box 1034, Sunderland SR1 3YZ
Fax 0191-567 0777   Tel 0191-567 3333
Music, local news, sport and information.
Parent company: Border Radio Holdings
Area: Sunderland, Washington, South tyneside and Co
Durham.
Dial: 103.4MHz

Sunrise Radio
Sunrise House, Sunrise Road, Southall, Middlesex
UB2 4AU
Fax 0181-813 9800   Tel 0181-574 6666
Music, news and information for the Asian community
Parent company: Sunrise Group
Starting date: 5.11.89
Area: Ealing, Hounslow area of London
Dial: 1458 kHz

Sunrise FM
30 Chapel Street, Little Germany, Bradford BD1 5DN
Fax 01274-728534   Tel 01274-735043
Music, news and information for the Asian community
Starting date: 9.12.89
Area: Bradford
Dial: 103.2 MHz

Sunshine 855
Sunshine House, Waterside, Ludlow, Shropshire SY8
1GS
Fax 01584-875900   Tel 01584-873795
Starting date: 18.10.92
Area: Ludlow, south Shropshire   Dial: 855 kHz

Swansea Sound (1170) Sound Wave 964
Victoria Road, Gowerton, Swansea, West Glamorgan
SA4 3AB
Fax 01792-511171   Tel 01792-511170
E-mail: sales@swanseasound.co.uk
Some Welsh language broadcasting
Parent company: The Radio Partnership
Starting date: 30.9.74
Area: Swansea
Dial: 96.4 MHz, 1170 kHz

Tay FM/Radio Tay AM
6 North Isla Street, Dundee, Tayside DD3 7JQ
Fax 01382-593252   Tel 01382-200800
E-mail: tayfm@srh.co.uk and tayam@srh.co.uk
Parent company: Scottish Radio Holdings
Starting date: 17.10.80 (Tay FM), Radio Tay AM (to be
advised)
Area: Dundee, Perth
Dial: 102.8 MHz (Dundee), 96.4 MHz (Perth) Tay FM/
1161 kHz (Dundee), 1584 kHz (Perth), Radio Tay AM

Ten 17
Latton Bush Centre, Southern Way, Harlow, Essex
CM18 7BL
Fax 01279-445289   Tel 01279-432415
E-mail: studios@ten17.co.uk
Website: http://www.ten17.co.uk
Parent company: Essex Radio, a subsidiary of DMG
Radio
Starting date: 1.5.93
Area: Harlow.
Dial: 101.7 MHz

TFM
Yale Crescent, Stockton-on-Tees, TS17 6AA
Fax 01642-868290   Tel 01642-888222
Parent company: Emap Radio
Starting date: 24.6.75
Area: Teesside.
Dial: 96.6 MHz

Thanet Local Radio
Imperial House, 2-14 High Street, Margate, Kent CT9
1DH
Fax 01843-299666   Tel 01843-220222
E-mail: general@tlrfm.co.uk
Starting date: 17.01.98
Area: Thanet, east Kent
Dial: 107.2 MHz

Touch AM
West Canal Wharf, Cardiff CF1 5XL
Fax 01222-384014   Tel 01222-237878
E-mail: mail@rdfm.co.uk
Website: http://www.rdfm.co.uk
Parent company: Emap
Starting date: 15.7.90
Dial: 1359 kHz (Cardiff), 1305 kHz (Newport)

Townland Radio/Goldbeat 828
2c Park Avenue, Cookstown, Co. Tyrone BT80 8AH
Fax 016487-63828   Tel 016487-64828
Starting date: 15.4.95
Area: Mid Ulster.
Dial: 828 kHz

Trent FM
29 Castle Gate, Nottingham NG1 7AP
Fax 0115-912 9302   Tel 0115-952 7000
E-mail: admin@trentfm.musicradio.com
Parent company: GWR Group
Starting date: 3.7.75
Area: Nottingham.
Dial: 96.2 MHz

Valleys Radio
Festival Park, Victoria, Ebbw Vale NP3 6XW
Fax 01495-300710   Tel 01495-301116
Starting date: 23.11.96
Area: Heads of south Wales valeys.
Dial: 999 & 1116MW

Vibe FM
Reflection House, Olding Road, Bury St Edmunds,
Suffolk IP33 3TA
Fax 01284-718839   Tel 01284-718800
E-mail: studios@vibefm.co.uk
Website: http://www.vibefm.co.uk
Parent company: Essex Radio, subsiduary of DMG
Radio
Starting date: 22.11.97
Area: East of England
Dial: 106.4 MHz(Suffolk), 105.6 MHz(Cambridge),
106.1 MHz(Norwich), 107.7 MHz(Peterborough)

Viking FM
Commercial Road, Hull, HU1 2SG
Fax 01482-587067   Tel 01482-325141
Parent company: Emap Radio
Starting date: 17.4.84
Area: Yorkshire-Lincolnshire
Dial: 96.9 MHz

Virgin Radio London
1 Golden Square, London W1R 4DJ
Fax 0171-434 1197   Tel 0171-434 1215
E-mail: virgin@vradio.co.uk
Website: http://www.virginradio.co.uk
Parent company: Ginger Productions
Starting date: 10.4.95
Area: Greater London
Dial: 1197 AM, 105.8 FM

The Wave
965 Mowbray Drive, Blackpool, Lancs FY3 7JR
Fax 01253-301965   Tel 01253-304965
E-mail: sales@thewavefm.co.uk
Website: http://www.thewave.co.uk
Starting date: 25.5.92
Area: Blackpool and the Fylde coast   **Dial:** 96.5 MHz

Wessex FM
Radio Ho, Trinity Street, Dorchester, Dorset DT1 1DJ
Fax 01305-250052   Tel 01305-250333
Starting date: 4.9.93
Area: Dorset
Dial: 97.2 MHz & 96.0 MHz

West Sound
Radio House, Holmston Road, Ayr KA7 3BE
Fax 01292-283662   Tel 01292-283662
E-mail: GordonM@SRH.co.uk
Web: http://www.tukonline.co.uk/wsradio.h
Starting date: 16.10.81
Area: South west Scotland
Dial: 97, 103, 96.5 MHz, 1035 kHz AM

West FM
Radio House, Holmston Road, Ayr KA7 3BE
Fax 01292-283662   Tel 01292-283662
E-mail: BrianP@SRH.co.uk
Web: http://www.westfm.mcmail.com
Starting date: 1.1.97
Area: Ayrshire   **Dial:** 96.7, 97.5 MHz

Wey Valley Radio
Prospect Place, Mill Lane, Alton, Hants GU34 2SY
Fax 01420-544044   Tel 01420-544444
E-mail: wvr@dial.pipex.com
Website: http://www.cableol.net/ukrd/
Parent company: UK Radio Development
Starting date: 22.11.92
Area: NE Hampshire
Dial: 101.6 & 102 MHz

Wish 102.4
Orrell Lodge, Orrell Road, Orrell, Wigan WN5 8HJ
Fax 01942-620222   Tel 01942-761024
Parent company: Independent Radio Group
Starting date: 1.4.97
Area: Wigan, St Helens, Skelmersdale
Dial: 102.4 MHz

107.7 The Wolf
10th Floor, Mander House, Wolverhampton WV1 3NB
Fax 01902-571079   Tel 01902-571070
E-mail: studio@thewolf.co.uk
Website: http://www.thewolf.co.uk
Starting date: 7.10.97
Area: Wolverhampton
Dial: 107.7 MHz

Wyvern FM/Classic Gold
5 Barbourne Terrace, Worcester WR1 3JZ
Fax 01905-613549   Tel 01905-612212
Area: Hereford, Worcester, Kidderminster
Dial: 97.6 Mhz (Hereford), 102.8 MHz (Worcester),
96.7 Mhz (Kidderminster); Classic Gold - 954 Khz
(hereford), 1530 Khz (Worcester)

XFM
97 Charlotte Street, London W1P 1LB
Fax 0171-299 4050   Tel 0171-299 4000
Starting date: 9.97
Area: Greater London   **Dial:** 104.9 MHz

Yorkshire Coast Radio
PO Box 962, Scarborough, Yorkshire YO12 5YX
Fax 01723-501050   Tel 01723-500962
Parent company: Minster Sound Radio
Starting date: 7.11.93
Area: Scarborough   **Dial:** 96.2 & 103.1 MHz

CABLE RADIO

Bantams 1566AM
2 Forster Square, Bradford, West Yorkshire BD1 1DQ
Fax 01274-771680   Tel 01274-771677
E-mail: info@bcb.yorks.com
Website: http://www.bcb.yorks.com
Match day service on behalf of Bradford City FC.
Area: Bradford   **Dial:** 1566 AM

BCB (Bradford Comunity Broadcasting)
2 Forster Square, Bradford, West Yorkshire BD1 1DQ
Fax 01274-771680   Tel 01274-771677
E-mail: info@bcb.yorks.com
Website: http://www.bcb.yorks.com
Community radio for Bradford. Special event RSL
broadcaster. Radio production skills training.
Area: Bradford
Dial: 104 FM on the Yorkshire Cable Network
107.4 FM or 1566 AM during RSL broadcasts.

Birmingham's BHBN
Dudley Road, Birmingham B18 7QH
Fax 0121-554 2255   Tel 0121-554 5522
Hospital info, easy listening music, local news and features
Starting date: 5.9.94
Cable Radio Milton Keynes
14 Vincent Avenue, Crownhill, Milton Keynes MK8 0AB
Fax 01908-564893   Tel 01908-265266
Commmunity radio for Milton Kenyes
Starting date: 7.79
Area: Milton Keynes
Cruise FM
Cricklade College, Charlton Road, Andover, Hants SP10 1EJ
Tel 01264-393333
Area: Andover, Salisbury, Romsey
Lite FM
2nd Floor, 5 Church Street, Peterbrough PE1 1XB
Fax 01733-898107   Tel 01733-898106

Max FM
PO Box 6000, Southampton SO16 4XD
Fax 01703-223388   Tel 01703-222122
Music Choice Europe
16 Harcourt Street, London W1H 2AU
Fax 0171-724 0404   Tel 0171-724 9494
E-mail: sales@musicchoice.co.uk
Website: http://www.musicchoice.co.uk
Radio City
Singleton Hospital, Sketty Lane, Swansea SA2 8QA
Tel 01792-205666 x 5264
E-mail: Radio.City@btinternet.com
Starting date: 31.12.6
Radio Phoenix
Neath General Hospital, Neath SA11 2LQ
Tel 01639-762029/762333
Starting date: 25.3.88   **Area:** Neath & Port Talbot
Radio Victory
Media House, Tipner Wharf, Twyford Avenue, Portsmouth Hants HP2 8PE
Fax 01705-358863   Tel 01705-358853

INDEPENDENT RADIO PRODUCERS

Independent Association of Radio Producers
29 Foley Street, London W1P 7LB
Fax 0171 436 0132   Tel 0171 402 1011

A
Aggelon Radio   01278-732848
All Out Productions   0171-831 8707
Armada Theatre   0171-831 1814
Arthur Johnson   0181-202 0274
B
BGB   0171-385 4501
Blanket Productions   0181-342 9700
Bona Lattie Productions
                       01843-290944
Business Sound   01483-898868
C
Celador Productions   0171-240 8101
Children's Voices   01364-642787
CSA Telltapes   0181-960 8466
D
David Ness   0131-556 4764
Davina Greenspan   0171-372 6311
E
Excalibur Productions
                       01422-843871
F
The Fiction Factory   0181-853 5100
First Writes   01223-264 129
Floating Earth   0181-997 4000
G
Greeh Audio   0171-240 3456
Green Mann Productions
                       0181-341 6754
H
Harry Schneider   0181-959 1695
Heavy Entertainment
                       0181-960 9001

Human Horizons   0171-704 8583
J
Jo Phillips   0227-455618
Jon Glover Partnership
                       09932-864426
Jude Habib   0181-455 6431
K
Kirsten Lass   0181-996 9960
L
Ladbroke Productions
                       0171-580 8864
Leisure Time Productions
                       0171-837 8777
Liba Productions   0181-904 8136
Loftus Productions   0181-740 4077
Louise Armitage   0171-243 0456
Louise Lawson   0181-801 0650
M
Mandy Wheeler   0171-437 8121
Mediatracks   01254-691197
P
Palace Radio   0171-415 7136
Partners in Sound   0171-485 0873
Peartree Productions
                       01905-351748
Pier Productions   01273-691401
Planet 24   0171-345 2424
Presentable Productions
                       01222-575729
Printz P Holman   01298-27975
Q
Quantum Radio Productions
                       0181-875 9999

R
Radio Star   0171-717 1257
Revolution Recordings
                       01603-433566
Rewind Productions   0171-577 7772
Robin Quinn   01892-669346
Rosemary Hartill   01665-578 543
Ruth Prince   01633-450351
S
Screen Play   01273-708610
Somethin Else Sound Direction
                       0171-613 3211
Sound Visual   01380-726831
T
Testbed Productions
                       0171-436 0555
Track Record   0171-431 3834
Tumble Hill Productions
                       01222-594044
U
Unique Broadcasting
                       0171-453 1646
V
VERA   0171-436 6116
The Vocal Suite   0171-437 2455
W
Watchmaker   0171-456 6000
Watermill Productions
                       01784-442625
Weigall Productions   0171-229 5725
Whirlwind Prods
                       01203-382633
WKD Productions   0181-748 1413

Digital radio

The Broadcasting Act 1996 provides for the licensing of at least 12 digital radio services on two national multiplexes, with at least one multiplex for local services in most parts of Britain. As with digital TV, multiplexing combines the signals of several broadcasters into a single stream on a single-frequency channel. Thus there is no longer a direct one-to-one relationship between a programme service and a frequency.

In March 1998 the Radio Authority advertised the sole national commercial radio multiplex, inviting applications from those interested in operating the multiplex for a 12 year licence term. Once the national multiplex has been awarded, the Radio Authority will advertise local multiplexes, first around major conurbations. "This pace of national and local progress," says the Radio Authority, "could bring listeners in major areas up to 24 digital radio services (London 32), plus a further selection on the BBC's own separate national multiplex." The BBC has had an experimental digital radio broadcast covering 60 per cent of the country since September 1995.

The costs are considerable. Broadcasters, judging by the levels of BBC investment, will face a likely cost of £20 million for establishing a national service. Consumers will have to pay some £500 for the first generation of digital audio broadcast receivers, devices which may contain a small screen carrying pictures and text along with the programme.

Despite the expense, the government is doing all it can to promote digital radio. Within the next two decades it will most likely have forced companies to back it by switching off the analogue frequencies to free them for mobile telephones and the like. Tim Schoonmaker, chief executive of Emap Radio, says: "There is no doubt the future is digital. We just don't know when the future is going to arrive."

We do know that only one application was made for the one and only national commercial digital multiplex licence. The Radio Authority's sole non-returnable £50,000 application fee came from Digital One, a consortium made up of GWR (57 per cent), NTL Digital Radio (33 per cent) and Talk Radio (10 per cent).

THE TECHNOLOGY

A conventional FM/AM transmitter sends radio waves into the air modifying them in a way which directly mimics the original sounds sent by the radio studio. Radios interpret this modulation and reproduce the original electronic mimicry of a microphone or other sound source to drive a speaker. Instead of using electronic circuits to mimic sounds directly, digital radio translates sounds into a rapid sequence of binary digits. These are converted back to analogue prior to hitting the radio speakers.

The older methods of transmission are prone to distortion and interference, whereas digital radio listeners will either get a clear signal or nothing at all. The advantage to listeners, once they have invested in decoders, is reception quality to match a CD.

The principles for broadcasting digitally is like digital TV, where multiplexing combines the signals of several broadcasters into a single stream on a single-frequency channel. There is no longer a direct one-to-one relationship between a programme service and a frequency.

Digital One
Classic FM House, 7 Swallow Place, London W1R 7AA
Tel: 0118 928 4316
Its ten proposed channels are as follows:
24 hours/day: Classic FM; Virgin Radio; Talk Radio; Classic Gold Rock; Soft AC; Teen and Chart Hits.
1900-0600: Club Dance
0600-1900: Plays/Books/Comedy
0600-0000: Rolling News
1900-000: weekdays & **1200-1900:** weekend Sports Channel

Publications about broadcasting

MAGAZINES

Airflash
15 Paternoster Row, Sheffield S1 2BX
Fax 0114-279 8976   Tel 0114-279 5219
E-mail CRA@gn.apc.org
Website: http://www.commedia.org.uk
Publisher: Community Media Association
Editor: Tony Harcup.
£1.00. Quarterly journal about community media.

Ariel
Room 123, Henry Wood House, 3 Langham Place,
London W1A 1AA
Fax 0171-765 3621   Tel 0171-765 3623
E-mail: ARIEL@bbc.co.uk
Publisher: BBC
Internal weekly staff magazine of the BBC.

Asia Image
6 Bell Yard, London WC2A 2JR
Fax 0171-520 5226   Tel 0171-520 5244
Publisher: Partners in Media
Monthly magazine for people in broadcasting,
production and post production in Asian TV.

Audio Media
Atlantica House, 11 Station Road, St Ives, Cambs
PE17 4BH
Fax 01480-461550   Tel 01480-461555
E-mail: mail@audiomedia.com
Website: http://www.audiomedia.com
Publisher: AM Publishing
£3.60. A monthly publication aimed at audio
professionals in the fields of recording, broadcast, post-
production, live sound and multi-media.

AV Magazine
Quantum House, 19 Scarbrook Road, Croydon CR9
1LX
Fax 0181-565 4282   Tel 0181-565 4200
E-mail: peter@av-magazine.co.uk
Publisher: Quantum
Monthly news on the audio-visual business.

BBC On Air
Room 227 NW, Bush House, Strand, London WC2B
4PH
Fax 0171 240 4899   Tel 0171-257 2875
E-mail: on.air.magazine@bbc.co.uk
Website: http://www.bbc.co.uk/worldservice/onair
Publisher: BBC World Service.
£2. Monthly programme guide to the BBC World
Service radio, BBC World and BBC Prime international
television channels.

Better Satellite
57 Rochester Place, London NW1 9JU
Fax 0171-331 1241   Tel 0171-331 1000
E-mail: bettersat@aol.com
Publisher: WV Publications
Editor: Mark Newman
£2.50. Quarterly magazine for consumers buying
satellite products.

Books in the Media
15-Up, East Street, Lewins Yard, Chesham, Bucks
HP5 1HQ
Fax 01494-784850   Tel 01494-792269
E-mail: 100615.1643@compuserve.com
Publisher: Bookwatch.
£102 p.a. members, £112 non-members. Weekly
resource newsletter keeping bookshops and libraries
informed of books appearing in the media. Bookwatch
carries out book-related research for newspapers, TV
and radio. Editor: Claire MacRae.

Braille Radio/TV Times
Orton Southgate, Peterborough, Cambs PE2 0XU
Fax 01733-371555   Tel 01733-370777
Publisher: Royal National Institute for the Blind.
Radio: 23p UK discount 60p UK cost. TV Times: £1.25
UK discount, 40p UK cost. Two braille weeklies
summarising programmes.

British Journal of Photography
39 Earlham Street, London WC2H 9LD
Fax 0171-306 7017   Tel 0171-306 7000
E-mail: bjp@benn.co.uk
Website: http://www.bjphoto.demon.co.uk
Publisher: Bouverie Publishing.
£1.50. The leading weekly professional photographic
magazine which was established 1854.

British Journalism Review
John Libbey Media, University of Luton,
75 Castle Street, Luton LU1 3AJ
Fax 01582-743298   Tel 01582-743297
E-mail: ulp@luton.ac.uk
Publisher: John Libbey Media/BJR Publishing.
Scholarly quarterly, providing a critical forum for
discussion of media topics.

Broadcast
33-39 Bowling Green Lane, London EC1R 0DA
Fax 0171-505 8050   Tel 0171-505 8014
E-mail bcast@media.emap.co.uk
Publisher: Emap Media.
£2.10. The leading weekly newspaper on the TV and
radio industry, with news, features and comments.
Emap also publishes: International Broadcasting, a
specialist monthly for technical equipment managers
and engineers; International Broadcasting Asia and TV
World, 9x pa, on international television; and Television
Buyer, a monthly for buyers of technical equipment.

Cable Guide
172 Tottenham Court Road, London W1P 0JJ
Fax 0171-419 7299   Tel 0171-419 7300
Publisher: Cable Guide .
Editor: Robin Jarossi
£3.25 monthly. Cable listings magazine with editorial
coverage of major film, drama and sports events for the
month ahead.

Cable & Satellite Communications International
Queensway House, 2 Queensway, Redhill, Surrey
RH1 1QS
Fax 01737-855470   Tel 01737-768611
Web: http://www.dmg.co.uk
Monthly magazine, target readership senior
management with purchasing influence working in
cable and satellite technology industry.

Cable & Satellite Europe
Maple House, 149 Tottenham Court Road, London
W1P 9LL
Fax 0171-896 2256   Tel 0171-896 2700
E-mail: ftmediasub@pearsonpro.com
Publisher: FT Media & Telecommunications
£115. The journal of international satellite and cable
communications.

CGI
30-31 Islington Green, London N1 8DU
Fax 0171-226 8586   Tel 0171-226 8585
E-mail: joeo@mdi-uk.com
Publisher: Media Directories International
£3.95. monthly. Art technology and ideas, a complete
monthly guide to the latest developments in digital
content creation.

Convergence
University of Luton Press, 75 Castle Street, Luton,
Beds LU1 3AJ
Fax 01582-743298   Tel 01582-743297
E-mail: convergence@luton.ac.uk
Quarterly. Journal on new media technology and
research.

Creation
30-31 Islington Green, London N1 8DU
Fax 0171-226 8586   Tel 0171-226 8585
E-mail: clarem@mdi-uk.com
Publisher: Media Directories International
£2.50. monthly. Modern magazine for creative people
in film, television and new media.

Crosstalk
PO Box 124, Westcliff on Sea, Essex SS0 0QU
Fax 01702-305121   Tel 01702-348369
E-mail: office@caclb.org.uk
Website: http://www.caclb.org.uk
Publisher: Churches Advisory Council for Local
Broadcasting (CACLB)
Quarterly news bulletin about the church and local
radio and television.

Cuts Magazine
48 Carnaby Street, London W1V 1PF
Fax 0171-437 3259   Tel 0171-437 0801
E-mail: CUTS@compuserve.com
Website: http://www.demon.co.uk/interactive/cuts/
Publisher: Sound & Vision Publishing.
Editor: George Jarrett
£30 p.a.Europe-oriented TV and film production and
post-production monthly.

Eyepiece
Studio 15, 65 Maygrove Road, London NW6 2EG
Fax 0171-372 8319   Tel 0171-328 2210
E-mail: film+video@studio22ten.cemon.co.uk
Publisher: Guild of British Camera Technicians
Editors: Kerry Anne Burrows, Charles Hewitt
Magazine for film and television people featuring
location reports, new equipment reports, news,
interviews with filmmakers past and present.

Financial Times Newsletters
Maple House, 149 Tottenham Court Road, London
W1P 9LL
Fax 0171-896 2256   Tel 0171-896 2072
E-mail: ftmediasubs@pearsonpro.com
Publisher: FT Media & Telecoms Publishing.
Produces the following newsletters: Asia-Pacific
Telecoms Analyst; Mobile Communications; Music &
Copyright; New Media Markets; Screen Finance;
Telecom Markets and related management reports.

Free Press
8 Cynthia Street, London N1 9JF
Fax 0181-837 8868   Tel 0171-278 4430
Publisher: Campaign for Press and Broadcasting
Freedom.
50p non-members. Free members news magazines.
Published eight times a year.

Historical Journal of Film, Radio and Television
PO Box 25, Abingdon, Oxfordshire OX14 3UE
Fax 01235-401550   Tel 01235-401000
E-mail: enquiries@carfax.co.uk
Website: http://www.carfax.co.uk
Publisher: Carfax Publishing Co.
Quarterly academic journal.

HotShoe International
Fairmeadow, Maidstone, Kent ME4 1NG
Fax 01622 757464   Tel 01622-687031
Publisher: Datateam Publishing
Editor: Jon Tarrant
£2.95. monthly. Magazine for the upper echelons of
creative professional photography.

Image
81 Leonard Street, London EC2A 4QS
Fax 0171-253 3007   Tel 0171-608 1441
E-mail: aop@dircon.co.uk
Publisher: Association of Photographers.
£2.00. High quality, monthly photography magazine,
with news, reviews, events and ads. Also published is
The Awards Book, an annual of top advertising and
editorial photography.

Image Technology
63-71 Victoria House, Vernon Place, London WC1B
4DA
Fax 0171-405 3560   Tel 0171-242 8400
E-mail: movimage@bksts-demon.co.uk
Website: http://www.bksts.demon.co.uk
Publisher: BKSTS.
Monthly technical journal for members of the British
Kinematograph Sound and TV Society. Also publishes
Cinema Technology.

Information World Review
Woodside, Hinksey Hill, Oxford OX1 5BE
Fax 01865-736354   Tel 01865-388000
E-mail: iwr@learned.co.uk
Website: http://www.iwr.vnu.co.uk
Publisher: Learned Information.
Monthly newspaper on the information industry, for users and producers of electronic information services.

Inside Cable & Telecoms Europe
PO Box 5 Church Stretton, Shropshire SY6 6ZZ.
Fax 01694-724135   Tel 01694-722504
E-mail: editor@dflair.demon.co.uk
Website: http://www.inside-cable.co.uk
Free-access web-news service covering the European cable TV and telecoms industry. Also maintains key data and statistics files on cable industry.

InterMedia
Tavistock House South, Tavistock Square, London WC1H 9LF
Fax 0171-380 0623   Tel 0171-388 0671
Website: http://www.iicom.org/
Publisher: International Inst of Communications
Discussion journal covering issues affecting international telecommunications, broadcasting and media. 6x pa.

International Broadcast Engineer
Queensway House, 2 Queensway, Redhill, Surrey RH1 1QS
Fax 01737-855470   Tel 01737-768611
E-mail: 100553.151@compuserve.com
Website: http://www.dmg.co.uk/ibex
Publisher: International Trade Publications
Looking at broadcast technology, for senior engineering and operational staff. 6x pa.

International Broadcast ing
See Broadcast, above

Journal of Educational Media
37 Monkgate, York YO31 7PB
Fax: 01904-639212   Tel 01904-639212
E-mail: josie.key@etma.u-net.com
Website: http://www.etrc.ox.ac.uk/ETMA.html
Publisher: Carfax Publishing Co..
Academic journal, published 3x pa, providing forum for discussing developments in TV and related media in education.

Kagan World Media
524 Fulham Road, London SW6 5NR
Fax 0171-371 8715   Tel 0171-371 8880
E-mail: kwm.research@kagan.com
Kagan is an international company specialising in analysis of the media and communications industries. It publishes a range of Europe-oriented monthly newsletters, covering topics around TV, cable, video and radio, and special reports.

Line Up
27 Old Gloucester Street, London WC1N 3XX
Fax 01323-491739   Tel 01323-491739
Publisher: Institute of Broadcast Sound.
Journal mixing technical information, news and articles by practitioners in sound. 6x pa.

Media Action UK
21 Stephen Street, London W1P 2LN
Fax 0171-636 6568   Tel 0171-957 8947
Publisher: UK Media Desk, BFI
Internal newsletter of the Media Desk, keeping members informed about the Media II Programme, the European Union initiative for the support and development of the audiovisual industry.

Media, Culture & Society
6 Bonhill Street, London EC2A 4PU
Fax 0171-374 8741   Tel 0171-374 0645
E-mail: market@sagepub.co.uk
Website: http://www.sagepub.co.uk
Publisher: Sage Publications.
Quarterly, £40. An international forum for the presentation of research concerning the media within their political, economic, cultural and historic context.

Media Education Journal
74 Victoria Crescent Road, Glasgow G12 9JN
Fax 0141-334 8132   Tel 0141-334 4445
Publisher: Association for Media Education in Scotland.
2x pa. Educational journal covering media theory, and ideas for teaching from primary one to adult. Also teaching packs and newsletters.

Media Track
Aztec Media Systems, 10-12 John Marshall House, 246-254 High Street, sutton, surey SM1 1PA
Fax 0181-288 9793   Tel 0181-288 9795
E-mail: info@mediatrack.com
Web: http://www.mediatrack.com
Published every 12 weeks on CD-ROM. More than 90,00 entries in 800 categories, covering advertising, film, television, print, multimedia, radio and music.

Media Week
Quantum Ho, 19 Scarbrook Road, Croydon CR9 1LX
Fax 0181-565 4394   Tel 0181-565 4200
Publisher: Quantum
Weekly news magazine linking media and advertising .

Middle East Broadcast & Satellite
Chancery House, St Nicholas Way, Sutton , Surrey SM1 1JB
Fax 0181-642 1941   Tel 0181-6421117
Publisher: Icom Publications Ltd.
E-mail: fwah@icompub.demon.co.uk
£65. 6x.pa magazine on broadcast in the Middle East & S Asia. Also publishes Middle East Communications.

Moving Pictures International
6 Bell Yard, London WC2A 2JR
Fax 0171-520 5212   Tel 0171-520 5200
E-mail: mopix@compuserve.com
Website: http://www.filmfestivals.com
Publisher: Moving Pictures International
Monthly coverage of the international film, televison and video industry.

Off-Air
5 Market Place, London W1N 7AH
Fax 0171-255 2020   Tel 0171-255 2010
E-mail: info@radacad.demon.co.uk
Website: http://www.radacad.cemon.co.uk
Publisher: The Radio Academy.
Monthly journal of the Radio Academy.

The Pact Magazine
30-31 Islington Green, London N1 8DU
Fax 0171-226 8586   Tel 0171-226 8585
E-mail: michaelt@mdi-uk.com
Publisher: Media Directories International
Members magazine for the Producers Alliance for Cinema and Television.

The Photographer
Fox Talbot House, Amwell End, Ware, Herts SG12 9HN
Fax 01920-487056   Tel 01920-464011
E-mail: bavister@easynet.co.uk
Website: http://www.epicentre.co.uk
Publisher: British Institute of Professional Photography.
Editor: Steve Bavister
£2.75, free to members. 10 issues p.a. The British Institute of Professional Photography's journal of professional images and imaging technology, with news from the industry.

Post Update
30-31 Islington Green, London N1 8DU
Fax 0171-226 8586   Tel 0171-226 8585
E-mail: rebeccah@mdi-uk.com
Publisher: Media Directories International
£2.50. monthly. The European post-production magazine, features regular, detailed product reviews and technology updates.

Production Europe
33-39 Bowling Green Lane, London, EC1R 0DA
Fax 0171-505 8076   Tel 0171-505 8000
E-mail: Catherineb@media.emap.co.uk
Technological monthly magazine covering European issues in production. Aimed at audience in Europe, Africa and the Middle-East.

Production Solutions
33-39 Bowling Green Lane, London, EC1R 0DA
Fax 0171-505 8076   Tel 0171-505 8000
E-mail: catherineb@media.emap.co.uk
Monthly magazine aimed at people working in television, production and film. Covers new technology, film issues, training and features a buyers guide to technology . Cover price £4.50

The Radio Magazine
Crown House, 25 High Street, Rothwell, Northants NN14 6AD
Fax 01536-418539   Tel 01536-418558
radiomazine-goldcrestbroadcasting@btinternet.com
Website: http://www.theradiomagazine.co.uk
Publisher: Goldcrest Broadcasting.
Weekly, glossy on the radio world.

Radio Review
PO Box 46, Romford RM7 8AY
Newsletter about Radio Caroline, Radio London, Dutch radio, pirate sations etc.

Radio Times
Woodlands, 80 Wood Lane, London W12 0TT
Fax 0181-576 3160   Tel 0181-576 2000
E-mail: radio.times@bbc.co.uk
Website: http://www.rtguide.beeb.com
Publisher: BBC Worldwide
Editor: Sue Robinson
Weekly, 79p. The BBC's money-spinning mag detailing all TV programmes, plus radio.

Satellite TV Europe
531-3 Kings Road, London SW10 0TZ
Fax 0171-352 4883   Tel 0171-351 3612
E-mail: stv1@compuserve.com
Website: http://www.satellite-tv.co.uk
Publisher: Millenium Consumer Magazines
£2.40. Monthly.
Satellite TV listings.

Satellite Times
The Stables, West Hill Grange, North Road, Horsforth, Leeds LS18 5HJ
Fax 0113-258 9745   Tel 0113-258 5008
E-mail: stimes@cix.uk
Publisher: Everpage
£2.20. Listings magazine.

Screen Digest
Lyme House Studio, 38 Georgiana Street, London NW1 0EB
Fax 0171-580 0060   Tel 0171-482 5842
E-mail: screendigest@compuserve.com
Publisher: Screen Digest.
£295 p.a. Monthly round-up of international news, research and statistics on film, video, multimedia and television, aimed at executives.

Screen International
33 Bowling Green Lane, London EC1R 0DA
Fax 0171-505 8117   Tel 0171-505 8080
E-mail: screeninternational@compuserve.com
Website: http://www.emap.com/media
Publisher: Emap Media
Editor: Boyd Farrow
£2. Weekly magazine on the international cinema business.

Short Wave Magazine
Arrowsmith Court, Station Approach, Broadstone, Dorset BH18 8PW
Fax 01202-659950   Tel 01202-659910
E-mail: dick@pwpub.demon.co.uk
Publisher: PW Publishing.
£2.75. Monthly magazine for enthusiasts of all types of listening.

Sight & Sound
21 Stephen Street, London W1P 1PL
Fax 0171-436 2327   Tel 0171-255 1444
Publisher: British Film Institute.
E-mail s&s@bfi.org.uk
£2.90. The leading monthly magazine covering the film world.

Stage, Screen & Radio
111 Wardour Street, London W1V 4AY
Fax 0171-437 8268   Tel 0171-437 8506
E-mail: bectu@geo2.poptel.org.uk
Publisher: BECTU.
£1.60, free to members. Monthly journal of the largest trade union in film and broadcasting.

The Stage (incorporating Television Today)
47 Bermondsey Street, London SE1 3XT
Fax 0171-357 9287   Tel 0171-403 1818
90p. The independent weekly newspaper of the theatre and light entertainment world, with TV coverage. The publishers also produce Showcall, a light entertainment directory.

Television
100 Grays Inn Road, London WC1X 8AL
Fax 0171-430 0924   Tel 0171-430 1000
E-mail: royalsociety@btinternet.com
Website: http://ww.rts.org.uk
Publisher: Royal Television Society
Editor: Peter Kiddick
8x pa, £63 pa. Covers all aspects of the TV industry.

Television
Quadrant House, Sutton, Surrey SM2 5AS
Fax 0181-652 8956   Tel 0181-652 8120
E-mail: john.reddihough@rbi.co.uk
Publisher: Reed Business Information
Editor: John Reddihough
£2.50. Specialist monthly. Technical news and features
for the TV/video servicing engineer.

Television Asia
6 Bell Yard, London WC2A 2JR
Fax 0171-520 5226   Tel 0171-411 2541
E-mail: pimasia@pacific.net.sg
Web: http://www.home.pacific.net.sg/mtvasia
Publisher: Cahners Publishing
Monthly glossy magazine looking at the TV business
across Asia.

Televisual
49-50 Poland Street, London W1V 4AX
Fax 0171-970 4199   Tel 0171-970 4000
E-mail: televisual@centaur.co.uk
Publisher: Centaur Communications
Editor: Mundy Ellis
£2.95. Monthly business magazine for independent
producers, facility providers and the TV industry.

TV Quick
Shirley House, 25-27 Camden Road, London NW1
9LL
Fax 0171-284 0593   Tel 0171-284 0909
E-mail: lorimiles@tvquick.demon.co.uk
Publisher: H Bauer Publishing
£0.60. Weekly witty TV listings magazine geared to
women's interests.

TV & Satellite Week
Kings Reach Tower, Stamford Street, London SE1 9LS
Fax 0171-261 7525   Tel 0171-261 7534
E-mail: TVandSatweek@ipc.co.uk
Website: http://www.ipc.co.uk
Publisher: IPC Magazines.
£0.75. Weekly consumers guide to what's on satellite,
terrestrial and cable TV.

TV Times
Kings Reach Tower, Stamford Street, London SE1 9LS
Fax 0171-261 7777   Tel 0171-261 5000
Website: http://www.ipc.co.uk
Publisher: IPC Magazines.
Weekly details of television programmes. Sales of the
TV Times have now been overtaken by IPC's mass-
market magazine What's On TV, operating out of the
same offices.

TV Zone
9 Blades Court, Deodar Road, London SW15 2NU
Fax 0181-875 1588   Tel 0181-875 1520
E-mail: tvzone@visimag.com
Publisher: Visual Imagination

Longest running magazine dedicated to cult television.
Monthly plus 4 quarterly specials with features and
interviews on past and current TV with an emphasis on
science fiction and fantasy.

UK Press Gazette
See Press Gazette

Vertigo
20 Goodge Place, London W1P 1FN
Fax: 0171-631 1040   Tel 0171-436 3050
E-mail: vertigo@dial.pipex.com
Editor: Marc Karlin
£3.75, tri-annual. Vertigo gives independent film, video
and television works outside the mainstream the
attention they deserve, considering them in their wider
European and global perspectives.

Viewfinder
77 Well Street, London W1P 3RE
Fax 0171-393 1555   Tel 0171-393 1500
E-mail: bufvc@open.ac.uk
Website: http://www.bufvc.ac.uk/
Publisher: British Universities Film & Video Council
News and features published three times a year by the
British Universities Film/Video Council, which exists to
promote the production, study and use of film,
television and related media for higher education and
research.

Voice of the Listener & Viewer
101 Kings Drive, Gravesend, Kent DA12 5BQ
                         Tel 01474-352835
E-mail: vlv@btinternet.com
Publisher: Voice of the Listener and Viewer.
Quarterly newsletter of the independent watchdog,
which bills itself as "the citizen's voice in broadcasting
and the only consumer body speaking for listeners and
viewers on the full range of broadcasting issues".

What Satellite TV
57 Rochester Place, London NW1 9JU
Fax 0171-331 1241   Tel 0171-331 1000
E-mail: wwhatsat@aol.com
Website: http://www.membersaol.com/wotsat
Publisher: WV Publications
Editor: Geoff Bains
£2.85. Monthly consumer magazine with news on "the
equipment to buy and the programmes to watch".

World Media
BBC Worldwide Monitoring, Caversham Park,
Reading, Berks RG4 8TZ
Fax 0118-946 3823   Tel 0118-946 9289
E-mail: marketing@mon.bbc.co.uk
Website: http://www.monitor.bbc.co.uk
Weekly publication, also available via Internet,
containing all the latest news and developments in the
international broadcasting scene, reporting on satellite,
cable and terrestrial radio and TV, together with
multimedia applications within broadcasting. Annual
subscription £410.

Zerb
Church Barn, Harberton, Totnes, Devon TQ9 2SQ
Fax 01803-868444   Tel 01803-868652
E-mail: samps@easynet.co.uk
Web: http://www.easyweb.easynet.co.uk/~guildtvc
Publisher: Guild of TV Cameramen.

MAGAZINES

BAPLA Directory
18 Vine Hill, London EC1R 5DX
Fax 0171-713 1211   Tel 0171-713 1780
Publisher: British Association of Picture Libraries &
Agencies
Contact: Linda Royles
£20. An invaluable guide to picture sources by Britain's
leading association. With full details of all members,
a description of their stock, a subject index and hints
for library users.

Benn's Media
Riverbank House, Angel Lane, Tonbridge, Kent TN9
1SE
Fax 01732-367301   Tel 01732-362666
Publisher: Miller Freeman Information Services
3 vols £297, 2 vols £266, 1 vol £133.
Benn's has the most comprehensive listings amongst
the general media directories. It comes in three
volumes, covering the UK, Europe and the rest of the
world.

Blue Book of British Broadcasting
Communications House, 210 Old Street, London
EC1V 9UN
Fax 0171-566 3142   Tel 0171-490 1447
Publisher: Tellex Publications Dept.
£75
A contacts book for radio, TV and satellite containing
thousands of names,addresses and phone numbers.

Bowkers Complete Video Directory
Bowker-Saur   Tel 01342-323650
£210, three vols.
Only source of info covering over 107,000 video titles.

**British Film Institute Film and Television
Handbook**
21 Stephen Street, London W1P 2LN
Fax 0171-436 7950   Tel 0171-255 1444
Publisher: BFI
£17.99. Combines hundreds of film and broadcasting
facts and figures with an extensive directory of
thousands of contacts and addresses.

Cable & Satellite Yearbook
Maple House, 149 Tottenham Court Road, London
W1P 9LL
Fax 0171-896 2749   Tel 0171-351 3612
E-mail: info@ftmedia.com
Publisher: FT Media & Telecoms
£250 for yearbook, £295 for TV Business International
Comprehensive details of the industry in all European
countries, covering manufacturers, distributors and
broadcasters, plus a breakdown of each nation. Also
published is: TV Business International, with all the
world's TV stations and prices.

Cable TV & Telecom Yearbook
Forum Chambers, The Forum, Stevenage,
Hertfordshire SG1 1EL
Fax 01438-740154   Tel 01438-742424
E-mail: sandymaclean@dial.pipex.com
Publisher: Philips Business Information
Contact: Karen Milton
£95.
Industry facts, figures analysis and information.

Commonwealth Broadcasters' Directory
Room 312, BBC Yalding House, 152-156 Great
Portland Street, London W1N 6AJ
Fax 0171-765 5152   Tel 0171-765 5151
E-mail: cba@cba.org.uk
Website: http://www.oneworld.org/cba/
Publisher: Commonwealth Broadcasting Assocation
£20. non-members, UK; £23 non-members Europe.
Details of Commonwealth broadcasting organisations,
with names of top executives, phones, faxes and
addresses.

The Creative Handbook
34-35 Newman Street, Londn W1P 3PD
Fax 0171-580 5559   Tel 0171-637 3663
Publisher: Variety Media Publications
Contact: Jerry Odlin
£124
For the the commercial arts. Also publishes the
International Creative Handbook, £99.

Directors' Guild Directory
15-19 Great Titchfield Street, London W1P 7FB
Fax 0171-436 8646   Tel 0171-436 8626
E mail: guild@dggb.co.uk
Publisher: Directors Guild of Great Britain
£20.
A-Z of Britain's TV, film, radio and theatre directors.

Directors and Producers Directory
111 Wardour Street, London W1V 4AY
Fax 0171-437 8268   Tel 0171-437 8506
E-mail: bectu@geotv.poptel.org.uk
Publisher: BECTU
£10.95 (free to members).
Contains the names and addresses of over 1,000
producers and directors who are members of the
London Production Division of the main broadcasting
trade union BECTU.

Directory of British Film & TV Producers
45 Mortimer Street, London W1N 7TD
Fax 0171-331 6700   Tel 0171-331 6000
Publisher: Pact
£25.
Full details of PACT members.

**Directory of International Film & Video
Festivals**
11 Portland Place, London W1N 4EJ
Fax 0171-389 3041   Tel 0171-389 3065
Publisher: British Council
£12
Lists all international film and video festivals.

WHATEVER THE MEDIA, WHEREVER IT IS...

● *Over 44,000 listings* ● *Three Volumes* ●
● *The whole World* ●

Benn's Media is the essential reference source to media in the
UK, Europe and throughout the world. It will provide you with
comprehensive and accurate information on the press, television,
radio and other media related organisations.

The UK Volume:
● 16,000 entries

The European Volume:
● 11,500 entries

The World Volume:
● 17,000 entries

●**Advertising and editorial contact
details including:**

✔ e-mail numbers
✔ advertising rates
✔ readership data
✔ frequency and circulation data

● ***Benn's Media Guide*** is the *complete*
guide to national, regional and
international newspapers, consumer
and business periodicals, reference
publications and broadcasting.

... BENN'S MEDIA
HAS IT COVERED.

f you would like to purchase a copy of *Benn's Media* or would like some
additional information please phone: **01732 377591**, or fax, **01732 367301.**
Alternatively, write to us at: Miller Freeman Information Services, Miller Freeman UK Ltd, Riverbank House,
Angel Lane, Tonbridge, Kent, TN9 1SE. Internet: http://www.mfplc.co.uk/mfinfo E-mail:bennsmedia @unmf.com

DPA   **un** Miller Freeman   European Association of Directory Publishers
A United News & Media publication

IPO Directory
PO Box 30, Wetherby, West Yorkshire LS23 7YA
Fax 01937-541083   Tel 0171-261 8534
£13 annual subscription.
The official directory of the information and PRs in
government departments and public corporations.
Published bi-annually.

Kays UK Production Manual
8 Golden Square, London W1R 3AF
0171-437 0884   Tel 0181-749 1214
Publisher: Kays Publishing
£70.
With its Crew Directory, this is one of the most
comprehensive and reliable manuals of people and
organisations in the production side of the film, TV and
broadcast industry. Contains 15,000 names and
addresses in over 250 classifications. Also available is its
European equivalent the European Production Manual
(£85), plus the Art Diary (£30) listing the art business.

Kemps Film, TV & Video Yearbook
34-35 Newman Street, London W1P 3PD
Fax 0171-580 5559   Tel 0171-637 3663
E-mail: odlin@aol.com
Publisher: Variety Media Publications
£35 UK; £75 International
Long-established directory of the film and television
production industries in nearly every country.

The Knowledge
Riverbank House, Angel Lane, Tonbridge, Kent TN9
1SE
Fax 01732-367301   Tel 01732-362666
Publisher: Benn Business Information Services
Book £76; CD rom £86
The leading guide to the products and services of the
UK film, TV and video industry. Over 10,000 A-Z
listings of equipment, technicians and specialist
services, plus features on codes of conduct, procedures,
specifications, and more.

The Media Guide
Fourth Estate, for The Guardian
                    Tel 0171-727-8993
Bingo.

Multimedia and CD-ROM Directory
6-14 Underwood Street, London N1 7JQ
Fax 0171-324 2312   Tel 0171-324 2345
E-mail: gbuecker@waterlow.com
Publisher: Waterlow Publishing
Contact: Gesche Beucker
3 CD roms: CD rom annual sbscription - £229
Vol 1. The Marketplace - £149
Vol 2. The Titles - £149

Pims Media Directories
Pims House, Mildmay Avenue, London N1 4RS
Fax 0171-354 7053   Tel 0171-226 1000
E-mail: press@pims.co.uk
Publisher: Pims International
Contact: Susan Mears
Pims produces a range of detailed, loose-leaf guides to
editorial media contacts, all regularly updated, aimed
mainly at the public relations sector. Titles include: UK
Media Directory £120, A-Z Towns Directory £125 and
several USA/European directories.

The Production Guide
33-39 Bowling Green Lane, London EC1R 0DA
Fax 0171-505 8293   Tel 0171-505 8000
E-mail: dougm@media.emap.co.uk
Publisher: Emap Media
Contact: Doug Marchall
£75
Annual details of technical contacts, services and
equipment, from the publishers of the prominent
weekly magazine Broadcast. Also available:
International Broadcasting Directory, £40, guide to
international broadcasting hardware and services;
Broadcast Diary, £40, desk diary with extensive industry
information; Screen International Film & TV Directory,
three volumes of data on companies, people and
countries, £60; and TV Buyer Handbook, £40, the
producers guide to the global TV market.

Programme News
32-38 Saffron Hill, London EC1N 8SH
Fax 0171-430 1089   Tel 0171-405 4455
Publisher: The Profile Group
From £324 p.a. 12x p.a. An information service in
directory format. Independent broadcast listings. The
UK industry guide for advance broadcast lanning.

Radio Academy Yearbook
5 Market Place, London W1N 7AH
Fax 0171-255 2029   Tel 0171-255 2010
E-mail: info@radacad.demon.co.uk
Website: http://www.radacad.demon.co.uk/
Publisher: The Radio Academy.
£25.00. Annual directory/listings guide of the radio
industry's leading professional society.

Radio Advertising Handbook
77 Shaftesbury Avenue, London W1V 7AD
0171-306 2505   Tel 0171-306 2500
E-mail: rab@rab.co.uk
Publisher: Radio Advertising Bureau
Free
Handbook of radio advertising, providing an overview
of the independent radio industry, with masses of data
and listings information.

Radio Authority Pocket Guide
Holbrook House, 14 Great queens Street, London
WC2B 5DG
Fax 0171-405 7062   Tel 0171-430 2724
Publisher: Radio Authority
Free
Regularly updated reference booklet to the independent
radio business. The authority also produces a free video
called "The Radio Authority - What It Is, What It Does",
which is aimed at students.

Radio Listener's Guide
PO Box 151 Abingdon, Oxon OX13 5DP
                    Tel 01865-820387
Publisher: PDQ Publishing
Contact: Clive Woodyear
£4.95.
Pocket guide to all the UK radio stations, detailing
which wavelengths they are on, and explaining clearly
how to tune in. This is an invaluable aid to those trying
to find their way around the radio dial.

Royal Television Society Handbook
Holborn Hall, 100 Grays Inn Road, London WC1X
8AL
Fax 0171-430 0924   Tel 0171-430 1000
E-mail: royaltvsociety@btinternet.com
Publisher Radio Television Society
£7
Guide to the society, with directory of its many
members, leading figures in the TV world.
Satellite Broadcasting Guide
23 Ridgmount Street, London WC1E 7AH
Fax 0171-323 2314   Tel 0171-323 6686
E-mail: alisonsmith@bpicomm.com
Publisher: Billboard
£21.50
Details of installation methods, satellite global coverage
and satellite broadcasters.
The Television Book
24 Neal Street, London WC2H 9PS
0171-836 0702   Tel 0171-379 4519
E-mail: geitf@festival.demon.co.uk
Publisher: Edinburgh International Television Festival
£7.99.
Published to tell people of the profusion of
programmes and programme-making issues arising at
the annual August festival in Edinburgh.
Television Business International Yearbook
Yearbooks Dept., Maple House, 149 Tottenham Court
Road, London W1P 9LL
Fax 0171-896 2710   Tel 0171-896 2700
Publisher: FT Media and Telecoms
£295.
Handbook for international TV executives.
**University of Manchester Broadcasting
Symposia**
75 Castle Street, Luton LU1 3AJ
Fax 01582-743298   Tel 01582-743297
E-mail: ulp@luton.ac.uk
Publisher: University of Luton Press
£14.95
Each year all sides of the broadcasting industry meet for
a symposium organised by the University of
Manchester. The proceedings are published later in
book form. The latest publication is What Price
Creativity?.
The White Book
The White Book
                    Tel 01932-572622
£50.
The key international production directory.

Who's Who in Cable & Satellite UK
Forum Chambers, The Forum, Stevenage,
Hertfordshire SG1 1EL
Fax 01438-740154   Tel 01438-742424
E-mail: sandymaclean@dial.pipex.com
Publisher: Philips Business Information
Contact: Karen Milton
Single edition £24.95; years sub £44.95
Contact details for more than 3000 key personnel from
over 1100 companies. Published in January and July.
Who's Who in Cable & Satellite Europe
Forum Chambers, The Forum, Stevenage,
Hertfordshire SG1 1EL
Fax 01438-740154   Tel 01438-742424
E-mail: sandymaclean@dial.pipex.com
Publisher: Philips Business Information
Contact: Karen Milton
Single edition £34.95; years sub £64.95
Covers over 30 countries, more than 4000 key
personnel from over 1900 cmpanies. Published in
April and October.
World Radio & TV Handbook
23 Ridgmount Street, London WC1E 7AH
Fax 0171-323 2314   Tel 0171-323 6686
E-mail: alisonsmith@bpicomm.com
£21.50.
World broadcasting stations, by frequency, time and
language.
World Satellite Yearly
24 River Gardens, Purley, Reading RG8 8BX
Faxl 0118-9414468   Tel 0118-9414468
E-mail: www.baylin.com
Publisher: Baylin Publications
£59.
American technical manual and guide to satellites.

Broadcast support organisations

All-Party Media Group
c/o Good News Communications, Suite 228, Premier House, 10 Greycoat Place, London SW19 1SB
Fac 0171-222 4189   Tel 0171-222 4179
Cross party forum of 100 MPs and peers with an interest in media issues.

AMARC
15 Paternoster Row, Sheffield, Yorkshire S1 2BX
Fax 0114-279 8976   Tel 0114-221 0592
E-mail amarc@gn.apc.org
AMARC, the World Association of Community Radio Broadcasters, is a world-wide network of local radios which operate for social purposes and are independent of governments and large media corporations.

Amnesty International: Journalists' Network
202 Mansfield Road, Nottingham NG1 3HX
Fax 0115-924 5055   Tel 0115-924 5100
E-mail: nottm@amnesty.org.uk
This division of Amnesty International campaigns on behalf of media workers who have disappeared, been imprisoned, tortured or threatened with death. It holds meetings and publishes a quarterly newsletter.

Amsat-UK
40 Downsview, Small Dole, West Sussex BN5 9YB
Fax 01273-492927   Tel 01273-495733
E-mail: g3aaj@amsat.org
National society specialising in amateur radio satellite matters. Publishes Oscar News 6x pa.

Article 19, the International Centre Against Censorship
Lancaster House, 33 Islington High Street, Islington London N1 9LH
Fax 0171-713 1356   Tel 0171-278 9292
E-mail article19@gn.apc.org.
International human rights organisation campaigning for the right to freedom of expression and information. The organisation promotes improved legal standards for freedom of expression and defends victims of censorship. It publishes regular newsletter and a range of country and theme reports, with emphasis on media freedom.

Aslib
Staple Hall, Stone House Court, London EC3A 7PB
Fax 0171-903 0011   Tel 0171-903 0000
E-mail: members@aslib.co.uk
Website: http://www.aslib.co.uk/aslib/
The Association for Information Management is the leading corporate membership information management association. It gives advice on information sources and strategy. There is also a network of special interest groups.

Association of Broadcasting Doctors
PO Box 15, Sindalthorpe House, Ely, Cambridge CB7 4SG
Fax 01353-688451   Tel 01353-688456
E-mail: peter.petts@btinternet.com
Represents practising doctors who also broadcast, providing training, data and media liaison. Publishes

monthly newsletter and briefings. Contact point for broadcasters seeking medical contributors.

Association of Independent Radio Companies
see Commercial Radio Companies Association

Audio Visual Association
156 High Street, Bushey, Hertfordshire WD2 3DD
Fax 0181-950 7560   Tel 0181-950 5959
Website: http://www.thebiz.co.uk/ava.htm
Special interest group of the British Institute of Professional Photography representing people working to sub-broadcast standard in audio visual and multi-media. The association evolves with new technical developments.

Barb
See Broadcast Audience Research Board

British Academy of Film and Television Arts
195 Piccadilly, London W1V 0LN
Fax 0171-734 1792   Tel 0171-734 0022
BAFTA North   Tel 0161-831 9733
BAFTA Scotland   Tel 0141-357 4317
BAFTA Wales   Tel 01222-223898
Website: http://www.bafta.org
BAFTA was formed in 1947 and promotes high creative standards in film and television production, and encourages experiment and research. It organises awards ceremonies for film, television, children's films and programmes and interactive entertainment and has an extensive programme of seminars, lectures etc. It has 3000 members and provides screenings and previews and publishes a monthly newsletter. It also offers a range of educational and training initiatives.

British Academy of Songwriters, Composers & Authors
The Penthouse, 4 Brook Street, London W1Y 1AA
Fax 0171-629 0993   Tel 0171-629 0992
E-mail: basca@basca.org.uk
BASCA was founded in 1947 and is the largest trade association for songwriters and composers. It lobbies for developments in copyright legislation, produces BASCA News, holds a regular forum for legal advice and presents annual Ivor Novello awards. The Academy is represented on all the major music industry boards.

British Amateur Television Club
Church Road, Harby, Notts NG23 7ED
Fax 01522-703348   Tel 01522-703348
E-mail: secretary@batc.org.uk
Website: http://www.batc.org.uk
Founded in 1948 to inform, instruct, co-ordinate and represent the activities of television enthusiasts in the UK and worldwide. Publishes quarterly technical magazine CQ-TV

British Board of Film Classification

3 Soho Square, London W1V 6HD
Fax 0171-287 0141   Tel 0171-439 7961
The body responsible for classifying publicly shown films:

U (Universal)
PG (Parental Guidance)
12 (age 12 and over only)
15 (age 15 and over only)
18 (age 18 and over only)
R18 (restricted to premises barred to under 18s)

British Film Commission

70 Baker Street, London W1M 1DJ
Fax 0171-224 1013   Tel 0171-224 5000
E-mail: press@britfilmcom.co.uk
Website: http://www.britfilmcom.co.uk

Bath Film Office	01225-477711
Cardiff Film Commission	
	01222-590240
Central England Screen Commission	
East Midlands Office	01159-527870
Eastern Screen	01603-767077
Edinburgh and Lothian	
Screen Industries	0131-622 7337
N Wales Film Commission	
	01286 679685
Isle of Man Film Commission	
	01624-685864
Lancashire Film & Television Office	
	01772-203020
Liverpool Film Office	0151-291 9191
London Film Commission	
	0171-387 8787
Manchester Film Office	
	0161-238 4537
North West Commission	
	0151-330 6666
N Ireland Film Commission	
	01232-232444
Northern Screen Commission	
	0191-204 2311
Scottish Screen Locations	
	0141-302 1700
Sgrin	01222-333300
SW Film Commission	01752 841199
SW Scotland Screen Commission	
	01387-263666
Southern Screen Commission	
	01705-650779
Yorkshire Screen Commission	
	01142-799115

Set up by the government in 1991, the BFC is funded through the Department of Culture, Media and Sport. It promotes the UK as an international production centre and provides support to those filming in the UK. BFC publications include Check Book, a UK production guide for overseas film-makers and the newsletter Framework. The BFC also participates in industry trade events abroad and helps foreign film makers considering production in the UK. It also works in association with the UK Film Commission Network.

British Film Institute

21 Stephen Street, London W1P 2LN
Fax 0171-436 7950   Tel 0171-255 1444
Website: http://www.bfi.org.uk.
The BFI is Britain's leading moving image resource. It encourages the development of film, TV and video, both as an art and as a medium of record. The institute runs the London Film Festival, Museum of the Moving Image, National Film Archive and National Film Theatre . The BFI helps in film production, runs a library and information services, provides training advice and organises events. It publishes many books and periodicals (including the annual BFI Film Handbook and the monthly mag Sight and Sound). The institute supports regional and local film theatres and societies. BFI funding comes partly from its commercial activities and partly from the government.

British Interactive Multimedia Association

5-6 Clipstone Street, London W1P 7EB
Fax 0171-436 8251   Tel 0171-436 8250
E-mail: enquiries@bima.co.uk
The trade body for the multimedia industry. Publishes directory of members and newsletter. Meets ten times a year.

British Kinematograph, Sound and Television Society (BKSTS)

63-71 Victoria House, Vernon Place, London WC1B 4DA
Fax 0171-405 3560   Tel 0171-242 8400
E-mail: movimage@bksts.demon.co.uk
Website: http://www.bksts.demon.co.uk
BKSTS was founded in 1931 and is the only European society covering all technical aspects of film, television, sound and associated industries. It plays a leading role in the development and implementation of technical standards. The main aim is to keep members abreast of the continually changing technology in the industry and its implications. The society achieves this through its journals, Cinema Technology and Image Technology (10x pa) and by holding seminars and conferences. Many training courses are held.

British Library National Sound Archive

96 Euston Road, London NW1 2DB
Fax 0171-412 7441   Tel 0171-412 7440
E-mail: nsa@bl.uk
Website: http://www.bl.uk/collections/sound-archive
The national collection of sound recordings, covering all topics since the 1890s. Provides library, information, listening and transcription services. Publishes newsletter Playback and range of print and audio titles.

British Radio & Electronic Equipment Manufacturers' Association

Landseer House, 19 Charing Cross Road, London WC2H 0ES
Fax 0171-839 4613   Tel 0171-930 3206
E-mail: @brema.org.uk
Trade association for the TV and radio manufacturers.

British Screen Advisory Council

19 Cavendish Square, London W1M 9AB
Fax 0171-306 0329   Tel 0171-499 4177
E-mail BSACouncil@aol.com.

Independent, industry funded, advisory body to government and policy makers at national and European level. It provides a forum for the audiovisual industry to discuss major issues. It commissions research and organises conferences and seminars.

British Screen Finance

14 -17 Wells Mews, London W1P 3FL
Fax 0171-323 0092   Tel 0171-323 9080
E-mail: info@britishscreen.co.uk

The company receives some government funding and provides loans to film makers for developing and producing commercial feature films. Administrates the European Co-production Fund on behalf of the Department of Culture, Media and Sport.

British Society of Cinematographers

11 Croft Road, Chalfont St Peter, Gerrards Cross, Bucks SL9 9AE
Fax 01753-891486   Tel 01753-888052
E-mail: BritCinematographers@compuserve.com

Society of motion picture cinematographers. Arranges technical meetings, social events, film shows etc. Publishes directory biennially.

Broadcasters Audience Research Board (Barb)

Glenthorne House, Hammersmith Grove, London W6 0ND
Fax 0181-741 1943   Tel 0181-741 9110

Barb provides information to all elements of the TV industry, broadcasters, advertising/media buying agencies and advertisers. Barb uses professional research suppliers to conduct and report on audience research. It produces statistical research on TV audiences for its subscribers. Audiences for TV programmes are measured by electronic meters attached to television sets in 4,485 homes. This panel, which is one of the largest of its kind in the world, includes some 10,500 people. The meters record the state of each TV set or video. The information is transmitted automatically each night by telephone into a central computer and is used to calculate the size of the audience. Since 1991, the meters have been able to record video playback.

Broadcasting Complaints Commission

merged with Broadcasting Standards Commission

Broadcasting, Entertainment, Cinematograph Theatre Union (BECTU)

111 Wardour Street, London W1V 4AY
Fax 0171-437 8258   Tel 0171-437 8506
E-mail: bectu@geo2.poptel.org.uk
Website: http://www.bectu.org.uk
   Midlands office   Tel 0121-632 5372
   North west office   Tel 0161-274 3174
   Scottish office   Tel 0141-248 9558
   Wales office   Tel 01222-666557

BECTU is the main trade union for workers in broadcasting, film, theatre and other sectors of the entertainment and media industry. It offers a Student Link-up Scheme to arts and media students, and a special introductory membership rate to course graduates. It can give some careers advice (SAE please) but works with Skillset, regional training consortia and FT2 in promoting acess, opportunity, training and employment prospects. Publishes a journal Stage, Screen & Radio.

Broadcasting Press Guild

Tiverton, The Ridge, Woking, Surrey GU22 7EQ
Fax 01483-764895   Tel 01483-764895

Association of 90+ journalists writing about the media in the national and trade press. Holds monthly lunches addressed by top broadcasting executives. Each spring it presents the BPG TV and Radio Awards.

Broadcasting Research Unit

see Voice of the Listener and Viewer

Broadcasting Standards Commission

7 The Sanctuary, London SW1P 3JS
Fax 0171-233 0397   Tel 0171-233 0544

The BSC is the statutory body for both standards and fairness in broadcasting. It is the only organisation within the regulatory framework of UK broadcastng to cover all tv and radio. this includes BBC and commercial broadcasters as well as text, cable, satellite and digital services. As an independent organisation representing the interests of the consumer, the Broadcasting Standards Commission considers the portrayal of violence, sexual conduct and matters of taste and decency. As an alternative to a court of law it provides redress for people who believe they have been unfairly treated or subjected to unwarranted infringement of privacy. Its three main tasks are set out in the 1996 Broadcasting Act:

* to produce codes of practice relating to standards and fairness;
* to consider and adjudicate on complaints;
* to monitor, research and report on standards and fairness in broadcasting

Cable Communications Association
Artillery House, Artillery Row, London SW1P 1RT
Fax 0171-799 1471   Tel 0171-222 2900
Website: http://www.cable.co.uk
The CCA is the trade body for Britain's cable
communications industry. It produces summaries of
statistics and other information on the growth of
broadband cable services, runs the 'Cable Hotline' -
0990 111777 - to provide consumers with advice on the
availability of cable television and telephone services in
their area, and acts as a lobbying organisation to
influence government and regulatory decisions
affecting the future of the telecomms and broadcasting
industries. The CCA also organises the European Cable
Convention, Europe's largest exhibition for suppliers of
programmes, equipment and other services.

Campaign for Freedom of Information
Suite 102, 16 Baldwins Gardens, London EC1N 7RJ
Fax 0171-831 7461   Tel 0171-831 7477
E-mail: admin@cfoi.demon.co.uk
Website: http://www.cfoi.org.uk
The campaign is pressing for a Freedom of Information
Act which would create a general right of access to
official records subject to exemptions protecting
information whose disclosure would cause real harm to
essential interests such as defence, law enforcement
and privacy. Campaigns for a public interest defence
under the Official Secrets Act. It also seeks disclosure
in the private sector on issues of public interest. It
publishes the newspaper Secrets, plus briefings and
other publications.

**Campaign for Press and Broadcasting
Freedom**
See Press Support, page 139

Celtic Film and Television Association
1 Bowmont Gardens, Glasgow G12 9LR
Fax 0141-342 4948   Tel 0141-342 4947
E-mail: mail@celticfilm.co.uk
Organises the annual International Celtic Festival of
Film and Television, peripatetic in Scotland, Wales,
Cornwall, Ireland and Brittany, including awards and
conference. It supports development of TV and film in
Celtic nations and indigenous languages.

Children's Film & Television Foundation
Elstree Film Studios, Borehamwood, Herts WD6 1JG
Fax 0181-207 0860   Tel 0181-953 0844
Non-profitmaking organisation which funds script
development for quality television projects aimed at 5-12
year old children. Holds an extensive film library, with a
wide range of films made for children/family viewing.
Founded 1951.

**Churches Advisory Council for Local
Broadcasting (CACLB)**
PO Box 124, Westcliffe-on-Sea, Essex SS0 0QU
Fax 01702-305121   Tel 01702-348369
E-mail: office@caclb.org.uk
Website: http://www.caclb.org.uk
A charity bringing together the main Christian
churches for the advancement of Christianity through
radio and TV. Has an Association of Christian
broadcasters, quarterly news bulletin, annual
conference and awards.

Cinema and TV Benevolent Fund
22 Golden Square, London W1R 4AD
Fax 0171-437 7186   Tel 0171-437 6567
Trade charity for retired and serving employees and
their dependents needing caring help, support and
financial aid.

Commercial Radio Companies Association
77 Shaftesbury Avenue, London W1V 7AD
Fax 0171-470 0062   Tel 0171-306 2603
E-mail: info@crca.co.uk
The trade body for UK commercial radio. It represents
commercial radio to Government, the Radio Authority,
Copyright Societies and other organisations concerned
with radio. CRCA gives advice to members and acts as a
clearing house for radio information. The CRCA jointly
owns Radio Joint Audience Research (RAJAR) with the
BBC, owns the Network Chart Show and is a member
of the Association of European Radios which lobbies
European institutions on behalf of commercial radio.

Commonwealth Broadcasting Association
Room 312, Yalding House, 152-156 Great Portland
Street, London W1N 6AJ
Fax 0171-765 5152   Tel 0171-765 5144
E-mail: cba@cba.org.uk
Non-profit association of broadcasters with a
commitment to public service broadcasting in
Commonwealth countries. Activities include training
programmes and conferences.

Communication Workers Union
150 The Broadway, Wimbledon, London SW19 1RX
Fax 0181-971 7437   Tel 0181-971 7200
E-mail: LQuinn@cwu.org
Website: http://www.cwu.org
The largest trade union in posts, telecommunications
and financial services. The CWU Voice is published
monthly.

Community Media Association
15 Paternoster Row, Sheffield, S Yorks S1 2BX
Fax 0114-279 8976   Tel 0114-279 5219
E mail: cra@gn.apc.org
Website: http://www.commedia.org.uk
London Development Unit: The Resource Centre, 356
Holloway Road, London N7 6PA
Fax 0171-700 0099   Tel 0171-700 8161
UK membership body, developing and campaigning for
community-based media. It offers information, advice,
training and consultancy, holds conferences and events
and publishes the quarterly journal Airflash.

Confederation of Aerial Industries
Fulton Road, Wembley Park, Middlesex HA9 0TF
Fax 0181-903 8719   Tel 0181-902 8998
E-mail: office@cai.org.uk
Trade association for aerials and satellite dish
manufacturers.

Coopers & Lybrand Media Group
1 Embankment Place, London WC2N 6NN
Fax 0171-213 2411   Tel 0171-213 5353
C & L "audits and advises more UK TV broadcasters
than any other firm".

CSV Media
237 Pentonville Road, London N1 9NJ
Fax 0171-278 7912   Tel 0171-278 6601
E-mail 100141.3615@compuserve.com
CSV Media, part of the national charity Community
Service Volunteers, specialises in social action
broadcasting, media support services and media
training. Services range from TV and radio programme
production, broadcast back-up , including telephone
helplines and training in TV and radio production.

Deaf Broadcasting Council
70 Blacketts Wood Drive, Chorleywood,
Rickmansworth, Herts WD3 5QQ
Fax 01923-283127
E-mail dmyers@cix.co.UK
Website: http://www.waterlow.com/dbc
An umbrella organisation to which all the major
national bodies for and on behalf of deaf, deafened and
hard of hearing people are affiliated. Ensures that TV
companies and broadcasters are aware of their needs.
Publishes newsletter Mailshot 3-4x pa.

Different Voices
108 Portnall Road, London W9 3BG
Fax 0181-968 0991   Tel 0181-969 0109
E-mail: voices@twiza.demon.co.uk
Website: http://www.twiza.demon.co.uk/
Non-profit making information and support network
working for greater cross-cultural understanding and
wider media access for under-represented groups.
Different Voices is a OneWorld online partner.

Directors Guild of Gt Britain
15-19 Great Titchfield Street, London W1P 7FB
Fax 0171-436 8646   Tel 0171-436 8626
E-mail: guild@dggb.co.uk
Website: http://www./dggb.co.uk
Union for directors in all media, including TV, film,
theatre and radio. Issues an advised schedule of rates,
code of practice and contract guides. Gives contractual
advice and holds workshops, conferences, public events
and social events. Publishes a magazine, Direct and an
annual directory of all members.

Directors and Producers' Rights Society
15-19 Great Titchfield Street, London, W1P 7FB
Fax 0171-631 1019   Tel 0171-631 1077
E-mail: dprs@dial.pipex.com
A collecting society which administers authorial rights
payments on behalf of British film and television
directors.   -

Eclipse
18-20 Highbury Place, London N5 1QP
Fax 0171-354 8106   Tel 0171-354 5858
Website: http://www.irseclipse.co.uk
Provides information on industrial relations practice,
health and safety legislation and employment law as
well as publishing journals and reports.

Edinburgh Television Trust
The Retreat, Manse Road, Dirleton, East Lothian
EH39 5EP
Fax 01620-850408   Tel 01620-850408
E-mail: 101501@compuserve.com
Local charity set up to provide training for TV access via
restricted television services and cable.

Equity
Guild House, Upper St Martins Lane, London WC2H
9EG
Fax 0171-379 7001   Tel 0171-379 6000
E-mail: equity@easynet.co.uk
Website: http://www.equity.org.uk/equity
British Actors' Equity Association is the trade union for
actors, stage managers, opera singers, dancers,
directors, designers, choreographers, variety artistes
and stunt performers working in theatre, film,
television, radio and variety venues. The union
publishes the quarterly magazine Equity which is
distributed to the membership of 35,000.

FACT
7 Victory Business Centre, Worton Road, Isleworth,
Middlesex TW7 6DB
Fax 0181-560 6364   Tel 0181-568 6646
FACT, Federation Against Copyright Theft, is an
investigative organisation funded by its members to
combat counterfeiting piracy and misuse of their
poroducts.

Federation of Communication Services
Keswick House, 207 Anerley Road, London SE20
8ER
Fax 0181-778 8402   Tel 0181-778 5656
E-mail: fcs.london@dial.pipex.com
Website: http://www.fcs.org.uk
The FCS is the representative body for the UK mobile
communications industry. It is the focus for
developments, issues and legislation affecting moblie
communications.

Federation of the Electronics Industry
10-12 Russell Square, London WC1B 5EE
Fax 0171-331 2040   Tel 0171-331 2000
E-mail feedback@fei.org.uk
Website: http://www.fei.org.uk/fei
Trade association for information technology,
electronics, communication, office equipment. and
office furniture. Represents the industry's interests on
major European and international standards and
regulatory bodies, satellite and broadcasting groups. It
publishes annual statistics on electronic components.

Federation of Entertainment Unions
1 Highfield, Twyford, near Winchester, Hants SO21
1QR
Fax 01962-713288   Tel 01962-713134
E-mail: harris@interalpha.co.uk
Collective body of trade unions, representing the
interests of 140,000 members in the broadcasting and
entertainment industries. The unions are: BECTU,
Equity, Musicians Union, NUJ, Writers Guild, AEEU. It
provides liaison, representation, lobbying and co-
ordination services on issues of common concern.

Film Artistes Association
111 Wardour Street, London W1 4AY
Fax 0171-287 8984   Tel 0171-437 8506
E-mail: bactu@geo2.poptel.org.uk
The trade union representing crowd artistes, stand-ins
and doubles.

FOCAL: Federation of Commercial Audio Visual Libraries
Pentax House, South Hill Avenue, Northolt Road, South Harrow HA2 0DU
Fax 0181-423 5853   Tel 0181-423 5853
E-mail anne@focalltd.demon.co.uk
Website: http://www.focalltd.demon.co.uk/
FOCAL is the international trade association for audio visual libraries, researchers and producers. It promotes the use of library footage, stills and sound in programming and holds regular seminars and meetings.

405-Line Group
71 Falcutt Way, Northampton, Northants NN2 8PH
Fax 01604-821647   Tel 01604-844130
E-mail midshires@cix.compulink.co.uk
Promotes the study of television history. Publishes quarterly magazine 405 Alive and holds occasional displays of old TV equipment. In 1996 it celebrated 60 years of real TV in the UK.

Gaelic Broadcasting Committee
4 Harbour View, Cromwell St Quay, Stornoway, Isle of Lewis HS1 2DF
Fax 01851-706432   Tel 01851-705550
E-mail: comataidh@compuserve.com
Statutory body grant-funding Gaelic television sound programmes, development and training.

Guardian Edinburgh International TV Festival
24 Neal Street, London WC2H 9PS
Fax 0171-836 0702   Tel 0171-379 4519
E-mail: GEITF@festival.demon.co.uk
Britain's biggest international forum for the TV industry attracts prominent speakers, many delegates and widespread interest. Held over the English August bank holiday, for four days, during the Edinburgh Festival. Publishes an annual magazine.

Guild of British Animation
26 Noel Street, London W1V 3RD
Fax 0171-434 9002   Tel 0171-434 2651
E-mail: afvpa@easynet.co.uk
The Guild represents the interests of the growing number of British animation companies.

Guild of British Camera Technicians
5-11 Taunton Road, Metropolitan Centre, Greenford, Middlesex UB6 8UQ
Fax 0181-575 5972   Tel 0181-578 9243
The Guild represents film and video camera technicians working in the UK entertainment industry. It publishes the bimonthly news magazine Eyepiece.

Guild of British Film Editors
Travair, Spurlands End Road, Great Kingshill, High Wycombe, Bucks HP15 6HY
Fax 01494-712313   Tel 01494-712313
The Guild of British Film Editors organises film shows and technical visits for its members. It presents awards for film and sound editing. It maintains a dialogue with other technical guilds at home and abroad, publishes newsletters.

Guild of Local Television
c/o The Food Channel, Hagley Hall, Stourbridge, W Midlands
Fax 01562-883386   Tel 01562-882633
Promotes locally-originated TV, and supports groups and individuals involved in local TV. Organises conferences, seminars, workshops and publications. Promotes the skills of its members and undertakes research on their behalf. Aims to identify and accredit training opportunities.

Guild of Television Cameramen
1 Churchill Road, Tavistock, Devon PL19 9BU
Fax 01822-614405   Tel 01822-614405
Website:
http://www.easyweb.easynet.co.uk/~guildtvc
Professional association aiming to preserve the working status of TV camera operators. Publishes bi-annual Zerb Magazine and newsletter. Holds regular workshops.

Hospital Broadcasting Association
PO Box 2481, London W2 1JR
                       Tel 01324-611996
The HBA is the national representative association for hospital broadcasting. It is responsible for providing advice and support to hospital radio stations, and for promoting hospital broadcasting nationwide.

Independent Television Commission (ITC)
HQ: 33 Foley Street, London W1P 7LB
Fax 0171-306 7800   Tel 0171-255 3000
Kings Worthy Court, Kings Worthy, Winchester, Hants SO23 7QA.
Fax 01962-886141   Tel 01962-848600
E mail: 100731.3515@compuserve.com
Website: http://www.itc.org.uk
National and regional offices:

Northern Ireland	01232-248733
Scotland	0141-226 4436
Wales	01222-384541
East of England	01603-623533
Midlands - Birmingham	0121-693 0662
Midlands - Nottingham	0115-952 7333
North East England	0191-261 0148
North of England	0114-276 9091
North West England	0161-834 2707
S of England, Winchester	01962-883950
S of England, Plymouth	01752-663031

The ITC is the public body responsible for licensing and regulating commercially funded television services provided in and from the UK. These include Channel 3 (ITV), Channel 4, Channel 5, public teletext and a range of cable, local delivery and satellite services. They do not include services provided by the BBC or by S4C, the fourth channel in Wales. The ITC replaced the Independent Broadcasting Authority and the Cable Authority in 1991. It publishes the quarterly magazine Spectrum.

Institute of Broadcast Sound

27 Old Gloucester Street, London WC1N 3XX
Fax 0181-887 0167   Tel 01923-270888
E-mail http://www.wrn.org/ibs/
Professional body for people responsible for the sound broadcast on TV and radio. Publishes the industry's bi-monthly trade magazine Line Up.

Institute of Local Television

13 Bellevue Place, Edinburgh EH7 4BS
Fax 0131-557 8608   Tel 0131-557 8610
E-mail: instituteoflocaltv@msn.co.uk
Aims to increase local TV programming and maintain high quality local service on cable.Through research and consultancy supports development of the new resticted service TV licence and the introduction of local digital TV. Runs courses and conferences. Launched Channel 6 as first local terrestrial TV service in Edinburgh in spring 1997.

International Broadcasting Trust

2 Ferdinand Place, London NW1 8EE
Fax 0171-284 3374   Tel 0171-482 2847
E-mail: ibt@gn.apc.org
An independent TV company with charitable status specialising in making programmes on development, environment and human rights issues. Its aim is to promote a wider understanding of these issues through the use of the media. IBT is backed by a consortium of 70 aid and development agencies, educational bodies, churches and trade unions. It publishes the bi-annual newsletter Fast Forward and a range of back-up material.

International Institute of Communications

Tavistock Square, London WC1H 9LF
Fax 0171-380 0623   Tel 0171-388 0671
E mail: enquiries@iicdm.org
Website: http://www.iicom.org
Promotes the open debate of issues in the communications field worldwide, in the interest of human and social advancement. Specialises in broadcasting, telecommunications and communications policy. It publishes books, bimonthly journal Intermedia, newsletter, reports, etc.

International Visual Communications Association

5-6 Clipstone Street, London W1P 8LD
Fax 0171-436 2606   Tel 0171-580 0962
E-mail: info@ivca.org
A trade association representing the users and suppliers of the corporate visual communications industry. It publishes magazine and guides and organises regular professional and social events. Provides legal and information help.

ITV Association

200 Grays Inn Road, London, WC1X 8HF
Fax 0171-843 8155   Tel 0171-843 8000
The corporate political arm for the ITV. It lobbies MPs about broadcasting standards and seeks to improve or amend broadcasting bills.

ITV Network Centre

200 Grays Inn Road, London WC1X 8HF
Fax 0171-843 8158   Tel 0171-843 8000
Represents the interests of the regional ITV companies.

Set up in late 1992 to commission and schedule ITV's networked programmes from 1 January 1993, as required by the 1990 Broadcasting Act. Also responsible for research, programme acquisitions and financial, legal and business matters for ITV. The Centre also clears advertisements prior to transmission.

JICRAR (Joint Industry Committee for Radio Audience Research)

See RAJAR

London Film Commission

20 Euston Centre, Regent's Place, London NW1 3JH
Fax 0171-387 8788   Tel 0171-387 8787
E-mail: lfc@london-film.co.uk
The Commission encourages and assists film and TV production in London and holds databases of locations, personnel and facilities. It works to promote London as a first choice destination for overseas film makers.

Mechanical-Copyright Protection Society

41 Streatham High Road, London SW16 1ER
Fax 0181-769 8792   Tel 0181-664 4400
E mail: corpcomms@mcps.co.uk
Websitew: http://www.mcps.co.uk
Organisation of music publishers and composers, collecting and distributing royalties from the recording of copyright music onto CDs, cassettes, audio-visual and broadcast material. The society's National Discography, a database of commercial music and records, offers a wide range of music information. Publishes On the Right Track (a guide to starting in the music business) and the magazine For the Record.

Media Antenna Scotland

74 Victoria Crescent Road, Glasgow G12 9JN
Fax 0141-357 2345   Tel 0141-302 1777
E-mail: louisescott@dial.pipex.com
Office in Scotland for the European Commission's media programme.

Media Agency for Wales

see Sgrin

Media Research Group

Telmar,46 Chagford Street, London NW1 6EB
Fax 0171-723 5265   Tel 0171-224 9992
Provides forum for debating issues relating to media planning and research. Holds bi-annual conference.

MediaTel

52 Poland Street, London W1V 4LQ
Fax 0171-734 0940   Tel 0171-439 7575
E-mail: info@mediatel.co.uk
Website: http://www.mediatel.co.uk
MediaTel is an on-line media news and information database. There is free access to daily media news and walkthrough screens but the media databases are only available on an annual company subscription.

Media Trust

3-6 Alfred Place, London WC1E 7EB
Fax 0171-637 5757   Tel 0171-637 4747
E-mail: mediatrust@easynet.co.uk
Website: http://www.mediatrust.co.uk
The Trust builds partnerships between the media and the voluntary sector. It provides information, training services, and on-line material. It also runs Media Resource to match voluntary organisations with skills and resources donated by the media.

Mobile Data Association
22-24 Worple Road, London SW19 4DD
Fax 0181-947 9042   Tel 0181-947 5991
E-mail: mda@dial.pipex.com
Website: http://dialspace.dial.pipex.com/mda/
The mobile phone trade body.

Museum of the Moving Image
South Bank, Waterloo, London SE1 8XT
Fax 0171-815 1419   Tel 0171-815 1331
E-mail: wendy.taylor@bfi.org.uk
Website: bfi.org.uk/museum/
The national museum of TV and cinema including pre-cinema film, TV, video and new technologies. It is run by the British Film Institute. It hosts exhibitions, screenings, press previews and photocalls.

Musicians' Union
60-62 Clapham Road, London SW9 0JJ
Fax 0171-582 9805   Tel 0171-582 5566
The trade union which looks after the interests all styles of musician. It publishes the quarterly journal Musician plus a range of leaflets on the music biz.

National Communications Union
see Communication Workers Union

National Film and Television Archive
21 Stephen Street, London W1P 2LN
Fax 0171-580 7503   Tel 0171-255 1444
Founded in 1935 as a division of the British Film Institute. It acquires, preserves, catalogues and makes permanently available for study, research and screening a national collection of moving images of all kinds. Now holds over 350,000 titles, starting from 1895. Covers TV, documentary and feature films.

National Film Theatre
South Bank, Waterloo, London SE1 8XT
Fax 0171-633 9323   Tel 0171-928 3535
E-mail: bri.robinson@bfi.org.uk
Three cinemas owned by the British Film Institute (cf) showing the widest possible range of film and television from around the world.

National Sound Archive
see British Library National Sound Archive

National Viewers and Listeners Association
All Saints House, High Street, Colchester, Essex CO1 1UG
Fax 01206-766175   Tel 01206-561155
Organisation founded by Mary Whitehouse. It campaigns to make the Obscene Publications Act 1959 and 1964 effective, and encourages discussion and debate about the effects of the media on individuals, family and society. Publishes reports and the magazine The Viewer & Listener x3 p.a.

Networking
Vera Media, 30-38 Dock Street, Leeds, West Yorks LS10 1JF
Fax 0113-245 1238   Tel 0113-242 8646
E mail: networking@vera-media.demon.co.uk
Membership organisation for women involved in any way, or hoping to work in film, video or television. Media departments, libraries,careers offices are welcome. It publishes a newsletter and contacts index and provides information and advice.

NTL
Crawley Court, Winchester, Hants SO21 2QA
Fax 01962-822378   Tel 01962-823434
E-mail: marcom@ntl.co.uk
Provides the transmission service for ITV, Channel 4, S4C, Channel 5 and most independent radio stations. Services include a digital telecoms network, mobile radio cmmunications and satellite uplinking (including Occasional Services).

OneWorld Online
Hedgerley Wood, 4 Red Lane, Chinnor Oxon OX9 4BW
Fax 01494-481751   Tel 01494-481629
E-mail: justice@oneworld.org
Website: http://www.oneworld.org
OneWorld is a community of over 100 websites devoted to human rights and sustainable development. It includes a library, a discussion forum, a news wire and a radio station offered free to local communities for rebroadcasting.

Pact (Producers Alliance for Cinema & Television)
45 Mortimer Street, London W1N 7TD
Fax 0171-331 6700   Tel 0171-331 6000
E-mail: enquiries@pact.co.uk
Website: http://www.pact.co.uk
Trade association and employers' body for feature film and independent TV producers. Formed in 1991 from the Independent Programme Producers Association and the British Film and TV Producers Association. Provides a range of services, including information and production advice.

Production Managers Association
Ealing Studios, Ealing Green, London W5 5EP
Fax 0181-758 8647   Tel 0181-758 8699
E-mail: pma@pma.org.uk
Website: http://www.pma.org.uk
Offers a professional voice for both freelance and permanently employed production managers. Provides regular workshops, training courses and an employment register.

Radio Academy
5 Market Place, London W1N 7AH
Fax 0171-255 2029   Tel 0171-255 2010
E-mail: radacad@radacad.demon.co.uk
Website: www.radacad.demon.co.uk
Professional membership organisation for the radio industry. Organises the industry's annual conference, the Radio Festival plus seminars and workshops. Regional centres organise their own programme of events. Makes a number of awards for outstanding contributions to the radio industry.

Radio Advertising Bureau
77 Shaftesbury Avenue, London W1V 7AD
Fax 0171-306 2505   Tel 0171-306 2500
Website: http://www.rab.co.uk
The RAB is the marketing arm of the commercial radio industry. It aims to increase the levels of familiarity and favourability towards commercial radio as an advertising medium.

Radio Advertising Clearance Centre
46 Westbourne Grove, London W2 5SH
Fax 0171-229 0352   Tel 0171-727 2646
E-mail: adclear@racc.co.uk
Clears advertisements for radio.

Radio Authority
Holbrook House, 14 Great Queen Street, London
WC2B 5DG
Fax 0171-405 7062   Tel 0171-430 2724
Statutory body licensing and regulating independent
radio (all non-BBC services). Started in 1991, replacing
part of the Independent Broadcasting Authority (see
also Independent Television Commission). Publishes
the annual Radio Authority Pocket Book, detailing the
independent radio industry, and The Radio Authority
and the Listener, explaining how to complain.

Radio
PO Box 14880, London NW1 9ZD
    Tel 0171-485 0873
A recently-formed trade body representing independent
radio producers. It is a lobbying organisation that
negotiates with the radio network, government and the
unions. One of its aims is to increase the BBC's quota
of independently produced programmes from around
10 per cent to some 25 per cent of output.

Radio Joint Audience Research (RAJAR)
Collier House, 163-169 Brompton Road, London
SW3 1PY
Fax 0171-589 4004   Tel 0171-584 3003
Joint body involving the BBC and commercial radio
which is responsible for controlling a system of
audience research for radio in the UK.

Radio Society of Great Britain
Lambda House, Cranborne Road, Potters Bar, Herts
EN6 3JE
Fax 01707-645105   Tel 01707-659015
E-mail: ar.dept@rsgb.org.uk
The leading national organisation for amateur radio
enthusiasts, offering a range of services to members.
The society publishes: the monthly magazine Radio
Communication, full of news, features, etc; and the
annual Amateur Radio Call Book and Information
Directory, a comprehensive guide to all organisations
and the holder of every G call-sign.

Radiocommunications Agency
New King's Beam House, 22 Upper Ground, London
SE1 9SA
Fax 0171-211 0507   Tel 0171-211 0211
E-mail: library@ra.gtnet.gov.uk
Website: http://www.open.gov.uk/radiocom/
An executive agency of the DTI. It is responsible for the
management of the civilian radio spectrum within the
UK. It also represents UK radio interests
internationally. Publishes an annual report and many
useful information sheets on radio-related topics.

RAJAR
see Radio Joint Audience Research

Reel Women
57 Holmewood Gardens, London SW2 3NB
Fax 0181-678 7404   Tel 0181-678 7404
E-mail: rawlinj@uwest.ac-uk
Brings together women working in television, film and
video for discussions, seminars, screenings and
workshops.

Researcher's Guide to British Film and TV Collections
British Universities Film and Video Council, 77 Well
Street, London W1P 3RE
    Tel: 0171-393 1500
E-mail: bufvc@open.ac.uk
Website: http://www.bufvc.ac.uk

Ricardo-Hall Carnegie
The Deanery, 7 Deanery Street, London W1Y 5LH
Fax: 0171-495 7003   Tel 0171-495 7002
A film and broadcast consultancy.

Royal Television Society
100 Grays Inn Road, London WC1X 8AL
Fax 0171-430 0924   Tel 0171-430 1000
E-mail: royaltvsociety@btinternet.com
Promoting the art and science of television
broadcasting. The Society is at the heart of the British
television world. It provides a unique forum where all
branches of the industry can meet and discuss major
issues. Organises conferences, lectures, workshops,
masterclasses and awards ceremonies. The RTS has
regional centres each running their own programme of
events. Publishes journal Television eight times a year,
annual handbook, Membership £57 pa, students £13.

Satellite & Cable Broadcasters' Group
64 West End, Northwold, Thetford, Norfolk IP26 5LG
Fax 01366-727411   Tel 01366-728795
Association of cable and satellite TV programme
providers.

Satellite Media Services
Lawford Heath, Rugby, Warwickshire CV23 9EU
Fax 01788-523001   Tel 01788-523000
E mail info@sms.co.uk
SMS uses its dedicated lines, digital satellite and ISDN
networks to distribute commericals, programmes, IRN
and PA news services and record releases to
independent commercial radio. It is also active in retail
broadcasting, data communications networks and other
commercial services distributed via satellite.

Scottish Assoc. of Smallscale Broadcasters
Struan House, The Square, Aberfeldy, Perthshire
PH15 2DD
Fax 01887-820038   Tel 01887-820956
E-mail: wwright@sol.co.uk
Co-operative umbrella for all individuals and
organisations concerned with smallscale broadcast
operations, RSLs (restricted service licences), training
workshops, etc. Publishes quarterly newsletter.
Formerly called the Scottish Community Broadcasting
Group, set up in 1985.

Scottish Screen
74 Victoria Crescent Road, Glasgow G12 9JN
Fax 0141-302 1711   Tel 0141-302 1700
E-mail: info@scottishscreen.demon.co.uk
Website: http://www.scottishscreen.demon.co.uk
Government-backed body encouraging film
development and education in Scotland. Provides wide
range of information and support services. Runs the
Scottish Film Archive, preserving Scotland's moving
image heritage. Created in 1997.

Services Sound and Vision Corporation
Chalfont Grove, Gerrards Cross, Bucks SL9 8TN
Fax 01494-872982   Tel 01494-874461
Website: http://www.ssvc.com
Broadcasts radio and TV to the British armed forces via
BFBS (British Forces Broadcasting Service) around the
world. TLI (Teleport London International) provides
satellite services and Visua gives audiovisual and
multimedia help.

Sgrin - Media Agency for Wales
The Bank, 10 Mount Stuart Square, Cardiff Bay,
Cardiff CF1 6EE
Fax 01222-333320   Tel 01222-333304
The Welsh national information centre for European
audivisual funding and policy in Wales. It promotes the
EU action programme for the audiovisual industry.

Society of Cable Telecommunication Engineers
Fulton House Business Centre, Fulton Road,
Wembley Park, Middlesex HA9 0TF
Fax 0181-903 8719   Tel 0181-902 8998
E-mail: office@scte.org.uk
Technical body aiming to raise the standards of cable
telecommunication engineering, improve the status of
cable engineers and offer members opportunities to
attain further skills. Publishes journal Cable
Telecommunication Engineering.

Society of Television Lighting Directors
Tel 0973-249432
The Society promotes discussion on techniques and on
the use and design of equipment. It organises meetings
and produces a journal: Television Lighting.

Student Radio Association
c/o The Radio Academy, 5 Market Place, London
W1N 7AH
Fax 0171-255 2029   Tel 0171-255 2010
E-mail: sra@radacad.demon.co.uk
The SRA represents student radio stations. It holds an
annual conference and organises the Radio 1 Student
Radio Awards.

Telecommunications Users' Association
Woodgate Studios, 2-8 Games Road, Cockfosters
EN4 9HN
Fax 0181-447 4901   Tel 0181-449 8844
E-mail: tua@dial.pipex.com
Website: http://www.tua.co.uk
An independent organisation representing its members
interests within the world's telecommunications
companies. Membership includes a help line,
consultancy, training, workshops and publications.

Television & Radio Industries Club
2 Duckling Lane, Sawbridgeworth, Herts CM21 9QA
Fax 01279-723100   Tel 01279-721100
Founded 1931 to promote goodwill amongst those
engaged in the audio, visual and allied industries. Its
primary role is arranging social events and it also
publishes a yearbook and organises annual Celebrity
Awards.

3WE (Third World & Environmental Broadcasting Project)
2 Ferdinand Place, London NW1 8EE
Fax 0171-284 3374   Tel 0171-482 2847
E-mail: ibt@gn.apc.org
3WE works for sustained and imaginative coverage of
global affairs on UK TV on behalf of Oxfam, WWF,
Amnesty International and a consortium of other
leading voluntary agencies.

Voice of the Listener and Viewer
101 King's Drive, Gravesend, Kent DA12 5BQ
Tel.01474-352835
E-mail: vlv@btinternet.com
Non-profit making, independent society representing
the citizen's voice in broadcasting. The only consumer
body speaking for viewers and listeners on all
broadcasting issues. Publishes quarterly newsletter,
reports and briefings on broadcasting developments.
Arranges public seminars, debates and conferences
throughout the UK. Holds the archives of the former
Broadcasting Research Unit and British Action for
Children's Television.

White Dot
PO Box 2116, Hove, East Sussex BN3 3LR
E-mail: whitedot@mistral.co.uk
A campaign against television which encourages people
to get a life and turn off their sets. It organises an
annual Turn Off TV Week.

Wireless Preservation Society
52 West Hill Road, Ryde, Isle of Wight PO33 3LN
Fax 01983-564708   Tel 01983-567665
The society and the linked Communications and
Electronics Museum preserve a reference collection of
radio, TV and other electronic equipment in Museums
at Arreton Manor and Puckpool on the Isle of Wight
and at Bletchley Park, near Milton Keynes.

Women in Film and Television
11-15 Betterton Street, London WC2H 9BP
Fax 0171-379 1625   Tel 0171-379 0344
E-mail wftv@easynet.co.uk
Professional membership organisation for women
working in the film and TV industries. Provides
information and support to members. Campaigns and
lobbies on issues pertinent to membership. Publishes a
quarterly magazine and runs a programme of events
and an annual awards ceremony.

The Writers' Guild of Great Britain
430 Edgware Road, London W2 1EH
Fax 0171-706 2413   Tel 0171-723 8074
E-mail: tostia@wggb.demon.co.uk
The writers' union. It has agreements with Pact, BBC,
ITV, ITC, TMA and TAC. Provides support for
members, organises events and publishes a bi-monthly
magazine.

Republic of Ireland media

Media in the Irish Republic is an oddity in that much of it comes from overseas. Nearly half its television viewing originates in the UK, and a third of the Sunday papers plus half the dailies are London-based titles. Other small and prosperous cosmopolitan states - Switzerland and Belgium, for example - don't have this degree of saturation from foreign press and broadcasting. But then the Swiss and Belgians do not share a language or so many cultural values with their neighbours. When it comes to near identical appetites for soccer and soap operas, there is unity between the British and Irish nations.

There is, however, a thriving indigenous media which is most heavily Irish where it's for the most educated. The Irish Independent and Irish Times have a combined daily circulation of over 250,000 for a population of four million. Approximately one in 14 of Irish people buys a heavyweight daily, compared with one in 24 in the UK. Of the two, the Irish Independent has the bigger sale with a large farming readership making it the stronger outside Dublin. The Irish Times is close in spirit to the Guardian, from which it takes syndicated features: it is liberal left, urban and owned by a trust.

A large well educated readership in a tigerish economy ensures the Independent and Times do well, despite VAT and competition from cheaper British rivals. The latest trading figures from the Irish Times reveal a £12 million profit on a £140 million turnover and Independent Newspapers operations are funding Tony O'Reilly's expansion into the UK Independent. More of which later.

To a Brit's eyes the two big Dublin dailies seem old fashioned - the Irish Times clutters its back page with small ads and the Irish Independent has quaint production values. They're old fashioned, too, in not having gone down the broadloid route, sticking, instead, with the ideal that newspapers are about informing and educating as well as entertaining. Perhaps it's something to do with the Irish press' role in nation building.

For another mark of a nation which takes its media seriously, the daily broadsheets outsell the tabloids. The tabloid part of the market belongs to UK interests, with a lightly regionalised Sun and Mirror and a very different Dublin-based Daily Star outselling Irish owned and produced rivals. The Sunday market is led by the Sunday Independent and Sunday World with the new Ireland on Sunday gaining readers from the Sunday Independent. Next come Rupert Murdoch's News of the World and Sunday Times, flown in by Ryan Air on a plane which

Irish national newspaper circulations

DAILIES	1988	1996	1997	change since 1996
1 Irish Independent	153,054	158,712	160,137	+1.40%
2 Evening Herald	108,702	115,983	112,546	-2.66%
3 Irish Times	87,855	101,841 1	107,839	+7.72%
4 The Star	69.819	85,976	88,840	+7.56%
5 Examiner	58,227	55,194	56,628	+2.60%
6 Evening Echo	32,450	25,697	26,520	+2.00%
SUNDAYS				
1 Sunday Independent	230,794	339,501	327,153	-6.38%
2 Sunday World	360,138	296,085	307,162	+3.28%
3 Sunday Tribune	96,871	77,817	86,766	+16.9%
4 Ireland on Sunday			66,863	
5 Sunday Business Press		37,429	43,698	+20.4%

Source: ABC

doubles as a flying billboard advertising the Super Sunic.

Talk of the Sunday papers has a familiar ring to Brit ears, with commentators lamenting a trudge downmarket with flash layouts hyping up opinionated style tosh. At its best an undisguised push for readers has led to some valuable exposés, most notably by the late Veronica Guerin. She was murdered during her investigations into gangsterism for the Sunday Independent. Her death in June 1996 led first to her being lionised as a crime fighter and all round Joan of Arc. Then, in May 1998, Guerin was subject of a revisionist book. The Life and Death of Crime Reporter is by Emily O'Reilly and is billed by its publisher as a "ruthless, sensitive, highly controversial and disturbing read". Saint was turned into a sinner and Vincent Brown, editor of Magill (a New Statesman-like mag), concluded "Regrettably, the political legacy [Guerin] left - in terms of the atavistic response to crime - is far less happy than the memory or her."

The other hardy perennial media story about the media dwells on Guerin's employer, Tony O'Reilly. The ex-international rugby star and ex-Heinz star executive controls Independent Newspapers and is proprietor of the Irish Independent, the Evening Herald, the Sunday Independent, the Sunday Tribune and ten local papers. Another non-anglophile spin on newspaper sales figures (and another oddity) tells of a press more heavily dominated by one owner than any other liberal democracy. O'Reilly's papers account for two thirds of Irish national morning and evening papers and 95 per cent of the home-produced Sundays. Add in ten local papers with average sales of 10,000 each and O'Reilly has the potential influence on public opinion which Rupert Murdoch would envy.

O'Reilly's business reputation is based on marketing acumen and he made his commercial name by dispelling British prejudice about Irish food and making Kerrygold butter an acceptable brand name. Michael Foley, the Irish Times' media correspondent, thinks O'Reilly will pull off the same trick now he has control of the UK Independents. "I'm convinced he'll do well with the Independent in London. He'll market it.".

News is scarce about local newspapers. The demise of the Irish Press saw several old titles go to the wall in 1995, part of a shakeout which left many papers in their original family ownership. Not much to say about magazines either: the RTÉ TV guide is the biggest seller; otherwise there is the normal range of consumer titles

Share of TV audience	
RTE	34%
Network 2	19%
UTV	11%
BBC1	10%
C4	6%
BBC2	5%
TNAG	1%
Others*	15%

* mostly Sky channels
Source: RTE, for 12 months to December 1997

Share of radio audience	
Independents	43%
RTE Radio 1	33%
2FM	22%
Today FM	2%

Source: IRTC

including a new lad-mag called Himself; Magill has been resurrected and the satirical magazine Phoenix is well above the ashes.

As in Britain, broadcasting is highly regulated. The 1960 Broadcasting Act established Radio Telefís Eireann (RTÉ) as a licence fee and advertising revenue hybrid. RTÉ runs two English language TV stations (RTÉ 1 and Network 2), three national English language radio stations (Radio 1, 2FM, FM 3), a Gaelic TV station (Teilifís Na Gaeilge or TNAG) and a Gaelic radio station (Raidió Na Gaeltachta).

Late in 1998 TV3 will start broadcasting as the first fully commercial Irish TV station. Its major shareholder is CanWest, a Canadian cable company which is the world's biggest single purchaser of Hollywood movies. CanWest also has a stake in UTV and its strategy is to build upon an island of Ireland commercial TV tradition. While there is little sale of Belfast papers in Dublin (and vice versa) there is a clear demand for cross border television with UTV being the state's de facto third channel. UTV - which in recent years has favoured initials for its title instead of the more politically loaded Ulster TV - has 11 per cent of the Republic's viewing

figures and is in the unique position of having more viewers outside its franchise area than in.

Dublin is a world capital of cable following investment by Telecom Eireann and RTÉ. It can thus receive all the terrestrial channels from the UK, and the republic's TV has a British feel with TV listings including BBC 1 and 2, plus Channels 4 and 5 and Sky.

Radio divides into three sections: state owned channels from RTÉ; commercial channels led by Today FM (formerly 100FM) plus the 22 local stations which came into existence after the 1988 Broadcasting Act; and community radio for which the Independent Radio and Television Commission started awarding licences in spring 1998. Commercial radio, with the exception of Today FM, has proved very successful. The stations typically have more talk than their UK counterparts and provide sought after platforms for politicians to get their messages across.

There is as much interest in the web as anywhere else. Most noteworthy is the Irish Times site which gets 20 million hits a month, 70 per cent of them from North America. The Times is considering charging for its electronic edition in the near future.

UK newspaper circulations in the Republic of Ireland			
DAILIES	Jul-Dec 96	Jul-Dec 97	CHANGE
1 Sun	89,942	75,522	-16.03%
2 Mirror	66,218	42,365	-36.02%
3 Daily Mail	4,497	6,127	+36.25%
4 Times	16,970	5,811	-65.76%
5 Express	4,017	4,307	+7.22%
6 Daily Telegraph	6,636	3,979	-40.04%
7 Financial Times	3,454	3,826	+10.77%
8 Guardian	4,974	3,015	-39.38%
9 Independent	4,405	2,307	-47.63%
10 Daily Record	1,480	1,189	-19.66%
SUNDAYS			
1 News of the World	181,038	153,532 -	-15.19%
2 Sunday Times	89,864	76,018	-15.41%
3 The People	120,138	73,689	-38.66%
4 Sunday Mirror	88,188	46,783	-46.95%
5 Mail on Sunday	10,499	10,483	-0.15%
6 Express on Sunday	9,806	9,540	-2.71%
7 Observer	17,861	9,038	-49.40%
8 Independent on Sunday	13,527	7,049	-47.89%
9 Sunday Telegraph	8,166	4,370	-46.49%

Source: ABC

Republic of Ireland press

NATIONAL NEWSPAPERS

Evening Echo
Academy Street, Cork
Fax 00-353 21-275112 Tel 00-353 21-272722
Editor: Brian Feeney
Deputy editor: Maurice Gribbins
Arts editor: Declan Hassett
Features editor: Eughan Dinan
News editor: Vincent Kelly
Picture editor: Norma Cuddihy
Political editor: Liam O'Neill
Sports editor: Mark Woods
Advertisement manager: Paudraig Mallon
Head of marketing : Nigel O'Mahony
Owner: Examiner Publications

Evening Herald
Middle Abbey Street, Dublin 1
Fax 00-353 1-873 1787 Tel 00-353 1-873 1666
E-mail: herald.letters@independent.ie
Editor: Paul Drury
Deputy editor: Noirin Hegarty
Arts editor: Maurice Haugh
Features editor: David Robbins
Finance editor: Bill Tyson
News editor: Martin Brennan
Picture editor: Liam Mulcahy
Political editor: Kate Hannah
Sports editor: David Courtney
Advertisement manager: Karen Preston
Marketing manager: Barry Brennan
Owner: Independent Newspapers (Ireland)

The Examiner
PO Box 21, Academy Street, Cork
Fax 00-353 21-275112 Tel 00-353 21-272722
Dublin office: 96 Lower Baggot Street, Dublin 2
Fax 00-353 1-661 2737 Tel 00-353 1-661 2733
Editor: Brian Looney
Deputy editor: Tim Vaughan
Arts editor: Declan Hassett
Features editor: Dan Buckley
Finance editor: Kevin Mills
News editor: Ann Cahill
Picture editor: Norma Cuddihy
Political editor: Liam O'Neill
Sports editor: Tony Leer
Advertisement manager: Paudraig Mallon
Marketing Manager: Nigel O'Mahony
Owner: Examiner Publications

Irish Independent
Middle Abbey Street, Dublin 1
Fax 00-353 1-873 1787 Tel 00-353 1-873 1333
Website: http://www.independent.ie
Editor: V Doyle
Deputy editor: Michael Wolsley
Arts editor: Tom Brady
Business editor: F Mulrennan
Features editor: John Spain
Finance editor: Brendan Keenan
News editor: P Molloy
News analysis editor: Brian Brennan
Picture editor: Dedraig Breine
Political editor: Chris Lennon
Sport editor: PJ Cunningham
Advertisement manager: Brendan McCabe
Marketing manager: Barry Brennan
Owner: Independent Newspapers (Ireland)

The Irish Times
PO Box 74, 10-16 D'Olier Street, Dublin 2
Fax 00-353 1-679 3910 Tel 00-353 1-679 2022
E mail: postmaster@irish-times.ie
        lettered@irisht-times.com
Website: http://www.irish-times.com
Editor: Conor Brady
Managing editors: Pat O'Hara, Eoin McVey
Arts editor: Victoria White
Chief news editor: Don Buckley
Finance editor: Cliff Taylor
Features editor: Sheila Wayman
Foreign editor: Paul Gillespie
News editor: Niall Kiely
Night editors: John Armstrong, Eugene McEldowney
Picture editor: Dermot O'Shea
Political editor: Dick Walsh
Sports editor: Malachy Logan
Advertising and marketing director: Maeve Donovan
Chief executive: Louis O'Neill
Owner: Irish Times Trust

The Star
62A Terenure Road North, Dublin 6W
Fax 00-353 1-490 2193   Tel 00-353 1-490 1228
E mail: news@the-star.ie
Editor: Gerard O'Regan
Deputy editor: Danny Smyth
Arts editor: Jim Dunne
Features editor: Danny Smyth
Finance editor: F McMillan
News editor: D O'Connell
Picture editor: James Dunne
Political editor: John Donlon
Sports editor: Des Gibson
Advertising manager: Ken Grace
Marketing manager: Conner Mahon
Owner: Examiner Publications

SUNDAY NEWSPAPERS

Ireland on Sunday
50 City Quay, Dublin 2
Fax 00-353 1-671 8882 Tel 00-353 1-671 8255
E mail: info@irelandonsunday.iol.ie
Editors: Liam Hayes, Cathal Dervan
Arts editor: Eugene Masterson
Features editor: Fiona Ryan
Finance & business editor: David O'Riordan
News editor: Mairead Cavey
Picture editor: Fiomuala McCarthy
Political editor: Mary Kerrigan
Sports editor: Cathal Dervan
Advertising & marketing manager: Kari Louwrens
Owner: Title Media

Sunday Business Post
27-30 Merchants Quay, Dublin 8
Fax 00-353 1-679 6496 Tel 00-353 1-679 9777
E-mail: sbpost@iol.ie
Website: http://www.sbpost.ie
Editor: Damien Kiberd
Deputy editor: Aileen O'Toole
Arts & features editor: Marion Mckeon
Finance editor: Gail Seekamp
News editor: Nick Mulcahy
Picture editor: Emily O'Reilly
Political editor: Eoghan Corry
Advertising manager: Shiobhan Lennon
Marketing manager: Fiachra O'Riordan

Sunday Independent
Middle Abbey Street, Dublin 1
Fax 00-353 1-873 1787 Tel 00-353 1-873 1333
E-mail: sunday.letters@independent.ie
Website: http://www.independent.ie
Editor: Aengus Fanning
Deputy editor: Anne Harris

Arts editor: Ronan Farren
Features editor: Anne Harris
Finance editor: Shane Ross
News editor: Nick Mulcahy
Deputy news editor: Liam Collins
Picture editor: Brian Farrell
Political editor: Joseph O'Malley
Sports editor: Adhmhain O'Sullivan
Owner: Independent Newspapers (Ireland)

Sunday Tribune
15 Lower Baggot Street, Dublin 2
Fax 00-353 1-661 5302 Tel 00-353 1-661 5555
E-mail: stribune@indigo.ie
Editor: Matt Cooper
Deputy editor: Richard Curran
Arts editor: K Carty
Business editor: Shane Coleman
Features editor: R Deeb
News & finance editor: Miriam Binohae
Northern editor: Ed Moloney
Political correspondent: Stephen Collins
Sports editor: Eoghan Curry

Sunday World
Newspaper House, Rathfarnham Road, Dublin 6
Fax 00-353 1-490 1838 Tel 00-353 1-490 1980
Editor: Colm MacGinty
Deputy editor: J P Thompson
Deputy editor (content): John Sheils
Arts editor: Val Sheehan
Features editor: John Sheils
Finance editor: Aileen Hickie
News & political editor: Sean Boyne
Picture editor: Val Sheehan
Sports director: Pat Quigley
Advertising manager: Gerry Lennon
Marketing manager: Jerry McGettigan
Owner: Sunday Newspapers

MAGAZINES

When phoning from the UK, Republic of Ireland telephone numbers begin: 00-353

Accountancy Ireland	1-668 0400
Administration	1-269 7011
Afloat Magazine	1-284 6161
Aisling Magazine, The	99-61245
Amnesty International	1-677 6361
AMT Magazine	1284 7777
Angling Holidays in Ireland	1-454 2717

Arena	1661-5588
Aspect	1-676 0774
Astronomy & Space	1-459 8883
audIT	21-313855
Bakery World	1-280 0000
Big Issue, The	1-855 3969
Books Ireland	1-269 2185
An Bord Altranais News	1-676 0226
Bulletin	1-838 4167
Business & Finance	1-676 4587
Business Contact	1-855 0477
Buy & Sell	1-6080707
Car Driver Magazine	1-2600899
Cara	1-662 3158

Catholic Standard	1-8555619
Celtic Journey	1-296 0000
Checkout Magazine	1-280 2933
CIF Blue Pages	1-667-2885
CIRCA Art Magazine	1-676 5035
CIS Report	1-668 9494
Clar na nOg	1-478 4122
Comhar	1-678 5443
Commercial Law Practitioner	1-873 0101
Communications Today	1-284 7777
Communications Worker	1-18366388
ComputerScope	1-830 3455
Construction	1-671 9244

Construction & Property News
1-855 6265
Consultant, The   1-671 3500
Consumer Choice 1-668 6836
An Cosantoir   1-804 2690
CPA Journal of Accountancy
1-676 7353
Cuba Today   1-676 1213
Decision   1-283 6466
Doctor Desk Book
1-492 4034
Economic & Social Review
1-667 1525
Economic Series   1-661 3111
Education   1-880563
Education Today   1-872 2533
Employment Law Reports
1-873 0101
Engineers Journal 1-855 0477
Environmental Management
Ireland   1-872 0734
Farm Week   801762-
339421
Feasta   1-475 7401
Finance   1-660 6222
Finance Dublin   1-660 6222
Focus on Ireland in the Wider
World   1-478 3490
Food Ireland   1-671 9244
Forum   1-280 3967
Futura   1-283 6782
Gaelic Sport   1-837 4311
Gaelic World   1-679 8655
Gaelsport Magazine
1-478 4322
Garda Review   1-830 3533
Gay Community News
1-671 9076
Golfers Companion
1-2804077
Guidelines   1-676 1975
Hardware & DIY   1-767018
Health & Safety   1-671 3500
Health Service News
1-668 6233
History Ireland   1-453 5730
Hot Press   1-679 5077
Hotel & Catering Review
1-280 0000
IMAGE   1-280 8415
IMPACT News   1-855 0873
In Dublin   1-478 4322
Industrial Relations News Report
1-497 2711
Industry & Commerce
1-671 3500
Inside Business   1-855 0477
Inside Ireland   1-493 1906
Insight Magazine   1-205 7200
IPA Journal   1-671 3500

IPU Review   1-493 1801
Ireland of the Welcomes
1-602 4000
Ireland's Eye   44-48868
Ireland's Own   53-22155
Iris Oifigiuil   1-661 3111
Irish Architect   1-295 8115
Irish Banking Review, The
1-671 5299
Irish Building Services News
1-288 5001
Irish Catholic   1-8555169
Irish Competition Law Reports
88-557584
Irish Computer   1-280 0424
Irish Criminal Law Journal
1-873 0101
Irish Current Law Monthly Digest
1-873 0101
Irish Dental Association, Journal of
1-283 0496
Irish Electrical Review
1-283 6755
Irish Emigrant, The 91-569158
Irish Family Law Reports
88-557584
Irish Farmers' Journal
1-450 1166
Irish Farmers' Monthly
1-289 3305
Irish Field, The   1-679 2022
Irish Food   1-289 3305
Irish Forestry   1-278 1874
Irish Geography   1-708 3938
Irish Hardware Magazine
1-280 0000
Irish Homes Magazine
1-878 0444
Irish Journal of European Law
1-873 0101
Irish Marketing Journal
1-295 0088
Irish Medical Journal
1-676 7273
Irish Medical News 1-296 0000
Irish Medical Times1-4757461
Irish Pharmacy Journal
1-660 0551
Irish Racing Calender 45-441599
Irish Skipper, The 1-296 0000
Irish Social Worker 1-677 4838
Irish Travel Trade News
1-450 2422
IT   1-6623158
Journal, The   1-478 4141
LAN   1-872 0734
Law Society Gazette
1-671 0711
Licensing World   1-280 0000
Local Authority Times
1-668 6233

Magill   1-670 3722
Management   1-280 0000
Marketing   1-280 7735
Medico-Legal Journal of Ireland
1-873 0101
Motoring Life   1-878 0444

When phoning from the UK, Republic
of Ireland telephone numbers begin:
00-353

New Music News 1-661 2105
Newmarket Business Report
1-668 9494
NODE News   1-475 1998
North County Leader
1-840 0200
Off Licence   1-280 0000
PC Live!   1-830 3455
Phoenix   1-661 1062
Plan-The Business of Building
1-295 8115
Poetry Ireland Review
1-671 4632
Provincial Farmer 46-21442
Public Sector Times
1-286 9111
Public Service Review
1-676 7271
Retail News   1-671 9244
RTE Guide   1-208 3111
Running Your Business
1-296 2244
Runway Airports   1-704 4170
Saol na nOilean   99-75096
Shelflife   1-284 7777
Socialist Voice   1-671 1943
Sporting Press   52-21422
Sportsworld   1-878 0444
Taxi News   1-855 5682
Technology Ireland
1-808 2287
Tillage Farmer, The
503-31487
Today's Farmer   1-668 8188
Today's Grocer   1-2809466
Trade-Links Journal
1-454 2717
Tuarascail   1-872 2533
U Magazine   1-662 3158
Unity   1-671 1943
Updata   1-872 8800
Visitor   1-296 0000
WHERE Killarney   64-31108
Wicklow Times   1-286 9111
Wings   1-280 4322
Woman's Way   1-662 3158

LOCAL PAPERS

CAVAN
The Anglo-Celt Weekly w
00-353-49-31100

CARLOW
Nationalist and Leinster Times w
00-353-503-31731
The Carlow People w
00-353-503-41877

CLARE
Clare Champion w
00-353-65-28105

CORK
The Corkman w
00-353-66-21666
Southern Star w
00-353-28-21200

DONEGAL
Derry People and Donegal News w
00-353-74-21014
Donegal Democrat w
00-353-72-51201
Donegal People's Press w
00-353-74-28000

CO. DUBLIN
Inner City News f 6xpa
00-353-1-836 3832
Local News Publications
00-353-1-453 4011
The Southside People (East) f
00-353-1-294 2494
The Southside People (West) f
00-353-1-294 2494

GALWAY
The Connacht Sentinel w
00-353-91-567251
The Connacht Tribune w
00-353-91-567251
Galway Advertiser w
00-353-91-567077
Tuam Herald w
00-353-93-24183

KERRY
The Kerryman w
00-353-66 21666
Kerry's Eye w
00-353-66-23199

KILDARE
Kildare Nationalist
00-353-45-432147
Leinster Leader w
00-353-45-897302
Liffey Champion
00-353-1-624 5533

KILKENNY
Kilkenny People w
00-353-56-21015

LEITRIM
Leitrim Observer w
00-353-78-20025

LEIX
Laois Nationalist w
00-353-502-60265
Leinster Express w
00-353-502-21666

LIMERICK
Limerick Chronicle w
00-353-61-315233
Limerick Leader 4xw
00-353-61-315233
Limerick Post
00-353-61-413322

LONGFORD
The Longford Leader w
00-353-43-45241
Longford News w
00-353-43-46342

LOUTH
The Argus w
00-353-801849-462624
Drogheda Independent w
00-353-41-38658
Dundalk Democrat w
00-353-42-34058

MAYO
Connaught Telegraph w
00-353-94-21711
Mayo News w
00-353-98-25311
The Western People w
00-353-96-21188

MEATH
Meath Chronicle w
00-353-46-21442
Cavan and Westmeath Herald w
00-353-46-21442
Meath Topic w
00-353-44-48868

MONAGHAN
Northern Standard w
00-353-47-81867

OFFALY
The Midland Tribune w
00-353-509-20003
Offaly Express w
00-353-506-21744
Offaly Independent
00-353-902-21403
Offaly Topic w
00-353-506-41182
Tullamore Tribune w
00-353-506-21152

ROSCOMMON
Roscommon Champion w
00-353-903-25051
Roscomon Herald w
00-353-79-62622

SLIGO
Sligo Champion w
00-353-71-69222
Sligo Weekender
00-353-71-42140

TIPPERARY
Nationalist Newspaper w
00-353-52-22211
Nationalist & Munster Advertiser
00-353-52-22211
Nenagh Guardian w
00-353-67-31214
Tipperary Star w
00-353-504-21122

WATERFORD
Dungarvan Leader and Southern Democrat w
00-353-58-41203
Dungarvan Observer and Munster Industrial Advocate w
00-353-58-41205
The Munster Express wx2
00-353-51-872141
Waterford News & Star e
00-353-51-874951

WESTMEATH
The Westmeath Examiner w
00-353-44-48426
Westmeath Independent
00-353-902-72003
Westmeath Topic w
00-353-44 48868

WEXFORD
The Echo w
00-353-54-33231
Enniscorthy Guardian w
00-353-53-22155
Gorey Echo w
00-353-54-33231
The Guardian w
00-353-54-33833
New Ross Echo w
00-353-54-33231
New Ross Standard
00-353-51-21184
The People w
00-353-53-22155
Wexford Echo w
00-353-54-33231

WICKLOW
Wicklow People w
00-353-404-67198
Bray People w
00-353-1-286 7393

Republic of Ireland broadcasting

TELEVISION

RTE - Radio Telefis Eireann
Donnybrook, Dublin 4
Fax 00-353 1-208 3080 Tel 00-353 1-208 3111
Website: http://www.rte.ie
RTE is the Irish national broadcasting organisation. It is a statutory corporation, created under the Broadcsting Authority Act, 1960. There are separate but interlinked divisions catering for radio and television programmes, news, engineering, sales and marketing, personnel, finance and public affairs. RTE's expenditure is funded from television licence fee income and from commercial revenue.
RTE executive board
Director-general: Bob Collins
MD - organisation and development: Liam Miller
Managing director - television: Joe Mulholland
Managing director - commercial: Conor Sexton
Director of radio: Helen Shaw
Director of news: Edward Mulhall
Director of finance: Gerard O'Brien
Director of public affairs: Kevin Healy
Director of corporate affairs/secretary: Tom Quinn

Province 5 Television
Clogherboy House, Commons Road, Navan, Co Meath
Fax 00-353 46-27880   Tel 00-353 46-27880
E-mail:
Website:
Province 5 Television is a voluntary organsiation and is Ireland's only community television station. It operates under Cable Management in the Meath and north Dublin area. It provides 12 hours of local television and a 24 hour 7 day text service. The station is funded by sponsorship and fund-raising activities.
Station director: Kevin Mac Namidhe

TV3
Unit 5, Westgate Business Park, Ballymount, Dublin 4
Fax 00-353 1-456 9280 Tel 00-353 1-456 9263
E-mail: rick.hetherington@tv3.ie
Chief exec/anaging director: Rick Hetherington
Chief financial officer: Ken Scott
Director of programming: Michael Murphy
Director of news: Andrew Hanlon
Personnel: Michal Cahole

RADIO

3R Productions
36 Lower Leeson Street, Dublin 2
Fax 00-353 1-676 2984   Tel 00-353 1-676 8408
96 FM
Broadcasting House, Patrick's Place, Cork
Fax 00-353 21-551500 Tel 00-353 21-551596
103 FM
Mallow, Co Cork
Fax 00-353 22-42488   Tel 00-353 22-42103
103FM
Bandon, co Cork
Fax 00-353 23-44294   Tel 00-353 23-43103
Anna Livia FM
3 Grafton Street, Dublin 2
Fax 00-353 1-677 8150 Tel 00-353 1-677 8103
Area: Dublin
Dial: 103.8FM
Atlantic 252
Radio Tara, Mornington House, Summerhill Road, Trim, co Meath
Fax 046-36704   Tel 046-36655
Carlow Kildare Radio
Lismard House, Tullow Street, Carlow
Fax 00-353 503-41047 Tel 00-353 503-41044
ACC House, 51 South Main Street, Naas, Co Kildare
Fax 00-353 45-897611 Tel 00-353 45-879666
Area: Leinster
Dial: 97.3FM, 97.6FM 107.4FM
CKR FM
Carlow Kildare Radio, Lismard House, Tullow Street, Carlow, Co Kildare
Fax 00-353 503-41047 Tel 00-353 503-41044
Clare FM
The Abbeyfield Centre, Francis Street, Ennis, Co Clare
Fax 00-353 65-29392   Tel 00-353 65-28888
Classic Hits 98 FM
8 Upper Mount Street, Dublin 2
Fax 00-353 1-670 8969 Tel 00-353 1-670 8970
Community Radio Castlebar
New Antrim Street, Castlebar, Co Mayo
Fax 00-353 94-25989   Tel 00-353 94 25555
Area: Castlebar
Dial: 102.9 FM
Community Radio Youghal
League of the Cross Hall, Catherine Street, Youghal, Co Cork
Fax 00-353 24-91199   Tel 00-353 24-91199
Area: Youghal
Dial: 105.1 FM
CRC FM
Community Radio Castlebar, New Antrim Street, Castlebar, Co Mayo
Fax 00-353 94-25989   Tel 00-353 94-25555
Area: Castlebar Town
Dial: 102.9 FM

Connemara Community Radio
Connemara West Centre, Letterfrack, co Galway
Fax 00-353 95-41628   Tel 00-353 95- 41616
Area: North west Connemara
Dial: 106.1 FM

Cork Campus Radio
Level 3, Aras na MacLeinn, UCC, Cork
Fax 00-353 21-903108 Tel 00-353 21-902008
E-mail: s.wylde@ucc.ie
Website: http://www.ucc/ccr
Area: Cork city
Dial: 97.4 FM

Donegal Highland Radio
Pinehill, Letterkenny, Co Donegal
Fax 00-353 74-25344   Tel 00-353 74-25000

Dublin South Community Radio
The Old School, Loreto Avenue, Rathfarnham, Dublin 14
Fax 00-353 1-493 0520 Tel 00-353 1-493 0377
Area: Dublin south, west side of Dun Laoghaire
Dial: 104.9 FM

Dublin Weekend Radio
Dublin City University, Glasnevin, Dublin 11
Fax 00-353 1-704 5968 Tel 00-353 1-704 5203
Area: Dublin city and county
Dial: 102.2 FM

East Coast Radio
9 Prince of Wales Terrace, Quinsboro Road, Bray, Co Wicklow
Fax 00-353 1-286 1219 Tel 00-353 1-286 6414

Flirt FM
c/o The Porter's Desk, Concourse, University College Galway, Galway
Fax 00-353 91-525700 Tel 00-353 91-750445
Area: Galway city
Dial: 105.6 FM

FM 104
Ballast Office, O'Connell Bridge, Dublin 2
Fax 00-353 1-671 1797 Tel 00-353 1-677 7111

Galway Bay FM
Sandy Road, Galway
Fax 00-353 91-752689 Tel 00-353 91-770000
Area: Galway city and county
Dial: 95.8, 96.0, 96.8, 97.4 FM

Ireland Radio News
8 Upper Mount Street, Dublin 2
Fax 00-353 1-670 8968 Tel 00-353 1-670 8989

Limerick 95
100 O'Connell Street, Limerick
Fax 00-353 61-419890 Tel 00-353 61-319595

LMFM Radio
Boyne Centre, Drogheda, Co Louth
Fax 00-353 41-32957   Tel 00-353 41 32000

Long Wave Radio Atlantic 252
Mornington House, Summmerhill Road, Trim, Co Meath
Fax 00-353 46 36644   Tel 00-353 46 36655

Mid and North West Radio
Corporate Head Office, Abbey Street, Ballyhsunis, Co Mayo
Fax 00-353 907-30285 Tel 00-353 907-30553
Area: Connaught, Donegal

Midlands Radio 3
the Mall, William Street, Tullamore, Co Offaly
Fax 00-353 506-52546 Tel 00-353 506-51333
Area: Westmeath, Laois, Offaly

N.E.A.R 101.6FM
The Development Centre, Bunratty Drive, Dublin 17
Fax 00-353 1-848 6111 Tel 00-353 1-848 5211
Area: North east Dublin
Dial: 101.5 FM

Radio County Sound
Broadcast House, Patricks Place, Cork, Co Cork
Fax 00-353 21-551500 Tel 00-353 21-551596
Area: Cork city and county
Dial: 96-103FM

Radio Kilkenny
Hebron Road, Kilkenny
Fax 00-353 56-63586   Tel 00-353 56-61577
Area: Kilkenny city and county
Dial: 96.6, 96, 106.3 FM

Radio Kerry
Maine Street, Tralee, Co Kerry
Fax 00-353 66-22282   Tel 00-353 66-23666
Area: Kerry and the south-west
Dial: 97, 97.6, 96.2 FM

Radio Telefis Eireann
Donnybrook, Dublin 4
Fax 00-353 1-208 3080 Tel 00-353 1-208 3111

Radio na Gaeltachta
Cashla, Co Galway
Fax 00-353 91-506666 Tel 00-353 91-506677
Area: National
Dial: 92-94 agus, 102.7 FM

Radio na Life 102 FM
7 Cearnog Mhuirfean, Baile Atha Cliath 2
Fax 00-353 1-661 3966 Tel 00-353 1-661 6333

South East Radio
Custom House Quay, Wexford
Fax 00-353 53-45295   Tel 00-353 53-45200

Tipp FM
Co Tipperary Radio, Davis Road, Clonmel, Co Tipperary
Fax 00-353 52-25447   Tel 00-353 52-25299
Area: Tipperary
Dial: 97.1 FM, 103.9FM

Tipperary Mid-West Radio
St Michael's Street, Tipperary Town
Fax 00-353 62-52671   Tel 00-353 62-52555
Dial: 104.8 FM

West Dublin Community Radio
Ballyfermot Road, Dublin 10
Fax 00-353 1-626 1167 Tel 00-353 1-626 1160
Area: Dublin west
Dial: 104.9 FM

Wired 103FM
South Circular Road, Limerick
Fax 00-353 61-315776 Tel 00-353 61-315103
Area: Limerick city
Dial: 96.8 FM

WLR FM
The Radio Centre, George's Street, Waterford
Fax 00-353 51-77420   Tel 00-353 51-72248

Republic support orgs and agencies

SUPPORT ORGANISATIONS

Association of Advertisers in Ireland
Rock House, Main Street, Blackrock, Dublin
Fax 00-353 1-278 0488 Tel 00-353 1-278 0499
Advisory and information service for advertisers, to
ensure the highest ethical standards.
Broadcasting Complaints Commission
PO Box 913, Dublin 2
Tel 00-353 676 7571
The Broadcasting Complaints Commission was
established in 1977. The objectives of the comission are
to deal with complaints relating to news, current affairs,
ministerial prohibitions, invasion of privacy, advertising
and published matters broadcast by RTE and local radio
stations.
Cable Link
10 Pembroke Place, Dublin 4
Tel 00-353 1-799 8400
**The Independent Radio and Television
Commission**
Marine House, Clanwilliam Place, Dublin 2
Fax 00-353 1-676 0948 Tel 00-353 1-676 0966
The objectives of the Independent Radio and Television
Commission (IRTC) are to ensure the creation, and
monitoring of independent broadcasting. There are 21
local/regional stations operating in the country as well
as a community/special interest radio station and an
Irish language radio station in the Dublin area.
Working with the stations' management, the IRTC
seeks to ensure compliance with the laws of the land
and the maintenance of broadcasting and advertising
standards. The IRTC is a self-financing agency, drawing
its income from the levies paid by franchised stations.
**Institute of Advertising Practioners
in Ireland**
8 Upper Fitzwilliam Street, Dublin 2
Fax 00-353 1-661 4589 Tel 00-353 1-676 2991
Professional body representing advertising agencies,
providing a members advisory and information service.
Available to non-members.
Public Relations Institute of Ireland
62 Merrion Square, Dublin 2
Fax 00-353 1-764562   Tel 00-353 1-618004
Publicity Club of Ireland
4 Woodbine Avenue, Stillorgan, Dublin
Tel 00-353 1-269 3047
Regional Newspapers Advertising Network
33 Parkgate Street, Dublin 8
Fax 00-353 1-677 9144 Tel 00-353 1-677 9049
**Regional Newspapers Association of
Ireland**
33 Parkgate Street, Dublin 8
Fax 00-353 1-677 9144 Tel 00-353 1-677 9049
Windmill Lane Pictures
4 Windmill Lane, Dublin 2
Fax 00-353 1-671 8413 Tel 00-353 1-671 3444
Ireland's leading independent television facility
company.

NEWS AGENCIES

AP-Dow Jones News Services
Longport House, Earlsfort Centre, Lower Leeson
Street, Dublin 2
Fax 00-353 1-662 1389 Tel 00-353 1-676 2189

BBC Dublin Office
Leo Enright/Shane Harrison
Fax 00-353 1-662 5712 Tel 00-353 1-662 5500

Belfast Telegraph Press Office
156 Vernon Avenue, Clontarf, Dublin 3
Fax 00-353 1-833 3771 Tel 00-353 1-833 3771

Financial Times
20 Upper Merrion Street, Dublin 2
Fax 00-353 1-676 2125   Tel 00-353 1-676 2071

The Independent (London)
47 South William Street, Dublin 2
Fax 00-353 1-679 7675 Tel 00-353 1-679 5558

Independent Network News
62 Lower Mount Street, Dublin 2
Tel 00-353 1-662 9563
News syndicate for local radio stations.

Ireland International News Agency
51 Wellington Quay, Dublin 2
Fax 00-353 1-679 6586 Tel 00-353 1-671 2442
E-mail: iina@indigo.ie

PA News
41 Silchester Road, Glenageary, co Dublin
Fax 00-353 1-280 0936   Tel 00-353 1-280 0936

Reuters Ireland
Kestrel House, Clanwilliam Place, Lower Mount Street,
Dublin 2
Fax 00-353 1-676 9783   Tel 00-353 1-660 3377

Department for Culture, Media & Sport

The Labour government renamed the Department of National Heritage as the Department for Culture, Media and Sport. The secretary of state, Chris Smith, said: "Heritage only described a tiny bit of what we do and was backward looking. The new name gives a good sense of overall responsibilities but isn't afraid to use the word culture."

On taking office, Smith immediately ruled out major changes, saying: "We have no current plans to change the legislation that has been put in place by the previous government and to a certain extent I want to see how those rules bed down before making any changes. The only proviso I would add is that because the whole world of media is so fast-moving and fast-changing, putting legislation in place and hoping it will last forever is not necessarily the right way to approach these things. You have to make sure that you are aware of the way the present system works, we have to listen to what the media industry has to say as the present year proceeds and in due course it might be necessary to respond to new media and the explosion of further media outlets, but I don't envisage that at present."

Since then Smith has remained a hands off style minister. With the press, the Department of Culture, Media and Sport takes the same line as the old DNH with the 1998 annual report stating: "The government's policy for the press is that effective self-regulation is much preferable to statutory control or a law of privacy. It therefore welcomed proposals from Lord Wakeham, chairman of the Press Complaints Commission on 25 September 1997 for improvements to the newspaper industry's code of practice. Most of these proposals were incorparated in the new code publihsed on 19 December. The government expects the press to abide by all agreements in the spirit and the letter, and will be discussing further improvements to protect people in all walks of life with Lord Wakeham." So, in this case the old DNH initials still apply: Department where Nothing Happens.

Elsewhere in the department's broad media remit, the highlights are:

AUGUST 1997: C4 FUNDING
The Channel 4 Funding Formula was scrapped. Chris Smith said: "There is no continuing need, or real justification, for the C4 Funding Formula now that C4 is a well-established broadcaster with a steady income stream. There should be one transitional year (1998) under the Formula - with the payment set at a lower rate to soften the financial impact on Channel 3 companies."

SEPTEMBER: DIGITAL TV
Chris Smith told a Royal Television Society audience that he wanted digital TV to develop on the basis of fair competition rather than as a war betweeen different delivery systems. "In broadcasting," he said, "we are talking about an industry which plays a crucial role in determining individuals' sense of their own identity, moulding their tastes, interests and consumer preferences. It is more important than regulating competition in the provision of goods on the supermatrket shelves. We are also, crucially if more prosaically, talking about an industry which has always been very heavily regulated. The transistion from that regulated past to a more abundant and unconstrained future is a process which itself needs to be carefully managed."

FEBRUARY 1998: DIGITAL TV
The government invited responses to a report it commissioned from National Economic Research Associates and Smith System Engineering. The report concluded:
* consumer take-up of digital TV services should mean that the analogue network could be closed down within 10-15 years time.
* there are benefits to the economy - and for the speed of digital take-up - if the government announces within two years of the launch of digital terrestrial TV a firm indication of the date and process they intend to follow in encouraging the switch.

MARCH 1998: BBC GOVERNORS

Chris Smith advertised BBC governorships for the first time. He said: "I am determined to see more openness and transparency introduced into the process for making key public appointments including the BBC Governors. I therefore hope that the advertisments will encourage applications from the many well-qualified people who might not otherwise have considered a public appointment and increase the pool of candidates from which these key positions will be filled."

The papers chosen to carry the adverts were: the Sunday Times; the Times; the Guardian, the Glasgow Herald, the Western Mail; and the Belfast Telegraph.

OFFICIAL MEDIA GUIDES

Department for Culture Media and Sport 1998 Annual Report

The government's expenditure plans for the Department of National Heritage, the Office of the National Lottery and the Charity Commission.

Media Ownership Regulations

Details of the 1996 Broadcasting Act cross media ownership rules with definitions of control of an enterprise.

Digital Broadcasting

Licencing arrangements and the role of the multiplex provider.

The latter two are available on the Internet at: http://www.heritage.gov.uk

CHRIS SMITH:
MINISTER FOR CULTURE, MEDIA AND SPORT
"I take a wholly robust view about what the interests of the viewers are, and that's where I start from, not the interests of a particular proprietor or organisation. What viewers watch are programmes and content, not delivery platforms. We shouldn't be saying: 'Oh, wow! look at all this new gadgetry, we must change everything we do in regulation to suit the gadgetry.' We need to change regulation ... to suit viewers."

Department for Culture, Media and Sport
2-4 Cockspur Street, London SW1Y 5DH
Press office:
Fax 0171-211 6270   Tel 0171-211 6266
Head of Division: Paul Bolt   0171-211 6463
General policy branch
(includes broadcasting appointments, BSC and broadcasting standards, sports rights):
Harry Reeves   0171-211 6461
International policy branch:
Carolyn Morrison   0171-211 6444
Commercial broadcasting branch
(includes digital broadcasting, Channel 4 & S4C):
Niall Mackenzie: 0171-211 6456
BBC policy branch: Paul Heron   0171-211 6468
Head of media division: Janet Evans 0171-211 6424
Policy on press freedom & regulation, cross media
ownership: Philip Stevens   0171-211 6432
Films branch, UK film industry and film culture:
Alan Sutherland   0171-211 6447
National film and television school, film industry training, British Film Commission, media & media programmes:
John Zeff   0171-211 6434

Labour's news management

A hundred years of lobby secrecy ended on 27 November 1997 when Tony Blair announced that lobby briefings by government spokesmen would be on the record and no longer subject to a tradition of spurious secrecy. The 120 accredited lobby correspondents could now attend lobby briefings armed with tape recorders.

Henceforth Blair's chief press secretary Alastair Campbell was to be officially known as "the PM's official spokesman" though Campbell said he'd prefer not to be named to avoid becoming the public figure that his White House counterpart has become. The shy and retiring Campbell would certainly have preferred a letter to government press officers had remained anonymous when he made explicit the business of imparting media spin. "My sense is that in many departments policy is discussed and developed on a completely separate track, and the media plan is added on at a later stage. We need to be in there at the start," he wrote. "Decide your headlines. Sell your story and, if you disagree with what is being written, argue your case. If you need support from here, let me know."

Campbell's government department press officers needed support and reassurance about their job security with seven ministries losing their directors of information in the four months since Labour was elected. In December Jill Rutter, a former Treasury PR/civil servant who was ousted by Gordon Brown's staff, accused Labour of "politicising the Whitehall media machine". She called for "a strict code of conduct in handling government information. It is one thing for parties to manipulate, but should government do it at the taxpayer's expense?"

Criticism of Labour news management came from opposition MPs, including the Lib Dem's Steven Webb who tabled a question asking how many ministerial decisions had first been reported in the press. Betty Boothroyd, the speaker of the House of Commons, responded saying the government shouldn't use the press to make its announcements. "What is happening is that this House and the status of this House is being devalued and I deprecate it most strongly. I hope that those on the front bench will note what I have said and see there is no recurrence of this."

Campbell was back in the news in December following an interview that Harriet Harman, then social security secretary, gave to John Humphrys on Radio 4's Today programme. He wrote to the Guardian saying: "There is a problem. It is that Mr Humphrys is incapable of imagining that politicians might tell the truth, or of allowing them to explain complex points. He and his colleagues complain that politicians speak only in soundbites, and yet barely is half a sentence out of the politician's mouth than Mr Humphrys interrupts." On Christmas Eve another letter to the Guardian had him wondering whether the political commentator Ian Aitken "doesn't ... sometimes lament the state of the Guardian ... and its stereotypical views of politics, politicians and the poor".

Then Campbell switched on his television and found the BBC to be "dumbed down and overstaffed". Fifty-nine MPs put down a Commons motion to rebut Campbell's criticism, saying the BBC should "resist pressure from those who can otherwise not get their own way". In March Campbell yet again emerged from his preferred anonymity with another leaked message, this one a fax urging ministers to stop speaking to reporters during what he called a "pre-budget purdah ... I should also be grateful for an explanation of why interviews with the Guardian, Women's Hour and World at One were not cleared through this office," he huffed.

The nature of Campbell's role was queried by the Commons public administration select committee where it was revealed the press secretary attends Cabinet meetings. Rhodri Morgan MP, the Labour chairman of the committee, said: "Alastair Campbell's attendance at Cabinet meetings is perhaps another step down the path towards a presidential system. This tells you how the British constitution is being dangled halfway between the traditional description of prime minister plus cabinet, and a presidential system." The Tory MP David Ruffley said: "He is the 23rd member of the cabinet and yet he is unelected. He is more powerful than most cabinet ministers but is not accountable to parliament."

Campbell again made the news during the Spring-time row about Tory allegations that he had lied to cover cover up a phone conversation between Tony Blair and the Italian prime minister Romano Prodi. This prime minsiterial chat had allegedly touched on Rupert Murdoch's commercial plans in Italy and Campbell denied Blair had "intervened" on Murdoch's behalf. "A complete joke," Campbell said. "Crap." When Murdoch said a subsequent chat with Blair had influenced his decision to call off a bid for the Italian TV company Mediaset, Campbell admitted the conversation had been a matter of legitimate public interest. In June Campbell appeared before the public administration committee to be questioned about this incident plus accusations of "control feakery". He denied he had been misleading about the Blair/Prodi/Murdoch axis and also said: "I happen to think you can put across the government case in a coherent way without briefing against anybody."

The spin-doctor story got extra spin when Derek Draper and Roger Liddle emerged with some extraordinary boasts. Liddle, a member of Blair's in-house policy unit, boasted to an Observer journalist: "Just tell me what you want and who you want to meet and Derek and I will make the call for you." Draper, an ex-Peter Mandelson aide, topped the boast with ludicrous hubris. "There are 17 people who count and to say I am intimate with every one of them is the understatement of the century."

In April two of Labour's press staff moved on to more lucrative commercial jobs. David Hill, Labour's chief spokesman, resigned to begin working for the Thatcherite PR man Tim Bell. Then Tim Allan, Campbell's deputy become director of corporate communications at BSkyB on more than £100,000 a year. A man who sold Labour to the middle class is now selling the same people BSkyB.

Alastair Campbell, the man who makes sure that Tony Blair doesn't have to catch it on the chin.

Privacy legislation

Princess Di's death in August 1997 sparked the bitterest argument over the rights and wrongs of the British media. Centre-stage in the first few days were photographers, then believed to be responsible for her death, and their alleged behaviour provoked demands for a privacy law. Newspaper chiefs knew they had to fight this and instead went for changes in their own self-governing rule book, the code of conduct of the Press Complaints Commission (PCC).

Several other scenes were also taking place. Two new Euro-based laws were going through Parliament, one with wide-ranging powers on both anti-press privacy and press freedom and the other, the Data Protection Bill, threatening to place another gag on the media. In a third scene the media was promised a Freedom of Information Act. Taken together, these four scenes added up to a media show whose central theme was knowledge control - who or what is going to decide how much (or how little) the public is told. While media owners know that Knowledge = Power, they also know there are profits to be made out of selling at least some of the upper echelons' sensitive secrets to the masses, as Princess Di discovered. So Knowledge also = Profit. This contradiction shaped and twisted events.

Within a few weeks of Di's death it became clear that the paparazzi were less villainous than first thought, and this defused anti-media anger by the end of the year. But during September 1997 there was a fierce debate about how to bring the media under some form on public control.

By early October two media camps had formed. Only the Daily Telegraph and Guardian were supporting a privacy law. Opposing were the Mail, Express and Sun/Times, although their editors shared a sense of shame. But then Rupert Murdoch spoke out, making a strong self-defence speech for the press: "Privacy laws are for the protection of people who are already privileged. They are not for the ordinary man and woman. The talk of privacy laws is to see if we can get a new privilege for the already privileged, and that should be resisted." David Barclay, proprietor of The European, took an even tougher line: "The abuse of press power is unacceptable. I believe that far worse, however, would be a new statute law in Britain that interferes with the freedom of the press. A free press is essential. It is the only effective opposition to over-powerful government, and the guardian of democracy. The abuse of power by the State is the road to dictatorship."

An opinion poll in early November found 87 per cent of people wanted a privacy law. But by that time the government had made up its mind and stuck to the line that the European Convention on Human Rights would create a satisfactory judge-run law on privacy. In January 1998 Earl Spencer failed at the European Commission to obtain a judgement forcing the UK government to bring in a statutory law. Then, in early February, the Guardian produced its own draft Privacy and Defamation Bill "to establish a right to respect for private and family life, home and correspondence and to amend the law of defamation". The Guardian editor Alan Rusbridger said the government should "do more than simply make reassuring noises about privacy". The Bill would give people concrete defences, rather than forcing them to rely on unpredictable rulings by judges. The Bill would also tackle the libel laws, described by Rusbridger as "a disgrace".

Most of the media hoped to dodge the possibility of any privacy law by tightening and reshaping their codes of conduct. This would help the press appear more responsible and less biased, although without having any legal obligation to be so. TV and radio were already controlled by the Broadcasting Acts of 1990 and 1996, but the press is less restricted and wished to remain so, free of profit-restricting legal shackles.

Less than three weeks after Diana's death, a meeting of the PCC agreed to end "deplorable practices". The PCC's main weakness was that it had no sanctions other than the ability to demand newspaper offendors breaking the code should publish some kind of apology. Members feared this ineffective self-regulation - denounced by Geoffrey Robertson QC as "an enormous confidence trick" - would be replaced by a privacy law. An urgent review of the whole code was launched. Small changes were announced with a big fanfare by PCC chairman Lord Wakeham on 25 September. The proposals were aimed directly at the paparazzis, still at that time carrying the blame for the accident. The NUJ dismissed the revised code as "a sham to placate public opinion". Over following weeks the code was given a complete overhaul, while responsibility for the accident began to switch away from the paparazzi and on to Diana's driver. The revised PCC code was published on 18 December and came into force on 1 January 1998. Described by Lord Wakeham as "the toughest in Europe", the code was no stronger than its September draft, but was tough enough, given that public hostility to the press was declining following the rewriting of Di's death story.

New code provisions focused on privacy, treatment of children and intrusion into grief. There were new controls on the investigation of stories, with journalists banned from being involved in the "persistent pursuit" of people - their crime in the Princess Diana case. The government welcomed the new code, saying self-regulation was preferable to statutory legislation. The Campaign for Press and Broadcasting Freedom (CPBF) said mere reform of the code would have little effect, as in the past. "We are convinced that the absence of a statutory framework which enables the press to exercise its freedoms whilst at the same time encouraging high standards and providing fast, effective and inexpensive redress for members of the public is the right way forward for press reform. Self-regulation has survived because the press is so powerful. It can, and does, hold politicians to ransom."

Another code of conduct was under examination after Diana's death. The Broadcasting Standards Commission (BSC) had been required under the 1996 Broadcasting Act to produce its first-ever set of codes and this was duly published in late November 1997. The BSC code has statutory effect, while the PCC's does not and its effect is to strengthen the public's right to privacy and tighten controls on programme makers. Other codes in operation are those of the NUJ, BBC, ITC, Radio Authority, Institute of Journalists and International Federation of Journalists.

In the backgound of the debates over privacy laws and codes of conduct loomed the European Convention of Human Rights (ECHR). All EU states had to introduce the ECHR directive, giving a statutory right of privacy, the first such law in the UK. In late October 1997 the government published its new Human Rights Bill, incorporating the ECHR. This wide-ranging bill enshrined a code of fundamental rights in British law making it illegal for public authorities, including the government, courts and private bodies exercising public functions, to act in a way incompatible with the convention's rights to liberty and security, to a fair and public hearing, to respect for private and family life, to freedom of thought and expression. Article 8 states that everyone has the right to respect for private and family life, and there should be no interference by a public authority, except in specific cases. Under Article 10 there is a right to freedom of expression, including freedom to "receive and impart information and ideas without interference by public authority". Article 10 in theory upholds the freedom of the press against efforts by the state to restrict it. The best-known example is the 1979 case concerning the Sunday Times, where the European Court found that an injunction preventing publication by the newspaper of material on the thalidomide disaster amounted to a violation of Article 10.

But it would be down to judges to decide whether privacy had been invaded illegally, or if public authorities had failed to provide the public with redress. As the bill started going through parliament in November 1997, the media launched a campaign against it seeking assurances that it would not stop legitimate newspaper investigations. Either newspapers should be exempted from the directive in some way, or the bill should at least give some direction to the judiciary on how to interpret privacy and the right to disclosure. Lord Wakeham declared: "This back door privacy law is a threat to all our freedoms." Leslie Hinton, executive chairman of News International, said: "Members of the government have on numerous occasions said they did not intend to introduce privacy legislation and yet Article 8 of the convention could do just that." He added that Article 10 enshrined the right of freedom of speech. "The balance of these two rights - privacy and free speech - are at the heart of our concern." Alan Rusbridger of the Guardian said: "We seem to be striding blindly into a situation where a privacy law is going to be introduced by the back door, with no parliamentary debate, and no definition of what constitutes public interest. It is surely in the interests of editors and proprietors to take initiative instead of waiting for judges to do their worst."

Lord Irvine, the Lord Chancellor, tried to calm media fears by telling the House of Lords: "Press freedom will be in safe hands with our British judges." But behind the scenes the government began lengthy discussions with the press, seeking a mutually agreed way of amending the bill. Then in early February Lord Irvine was publicly rebuked by 10 Downing Street when he told the Lords he hoped future press curbs would prevent disclosures such as the one about the Foreign Secretary's affair with his secretary.

A fortnight later the bill came before the Commons. The home secretary Jack Straw announced the government had "reached an understanding" with the PCC, whereby its code would effectively be enshrined in the bill. Judges would be asked to rule on privacy claims using the PCC's code as its bible. In late June Straw promised strict guidelines on the powers of the courts to restrict reporting. Courts will have to pay "particular regard" to the right to freedom of expression when considering the right to privacy. The amendment

means Parliament retains much more influence over what judges will be allowed to do. Lord Wakeham said the amendment had the wide support of the newspaper industry. "We have enshrined the principle of freedom of expression and restrained the judges."

Another Euro-threat to press freedom was the 1998 Data Protection Act. Like the ECHR, this was the offspring of an EU directive that had to be turned into UK law. It shared the same balancing problem as the ECHR: how to reveal public information while defending personal privacy. The white paper for the act was published in late July 1997, a month before Di's death. Sweeping proposals in the directive tightened up control over the use of personal information, describing the way such data should be gathered, processed and stored. The directive ruled the new law had to be in force by late October 1998. It would replace the 1984 Data Protection Act.

Media owners feared the new act would inhibit normal reporting but the white paper was sufficiently vague to signal that negotiations were on the agenda. The death of Di tore up that agenda, forcing all parties to argue simultaneously about data protection, the PCC code, an actual privacy law, European human rights and basic media morals - if any existed. The Data Protection Bill was finally published on 15 January 1998 and - surprise, surprise - the government had done a deal with the press. The difference between the white paper and the bill was a specific exemption stopping courts issuing injunctions if the media reasonably believe, in the light of "the special importance of freedom of expression", that publication would be in the public interest. A key test would be compliance with the PCC code. The Home Office said: "The legitimate activities of a free press, including investigative journalism, will be able to continue." In charge of it all will be the Data Protection Commissioner, the renamed Data Protection Registrar.

The Act has been criticised by civil liberties groups for being too weak, and especially for the sweeping exemptions to many state-run bodies. There were also fears that taking any action would be so bureaucratic, complex and expensive that few members of the public would be able to do anything. But the press was not complaining.

As the battle between new media laws, rules and emotions was taking place on centre-stage following Di's death, a new act appeared in the wings. The white paper "Your Right to Know - The government's proposals for a Freedom of Information Act" was published on 11 December, at the moment the PCC code of conduct arguments reached their climax. The long-delayed proposals were broadly welcomed by even the strongest critics of Whitehall secrecy. The white paper proposed to "provide the people of this country, for the first time, with a statutory right of access to the information held by public authorities". Individuals would be able to appeal to a new, independent Information Commissioner, who would have the power to order recalcitrant Whitehall and public authorities to disclose documents on a range of policy issues. However, the commissioner's decisions would not be subject to appeal in the courts.

David Clark, then Chancellor of the Duchy of Lancaster, said: "Openness is fundamental to the political health of a modern state. This white paper marks a watershed in the relationship between the government and people of the UK. At last there is a government ready to trust the people with a legal right to information." The people were not to be trusted completely, however. "There are matters, such as national security or personal privacy, where information has to be protected. Government itself needs some protection for its internal deliberations."

Whitehall was prepared to swap some external looseness in return for more internal security. A member of the public wanting to know something about the NHS or local education would be suitably rewarded if they were clever enough to work out which unmarked Whitehall door to knock on - and had some money to give as an entrance fee. But all doors to policing, immigration, law enforcement by government departments, public sector employees and the security and intelligence services would be firmly shut.

The white paper was thrown back into Cabinet and the bill-making process. While in opposition before May 1997, Labour had promised the bill would have speedy priority. But as time went by the Cabinet's anti-freedom wing became stronger, initially delaying the white paper until December 1997, and then in the first half of 1998 trying to shoot it down before it made real progress. They thought that having a better information management system was not enough compensation for actually having to open even a just a very few of the firmly-closed Whitehall doors.

In early July a Cabinet committee met to decide the future of the bill. During a two-hour battle the freedom fighters just managed to force through an agreement to produce a draft bill by September. But the secreteers - led by Home Secretary Jack Straw, backed by Peter Mandelson - insisted that no decision should be made at that moment on whether it would be in November's Queen's Speech. This would delay it yet another year. The July Cabinet reshuffle confirmed this position with David Clark deposed and Jack Straw firmly in an ascendancy. The chances of a bill appearing in the November Queen's Speech were said to be "absolute zero".

In the days immediately following Diana's death, Britain's media owners hit panic buttons. For the first time ever, they feared the public might actually force the government to do something about the tabloid trash. A year later the points score-card showed the media as the winners. The privacy law had sunk without trace; the PCC code of conduct looked better to the public but in reality was little different; Euro-citizens had more rights but not many affected the media; data had some new protection but not enough to worry about; and official information would probably remain under Whitehall padlocks. As the curtain came down, it had been a good show for the media. Pity about Di.

Law and the media

The media operates under many legal restraints. Broadcasters are governed by several statutory controls specific to them and operated via the Broadcasting Standards Council, the BBC Charter, the ITC and the Radio Authority. Although newspapers and magazines are not so tightly regulated as TV and radio, all forms of media must prepare material within five legally defined boundaries. These are:

DEFAMATION
OBSCENE PUBLICATION
INCITEMENT TO RACIAL HATRED
BLASPHEMY
SEDITION

DEFAMATION is the aspect of law which most affects journalists and it covers a multitude of sins. A statement is defamatory if it damages reputation by exposing a person to hatred, contempt, shame or ridicule or makes a person likely to be avoided or shunned. It is defamatory to attack a person's honour, to injure them (or a company) in following their trade. It is also defamatory to wrongly accuse somebody of criminal activity, dishonesty, cruelty, hypocrisy, incompetence, inefficiency or stupidity.

There are two sorts of defamation: slander is non-published and libel is published. There are five defences to accusations of defamatory libel:
    justification/truth
    fair comment
    privilege
    "innocent" defamation
    apology
Justification: truth is the first defence against a libel action. It is for the journalist to prove that what has been published or broadcast is true, rather than for a plaintiff to disprove it. Therefore, keep notes and background material for at least three years, after which libel claims are barred by statute through lapse of time.

Fair comment: this is a journalist's genuinely held opinion and one which is held without malice and in good faith on a matter of public interest. Malice means dishonest or improper motives as well as personal spite.

Privilege: defamation laws are, under certain circumstances, suspended. These are reports of public judicial proceedings; statements made in Parliament; and public meetings. To avoid libel, a court would need to be convinced that a report of a privileged event was fair accurate and contemporaneous.

"Innocent" defamation: the mere absence of an intention to defame is not defence enough against a charge of libel. However the 1952 Defamation Act allows journalists the defence of saying they did not know the circumstances which make a statement libellous. An offer of a correction and apology is a key to this defence.

Apology: this admits a libel without malice or gross negligence and offers recompense via published apology and sometimes a payment. It originates from the mid-19th century, and is a dangerous defence which must be met to the letter if a court is not to move immediately to its own assessment of damages.

OBSCENE PUBLICATION legislation makes it illegal to publish material which will tend to deprave and corrupt persons who are likely to read, see or hear it. The 1950 Obscene Publications Act allows expert evidence to be given using artistic, literary, scientific or other merits as a defence.

INCITEMENT TO RACIAL HATRED legislation is framed in the 1986 Public Order Act forbids publication of material likely to incite hatred against any racial group.

BLASPHEMY- aka blasphemous libel - only applies where a piece of work is "so scurrilous and offensive as to pass the limit of decent controversy and to outrage Christian feeling". Under this law, only Christians can be outraged.

SEDITION is a little used catch-all to ban publication of material which either incites contempt or hatred for Parliament or the Monarch, or promotes reforms by violent or otherwise unconstitutional means.

Law for journalists is no laughing matter

. . . but cartoonist Barry Knowles is doing his best to stop us from bursting into tears

Media Lawyer, a bi-monthly newsletter, is for editors, reporters, journalism trainers, lawyers and all concerned with media law. Subscription is £30 a year.

Get a free sample from the editor, Tom Welsh, at 3 Broom Close, Broughton-in-Furness, Cumbria LA20 6JG

Phone 01229 716622, fax 01229 716621

E-mail media_lawyer@compuserve.com

Website http://ourworld.compuserve.com/homepages/media_lawyer

MEDIA LAW FIRMS

The definitive guide to British law firms is The Legal 500 which is published by Legalease (0171-396 9292). The media related law firms listed below have been culled from the book's 1,300 pages under the following specialities. defamation; digital mixed media; publishing and literary; entertainment and media (for the minority of out of London media practices) and TV. TV is subdivided into content (law firms acting for programme makers) and carriers (firms acting for satellite, cable and TV channels). But, as The Legal 500 points out: "Nearly all the major newspapers and publishers have established legal departments in the last few years. As a result, at least 50 per cent of all defamation defence work is now handled in-house, and the private practice defamation field has become fiercely competitive."

Allen & Overy
One New Change, London EC4M 9QQ
Fax 0171-330 9999   Tel 0171-330 3000
Defamation; TV carrier.
Clients include: Independent Television Commission.

Allison & Humphreys
See Field, Fisher, Waterhouse

Anderson Strathern WS
48 Castle Street, Edinburgh EH2 3LX
Fax 0131-226 7788   Tel 0131-220 2345
Entertainment and media.

Ashurst Morris Crisp
Broadwalk House, 5 Appold Street, London EC2A 2HA
Fax 0171-972 7990   Tel 0171-638 1111
E-mail: postbox@ashurst.com
TV carrier.

Baker & McKenzie
100 New Bridge Street, London EC4V 6JA
Fax 0171-919 1999   Tel 0171-919 1000
Website: http://www.bakerinfo.com
Digital mixed media.

Bannatyne Kirkwood France & Co
16 Royal Exchange Square, Glasgow G1 3AG
Fax 0141-221 5120   Tel 0141-221 6020
E-mail: martin@b-k-f
Entertainment and media.
Clients include: Associated Newspapers, Scotsman Publications, Scottish & Universal Newspapers, Equity.

Bell & Scott WS
16 Hill Street, Edinburgh EH2 3LD
Fax 0131-226 7602   Tel 0131-226 6703
E-mail: maildesk@bellscott.co.uk
Entertainment and media.

Berwin Leighton
Adelaide House, London Bridge, London EC4R 9HA
Fax 0171-623 4416   Tel 0171-623 3144
Website: http://www.berwinleighton.com
TV carrier; TV content.
Clients include: United News & Media, Walt Disney, Dream Works SKG, Endemol.

Bevan Ashford
35 Colston Avenue, Bristol BS1 4TT
Fax 0117-929 1865   Tel 0117-923 0111
Entertainment and media.

Biddle
1 Gresham Street, London EC2V 7BU
Fax 0171-606 3305   Tel 0171-606 9301
E-mail: law@biddle.co.uk
Defamation.
Clients include: Vanity Fair.

Bindman & Partners
275 Grays Inn Road, London WC1X 8QF
Fax 0171-837 9792   Tel 0171-833 4433
Defamation

Bird & Bird
90 Fetter Lane, London EC4A 1JP
Fax 0171-415 6111   Tel 0171-415 6000
Website: http://www.twobirds.com
Digital mixed media.

Bristows
3 Lincolns Inn Fields, London WC2A 3AA
Fax 0171-400 8050   Tel 0171-400 8000
E-mail: info@bristows.co.uk
Computer games.

Burness Solicitors
50 Lothian Road, Festival Square, Edinburgh EH3 9WJ
Fax 0131-473 6006   Tel 0131-473 6000
E-mail: edinburgh@burness.co.uk
Entertainment,media, defamation, intellectual property, publishing.

Campbell Hooper
35 Old Queen Street, London SW1H 9JD
Fax 0171-222 5591   Tel 0171-222 9070
E-mail: ch@campbell-hooper.co.uk
TV carrier; TV content. Clients include: Virgin Television.

Charles Russell
8-10 New Fetter Lane, London EC4A 1RS
Fax 0171-203 0200   Tel 0171-203 5000
Website: http://www.charlesrussell.co.uk
TV carrier; TV content.

Clifford Chance
200 Aldersgate Street, London EC1A 4JJ
Fax 0171-600 5555   Tel 0171-600 1000
Defamation; digital mixed media; TV carrier.
Clients include: Reuters, Carlton, TeleWest.

Crockers Oswald Hickson
10 Gough Square, London EC4N 3NJ
Fax 0171-583 1417   Tel 0171-353 0311
Defamation
Clients include: Birmingham Post, The Economist, FT, Hello magazine, International Herald Tribune, Jewish Chronicle, Liverpool Echo, Liverpool Institute for Performing Arts, Magnum,Observer, Telegraph Group.

Davenport Lyons
1 Old Burlington Street, London W1X 2NL
Fax 0171-437 8216   Tel 0171-468 2600
Defamation; TV content; publishing and literary
Clients include Private Eye, Daily Telegraph, Express,
MGN.

David Price & Co
5 Great James Street, London WC1N 3DA
Fax 0171-916 9910   Tel 0171-916 9911
Defamation.

Denton Hall
Five Chancery Lane, Clifford's Inn, London EC4A 1BU
Fax 0171-404 0087   Tel 0171-242 1212
Digital mixed media; TV carrier; TV content;
publishing/literary.

DJ Freeman
43 Fetter Lane, London EC4A 1JU
Fax 0171-353 7377   Tel 0171-583 4055
Website: http://www.djfreeman.co.uk

Dundas & Wilson CS
20 Castle Terrace, Edinburgh EH1 2EN
Fax 0131-228 8888   Tel 0131-228 8000
Entertainment and media.

Edwards Geldard
Dumfries House, Dumfries Place, Cardiff CF1 4YF
Fax 01222-237268   Tel 01222-238239
Intellectual property.

Eversheds
Fitzalan House, Fitzalan Road, Cardiff CF2 1XZ
Fax 01222-464347   Tel 01222-471147
Intellectual property.

Farrer & Co
66 Lincoln's Inn Fields, London WC2A 3LH
Fax 0171-831 9748   Tel 0171- 242 2022
E-mail: postmaster@farrer.co.uk
Defamation.
Clients include: Sun, News of the World, Haymarket
Publishers, Daily Telegraph, Sunday Telegraph.

Field, Fisher, Waterhouse
41 Vine Street, London EC3N 2AA
Fax 0171-488 0084   Tel 0171- 481 4841
Merged with Allison & Humphreys. Clients include
BBC.

Foot & Bowden
Pynes Hill, Rydon Lane, Exeter EX2 5AZ
Fax 01392-203981   Tel 01392-203980
Defamation, contempt, court secrecy, challenges,
promotions.
Clients include: Northcliffe Newspapers, regional
newspapers, publishers.

Frere Cholmeley Bischoff
4 John Carpenter Street, London EC4Y 0NH
Fax 0171-615 8080   Tel 0171-615 8000
E-mail: mel@freres.com
Website: http://www.freres.com
Defamation; TV carrier; TV content; publishing and
literary.

Freshfields
65 Fleet Street, London EC4Y 1HS
Fax 0171-832 7001   Tel 0171-936 4000
E-mail: email@freshfields.com
TV carrier.

Garrett & Co
180 Strand, London WC2R 2NN
Fax 0171-438 2518   Tel 0171-344 0344
Digital mixed media.

Goodman Derrick
90 Fetter Lane, London EC4A 1EQ
Fax 0171-831 6407   Tel 0171-404 0606
Defamation; TV carrier; TV content; publishing and
literary.
Clients include: Carlton, Central, West Country,
Yorkshire, Granada, Daily Express, Daily Mirror, IPBC
magazines, News Group, Zenith Productions.

Hammond Suddards
7 Devonshire Square, Cutlers Gardens, London
EC2M 4YH
Fax 0171-655 1001   Tel 0171-655 1000
TV content; publishing and literary.

Harbottle & Lewis
14 Hanover Square, London W1R 0BE
Fax 0171-667 5100   Tel 0171-667 5000
E-mail: hal@harbottle.co.uk   .
Website: http://www.harbottle.co.uk
Defamation; digital mixed media; TV/fim/theatre
content; publishing/literary.

Hempsons
33 Henrietta Street, London WC2E 8NH
Fax 0171-836 2783   Tel 0171-836 0011
E-mail: londonhempsons@btinternet.com
Defamation.

Henderson Boyd Jackson WS
19 Ainslie Place, Edinburgh EH3 6AU
Fax 0131-225 1103   Tel 0131-226 6881
E-mail: hlog@hbj.co.uk
Website: http://www.hbj.co.uk
Entertainment and media.

Henry Hepworth
5 John Street, London WC1N 2HH
Fax. 0171-242 7998   Tel 0171-242 7999
E-mail: hh@medialaw.co.uk
Defamation; digital mixed media; entertainment and
media; TV carrier; TV content; publishing and literary.
Clients include: BBC, BFI, Express Newspapers, John
Wiley & Sons, Mirror Group Newspapers, S4C,
Yorkshire Tyne Tees Television, Zenith Productions.

Herbert Smith
Exchange House, Primrose Street, London EC2A
2HS
Fax 0171-374 0888   Tel 0171-374 8000
E-mail: londoncentre@herbertsmith.com
Defamation; TV carrier.
Clients include: WHSmith, Washington Post,
International Herald Tribune, BSkyB.

Hobson Audley Hopkins & Wood
7 Pilgrim Street, London EC4V 7DR
Fax 0171-450 4545   Tel 0171-450 4500
E-mail: lawyers@hobsonaudley.co.uk
Website: http://www.hobsonaudley.co.uk
Defamation, publishing, literary, electronic commerce.

Lee & Thompson
Green Garden House, 15-22 St Christopher's Place,
London W1M 5HD
Fax 0171-486 2391   Tel 0171-935 4665
E-mail: leeth@globalnet.co.uk
TV content.

Lewis Silkin
50 Victoria Street, London SW1H 0NW
Fax 0171-222 4633   Tel 0171-227 8000
Defamation, publishing and literary digital mixed
media, entertaiment. Plaintiff/defendant newspaper to
include contempt.

Lovell White Durrant
65 Holborn Viaduct, London EC1A 2DY
Fax 0171-248 4212   Tel 0171-236 0066
Website: http://www.lovellwhitedurrant.com
Defamation; digital media; TV content;
publishing/literary.
Clients include the Guardian.

Manches & Co
Aldwych House, 81 Aldwych, London WC2B 4RP
Fax 0171-430 1133   Tel 0171-404 4433
Defamation; digital mixed media, TV contents;
publishing and literary.
Clients include: Which? magazine, Conde Nast, OU.

Marriott Harrison
12 Great James Street, London WC1N 3DR
Fax 0171-209 2001   Tel 0171-209 2000
TV carrier; TV content.

Masons
30 Aylesbury Street, London EC1R 0ER
Fax 0171-490 2545   Tel 0171-490 4000
Website: http://www.masons.com
Digital mixed media.

McGrigor Donald
Pacific House, 70 Wellington Street, Glasgow G2 6SB
Fax 0141-204 1351   Tel 0141-248 6677
E-mail: enquiries@mcgrigors.com
Website: http://www.mcgrigors.com
Entertainment and media.

Mishcon de Reya
21 Southampton Row, London WC1B 5HS
Fax 0171-404 5982   Tel 0171-440 7000
E-mail: postmaster@mischon.co.uk
Defamation; digital mixed media; TV content;
publishing and literary.
Clients include: Associated Newspapers, United
Newspapers, Mirror Newspapers, Channel 4, Carlton,
Central, Yorshire.

Morgan Bruce
Princess House, Princess Way, Swansea SA1 3JL
                        Tel 01792-634634
E-mail: elewis@morgan_bruce.co.uk
Film and TV production and financing, animation, TV
content.
Clients include: HIT Entertainment, Agenda Group,
Aaargh! Animation

Nellen & Co
19 Albemarle Street, London W1X 3HA
Fax 0171-493 0146   Tel 0171-499 8122
E-mail: nellenco@compuserve.com
Specialists in buying and selling magazines. Authors of
PPA publication Guidelines for buying and Selling
Magazine Titles - The Legal Framework.

Norton Rose
Kempson House, 35-37 Cammomile Street, London
EC3A 7AN
Fax 0171-283 6500   Tel 0171-283 6000
Website: http://www.nortonrose.com
Computer games.

Olswang
90 Long Acre, London WC2E 9TT
Fax 0171-208 8800   Tel 0171-208 8888
Website: http://www.olswang.co.uk
Defamation; digital mixed media; TV carrier; TV
content; publishing, intellectual property.
Clients include: Guardian, Associated Newspapers,
Daily Mirror, Daily Telegraph, IPC Magazines, MTV,
Warner Bros, Channel 4, Granada, Nickleodeon, BBC
Worldwide.

Osborne Clarke
50 Queen Charlotte Street, Bristol BS1 4HE
Fax 0117-927 9209   Tel 0117-923 0220
26 Old Bailey, London EC4M 7HS
Fax 0171-248 9934   Tel 0171-600 0155
Aex Plaza, Reading RG1 1AX
Fax 0118-925 0038   Tel 0118-925 2000
E-mail: info@osborne-clarke.co.uk
Website: http://www.osborne-clarke.co.uk
Entertainment and media.

Peter Carter-Ruck & Partners
76 Shoe Lane, London EC4A 3JB
Fax 0171-353 5553   Tel 0171-353 5005
E-mail: lawers@carter-ruck.co.uk
Defamation.

Phil Fisher Waterhouse
41 Vine Street, London EC3N 2AA
Fax 0171-488 0084   Tel 0171-481 4841
TV carrier; TV content.
Clients include: BBC.

Reid Minty & Co
19 Bourdon Place, London W1X 9HZ
Fax 0171-318 4445   Tel 0171-318 4444
Defamation.

Richards Butler
Beaufort House, 15 St Botolph Street, London EC3A
7EE
Fax 0171-247 5091   Tel 0171-247 6555
Defamation; TV carrier; TV content.
Clients include: BBCWorldwide, Turner Broadcasting.

Rowe & Maw
20 Black Friars Lane, London EC4V 6HD
Fax 0171-248 2009   Tel 0171-248 4282
Publishing and literary.

Russell Jones & Walker
Swinton House, 324 Gray's Inn Road, London WC1X
8DH
Fax 0171-837 2941   Tel 0171-837 2808
Defamation.

Russells
Regency House, 1-4 Warwick Street, London W1R 6LJ
Fax 0171-494 3582   Tel 0171-439 8692
E-mail: media@russells.co.uk
TV content.

Schilling & Lom
Royalty House, 72-74 Dean Street, London W1V 6AE
Fax 0171-453 2600   Tel 0171-453 2500
E-mail: legal@schillinglom.co.uk
Entertainment and media, defamation; TV content.
Clients include: LWT, Granada, Carlton, Yorkshire.

Sheridans
14 Red Lion Square, London WC1R 4QL
Fax 0171-831 1982   Tel 0171-404 0444
E-mail: general@sheridans.co.uk
Website: http://www.sheridans.co.uk
Digital mixed media.

The Simkins Partnership
45-51 Whitfield Street, London W1P 6AA
Fax 0171-436 2744   Tel 0171-631 1050
E-mail: simkins@simkins.com
Defamation; digital media; TV content;
publishing/literary.
Clients include: Channel 4, The Financial Times.

Simmons & Simmons
21 Wilson Street, London EC2M 2TX
Fax 0171-628 2070   Tel 0171-628 2020
TV carrier.
Clients include: NYNEX, General Cable, Rapture Channel.

Simons Muirhead & Burton
50 Broadwick Street, London W1V 1FF
Fax 0171-734 3263   Tel 0171-734 4499
Defamation.
Clients include: Time Out, Random House.

SJ Berwin & Co
222 Grays Inn Road, London WC1X 8HB
Fax 0171-533 2000   Tel 0171-533 2222
E-mail: info@sjberwin.com
Digital mixed media; TV carrier; TV content.

Steedman Ramage WS
6 Alva Street, Edinburgh EH2 4QQ
Fax 0131-225 8329   Tel 0131-226 3781
E-mail: info@srws.co.uk
Entertainment and media.

Stephens Innocent
21 New Fetter Lane, London EC4A 1AP
Fax 0171-353 4443   Tel 0171-353 2000
Defamation, worls wide web, registration of media, film amd TV content, publishing.
Clients include: Wall Street Journal, Washington Post, Society of Authors, ITN.

Swepstone Walsh
9 Lincolns Inn Fields London WC2A 3BP
Fax 0171-404 1493   Tel 0171-404 1499
Defamation

Tarlo Lyons
Watchmaker Court, 33 St John's Lane, London EC1M 4DB
Fax 0171-814 9421   Tel 0171-405 2000
TV content.

Taylor Joynson Garrett
Carmelite, 50 Victoria Embankment, Blackfriars, London EC4Y 0DX
Fax 0171-936 2666   Tel 0171-353 1234
Digital mixed media; TV carrier; TV content; publishing and literary.

Theodore Goddard
150 Aldersgate Street, London EC1A 4EJ
Fax 0171-606 4390   Tel 0171-606 8855
Defamation; TV carrier; TV content, digital mixed media, media litigation, publishing.
Clients include: The Times, Mirror Group.

Titmuss Sainer Dechert
2 Serjeants' Inn, London EC4Y 1LT
Fax 0171-353 3683   Tel 0171-583 5353
Defamation; digital mixed media.

Tods Murray WS
66 Queen Street, Edinburgh EH2 4NE
Fax 0131-225 3676   Tel 0131-226 4771
Entertainment and media.

Wansbroughs Willey Hargrave
103 Temple Street, Bristol BS99 7UD
Fax 0117-929 1582   Tel 0117-926 8981
Entertainment and media.

Wiggin & Co
The Quadrangle, Imperial Square, Cheltenham, Gloucestershire GL50 1YX
Fax 01242-224223   Tel 01242-224114
E-mail: law@wiggin.co.uk
3 Albany Courtyard, Piccadilly, London W1V 9RA
Fax 0171-287 8628   Tel 0171-287 8833
Entertainment and media, defamation, digital mixed media, TV carrier, TV content, publishing and literary.

LEGAL PUBLICATIONS

The Incorporated Council of Law Reporting for England & Wales
3 Stone Buildings, Lincoln's Inn, London WC2A 3XN
Fax 0171-831 5247   Tel 0171-242 6471
The Council publishes the Weekly Law Reports etc and produces law reports for The Times, The Law Society Gazette and other titles.

The Legal 500
28-33 Cato Street, London W1H 5HS
Fax 0171-396 9300   Tel 0171-396 9292
Website: the_legal_500@link.org
Publisher of "The Client's Guide to UK Law Firms".

Media Lawyer
3 Broom Close, Broughton in Furness, Cumbria LA20 6JG
Fax 01229-716621   Tel 01229-716622
A newsletter for media lawyers, journalism trainers, journalists and all concerned with media law. Covers media law events and developments. Bi-monthly. £30 pa.

Nellen & Co
19 Albemarle Street, London W1X 3HA
Fax 0171-493 0146   Tel 0171-499 8122
Authors of PPA publication Guidelines for Buying and Selling Magazine Titles - The Legal Framework.

LIBEL INSURANCE

Libel damages have fallen in the past couple of years and for several reasons. Since 1990 the Court of Appeal has been able to substitute what a jury has awarded as happened, for example, when Elton John's original £350,000 libel award from the Mirror was reduced on appeal to £75,000. On a more general level the Court of Appeal has also ruled that juries may be directed to bear in mind the £50,000 to £125,000 awards for pain and suffering in cases of bodily injury. Another factor is a decision by the European Court of Human Rights that the £1.5 million award in 1995 to Lord Aldington against Nikolai Tolstoy over allegations that he sent Cossacks and Yugoslavs to their death in 1945, breached the freedom of expression guarantee in the European Convention on Human Rights.

While the days of the £1 million are probably over, existing libel laws are still an obstacle to investigative journalism. The Guardian editor Alan Rusbridger says there should be three changes. First, that judges should not be allowed to dismiss the jury and make the final decision, as happened in Jonathan Aitken's unsuccessful case against the Guardian. Second, that the innocent-until-guilty principle should apply instead of the defence having to prove its case. And third, the withdrawal of qualified privilege, which in some circumstances allows individuals to speak without fear of a defamation action.

Speaking some while after the Guardian had been vindicated after libel actions brought by the MPs Jonathan Aitken and Neil Hamilton, Rusbridger said: "I have some sympathy for Aitken and Hamilton because they were forced to use a process that isn't designed to get to the truth. It is a fight to the death and one side will end up with their lives destroyed. There must be a way we can get away from this. It is lengthy, unpleasant and destructive."

Meanwhile libel insurance is a booming business. The coverage typically provided within a media or libel policy includes libel, slander, malicious falsehood, passing off, infringement of copyright and trademark, false attribution of authorship, breach of confidence, trespass and invasion of privacy. Optional coverage may include withdrawal costs, errors and omissions or negligent statement and commercial printing exposures.

Policies can be written either on a claims made basis or occurrence wording with limits in the aggregate or on an each and every event basis. Jurisdictions are available for the UK, EC, USA/Canada or worldwide. To obtain a quote, full proposal information is usually required. Most of the insurers can either be contacted directly or via your insurance broker. Professional indemnity underwriters normally give a libel and slander extension where publishing or broadcasting is incidental to the main business of the Insured. However, specific libel policies are provided by the following London insurers.

LIBEL INSURERS

ERC Frankona
7/8 Philpot Lane, London EC3M 8AA
Fax 0171-617 6860   Tel 0171-617 6800
E-mail: sara.neale@ercgroup

Royal Sun Alliance
Leadenhall Court, 1 Leadenhall Street, London EC3V 1PP
Tel 0171-588 2345
Website: http://www.royal-and-sunalliance.com

Media/Professional UK Limited
New London House, New London Street, London EC3R 7QL
Fax 0171-680 1177   Tel 0171-626 0211
Website: http://www.mediaprof.com

RE Brown & Others (Lloyd's Syndicate 702)
84 Fenchurch Street, London EC3M 4BY
Fax 0171-480 6920   Tel 0171-265 0071

Denham Syndicate ((Lloyd's Syndicate 990)
Holland House, Berry Street, London EC3
Fax 0171-623 8223   Tel 0171-283 0045E-mail: denhamdirect@compuserve.com

Hiscox Underwriting Limited
52/54 Leadenhall Street, London EC3A 2BJ
Fax 0171-929 1251   Tel 0171-423 4000
Website: http://www.hiscox.co.uk

Newspapers Mutual Insurance Society
Bloomsbury House, 74-77 Great Russell Street, London WC1B 3DA
Fax 0171-631 5119   Tel 0171-636 7014
E-mail: ns@newspapersoc.org.uk

Complaints to the media

The first rule about complaining is to make objections fast and be prepared for a long drawn out resolution. For trivial complaints, write to the journalist who has caused offence. Sprinkle complaints with praise, and journalists will often write a follow up story if subtly persuaded their wrong needs to be righted. More serious complaints warrant a phone call to the editor responsible for the article or broadcast. Editors, especially if they sense lawyers looming, will be cagey. However, they are unlikely to be openly hostile and will invariably ask for the complaint to be put in writing. A decently phrased letter has a good chance of being printed and the smaller the offending newspaper or magazine, the more likely a letter is to get a public airing.

With small complaints about a BBC TV or radio programme, try going to journalists and then producers. If these direct routes are closed, try one of the BBC numbers on this page. Likewise with minor complaints about ITV programmes: try the producers, then the ITC. More serious complaints should go to the Broadcasting Standards Commission.

The alternative is to sue for libel and the best advice here is: don't. It takes strong nerves and deep pockets and litigants will be entering a treacherous territory where the opposition knows the best tricks.

PRESS COMPLAINTS

Advertising Standards Authority
2 Torrington Place, London WC1E 7HW
Fax 0171-323 4339   Tel 0171-580 5555
For complaints about newspaper and magazine advertisements.
National Newspapers Mail Order Protection Scheme (MOPS)
16 Tooks Court, London EC4A 1LB
Fax 0171-404 0106   Tel 0171-405 6806
For mail order rip-offs.
Press Complaints Commission
1 Salisbury Square, London EC4 8AE
Fax 0171 353 8355   Tel 0171-3531248
E-mail: pcc@pcc.org.uk
Website: http://www.pcc.org.uk
For complainants about the contents and conduct of newspapers and magazines. Upholds a Code of Practice and advises editors on journalistic ethics.

BROADCAST COMPLAINTS

BBC Information
BBC Television Centre, London W12 7RJ
0870 0100 222
0870 0100 212 (Minicom)
(Calls charged at national rate)
E-mail: info@bbc.co.uk
Website: http://www.bbc.co.uk/info/
Ceefax: page 695
For comments and queries.
BBC Reception Advice
BBC Television Centre, London W12 7RJ
0870 0100 123
0870 0100 212(Minicom)
(0800-1900 weekdays, calls charged at national rate)
E-mail: reception@bbc.co.uk
Website: http://www.bbc.co.uk/reception/
Ceefax: page 695 & 698
For radio and TV reception advice.
BBC Programme Complaints Unit
BBC Broadcasting House, London W1A 1AA
If you think a programme has included specific and serious injustice, a serious invasion of privacy, a specific and serious inaccuracy or breach of broadcasting standards write to Fraser Steel at the above address.
British Board of Film Classification
3 Soho Square, London W1V 6HD
Fax 0171-287 0141   Tel 0171-439 7961
The body responsible for classifying publicly shown films:
   U (Universal)
   PG (Parental Guidance)
   12 (age 12 and over only)
   15 (age 15 and over only)
   18 (age 18 and over only)
   R18 (restricted to premises barred to under 18s)
Broadcasting Standards Commission
7 The Sanctuary, London SW1P 3JS
Fax 0171-222 3172   Tel 0171-233 0544
The 1996 Broadcasting Act established the BSC to replace the Broadcasting Complaints Commission and the Broadcasting Standards Council. It starts work on 1 April 1997 for those complaining of a breach of privacy or unjust or unfair treatment on radio or TV.
Independent Television Commission
33 Foley Street, London W1P 7LB
Fax 0171-306 7800   Tel 0171-255 3000
E-mail: publicaffairs@itc.org.uk
Complaints about ITV, C4, C5 and licensed cable or satellite.
Radio Authority
Holbrook House, 14 Great Queen Street, London WC2B 5DG
Fax 0171-405 7064   Tel 0171-430 2724
Complaints about commercial radio. Ask for the RA leaflet titled How To Make A Complaint.

Sport and the media

Summer 1997: the new health minister, Frank Dobson, promised he would include sports sponsorship in his plans to ban tobacco advertising; and the sports minister Tony Banks promised to extend the number of sports events which the terrestrial broadcaster can transmit as of right.

Funny old game politics. You never know what will happen next. The marriage of media and sport meant both promises were broken within the year. Despite pressure from health lobbyists, even greater pressure from the Formula One motor racing authorities ensured that racing cars will continue doubling up as cigarette advertising hoardings.

The value of Banks' promise is shown in the comparison of the 1996 Broadcasting Act's listed events and the new 'A' list Crown Jewel events announced in June 1998 and tabulated below. A slight improvement and Tony Banks is as good as his word. However the truly committed armchair sportif won't get everything free-to-air and the new 'A' list is more a swap of a little rugby for a lot of cricket than a significant extension of consumer rights. Meanwhile leaving aside the 'A' list, the Department of Culture has allowed every other sport to put itself up for grabs - non-finals Wimbledon, Five Nations rugby, World Athletics Championships, Commonwealth Games, Open Golf, Ryder Cup.

"Sport absolutely overpowers film and everything else in the entertainment genre," said Rupert Murdoch and nobody in politics or the media would disagree. A quarter of all newspaper coverage is devoted to sport and nearly every national paper has a separate sports supplement. There are nearly 20,000 hours of sport a year on television and the BBC alone has an annual £100 million sports budget.

Sport delivers audiences and England's penalty shootout against Argentina was watched by a record ITV audience of 26 million. "Football of all sports is number one," Murdoch says. Which is why, from August 1997, Sky signed a £670 million four year deal to show twice-weekly live Premiership matches. At the time, a BBC spokesman said: "The BBC is just not willing to pay ever-escalating costs. We just can't justify it. The previous argument that sport was relatively cheap for the amount of programming you get out of it is simply not true any more."

As TV provision fragments, so the broadcasting deals will gather in complexity. In September 1997 Manchester United football club completed an arrangement with Granada and BSkyB to start a football-only digital TV channel. The channel won't show the big matches, only old games, reserve games, testimonials, friendlies and interviews.

SPORTS COUNCILS

English Sports Council   0171-273 1500
Sports Council for Wales   01244-822600
Scottish Sports Council   0131-317 7200
Sports Council for N Ireland 01232-381222

Sport and the media

1998 A LIST EVENTS	1996 BROADCASTING ACT LISTED EVENTS
Olympic Games	Olympic Games
World Cup finals	World Cup finals
FA Cup Final	FA Cup Final
Wimbledon	Wimbledon finals weekend
Grand National	Grand National
Derby	Derby
Scottish Cup Final	Scottish Cup Final
Rugby World Cup Final	Domestic cricket Tests
Rugby League Challenge Cup final	

Advertising and public relations

PRESS

Advertising in newspapers, magazines, posters, the cinema and direct mail is regulated by the Advertising Standards Authority, which is funded by a levy on display ads. It aims to enforce standards through a code which says ads should be: legal, decent, honest and truthful; prepared with a sense of responsibility to the consumer and society; and fair competition as generally accepted in business. The Authority's main sanction is to recommend that the ads it considers in breach of its code are not published. This is normally enough to make sure an offending ad is quashed. The Authority publishes monthly reports on the results of its investigations and, as a final resort, refers misleading adverts to the director general of fair trading who has the power to seek injunctions to prevent publication.

BROADCASTING

The advertising rules for broadcasting are more complex than for the press. Advertising is allowed on independent television and radio, subject to controls laid down by the ITC and the Radio Authority. Both can impose heavy penalties on companies failing to comply with their codes. Advertisers are not allowed to influence programme content and their ads must be distinct from programmes. TV advertising is limited to an average seven minutes an hour during the day and seven and a half minutes in the peak evening period. Ads are forbidden in religious and school broadcasts, though religious ads are now permitted. Political advertising is prohibited and gambling ads are restricted to the football pools and the National Lottery. All tobacco ads are banned on TV (with the exception of ones that just happen to appear on Formula One racing cars) and cigarette ads are banned on radio.

1997 advertising expenditure

TYPE	AMOUNT	TOTAL
National newspapers	£1,650m	12.6%
Regional newspapers	£2,237m	17%
Consumer magazines	£660m	-5%
Business & professional	£1,106m	8.4%
Directories	£737m	5.6%
Press production costs	£577m	4.4%
TOTAL PRESS	£6,967m	53%
Television	£3,651m	27.8%
Direct mail	£1,540m	11.72%
Outdoor & transport	£500m	3.8%
Radio	£393m	3%
Cinema	£88m	0.7%
TOTAL	£13,139m	100%

Source: The Advertising Association

AD/PR CONTACTS

AC Nielsen.MEAL
7 Harewood Avenue, London NW1 6JB
Fax 0171-393 5088   Tel 0171-393 5070
E-mail: john.purcell@acnielsen.co.uk
AC Nielsen.MEAL has provided the advertising industry's standard measure of above-the-line advertising expenditure since 1968, with electronic data available back to 1986 covering TV, press, radio, cinema and outdoor media.

Advertising Association
Abford House, 15 Wilton Road, London SW1V 1NJ
Fax 0171-931 0376   Tel 0171-828 2771
E-mail: aa@adassoc.org.uk
Website: http://www.adassoc.org.uk
The remit of the AA is to promote and protect the rights, responsibilities, and role of advertising. It is also committed to upholding the freedom to advertise in the UK and to uphold standards and principles of self-regulation. It povides and publishes information, research and statistics on the advertising business.

Advertising Film & Videotape Producers Assoc.
26 Noel Street, London W1V 3RD
Fax 0171-434 9002   Tel 0171-434 2651
TV commercials' production companies trade body.

Advertising Standards Authority
2 Torrington Place, London WC1E 7HW
Fax 0171-631 3051   Tel 0171-580 5555
Promotes and enforces high standards in all non-broadcast ads. It ensures that everyone who commissions, prepares and publishes advertisements observes the British Codes of Advertising and Sales Promotion by making them legal, decent, honest and truthful. The Authority is financed by a levy on advertising space.

British Independent Television Enterprises
TV Centre, Upper Ground, London SE1 9LT
Fax 0171-261 8162   Tel 0171-737 8603
Sells programmes worldwide for Granada, LWT and Yorkshire.
Broadcast Advertising Clearance Centre
200 Grays Inn Road, London WC1X 8HF
Fax 0171-843 8154   Tel 0171-843 8265
Ensures that TV commercials comply with ITC codes on behalf of the ITV and satellite companies.
Direct Marketing Association
1 Oxendon Street, London SW1Y 4EE
Fax 0171-321 0191   Tel 0171-321 2525
Website: http://www.dma.org.uk
The trade association for direct marketers, carrying out lobbying, setting standards, running many events and publishing leaflets, members' directory and code of practice.
History of Advertising Trust
Hat House, 12 Raveningham Centre, Raveningham, Norwich, Norfolk NR14 6NU
Fax 01508-548478   Tel 01508-548623
Website: http://www.lib.uea.ac.uk/HAT/
An archive of advertising material from the beginning of the nineteenth century to the present day. The collection contains over one million items.
Incorporated Society of British Advertisers
44 Hertford Street, London W1Y 8AE
Fax 0171-629 5355   Tel 0171-499 7502
Website: http://www.isba.org.uk
Association representing major advertisers' interests across the industry on all marketing communication issues.
Institute of Practitioners in Advertising
44 Belgrave Square, London SW1X 8QS
Fax 0171-245 9904   Tel 0171-201 8211
E-mail: tessa@ipa.co.uk
Website: http://www.ipa.co.uk
Trade and professional body for advertising agencies in the UK.
Institute of Public Relations
15 Northburgh Street, London EC1V 0PR
Fax 0171-490 0588   Tel 0171-253 5151
E-mail: info@ipr1.demon.co.uk
Website: http://www.ipr.press.net
The main professional association for all working in PR.
Market Research Society
15 Northburgh Street, London EC1V 0AH
Fax 0171-490 0608   Tel 0171-490 4911
E-mail: mrs@dial.pipex.com
Website: http://www.marketresearch.org.uk
Publishes a monthly magazine called the Journal of Market Research Society and runs trainingcourses and seminars, and holds an annual conference every March.

National Newspapers Mail Order Protection Scheme (MOPS)
16 Tooks Court, London EC4A 1LB
Fax 0171-404 0106   Tel 0171-405 6806
Reimburses readers of member newspapers who lose money when approved mail order advertisers enter liquidation or bankruptcy, or cease to trade.
Public Relations Consultants' Association
Willow House, Willow Place, London SW1P 1JH
Fax 0171-828 9797   Tel 0171-233 6026
Website: http://www.prca.org.uk
Radio Advertising Bureau
77 Shaftesbury Avenue, London W1V 7AD
Fax 0171-306 2505   Tel 0171 306 2500
E-mail: rab@rab.co.uk
Website: http://www.rab.co.uk
Marketing company set up by the commercial radio industry to provide advice and planning services to advertisers and advertising agencies.
Radio Advertising Clearance Centre
46 Westbourne Grove, London W2 5SH
Fax 0171-229 0352   Tel 0171-727 2646
E-mail: adclear@racc.co.uk
Clears radio advertisement scripts for commercial radio and ensures compliance with the Radio Authority's Advertising Code.

AD/PR MAGAZINES

Campaign
174 Hammersmith Road, London W6 7JP
Fax 0171-413 4507   Tel 0171-413 4036
Website: http://www.campaignlive.com
Publisher: Haymarket.
£2. Leading weekly news magazine for the advertising industry.
Creative Review
50 Poland Street, London W1V 4AX
Fax 0171-970 4498   Tel 0171-439 4222
Publisher: Centaur Communications.
Monthly looking at the best in advertising and design.
Marketing
174 Hammersmith Road, London W6 7JP
Fax 0171-413 4504   Tel 0181-943 5000
E-mail: editor@marketing.haynet.com
Website: http://www.marketing.haynet.com
Publisher: Haymarket Business Publications
£1.90. The weekly business newspaper for marketing.
Media International
The Quadrant, Sutton, Surrey SM2 5AS.
Fax 0181-652 8961   Tel 0181-652 4943
E-mail: peny.wilson@rbp.co.uk
Publisher: Reed Business Publishing.
Monthly media and marketing magazine.

Media & Marketing Europe
33-39 Bowling Green Lane, London EC1R 0DA
Fax 0171-505 8320   Tel 0171-505 8312
Publisher: Emap Media.
E-mail traceyt@media-emap.co.uk
£5.00. Monthly mag aimed at advertising and
marketing execs.

Media Week
Quantum House, 19 Scarbrook Road, Croydon CR9
1LX
Fax 0181-565 4394   Tel 0181-565 4200
Publisher: Quantum
Weekly news magazine linking media and advertising .

PR Week
174 Hammersmith Road, London W6 7JP
Fax 0171-413 4509   Tel 0171-413 4429
E-mail: prweek@sol.co.uk
Publisher: Haymarket.
£1.70. The weekly news magazine for the PR industry.

AD/PR YEARBOOKS & GUIDES

Advertisers Annual/Blue Book
Harlequin House, 7 High Street, Teddington,
Middlesex TW11 8EL
Fax 0181-977 1133   Tel 01342-326972
E-mail: hollis-pr.co.uk
Publisher: Hollis Directories
Contact: Mr Hollis
£185. An ad directory from same stable as Willings
Press Guide. Covers: Agencies/advertisers; UK media;
Overseas media.

Benn's Media
Riverbank House, Angel Lane Tonbridge, Kent TN9
1SE
01732-367301   Tel 01732-362666
Publisher: Benn Business Information Services
Contact: Sarah Creech
3 vols £297, 2 vols £266, 1 vol £133
Benn's has the most comprehensive listings and is the
most commonly stocked in public libraries. Its three
volumes, cover the UK, Europe and the rest of the
world. Established 1846.

Brad (British Rate & Data)
33-39 Bowling Green Lane, London EC1R 0DA
Fax 0171-505 8293   Tel 0171-505 8246
E-mail: dougm@media.emap.co.uk
Publisher: Emap Media
Contact: Doug Marshall
BRAD contains over 11,000 entries, covering all forms
of media. BRAD £475 2 vols, £250 1 vol. Also
published: Agencies and Advertisers, £295
subscription, £125 single; Direct Marketing, £99;for a
print out or CD, or £140 for both.

Editors
9-10 Great Sutton Street, London EC1V 0BX
Fax 0171-251 3738   Tel 0171-251 9000
Publisher: PR Newslink
Contact: James Scott
6 volumes for £470 pa.subscription
Directory of media contacts for the PR industry.

Hollis Press & PR Annual
Harlequin House, 7 High Street, Teddington,
Middlesex TW11 8EL
Fax 0181-977 1133   Tel 01342-326972
E-mail: hollis-pr.co.uk
Publisher: Hollis Directories
Contact: Sarah Hughes
£82.50.Contacts throughout industry plus voluntary
organisations, PR consultancies and major media titles.

Institute of Public Relations Handbook
120 Pentonville Road, London N1 9JN
Fax 0171-837 6348   Tel 0171-278 0433
E-mail: kpinfo@kogan-page.co.uk
Publisher: Kogan Page
Contact: Don Edwards
£135. List of over 5,000 IPR members, plus other
information and articles.

Media Pocket Book
Farm Road, Henley on Thames, Oxfordshire RG9 1EJ
Fax 01491-571188   Tel 01491-574671
Publisher: Advertising Association
£24, each May. Key facts and figures on the media and
advertising, from newspaper circulations to TV
ownership. Other titles in this series, are the Marketing,
Retail and Lifestyle Pocket Books.

PR Planner
Hale House, 290-296 Green Lanes, London N13 5TP
Fax 0181-886 0703   Tel 0181-882 0155
Publisher: Romeike Group
Loose-leaf guide to contacts in all media. The UK
edition is updated monthly and costs £315 pa. The Euro
edition is updated every other month and costs £350 pa

UK Media Yearbook
63-65 Bishops Bridge Road, London W2 1LA
Fax 0171-706 2650   Tel 0171-224 8500
Publisher: Zenith Media
£225. An analysis, for advertisers, of media data.

World Advertising Trends
Farm Road, Henley on Thames, Oxfordshire RG9 1EJ
Fax 01491-571188   Tel 01491-574671
Publisher: Advertising Association
Contact: Toby Howard
£115. Statistical analysis of ad spends from 57 countries.

MEDIA AGENCIES

Top twenty media agencies by billings

1 Zenith Media
2 TMD Carat
3 Mediavest (London)
4 BMP Optimum
5 Mediapolis
6 Universal McCann
7 Initiative
8 New PHD
9 Mediacom
10 CIA Medianetwork
11 The Media Business Group
12 The Network (now MindShare)
13 Leo Burnett
14 Optimedia UK
15 JWT (now MindShare)
16 BBJ Media Services
17 Western International Media
18 IDK Media
19 Motive
20 Manning Gottlieb Media

The advertising market used to be controlled by the advertising agencies, but has since been broken down into divisions. The media agency emerged to specialise in buying advertising space leaving the creative side to the advertising agencies.

Media agencies negotiate prices with media owners and buy advertising space on television, press, radio, cinema and outdoor. Last year Initiative Media took over buying on the PSA Peugeot Citroen account which belonged to Mediapolis. This was the largest account to move at £90 million and increased Initiative's billings by 14 per cent. Mediapolis will have a long way to go to replace the loss of the PSA billings.

Some agencies have merged to become stronger in the advertising market. JWT and The Network merged together to form MindShare which means that their combined billings would put them at number three in the top 20.

BBJ Media Services
Orion House, 5 Upper St Martins Lane, London, WC2H 9EA
Fax 0171-497 1177   Tel 0171-379 9000
Clients include Cable and Wireless and Audi.

BMP Optimum
12 Bishops Bridge Road, Paddington, London, W2 6AA
Fax 0171-258 4545   Tel 0171-893 4189
Website: www.bmpddb.com
Formerly known as BMP DDB. Clients include Barclaycard, Boots and Alliance and Leicester.

Carat
Parker Tower, 43-49 Parker Street, London, WC2B 5PS
Fax 0171-430 6155   Tel 171-430 6000
Clients include Cadburys, American Express and Courts.

CIA Medianetwork
1 Paris Garden, London, SE1 8NU
Fax 0171-803 2080   Tel 0171-633 9999
Clients include Odeon, Early Learning Centre and Llyods/TSB.

IDK Media
1 Paris Garden, London, SE1 8NU
Fax 0171-803 2086   Tel 0171-803 2400
Clients include Microsoft, Lego and DHL.

Leo Burnett
The Leo Burnett Building, 60 Sloane Avenue, London, SW3 3XE
Fax 0171-591 9126   Tel 0171-591 9111
Clients include McDonalds and McVities.

Manning Gottlieb Media
Seymour Mews House, Wigmore Street, London, W1H 0AA
Fax 0171-412 0244   Tel 0171-470 5300
Clients include Eurostar, Nike and Virgin Direct.

The Media Business Group
70 North Road, Park Lane, London, W1R 1DE
Fax 0171-499 7279   Tel 0171-408 4400
Clients include Mothercare and Polygram.

Mediacom
1 Livonia Street, London, W1V 3PG
                           Tel   0171-872 9928
Clients include Ben Sherman, BP and Nokia.

Mediapolis
Commonwealth House, 1-19 New Oxford Street, London, WCA 1NQ
Fax 0171-393 2525   Tel 0171-393 9000
Clients include Colgate, Mercedes Benz and Our Price.

Mediavest
123 Buckingham Palace Road, London, SW1W 9DZ
Fax 0171-630 0033   Tel 0171-233 5678

MindShare
40 Strand, London, WC2N 5HZ
Fax 0171-969 4000   Tel 171-969 4040
The product of a merger between JWT and The Network. Clients include Kelloggs, Ford and Nestle Rowntree.

Motive
24-27 Great Pulteney Street, London, W1R 3DB
Fax 0171-437 2401   Tel 0171-453 4444
Clients include Levi Strauss, Golden Wonder and Electrolux.
New PHD
5 North Crescent, Chenies Street, London, WC1E 7PH
Fax 0171-446 7100   Tel 0171-446 0555
Clients include Midland Bank, BT and Toshiba.
Optimedia UK
84-86 Baker Street, London, W1M 1DL
Fax 0171-486 1985   Tel 0171-935 0040
Clients include Renault, British Airways and Mastercard.
Universal McCann
36 Howland Street, London, W1A 1AT
Fax 0171-323 2883   Tel 0171-436 7711
Website: www.mccann.co.uk
Clients include Coca-Cola, Post Office and Black&Decker.
Western International Media
Bowater House, 68-114 Knightsbridge, London, SW1X 7LT
Fax 0171-823 7115   Tel 0171-581 1455
Clients inlcude Vauxhall and Smirnoff.
Zenith Media
63-65 North Wharf Road, London, W2 1LA
Fax 0171-706 4028   Tel 0171-224 8500
Website: www.zenithmedia.co.uk
Clients include BMW, Rover and B&Q.
Zenith is jointly owned by Saatchi & Saatchi and Cordiant Communications. It is the largest buyer of media in the UK and has offices in 25 countries across Europe. Publishes various media guides including UK Media Yearbook, Top 50 European Media Owners, Digital Media and Television in Europe to 2007.

ADVERTISING AGENCIES

Top ten ad agencies

| 1 Abbott Mead Vickers BBDO |
| 2 Ogilvy and Mather |
| 3 Saatchi & Saatchi |
| 4 J Walter Thompson |
| 5 BMP DDB |
| 6 Grey |
| 7 Bates Dorland |
| 8 M&C Saatchi |
| 9 Publicis |
| 10 McCann-Erickson |

Source: The Advertising Association

Abbott Mead Vickers BBDO
191 Old Marylebone Road, London NW1 5DW
                    Tel 0171-402 4100
Clients include: BT, Cellnet, Granada, Kiss FM
BMP DDB
12 Bishop's Bridge Road, London W2 6AA
Fax 0171-402 4871   Tel 0171-258 3979
Grey
215-227 Great Portland Street, London W1N 5HD
                    Tel 0171-636 3399
McCann-Erickson
36 Howland Street, London W1A 1AT
                    Tel 0171-580 6690
Ogilvy and Mather
10 Cabot Sq, Canary Wharf, London E14 4QB
Fax 0171-345 9000   Tel 0171-345 3000
Publicis
82 Baker Street, London W1M 2AE
Fax 0171-487 5351   Tel 0171-935 4426
M&C Saatchi
36 Golden Square, London W1R 4EE
Fax 0171-543 4501   Tel 0171-486 1100
Saatchi and Saatchi
80 Charlotte Street, London W1A 1AQ
Fax 0171-637 8489   Tel 0171-636 5060
J Walter Thompson
40 Berkeley Square, London W1X 6AD
Fax 0171-493 8432   Tel 0171-499 4040

PR AGENCIES

Top ten PR agencies
1 Shandwick
2 Bell Pottinger
3 Hill & Knowlton
4 Countrywide Porter Novelli
5 Dewe Rogerson
6 The Incepta Group
7 Weber PR Worldwide
8 Euro RSCG International Communications
9 Edelman
10 The Grayling Group
Source: PR Week

Bell Pottinger Communications
7 Hertford Street, London W1Y 9LP
Fax 0171-629 1277   Tel 0171-495 4044
Burson-Marsteller
24-28 Bloomsbury Way, London WC1A 2PX
Fax 0171-430 1033   Tel 0171-831 6262
Website: http://www.bm.com
Charles Barker
56 Dean Street, London W1V 6HX
Fax 0171-439 1071   Tel 0171-494 1331
Website: http://www.charles.co.uk
Citigate Communications
26 Finsbury Square, London EC2A 1DS
Fax 0171-282 8010   Tel 0171-282 8000
Website: http://www.citigate.com
Countrywide Porter Novelli
South Bar, Banbury, Oxfordshire OX16 9AD
Fax 01295-224444   Tel 01295-224400
Website: http://ww.countrywidepn.co.uk
Dewe Rogerson Corporate Publications
3 London Wall, London EC2M 5SY
Fax 0171-628 3444   Tel 0171-638 9571
E-mail: gell@dewrog.co.uk
Edelman PR Worldwide
28-29 Haymarket, London SW1Y 4SP
Fax 0171-344 1222   Tel 9171-344 1200
Financial Dynamics
30 Furnival Street, London EC4A 1JE
Fax 0171-831 6038   Tel 0171-831 3113
Hill and Knowlton
5 Theobalds Road, London WC1X 8SH
Fax 0171-413 3111   Tel 0171-413 3000
E-mail: info@hillandknowlton.com
Website: http://www.hillandknowlton.com
Grayling Group
4 Bedford Square, London WC1B 3RA
Fax: 0171-631 0602   Tel: 0171-255 1100
Shandwick Marketing
18 Dering Street, London W1R 9AF
Fax 0171-499 1752   Tel 0171-950 2000
E-mail: gboyd@shandwick.com
Website: http://www.shandwick.co.uk

MEDIA ANALYSTS

Media analysts study media companies on the stock market. We're not sure whether they are bad journalists who write widely-spaced copy for ring bound reports or smart journalists who know where the money is. What's more certain to us is that this book makes free with quotes from media-watchers and those in the listing below have all been quoted somewhere in this book.

Credit Lyonnais Laing
Broadwalk House, 5 Appold Street, London, EC2A 2DA
Fax 0171-214 5274   Tel 0171-588 4000
Media analyst: Nick Ward
CS First Boston
1 Cabot Square, London, E14 4QJ
Fax 0171-888 1600   Tel 0171-516 1616
Media analyst: Vighnesh Padiachy
Goldman Sachs
Peterborough Court, 133 Fleet Street, EC4A 2BB
Tel 0171-774 1000
Media analyst: Guy Lamming
Henderson Crosthwaite
32 St Mary at Hill, London, EC3P 3AJ
Fax 0171-528 0884   Tel 0171-623 9992
Media analyst: Matthew Horsman
Kleinwort Benson
20 Fenchurch Street, London, EC3P 3DB
Fax 0171-623 8000   Tel 0171-623 4069
Media analyst: Michael Hilton
Merrill Lynch
Ropemaker Place, 25 Ropemaker Street, London, EC2Y 9LY
Fax 0171-867 2867   Tel 0171-867 2000
Media analyst: Neil Blackley
Panmure Gordon
New Broad Street House, 35 New Broad Street, London, EC2M 1ND
Fax 0171-920 9305   Tel 0171-638 4010
Media analyst: Lorna Tilbian
Salomon Smith Barney
Victoria Plaza, 111 Buckingham Palace Road, London, SW1W 0SB
Fax 0171-222 7062   Tel 0171-721 2000
Media analyst: Richard Dale
SBC Warburg Dillon Read
Swiss Bank House, 1 High Timber Street, London, EC4V 3SB
Fax 0171-567 8700   Tel 0171-567 8000
Media analyst: Colin Tennant
Schroder
120 Cheapside, London, EC2V 6DS
Fax 0171-658 3950   Tel 0171-658 6000
Media analyst: Patrick Wellington

Media training

A recent survey revealed that half of all students - yes, one in every two - said some kind of job in journalism would be their favoured career. That desire is reflected in the numbers applying for a plethora of courses which have sprung up to meet this demand. A decade ago students of journalism picked from 100 courses whereas there are now more like 1,500. In consequence the number doing journalism and media studies courses has increased from 6,000 in 1990 to nearly 35,000 today. The job market has not expanded in proportion and the National Union of Journalists estimates there are about four times as many accepted at the institutions listed in the next pages as can possibly expect work in anything remotely connected to the media. So, be warned.

To earn a living in print journalism requires no compulsory qualifications and thus journalism is not really a profession. Once you've got started many - perhaps most - editors hire on the basis of hunch and evidence of past work. Formal qualifications don't count for much. The problem is getting started and a vocational postgraduate course - not a media studies first degree - is increasingly the best way to start, particularly in local papers or magazines. Local papers are once again a good place to start a career. Half run their own training departments, as do many magazine companies. The national papers hardly pay lip service to formal training and are more than happy to draw in the most talented recruits from magazines and locals.

Broadcasting demands specific technical skills which are not taught during a normal education. A more coherent and universally recognised training structure, which is coordinated by Skillset, is therefore in place. The best way into broadcasting is via one of the BBC or ITV in-house courses. Competition for places is intense and intensifies when even the best qualified are looking for work in an area where only about 5,000 people make a living as broadcast journalists. The BBC receives 80,000 enquiries a year about broadcasting jobs, and takes on around 2,000 a year at all grades. That said, the increase in channels is creating new jobs.

At the non-university end of the scale are National Vocational Qualifications, the closest the media has come to a start-off educational standard. NVQs are awarded by the RSA Examinations Board in partnership with the Newspapers Qualifications Council for newspapers, the Periodicals Training Council for magazines and Skillset in partnership with the Open University for broadcast journalism. They are open to those without formal qualifications (hence the nickname Not Very Qualified) and, being based on practical work and continual assessment, can be done at the candidate's pace. NVQs come in five levels. In newspaper journalism NVQs are at Level 4 in writing, production and press photography, and Level 3 in graphics journalism; in magazine journalism they are at Level 4 for writing and subbing; in broadcast journalism there is a single Level 4.

Then there are media studies degrees. Some take the line they are valuable because they give systematic study to the way information mutates during the process of mediation. Within a business led by people who graduated - in what they regard as more rigorous liberal arts degrees during the seventies and eighties - "media studies" is a phrase to evoke an automatic sneer. Most journalists over 30 tend to agree with Roger Scruton who said: "Media studies course content is sub-Marxist gobbledegook and courses are taught by talentless individuals who can't get jobs in the media, so they teach instead. There's nothing really to learn except by way of apprenticeship on the job."

Whether trained in some way or not, the iron law of the trade is that you are only as good as your last by-line. The best places for a first by-line are school and university newspapers, or by making a close study of the stories your local paper runs and offering them something similar for nothing. Ditto your favourite magazines. The rule in all cases is that the smaller the publication, the better the chance of a byline. Aspiring journalists will find a degree in any subject is more or less mandatory. After that the ways into employment are many and vague, usually mundane, and always badly paid.

skill|set

91-101 Oxford Street, London W1R 1RA
Tel: 0171 534 5300 Fax: 0171 534 5333
Email: info@skillset.org Website: www.skillset.org

Skillset is the National Training Organisation for Broadcast, Film, Video and Multimedia. Skillset exists to encourage the delivery of informed training provision so that the British broadcast, film, video and multimedia industry's technical, creative and economic achievements are maintained and improved.

Supported by the BBC; Channel 4; Channel 5; ITV Association; Producers Alliance for Cinema & Television; Advertising, Film & Videotape Producers Association, International Visual Communications Association and the Federation of Entertainment Unions, Skillset operates at a strategic level to:

- provide labour market, training and careers information,
- encourage higher levels of investment in training,
- develop and implement occupational standards and vocational qualifications,
- influence national and international education and training policies,
- create greater and equal access to training and career development.

Contact Skillset for more information on training courses, careers information, labour market research into employment trends, NVQ/SVQ and other industry training issues.

TRAINING GUIDES

Skillset Careers Pack
Skillset, free   Tel 0171-534 5300
Website: http://www.skillset.org
The full directory is on the internet.
Media Courses UK 99
BFI, £10.99   Tel 0171-255 1444
Careers in Journalism
NUJ   Tel 0171-278 7916
How to be a Journalist
Newspaper Society   Tel 0171-636 7014
Includes lists of accredited courses.
Media & Multimedia Short Courses
Compiled by Lavinia Orton
BFI, £3   Tel 0171-255 1444
Lights, Camera, Action!
BFI, £9.99   Tel 0171-255 1444
A useful book.
Education, Training and Working in Film, Television and Broadcasting
BKSTS, free   Tel: 0171-242 8400
The Big Official Guide to University and College Entrance
UCAS, £19.95   0171-702 9799
Book and CD Rom
Courses in Radio Training
Commercial Radio Companies Association
      Tel 0171-727 2646
A computer database of radio training opportunities.
The BFI and Skillset Training Database
At Arts Council Regional Arts Boards:
London Film and Video   0171-383 7755
South East Arts Board   01892-515210
Southern Arts Board   01962-855099
South West Arts Board   01392-218188
Eastern Arts Board   01223-215355
East Midlands Arts Board
      01509-218292
Virgin 1999 Alternative Guide to British Universities
Virgin, £19.95   01483 204457

RECOMMENDED READING

McNae's Essential Law for Journalists
Tom Welsh and Walter Greenwood, Butterworth
Journalists' legal bible

Modern Newspaper Practice
FW Hodgson, Focal Press
Everything from style to page planning to freedom of the press

News Journalism
Nick Varley, Fourth Estate
One of a range of career guides and a good solid intro.

See also page III for a list of Waterstone's best-selling books about the media

TRAINING CONTACTS

BBC Centre for Broadcast Skills Training
Wood Norton, Evesham, Worcestershire WR11 4TB
Fax 01386-420145   Tel 01386-420216
E-mail: cbst.admin@bbc.co.uk
Website: http://www.bbc.co.uk/woodnorton
CBST offers a range of residential courses in television and radio operations and engineering, as well as satellite and transmitter training. Courses range from foundation through to short course updates, though courses are mainly for those already in the industry.
BBC Training
379 Euston Road, Grafton House, London NW1 3AU
Fax 0171-935 6382   Tel 0171-765 0005
E-mail: training@bbc.co.uk
BBC Training is the umbrella unit set up to provide information on all of the training offered by the BBC.
British Kinematograph Sound and Television Society
Victoria House, Vernon Place, London WC1B 4DA
Fax 0171-405 3560   Tel 0171-242 8400
E-mail: movimage@bksts.demon.co.uk
The BKSTS publishes a regularly updated collection of documents called Education, Training and Working in Film, Television and Broadcasting. It accredits courses and runs its own courses.
British Film Institute
21 Stephen Street, London W1P 2LN
Fax: 0171-436 7950   Tel 0171-255 1444
Website: http://www.bfi.org.uk
The BFI has an active involvement in film and TV training and runs an education section which publishes the career books listed opposite.
British Universities Film & Video Council
77 Well Street, London W1P 3RE
Fax 0171-393 1555   Tel 0171-393 1500
E-mail bufvc@open.ac.uk
Website: http://www.bufvc.ac.uk
The Council promotes the study, production and use of TV film and related media in higher education. It runs an information service, has editing facilities, organises conferences and courses and provides research facilities. It publishes the Researcher's Guide to British Film and TV Collections, the Researcher's Guide to British Newsreels. Film and Television Collections in Europe: The MAP-TV Guide and the BUFVC magazine Viewfinder. Runs the Newsreel Project, compiling a database of all UK newsreel stories, 1910-1979.
Broadcast Journalism Training Council
39 Westbourne Gardens, London W2 5NR
Fax 0171-727 9522   Tel 0171-727 9522
E-mail: 100771.205@compuserve.com
Website: http://www.BJTC.org.uk
The BJTC is a registered charity and a company limited by guarantee, whose subscribers come from all sides of the radio and TV industry, the NUJ and colleges which offer courses in broadcast journalism. Its role is to advise and cooperate with the colleges and universities to maintain standards. The Council has worked on the NVQs and is represented on Skillset.

Broadcasting, Entertainment, Cinematograph and Theatre Union (BECTU)
111 Wardour Street, London W1V 4AY
Fax 0171-437 8258   Tel 0171-437 8506
E-mail: bectu@geo2.poptel.org.uk
Website: http://www.bectu.org.uk
BECTU is the main trade union for workers in broadcasting, film, theatre and other sectors of the entertainment and media industry. It offers a Student Link-up Scheme to arts and media students, and a special introductory membership rate to course graduates. It can give some careers advice (s.a.e. please), but works with Skillset, regional training consortia and FT2 in promoting access, equality of opportunity, quality training, trainees' safety and optimum employment prospects once training has ended. The union has regional offices in Glasgow, Cardiff, Manchester and Birmingham, and publishes a journal. Stage, Screen & Radio, ten times a year.

Cyfle
Gronant, Penrallt Isaf, Caernarfon, Gwynedd LL55 1NW
Fax 01286-678831   Tel 01286-671000
Website: http://www.cyfle-cyf.demon.co.uk
Training for the Welsh film and TV industry.

Educational Television and Media Association
37 Monkgate, York, YO31 7PB
Fax 01904-639212   Tel 01904-639212
E-mail Josie.key@etma.u-net.com
Brings together organisations and individuals using TV and other media for education and training. Holds annual conference and video competition. Publishes newsletter and academic-oriented Journal of Educational Media. New members welcome.

Film Education
27-31 Charing Cross Road, London WC2H 0AU
Fax 0171-839 5052   Tel 0171-976 2291
E-mail: film.ed@campus.bt.com
Film Education is a registered charity supported by the UK film industry. Its aims are to develop the use of film in the school curriculum and to facilitate the use of cinemas by schools. To this end it publishes a variety of free teaching materials, produces educational television programmes, organises screenings and runs a range of workshops, events and In Service Training courses.

FT2 - Film and Television Freelance Training
9 Warwick Street, London W1R 5RA
Fax 0171-287 9899   Tel 0171-734 5141
Website: http://www.ft2.co.uk
FT2 provides new entrant training in the junior construction, production and technical grades for the freelance sector of the film and television industry. It is funded by the Skillset Freelance Training Fund, European Social fund and C4 and runs three projects:
FT2 **New Entrant Technical Training** A two year course for young people to become technical assistants.
FT2 **Setcrafts Apprenticeship Training Scheme** For young people to enter the freelance features and commercials as carpenters, plasterers and set painters.
FT2 **Freelance Access to Skillset NVQ Assessment** To enable existing freelances to undertake subsidised assessments against the Skillset NVQs.

First Film Foundation
9 Bourlet Close,London W1P 7PJ
Fax 0171-580 2116   Tel 0171-580 2111
E-mail: info@firstfilm.demon.co.uk
A charity that works with first-time filmmakers in TV and feature film prodcution.

Guild of Editors
Bloomsbury House, 74-77 Great Russell Street, London WC1B 3DA
Fax 0171-637 2748   Tel 0171-436 2445
The Guild of Editors is the collective voice of more than three hundred newspaper editors, and their counterparts in broadcasting and the electronic media, on editorial freedom, independence standards and training.

Institute of Communications Studies
University of Leeds, West Yorkshire LS2 9JT
Fax 0113-233 5808   Tel 0113-233 5800
E-mail: 1csb@leeds.ac.uk
Britain's oldest media research body, originally the Centre for Television Research, looking mainly at the role of TV in political communications, now also a teaching department. Three year BA in Broadcasting Studies, four year Bachelor of Broadcasting and three year BA in Broadcast Journalism degree schemes in co-operation with the BBC and a three year broadly based BA in Communications.

National Association for Higher Education in the Moving Image (NAHEMI)
Yossi Bal, NAHEMI, Chair, Sir John Cass Department of Art, c/o London Guildhall University, Central House, 59-63 Whitechapel High Street, London E1 7PF
Tel 0171-320 1000 x 1956
Forum for debate on all aspects of film, video and TV education. Fosters links with industry, the professions and government. Represents all courses offering a major practical study in film, video or TV at higher education level.

National Council for the Training of Journalists
Latton Bush Centre, Southern Way, Harlow, Essex CM18 7BL
Fax 01279-438008   Tel 01279-430009
E-mail: NCTJ@itecharlow.co.uk
Website: http://www.itecharlow.co.uk/nctj/
The NCTJ is a charity which runs the most widely accepted independent training schemes for print journalists. It accredits courses at universities and colleges and should be the first point of contact for those who need to know more of the pre-entry, block and day release options for formal training. The NCTJ has three standard textbooks - Essential Law for Journalists, published by Butterworths, Essential Local Government for Journalists, and Essential Central Government for Journalists published by LGC Communications - and provides a mail order service of recommended books on many aspects of journalism. The Council's short course department has provided over 500 open courses for more than 7,000 journalists.

On Monday, Philip Braund set up a sting for The Cook Report. On Tuesday, he was training for PMA.

Ex-Daily Mirror news editor Philip Braund is typical of our trainers. We have 100 like him on our books. Whatever your media needs — from PR to editorial, from production to DTP, from the Internet to publishing management — we've got an expert on call. And it will be someone who's doing it now, rather than someone who's retired and vaguely remembers how it used to be.

It's not just the quality of trainers that explains why PMA Training is the largest editorial skills company in Europe — there are many other factors. We don't lecture you: we work with you. At our training suite near London's Barbican, we run personalised workshops with no more than six on a course. We use *your* material and address *your* needs with training that's sharp and intensive.

Talk to us or better still, come on one of our courses. (PMA is run by a working journalist, so we can talk your language.) And if you've got a scandal that needs the Cook treatment, we can probably put you in touch with the right person there too.

Tel: 0171 490 7280.
Email: admin@pma-group.com
Web: www.pma-group.co.uk

National Union of Journalists
Acorn House, 314-320 Grays Inn Road, London
WC1X 8DP
Fax 0171-837 8143   Tel 0171-278 7916
The NUJ's booklet Careers in Journalism is
recommended.
NCTBJ
see Broadcast Journalism Training Council
Newspaper Society
Bloomsbury House, 74-77 Great Russell Street,
London WC1B 3DA
Fax 0171-631 5119   Tel 0171-636 7014
E-ail: ns@newspapersoc.org.uk
The Society takes a broad interest in local newspaper
training acting as industry training organisation and
lead body. Although the Society leaves course
accreditation to the NCTJ, it is a prime source of
information on all aspects of newspaper training and its
leaflet Training to be a Journalist, is recommended.
Periodicals Training Council
55/56 Queen's House, Lincoln's Inn Fields, London
WC2A 3LJ
Fax 0171-404 4167   Tel 0171-404 4168
E-mail: training@ppa.co.uk
The PTC is the training arm of the Periodical
Publishers Association. It aims to enhance the
performance of the UK magazine industry and act as a
focus for training. It has recently been active in setting
up magazine NVQs and has accredited the vocational
courses in periodical journalism listed below. The
Council publishes PPA Training Programme,which has
full listings of all the courses run throughout the year at
the PPA; also A Career in Magazines, which is available
free.
RSA Examinations Board
Progress House, Westwood Way, Coventry CV4 8HS
Fax 01203-468080   Tel 01203-470033
Website: http://www.rsa.co.uk
The NVQ awarding body.
Scottish Daily Newspaper Society
48 Palmerston Place, Edinburgh EH12 5DE
Fax 0131-220 4344   Tel 0131-220 4353
E-mail: info@spef.org.uk
The major training co-ordinator in Scotland.
Scottish Newspaper Publishers Association
48 Palmerston Place, Edinburgh EH12 5DE
Fax 0131-220 4344   Tel 0131-220 4353
E-mail: info@spef.org.uk
Contact point for SVQ, the Scottish version of NVQs.
WAVES
4 Wild Court, London WC2B 4AU
Fax 0171-242 2765   Tel 0171-430 1076
Runs practical and theoretical training courses for
women in film, broadcast video and new digital media.

Skillset
91-10 Oxford Street, London W1R 1RA
Fax 0171-534 5333   Tel 0171-534 5300
E-mail: info@skillset.org
Website: http://www.skillset.org
The National Training Organisation for broadcast, film,
video and multi media. Recognised by Government as
the voice of the industry in training. Operates at a
strategic level to improve training and education policy
and provision. Publishes a careers pack, plus
employment and labour market trends, professional
standards and qualifications and much more. Set up in
1993, Skillset is managed and funded by Advertising
Film and Videotape Producers Association (AFVPA),
BBC, Channel 4, Channel 5, the Federation of
Entertainment Unions (FEU), International Visual
Communications Association (IVCA), ITVA and the
Producers Alliance for Film and Television (PACT).
Skillset Midlands:
Midlands Media Training Consortium
Studio 11, the Nottingham Fashion Centre,
Huntingdon Street, Nottingham NG1 3LF
Fax 0115-993 0151 Tel 0115-993 0151
Website: http://www.training@mmtc.co.uk
The Big Peg, 120 Vyse Street, The Jewellery
Quarter, Birmingham B18 6NF
Fax 0121-248 1616 Tel 0121-248 1515
Skillset North East:
Broadcasting Centre, Barrack Road, Newcastle U
Tyne NE99 2NE
Fax 0191-232 8871 Tel 0191-232 5484
E-mail: marion-mediaskill@watermans.net
Skillset North Wes
Campus Manor, Childwall Abbey Road,Liverpool
L16 0JP
Fax 0151-722 6839 Tel 0151-722 9122
Skillset Northern Ireland:
Northern Ireland Film Commission
21 Ormeau Avenue, Belfast BT2 8HD
Fax 01232-239918 Tel 01232-232444
Scottish Screen Training:
74 Victoria Crescent Road, Glasgow G12 9JN
Fax 0141-302 1715 Tel 0141-302 1761
E-mail: training@scottishscreen.demon.co.uk
Website: http://www.scottishscreen.demon.co.uk
Skillset South West:
59 Prince Street, Bristol BS1 4QH
Fax 0117-925 3511 Tel 0117-925 4011
Skillset Wales
Broadcast Training Wales, Gronant, Penrallt
Isaf, Caernarfon, Gwynedd LL55 1NW
Fax 01286-678890 Tel 01286-671000
or: Mount Stuart Square, Cardiff CF1 6EE
Fax 01222-463344 Tel 01222-465533
E-mail: cyfle@cyfle-cyf.demon.co.uk
Website: http://www.cyfle-cyf.emon.co.uk
Skillset Yorkshire
Yorkshire Media Training Consortium, Unit 72,
Carlisle Business Centre, 60 Carlisle Road,
Bradford BD8 9BD
Fax 01274-772257 Tel 01274-223216
E-mail: ymtc@globalnet.co.uk

PRESS COURSES

Newspaper training courses are accredited by the National Council for Training of Journalists, and magazine courses are accredited by the PPA's training wing, the Periodical Training Council. Both these trade bodies support NVQs.

Bell College of Technology
Almada Street, Hamilton, Lanarkshire ML3 0JB
Fax 01698-282131   Tel 01698-283100
E-mail: enquiries@bell.ac.uk
Website: http://www.bell.ac.uk
NCTJ accredited two year Higher National Diploma.

Bournemouth University
Talbot Campus, Poole, Dorset BH12 5BB
Fax 01202-595099   Tel 01202-595431
E-mail: emcallis@bournemouth.ac.uk
Website: http://www.bournemouth.ac.uk
NCTJ accredited degree course & PTC.

Brighton College of Technology
Pelham Street, Brighton BN1 4FA
Fax 01273-667703   Tel 01273-667788
E-mail: info@bricoltech.ac.uk
Website: http://www.bricoltech.ac.uk
NCTJ accredited

Centre for Journalism Studies
see University of Wales

City University
Department of Journalism, Northampton Square, London EC1V 0HB
Fax 0171-477 8594   Tel 0171-477 8221
E-mail: journalism@city.ac.uk
Web: http://www.city.ac.uk/journalism
NCTJ accredited postgraduate diploma in Newspaper Journalism and a PTC postgraduate diploma in Periodical Journalism. It also offers a Masters in Electronic Publishing.

Cornwall College
Centre for Arts, Media & Social Sciences, Redruth, Cornwall TR15 3RD
Fax 01209-718802   Tel 01209 712911
E-mail: enqiries@cornwall.ac.uk
BJTC-accredited postgraduate diploma in broadcast journalism.

Darlington College of Technology
Cleveland Avenue, Darlington, Co. Durham DL3 7BB
Fax 01325-503000   Tel 01325-503050
Website: http://www.darlington.ac.uk
NCTJ accredited pre-entry academic year, pre-entry calendar year and block release courses.

De Montfort University
The Gateway, Leicester LE1 9BH
Fax 0116-255 0307   Tel 0116-255 1551
E-mail: http://www.dmu.ac.uk
One-year postgraduate Diploma in Journalism, NCTJ accredited.

Gloucestershire College of Arts & Technology
Brunswick Campus, Brunswick Road, Gloucester GL1 1HU
Fax 01452-426607   Tel 01452-426600
NCTJ accredited pre-entry academic year course.

Greenhill College
Lowlands Road, Harrow, Middlesex HA1 3AQ
Fax 0181-423 5183   Tel 0181-869 8600
E-mail: enquiries@harrow.greenhill.ac.uk
NCTJ accredited college for pre-entry print journalism. Full time one year course.

Gwent Tertiary College
Pontypool Centre, Blaendare Road, Pontypool, Gwent NP4 5YE
Fax 01495-333110   Tel 01495-333100
Website: http://www.gwent-tertiary.ac.uk
BTEC Media, two years, full time. HND/HNC Graphic Design, a range of full and part time courses.

Harlow College
Velizy Avenue, Town Centre, Harlow, Essex CM20 3LH
Fax 01279-868260   Tel 01279-868000
NCTJ accredited pre-entry academic year and 20 week postgraduate programmes. Two year HND programme.

Highbury College, Portsmouth
School of Media & Journalism, Dovercourt Road, Cosham, Portsmouth, Hants PO6 2SA
Fax 01705-378382   Tel 01705-283287
E-mail: glenne.martin@highbury.ac.uk
NCTJ and PTC accredited courses in newspaper journalism (20 weeks) and magazine journalism.

Journalism Training Centre
Unit G, Mill Gren Business Park, Mill Green Road, Mitcham, Surrey CR4 4HT
Fax 0181-640 6266   Tel 0181-640 3696
Level IV NVQ foundation skills cetificate in journalism. PTC accredited. NUJ approved. 3 courses per year, duration 14 weeks.

Lambeth College
Vauxhall Centre, Belmore Street, Wandsworth, London SW8 2JY
Fax 0171-501 5490   Tel 0171-501 5424
Website: http://www.lambethcollege.ac.uk
NCTJ accredited pre-entry academic year course. One year post-graduate. Also run Access to Journalism course and Print Journalism course.

Leeds Trinity and All Saints College
Brownberrie Lane, University of Leeds, Leeds LS18 5HD
Fax 01132-837200   Tel 01132-837100
Website: http://www.tasc.ac.uk
NCTJ approved 10 month PG diploma in print journalism.

London College of Fashion
20 John Princes Street, London W1M 0BJ
Fax 0171-514 7484   Tel 0171-514 7400
Website: http://www.linst.ac.uk/li/seup.htm
PTC accredited fashion promotion degee with journalism, public relations and broadcast options.

London College of Printing
School of Media,10 Back Hill, Clerkenwell, London
EC1 5EN
Fax 0171-514 6848   Tel 0171-514 6500
E-mail: t.bodenham@lcpdlt.linst.ac.uk
PTC accredited BA and HND journalism courses and
media courses.

Napier University
Department of Print Media, Publishing and
Communications. Craighouse Campus, Craighouse
Road, Edinburgh EH10 5LG
                        Tel 0131-455 6150
E-mail: d.brand@napier.ac.uk
Degree and Masters programmes.

PMA Training
PMA House, Free Church Passage, St Ives,
Cambridgeshire PE17 4AY
Fax 01480-496022   Tel 01480-300653
E-mail: admin@pma-group.com
Website: http://www.pma-group.co.uk
PMA training was founded in 1980. It maintains close
links with the Periodicals Training Council and now
supplies most of the editorial training for the industry.
PMA is based in Clerkenwell, central London. PMA is
officially approved by the PTC, the Newspaper Society
and the BACB. The five training rooms are registered as
an NVQ assessment centre, and workshops are geared
to NVQs. There are over 500 workshops per year
covering editorial, internet, desktop publishing, law,
design, new technology, marketing, PR, production,
advertising, direct mail, radio and publishing
management. PMA also runs a nine week post
graduate course in magazine journalism every summer.

School of Communication
see University of Westminster

Sheffield College
Norton Centre, Dyche Lane, Sheffield S8 8BR
Fax 0114-2602 301   Tel 0114-2602 600
NCTJ accredited block release, pre-entry academic year
and January-December courses. 18 week "fast-track"
graduate course. Also photojournalism and press
photography.

South East Essex College
Carnarvon Road, Southend, Essex SS2 6LS
                        Tel 01702-220400
E-mail: learning@se-essex-college.ac.uk
BSc (hons) media production and technology - 3 years.
BSc (hons) multimedia technology - 3 years.
BTEC/GNVQ broadcast media -2 years; print media.2
years.

Strathclyde University
Livingstone Tower, 26 Richmond Street, Glasgow G1
1XH   ·
Fax 0141-552 3493   Tel 0141-553 4166
E-mail: gordon.j.smith@strath.ac.uk
NCTJ accredited one year postgradute course.

Surrey Institute of Art and Design
Falkner Road, Farnham, Surrey GU9 7DS
Fax 01252 733869   Tel 01252-722441
E-mail: registry@surrart.ac.uk
Website: http://www.surrart.ac.uk
BECTU and BKSTS accredited degrees in film and
video, media studies and in animation. BJTC
recognised first degree with radio and print options.
There is a BA (Hons) in journalism.

Sutton Coldfield College
Lichfield Road, Sutton Coldfield, B74 2NW
Fax 0121-355 0799   Tel 0121-355 5671
E-mail: SCSE@sutcol.ac.uk
NCTJ accredited.

University of Central Lancashire
Department of Journalism, Preston PR1 2HE
Fax 01772-892907   Tel 01772-893730
E-mail: n.atkinson@uclan.ac.uk
NCTJ and BJTC accredited courses: undergraduate BA
(Hons) course, multi-media two years,print, broadcast
or dissertation final year. New media option for '99.
Separate one year postgraduate diploma courses in
newspaper and broadcast journalism. New media
postgraduate diploma course in '99. IPR recognised
undergraduate BA (Hons) course in public relations.
Joint honours undergraduate BA (Hons) courses in
journalism and public relations.

University of Sheffield
171 Northumberland Road, Sheffield S10 2TZ
Fax 0114-266 8918   Tel 0114-222 2500
E-mail: jnlstudies@sheffield.ac.uk
NCTJ accredited.

University of Wales
School of Journalism, Media and Cultural Studies,
Centre for Journalism Studies, Bute Building, King
Edward V11 Avenue, Cardiff CF1 3NB
Fax 01222-238832   Tel 01222-874786
E-mail: PalserES@Cardiff.ac.uk
Website: http://www.cf.ac.uk/uwcc/jomec/jomec.html
NCTJ recognised postgraduate diploma in newspaper
journalism; BJTC recognised course in broadcast (bi-
media) journalism; PTC recognised course in magazine
journalism, IPR recognised course in public and media
relations. Course in photojournalism. Euro MA course.

University of Westminster
School of Communication, Harrow Campus, Watford
Road, Northwick Park, Harrow HA1 3TP
Fax 0171-911 5921   Tel 0171-911 5000
E-mail: hrw12@wmin.ac.uk
PTC accredited postgraduate diploma in periodical
journalism for ethnic minorities. Part-time MA in
Journalism Studies.

Warrington Collegiate Institute
Padgate Campus, Warrington WA2 0DB
Fax 01925-816077   Tel 01925-814343
E-mail: wci@warr.ac.uk
NCTJ accredited.

Wulfrun College
Paget Road, Wolverhampton WV6 0DU
Fax 01902-423070   Tel 01902-317700
Day-release/pre-entry. NCTJ, C &G and BTEC media
courses.

GROUP TRAINING (PRESS)

These are the in-house courses run by the local newspaper companies:

The Editorial Centre
Hanover House, Marine Court, St Leonards on Sea, East Sussex TN38 0DX
Fax 01424-445547   Tel 01424-435991
E-mail:editorial_centre@mistral.co.uk
Offers a wide range of journalism courses including pre-entry NVQ, starting 3 times a year.
Johnston Training Centre
Upper Mounts, Northampton NN1 3HR
Fax 01604-250186   Tel 01604-231528
Midland News Association
Rock House, Old Hill, Tettenhall Wolverhampton, West Midlands WV6 8QB
Fax 01902-759478   Tel 01902-742126
NCTJ accredited. Takes a few non-company trainees.
Trinity Editorial Training Centre
Groat Market, Newcastle upon Tyne NE1 1EO
Fax 0191-232 1724   Tel 0191-232 7500
Trinity International Holdings
Kingsfield Court, Chester Business Park, Chester, CH4 9RE
Fax 01244-687100   Tel 01244-350555
E-mail: trinity@trinity.plc.uk
United Provinicial Newspapers
Wellington Street, Leeds, West Yorks LS1 1RF
Fax 0113-244 3430   Tel 0113-243 2701
E-mai: up.newsdesk@upn.co.uk
Accredited courses: TV/radio

TV/RADIO COURSES

Bell College of Technology
Almade Street, Hamilton, Lanarkshire ML3 0JB
Fax 01698-282131   Tel 01698-283100
E-mail: enquiries@bell.ac.uk
Website: http://www.bell.ac.uk
BJTC recognised postgrad diploma in radio journalism.
Bournemouth & Poole College of Art & Design
Wallisdown, Poole, Dorset BH12 5HH
Fax 01202-537729   Tel 01202-538204/533011
E-mail: general@bmth-poole.ac.uk
BKSTS accredited HND in film and TV. BTEC HND course in Design (Film & TV Production) due to become a BA (Hons) Film & Animation course in October 1998.
Bournemouth University
Fern Barrow, Poole, Dorset BH12 5BB
Fax 01202-595099   Tel 01202-524111
E-mail: emcallis@bournemouth.ac.uk
Website: http://www.bournemouth.ac.uk
Degrees in Media Production, TV & Video Production. BJTC, NCTJ & PTC endorsed Multi-media journalism degree. Postgrad in TV and Video Production.
Centre for Journalism Studies
see University of Wales
City University
Department of Journalism, Northampton Square, London EC1V 0HB
Fax 0171-477 8594   Tel 0171-477 8221
E-mail: journalism@city.ac.uk
Web: http://www.city.ac.uk/journalism
BJTC postgrad diploma in broadcast journalism.
Falmouth College of Arts
Woodlane, Falmouth, Cornwall TR11 4RA
Fax 01326-211077   Tel 01326-211077
E-mail: reception@falmouth.ac.uk
BJTC recognised courses. Postgraduate diploma in broadcast journalism. BA Hons in Broadcasting Studies and Journalism Studies. Plus English with media studies and a postgrad diploma in professional writing.
Gwent Tertiary College
Blaendare Road, Pontypool, Gwent NP4 5YE
Fax 01495-333110   Tel 01495-333100
Website: http://www.gwent-tertiary.ac.uk
BTEC Media, two years, full time. Emphasis on digital and linear TV/video. HND/HNC Graphic Design, a range of full and part time courses.
Highbury College, Portsmouth
School of Media & Journalism, Dovercourt Road, Cosham, Portsmouth, Hants PO6 2SA
Fax 01705-378382   Tel 01705-283287
E-mail: glenne.martin@highbury.ac.uk
BJTC recognised post-graduate diploma in broadcast journalism.
Leeds Trinity and All Saints College
University of Leeds, Leeds LS18 5HD
Fax 01132-837200   Tel 01132-837100
Website: http://www.tasc.ac.uk
BJTC recognised postgraduate diploma in bi-media journalism, radio/television.

London College of Printing
10 Back Hill. Clerkenwell, London EC1R 5EN
Fax 0171-514 6848   Tel 0171-514 6500
E-mail: t.bodenham@lcpdt.linst.ac.uk
BJTC postgrad diploma in radio journalism.
London International Film School
24 Shelton Street, London WC2H 9HP
Fax 0171-497 3718   Tel 0171-836 9642
National Film and Television School
Beaconsfield Studios, Bucks HP9 1LG
Fax 01494-674042   Tel 01494-671234
E-mail: admin@nftsfilm-tv.ac.uk
10 full-time post graduate/post experience courses in all
aspects of film and television arts and scienes.
Nottingham Trent University
Clifton Lane, Nottingham NG11 8NS
Fax 0115-948 6632   Tel 0115-948 6677
Website: http://www.ntu.ac.uk
BJTC recognised degree in broadcast journalism; and
industry led MA in investigative journalism.
Plymouth College of Art and Design
Tavistock Place, Plymouth PL4 8AT
Fax 01752-203444   Tel 01752-203434
BKSTS accredited HND course in film and TV with
optional one year top up to BA (Hons).
Ravensbourne College of Design & Comms.
Walden Road, Chislehurst, Kent BR7 5SN
Fax 0181-325 8320   Tel 0181-289 4900
E-mail: info@rave.ac.uk
Website: http://www.rave.ac.uk
Full-time HND programmes in Technical Operations,
Production and Engineering. Degree courses in
Professional Broadcasting, Broadcast Engineering and
Communication and Technology.
Salisbury College
Southampton Road, Salisbury, Wilts SP1 2LW
Fax 01722-326006   Tel 01722-323711
E-mail: @salcol.com
BKSTS accredited HND in film and TV and BA (Hons)
degree in film and TV.
Sheffield Hallam University
Northern Media School, The Workstation, 15
Paternoster Row, Sheffield S1 2BX
Fax 0114-225 4606   Tel 0114-225 4648
BJTC post-graduate diploma in broadcast journalism.
South East Essex College
Carnarvon Road, Southend, Essex SS2 6LS
                              Tel 01702-220400
E-mail: learning@se-essex-college.ac.uk
BSc (hons) media production and technology - 3 years.
BSc (Hons) multimedia technology - 3 years.
BTEC/GNVQ broadcast media -2 years; print media.2
years.
South Thames College
Wandsworth High Street, London SW18 2PP
Fax 0181-918 7136   Tel 0181-918 7000
BKSTS accredited HNCs in TV production and AV.
Southampton Institute
East Park Terrace, Southampton SO14 0YN
Fax 01703-22259   Tel 01703-319000
E-mail: maureen.francis@solent.ac.uk
BSc (Hons) Media Technology.

Surrey Institute of Art and Design
Falkner Road, Farnham, Surrey GU9 7DS
Fax 01252 733869   Tel 01252-722441
E-mail: registry@surrart.ac.uk
Website: http://www.surrart.ac.uk
BECTU and BKSTS accredited degrees in film and
video, media studies and in animation. BJTC
recognised first degree with radio and print options.
There is a BA (Hons) in journalism.
University of Bradford
Richmond Road, Bradford BD7 1DP
Fax 01274-305340   Tel 01274-733466
BSc in electronic imaging and media communications.
University of Bristol
Woodland Road, Bristol BS8 1UP
Fax 0117-928 8251   Tel 0117-928 7838
University of Central England in B'ham
Perry Bar, Birmingham B42 2SU
Fax 0121-331 6501   Tel 0121-331 5719
E-mail: rod.pilling@uce.ac.uk
BJTC postgraduate course in broadcast journalism.
University of Central Lancashire
Department of Journalism, Preston PR1 2HE
Fax 01772-892907   Tel 01772-893730
E-mail: n.atkinson@uclan.ac.uk
NCTJ and BJTC accredited courses: undergraduate BA
(Hons) course, multi-media two years,print, broadcast
or dissertation final year. New media option for '99.
Separate one year postgraduate diploma courses in
newspaper and broadcast journalism. New media
postgraduate diploma course in '99. IPR recognised
undergraduate BA (Hons) course in public relations.
Joint honours undergraduate BA (Hons) courses in
journalism and public relations.
University of London
Goldsmith's College, London SE14 6NW
                              Tel 0171-919 7611
BJTC recognised course. MA Radio covering
journalism, drama and new sound technology.
University of Wales
School of Journalism, Media and Cultural Studies,
Centre for Journalism Studies, Bute Building, King
Edward V11 Avenue, Cardiff CF1 3NB
Fax 01222-238832   Tel 01222-874786
E-mail: PalserES@Cardiff.ac.uk
Website: http://www.cf.ac.uk/uwcc/jomec/jomec
NCTJ recognised postgraduate diploma in newspaper
journalism; BJTC recognised course in broadcast (bi-
media) journalism; PTC recognised course in magazine
journalism, IPR recognised course in public and media
relations. Course in photojournalism. Euro MA course.
University of Westminster
School of Communication, Harrow Campus, Watford
Road, Harrow HA1 3TP
Fax 0171-911 5939   Tel 0171-911 5000/5943
BJTC accredited postgraduate diploma with periodical
and broadcast pathways. Many other courses available.
West Herts College
Hempstead Road, Watford, Herts WD1 3EZ
Fax 01923-812667   Tel 01923-812662
E-mail: viscom@westherts.ac.uk
BKSTS accredited course in media production.

MEDIA STUDIES COURSES

The listing is of universities offering degree courses in media studies and related subjects like communication, journalism, broadcasting and cultural studies. It has been taken from: The Big Official Guide to University and College Entrance which is published by UCAS. Tel 0171-702 9799.

Anglia Polytechnic University
Fax 01223-576156   Tel 01223-363271

University of Wales, Bangor
Fax 01248-370451   Tel 01248-351151

Barnsley College
Fax 01226-298514·   Tel 01226-730191

University of Birmingham
Fax 0121-414 3850   Tel 0121-414 3697

Bournemouth University
Fax 01202-595099   Tel 01202-524111

University of Bradford
Fax 01274-236260   Tel 01274-733466

University of Brighton
Fax 01273-642825   Tel 01273-600900

University of the West of England, Bristol
Fax 0117-976 3804   Tel 0117-965 6261

Brunel: The University of West London
Fax 01895-232806   Tel 01895-274000

Bucks College
Fax 01494-524392   Tel 01494-522141

Christ Church College of Higher Education
Fax 01227-470442   Tel 01227-782422

Cardiff University of Wales
Fax 01222-874130   Tel 01222-874404

University of Central England in B'ham
Fax 0121-331 6740   Tel 0121-331 5595

University of Central Lancashire
Fax 01772-892935   Tel 01772-201201

Cheltenham and Glos College of Higher Ed
Fax 01242-256759   Tel 01242-532824

Chichester Institute of Higher Education
Fax 01243-816080   Tel 01243-865581

City University
Fax 0171-477 8559   Tel 0171-477 8028

Colchester Institute
Fax 01206-763041   Tel 01206-718000

Coventry University
Fax 01203-838638   Tel 01203-631313

Cumbria College of Art & Design
Fax 01228-514491   Tel 01228-400300

De Montfort University
Fax 0116-255 0307   Tel 0116-255 1551

University of Derby
Fax 01332-622754   Tel 01332-622289

University of East Anglia
Fax 01603-458596   Tel 01603-592216

University of East London
Fax 0181-590 7799   Tel 0181-590 7722

Edge Hill University College
Fax 01695-579997   Tel 01695-575171

Falmouth College of Arts
Fax 01326-211205   Tel 01326-211077

Farnborough College of Technology
Fax 01252-407041   Tel 01252-391212

University of Glamorgan
Fax 01443-480558   Tel 01443-480480

Glasgow Caledonian University
Fax 0141-331-3005   Tel 0141-331 3000

Goldsmiths College
Fax 0181-691 4490   Tel 0181-510 7171

University of Greenwich
Fax 0181-331 8385   Tel 0181-331 8000

University of Huddersfield
Fax 01484-516151   Tel 01484-422288

University of Humberside
Fax 01482-463532   Tel 01482-440550

King Alfred's College
Fax 01962-842280   Tel 01962-841515

Lancaster University
Fax 01524-846243   Tel 01524-65201

University of Leeds
Fax 0113-233 3991   Tel 0113-233 3999

Leeds, Trinity & All Saints
Fax 0113-283 7200   Tel 0113-283 7123

Leeds Metropolitan University
Fax 0113-283 3114   Tel 0113-283 2600

University of Leicester
Fax 0116-252 2200   Tel 0116-252 2522

University of Lincolnshire & Humberside
Fax 01482-463532   Tel 01482-440550

University of Liverpool
Fax 0151-708 6502   Tel 0151-794 2000

Liverpool John Moores University
Fax 0151-707 1938   Tel 0151-231 2121

London Guildhall University
Fax 0171-320 3462   Tel 0171-320 1000

London Institute
Fax 0171-514 6848   Tel 0171-514 6000

Loughborough University
Fax 01509-223905   Tel 01509-263171

University of Luton
Fax 01582-489323   Tel 01582-734111

Manchester Metropolitan University
Fax 0161-247 6311   Tel 0161-247 2000

Middlesex University
Fax 0181-362 5649   Tel 0181-362 5000

Napier University
Fax 0131-455 4329   Tel 0131-444 2266

Nene College of Higher Education
Fax 01604-720636   Tel 01604-735500

University of Wales College, Newport
Fax 01633-432850   Tel 01633-432432

NE Wales Institute of Higher Education
Fax 01978-290006   Tel 01978-290666

University of North London
Fax 0171-753 3272   Tel 0171-753 3355

University of Northumbria
Fax 0191-227 3009   Tel 0191-227 4777

Nottingham Trent University
Fax 0115-948 6063   Tel 0115-941 8418

University of Paisley
Fax 0141-848 3623   Tel 0141-848 3000

University of Plymouth
Fax 01752-232179   Tel 01752-600600

Queen Margaret College
Fax 0131-317 3256   Tel 0131-317 3240

University College of Ripon & York St John
Fax 01904-612512   Tel 01904-656771
University of Salford
Fax 0161-295 5258   Tel 0161-745 5000

University of Sheffield
Fax 0114-272 8014   Tel 0114-222 2000

Sheffield Hallam University
Fax 0114-253 2161   Tel 0114-272 0911

Southampton Institute
Fax 01703-332077   Tel 01703-319000

South Bank University
Fax 0171-815 8273   Tel 0171-815 6109

College of St Mark & St John
Fax 01752-761120   Tel 01752-777188

St Mary's University College
Fax 0181-240 4255   Tel 0181-240 4000

Staffordshire University
Fax 01782-292740   Tel 01782-294000

University of Stirling
Fax 01786-466800   Tel 01786-467044

University College Suffolk
Fax 01473-230054   Tel 01473-255885

University of Sunderland
Fax 0191-515 2423   Tel 0191-515 2082

Surrey Institute of Art & Design
Fax 01252-892616   Tel 01252-722441

University of Sussex
Fax 01273-678545   Tel 01273-678416

Swansea Institute of Higher Education
Fax 01792-481085   Tel 01792-481000

University of Teesside
Fax 01642-342067   Tel 01642-218121

Thames Valley University
Fax 0181-231 2900   Tel 0181-231 2902

Trinity College Carmarthen
Fax 01267-676766   Tel 01267-676767

University of Ulster
Fax 01265-324927   Tel 01265-324927

University of Wales Aberystwyth
Fax 01970-622831   Tel 01970-622828

University College Warrington
Fax 01925-816077   Tel 01925-814343

West Herts College
Fax 01923-812556   Tel 01923-684848

University of Westminster
Fax 0171-911 5118   Tel 0171-911 5000

Wirral Metropolitan College
Fax 0151-551 7701   Tel 0151-551 7926

University of Wolverhampton
Fax 01902-323379   Tel 01902-321000

Worcester College of Higher Education
Fax 01905-855132   Tel 01905-855111

Odds and ends

HACKED OFF

"Media and publishing professionals are feeling stressed, miserable and have a very poor work/life balance. Too many are taking their work pressures home and bringing their home pressures to work. Media and publishing people mention divorce and strain on relationships and not having or postponing children significantly more than other professionals."

So said Trevor Merriden in an introduction to a survey published by Management Today magazine. The survey also revealed:

Meeja grizzles

PERSONAL SACRIFICES MADE BY MEDIA PEOPLE

1 Missing children growing up (1)
2 Work before family/home (2)
3 Divorce/strain on relationship (6)
4 Missed leisure & holiday time (4)
5 Moving home for employer (3)
6 Not having/postponing children (9)
7 Away from home - long term (7)
8 Away from home - short term (5)
9 Time spent on work related education (8)
10 Unable to form relationships (10)

MEDIA PEOPLE'S WISH LIST

1 Work fewer hours (1)
2 Reduce or avoid commuting (4)
3 Change the culture of the company (2)
4 Work flexible hours (3)
5 Earn more (8)
6 Work from home (5)
7 More staff (7)
8 Change jobs or move (6)
9 Retire (9)
10 Reduce stress (10)

Figures in brackets compare with averages across other industries.

Source: WFD/Management Today

MEDIA FRAUDS

The Connection, an award winning Carlton Network First documentary faked up a drug runner's journey from Columbia to Britain. A Guardian investigation, published during May 1998, revealed: the drugs mule filmed by Carlton did not have drugs in his stomach when he flew to Britain; he did not get through Heathrow customs as was suggested but was deported; the man described as a senior member of the Cali drugs ring was a retired bank cashier; the mule's "contiguous" journey from Columbia was filmed in two stages, six months apart; the programme's producer, Marc de Beaufort, bought the coke smuggler's flight ticket.

Inside Castro's Cuba, another Network First programme, was another fraud. Carlton claimed its producer (none other than de Beaufort) had spent a "nerve shattering year" to gain "rare access" to President Castro. The nearest he got to an interview was government archive footage which was passed off as a chat chez Castro. "It's a fake," a Cuban diplomat confirmed.

There is some point on the scale of editorial values when fakery turns into hoax. A pair of News of the World journalists, for example, were carrying on a fine tradition when they reported proof of the Beast of Bodmin's existence. When the beast was revealed as a puma in Devon zoo, their outraged employers got rid of them. The posh version of a hoax is called a satire as when Julian Barnes fooled the New York art world with his account of a concept artist's tragic life. Then there are spoofs, though these can backfire. Associated Newspapers had to pay up to £250,000 in legal costs when Alan Clark MP was successful in his action preventing the Evening Standard from carrying a column called Alan Clark's Secret Political Diary. Its author, Peter Bradshaw, said: "This sets a worrying precedent that politicians could use to suppress satirical criticism of themselves. Is Tony Blair going to sue Rory Bremner for passing himself off as him? It's a victory for humourlessness."

MEDIA DEATHS

A total of 474 journalists have been killed in the last ten years and by the end of 1997 at least 129 were in prison in 24 countries and 26 had been murdered. Seven journalists died in India, four in Columbia, three in Mexico, two in Cambodia and one each in Argentina, Brazil, Guatemala, Indonesia, Iran, Pakistan, the Philippines, Rwanda, Sierra Leone and Ukraine.

These figures were produced in a survey of press freedom produced by Reporters Without Borders and the Committee to Protect Journalists. William Orme, the CPJ director,

says: "The ruthless persecution of local journalists in Nigeria was the single most troubling development. Although Turkey still holds more journalists in jail than any other country, we are encouraged it is less than half the number than the previous year."

Committee to Protect Journalists
12th Floor, 330 Seventh Avenue, New York 10001, USA
Tel: 001-212-465-1004
Website: www.cpj.org

MEDIA RICH

Top media owners

POSITION	WEALTH	NAME
13	£1,100m	Tony O'Reilly, Independent Newspapers
14	£1,000m	Viscount Rothermere, Daily Mail & General Trust
22	£650m	David and Frederick Barclay, European Press Holdings
29	£500m	Viscount Cowdray and the Pearson family (Financial Times)
51	£350m	David Sullivan, Roldvale and Conegate
77	£280m	David and Ralph Gold, Sullivan's partners
84	£270m	John Madejski, Hurst Publishing
93	£252m	Thomson family, Dundee (Sunday post & Dandy)
110	£200m	Felix Dennis, Dennis Publishing
134	£150m	Michael Heseltine, Haymarket
165	£125m	Freddie Johnston and family, Johnston Press
192	£105m	Paul Gibbons, Hurst Publishing
203	£100m	Douglas Graham and family, Claverly
233	£91m	Nicholas Forman Hardy and family
254	£85m	Michael Green, Carlton Communications
264	£80m	Paul Morgan and family, Romeike press cuttings
357	£60m	Richard Desmond, Northern & Shell
357	£60m	Peter Wilson, former owner of Estates Gazette
428	£50m	Michael Watt, CSI (satellite television racing coverage)
508	£45m	Lindsay Masters, Haymarket
557	£42m	Peter Field, Financial Engineering
562	£40m	Owen and Vicki Oyston, radio interests
562	£40m	Sir Ray Tindle, Tindle Newspapers
617	£35m	Sir Richard Storey and family
656	£34m	Mark Getty, Getty Communications
668	£30m	Tony Elliott, Time Out owner
668	£30m	Andrew Knight, ex Telegraph & News International
668	£30m	Eddy Shah, former publisher of Today

Source: Durrants

Rupert Murdoch

Rupert Murdoch has spoken on the record more than is usual in what, for him, has been an unusually eventful year. A trawl through the cuttings landed a haul of intertwining stories and quotes about his businesses, his political links and his family. Go to page 31 and 170 for more about Murdoch

BUSINESS

[News Corp is] "a small part of an ever-widening rainbow ... Our competitors cloak their pleas for protection and privilege in the language of public interest."
Rupert Murdoch at the European Audiovisual Conference in April 1998

"The only truly news and entertainment company."
Prince Alaweed Bin Talal Abdul Aziz Alsaud after buying 5% of News Corp in Nov 1997.

"When you look at what is coming down the line, News Corp is in a hell of a mess."
Anonymous City analyst

"The management is weak, it's just not the sort of company you should be playing family dynasties with."
Another anonymous City analyst

"At the root of Murdoch's financial power is his talent for manipulating tax laws ... in Britain, in the decade to 1996, Murdoch's News International paid virtually no tax on recorded profits of almost a billion pounds. None of this is against the law."
John Pilger in his book Hidden Agendas

"Rupert Murdoch's News Corporation is under examination by an international team of tax investigators as part of a drive to clamp down on multinational companies using international loopholes to avoid paying tax."
David Hencke, the Guardian 5 February, 1998

POLITICS

"The extent of the ties that developed between New Labour and News Corp has never been fully revealed. In addition to regular meetings between the two top men, a network of contacts has been established between senior company executives and Labour front benchers."
Andrew Neil, the former Murdoch editor in his autobiography Full Disclosure

"We were a bit concerned that the Italian government would not like a foreigner buying up such a politically sensitive company. Rupert said he would ring up the Prime Minister [Tony Blair] to see if he could help."
25 March 1998 - a News Corp spokesman on negotiations for the £4 billion bid for the Italian TV company Mediaset.

"Rupert Murdoch ... used information obtained directly from Tony Blair to inform his business decisions during his attempt to buy a controlling interest in Silvio Berlusconi's television interests in Italy. Despite a number of ambiguous statements from Downing Street spokesmen over the past few days it is now clear that last week Mr Murdoch rang the Prime Minister to see if he would find out what the political reaction might be."
27 March - a front page story in a News Corp newspaper, aka the Times

"Of course I understand the concerns. But the only issue is whether BSkyB was treated differently from any other media company or significant British company. The answer is no."
1 April - Tony Blair in the House of Commons

THE PATTEN AFFAIR

"Our people screwed it up .... There are no winners or losers in the current controversy; mistakes have been made and we all share responsibility."
6 March - Rupert Murdoch. Chris Patten emerged as a winner, having kept his £150k advance and taken his book to Macmillan.

"Faceless Stalinists."
The former Hong Kong governor, Chris Patten, writing about the Chinese leadership in his new book East and West

"Too boring"
A Harper Collins summary of Patten's book

"Harper Collins have unreservedly apologised for and withdrawn any suggestion that Chris Patten's book was rejected for not being up to proper professional standards or being too boring."
6 March - Harper Collins and Patten's lawyers

"I am leaving Harper Collins with extreme regret. I was told several times that Rupert Murdoch had called to express extreme displeasure that we had signed the book."
Stuart Proffitt, Patten's Harper Collins editor

"The Times has simply decided, because of Murdoch's interests, not to cover China in a serious way."
Jonathan Mirsky, ex-Times correspondent

THE SUCCESSION

"The succession at News Corporation depends on how long I remain compos mentis . I would say it is currently the children's consensus that Lachlan will take over. He will have to be first among equals, but they have to prove themselves."
Rupert Murdoch on career opportunities for his children. Lachlan M is chief executive of News Corp in Australia, James M looks after new media interests in the US and Elisabeth M is general manager of broadcasting at BSkyB. She clashed with her colleague Sam Chisholm.

"Elisabeth thought Sam would teach her everything, but he didn't. He tried to cut her out."
Rupert Murdoch. Mr Chisholm quit, Ms Murdoch kept her job.

"Unto every one that hath shall be given, and he shall have abundance; but from him that hath not shall be taken away even that which he hath."
Rupert Murdoch quoting from the parable of the talents in Matthew 25. He read it at Woodrow Wyatt's funeral in April 1998.

THE SEPARATION

"Privacy laws are for the protection of people who are already privileged. They are not for the ordinary man and woman. The talk of privacy laws is to see if we can get a new privilege for the privileged and that should be resisted."
October 1997 - Rupert Murdoch

"It is with some personal sadness that I announce the amicable separation of Rupert Murdoch and his beautiful wife, Anna, after 31 years of marriage and three children."
Liz Smith, gossip columnist on Murdoch's New York Post on 21 April, 1998.

"Rupert and I work very hard at seeing each other. I do a lot of travelling, otherwise I probably wouldn't see him."
Anna Murdoch in a 1991 Today interview.

"This separation may not be forever. My belief is that Anna has had enough of him working so hard and is saying this isn't how I want to spend the rest of our marriage."
A Friend, quoted in the Times.

"As Oscar Wilde said of Little Nell's death, you'd need a heart of stone not to laugh."
Francis Wheen, journalist.

1999 anniversaries

All events listed here took place in multiples of five years ago. 1999 is the:

25th anniversary of 1974
50th anniversary of 1949
75th anniversary of 1924

JANUARY

1 New Year's Day becomes a bank holiday throughout the UK for the first time, 1974. Rupert Murdoch beats Robert Maxwell in takeover battle for the News of the World, 1969. Sir Learie Constantine becomes UK's first black peer, 1969 Start of Top of the Pops on BBC1, with Jimmy Savile, 1964.

2 Start of trial of Sex Pistol singer Sid Vicious, 1979, accused of murdering his girlfriend Nancy Spungen in New York; he dies of a drug overdose 2 February, aged 21. Energy Crisis: About 730,000 workers now laid off because of the crisis caused by the miners dispute, 1974; electricity is rationed and businesses can only work three days a week. Fidel Castro proclaims new socialist government in Cuba after ousting the dictator Fulgencio Batista, 1959.

4 Civil rights march across Northern Ireland broken up by Protestants at Burntollet, 1969; large police escort fails to take effective action, setting the pattern for events in the coming months. World War Two: Allies launch attack on Monte Cassino in Italy, 1944.

5 The Winter of Discontent: Start of lorry drivers strike today is catalyst for many other strikes in coming weeks, 1979. Today and tomorrow see much IRA activity, with five bombs in London, including Earls Court Boat Show and Madame Tussauds, 1974. Nazi Party formed in Germany, 1919.

6 Two Sikhs are executed for the murder of Indian premier Indira Gandhi, 1989.

Energy Crisis: Professional football played on Sunday for first time ever, because of the crisis (four FA Cup games), 1974. First religious service broadcast on BBC radio, 1924.

8 Bantry Bay in Ireland rocked by huge explosion when 120,000 ton oil tanker blows up while unloading her cargo, killing 49 people, 1979.

9 Boeing 737 airliner with engine trouble crashes on the M1 as it approaches East Midlands airport, killing 44 people, 1989. Energy Crisis: Parliament renews the State of Emergency declared two months ago, 1974; prime minister Ted Heath is accused of "pyschological warfare" after shutting down all TV at 10.30pm nightly. Income tax introduced (at 10 per cent) to pay for Napoleonic War, 1799.

10 Leo the Lion, appearing with three lionesses in the pantomime Robinson Crusoe at Wolverhampton, is sent home in disgrace after his amorous nature gets the better of him in front of a capacity audience, 1974. First 45 rpm records go on sale, in the USA, 1949.

11 Energy Crisis: lighting on trunk roads is to be cut, 1974. Severe storms, with winds up to 106 mph, 1974. The first weatherman appears on TV, 1954; the BBC shows George Cowling sketching on a map pinned on an easel. Opening of Charing Cross rail station, 1864.

12 Anti-apartheid demonstrators try to storm Rhodesia House and the South African Embassy in London, 1969.

13 Four-year investigation finds Tory-run Westminster Council guilty of unlawful action in selling £27 million of council houses for political benefit, 1994; a criticized councillor commits suicide. British Nuclear Fuels wins injunction banning Greenpeace from interfering with its Sellafield waste pipe, 1984. Hurricane force winds kill six people, 1984.

14 An angry crowd of 1,000 Muslims publicly burns Salman Rushdie's book The Satanic Verses, in Bradford, 1989. Last Frost Fair held on the frozen River Thames in London, 1814.

15 The launch of Tyne Tees Television, the first ITV station for North East England, 1959. The start of commercially sponsored programmes from Radio Luxembourg, aimed at Britain, 1934.

16 Launch of Rupert Murdoch's Sky Channel, the UK's first satellite TV programme channel, 1984; initially available through cable systems. Launch of The Listener magazine, 1929.

18 Anglia Television is bought for £292 million by MAI, the parent company of the south coast's Meridian, 1994. Squatters take over the empty London West End office block Centre Point, a key symbol of the property speculation that has been rife for many months, 1974; they leave on the 20th.

19 Czech student Jan Palach commits suicide by fire in Prague's Wenceslas Square in protest at the USSR's 1968 invasion of his country, 1969. English Civil War: Scottish army invades England to support Parliamentarians, 1644.

20 Closure of Northern Star, one of the last surviving 1970s alternative radical news magazines, 1994.

21 Rupert Murdoch appoints Sun editor Kelvin MacKenzie as managing director of BSkyB, 1994; succeeded on Sun by Stuart Higgins; but MacKenzie resigns from BSkyB on 2 August and becomes executive director of Mirror Group Newspapers on 19 October 1994. Launch of the world's first nuclear submarine, USS Nautilus, 1954. Sixty nine Sinn Fein MPs elected in the British general election in December form their own Irish parliament, the Dail Eireann, 1919; they include the first British woman MP.

22 Peking captured by communists, 1949. Britain's first Labour prime minister, Ramsay MacDonald, takes office following resignation of Tory Stanley Baldwin, 1924.

24 Student demonstrations at the LSE, 1969; security gates are wrecked and police arrest 25 people. Ford unveils the Capri, 1969. English Civil War: Start of three-day Battle of Nantwich, 1644; ends in Royalist defeat, and Irish troops switch to Parliamentary side.

25 Pop singer Michael Jackson reaches out-of-court settlement with 14-year old boy who had accused him of sexual abuse, 1994. Energy Crisis: Revealed that the 10.30pm TV shutdown only saves 600 tons of coal daily, 1974. Founding of the League of Nations, forerunner of the UN, 1919.

26 Closure of Wales, West and North, the first ITV company to collapse, 1964. End of the two-year long Siege of Leningrad, 1944.

27 Radio 2 becomes the first BBC Radio network to start 24-hour service, 1979.

30 English Civil War: Beheading of King Charles I and setting up of the Commonwealth of England, 1649.

31 The last British-owned major car-maker, Rover, is sold to German firm BMW for £800m, 1994.

FEBRUARY

1 Labour MP Austin Mitchell sacked from shadow cabinet for appearing as a presenter on Sky TV, 1989. Government announces the halfpenny is to be phased out by end of the year, 1984. Ayatollah Khomeini greeted by three million people on returning to Iran following 16 years exile, 1979. Trevor Francis becomes England's first £1 million footballer when he signs for Notts Forest, 1969. Great Train Robber Ronald Biggs is found by the Daily Express and Scotland Yard, 1974. Attempts to extradite him fail because he has a Brazilian child.

3 Yasser Arafat becomes leader of the Palestine Liberation Organisation, 1969. London School of Economics closed by student protests. Deaths of pop musicians Buddy Holly and Richie Valens in aircrash in USA, 1959. The Queen becomes first reigning monarch to visit Australia, 1954. Tidal wave hits south coast of England, 1904.

4 Eleven people killed when IRA bomb explodes on coach carrying servicemen and their families on the M62 near Bradford, 1974. BBC makes first schools radio broadcast, 1924.

5 A semi-naked man wearing a motorised parachute lands on the roof of Buckingham Palace, 1994. Energy Crisis: CBI president Sir Michael Clapham warns UK facing a situation "almost as serious as the outbreak of war", 1974; police finalise contingency plans for dealing with mass picketing. Kidnapping of 19-year old heiress Patty Hearst in San Francisco by the Symbionese Liberation Front, 1974. The GMT signal (the "Pips") is broadcast for the first time, on BBC radio, 1924.

7 Energy Crisis: Ted Heath calls general election for 28 February, 1974; TV curfew is lifted, but the state of emergency is renewed. Launch of Morning Advertiser, the newspaper of the licensed trade, 1794; daily until February 1994, then twice weekly.

8 Hull trawler Gaul disappears in the Arctic Ocean with 36 crew, 1974; later it is believed the ship was involved in spying on the USSR. Maiden flight of the Boeing 747, 1969. Beatles in New York for start of first US tour, 1964.

10 Start of PAYE (Paye As You Earn) income tax, 1944.

11 In the USA, first-ever woman Anglican bishop is consecrated,1974; she is black. Revolutionary Islamic government formed in Iran by followers of Ayatollah Khomeini, 1979. Architect John Poulson and civil servant George Pottinger jailed for five years for corruption after one of the longest trials of its type, 1974.

13 Writer Alexander Solzhenitsyn expelled from USSR for exposing terrible conditions in Stalin's labour camps in his new novel The Gulag Archipelago, 1974. British doctors announce they have carried out the first fertilisation of human eggs in a test tube, 1969.

14 Iranian religious leader Ayatollah Khomeinin passes death sentence on British author Salman Rushdie for writing the book The Satanic Verses, 1989.

15 Last Soviet troops leave Afghanistan after nine-year occupation, 1989. Anti-Rushdie protesters attack UK embassy in Tehran; Rushdie goes into hiding. World War Two: Allies bomb Monte Cassino monastery in Italy, 1944.

16 A thousand security officers and police evict 300 anti-road protesters from three barricaded houses on the path of the M11 in East London, 1994.

17 The Big Ben daily time signal broadcast for the first time, on BBC radio, 1924.

22 Frank Winfield Woolworth opens his first store, New York, 1879. USA acquires Florida from Spain, 1819.

24 American space probe Mariner Six launched on trip to Mars, 1969.

25 Granada wins its takeover battle for LWT, paying £765 million, 1994; LWT chief exec Greg Dyke resigns. Muhammad Ali (then Cassius Clay) wins world heavyweight boxing title for first time, defeating Sonny Liston, 1964.

26 Eleven men killed when arsonist sets fire to cinema club in London showing sex films, 1994. First of Frederick West's many murder victims found in his house in Gloucester, 1994. First Grand National steeplechase run at Aintree, 1839.

28 National day of industrial protests against banning of trade unions at GCHQ, 1984; no national newspapers published in London.

General election, 1974; Labour wins 301 seats, Tories 297, giving minor parties the balance of power; Ted Heath spends four days trying to put together a coalition with the Liberals before resigning and handing over to Labour under Harold Wilson. American troops land in Honduras, 1924.

MARCH

1 Eddy Shah awarded £74,000 against the NGA, 1984, over the security costs incurred during the picketing of his Warrington print plant in November 1983. Prince Charles broadcasts for first time, on Radio Four, 1969. First hydrogen bomb test, carried out by the USA at Bikini Atoll in the Pacific, 1954.

2 First test flight of Concorde, in France, 1969. Completion of first non-stop flight round the world, by US Air Force plane, 1949.

3 World's worst air disaster to date: 345 people killed when Turkish Airlines DC10 en route to London crashes into wood near Paris, 1974.

4 Government says the August Bank Holiday will in future be on the last Monday in the month instead of the first, 1964. Founding of the Royal National Lifeboat Institute, 1824.

5 Warner Communications and Time announce merger plans, forming the largest media business in the world, 1989. Launch of Wales on Sunday newspaper, 1989. East End gangster twins Ronnie and Reggie Kray given life sentences for murdering Jack "The Hat" McVitie in a Whitechapel pub, 1969; judge recommends they serve 30 years.

6 Patenting of aspirin, 1899.

7 Opening of the London Underground's Victoria Line by the Queen, 1969.

9 IRA fires four mortar bombs at Heathrow Airport, 1994; eight more fired in coming days, but all fail to explode.

10 James Earl Ray sentenced to 99 years jail for murdering Martin Luther King, 1969. Suffragette Mary Richardson slashes Velasquez's masterpiece the Rokeby Venus at the National Gallery, 1914.

11 Eruption of Mount Etna volcano in Sicily, 1974. Energy Crisis: State of Emergency ends, although 50mph speed limit and other restrictions stay.

12 Freighter carrying cargo of drums of deadly chemicals sinks off Devon, 1989; most, but not all, are recovered over following weeks. Miners Strike: Start of the year-long national strike which is to prove the decisive battle in the government's campaign to remove the power of the trade unions, 1984. Beatle news: Paul McCartney marries Linda Eastman, George Harrison is arrested for possessing cannabis, 1969. Britain's first mainline electric train takes to the rails (Liverpool-Southport), 1904.

14 Sinn Fein leader Gerry Adams shot and injured in Belfast by Loyalists, 1984. Jack Ruby, murderer of President Kennedy's assassin Lee Harvey Oswald, was sentenced to death, 1964.

15 Opening of Britain's first department store, Selfridges, 1909.

17 MPs demand inquiry into possible links between alleged high class call girl Pamella Bordes and Libyan intelligence, 1989; Ms Bordes is a friend of prominent newspaper editors Andrew Neil and Donald Trelford. English Civil War: Oliver Cromwell declares England a Commonwealth and abolishes the monarchy, 1649.

18 Mirror Group Newspapers consortium buys the Independent and Independent on Sunday newspapers for £75 million from the founding company, 1994. The six Tolpuddle Martyrs were sentenced to deportation to Australia for forming a trade union for farm workers, 1834.

19 British troops and 40 police officers invade the Caribbean island of Anguilla to put down revolt, 1969; they meet no resistance.

20 Miners' Strike: Two Kent miners refused High Court injunction against police who will not let them leave the county to join pickets in other areas, 1984; the decision is condemned as a major infringement of civil liberties. After an unsuccessful attempt by an armed man to kidnap Princess Anne in The Mall, 1974 several people were seriously wounded by his shooting; he says he did it to highlight the shortage of mental health care facilities.

21 Australian premier Bob Hawke cries on TV after admitting adultery, 1989.

23 Civil servant Sarah Tisdall jailed for six months for passing military secrets to the Guardian, 1984.

24 Launch of the daily racing paper Sporting Life, 1859.

25 America's worst oil pollution disaster when tanker Exxon Valdez runs aground off the Alaskan coast, spilling 12 million gallons of oil, 1989.

27 Mod and Rocker riots: Nationwide moral panic as Clacton suffers rioting and damage in clashes between gangs of youths over Easter weekend 27-30 March, 1964; this is the prelude to a summer of disturbances in many seaside resorts.

28 BBC Radio Five goes on air for first time, at 5.00am, 1994. Serious accident at the Three Mile Island nuclear power plant in Pennsylvania halts the American nuclear programme, 1979. British radio is revolutionised with the launch of the first pirate radio station, Radio Caroline, on Easter Sunday, 1964; it broadcasts from a ship outside UK territorial waters (off Clacton). Spanish Civil War: Republican-held Madrid surrenders to

General Franco's Nationalist forces, 1939. Government announces plans to introduce driving tests for motorists, 30 mph speed limit in towns and pedestrian crossings, 1934. Start of the Crimean War between Britain and Russia, 1854.

29 London radio station LBC goes into receivership, 1994.

30 The Observer publishes unique Thursday edition detailing secret government report on the purchase of House of Fraser by the Al-Fayeds, arch rivals of Observer-owners Lonrho, 1989; the government wins an injunction to stop sale of the paper. The IRA assassinates the Tory MP Airey Neave with a car bomb as he drives out of the House of Commons car park, 1979.

31 The Dalai Lama flees Tibet because of repression by Chinese, 1959. Launch of the Daily Herald, 1919.

APRIL

1 Poll tax introduced in Scotland, 1989 (1990 in England and Wales). American pop singer Marvin Gaye shot dead by his father, 1984. English Civil War: Britain's first commune is created by the radical Diggers, or True Levellers, on St George's Hill, Walton-on-Thames, Surrey, 1649; it is quickly broken up.

2 Official ending of the Spanish Civil War, following defeat of the Republican movement by the right-wing Nationalists, 1939.

4 NATO comes into being with the signing of the North Atlantic Treaty, 1949. First national schools broadcast, on BBC radio, 1924.

5 Eamon de Valera elected president of Sinn Fein, 1919.

6 Fourteen IRA firebombs explode in shops in London, Manchester and Birmingham, 1974. The American Robert Peary becomes first known human to reach the North Pole, 1909.

7 The first televising of a British trial takes place, 1994 but the BBC broadcasts it in Scotland only, where the law is different. The highwayman Dick Turpin is hanged at York, 1739.

9 Launch of Sunday Daily Mail and Sunday Daily Telegraph, 1899; both close within two months because of religious hostility; Mail on Sunday starts in 1982, Sunday Telegraph in 1961.

10 Emiliano Zapata, leader of the Mexican revolution, killed by government forces, 1919.

11 Abbey National becomes first building society to convert into a bank when members vote for the changeover, 1989. Australia replaces God Save the Queen with Advance Australia Fair as its national anthem, 1984.

12 One of the first pop music sensations after Rock Around the Clock recorded by Bill Hailey and the Comets, 1954.

CIVIL WAR: 17 MARCH 1649
Oliver Cromwell declares England a
Commonwealth and abolishes the monarchy

13 Ian Botham fined £1,000 by the Test and County Cricket Board for his comments on Pakistan during a radio interview, 1984. Ian Botham fined £1,000 by the Test and County Cricket Board for his comments on Pakistan during a radio interview, 1984. Amritsar Massacre: British troops fire on political demonstration at Amritsar in India's Punjab, killing 379 people, 1919.

15 Britain's worst-ever football disaster leaves 95 Liverpool fans dead, crushed at Sheffield's Hillsborough stadium during an FA Cup semi-final match with Nottingham Forest, 1989; sales of the Sun slump in Liverpool amidst widespread hostility after the newspaper claims - without evidence - that Liverpudlian fans were drunk.

16 West German Geraldine Monk becomes first woman to fly alone round the world, 1964.

17 WPC Yvonne Fletcher shot dead in London during protest outside the Libyan Embassy, 1984; the government expels 30 diplomats - including the murderer - ten days later. Suffragettes blow up the pier at Great Yarmouth in Norfolk, 1914.

18 West Indian batsman Brian Lara scores highest-ever individual Test score: 375, in match against England in Antigua, 1994. Irish civil rights activist Bernadette Devlin wins by-election in Mid-Ulster at age 21, 1969. Opening of the first launderette, in Fort Worth, Texas, 1934.

19 SOGAT 82 and NGA fined £75,000 each for refusing to end sit-in at Robert Maxwell's company BPCC, 1984.

20 Catholic man shot dead in Belfast is the 1,000th victim of the five years of unrest, 1974. Fire bombs explode at many locations in Belfast, 1969; troops now guarding key sites.

21 BBC2 goes on the air for the first time, the first 625-line system in UK, 1964; it should have started yesterday but was postponed because of a power blackout in London; first programme is Play School, at 11am.

22 The cruise liner QE2 starts her maiden voyage, 1969.

23 Discovery of the Aids virus announced in USA, 1984. Schoolteacher Blair Peach killed during a demonstration in Southall against fascism, 1979. Birth of English playwright William Shakespeare, 1563 (died same day, 1616).

25 Army leads coup in Portugal against right-wing government, 1974. BBC radio serial Mrs Dale's Diary axed after 21 years, 1969.

26 The largest-ever art raid, 1974, nets £8 million of old masters stolen from a mansion in County Wicklow; all were recovered a week later; Rose Dugdale later jailed for her alleged role.

27 Students take control of Beijing's Tiananmen Square, posing major threat to the country's ruling communist party, 1989.

30 The design of the first "prefabs" (prefabricated homes) is unveiled, 1944; they become a familiar sight in the late 1940s and some remain standing to this day.

MAY

1 Ayrton Senna, three times world motor-racing champion, is killed in San Marino grand prix, 1994. Batman makes his first appearance, in Detective Comics, 1939.

2 Hungary opens its "iron curtain" when it begins dismantling the fences along its border with Austria, 1989. The luxury liner QE2 sails on her maiden voyage from Southampton, 1969.

3 Magistrates dismiss charges against six police officers arising from the disorder in 1986 during the picketing of News International's new Wapping plant, 1989.

4 Margaret Thatcher becomes Britain's first woman prime minister following Tory defeat of Labour at the general election, 1979. Work begins on the digging of the Panama Canal, 1904. Charles Rolls and Henry Royce form partnership to make cars, 1904.

6 Channel Tunnel formally opened by the Queen and President Mitterand, 1994. Roger Bannister becomes first person to run a mile in under four minutes, at an athletics meeting in Oxford, 1954. American Civil War: Confederates win the Battle of the Wilderness, 1864.

7 Dien Bien Phu in Vietnam captured from the French by the Vietminh, 1954; this was a key defeat for the French and they agreed peace terms in July to end the seven-year war.

8 Opening of the Thames Barrier at Woolwich by the Queen, 1984.

10 Nelson Mandela becomes president of South Africa, 1994. Completion of the American transcontinental railway when the Central Pacific and Union Pacific lines meet in Utah, 1869.

11 About 20,000 people killed by big earthquake in China's Sichuan province, 1974. Waterloo Bridge is closed because of subsidence, 1924; then rebuilt.

12 Labour leader John Smith dies of heart attack, 1994; Tony Blair elected on 21 July. Tory MP Keith Hampson resigns as PPS to the Defence Secretary after being arrested in a Soho gay strip club, 1984. Minimum voting age lowered from 21 to eighteen, 1969.

13 Social Democratic Party announces it will stop operating as a national party, 1989.

16 Soviet and Chinese leaders meet in Beijing's Great Hall of the People, while half a million demonstrate outside for greater democracy, 1989. Government sets up Selsdon Committee to investigate feasibility of launching a public television service, 1934; results in start of BBC on 2 November 1936.

17 Three car bombs explode during the rush hour in Dublin, killing 23 people, 1974. Finish of first solo trans-Atlantic crossing in rowing boat, by Tom McClean, 1969. Mods and Rockers riots: Whitsun weekend 17-18 May sees more disorder in seaside resorts, especially Brighton and Margate, 1964.

18 World War Two: Allies capture Monte Cassino in Italy, 1944. Napoleon Bonaparte becomes emperor of France, 1804.

19 English Civil War: England is declared a republican state for the first, and only, time in its history, 1649.

20 Chinese government imposes martial law to crush pro-democracy forces, 1989.

21 Court says the National Trust has the right to lease land in the Chilterns to the military to build a new NATO war bunker, 1984. Manchester Ship Canal opened by Queen Victoria, 1894.

23 Explosion kills 15 people at Abbeystead, Lancs, underground water treatment works, 1984.

24 BBC staff stage 24-hour strike over threatened cuts to wages and conditions, 1994; another strike on 9 June. Over 300 people killed during riot at international football match in Lima, Peru, 1964. Empire Day, created in 1902, is renamed Commonwealth Day, 1959. Derby Day: Leader in the Times gives the first three horses, 1929. Transmission of first morse telegraph message, by inventor Samuel Morse, from Washington to Baltimore, 1844. Opening of Dartmoor Prison, for French prisoners-of-war, 1809.

25 Death in Vietnam of American war photographer Robert Capa, 1954.

26 Shanghai captured by Chinese communists, 1949.

28 Eight-day general strike by Protestant workers in Northern Ireland ends with the collapse of the new power-sharing Executive, resignation of chief executive Brian Faulkner and the re-imposition of direct rule from Westminster, 1974.

29 Miners Strike: Orgreave coking plant in South Yorkshire is the scene of most violent clashes so far, 1984; miners' leader Arthur Scargill arrested next day for obstruction. Loss of the liner Empress of Ireland in Canada's St Lawrence River kills over 1,000 people,1914. First Bank Holiday in Britain (Whit Monday), 1879.

30 Launch of the world's first hovercraft, at Cowes, 1959. Labour wins the general election, 1929; Ramsay MacDonald becomes prime minister.

JUNE

1 Flixborough disaster: 28 people killed and hundreds injured when a chemical plant in Lincolnshire blows up, 1974; scores of houses destroyed or damaged. BBC starts Juke Box Jury, the first pop music quiz on television, 1959.

2 Nineteen of the most senior UK intelligence and security officers are killed when their helicopter, travelling between Belfast and Inverness crashes in fog in western Scotland, 1994. Palestine Liberation Organisation (PLO) formed, 1964.

3 British sailing ship Marques sinks in the Atlantic with the loss of 19 lives, 1984.

4 The People's Liberation Army of China crushes the country's pro-democracy movement by massacring over 2,000 of the people who have been occupying Beijing's Tiananmen Square, 1989; the military brutality stuns the world; it is followed by weeks of violent government retaliation against pro-democracy activists.

6 At least 700 people killed when Indian troops storm the Sikh holy shrine at Amritsar, following its seizure by Sikh militants, 1984; followed by violence in many areas. Launch of the Eurovision television network, 1954. World War Two: Allied forces start the D-Day landings in Normandy, the beginning of the campaign to recapture north-west Europe, 1944. Golf is shown on TV for first time, 1939; from Coombe Hill in Surrey.

7 Miners Strike: Miners lobby of parliament ends with 250 arrests, 1984. Vatican City established in Rome, 1929. Labour's Margaret Bondfield becomes first woman Cabinet minister.

8 First direct elections for the European parliament, 1979. Spain closes its border with Gibraltar after Britain refuses to concede its sovereignty, 1969. US government announces staged withdrawal of troops from Vietnam.

9 USA launches its first submarine armed with Polaris nuclear missiles, 1959.

10 British liner SS Slavonia sends out first radio SOS message when it is wrecked off the Azores, 1909.

12 The first disc-jockey led programme is broadcast on BBC radio, with Compton Mackenzie, 1924.

13 The Royal Navy was seriously embarrassed when its frigate Jupiter collides with London Bridge while turning in the Thames, 1984. The divorce law was liberalised by the Divorce Reform Bill, given its third reading in 1969. World War Two: The first German V1 flying bomb (the Doodlebug) lands in Britain, 1944.

14 Black activist Nelson Mandela sentenced to life imprisonment in South Africa, 1964.

15 European parliament elections: Green Party surprises everyone by taking 15 per cent of vote, their best performance in any election, 1989. Student Kevin Gateley killed by blow from police truncheon during anti-fascist demonstration in London's Red Lion Square, 1974; this year has seen an upsurge of fascism in Britain, and of protests against it. First non-stop trans-Atlantic flight made by Alcock and Brown, 1919.

17 IRA bomb devastates historic Westminster Hall at the Houses of Parliament, 1974. Iceland becomes independent, 1944. Opening of the Eiffel Tower in Paris, 1889.

19 Act of Parliament passed setting up the Metropolitan Police, 1829.

20 Britain's first interactive television news service is launched, for Videotron cable subscribers in London, 1994. First steamship to cross the Atlantic, the Savannah, arrives in Liverpool after a 27 day crossing, 1819.

21 Major police operation to stop hippies reaching Stonehenge for the solstice ends with 250 arrests, 1989. German sailors scuttle their battle-fleet at Scapa Flow in Orkney rather than surrender it to the British, 1919. Awarding of the first Victoria Cross, to seaman Charles Lucas, 1854.

22 Acquittal of the former Liberal leader Jeremy Thorpe on charges of plotting to kill Norman Scott, 1979. First match played at the new Lord's cricket ground (MCC vs Hertfordshire), 1814.

23 Newspaper price war: Daily Telegraph cuts its price from 48p to 30p to match the Times, which tomorrow goes down to 20p, 1994.

26 Miners Strike: Print unions demand national newspapers carry a statement supporting the striking miners, 1984; most agree, but three refuse and do not appear. Opening of the V&A Museum, 1909.

27 Police raid the gay Stonewall bar in New York, 1969; the occupants fight back, providing the spark for the start of the Gay Liberation movement. Opening of the first nuclear power station, at Obninsk near Moscow, 1954.

28 Assassination in Sarajevo of Archduke Franz Ferdinand of Austro-Hungary, to open World War One, 1914.

30 Official opening of Tower Bridge in London, 1894.

JULY

1 Investiture of Prince Charles as Prince of Wales, at Caernarvon, 1969 (also on this day, in 1961, his future wife Diana Spencer was born). Strike takes most ITV stations off the air until 6 July, 1964. BBC starts the radio receiving licence system, charging ten shillings (50p) annually, 1924; over a million issued in five months.

2 English Civil War: Parliamentarians score first big victory of the war with defeat of Royalists at Battle of Marston Moor near York, 1644.

3 The Rolling Stones guitarist Brian Jones is found dead in the swimming pool of his Sussex home, 1969; on 5 July the Stones stage a free rock concert in Hyde Park in his memory. Mick Jagger delivers some lines from Shelley. Last wartime rationing ends in Britain, 1954.

4 Government announces it is abolishing dog licences, 1984.

5 Start of the first daily television news service in the UK, BBC Television News and Newsreel, presented by Richard Baker, 1954; broadcast at 7.30pm, with newsreaders invisible for first 14 months.

6 The British airship R34 becomes the first to cross the Atlantic, 1919.

9 Respected BBC South Asia correspondent Mark Tully resigns after publicly criticising the corporation, 1994. York Minster seriously damaged by fire after being hit by lightning, 1984.

12 Robert Maxwell buys the Daily Mirror group of newspapers from Reed International for £113 million, 1984.

16 English Civil War: Three-month siege of York by Parliamentarians ends when Royalists surrender, 1644.

18 Scandal after Senator Edward Kennedy's car crashes into the Chappaquidick River, killing his passenger Mary Jo Kopechne, 1969; later Senator Kennedy says he will not stand for president.

19 Lone gunman shoots dead 22 people in a California restaurant before being shot himself by police, 1984. Britain suffers its worst earthquake in a century, 1984.

20 Turkish forces invade northern Cyprus following the pro-Greece coup there which deposed President Makarios, 1974; several weeks fierce fighting ends with peace talks, division of the island and an introduction of a United Nations peace-keeping force.

21 The Home Office switches on the brand new Police National Computer, 1974. The American astronaut Neil Armstrong makes his giant step for mankind and becomes first human to set foot on the Moon, 1969; live TV coverage, with 723 million viewers in 47 countries. World War Two: American troops invade Guam in the Pacific, 1944. Completion of the Trans-Siberian Railway, 1904. A car is driven at over 100mph for the first time, 1904.

25 First crossing of the English Channel by a hovercraft, 1959. First aircraft crossing of the English Channel, by France's Louis Bleriot, 1909.

26 Andreas Whittam Smith resigns as editor of the Independent, 1994; he is replaced by Ian Hargreaves. The Cable and Telecommunications Act is given Royal Assent to establish the legal framework determining the future of satellite and cable television trnsmissions, 1984.

27 Maiden flight of the world's first jet airliner, the British-built de Haviland Comet, 1949.

29 BBC TV starts its regular daily weather forecasts, initially just maps with captions, 1949.

30 Royal Assent given to the Television Act 1954; it authorises the setting up of the advertising-funded Independent Television (ITV) under the Independent Television Authority (ITA), which holds its first meeting on 4 August 1954.

31 Halfpennies cease to be legal tender, 1969. Death of American country-and-western singer Jim Reeves in an air crash, 1964.

BANK HOLIDAY BATTLES: 2 AUGUST 1964
Degenerate Coke-swigging, tea-swilling Rockers
prepare to do seaside battle with the Mods

AUGUST

1 Slavery officially abolished in the British Empire, 1834.

2 Mods and Rockers riots: More seaside violence over Bank Holiday weekend 2-3 August, especially at Hastings and Great Yarmouth, 1964.

3 World War One: Germany declares war on France, 1914; the British naval fleet is mobilised.

4 Maiden flight of the English Electric Lightning, Britain's first supersonic jet fighter, 1954. World War One: Germany invades Belgium and Britain declares war, 1914; USA says it will be neutral.

5 Watergate: President Richard Nixon admits withholding information about the 1972 political burglary by his aides at the Democrat Party headquarters, 1974; resigns 8 August, becoming the first American president to resign in office; succeeded by Gerald Ford.

6 Start of A Book at Bedtime, on BBC's Light Programme, 1949; first reading is the Sherlock Holmes novel The Speckled Band, by Sir Arthur Conan Doyle. Publication of first telegraphed news story, 1844, when the Times is honoured to report birth of Queen Victoria's son at Windsor.

8 First general election covered by both ITV and BBC, 1959. Passing of the Poor Law Amendment Act, creating the notorious Victorian workhouses, 1834.

9 Manson Murders: Actress Sharon Tate and four others murdered in Beverley Hills by Charles Manson, 1969. World War One: First ever air-raid on a town, by a German Zeppelin on Luneville, 1914.

10 Start of industrial action which blacks out ITV for 75 days, then the longest TV strike, 1979.

13 Two hot-air balloons collide in Australia, killing 12 people, 1989. The most recent British executions take place (of Peter Allen and John Walby), 1964.

14 Public order breaks down in Northern Ireland and British troops take over from the police, initially protecting the Catholic community in Derry from Protestant attack, 1969; this day is later seen as the symbolic start to "The Troubles" that continue into the 1990s. Radio transmission is first demonstrated publicly, by Professor Oliver Lodge at a meeting of the British Association in Oxford, 1894.

15 The famous Woodstock pop festival begins in New York state, 1969. Opening of the Panama Canal, 1914.

16 World War One: British Expeditionary Force lands in France, 1914. Peterloo Massacre: Troops kill 11 people and wound over 500 at a peaceful political demonstration in Manchester, 1819; a Times reporter is jailed later; followed by the passing of the repressive "Six Acts" of Parliament, including measures to stamp out radical newspapers.

18 South Africa banned from Olympic Games because of its apartheid policies, 1964. First Mini car unveiled by designer Alec Issigonis, 1959.

20 Thames pleasure boat Marchioness collides with dredger Bowbelle near Blackfriars Bridge, with the loss of 51 lives, 1989. Murder of 83-year old naturalist George Adamson, author of Born Free, 1989. First BBC transmission of 30-line experimental television, using John Logie Baird's studio, 1929.

22 BBC televises Match of the Day for the first time, 1964.

24 Hooliganism and pitch invasions at football grounds culminates in the fatal stabbing of an 18-year old fan at Blackpool, 1974. Anglo-American War: British troops capture Washington and burn White House, 1814.

25 French cargo ship carrying nuclear material sinks off the Belgian coast after colliding with a ferry, 1984. First experimental broadcasts of colour television in USA, 1949. Start of the BBC Monitoring Service, 1939.

27 Lord Louis Mountbatten killed by an IRA bomb while holidaying in Co Sligo in Ireland, 1979; another bomb at Warrenpoint in Co Down kills 15 soldiers. The world's first jet-propelled aircraft, the Heinkel 178, makes its maiden flight, 1939. First balloon ascent in Britain, 1784; it follows the first-ever balloon flight, in France in 1783.

29 Annual Windsor pop festival ends in eight-hour battle with the police, 1974.

30 American space shuttle Discovery makes maiden flight, 1984.

31 Announcement of separation of Princess Anne and husband Mark Phillips, 1989. Isle of Wight pop festival draws 150,000 people to see Bob Dylan, 1969.

SEPTEMBER

1 Libya becomes a socialist republic following coup led by Colonel Gaddafi, 1969. World War Two: Three-year old BBC TV suddenly closes down in middle of a Mickey Mouse cartoon, 1939, not reopening until 7 June 1946.

2 Yorkshire Ripper murders his 12th victim, a 20-year old woman at Bradford, 1979. English Civil War: Parliamentarians lose Cornwall following surrender of most of their troops at Lostwithiel, 1644.

3 World War Two: Britain and France declare war on Germany, 1939; British liner Athenia sunk by U-boat south of Iceland.

4 Opening by the Queen of the Forth Road Bridge, the longest in Europe, 1964; after the ceremony two Royal Navy ships collide. BBC televises the Moon for the first time, through a telescope, 1949.

5 ITV begins broadcasting in colour, 1969.

6 Opening of Britain's first telephone exchange, in the City of London, 1879.

8 The first charity advert (for Marie Curie Cancer Care) appears on British television, following a relaxation of the advertising regulations, 1989. Watergate: President Ford pardons Nixon for his role in the scandal, 1974. World War Two: First V2 rockets land in Britain, killing three people in Chiswick, 1944.

11 The 5.55pm weather forecast is the first sponsored national peak-time television programme, following a relaxation in the regulations, 1989.

12 Ethiopia's Emperor Haile Selassie deposed after 60 years in power, 1974.

13 English Civil War: Royalist troops loot Aberdeen, 1644.

14 Soviet spacecraft Lunik II becomes the first to land on the Moon, 1959. US national anthem The Star-Spangled Banner composed by Francis Key, 1814.

15 Pro-Labour Daily Herald relaunched as the Sun, 1964, calling itself new, independent and radical; bought by Rupert Murdoch in 1969.

16 The UK government drops its 1988 ban on the broadcasting of Sinn Fein, 1994; this follows the Irish government's abandoning of the rule on 19 January.

17 Launch of new quality broadsheet newspaper the Sunday Correspondent, 1989; closes (as tabloid) 27 November, 1990. Britain's first broadband cable television service is switched on, at Swindon, 1984.

18 Opening of the Blackpool Tower, at 518 feet the tallest structure in Britain, and modelled on the Eiffel Tower, 1894. Blackpool illuminations lit up for the first time, 1879.

20 Cromwell's government makes all newspapers illegal, passing the Act Against Unlicensed and Scandalous Books, 1649; Parliament then immediately launches two officially sanctioned titles. Ferdinand Magellan sails from Seville to start the first circumnavigation of the world, 1519.

21 Police storm a squatted mansion at 144 Piccadilly, arresting 150 occupants, 1969.

22 IRA bomb kills ten bandsmen at the Royal Marines school of music at Deal, 1989. Explosion at Gresford Colliery near Wrexham kills 262 miners, 1934.

23 All foreign exchange controls scrapped, allowing exodus of capital from UK, 1979. BBC starts Ceefax teletext service, 1974.

26 Launch of the liner Queen Mary on Clydebank, 1934.

27 Start of national rail strike, 1919; Whitehall fearful of Russian-style revolution in UK.

28 Chris Evans quits as star of Channel 4's morning show Big Breakfast, 1994.

30 Identity cards issued to all British civilians, 1939. Start of first daily service on television, 1929; BBC's 2LO London station transmits low-definition (30 line) programmes by John Logie Baird from Long Acre studio.

OCTOBER

1 Start of the Watergate trial in the USA, 1974. First McDonald's restaurant opens in Britain, in Woolwich, south east London, 1974. Peoples Republic of China comes into being following victory of communist revolution led by Mao Tse Tung, 1949; Nationalists retreat to Taiwan.

3 Fourteen-week occupation of Cammell Laird shipyard at Birkenhead ends with the workers surrendering to the police and then being jailed, 1984.

4 Unemployment reaches 3,283,640 in September, 1984. Launch of Britain's first commercial radio station, LBC, with news and chat, 1974; music station Capital follows a few days later; LBC closes on 5 October 1994, being replaced by London Radio.

5 US TV evangelist Jim Bakker convicted of wrongly taking $158 million from believers, 1989. BBC broadcasts the first episode of Monty Python's Flying Circus, 1969.

6 Turmoil as Chancellor Nigel Lawson raises base lending rates to 15 per cent, the highest for eight years, 1989; this signals the end to the boom years of the late 1980s.

7 First photos taken of the far side of the Moon, by the Russian Lunik III, 1959.

9 Two junior Tory government ministers deny accepting payment to ask parliamentary questions on behalf of lobbyists, but resign within days, 1994.

10 Labour wins the second general election of the year after six months with no overall majority, 1974; now it has a majority of just three over all other parties. English Civil War: Cromwell's army massacres 2,000 soldiers and civilians at Wexford City, Ireland, 1649.

12 IRA bombs the Grand Hotel in Brighton during the Tory Party conference, while many members of the Cabinet are inside, 1984; five people killed, 30 injured, with Margaret Thatcher only narrowly escaping injury. Launch of the R101, the largest airship in the world, 1929. Start of the Boer War in South Africa, 1899; ends 31 May 1902 with British victory.

13 BBC makes its first radio election broadcast (Ramsay MacDonald for Labour), 1924.

14 The 50p coin replaces the ten shilling note, 1969. World War Two: the suicide of the German military leader Field Marshal Erwin Rommel prior to his arrest for taking part in the plot to kill Adolf Hitler, 1944. World War Two: the British battleship Royal Oak is sunk by a U-boat at Scapa Flow with the loss of 883 sailors, 1939.

15 Miners Strike: Talks at ACAS aimed at settling the strike break down after four days, 1984; support for the strike is beginning to collapse. America sees its largest-ever peace demonstration, against the Vietnam War, 1969. Labour wins the general election with a majority of five; 1964; Harold Wilson becomes prime minister, ending 13 years of Tory government. Soviet leader Nikita Kruschev deposed while on holiday and replaced by Leonid Brezhnev.

16 World War Two: First German air attack on UK (Navy ships in the Firth of Forth), 1939. Houses of Parliament seriously damaged by fire, 1834.

18 Severe earthquake shakes San Francisco, killing 273 people, 1989. Communist rule ends in Hungary when it is declared a free republic, 1989. East German communist leader Eric Honecker forced to resign by the crisis in his country.

19 World War Two: American troops land in the Philippines, 1944. World War One: Start of the First Battle of Ypres, 1914. English Civil War: Scottish Parliamentary forces take Newcastle-upon-Tyne, 1644.

20 The Guardian exposes sleaze in the Tory government, 1994; this is the start of a long-running exposure that climaxes in victory for Labour in the May 1997 election. Irish gunboat sinks Spanish trawler off the coast of Cornwall when it refuses to heave to, 1984.

21 Pro-democracy demonstrators in Berlin form human chain across the city, 1989. Mao Tse Tung and his Communist army begin their Long March across China, 1934. Dogger Bank Incident: the Russian fleet, en route to fight Japanese, fires on British fishing boats in the North Sea, 1904; one boat sunk, two men killed.

BRITAIN'S FIRST MOTORWAY: 2 NOVEMBER 1959
A Jag in the outside lane and a Morris Minor in the slow lane. And all British made too

23 BBC report on famine in Ethiopia shocks world into action, 1984.

24 Start of the Wall Street Crash, 1929.

25 For the first time in its 21-year history, commercial radio takes a bigger audience share than the BBC, 1994. Lord Cardigan leads the Charge of the Light Brigade during Crimean War's Battle of Balaklava, 1854; war began May 1854, ends March 1856.

27 Anglia Television is launched, 1959. English Civil War: Battle of Newbury ends inconclusively 1644.

28 Bomb explodes under sports minister Denis Howell's car, 1974. Opening of the Royal Exchange by Queen Victoria, 1844.

30 Poland swept by demonstrations when the body of murdered Catholic priest Jerzy Popieluszko is found near Warsaw, 1979; he was a prominent government critic. World War One: Start of the Battle of Ypres, 1914.

31 Murder of Indian prime minister Indira Gandhi by member of her bodyguard, 1984. Ulster Television is launched, 1959. The radio valve is invented by John Fleming at London University, 1904.

NOVEMBER

2 Opening of the first section of the M1, Britain's first motorway, 1959. Start of top BBC series Hancock's Half Hour, 1954. First publication of a crossword in a British newspaper, the Sunday Express, 1924.

4 A million people march through East Berlin in biggest pro-democracy demonstration yet, 1989; travel to West made easier by loosening of restrictions starting today. US Embassy in Tehran stormed by Iranian revolutionary students, 1979; 53 hostages taken, whom President Carter unsuccessfully tries to release in a helicopter raid on 24 April 1980.

5 Anti-apartheid demonstrators halt Twickenham rugby match involving the South African Springboks, 1969.

6 Tories defeat Labour at the general election following the Daily Mail publishing the "Zinoviev letter", 1924; this was supposedly sent by Moscow Bolsheviks to British socialists urging them to organise a revolution, but was actually commissioned by MI6. Diamonds discovered at Kimberley in South Africa, 1869.

7 Granada sells What the Papers Say to the BBC, 1989. Lord Lucan disappears from his Belgravia home following the murder of his nanny, 1974; he has not been seen since. IRA bomb at pub near Woolwich Barracks kills two people and injures 34.

10 Pro-democracy movement in East German achieves biggest victory with the opening of the 28-mile long Berlin Wall at midnight last night, 1989; massive demonstrations; all border crossing points now clear.

11 Opening of the new Covent Garden vegetable and fruit market at Battersea, 1974.

12 World War Two: Sinking of the German battleship Tirpitz, 1944.

15 Colour television begins in UK, on BBC1 and some ITV stations, using 625-line UHF, 1969; the first colour is for Birds Eye peas. Winston Churchill taken prisoner in the Boer War while working as reporter for the Morning Post, 1899; he escapes soon after.

16 Opening of the Suez Canal, 1869.

17 Sunday Correspondent reporter David Blundy shot dead while covering fighting in San Salvador, 1989. Launch of the modern Sun newspaper under editor Larry Lamb, following purchase from IPC by Rupert Murdoch, 1969.

19 Britain's first National Lottery begins on BBC 1, 1994.

20 Anthony Blunt, Surveyor of the Queen's Pictures, is stripped of his knighthood following his confession to being a Soviet spy, 1979.

21 Televising of House of Commons begins, 1989; strict rules control the coverage. Miners Strike: there is chaos in House of Commons when the government announces families of striking miners will receive less social security benefit than other claimants, 1984. One of the worst ever IRA bomb explosions when 21 people die and 187 are injured in Birmingham when bombs go off in two city-centre pubs, 1974.

24 Resignation of the Czechoslovak communist leadership following massive popular demonstrations against them, 1989. American army says it will court martial Lt William Calley for killing 109 Vietnamese civilians at My Lai, 1969.

27 A fire in a disco in north-east China kills 233 people, 1994; on 9 December over 300 people are killed in a fire in a cinema in north-west China. House of Lords approves six-month trial of televising proceedings, 1984. World War Two: Underground munitions store explodes in Staffordshire, killing 68 people, 1944; the explosion is heard in London

29 The new Prevention of Terrorism Act becomes law, only eight days after the Birmingham pub bombings, 1974; it outlaws the IRA and gives police greater powers to interrogate people travelling between Britain and Ireland. Commander Byrd makes the first flight to the South Pole, 1929. First ever steam-powered newspaper printing press used to produce the Times, 1814.

30 British television's first 24-hour local news station is launched, 1994; Channel One is a cable service exclusively for viewers living in London.

DECEMBER

1 Lady Astor becomes the first woman MP to take her seat in the Commons, 1919.

2 Two men convicted of the £27 million Brinks Mat bullion haul, 1984.

3 Presidents Bush and Gorbachev agree big arms cuts, 1989. Over 2,000 people die when poisonous gas escapes from US-owned Union Carbide pesticide factory in Bhopal, India, 1984; another 180,000 seek hospital help.

4 The Independents begin publishing from Canary Wharf tower, 1994.

6 Gunman kills 14 women students at Montreal University, the worst massacre of its kind in Canadian history, 1989.

8 Richard Gott, literary editor of the Guardian, resigns following allegations he had been used as a Soviet spy by the KGB, 1994. Four hour gun battle in Los Angeles between 300 police and 12 members of the radical black organisation the Black Panthers, 1969. Government announces parking meters are to be introduced, 1954. Opening of IK Brunel's Clifton Suspension Bridge at Bristol, 1864.

12 Mid-Ulster MP Bernadette Devlin sentenced to six months prison for incitement to riot during the 12-14 August disturbances in Derry, 1969.

13 Start of the Battle of the River Plate off Uruguay, 1939; ends on 18 December with the scuttling of the German battleship Admiral Graf Spee. London's underground railway converted from steam to electric power, 1904.

14 Band Aid group of pop stars brought together by Bob Geldorf to raise funds for the famine in Ethiopia, 1984.

16 Death of the American band leader Glenn Miller, 1944; his plane crashes into the English Channel.

17 An estimated 2,000 pro-democracy demonstrators massacred in Romanian city of Timisoara, 1989. Labour Party abandons its traditional support for the closed shop, 1989.

21 First television broadcast of proceedings in the House of Commons, 1989. Government committee of inquiry recommends ending all restrictions on Sunday shopping, 1984. House of Commons votes to end capital punishment for most crimes, for experimental period of five years, 1964; made permanent 16 December, 1969.

22 President Ceausescu of Romania, the most tyrannical ruler in Eastern Europe, flees the country as the people rise against him, 1989; Romanian Army sides with them and joins battle against his secret police; much violence and bloodshed. IRA bomb explodes at home of Edward Heath, 1974.

24 Former Labour minister John Stonehouse found in Australia after disappearing in Miami, leaving his clothes on the beach, 1974. World War One: First ever bomb lands on British soil, dropped by a German aircraft above Dover, 1914.

25 Execution of Romanian dictator Nicolae Ceaucescu and his wife, 1989; they were convicted of "crimes against the people". Cyclone devastates the north Australian city of Darwin, leaving 49 dead, 1974. World War One: Informal Christmas Day truce in trenches on Western Front, 1914; fighting resumes at midnight.

28 Tay Bridge Disaster: Part of the Tay railway bridge collapses as a train is crossing, killing 75 people, 1879.

31 Britain's longest post-War strike comes to an end, 1994; all 41 staff have picketed Sheffield metal firm Keeton and Sons for 8 years, 5 months and 29 days, from 2 July 1986. Half-crowns cease to be legal tender, 1969. 70 children die in cinema fire in Paisley, 1929.

OUTSIDE CONTACTS

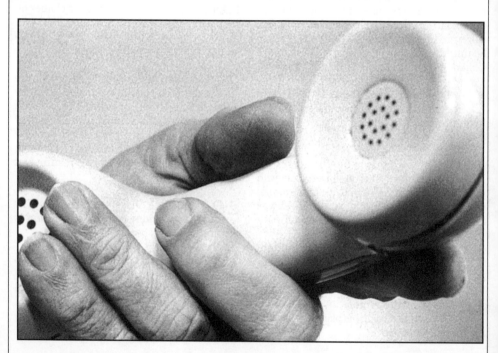

UK facts and figures

The main source of basic UK data is the Government Statistical Service (GSS), run by the Office for National Statistics (ONS). The ONS collects, compiles and makes public all Whitehall's statistical information. It was created in 1996 by merging the Central Statistical Office and the Office of Population Censuses and Surveys. Early in 1998 the government published a Green Paper, asking whether the ONS would be seen as more reliable if it were to become less dependent on Whitehall, being answerable to Parliament instead.

Data-hunters should start with the detailed annual catalogue *The Source* (free) and the *Guide to Official Statistics* (£35.95), explaining where to find all official sources of information. It is summarised in *A Brief Guide to Official Statistics* (free). The most compreh-ensive publication is the *Annual Abstract of Statistics* (£39.50), containing tables on most aspects of UK life. A condensed version is *Key Data* (£10.95), covering all essential material. Handiest of all is the detailed leaflet *UK in Figures* (free), crammed full of the main statistics. None of these publications are analytical; for this, look at *Family Spending, General Household Survey* and *Social Trends*, all three providing graphic pictures of UK life. Most readable is the annual hardback *Britain: An Official Handbook* (£32). All are published by the Stationery Office (formerly HMSO).

GSS began launching this data on Internet in July 1998. *StatBase* aims to give access to most official statistics, with much (but not all) of the wide-ranging service free of charge. ONS is based in London's Pimlico, near Vauxhall Bridge. It has its own shop, and a library, where all the above official titles - and many more - can be consulted; phone first. There is a second library in Newport.

All statistics below come from ONS sources, except where another organisation is quoted.
ONS/GSS, 1 Drummond Gate, London SW1V 2QQ.
Fax 0171-533 6261   Tel 0171-533 6363
Websites: ONS   www.ons.gov.uk
  Statbase   www.statistics.gov.uk
  Stationery Office   www.national-publishing.co.uk

GEOGRAPHY

Areas, 1998, in square kilometres:

England	30,410	Wales	20,758
Scotland	78,789	N Ireland	14,160
UK	244,101	(94,248 sq miles)	

Features, 1998, UK:
The longest river is the Severn, 220 miles.
The highest mountain is Ben Nevis, 4,406 feet. Nobody in Britain lives more than about 75 miles from the sea, which covers 29 per cent of the surface area of Earth.

POPULATIONS

World, 1999:
The population is expected to reach 6 billion in mid-June 1999, taking less than four decades to double from 3 billion in 1960. (Source: United Nations)
European Union, 1997:
373.3m, largest being Germany, 82.2m. (Source: UN)
UK, 1996:
Total 58.80m (38.24m in 1901), of which:

England	49.09m	Wales	2.92m
Scotland	5.13m	N Ireland	1.66m

The UK population is expected to rise to 62.2m by 2021, falling to 54.0m in 2061.
The next UK census is on Sunday 29 April 2001.
Cities, 1996, UK, in thousands:

London	7,074	Cardiff	294
Edinburgh	449	Belfast	297

Ethnic minorities, 1996, GB:
Total population 3.22m, the two largest of which being:

Black	992,000	Indian/	1.42m

PEOPLE

Sex, 1996, male/female:

UK 28.86m (49.1%)		29.97m (50.9%)
E&W	25.56m	26.45m
Scotland	2.49m	2.64m
N Ireland	812,000	851,000

Ages, 1996, UK:

Under 18: 13.56m, pensionable age: 10.67m, together making 41% of the population. Working age: 34.57m.

There is an ageing population, with the number of over-85s trebling between 1961 and 1996 to 1.1m.

By 2021, the proportion of over-65s will rise from 16% to 20% and the under-16s fall from 21% to 18%.

Births, 1996, UK:

Total 733,000, of which male 376,000, female 357,000.

Of these, 260,000 (35.5%) were born outside marriage, compared with 91,000 (12.4%) in 1981.

Women are having children later; the average of mothers was 26.4 in 1976, and 28.6 in 1996.

Contraception, 1995, GB:

28% of women aged 16-49 used no method of contra-ception, and of these half (14% of all women in the age range) did not have a sexual relationship.

Life expectancy, 1994-6, UK, in years:

Male   74.1   Female   79.4

Life expectancy increases about two years every decade.

At age 89 there were three UK women to every man.

Deaths, 1995, UK:

642,000, of which 3,701 in motor vehicle accidents.

Names, 1998, E&W:

The commonest forenames were, in descending order:

Male: John (1.472m), David and Michael

Female: Margaret (688,000), Mary and Susan.

The most popular names for babies born in 1997 were:

Male: Jack, James and Thomas

Female: Chloe, Emily and Sophie.

HOMES AND FAMILIES

Housing stock, 1996, GB:

Total: 23.83m homes, the tenure of which was:

66.9% owner-occupied (49% in 1971).

23.3% publicly rented (32% in 1971).

9.8% privately rented (15% in 1971).

Size of households, 1996-7, GB, compared with 1961:

The average size fell from 3.1 people to 2.4.

One person	27%	1961	14%
Two people	34%	1961	30%
Three or more	38%	1961	57%

The proportion of households consisting of a couple with dependent children fell from 38% in 1961 to 25%.

Marriages, 1995, UK: Total: 322,251, being 11.0 per thousand of population, the lowest figure since 1926. These were remarriages for both partners in 40.4% of cases, compared with 34.7% in 1985. The number of people cohabiting unmarried has more than doubled since 1981; then it was 9% of single women aged 18-49, in 1996/7 it was 27%.

Divorces, 1996, E&W, rate/1,000 of population:

Male: 1996	13.5	1961	2.1
Female: 1996	13.4	1961	2.1

Almost 75% of decrees are granted to wives.

Families, 1996, GB:

The number of one-parent families nearly trebled between 1971 (8%) and 1996 (21%).

DOMESTICITY

Household spending, 1996/7, UK:

Average weekly spending of households was £309.10, the largest elements being food at £55.10, leisure goods and services £49.10, housing £49.10, transport £48.70.

Total spending in 1996 was £464 billion, an increase of 83% on 1971 in real terms.

Machines, 1996/7, UK:

69% of households had a car or van, 99% a TV, 82% a video recorder, 75% a microwave oven, 80% central heating, 20% a dishwasher, 94% a telephone.

Time, 1995, GB:

The average adult spent 8.42 hours/minutes asleep every day, plus 2.33 watching TV and listening to radio. Low income people did more than professionals.

Petty things, 1996, UK:

Half of households owned a pet, with 8m cats, 7m dogs, over 1m budgerigar and over 3m homes with fish.

What a waste, 1995/6, E&W:

Only 6.5% of homes recycled or composted their garbage. Local councils collected 26m tonnes of waste, 90% of it from homes.

WORK/DOLE

Workforce, 1997, UK:
Total 28.7m. Of these, 26.5m were in employment:

14.3m males 12.2m female
3.1m self-employed 22.4m employees.

Unemployed, 1997, GB:
Rates were highest amongst young adults, including nearly 20% of 16-19 year old males and a seventh of females aged 16-19.
The unemployment rate for Black 16-24 year olds was more than double the rate for Whites.

Gender, 1997, UK:
Women outnumber male part-time workers by four to one, although the number of men working part-time more than doubled between 1984 and 1997.

Average wages for all full-time employees, 1997, GB: All adults
£367.6for 40.3 hours
 Men £408.7 for 41.8 hours
 Women £297.2 for 37.6 hours
Doctors were being paid £870 pw. But a fifth (20.8%) of all GB employees were receiving less than £4.00 per hour, including 41% of all workers in agriculture, fishing, hotels, restaurants and distribution.
Average wages in London were the highest, at just over £480 pw. Over a quarter of all employees in Wales, SW England and the North East were receiving less than £4.00 per hour..

Wealth, 1994, UK:
The richest 1% of adults owned 19% of marketable wealth; the poorest 50% owned only 7%.
The Sunday Times 1998 Rich List said Lord Sainsbury was Britain's wealthiest person (£3.3 billion); the top 1,000 people (only two of them black, and 64 female) had over £108 billion.
In 1997 on all the globe, eight million people (0.1% of the human race) owned $17,400,000,000,000, about £1.3m each; 59% of them lived in Europe and North America (Source: Merrill-Gemini Report).

TRAVEL

Length of public roads, 1996, GB:
All roads368,820 kms 1986 351,077 kms
Motorways 3,225 kms 1986 2,921 kms

Licensed motor vehicles, 1996, GB:
Total 26.30m 1986 21.70m
Private cars 21.17m 1986 16.98m
Small goods 2.27m Large goods 413,000
Buses/coaches75,900 1987 71,700

Traffic on all roads, 1996, GB, in billion kilometres:
All motor vehicles 443
Cars and taxis 362 Goods vehicles 71
Buses & coaches4.8 Bicycles 4.3
The average daily flow of traffic increased by half between 1981 and 1996; on motorways it doubled.

Road accidents, 1996, GB:
Total 235,939, involving 401,625 motor vehicles.
Deaths: 3,598 deaths (including 997 pedestrians and   203 cyclists), the lowest since records began, in 1926.

Rail and railtrack, 1995/6, GB:
Route open: 16,666 km. Passenger stations: 2,514.
1,753 accidents in 1996/7, with one death, 257 injured.

Air traffic, 1996, UK international:
Flights 992,300 Scheduled 763,000
Passengers 105.6m Scheduled 74.9m

Walkers, GB, miles:
The average distance walked per person has fallen steadily over many years:
 1985/6 244
 1994/6 200

Parliament and politics

OLD NATIONS ...

United Kingdom (UK): This is the official title for the state of Great Britain (the island comprising England, Wales and Scotland) and Northern Ireland. The Channel Islands and Isle of Man are not part of the UK, being direct dependencies of the Crown, and have a special relationship with the UK government. The UK is the result of colonialism originating in south-east England in Roman times, culminating in Acts of Union being passed in 1536-42 for Wales, 1707 for Scotland (creating the name "United Kingdom") and 1801 for all the island of Ireland.

England: The name England comes from the Angles, one of the Germanic tribes that succeeded the Romans in the 5th century. There were many autonomous Anglo-Saxon settlements until the single Kingdom of England was created in 954. The Welsh were the pre-Anglo-Saxon inhabitants of England who moved west. Many were also the original Britons. The Scots were the Irish people who settled in Argyll in the 6th century.

Britain: The original Anglo-Saxon descriptive term for the island of England, Wales and Scotland was Britain. The surrounding islands (including the Channel Islands and Isle of Man) were part of it, but not Ireland. Today the word Britain is used in a looser way, often referring to the UK in general. The UK government is also known as the British government, but strictly this is incorrect, as Britain does not include Northern Ireland.

Great Britain (GB): Great Britain, like Britain, consists of England, Wales and Scotland. It is the semi-official name that became common after the monarchies of Scotland and England merged in 1603. This event revived the Anglo-Saxon title of Britain that had fallen into disuse following the 11th century Norman invasion. "Great" Britain distinguished the new 17th century nation from both the old Anglo-Saxon island and from "Little" Britain (Britanny). Today Britain and Great Britain are synonymous.

Ireland: The 1921 Anglo-Irish Treaty gave near-independence to all Ireland except for the six counties in the north-east. These, with three other counties, had been known since the Middle Ages as Ulster, one of the four provinces of Ireland. The six counties are now called Northern Ireland officially, or Ulster unofficially by many people, especially non-Republicans. The other 26 counties of the island formed the Irish Free State from 1921 until 1937, when it achieved full independence, becoming Eire, aka the Republic of Ireland. The Republic is also often called just "Ireland" - but so is the whole island!

British Isles: This is the geographical term for all the islands forming old Britain, Northern Ireland and Eire. GB is the world's eighth-largest island; Ireland is 20th.

... NEW NATIONS

Wales and Scotland: In September, 1997, the people of Wales and Scotland voted for devolution. Scotland had a 60 per cent turnout of its 3.97m electorate, with 1.78m (74 per cent) voting yes. In Wales there were 1.11m votes, but the pro-majority was only 6,721, just 0.6 per cent. Both elections are scheduled for 1999, with the Scottish Parliament and Welsh Assembly both starting soon after. Scotland will have 129 MSPs, elected by a form of proportional representation for four years, with its home in Edinburgh. The Cardiff-based 60 Welsh members will have much less power than their Scotland counterparts.

England: The Wales/Scotland devolution raised the prospect of revived Anglo-Saxon nationalism, both anti-Europe and pro-Tory. Whitehall hoped to defuse and divert this new nativism by creating nine English regions.

Ireland: A referendum in May 1998 voted overwhelmingly for a new Northern Ireland Assembly of 108 members and a North-South Ministerial Council. In the north there was a 81.1 per cent turnout, 71.1 per cent saying yes; in Eire, a 55.6 per cent turnout, with 94.4 per cent yes. Elections took place in June, with

February 1999 scheduled as formal start-date. Alongside the Assembly will be the new Council of the Isles (CoI), with representatives from all the national ruling bodies in the British Isles. The CoI "will provide the harmonious and mutually beneficial development of the totality of relationships among the peoples of these islands". In practice, it would preserve some form of internal power for all the UK and Eire governing bodies if they joined the EU fully.

1997 ELECTION

The last UK general election was on 1 May 1997. The turnout was 31.3 million voters, 71.6 per cent of the 43.7 million registered electors. This was the lowest turnout since 1945. There was a 10.5 per cent national swing to Labour, which won 419 seats with 43.2 per cent of the turnout. But 77 per cent of the total UK population of 58.8m did not vote Labour. The Liberal Democrats had 12.1 per cent of the turnout, but only won 46 seats. The Labour majority was 177. In all by-elections to mid-1998 no seats changed hands. The results for the three main parties are shown below. Seats won by other parties were:

England: *Independent* (Martin Bell) 1
Wales: *Plaid Cymru* 4
Scotland: *Scottish National Party* 6
Northern Ireland: *Ulster Unionist* 10
   SDLP 3
   Democratic Unionist 2
   Sinn Fein 2
   UK Unionist 1

VOTING NATIONS

England has 529 seats; Labour won 329 of them, Tories 165 (all bar 17 of them in the South and Midlands), Liberal Democrats 34, Independent one. **Wales** has 40 seats; Labour won 34, Lib Dems 2, Plaid Cymru 4 (with 161,000 votes, 10 per cent of the total turnout in Wales), Tories none. **Scotland** has 72 seats; Labour won 56, Liberal Democrats 10, Scottish Nationalists 6 (8.3 per cent of the seats, but with 621,540 votes, 22 per cent of the total turnout in Scotland), Tories none. **Northern Ireland** has 18 seats, all won by indigenous parties (see above). The Ulster Unionists took 56 per cent of the seats with 33 per cent of the votes.

Labour's 418-seat win in 1997 was its highest-ever number; 1945 was next, with 393. A record number of woman MPs was elected: 120. The Tories had the lowest share of the vote since 1832 and the lowest number of MPs since 1906. The Lib Dems won their highest number of seats since 1929. The Referendum Party won 810,778 votes (2.6 per cent of the turnout) but no seats. The National Front's six candidates won a total of only 2,716 votes; the British National's 57 won 35,833.

Since the 1997 election it has been possible to drive east-west from the North Sea to the Irish Sea (Grimsby to Liverpool) without passing through a Tory seat, and north-south from John O'Groats to Lands End passing through only one (Ryedale, North Yorkshire). The most northerly Tory seat is Hexham.

AND NEXT?

General elections can be held at any time, but by law the House of Commons has to be dissolved not later than five years after its first meeting following an election. This usually takes place about two weeks after polling day. In addition, the election campaigns must last for at least 23 days. So the next election deadline is June 2002. The Conservatives will need a swing of 11.6 per cent to win. The gap between the 9 April 1992 and 1 May 1997 elections was the longest since the 1911 Parliament Act: five years and 22 days.

1997 General election results					
	seats won	% of all seats	votes	% of turnout	% of electorate
Labour	419	63.6%	13.52m	43.2%	30.1%
Conservatives	165	25.0%	9.60m	30.7%	22.0%
Liberal Democrats	46	7.0%	5.24m	16.7%	12.1%
Total + other parties	659	100%	31.29m	100%	71.6%

COMMONS CONTACTS

Main number (all MPs)	0171-219 3000
Information/press office	0171-219 4272
Night line	0171-219 3000
Committees office	0171-219 4300
Library	0171-219 4272
Official report (Hansard)	0171-219 3764
Parliamentary Bookshop	0171-219 3890
Parliamentary Archives	0171-219 3074
Press Gallery/Lobby: Secretary	0171-219 4395
Superintendent	0171-219 5371
Private bill office	0171-219 3250
Public bill office	0171-219 3251
Serjeant at Arms	0171-219 3030
Whips offices: Government	0171-219 4400
Opposition (Conservative)	0171-219 3237
Liberal Democrat	0171-219 5654
Website	www.parliament.uk

HOUSE OF LORDS

In mid-1998 the House of Lords had 1,175
active members, including 515 life peers, 759
hereditary and 26 spiritual. The parties were:

476 Conservatives
176 Labour
72 Liberal Democrat
323 cross-benchers

Main number	0171-219 3000
Press/information office	0171-219 3107
Private bill office	0171-219 3231
Public bill office	0171-219 3153
Committees office	0171-219 3218
Judicial business	0171-219 3111
Library	0171-219 5242
Official report (Hansard)	0171-219 3031
Serjeant at Arms (Black Rod)	0171-219 3100
Whips offices: Government	0171-219 3131
Opposition (Conservative)	0171-219 4770
Liberal Democrat	0171-219 3114
Website	www.parliament.uk

PARLIAMENTARY PARTIES

Labour Party	0171-802 1000
Press	0171-896 4140
Regional offices: Central	0115-943 1777
London	0171-490 4904
North & Yorkshire	01924-291221
North West	01925-574913
Scotland	0141-352 6900
South East	01473-228700
South West	01249-460011
Wales	01222-877707
West Midlands	0121-553 6601
Website	www.labour.org.uk
Conservative Party	0171-222 9000

Press	0171-896 4140
MEPs, London	0171-222 1720
Scottish Conservative Party	0131-555 2900
Primrose League	0171-976 7158
Website	www.conservative-party.org.uk
Liberal Democrats	0171-222 7999
Lib Dems Wales	01222-382210
Scottish Lib Dems	0131-337 2314
Alliance Party of N Ireland	01232-324274
Website	www.libdems.org.uk
Plaid Cymru	01222-646000
Website	www.plaidcymru.org.uk
Scottish National Party	0131-226 3661
Website	www.snp.org.uk
Sinn Fein	01232-323214
Social Democratic & Labour Party	01232-247700
Ulster Democratic Unionist Party	01232-471155
Ulster Unionist Party	01232-324601
UK Unionist Party	01247-272994

OTHER ORGANISATIONS

Anti-Nazi League	0171-924 0333
British National Party	0181-316 4721
Campaign for a Scottish Parliament	0131-225 7814
Campaign for an Independent Britain	0181-340 0314
Charter 88	0171-833 1988
Communist League Party	0171-401 2293
Communist Party of Britain	0171-275 8162
Conservatives Against a Federal Europe	0171-799 2655
Co-operative Party	0171-439 0123
Democratic Left	0171-278 4443
Electoral Reform Society	0171-928 1622
English National Party	0171-278 5221
Fabian Society	0171-222 8877
Freedom Association	0171-928 9925
Freemasons	0171-831 9811
Green Left	01904-672489
Green Party	0171-272 4474
Hansard Society	0171-955 7478
Islamic Party of Britain	01908-671756
Labour Campaign for Electoral Reform	0117-924 5139
Liberal Party (not Lib-Dems)	0171-233 2124
Monday Club	0171-2495368
Monster Raving Loony Party	01364-652205
National Front (also called National Democrats)	0181-471 6872
New Britain	0171-628 2843
Red Pepper Magazine	0171-281 7024
Referendum Movement	0990-110440
Referendum Party	0171-227 8500
Socialist Movement	0800-581611
Socialist Party (ex-Militant Labour)	0181-533 3311
Socialist Party of Gt Britain	0171-622 3811
Socialist Workers Party	0171-538 5821
Third Way	0171-373 3432
UK Independence Party	0171-434 4559
Western Goals Institute	0171-824 8634
Workers Revolutionary Party	0171-928 3218

Departments of state

PRIME MINISTER'S OFFICE

10 Downing Street, London SW1A 2AA
Main number   0171-270 3000
Press (24 hour)   0171-930 4433
Press Secretary   0171-930 7919
Website   www.number-10.gov.uk
Prime Minister   Tony Blair
Deputy Prime Minister   John Prescott
Press Secretary   Alastair Campbell

AG., FISHERIES & FOOD
Nobel House, 17 Smith Square, London SW1P 3JR
MAFF: main number   0171-238 6000
Information Division   0171-238 5603
Press Branch   0171-238 5599
  Eves   0171-270 8080
  Food safety, animal/plant health 0171-238 6044
  Fisheries, countryside, floods   0171-238 6001
  Agricultural/food industries, CAP 0171-238 6043
Publicity Branch   0171-270 3000
Helpline   0645-335577
Minister   Nick Brown
Minister of State   Jeff Rooker
Ministers: Fisheries/Countryside Elliot Morley
  Farming /Food Industry   Lord Donoughue

CABINET OFFICE

70 Whitehall, London SW1A 2AS
CO: main number   0171-270 1234
Head of Information   0171-270 0516
Press   0171-270 0635
Chancellor of the Duchy of Lancaster Jack Cunningham
Minister of State   Lord Falconer of Thoraton
Under Secretary, OPS   Peter Kilfoyle

CULTURE, MEDIA & SPORT

2-4 Cockspur Street, London SW1Y 5DH
DCMS: main number   0171-211 6000
Public enquiries   0171-211 6200
Information Division   0171-211 6263
Press   0171-211 6273
  Heritage, tourism, lottery   0171-211 6267
  Media, press regulation, arts   0171-211 6266
  Sport   0171-211 6275
Broadcasting & Media Group 0171-211 6410
  Broadcasting Policy Division   0171-211 6469
  Media Division   0171-211 6460
Secretary of State   Chris Smith
Minister for Film and Tourism Janet Anderson
Parliamentary Under Secs: Arts Alan Howarth
  Sport   Tony Banks

MINISTRY OF DEFENCE

Horseguards Avenue, London SW1A 2HB
MOD: main number   0171-218 9000
Director of Information & News 0171-218 5317
Press   0171-218 2906
  Eves   0171-218 7907
  Army   0171-218 3255
  Navy   0171-218 3257
  RAF   0171-218 3253
  Policy   0171-218 7931
  Procurement   0171-218 7714
Tri-Service Joint HQ   01923-846029
Army HQ, Wilton   01722-433345
Navy HQ, Northwood   01923-837336
RAF HQ, High Wycombe   01494-496131
Chief of Defence Staff   0171-218 2116
D-Notice Committee   0171-218 2206
Secretary of State   George Robertson
Ministers of State: Armed Forces Doug Henderson
  Defence Procurement   Lord Gilbert
Parliamentary Under Secretary John Spellar

EDUCATION & EMPLOYMENT

Great Smith Street, London SW1P 3BT
DfEE: main number   0171-925 5000
Information office   0171-925 5555
Press   0171-925 5615
  Employment, disability, learning 0171-925 6487
  Schools, regions, campaigns 0171-925 5105
Secretary of State   David Blunkett
Ministers of State:
  Employment and disability rights Andrew Smith
  School standards   Estelle Morris
  Further/higher education Baroness Blackstone
Ministers: School standards Charles Clarke
  Life-long learning   George Mudie
  Early years   Margaret Hodge

ENVIRONMENT, TRANSPORT, REGIONS

Eland House, Bressenden Place, London SW1E 5DU
DETR: main number   0171-890 3000
Communications Directorate 0171-890 3333
  Eves   0171-873 1985
Press: Environment   0171-890 4626
  Housing, local government 0171-890 4617
  Planning, London, construction 0171-890 4606
  Regions   0171-890 4614
  Transport   0171-890 3231
Secretary of State   John Prescott
Minister of Transport   John Reid
Environment Minister of State Michael Meacher
Environment/Transport/Regions Ministers of State:

Regions, Regeneration, Planning — Dick Caborn
Local Government, Housing — Hilary Armstrong
London and Construction — Nick Raynsford
Transport in London — Glenda Jackson
Roads — Lord Whitty, Alan Meale

FOREIGN &COMMONWEALTH

Downing Street, London SW1A 2AL
FCO: main number	0171-270 3000
Press	0171-270 3100
Europe/UN/human rights	0171-270 3119
Asia/Pacific/Americas/North Africa/	
Middle East/travel	0171-270 2861
Consular/drugs/crime/media	0171-270 3095
Information Dept	0171-270 6052
Public enquiries	0374-500900
Secretary of State	Robin Cook
Ministers of State	Derek Fatchett
	Joyce Quin, Tony Lloyd
Parliamentary Under Secretary	Baroness Symons

DEPARTMENT OF HEALTH

Richmond House, 79 Whitehall, London SW1A 2NS
DOH: main number	0171-210 3000
Eves	0171-210 5368
Press	0171-210 5225
Central desk	0171-210 5227
NHS: doctors/funds/licensing	0171-210 5226
NHS: hospitals/ambulances	0171-210 5230
Social care/mental illness/drugs	0171-210 5231
Public health/food safety/Aids	0171-210 5228
Media Initiatives	0171-210 5436
NHS Executive	0113-254 5000
Public enquiries	0171-210 4850
Health Information Service	0800-665544
Secretary of State	Frank Dobson
Minister for Public Health	Tessa Jowell
Ministers of State	Alan Milburn
Parliamentary Under Secretaries	Paul Boateng,
	Baroness Hayman

HOME OFFICE

50 Queen Anne's Gate, London SW1H 9AT
HO: main number	0171-273 4000
Eves	0171-273 4595
Director, Communication	0171-273 3757
Press: Chief press officer	0171-273 4117
Police/emergencies/terrorism	0171-273 4610
Criminal justice/crime	0171-273 4600
Immigration/asylum/ID cards	0171-273 4620
Constitution/data/drugs/fire	0171-273 4640
Prison Service	0171-217 6633
Secretary of State	Jack Straw
Ministers of State:	Alun Michael, Lord Williams
Parliamentary Under Secretaries:	Mike O'Brien
	George Howarth, Kate Hoey

INTERNATIONAL DEV'MENT

94 Victoria Street, London SW1E 5JL
DFID: main number	0171-917 7000
Eves	0171-917 0950
Information Dept	0171-917 0618
Press	0171-917 0435
Secretary of State	Clare Short
Parliamentary Under Secretary	George Foulkes

LAW OFFICERS' DEPT

Attorney General's Chambers, 9 Buckingham Gate,
London SW1E 6JP
Main number	0171-828 7155
Press	0171-233 7524
Attorney General	John Morris QC
Solicitor General	Ross Cranston QC

LORD ADVOCATE'S DEPT

2 Carlton Gardens, London SW1Y 5AA
25 Chambers Street, Edinburgh EH1 1LA
Main numbers: London	0171-210 1010
Edinburgh	0131-226 2626
Lord-Advocate	Andrew Hardie
Solicitor General for Scotland	Colin Boyd

LORD CHANCELLOR'S DEPT

54/60 Victoria Street, London SW1E 6QW
LCD: main number	0171-210 8500
Eves	0171-210 8512
Press	0171-210 8512/3
Lord Chancellor	Lord Irvine of Lairg
Parliamentary Secretary	Geoff Hoon

NORTHERN IRELAND OFFICE

11 Millbank, London SW1P 4QE
Stormont Castle, Belfast BT4 3ST
NIO: main numbers: Belfast	01232-520700
London (24 hr)	0171-210 3000
NI Information Service, Belfast	01232-528211
Press	01232-528233
London press office	0171-210 6473
Public enquiries	0171-210 6454
Agriculture Dept	01232-520100
Economic Development Dept	01232-529900
Education Dept	01247-279279
Environment Dept	01232-540540
Finance Dept	01232-520400
Health & Social Services Dept	01232-520500
Police Authority	01232-230111
Secretary of State	Marjorie Mowlam
Ministers of State:	Adam Ingram, Paul Murphy
Parlt Under Secretaries	Lord Dubs, John McFall

OFFICE OF PUBLIC SERVICE

Cabinet Office, 70 Whitehall, London SW1A 2AS
OPS: main number   0171-270 1234
Press   0171-270 0635
Chancellor of the Duchy of Lancaster Jack Cinningham
Parliamentary Secretary   Peter Kilfoyle

PRIVY COUNCIL OFFICE

68 Whitehall, London SW1A 2AT
Office   0171-270 0472
Judicial Committee   0171-270 0485
President of the Council and Leader of the
House of Commons   Margaret Beckett
Lord Privy Seal and Leader of the House of Lords and
Minister for Women   Baroness Jay of Paddington

SCOTTISH OFFICE

Dover House, Whitehall, London SW1A 2AU
St Andrew's House, Regent Road, Edinburgh EH1
3DG
Main numbers: Edinburgh   0131-556 8400
  London   0171-270 3000
Information Directorate   0131-244 1111
  Eves   0131-556 8400
  Press   0131-244 2718/2661
  Press: London   0171-270 6745
Enquiry Point   0345-741741
Secretary of State   Donald Dewar
Ministers of State:
  Home affairs and devolution   Henry McLeish
  Campaigns   Helen Liddell
Ministers:
  Agriculture, environment, fisheries   Lord Sewel
  Health and arts   Sam Galbraith
  Local goverment/transport   Calum MacDonald
  Industry   Gus MacDonald

DEPT OF SOCIAL SECURITY

79 Whitehall, London SW1A 2NS
DSS: main number   0171-238 3000
Press   0171-238 0800
  Eves   0171-238 0761
  Chief press officer   0171-238 0748
  Welfare reform   0171-238 0750
  Child support/disability   0191-238 0749
  Benefit/support/poverty   0171-238 0752
  Fraud/pensions/insurance   0171-238 0754
  Contributions Agency   0191-225 3502
  Benefits Agency   0113-232 4499
  Child Support Agency   01384-488000
Freeline help   0800-666555
Secretary of State   Alistair Darling
Social Security and Welfare Reform   John Denham
Parliamentary Under Secretaries   Baroness Hollis
    of Heigham, Angela Eagle, Stephen Timms

TRADE AND INDUSTRY

1 Victoria Street, London SW1H 0ET
DTI: main number   0171-215 5000
Eves   0171-215 4657
Information Director   0171-215 5951
News Director   0171-215 5954
Press: Energy/industry/regions   0171-215 6424
  Consumer/corporate/trade   0171-215 5970
Secretary of State   Peter Mandelson
Ministers of State: Lord Simon of Highbury, Ian
        McCartney, Brian Wilson, John Battle
Parliamentary Under Secretaries :   Barbara Roche,
    Kim Howells, Lord Sainsbury of Turville

TREASURY

Parliament Street, London SW1P 3AG
HMT: main number   0171-270 3000
Public enquiries   0171-270 4860
Press   0171-270 5238
  Public finances   0171-270 5245
  Private finance   0171-270 5192
  Taxation   0171-270 5187
Chancellor of the Exchequer   Gordon Brown
Chief Secretary   Stephen Byers
Paymaster General   Geoffrey Robinson
Financial Secretary   Dawn Primarolo
Economic Secretary   Patricia Hewitt

WELSH OFFICE

Gwydyr House, Whitehall, London SW1A 2ER
New Crown Building, Cathays Park, Cardiff CF1 3NQ
WO: main numbers: Cardiff   01222-825111
  London   0171-270 3000
Information Division: Enquiries   01222-825724
Press: Cardiff   01222-825648
  London   0171-270 0558
Secretary of State   Ron Davies
Parliamentary Under Secretaries   Win Griffiths
                                      Peter Hain

INTERNET

Cross departmental website   www.open.gov.uk

Public contacts

The corridors of Whitehall have always been shrouded in secrecy, but since 1994 some glimpses along them have been possible using the *Code of Practice on Access to Government Information*. The code - also called **Open Government** - says there is a "common set of standards governing the disclosure of information". Almost all government departments and bodies must respond to requests for information; notable exemptions are policing, defence and the security and intelligence services. Departmental contact points are listed below, under Openness Contacts. You may be told you have to write to the appropriate office; detailed replies should come within 20 days. There may be a charge, although usually there is not. Copies of the code are available from the Citizen's Charter Publication Line: 0345-223242.

The Labour government promised a **Freedom of Information Act** soon after election Its White Paper, published in December 1997, said the purpose was to "encourage more open and accountable government by establishing a general statutory right of access to official records and information". The public would have new legal rights, but Whitehall would also retain - and in some cases would tighten - its formal control over sensitive areas. The Act was scheduled for 1999. Media cynics believe its main aim will be the stricter management of information processing, rather than making it freer. The Act is being formulated by the Cabinet Office's FoI Unit: 0171-270 1880.

The main Whitehall knowledge managing machine is the **Central Office of Information**. The COI's main role is "the publicity procurement Agency for government". It has a wide remit, handling the flow of all information in and out of the government. Professional information officers in Whitehall departments make up the **Government Information Service**. This elusive body can be contacted via the Cabinet Office's Information Office Management Unit: 0171-276 2709.

The data and news that all these official organisations and people are processing comes from many internal sources. The best one of these open to the public is the **Office for National Statistics**, with its own library.

OPENNESS CONTACTS

Agriculture, Fisheries & Food	
Paul Fildes	0645-335577
Central Office of Information	
Mike Wheeler	0171-261 8488
Charity Commissioners	
Frances Grey	0171-210 4647
Culture, Media & Sport, Dept of	
Enquiry Unit	0171-211 6200
Customs & Excise	
David Rennie	0171-865 5777
Data Protection Registrar	
Ruth Robinson	01625-545700
Defence, Ministry of	
Secretary of State's office	0171-218 6432
Education & Employment, Dept for	
Enquiry unit: John Quinn	0171-925 5555
Electricity Regulation, Office of (OFFER)	
Ian Bickley	0121-456 6208
Employment Service	
Dean Weston	0171-389 1529
Environment, Transport & Regions, Dept of	
Public Enquiry Point	0171-890 3000
Fair Trading, Office of	
Public Liaison Unit	0171-269 8904
Foreign & Commonwealth Office	
Enquiry Unit: Kate Crowe	0171-270 3865
Gas Supply, Office of (OFGSA)	
Public Affairs	0171-828 0898
Health, Dept of	
Sarah Armstrong	0171-210 5787
Health & Safety Executive	
Infoline	0541-545500
Home Office	
Info Services: Jane Humphreys	0171-273 3072
Inland Revenue	
Jen Morgan	0171-438 6879
International Development, Dept for	
Anne Fraser	01355-843167
HM Land Registry	
Denise Reynolds	0171-917 8888
Legal Aid Board	
Jackie Collins	0171-813 1000
Lord Chancellor's Dept	
Kevin Fraser	0171-210 8533
National Lottery, Office of	
John Park	0171-227 2030
National Savings	
A Johnson	0191-374 5656

National Statistics, Office for
Landis Land — 0171-270 5973
Northern Ireland Office
Denis Carson — 01232-527015
Ordnance Survey
Mr A Warmington — 01703-792605
Passenger Rail Franchising
Gareth Williams — 0171-799 8823
Public Record Office
Ms A Crawford — 0181-392 8289
Public Service, Office of
Robert Cayzer — 0171-270 1875
Rail Regulator, Office of
Ian Cooke — 0171-282 2002
Royal Mint
Linda Viner — 01443-222111
Scottish Office
Craig Russell — 0131-244 0102
Social Security, Dept of
Disclosure of Info Unit — 0171-962 8142
Benefits Agency — 0113-232 7932
Contributions Agency — 0191-225 5492
Child Support Agency — 0191-225 3154
Trade & Industry, Dept of
Open Govt Enquiry Point — 0171-215 6668
Transport, Dept of
Tracey Wallace — 0171-271 5262
DVLA: Janice Jones — 01792-782965
Highways Agency: David Buxton — 0171-921 4031
HM Treasury
Charles Keseru — 0171-270 5188
Water Services, Office of (OFWAT)
Jane Fisher — 0121-625 1361
Welsh Office
Tom Hunter — 01222-825275

CENTRAL OFFICE OF INFORMATION

COI, Hercules Road, London SE1 7DU
Main number — 0171-928 2345
Enquiries — 0171-261 8241
Press — 0171-261 8815
Eves — 0171-261 8820
Email — coipress@gtnet.gov.uk
Marketing communications — 0171-261 8744
Films, radio and events — 0171-261 8598
New media — 0171-261 8406
News distribution service — 0171-261 8445

OFFICE FOR NATIONAL STATISTICS

ONS, 1 Drummond Gate, London SW1V 2QQ
Main number — 0171-233 9233
Enquiries — 0171-533 6363
Press — 0171-533 5697
Social statistics, labour — 0171-533 5712
Business — 0171-533 5725
Email — info@ons.gov.uk

ESSENTIAL GUIDES

Britain: An Official Handbook
ONS/Stationery Office — Tel 0171-873 9090
The official annual picture of the British government .

Civil Service Yearbook
Stationery Office — Tel 0171-873 9090
The twice-yearly Whitehall directory of ministries, civil service bodies and Next Steps agencies, with addresses, numbers and top personnel. With CD-ROM.

IPO Directory
Central Office of Information — Tel 0171-928 2345
Twice-yearly directory of information and press officers everywhere in and around Whitehall. Only available to journalists.

Parliamentary Companions
Vachers Publications — Tel 01442-876135
PMS Publications — Tel 0171-233 8283
Guides to Westminster and Whitehall. Both Vachers and PMS publish a quarterly European Companion describing the EU in the same detail.

Register of Members Interests
Stationery Office — Tel 0171-873 9090
Annual confessions of MPs about their financial interests.

GOVERNMENT HELPLINES

Citizen's Charter — 0345-223242
Crown Prosecution Service — 0171-334 8505
Customs & Excise — 0171-202 4227
VAT helpline — 0171-202 4087
Education, OFSTED — 0171-421 6664
Employment, Just the Job — 0800-250200
Industrial tribunals — 0345-959775
Fisheries & food (MAFF) — 0645-335577
Foreign & Commonwealth Office — 0374-500900
Travel advice — 0171-270 4129
Health & Safety Exec — 0114-289 2345
Health Info Service — 0800-665544
Home Office publications — 0171-273 3072
Inland Revenue Taxback — 0800-660800
National Rivers Authority: emergency — 0800-807060
Post Office — 0345-223344
Royal Mail Customer Service — 0345-740740
Scottish Office enquiries — 0345-741741
Social Security — 0800-666555
Trade & Industry — 0171-215 5000
Business in Europe — 0117-944 4888
Business Links — 0345-567765
Transport, DVLA driver — 01792-772151
DVLA vehicle — 01792-772134
Highways Agency — 0345-504030

Quangos

Quangos are public service bodies run as private businesses. The word "quango" is an abbreviation of "**QU**asi-**A**utonomous **N**on-**G**overnmental **O**rganisation". The Tory government began the privatisation process in 1988, aiming to transfer three-quarters of the Civil Service to quangoland within about ten years. This was achieved early in 1998, by which time the new Labour government had also become happier with the concept, and tried to improve it rather than abolish it.

The government officially calls most quangos either **Non-Departmental Public Bodies** (NDPBs) or **Next Steps Executive Agencies** (NSEAs). The NDPBs are almost separate from the government, while NSEAs are semi-detached subsidiaries of departments.

Whitehall defines an **NDPB** as: "A body which has a role in the process of national government, but is not a government department or part of one, and which accordingly operates to a greater or lesser extent at arms length from ministers". In 1997 there were over 107,000 staff in 1,200 NDPBs. Only a third of their 38,000 governors were women, an imbalance Whitehall promised to correct.

NSEAs are commonly known as *Executive Agencies*, or just *agencies*. They are the Next Steps Programme which was launched in 1988. NSEAs are less autonomous than the NDPBs. They are partially-independent organisations performing executive functions of government, while staying part of the civil service. Examples are the Prison Service, Land Registry, Meteorological Office and Ordnance Survey. There were 138 NSEAs by the beginning of 1998, employing 384,000 civil servants, with another 16 agencies and 7,300 staff in the pipeline.

At a local level, NDPBs, NSEAs and other types of quangos have taken over many services previously run by local authorities or by elected regional/national bodies, such as NHS hospitals, education and housing.

A major problem in understanding quangos is the similarity between semi-privatised and fully privatised bodies such as former gas, water and electricity boards, now the property of shareholders. It is often difficult to discover what formal status a quango has: an NSEA, private company, government department, trust, NDPB, public company or a mixture of some of these ingredients. In addition, public accountability is hard to define, often being a personal one where chief execs are responsible to the minister of the sponsoring government department. In Whitehall, the quangos and Civil Service come under the Office of Public Service (OPS), part of the Cabinet Office. The Cabinet Office has two basic roles: providing ministers with the bureaucracy services they need; and ensuring the Cabinet has managerial power over all public services, via the OPS. The OPS is headed by the Chancellor of the Duchy of Lancaster.

QUANGO GUIDES

Next Steps Briefing Note
Office of Public Service   0171-270 1234
Website   www.open.gov.uk/co
An informative newsletter containing an up-to-date list of all NSEAs. Enquiries about quangos should start with the OPS, which is part of the Cabinet Office.

Councils, Committees and Boards
CBD Research, £135   0181-650 7745
The nearest thing to a general quango directory is this biennial listing of 1,300 hard-to-find bodies.

Secret Services: A Handbook for Investigating Local Quangos
Local Govt Info Unit, free   0171-608 1051
A guide to what local authorities and others can do to investigate and expose the activities of non-elected service providers in their areas.

Next Steps Report
HMSO/Stationery Office £45   01603-622211
An annual directory and overview.

Citizen's Charter - The Facts and Figures
HMSO/Stationery Office, £13.50   01603-622211

Public Bodies
HMSO/Stationery Office, £15.50   01603-622211
A thin annual catalogue listing some basic NDPB data.

OFFICIAL BODIES

Organisations which are still part of the civil service, and therefore not quangos.

British Standards Institution	0181-996 9000
Charity Commission	0171-210 4477
Commonwealth Secretariat	0171-839 3411
Crown Estate	0171-210 4210
Export Credit Guarantee Dept	0171-512 7000
Law Commission: England	0171-453 1220
Scotland	0131-668 2131
National Audit Office	0171-798 7000
National Savings Department	0171-605 9300
International Development	0171-917 7000
Press	0171-917 0950
Post Office	0171-490 2888
Press 24 hrs	0171-250 2468
Queens Awards Office	0171-222 2277
Registry of Friendly Societies	0171-663 5000
Royal Commission on Environmental	
Pollution	0171-276 2080
Royal Mail	0171-250 2888
Royalty - press offices:	
Buckingham Palace	0171-930 4832
Clarence House	0171 930 3141
Duchy of Cornwall	0171-834 7346
Duchy of Lancaster	0171-836 8277
Trade Unions & Employers Associations	
Certification Office	0171-210 3734
Welsh Development Agency	0345-775577

UK AND ENGLISH QUANGOS

Below are NDPBs, NSEAs and other bodies run by the quangocracy in some form. Many national quangos cannot be asked questions over the phone because they come under the wings of a government department, and are only in the phone books under the department's name, not their own. Where no phone number is given here, inquiries should be made to the sponsoring department. The initials after each name are of these departments. The asterisked entries (*) are NSEAs.

ACAS - Advisory, Conciliation & Arbitration	
Service (DfEE)	0171-396 0022
ADAS* (MAFF)	01865-842742
Advisory Committees on:	
NHS Drugs	0171-210 5221
Novel Foods	0171-210 5221
Telecommunications	0171-215 0319
Advisory Councils on:	
Public Records (LCD)	0181-876 3444
Science & Technology	via CO
The Misuse of Drugs	via HO
Agricultural Land Tribunals	via MAFF
Agricultural Wages Board	via MAFF

Arts Council (DCMS)	0171-333 0100
Audit Commission for Local Authorities and	
the NHS (DETR)	0171-828 1212
Bank of England (HMT)	0171-601 4444
Press	0171-601 4411
BBC (Press)	0181-576 1865
Biotechnology and Biological Research	
Council (CO)	01793-413200
Boards of Visitors to Prisons	0171-217 8388
Boundary Commissions - Local Government:	
England	0171-430 8400
Wales	01222-395031
Scotland	0131-244 1111
Boundary Commissions - Parliamentary:	
England & Wales	0171-533 5177
Scotland	0131-244 2660
Northern Ireland	0171-210 6527
British Antarctic Survey	01223-361188
British Coal (DTI)	01782-662052
British Council (FCO)	0171-930 8466
Press	0171-389 4878
British Energy	0171-389 3406
British Film Institute (DCMS)	0171-255 1444
Press	0171-957 8920
British Library (DCMS)	0171-412 7000
Press	0171-412 7116
British Museum (DCMS)	0171-636 1555
Press	0171-323 8779
British National Space Centre	0171-215 0806
British Nuclear Fuels (DTI)	01925-832000
Sellafield (press)	01946-785838
British Overseas Trade Board (DTI)	0171-215 4936
British Tourist Authority (DCMS)	0181-846 9000
Press	0181-563 3034
British Waterways (DETR)	01923-226422
Broadcasting Complaints/Standards Commission	
(DCMS)	0171-233 0544
Building Regulations Advisory Cttee	0171-890 5742
Building Research Establishment*	
(DETR)	01923-894040
Building Societies Commission	0171-663 5000
CCTA*: Central Computer & Telecommunications	
Agency (OPS)	01603-704874
Central Fire Brigades Advisory Council	via HO
Central Office of Information* (OPS)	0171-928 2345
Press	0171-261 8815
Emergency Planning	0171-261 8221
Films & Radio	0171-261 8598
New Media	0171-261 8406
News Distribution Service	0171-261 8445
Press & Pictures	0171-261 8650
Central Rail Users Consultative Committee	
(DETR)	0171-505 9090
Central Science Laboratory* (MAFF)	01904-462000
Centre for Environment, Fisheries & Aquaculture	
Science* (MAFF)	01502-562244
Chemical & Biological Defence Establishment	
(MOD)	01980-613000
Citizens Charter Unit (CO)	0171-270 6303
Civil Aviation Authority (DETR)	0171-379 7311
Press	0171-832 5335

Civil Service College* (CO)	01344-634000
Coastguard & Marine Safety Agency*	
(DETR)	01703-329100
Commission for Racial Equality (HO)	0171-828 7022
Press	0171-932 5354
Commissioner for the Rights of Trade Union	
Members (DfEE)	01925-415771
Press	0161-952 4508
Committee for Monitoring Agreements on Tobacco	
Advertising/Sponsorship	0171-210 5221
Committees on:	
Carcinogenicity Food Chemicals	0171-210 5221
Medical Aspects of Food Policy	0171-210 5221
Safety of Medicines (DOH)	0171-273 0451
Standards in Public Life	0171-270 6345
Toxicity of Chemicals in Food	0171-210 5221
Commonwealth Institute (FCO)	0171-603 4535
Community Development Foundation	
(HO)	0171-226 5375
Companies House* (DTI)	01222-388588
Press	01222-380526
Consultative Panel on Badgers and	
Tuberculosis	via MAFF
Copyright Tribunal	0171-438 4776
Council on Tribunals (LCD)	0171-936 7045
Countryside Commission	01242-521381
Court Service* (LCD)	0171-210 2092
Customer service	0171-210 1775
Press	0171-210 8512
Crafts Council (DCMS)	0171-278 7700
Criminal Injuries Compensation Board	
(HO)	0171-842 6800
Crown Agents (FCO)	0171-834 3644
Crown Prosecution Service*	0171-273 8000
Customs & Excise (HMT)	0171-620 1313
Press	0171-865 5665
Investigations: press	0171-665 7829
Data Protection Registrar (HO)	01625-545700
Defence Agencies (MOD):	
Armed Forces Personnel Admin*	01452-712612
Army Base Storage*	01264-382424
Army Personnel*	0141-224 2070
Army Technical Support	01264-383753
Defence Analytical Services	0171-218 7950
Defence Animal Centre*	0171-218 7950
Defence Estates*	0171-218 6131
Defence Intelligence & Security*	01462-752101
Defence Vetting *	0171-218 80232
Disposal Sales Agency*	0171-218 7950
Joint Air Reconnaissance Intelligence	
Centre*	01480-52151x7230
Logistic Information*	01264-382832
Military Survey*	0181-890 3622
MOD Police*	01371-854000
Naval Recruiting & Training *	01705-727600
RAF Maintenance Group*	01480-52151
RAF Training Group*	01452-712612
Specialist Procurement*	0117-913 2724
Design Council (DTI)	0171-208 2121
Doctors/Dentists Review Body	0171-467 7217
Driver & Vehicle Licensing Agency*	
(DOT)	01792-782318
Driving Standards Agency* (DETR)	0115-901 2500
Economic and Social Research Council	
(CO)	01793-413000
Press	01793-413122
Education Assets Board	0113-234 8888
Employment Appeal Tribunal (DfEE)	0171-273 1041
Employment Service* (DfEE)	0171-273 6060
Engineering & Physical Science Research	
Council (CO)	01793-444000
English Heritage (DCMS)	0171-973 3000
Press	0171-973 3250
English Nature (DETR)	01733-455000
Press	01733-455193
English Tourist Board (DCMS)	0181-846 9000
Press	0181-563 3038
Environment Agency (DETR)	01454-624400
Press	0171-840 6144
Equal Opportunities Commission (DfEE)	0161-833 9244
Press	0171-222 1110
Farm Animal Welfare Council (MAFF)	0181-330 8077
Farming & Rural Conservation* (MAFF)	0171-238 5432
Fire Service College* (HO)	01608-650831
Fisheries Research* (SO)	01224-876544
Food Advisory Committee (MAFF)	0171-238 6267
Food From Britain (MAFF)	0171-233 5111
Football Licensing Authority (DCMS)	0171-491 7191
Forensic Science Service* (HO)	0171-230 6654
Forest Enterprise* (SO)	0131-334 0303
Forestry Commission Research*	0131-334 0303
Further Education Development Agency	
(DfEE)	0171-962 1280
Further Education Funding Council	
(DfEE)	01203-863000
Gaming Board (HO)	0171-306 6200
Government Car & Despatch* (OPS)	0171-217 3838
Govt Property Lawyers* (HMT)	01823-345200
Health & Safety Commission & Executive	
(DfEE)	0171-717 6000
Press	0171-717 6700
Health Education Authority (DOH)	0171-222 5300
Healthcare Advisory Service	0118-972 2696
Highways Agency* (DETR)	0171-921 4443
Historic Royal Palaces* (DCMS)	0181-781 9750
HMSO*	01603-723014
Press	0171-270 0375
Copyright section	01603 723001
Housing Corporation (DETR)	0171-393 2000
Hydrographic Office* (MOD)	01823-337900
Immigration Appellate Auth (LCD)	0171-862 4200
Independent Television Commission	
(DCMS)	0171-255 3000
Industrial Development Advisory Board	via DTI
Industrial Injuries Advisory Council	
(DSS)	0171-962 8065
Industrial Tribunals:	
National Enquiry Line (DfEE)	0345-959775
Press	0171-215 5964
Inland Revenue (HMT)	0171-438 6622
Press	0171-438 6692
Innovation Unit (DTI)	0171-215 1705
Insolvency Service* (DTI)	0171-637 1110
Intelligence Services Tribunal	0171-273 4383

Interception of Communications Tribunal	
(HO)	0171-273 4096
Intervention Board* (MAFF)	0118-958 3626
Joint Nature Conservation Committee	
(DETR)	01733-562626
Laboratory of the Government Chemist*	
(DTI)	0181-943 7000
HM Land Registry* (LCD)	0171-917 8888
Lands Tribunal (LCD)	0171-936 7200
Law Commission (LCD)	0171-453 1220
Legal Aid Board (LCD)	0171-813 1000
Library & Information Commission	via DCMS
London Docklands Urban Development	
Corporation (DETR)	abolished 1998
London Transport (DETR)	0171-222 5600
Maritime & Coastguard* (DETR)	01703-329467
Meat Hygiene Service* (MAFF)	01904-455501
Meat/Livestock Commission (MAFF)	01908-677577
Medical Devices Agency* (DOH)	0171-972 8000
Medical Practices Committee (DOH)	0171-972 2930
Medical Research Council (CO)	0171-636 5422
Medicines Commission/Control Agency*	
(DOH)	0171-273 0392
Mental Health Act Commission	0171-211 8061
Mental Health Review Tribunal	0171-210 5010
Meteorological Office* (MOD)	01344-420242
Press	01344-856655
Monopolies and Mergers Commission	
(DTI)	0171-324 1467
Press	0171-324 1407
Museums & Galleries Commission	
(DCMS)	0171-233 4200
National Consumer Council (DTI)	0171-730 3469
National Council for Vocational Qualifications	
(DfEE)	0171-229 1234
National Food Survey Committee	
(MAFF)	0171-270 8563
National Health Service Tribunal	via DOH
National Heritage Memorial Fund	
(DCMS)	0171-591 6000
National Physical Laboratory (DTI)	0181-977 3222
National Radiological Protection Board	
(DOH)	01235-831600
National Weights & Measures Laboratory*	
(DTI)	0181-943 7272
National Youth Agency	0171-925 5055
Natural Environment Research Council	
(CO)	01793-411500
Natural Resources Institute* (FCO)	01634-880088
NHS Estates* (DOH)	0113-254 7000
Nuclear Electric plc (DTI)	01452-652222
Press	01452-652793
Nuclear Powered Warships Safety Cttee	via MOD
Nuclear Weapons Safety Committee	via MOD
Occupational Health & Safety* (CO)	0131-220 9700
Office for National Statistics* (HMT)	0171-533 6207
Ordnance Survey* (DETR)	01703-792000
Parliamentary Boundary Commission	0171-533 5177
Parole Board (HO)	0171-217 3000
Particle Physics & Astronomy Research	
Council	01793-444000
Passport Agency* (HO)	0990-210410

Patent Office* (DTI)	01633-814000
Paymaster General*	01293-560999
Pesticides Safety Directorate* (MAFF)	01904 640500
Planning Inspectorate* (DETR)	0171-890 3043
Poisons Board	via HO
Police Advisory Board	via HO
Police Complaints Authority (HO)	0171-273 6450
Political Honours Scrutiny Committee	
(CO)	0171-219 4272
Post Office (DTI)	0171-490 2888
Press 24 hrs	0171-250 2468
Post Office Users National Council (DTI)	0171-928 9458
Prescription Pricing Authority	0191-232 5371
HM Prison Service* (HO)	0171-217 6633
Property Advisers to Civil Estate (CO)	0171-271 2610
Public Health Laboratory (DOH)	0181-200 1295
Public Lending Right	01642-604699
Public Record Office* (LCD)	0181-876 3444
Public Trust Office* (LCD)	0171-664 7000
QEII Conference Centre*	0171-798 4000
Radio Authority (DCMS)	0171-430 2724
Radioactive Waste Management Advisory	
Committee	0171-276 8121
Radiocommunications Agency* (DTI)	0171-211 0211
Railway Inspectorate	0113-483 4200
Recruitment & Assessment Services*	01256-869555
Renewable Energy Advisory Committee	via DTI
Royal Commission on Environmental	
Pollution (DETR)	0171-276 2109
Royal Commission on Historical Monuments	
(DCMS)	0171-208 8200
Royal Fine Art Commission (DCMS)	0171-839 6537
Royal Mint* (HMT)	01443-222111
Royal Parks Agency*(DCMS)	0171-298 2000
Rural Development Commission	
(DETR)	0171-340 2906
School Curriculum & Assessment Authority	
(DfEE)	0171-925 5001
Sea Fish Industry Authority (MAFF)	0131-558 3331
Securities & Investments Board	0171-676 1000
Security Committee	via CO
Security Facilities Executive* (DETR)	0171-921 4813
Security Services Tribunal	0171-273 4095
Serious Fraud Office*	0171-239 7272
Social Security (DSS):	
Advisory Committee	0171-412 1506
Benefits Agency*	0113-232 4000
Child Support Agency*	0345-133133
Contributions Agency*	0191-225 7665
War Pensions Agency*	01253-858858
Sports Council (DCMS)	0171-273 1500
Standing Advisory Committee on Trunk	
Road Assessment	0171-271 5766
Street Works Advisory Committee	via DETR
Top Salaries Review Body	0171-467 7217
Traffic Director for London (DETR)	0171-222 4545
Transport Research Lab* (DETR)	01344-773131
Treasury Solicitor's Dept (HMT)	0171-210 3079
Trinity House (DETR)	0171-480 6601
UK Atomic Energy Authority (DTI)	01235-821111
UK Nirex	01235-825500
Valuation Office (HMT)	0171-324 1033

Value Added Tax Tribunals (LCD)	0171-631 4242
Vehicle Certification Agency* (DETR)	0117-951 5151
Vehicle Inspectorate* (DETR)	0117-954 3200
Veterinary Laboratories Agency*	
(MAFF)	01932-341111
Veterinary Medicines Directorate	
(MAFF)	01932-336911
Wilton Park Conference Centre (FCO)	01903-815020
Womens National Commission (DfEE)	0171-712 2443

WELSH QUANGOS

Arts Council of Wales	01222-394711
Boundary Commission	0171-533 5177
Cadw: Historic Monuments*	01222-500200
Countryside Council for Wales	01248-370444
Development Board for Rural Wales	01686-626965
Fourth Channel Authority	01222-747444
Health Promotion Authority	01222-752222
Hill Farming Advisory Cttee	01222-825735
Housing for Wales	01222-741500
Land Authority for Wales	01222-223444
Local Government Boundary	01222-395031
National Library of Wales	01970-632800
National Museums of Wales	01222-397951
Patent Office*	01633-814000
Sports Council for Wales	01222-300500
Tai Cymru Housing for Wales	01222-741500
Wales Tourist Board	01222-499909
Welsh Development Agency	0345-775577
Welsh Funding Councils	01222-761861
Welsh Language Board	01222-224744
Youth Agency	01222-880088

SCOTTISH QUANGOS

Community Education Council	0131-313 2488
Council on the Curriculum	01382-455053
Crofters Commission	01463-663450
Deer Commission	01463-231751
Fisheries Research Services*	01244-876544
Forest Enterprise*	0131-334 0303
Forestry Commission Research*	0131-334 0303
Health Board	0131-244 3574
Health Service Committee	0131-244 2750
Highlands & Islands Enterprise	01463-234171
Hill Farming Advisory Cttee	0131-244 6417
Historic Buildings Council	0131-244 4999
Historic Scotland*	0131-668 8600
Lands Tribunal	0131-225 7996
Law Commission	0131-668 2131
Legal Aid Board	0131-226 7061
Mental Welfare Commission	0131-222 6111
National Galleries	0131-556 8921
NHS Tribunal	0131-244 4999
National Library	0131-226 4531
National Museums	0131-225 7534
Parliamentary Boundary Commission	0131-244 2196
Parole Unit	0131-244 8528
Pensions Appeal Tribunal	0131-220 1404
Police Advisory Board	0131-244 2143

Registers of Scotland*	0131-659 6111
Royal Fine Art Commission	0131-556 6699
Scottish Agricultural Science *	0131-244 8890
Scottish Arts Council	0131-226 6051
Scottish Court Service*	0131-229 9200
Scottish Enterprise	0141-248 2700
Scottish Environment Protection	01786-457700
Scottish Fisheries Protection*	0131-244 6059
Scottish Homes	0131-313 0044
Scottish Nuclear	01355-262000
Scottish Natural Heritage	0131-447 4784
Scottish Prison Service*	0131-244 8745
Scottish Qualifications Authority	0141-248 7900
Scottish Record Office*	0131-535 1314
Scottish Screen	0141-334 4445
Sports Council	0131-317 7200
Tourist Board	0131-332 2433

NORTHERN IRISH QUANGOS

Arts Council	01232-385200
NI Child Support Agency*	01232-896666
Citizen's Charter Unit	01232-521722
Commission for Police Complaints	01232 244821
Compensation Agency*	01232-249944
Construction Service*	01232-250284
Court Service*	01232-328594
Curriculum Council	01232-261200
Driver & Vehicle Testing*	01232-681831
Economic Council	01232-232125
Environment & Heritage Service*	01232-546569
Fishery Harbour Authority	01396-613844
Forensic Science Agency of NI*	01232-365744
Government Purchasing Service*	01232-526538
Health Estates*	01232-520025
Historic Monuments Council	01232-235000
Housing Executive	01232-240588
Human Rights	01232-243987
Industrial Court	01232-327666
Industrial Development Board	01232-233233
Industrial Research & Tech*	01232-529533
Land Registers of NI*	01232-251515
Law Reform Advisory Committee	01232-542900
NI Prison Service	01232 520700
Ordnance Survey of NI*	01232-255755
Parliamentary Boundary Commission	01232-311210
Police Complaints	01232-244821
Planning Service*	01232-540677
Police Authority	01232-230111
Probation Board	01232-262400
Public Record Office of NI*	01232-251318
Rate Collection Agency*	01232-252252
NI Council for the Curriculum	01232-261200
Social Security Agency NI*	01232-520520
Sports Council	01232-381222
Statistics and Research Agency	01232 520700
Tourist Board	01232-231221
Training/Employment Agency *	01232-257777
Transport Holding Company	01232-243456
Valuation & Lands Agency*	01232-250700
Water Service*	01232-244711

Local and regional government

Local government was transformed by the creation of unitary authorities from 1995 to 1998. These single-tier authorities, responsible for all local government services, replaced much of the two-tier structure set up in 1974/5. **Wales and Scotland** had new unitary systems imposed on them in 1996 without prior consultation, replacing all existing authorities. In Wales, 22 unitaries took over from all eight county councils and 37 district councils. In Scotland, the nine regional and 53 district councils were replaced by 29 unitaries. The only authorities that survived these reorganisations unchanged were Scotland's three islands councils (Orkney, Shetland and Western Isles), which were already unitary.

In **England** the public were consulted, producing wide-ranging views. This resulted in a confusing and illogical mixture of authorities with differing structures and powers, in marked contrast to Wales and Scotland. The first of the new English unitaries - the Isle of Wight - came into existence in April 1995, followed by another 45 from 1996-98. Three of 1974's new county councils - Avon, Cleveland and Humberside - were abolished, along with the traditional county of Berkshire. Herefordshire and Worcestershire were split, becoming separate counties again. By mid-1998 England had 387 authorities: 34 county councils, 238 district councils, 36 metropolitan districts, 32 London boroughs (plus the City of London), 46 new unitary councils and 4 existing island unitaries.

Northern Ireland has remained unchanged during the mainland's unitary upheavals. Since 1973 it has had 26 single-tier district councils, but these have fewer functions than the new mainland unitaries.

FUTURES

Radical changes in the way local government is run were proposed in a **white paper** published in July 1998. Downing Street is pressing ahead with plans to install a number of powerful elected mayors or cabinets in town halls, endorsed by voters in local referenda.

A new ethical framework for England's 20,000 councillors is proposed, with strict codes of conduct. The top-performing councils may be given more financial freedom, while annual elections could become the norm. At the heart of the plans is a requirement for councils to draw up plans streamlining procedures and introducing an executive, or cabinet-style of government.

A prototype of **regional government** should appear in England during 1999. The granting of new forms of independence to Wales, Scotland and Northern Ireland during 1997/8 produced sudden fears in Whitehall of the Tories galloping through the next general election riding an updated high-technology warhorse of revived English nationalism. Labour's response was to subdivide England into nine regions, each of will be the home to a Regional Development Agency (RDA) from the spring of 1999. They will be run by small boards of local notables, appointed by the Minister for the Regions, with only a third of them councillors. London is to be home of both an RDA and a pioneering large-scale authority. The Greater London Authority is due to start 31 March 2000, when the mayor and a 25-strong assembly will be elected.

ELECTIONS

Most UK councillors are elected for four years. In **England** county council seats are all polled at the same time, once every four years (next: 2001). In that year there are no district council elections. In district councils each authority can choose whether to elect all seats together once every four years, or ballot a third of seats every year, except in the year of county council elections. All London boroughs and the Corporation of London are held together every four years (next: 2002). Metropolitan authority elections are in thirds (next: 1999, 2000, not 2001). Unitary authority elections will be four years after their founding elections, being held in different years in England, starting in 1999.

Elections are also four-yearly in Wales

(next: 1999) and Northern Ireland (next: 2001), but in Scotland they are three-yearly (next: 1999). Most elections are on the first Thursday in May. In the Isle of Man, the House of Keys vote is held every five years, on the third Thursday in November (next: 2001).

The leading annual directory is the *Municipal Year Book*. The Local Government Information Unit produces many useful publications. Local finances can be examined using legal rights, spelled out in the Audit Commission's free booklet *Local Authority Accounts: The Rights of the Public*. Once an authority's accounts for the previous financial year are completed, it must advertise they are available for inspection for 15 days.

REGIONALISM

Ten Government Offices (GOs) for the Regions were set up in England in 1994. The GOs run the regional programmes of the DTI, DfEE, DETR and Home Office. Each regional director reports to the relevant Secretary of State for each department. The GOs Central Unit acts as the main coordinating point. The DETR is the leader.

GOs Central Unit	0171-890 5005
East Midlands (GOEM, Nottingham)	0115-971 2753
Eastern Region (GOER, Cambridge)	01223-346766
London (GOL, Millbank)	0171-217 3456
Merseyside (GOM, Liverpool)	0151-224 6302
North East (GONE, Newcastle)	0191-201 3300
North West (GONW, Manchester)	0161-952 4000
South East (GOSE, Guildford)	01483-882255
South West (GOSW, Bristol)	0117-900 1700
West Midlands (GOWM, Birmingham)	0121-212 5050
Yorks & Humber (GOYH, Leeds)	0113-280 0600

LOCAL GOVT. CONTACTS

Assoc Electoral Administrators	0116-267 2015
Assoc of London Government	0171-222 7799
Audit Commission for Local Auths	0171-828 1212
Publications	0800-502030
Convention of Scottish Local Auths	0131-474 9200
DETR	0171-890 3000
Public enquiries	0171-890 3333
Press (regions)	0171-890 3045
Institute of Revenues Rating and Valuation	0171-831 3505
Local Government Association	0171-834 2222
Press office	0171-664 3331

Website	www.lga.gov.uk
Local Government Commission for England	0171-430 8400
Local Government Boundary Commissions:	
Scotland	0131-538 7510
Wales	01222-395031
Local Govt Information Unit	0171-608 1051
Website	www.lgiu.gov.uk
Local Govt International Bureau	0171-664 3100
Local Govt Management Board	0171-296 6600
Municipal Yearbook	0171-973 6400
National Assoc of Local Councils	0171-637 1865
Ombudsmen: England	0171-915 3210
Wales	01656-661325
Scotland	0131-556 5574
Northern Ireland	01232-233821

ENGLISH TWO-TIER

County and district authorities, in shire areas.

Bedfordshire	**01234-363222**
Mid Bedfordshire	01525-402051
Bedford	01234-267422
South Bedfordshire	01582-472222

Berkshire
Abolished 1998. The former district councils are now unitary; see under Other English Unitary Councils.

Buckinghamshire	**01296-395000**
Aylesbury Vale	01296-585858
Chiltern	01494-729000
South Bucks	01753-533333
Wycombe	01494-461000

Cambridgeshire	**01223-717111**
Cambridge	01223-457000
East Cambridgeshire	01353-665555
Fenland	01354-654321
Huntingdonshire	01480-388388
South Cambs	01223-443000

Cheshire	**01244-602424**
Chester	01244-324324
Congleton	01270-763231
Crewe & Nantwich	01270-537777
Ellesmere Port & Neston	0151-356 6789
Macclesfield	01625-500500
Vale Royal	01606-862862

Cornwall	**01872-322000**
Caradon	01579-341000
Carrick	01872-278131
Kerrier	01209-614000
North Cornwall	01208-893333
Penwith	01736-362341
Restormel	01726-74466

Cumbria	**01228-606060**
Allerdale	01900-604351
Barrow-in-Furness	01229-825500
Carlisle City	01228-817000
Copeland	01946-693111
Eden	01768-864671
South Lakeland	01539-733333
Derbyshire	**01629-580000**
Amber Valley	01773-570222
Bolsover	01246-240000
Chesterfield	01246-345345
Derbyshire Dales	01629-580580
Erewash	0115-944 0440
High Peak	01663-751751
North East Derbyshire	01246-231111
South Derbyshire	01283-221000
Devon	**01392-382000**
East Devon	01395-516551
Exeter	01392-277888
Mid Devon	01884-255255
North Devon	01271-327711
South Hams	01803-861234
Teignbridge	01626-361101
Torridge	01237-476711
West Devon	01822-615911
Dorset	**01305-251000**
Christchurch	01202-495000
East Dorset	01202-886201
Purbeck	01929-556561
West Dorset	01305-251010
Weymouth & Portland	01305-761222
Durham	**0191-386 4411**
Chester-le-Street	0191-387 1919
Derwentside	01207-218000
Durham City	0191-386 6111
Easington	0191-527 0501
Sedgefield	01388-816166
Teesdale	01833-690000
Wear Valley	01388-765555
East Sussex	**01273-481000**
Brighton & Hove	01273-290000
Eastbourne	01323-410000
Hastings	01424-781066
Lewes	01273-471600
Rother	01424-787878
Wealden	01892-653311
Essex	**01245-492211**
Basildon	01268-533333
Braintree	01376-552525
Brentwood	01277-261111
Castle Point	01268-792711
Chelmsford	01245-606606
Colchester	01206-282222
Epping Forest	01992-564000
Harlow	01279-446611
Maldon	01621-854477

Rochford	01702-546366
Tendring	01255-425501
Uttlesford	01799-510510
Gloucestershire	**01452-425000**
Cheltenham	01242-262626
Cotswold	01285-643643
Forest of Dean	01594-810000
Gloucester City	01452-522232
Stroud	01453-766321
Tewkesbury	01684-295010
Hampshire	**01962-841841**
Basingstoke	01256-844844
East Hampshire	01730-266551
Eastleigh	01703-614646
Fareham	01329-236100
Gosport	01705-584242
Hart	01252-622122
Havant	01705-474174
New Forest	01703-285000
Rushmoor	01252-516222
Test Valley	01264-364144
Winchester	01962-840222
Herefordshire	

Not a county council. See under Other English Unitary
Councils.

Hertfordshire	**01992-555555**
Broxbourne	01992-631921
Dacorum	01442-260161
East Hertfordshire	01279-655261
Hertsmere	0181-207 2277
North Hertfordshire	01462-474000
St Albans	01727-866100
Stevenage	01438-356177
Three Rivers	01923-776611
Watford	01923-226400
Welwyn Hatfield	01707-357000
Kent	**01622-671411**
Ashford	01233-637311
Canterbury	01227-763763
Dartford	01322-343434
Dover	01304-821199
Gravesham	01474-564422
Maidstone	01622-602000
Sevenoaks	01732-741222
Shepway	01303-850388
Swale	01795-424341
Thanet	01843-225511
Tonbridge & Malling	01732-844522
Tunbridge Wells	01892 526121
Lancashire	**01772-254868**
Burnley	01282-425011
Chorley	01257-515151
Fylde	01253-721222
Hyndburn	01254-388111
Lancaster	01524-582000
Pendle	01282-661661

Preston	01772-254881
Ribble Valley	01200-425111
Rossendale	01706-217777
South Ribble	01772-421491
West Lancashire	01695-577177
Wyre	01253-891000
Leicestershire	**0116-232 3232**
Blaby	0116-275 0555
Charnwood	01509-263151
Harborough	01858-410000
Hinckley & Bosworth	01455-238141
Melton	01664-567771
North West Leicestershire	01530-833333
Oadby & Wigston	0116-288 8961
Lincolnshire	**01522-552222**
Boston	01205-314200
East Lindsey	01507-601111
Lincoln	01522-511511
North Kesteven	01529-414155
South Holland	01775-761161
South Kesteven	01476-406080
West Lindsey	01427-615411
Norfolk	**01603-222222**
Breckland	01362 695333
Broadland	01603-431133
Gt Yarmouth	01493-856100
Kings Lynn & West Norfolk	01553-692722
North Norfolk	01263-513811
Norwich	01603-622233
South Norfolk	01508-533633
Northamptonshire	**01604-236236**
Corby	01536-402551
Daventry	01327-871100
East Northants	01832-742000
Kettering	01536-410333
Northampton	01604-233500
South Northants	01327-350211
Wellingborough	01933-229777
Northumberland	**01670-533000**
Alnwick	01665-510505
Berwick-upon-Tweed	01289-330044
Blyth Valley	01670-542000
Castle Morpeth	01670-514351
Tynedale	01434-652200
Wansbeck	01670-814444
North Yorkshire	**01609-780780**
Craven	01756-700600
Hambleton	01609-779977
Harrogate	01423-568954
Richmond	01748-850222
Ryedale	01653-600666
Scarborough	01723-232323
Selby	01757-705101
York	01904-613161

Nottinghamshire	**0115-982 3823**
Ashfield	01623-450000
Bassetlaw	01909-533533
Broxtowe	0115-917 7777
Gedling	0115-901 3901
Mansfield	01623-656656
Newark & Sherwood	01636-605111
Rushcliffe	0115-981 9911
Oxfordshire	**01865-792422**
Cherwell	01295-252535
Oxford	01865-249811
South Oxfordshire	01491-835351
Vale of White Horse	01235-520202
West Oxfordshire	01993-702941
Shropshire	**01743-251000**
Bridgnorth	01746-713100
North Shropshire	01939-232771
Oswestry	01691-671111
Shrewsbury & Atcham	01743-232255
South Shropshire	01584-874941
Somerset	**01823-355455**
Mendip	01749-343399
Sedgemoor	01278-435435
South Somerset	01935-462462
Taunton Deane	01823-356356
West Somerset	01984-632291
Staffordshire	**01785-223121**
Cannock Chase	01543-462621
East Staffs	01283-508000
Lichfield	01543-414000
Newcastle-under-Lyme	01782-717717
South Staffs	01902-696000
Stafford	01785-223181
Staffs Moorlands	01538-483409
Tamworth	01827-311222
Suffolk	**01473-583000**
Babergh	01473-822801
Forest Heath	01638-719000
Ipswich	01473-262626
Mid Suffolk	01449-720711
St Edmundsbury	01284-763233
Suffolk Coastal	01394-383789
Waveney	01502-562111
Surrey	**0181-541 8800**
Elmbridge	01372-474474
Epsom & Ewell	01372-732000
Guildford	01483-505050
Mole Valley	01306-885001
Reigate & Banstead	01737-276000
Runnymede	01932-838383
Spelthorne	01784-451499
Surrey Heath	01276-686252
Tandridge	01883-722000
Waverley	01483-861111
Woking	01483-755855

Warwickshire	**01926-410410**
North Warwicks	01827-715341
Nuneaton & Bedworth	01203-376376
Rugby	01788-533533
Stratford-on-Avon	01789-267575
Warwick	01926-450000
West Sussex	**01243-777100**
Adur	01273-455566
Arun	01903-716133
Chichester	01243-785166
Crawley	01293-438000
Horsham	01403-215100
Mid Sussex	01444-458166
Worthing	01903-239999
Wiltshire	**01225-713000**
Kennet	01380-724911
North Wiltshire	01249-443322
Salisbury	01722-336272
West Wiltshire	01225-776655
Worcestershire	**01905-763763**
Bromsgrove	01527-873232
Malvern Hills	01684-892700
Redditch	01527-64252
Worcester City	01905-723471
Wychavon	01386-565000
Wyre Forest	01562-820505

ENGLISH UNITARY COUNCILS

London boroughs

Barking & Dagenham	0181-592 4500
Barnet	0181-359 2000
Bexley	0181-303 7777
Brent	0181-904 1244
Bromley	0181-464 3333
Camden	0171-278 4444
Croydon	0181-686 4433
Ealing	0181-579 2424
Enfield	0181-366 6565
Greenwich	0181-854 8888
Hackney	0181-356 5000
Hammersmith & Fulham	0181-748 3020
Haringey	0181-975 9700
Harrow	0181-863 5611
Havering	01708-772222
Hillingdon	01895-250111
Hounslow	0181-570 7728
Islington	0171-226 1234
Kensington & Chelsea	0171-937 5464
Kingston-upon-Thames	0181-546 2121
Lambeth	0171-926 1000
Lewisham	0181-695 6000
Merton	0181-543 2222
Newham	0181-472 1430
Redbridge	0181-478 3020
Richmond-upon-Thames	0181-891 1411
Southwark	0171-237 6677
Sutton	0181-770 5000

Tower Hamlets	0171-364 5000
Waltham Forest	0181-527 5544
Wandsworth	0181-871 6000
Westminster	0171-641 6000
Corporation of London	0171-606 3030

Metropolitan district councils

The six metropolitan counties (Greater Manchester, Merseyside, South Yorkshire, Tyne & Wear, West Midlands and West Yorkshire) have the 36 districts councils below, but no county councils.

Barnsley	01226-770770
Birmingham	0121-303 9944
Bolton	01204-522311
Bradford	01274-752111
Bury	0161-253 5000
Calderdale	01422-357257
Coventry	01203-833333
Doncaster	01302-734444
Dudley	01384-818181
Gateshead	0191-477 1011
Kirklees	01484-221000
Knowsley	0151-489 6000
Leeds	0113-234 8080
Liverpool	0151-227 3911
Manchester	0161-234 5000
Newcastle/North Tyneside	0191-200 5151
Oldham	0161-911 3000
Rochdale	01706-647474
Rotherham	01709-382121
Salford	0161-794 4711
Sandwell	0121-569 2200
Sefton	01704-533133
Sheffield	0114-272 6444
Solihull	0121-704 6000
South Tyneside	0191-427 1717
St Helens	01744-456000
Stockport	0161-480 4949
Sunderland	0191-553 1000
Tameside	0161-342 8355
Trafford	0161-912 1212
Wakefield	01924-306090
Walsall	01922-650000
Wigan	01942-244991
Wirral	0151-638 7070
Wolverhampton	01902-556556

Other English unitary councils

Bath & North East Somerset	01225-477000
Blackburn with Darwen	01254-585585
Blackpool	01253-477477
Bournemouth	01202-451451
Bracknell Forest	01344-424642
Brighton & Hove	01273-290000
Bristol	0117-922 2000
Darlington	01325-380651
Derby	01332-293111
East Riding of Yorkshire	01482-887700
Guernsey	01481-717000
Halton	0151-424 2061

Hartlepool	01429-266522
Herefordshire	01432-260000
Isle of Man	01624-685685
Isle of Wight	01983-821000
Jersey	01534-603000
Kingston upon Hull	01482-610610
Leicester	0116-254 9922
Luton	01582-746000
Medway Towns	01634-306000
Middlesbrough	01642-245432
Milton Keynes	01908-691691
North East Lincolnshire	01472-313131
North Lincolnshire	01724-296296
North Somerset	01934-888888
Nottingham	0115-915 5555
Peterborough	01733-563141
Plymouth	01752-668000
Poole	01202-633633
Portsmouth	01705-822251
Reading	0118-939 0900
Redcar & Cleveland	01642-444000
Rutland	01572-722577
Scilly Isles	01720-422537
Slough	01753-523881
South Gloucestershire	01454-868686
Southampton	01703-223855
Southend-on-Sea	01702-215000
Stockton on Tees	01642-393939
Stoke-on-Trent	01782-234567
Swindon	01793-463000
Thurrock	01375-390000
Torbay	01803-201201
Warrington	01925-444400
West Berkshire	01635-42400
Windsor & Maidenhead	01628-798888
Wokingham	0118- 974 6000
The Wrekin	01952-202100
York	01904-613161

WELSH UNITARY COUNCILS

Blaenau Gwent	01495-350555
Bridgend	01656-643643
Caerphilly	01443-815588
Cardiff	01222-872000
Carmarthenshire	01267-234567
Ceredigion	01545-570881
Conwy	01492-574000
Denbighshire	01824-706000
Flintshire	01352-704476
Gwynedd	01286-672255
Isle of Anglesey	01248-750057
Merthyr Tydfil	01685-725000
Monmouthshire	01633-644644
Neath Port Talbot	01639-763333
Newport	01633-244491
Pembrokeshire	01437-764551
Powys	01597-826000
Rhondda Cynon Taff	01443-424000
Swansea	01792-636000
Torfaen	01495-762200
Vale of Glamorgan	01446-700111
Wrexham	01978-292000

SCOTTISH UNITARY

Aberdeenshire	01467-620981
Angus	01307-461460
Argyll & Bute	01546-602127
Clackmannanshire	01259-450000
Dumfries & Galloway	01387-261234
Dundee City	01382-434000
East Ayrshire	01563-576000
East Dunbartonshire	0141-776 9000
East Lothian	01620-827827
East Renfrewshire	0141-577 3000
Edinburgh	0131-200 2000
Falkirk	01324-506070
Fife	01592-414141
Glasgow	0141-287 2000
Highland	01463-702000
Inverclyde	01475-724400
Midlothian	0131-663 2881
Moray	01343-543451
North Ayrshire	01294-324100
North Lanarkshire	01698-302222
Orkney Islands	01856-873535
Perth & Kinross	01738-475000
Renfrewshire	0141-842 5000
Scottish Borders	01835-824000
Shetland Islands	01595-693535
South Ayrshire	01292-612000
South Lanarkshire	01698-454444
Stirling	01786-443322
West Dunbartonshire	01389-737000
West Lothian	01506-777000
Western Isles	01851-703773

NI DISTRICT COUNCILS

Antrim	01849-463113
Ards	01247-824000
Armagh	01861-529600
Ballymena	01266-660300
Ballymoney	01265-662280
Banbridge,	01820-662991
Belfast City	01232-320202
Carrickfergus	01960-351604
Castlereagh	01232-799021
Coleraine	01265-52181
Cookstown	01648-762205
Craigavon	01762-341199
Down	01396-610800
Dungannon	01868-725311
Fermanagh	01365-325050
Larne	01574-272313
Limavady	01504-722226
Lisburn	01846-682477
Londonderry	01504-365151
Magherafelt	01648-32151
Moyle	01265-762225
Newry & Mourne	01693-65411
Newtownabbey	01960-352681
North Down	01247-270371
Omagh	01662-245321
Strabane	01504-382204

European Union

The European Union grew out of trading organisations created by Belgium, France, Germany, Italy, Luxembourg and the Netherlands in the 1950s. These USA-backed anti-Communist groupings created the **European Economic Community** (EEC) in 1957. It was also known as the Common Market, now the Single Market. During the 1970s member countries often dropped the word "Economic" from the title, but it did not officially become the **European Community** (EC) until late 1980. The title **European Union** (EU) was adopted in November 1993 when the Maastricht Treaty was ratified. The UK, Denmark and Ireland joined in 1973, Greece in 1981, Spain and Portugal in 1986, and Austria, Finland and Sweden in 1995. This brought membership to 15, with 371m citizens living in 146m households on 3.24m square kilometres.

The EU says: "The aims of the Union are essentially economic. They are to create a single economic region in which goods, services, people and capital can move as freely as they do within national boundaries." But the EU has been given broader social and political powers by the Single European Act of 1986 and the 1992 Maastricht Treaty, aimed at eventually creating a single European state. The Euro currency starts formally in January 1999, with coins and notes going into circulation in January 2002. The UK has not joined.

The Maastricht Treaty gave the EU three "pillars". The first is made up of the then-established institutions and decision-making processes, described below. The second pillar consists of defence and foreign policy, while the third encompasses policing, immigration, terrorism and legal co-operation. The second and third pillars are intergovernmental and therefore outside EU parliamentary control.

The EU is run by the six organisations forming the first pillar: the Council of Ministers, European Council, Parliament, Commission, Court of Justice and Court of Auditors.

The **Council of Ministers** (CoM) is the most powerful decision-making body in the EU. Also known as the *Council of the European Union*, the CoM, consists of ministers from

Inside the European Parliament in Strasbourg

each state, whose meetings take place behind closed doors. The presidency rotates every six months. The UK then Austria presided in 1998, followed by Germany and Finland in 1999, and Portugal and France in 2000.

Separate from the CoM is the **European Council**, comprising heads of state of each member country meeting two or three times a year. It sets political guidelines for the Council of Ministers. The European Council and CoM should not be confused with the similarly-named *Council of Europe* (CoE). This is a political institution outside the EU, set up by ten states in 1949, and today having 39 members. Alongside the CoE is the European Court of Human Rights, based in the Parliament building in Strasbourg.

The **European Parliament** draws up new law, rather than initiating it. Its main role is to scrutinise the activities of the CoM and the staff-run Commission. An Ombudsman, appointed by Parliament, investigates maladministration throughout the EU. Parliament has 626 members (MEPs), 87 of them in the UK. Elections have been held every five years since 1979, with the next taking place in June 1999 using a new form voting, where the electorate votes for parties, not individual candidates. The UK will be split into 12 regions, each with between four and 11 MEP seats. The UK result of the last election (June 1994) was:

Labour 63
Conservatives 18
Liberal-Democrats 2
Scottish Nationalist Party 2
Northern Ireland: one each to the SDLP,
the Democratic Unionist Party and the
Ulster Unionist Party.

Parliament meets 17 times each year. MEPs sit in political rather than national groupings. The largest are the Party of European Socialists with 217 members (including UK MEPs) and the European People's Party with 173 (including the UK Tories).

The main driving force of the EU is the **European Commission**, being both the EU's executive civil service and its legislature. The Commission drafts proposals, which are looked at by Parliament and decided by the CoM. In charge are 20 commissioners, non-MEPs recommended by member states for five-year renewable terms. The British commissioners until 2000 are Sir Leon Brittan and Neil Kinnock. The work is carried out by 30 Directorates-General and similar departments, employing 15,000 officials.

The **Court of Justice** is the legal administrator. Its 15 judges sit in Luxembourg. Their judgements are binding on member states and have primacy over national law. The **Court of Auditors** controls the EU's financial activities. Other influential EU bodies are the Economic and Social Committee, giving advice to the Commission; the Committee of the Regions, which must be consulted about regional interests; and the European Investment Bank, the EU's financing institution.

The EU's institutions are spread between Brussels; Luxembourg, where Commission and Parliament have offices and the Court of Justice is based; and Strasbourg, where Parliament meets a week a month. The CoM has meetings in Luxembourg two months a year. The committees meet in Brussels.

RESEARCH

Information about the EU can be hard to find. A starting point could be the Westminster alleyway called Lewisham Street, at the opposite ends of which are the London offices of the Commission and Parliament. Both are on the web. The official EU guidebook is the *Interinstitutional Directory of the European Union*, the Brussels equivalent to the UK's *Civil Service Yearbook*. More detail is in the quarterly handbook *Vacher's European Companion*, the standard work.

EU press officers are elusive; try their main switchboards, especially the Commission in Brussels. There is no single EU press office. Many journalists reporting on the EU are based in a Brussels building called the International Press Centre. The only independent body in Europe monitoring the EU's secret activities and their effects on civil liberties Europe-wide is Statewatch, based in London. It publishes a regular bulletin, plus special reports, and is on Internet.

COUNCIL OF MINISTERS

Secretariat, Brussels	00-322 2856111
UK Representation, Brussels	00-322 2878211

EUROPEAN PARLIAMENT

UK Information Office	0171-227 4300
Secretariat, Luxembourg	00-352 43001
Parliament, Strasbourg	00-33 388174488
Parliament, Brussels	00-322 2842111
Ombudsman	00-33 388174427
Website	www.europarl.eu.int

EUROPEAN PARTIES

Party of European Socialists (217 members):	
Brussels	00-322 2842111
Strasbourg	00-33 388174188
Labour MEPs, London	0171-222 1719
European People's Party (173):	
Brussels	00-322 2842111
Luxembourg	00-352 43001
Tory MEPs, London	0171-222 1994
Union for Europe (54)	00-322 2843920
European Liberal, Democratic and Reformist	
Party (52)	00-322 2842111
European United Left (33)	00-322 2842683
Greens (27)	00-322 2843045
European Radical Alliance (20)	00-322 2843324
Europe of Nations (19)	00-322 2842111
Non-attached (31)	00-322 2842579

EUROPEAN COMMISSION

HQ general	00-322 2991111
Luxembourg	00-352 43011
Press	00-322 2911111
UK offices: London	0171-973 1992
Cardiff	01222-371631
Edinburgh	0131-225 2058
Belfast	01232-240708
UK Commissioners: Neil Kinnock	00-322 2963220
Sir Leon Brittan	00-322 2952514
Website	www.cec.org.uk

OTHER EU OFFICIAL BODIES

Committee of the Regions	00-322 2822211
Economic/Social Committee	00-322 5469011
European Court of Auditors	
Secretariat, Luxembourg	00-352 43981
European Court of Justice	
Secretariat, Luxembourg	00-352 43031
European Investment Bank	0171-343 1200
European Monitoring Centre for Drugs and	
Drug Addiction	00-3511 8113000
Office for Official Publications	00-352 29291

OTHER ORGANISATIONS

Business in Europe - DTI Info Service	0117-944 4888
Consumers in Europe Group	0171-881 3021
Council of Europe	00-333 88412000
European Aid Intelligence Unit	0171-588 7070
European Disability Forum	00-322 2824609
European Broadcasting Union	
(Geneva)	00-4122 7172111
European Cultural Foundation	00-3120 6760222
European Free Trade Association	
EFTA (Geneva)	00-4122 7491111
European Institute. for the Media	00-49211 90104
European Movement	0171-233 1422
European Patent Office (Munich)	00-4989 2399
European Policy Forum	0171-839 7565
European Round Table	00-322-5343100
European Space Agency (Paris)	00-311 53697654
European Trade Union Confederation	
(Brussels)	00-322 240121
GATT (Geneva)	00-4122 7395111
House of Commons Select Committee on	
European Legislation	0171-219 5465
International Federation of Newspaper	
Publishers (Paris)	00-331 47428500
International Press Centre	00-322 2850800
Local Govt International Bureau	0171-222 1636
London Europe Society	01438-712999
NATO (Brussels)	00-322 7074111
Nordic Council (Stockholm)	00-468 111142
OECD (Paris)	00-331 45248200
Solidar	00-322 5001020
Statewatch	0181-802 1882
Website	www.poptel.org.uk/statewatch
TUC European Information Service	0171-636 4030
United Nations (London)	0171-630 1981
Western European Union	00-322 5004411

EURO-SCEPTICS

Bruges Group	0171-287 4414
Campaign Against Euro Federalism	0151-638 2780
Campaign for an Independent Britain	0181-340 0314
Conservatives Against a Federal	
Europe	0171-799 2655
Euro Facts	0181-746 1206
European Foundation	0171-930 7319
Freedom Association	0171-928 9925
Labour Euro Safeguards Campaign	0171-928 9925
New Britain Party	0171-628 2843
Referendum Movement	0171-834 6511
Save Britain's Fish	01472-317686
UK Independence Party	0171-434 4559
Youth Against the EU	01795-539227

The legal system

The Lord Chancellor's Department oversees the courts system. The Lord Chancellor is a government minister and head of the judiciary, responsible for administering civil courts, considering reforms, appointing magistrates, and advising on the appointment of judges. The Attorney General, assisted by the Solicitor General, is the governments chief legal adviser and prosecutor. The Home Secretary has many legal responsibilities, especially concerning criminal law and the administration of justice.

There are two separate kinds of law: *criminal* (offences against state laws) and *civil* (disputes between individuals or organisations). In **England and Wales** every criminal case starts in juryless magistrates courts, where most are also settled. Serious crimes move on to the 93 crown courts, where they are heard in front of a judge and jury. The leading crown court is the Central Criminal Court, best-known as the Old Bailey. Civil actions start in: the many local county courts; the magistrates courts in certain limited actions; or the Queens Bench, Chancery or Family Divisions of the High Court in more complicated cases. The High Court is based in the Royal Court of Justice in London's Strand.

Appeals are heard by the Criminal or Civil Divisions of the Court of Appeal, housed in the Royal Court of Justice. From the Court of Appeal, cases involving important points of law can ask to be heard by the House of Lords. The Criminal Cases Review Commission, an independent body set up in 1997, investigates suspected miscarriages of justice in England, Wales and Northern Ireland.

In **Scotland**, district courts are the equivalent of the magistrates courts. Above the districts are the sheriff courts, arranged in six sheriffdoms. They hear both criminal and civil cases, combining the roles of the crown and county courts south of the border. The Procurator Fiscal Service conducts public prosecutions. The final criminal court is the High Court of Justiciary, which is both a trial and appeal court; there is no appeal to the House of Lords. The supreme civil court is the Court of Session, but subject to the Lords.

The **Northern Ireland** legal system is similar to England and Wales, with magistrates, crown and county courts. The main difference is that terrorism cases are usually heard before judges without juries. Crown court appeals go to the Northern Ireland Court of Appeal, and then the House of Lords.

There are too many magistrate and county courts to include below, though county court administration offices are given.

LAW OFFICERS

Lord Chancellor's Dept	0171-210 8500
Press	0171-210 8512
Attorney General & Solicitor General	0171-828 7155
Press	0171-233 7524
Scotland: Lord Advocate/Sol. Gen.	0171-276 3000
Northern Ireland: Law Barristers	01232-241523

APPEAL COURTS

Judicial Committee of Privy Council	0171-270 0483
House of Lords Appellate Committee	0171-219 3000
Lord Chancellor's secretary	0171-219 3232
Scotland: High Court	0131-225 2595
Court of Appeal, Royal Courts of:	
Justice	0171-936 6000
Civil Division	0171-936 6409
Criminal Division	0171-936 6011

SUPREME COURTS

England/Wales

High Court, Strand	0171-936 6000
Crown Office	0171-936 6205
Lord Chief Justices clerk	0171-936 6001
Master of the Rolls clerk	0171-936 6371
Chancery Division	0171-936 6167
Family Division	0171-936 6540
Queens Bench Division	0171-936 6000
Court Service	0171-210 2092

Scotland

Court of Session and High Court of Justiciary	0131-225 2595
Crown Office (HQ, Procurator Fiscal)	0131-226 2626
Scottish Courts Administration	0131-229 9200

Northern Ireland

Supreme Court of Judicature	01232-235111
Court Service	01232-328594

CROWN COURTS

Crown Courts handle the most serious criminal cases. There are six circuits, each under an administrator responsible to the Lord Chancellor. The main court is the Central Criminal Court (Old Bailey) in the South East Circuit.

Midland and Oxford Circuit

Circuit Administrator (Bham)	0121-681 3200
Birmingham	0121-681 3300
Coventry	01203-536166
Derby	01332-622600
Grimsby	01472-311811
Hereford	01432-276118
Leicester	0116-222 2323
Lincoln	01522-883000
Northampton	01604-470400
Nottingham	0115-910 3500
Oxford	01865-264200
Peterborough	01733-349161
Shrewsbury	01743-355775
Stafford	01785-255217
Stoke-on-Trent	01782-854000
Warwick	01926-495428
Wolverhampton	01902-481000
Worcester	01905-730800

North Eastern Circuit

Circuit Administrator (Leeds)	0113-2511200
Bradford	01274-840274
Doncaster	01302-322211
Durham	0191-386 6714
Hull	01482-586161
Leeds	0113-283 0040
Newcastle-upon-Tyne	0191-386 4319
Sheffield	0114-281 2400
Teeside	01642-340000
York	01904-645121

Northern Circuit

Circuit Administrator	0161-833 1005
Barrow-in-Furness	01772-832300
Bolton	01204-392881
Burnley	01282-416899
Carlisle	01228-520619
Lancaster	01524-32454
Liverpool	0151-473 7373
Manchester	0161-954 1800
Preston	01772-832300

South Eastern Circuit

Circuit Administrator (London)	0171-936 7232
Aylesbury	01296-434401
Bury St Edmunds	01284-762676
Cambridge	01223-364436
Canterbury	01227-819200
Chelmsford	01245-603000
Chichester	01243-520700
Guildford	01483-506808
Ipswich	01473-213841
Kings Lynn	01553-760847
Lewes	01273-480400
London: Old Bailey	0171-248 3277
Croydon	0181-410 4700
Harrow	0181-424 2294
Inner London Sessions, SE1	0171-234 3100
Isleworth	0181-568 8811
Kingston-upon-Thames	0181-240 2500
Knightsbridge, SE1	0171-922 5800
Middlesex Guildhall, SW1	0171-799 2131
Snaresbrook, E11	0181-982 5500
Southwark, SE1	0171-522 7200
Wood Green, N22	0181-881 1400
Woolwich, SE28	0181-312 7000
Luton	01582-522000
Maidstone	01622-202000
Norwich	01603-761776
Reading	0118-9674400
St Albans	01727-834481
Southend	01268-458000

Wales and Chester Circuit

Circuit Administrator (Cardiff)	01222-396925
Caernarfon	01286-675200
Cardiff	01222-345931
Carmarthen	01267-236071
Chester	01244-317606
Dolgellau	01286-675200
Haverfordwest	01437-764782
Knutsford	01244-317606
Merthyr Tydfil	01685-388307
Mold	01352-754343
Newport	01633-266211
Swansea	01792-510200
Warrington	01925-572192
Welshpool	01244-317606

Western Circuit

Circuit Administrator (Bristol)	0117-974 3763
Barnstaple	01271-373286
Bournemouth	01202-502800
Bristol	0117-976 3030
Dorchester	01305-778684
Exeter	01392-210655
Gloucester	01452-529351
Newport	01983-526821
Plymouth	01752-208284
Portsmouth	01705-822281
Salisbury	01722-325444
Southampton	01703-228586
Swindon	01793-614848
Taunton	01823-335972
Truro	01872-222340
Winchester	01962-841212

N IRELAND CROWN COURTS

Court Service	01232-328594
Armagh	01861-522816
Ballymena	01266-49416
Belfast	01232-754741
Craigavon	01762-341324
Derry	01504-363448
Downpatrick	01396-614621
Enniskillen	01365-322356
Newtownards	01247-814343
Omagh	01662-242056

COUNTY COURTS

Midlands/Oxford

Birmingham	0121-681 3000
Nottingham	0115-910350
Stafford	01785-255217

North Eastern

Leeds	0113-245 9611
Newcastle-upon-Tyne	0191-201 2000
Sheffield	0114-281 2400

Northern

Liverpool	0151-473 7373
Manchester	0161-954 1800
Preston	01772-832300

South Eastern

Chelmsford	01245-264670
Kingston-upon-Thames	0181-546 8843
London	0171-917 5000
Maidstone	01622-202000

Wales & Chester

Cardiff	01222-376400
Chesterfield	01246-501200

Western

Bristol	0117-929 4414
Exeter	01392-210655
Winchester	01962-841212

SCOTTISH SHERIFF COURTS

Glasgow & Strathkelvin

Regional office	0141-429 5566
Sheriff courts	0141-429 8888

Grampian, Highlands & Islands

Regional office	01463 230782
Aberdeen	01224-648316
Banff	01261-812140
Dingwall	01349-863153
Dornoch	01862-810224
Elgin	01343-542505
Fort William	01397-702087
Inverness	01463-230782
Kirkwall	01856-872110
Lerwick	01595-693914
Lochmaddy	01876-500340
Peterhead	01779-476676
Portree	01478-612191
Stonehaven	01569-762758
Stornoway	01851-702231
Tain	01862-892518
Wick	01955-602846

Lothian & Borders

Regional office	0131-225 2525
Duns	01835-863231
Edinburgh	0131-225 2525
Haddington	01620-822936
Jedburgh	01835-863231
Linlithgow	01506-842922
Peebles	01721-720204
Selkirk	01750-21269

North Strathclyde

Regional office	0141-887 5225
Campbeltown	01586-552503
Dumbarton	01389-763266
Dunoon	01369-704166
Greenock	01475-787073
Kilmarnock	01563-520211
Oban	01631-562414
Paisley	0141-887 5291
Rothesay	01700-502982

South Strathclyde, Dumfries & Galloway

Regional office	01698-284000
Airdrie	01236-751121
Ayr	01292-268474
Dumfries	01387-262334
Hamilton	01698-282957
Kirkcudbright	01557-330574
Lanark	01555-661531
Stranraer	01776-702138

Tayside, Central & Fife

Regional office	01382-229961
Alloa	01259-722734
Arbroath	01241-876600
Cupar	01334-652121
Dundee	01382-229961
Dunfermline	01383-724666
Falkirk	01324-620822
Forfar	01307-462186
Kirkcaldy	01592-260171
Perth	01738-620546
Stirling	01786-462191

PROSECUTIONS

The Serious Fraud Office carries out the prosecution of the most important criminal cases. Others are handled by the Crown Prosecution Service, which takes over many of the criminal investigations started by the police in England and Wales. It has 6,000 staff in over 100 offices, handling 1.5 million cases a year.

Serious Fraud Office	0171-239 7272	
Enquiries	0171-239 7004	
Out-of-hours	0171-273 8341	
CPS headquarters	0171-273 8000	
Enquiries	0171-334 8505	
Press	0171-273 8106	
Central casework	0171-273 1217	
CPS areas:		
Anglia	01727-818100	
East Midlands	0115-948 0480	
Humber	0114-291 2000	
London	0171-915 5700	
Mersey/Lancashire	0151-236 7575	
Midlands	0121-629 7202	
North	0191-201 2390	
North West	0161-869 7402	
Severn/Thames	01905-795477	
South East	01483-882600	
South West	01392-422555	
Wales	01222-783000	
Yorkshire	01904-610726	

LEGAL BODIES

The Law Society is the professional organisation for lawyers. The Legal Action Group works to improve legal services for disadvantaged people and deprived areas. Liberty is the campaigning body (formerly the NCCL). Statewatch monitors the legal activities of the state, focusing especially on Europe.

Childrens Legal Centre	01206 873820
Criminal Cases Review Commission	0121-633 1800
Disability Law Service	0171-831 8031
Earthrights	0171-278 1005
Environmental Law Foundation	0171-404 1030
Free Representation Unit	0171-831 0692
Immunity Legal Centre	0171-388 6776
Inquest	0181-802 7430
Justice	0171-329 5100
Law Centres Federation	0171-387 8570
Law Society	0171-242 1222
Solicitors Supervision Office	01926-820082
Legal Action Group	0171-833 2931
Legal Aid Board	0171-813 1000
Liberty	0171-403 3888
Magistrates Association	0171-387 2353
Release	0171-729 9904
Rights of Women	0171-251 6577
Statewatch	0181-802 1882

LAW CENTRES

Law centres provide free legal advice and representation. They are run by voluntary committees of local people, and are usually financed by local authorities. The centres are members of the Law Centres Federation:

Law Centres Federation
18-19 Warren St, London W1P 5DB
Fax 0171-387 8368   Tel 0171-387 8570
Sheffield office   0114-278 7004

Local law centres

Avon & Bristol	0117-924 8662
Birmingham (Saltley)	0121-328 2307
Bradford	01274-306617
Cardiff	01222-498117
Carlisle	01228-515129
Chesterfield	01246-550674
Coventry	01203-223051
Derby	01332-344557
Gateshead	0191-477 1109
Glasgow (SCastlemilk)	0141-634 0313
Gloucester	01452-423492
Humberside	01482-211180
Huddersfield (Kirklees)	01484-518525
Ireland: North (Belfast)	01232-321307
South (Dublin)	00-353-1679 4239
Leeds (Harehills)	0113-249 1100
Leicester	0116-255 3781
Leicester (Highfields)	0116-253-2928
Liverpool Eight	0151-709 4996
London: Brent	0181-451 1122
Brixton	0171-737 0440
Camberwell	0171-701 9499
Camden	0171-485 6672
Central London	0171-839 6158
Greenwich	0181-853 2550
Hackney	0181-985 8364
Hammersmith & Fulham	0181-741 4021
Hillingdon	0181-561 9400
Hounslow	0181-570 9505
Newham	0181-555 3331
North Islington	0171-607 2461
North Kensington	0181-969 7473
North Lambeth	0171-582 4373
North Lewisham	0181-692 5355
Paddington	0181-960 3155
Plumstead	0181-855 9817
Southwark	0171-732 2008
Springfield	0181-767 6884
Stockwell & Clapham	0171-720 6231
Tottenham	0181-802 0911
Tower Hamlets	0171-791 0741
Vauxhall	0151-207 2004
Wandsworth & Merton	0171-228 9462
Luton	01582-481000
Manchester: North	0161-205 5040
South	0161-225 5111
Wythenshawe	0161-498 0905
Middlesbrough	01642-223813
Newcastle	0191-230 4777
Nottingham	0115-978 7813
Oldham	0161-627 0925
Rochdale	01706-57766
Salford	0161-736 3116
Scottish Association	0141-445 6451
Sheffield	0114-273 1888
Warrington	01925-651104
Wiltshire	01793-486926

Prisons

There are 133 prisons in England and Wales, plus 22 in Scotland and 4 in Northern Ireland. Since the passing of the 1991 Criminal Justice Act, the prison services have been managed by the three agencies - government quangos - listed below. Most new prisons are now run by private companies.

The number of prisoners has escalated since 1993, passing the landmark figure of 60,000 in April 1997, and topping 64,000 just 9 months later. This was a rise of 20,000 in five years. The reasons for this are a higher crime rate by the unemployed, a more prison-oriented attitude in courts and tougher laws. Britain has one of the highest imprisonment rates in western Europe, 116 per 100,000. All prisons are full to overflowing.

The 1997 Labour government in its first year had to boost the prison budget by £133 million The Home Office warned that the numbers in jail could rise to nearly 93,000 by 2005. A further 24 prisons costing £2 billion would have to be built. A prison ship was bought from the USA in 1997 and is now in Portland, Dorset. On average it costs over £24,000 per year to keep any prisoner.

Prisoners are housed in establishments ranging from open prisons to high security buildings. Nearly 96 per cent of prisoners are male. Women are held in separate prisons or in separate accommodation in mixed prisons.

PRISON AGENCIES

HM Prison Service	0171-217 3000
Press	0171-217 6633
Outside office hours	0181-840 6633
Security Group	0171-217 5574
Operations - North	0171-217 6677
Operations - South	0171-217 6447
Scottish Prison Service	0131-244 8475
Press	0131-244 8476
Prisons - South & West	0131-244 8546
Prisons - North & East	0131-244 8741
N Ireland Prison Service	01232-520700

GOVT DEPARTMENTS

Home Office: Main number	0171-273 4000
Press	0171-217 4600
HM Prison Service	0171-217 6000
Boards of Visitors	0171-217 8292
Prison Inspectorate	0171-273 3702
Prisons Ombudsman	0171-389 1527
Scottish Office: Main number	0131-556 8400
Press	0131-244 1111
Parole Board	0131-244 8755
Prison Inspectorate	0131-244 8481
Northern Ireland Office: Press	01232-528233

PRISON SUPPORT BODIES

Howard League for Penal Reform	0171-281 7722
Irish Commission Prisoners Overseas	0171-272 9843
Justice	0171-329 5100
NACRO	0171-582 6500
National Assoc of Prison Visitors	01234-359763
National Assoc of Probation Officers	0171-223 4887
National Council for Prisoners Abroad	0171-8333467
National Prisoners Movement	0181-542 3744
Prison Charity Shop Trust	0171-437 4334
Prison Governors Association	0171-217 8591
Prison Officers Association	0181-803 0255
Prison Reform Trust	0171-251 5070
Prison Watch	01332-753515
Prisoners Advice & Info Network	0181-542 3744
Prisoners Advice Service	0171-405 8090
Prisoners Families and Friends	0171-403 4091
Prisoners' Wives & Families Society	0171-278 3981
Prisons Ombudsman	0171-273 6060
Women in Prison	0171-226 5879
Women Prisoners' Centre	0181-968 3121

MALE PRISONS (E & W)

O = open prison

Acklington, Northumberland	01670-760411
Albany, Isle of Wight	01983-524055
Aldington, Kent	01233-720436
Ashwell, Leics	01572-774100
Bedford	01234-358671
Belmarsh, London SE28	0181-317 2436
Birmingham, Winson Green	0121-554 3838
Blakenhurst, Worcs	01527-543348
Blantyre House, Kent	01580-211367
Blundeston, Suffolk	01502-730591
Brinsford, Wolverhampton	01902-791118
Bristol	0117-980 8100
Brixton, London SW2	0181-674 9811
Brockhill, Worcs	01527-550314
Buckley Hall, Lancs	01706-861610
Bullingdon, Oxon	01869-322111
Camp Hill, Isle of Wight	01983-527661
Canterbury, Kent	01227-762244

Cardiff	01222-433100
Channings Wood, Devon	01803-812361
Chelmsford, Essex	01245-268651
Coldingley, Surrey	01483-476721
Dartmoor, Devon	01822-890261
Doncaster	01302-760870
Dorchester, Dorset	01305-266021
Downview, Surrey	0181-770 7500
Durham	0191-386 2621
Elmley, Kent	01795-880808
Erlestoke, Wilts	01380-813475
Everthorpe, Humberside	01430-422471
Exeter, Devon	01392-278321
Featherstone, Wolverhampton	01902-790991
Feltham, Middlesex	0181-890 0061
Ford (O), West Sussex	01903-717261
Frankland, Co Durham	0191-384 5544
Full Sutton, York	01759-375100
Garth, Lancs	01772-622722
Gartree, Leics	01858-410234
Glen Parva, Leics	0116-264 3100
Gloucester	01452-529551
Grendon & Spring Hill, Bucks	01296-770301
Guernsey, Channel Islands	01481-48376
Haslar, Hants	01705-580381
Haverigg, Cumbria	01229-772131
Hewell Grange (O), Worcs	01527-550843
High Down, Surrey	0181-643 0063
Highpoint (O), Suffolk	01440-823100
Hindley, Lancs	01942-866255
Holme House, Cleveland	01642-673759
Hull, N Humberside	01482-320673
Isle of Man	01624-621306
Jersey, Channel Islands	01534-44181
Kingston, Hants	01705-891100
Kirkham (O), Lancs	01772-684343
Kirklevington Grange, Cleveland	01642-781391
Lancaster	01524-385100
Latchmere House, Surrey	0181-948 0215
Leeds, West Yorks	0113-263 6411
Leicester	0116-254 6911
Lewes, East Sussex	01273-405100
Leyhill (O), Glos	01454-260681
Lincoln	01522-533633
Lindholme, South Yorks	01302-848700
Littlehey, Cambs	01480-812202
Liverpool	0151-525 5971
Long Lartin, Worcs	01386-830101
Low Newton, Co Durham	0191-386 1141
Maidstone, Kent	01622-755611
Manchester	0161-834 8626
Moorland, South Yorks	01302-351500
Morton Hall (O), Lincs	01522-866700
The Mount, Herts	01442-834363
North Sea Camp (O), Lincs	01205-760481
Norwich	01603-437531
Nottingham	0115-962 5022
Parkhurst, Isle of Wight	01983-523855
Pentonville, London N7	0171-607 5353
Preston, Lancs	01772-257734
Ranby, Notts	01777-706721
Reading, Berks	0118-958 7031
Risley, Cheshire	01925-763871
Rochester, Kent	01634-838100
Send, Surrey	01483-223048

Shepton Mallet, Somerset	01749-343377
Shrewsbury, Salop	01743-352511
Stafford	01785-254421
Standford Hill (O), Kent	01795-880441
Stocken, Leics	01780-410771
Sudbury (O), Derbys	01283-585511
Swaleside, Kent	01795-884100
Swansea	01792-464030
Usk, Gwent	01291-672411
Verne, Dorset	01305-820124
Wakefield, West Yorks	01924-378282
Wandsworth, London SW18	0181-874 7292
Wayland, Norfolk	01953-858100
Wealston (O), West Yorks	01937-844844
Wellingborough, Northants	01933-224151
Whatton, Notts	01949-850511
Whitemoor, Cambs	01354-660653
Winchester, Hants	01962-854494
Wolds, Humberside	01430-421588
Woodhill, Bucks	01908-501999
Wormwood Scrubs, W12	0181-743 0311
Wymott, Lancs	01772-421461

FEMALE PRISONS (E & W)

Askham Grange (O), York	01904-704236
Bullwood Hall, Essex	01702-202515
Cookham Wood, Kent	01634-814981
Drake Hall (O), Staffs	01785-850621
Durham	0191-386 2621
East Sutton Park (O), Kent	01622-842711
Eastwood Park	01454-262100
Exeter, Devon	01392-278321
Holloway, London N7	0171-607 6747
Low Newton, Co Durham	0191-386 1141
New Hall, West Yorks	01924-848307
Risley, Cheshire	01925-763871
Styal, Cheshire	01625-532141

SCOTTISH PRISONS

Aberdeen	01224-876868
Barlinnie, Glasgow	0141-770 2000
Cornton Vale, Stirling	01786-832591
Dungavel, Lanarkshire	01357-440371
Edinburgh	0131-444 2000
Friarton, Perth	01738-625885
Glenochil, Clackmannanshire	01259-760471
Inverness	01463-233320
Longriggend, Lanarkshire	01236-830392
Low Moss, Glasgow	0141-762 4848
Noranside, Angus	01356-650217
Penninghame, Wigtownshire	01671-402886
Perth	01738-622293
Peterhead, Aberdeenshire	01779-479101
Shotts, Lanarkshire	01501-822622

N IRELAND PRISONS

Belfast: Crumlin Road	01232-741100
Maghaberry, Co Antrim	01846-611888
Magilligan, Co Londonderry	01504-763311
Maze, Co Antrim	01846-683111

International

EMBASSIES

Em = Embassy, HCom = High Commission,
Con = Consulate

Afghanistan: London Em	0171-589 8891
Albania: London Em	0171-730 5709
Algeria: London Em	0171-221 7800
UK Em, Algiers	00-2132 692411
Angola: London Em	0171-495 1752
UK Em, Luanda	00-2442 334582
Antigua: London HCom	0171-486 7073
UK HCom, St Johns	00-1809 4620008
Argentina: London Em	0171-318 1300
UK Em, Buenos Aires	00-541 8037070
Australia: London HCom	0171-379 4334
UK HCom, Canberra	00-616 2706666
UK Con, Melbourne	00-613 96504155
UK Con, Perth	00-619 2215400
UK Con, Sydney	00-612 2477521
Austria: London Em	0171-235 3731
UK Em, Vienna	00-431 716130
Azerbaijan: London Em	0171-938 5482
Bahamas: London HCom	0171-408 4488
UK HCom, Nassau	00-1242 3257471
Bahrain: London Em	0171-370 5132
UK Em, Bahrain	00-973 534404
Bangladesh: London Em	0171-584 0081
UK HCom, Dhaka	00-8802 882705
Barbados: London HCom	0171-631 4975
UK HCom, Bridgetown	00-1246 4366694
Belarus: London Em	0171-937 3288
Belgium: London Em	0171-470 3700
UK Em, Brussels	00-322 2876211
Belize: London HCom	0171-499 9728
UK HCom, Belmopan	00-5018 22146
Bolivia: London Em	0171-235 4248
UK Em, La Paz	00-5912 433424
Bosnia: London Em	0171-255 3758
UK Em, Sarejevo	00-38771 444429
Botswana: London HCom	0171-499 0031
UK HCom, Gaborone	00-267 352841
Brazil: London Em	0171-499 0877
UK Con, Rio	00-5521 5533223
Brunei: London HCom	0171-581 0521
UK HCom, Begawan	00-6732 222231
Bulgaria: London Em	0171-584 9400
UK Em, Sofia	00-3592 4923335
Burma: London Em	0171-499 8841
UK Em, Rangoon	00-951 81700
Burundi: UK Con, Bujumbura	00-2572 23711
Cameroon: London HCom	0171-727 0771
UK Em, Yaounde	00-237 220545
Canada: London HCom	0171-258 6600
UK HCom, Ottawa	00-1613 2371530
UK Con,Vancouver	00-1604 6834421

Chad: UK Em, Ndjamena	00-235 513064
Chile: London Em	0171-580 6392
UK Em, Santiago	00-562 2313737
China: London Em	0171-636 9375
UK Em, Beijing	00-8610 65321961
UK Em, Hong Kong	00-852 25232031
Colombia: London Em	0171-589 9177
UK Em, Bogota	00-571 2185111
Costa Rica: London Em	0171-706 8844
UK Em, San Jose	00-506 2215566
Cote d'Ivoire: London Em	0171-235 6991
UK Em, Abidjan (via operator)	225-226850
Croatia: London Em	0171-387 2022
UK Em, Zagreb	00-3851 4555310
Cuba: London Em	0171-240 2488
UK Em, Havana	00-537 331771
Cyprus: London HCom	0171-499 8272
UK HCom, Nicosia	00-3572 473131
Czech Republic: London Em	0171-243 1115
UK Em, Prague	00-422 24510439
Denmark: London Em	0171-333 0200
UK Em, Copenhagen	00-45 35264600
Dominican Republic:UK HCom	0171-370 5194
UK Em, Santo Domingo	00-1809 4727111
Eastern Caribbean: London HCom	0171-937 9522
UK HCom, Castries	00-1758 452248
Ecuador: London Em	0171-584 1367
UK Em, Quito	00-5932 560669
Egypt: London Em	0171-499 2401
UK Em, Cairo	00-202 3540850
El Salvador: London Em	0171-436 8282
UK Em, San Salvador	00-503 2981763
Estonia: London Em	0171-589 3428
UK Em, Tallinn	00-3722 6313353
Ethiopia: London Em	0171-589 7212
UK Em, Addis Ababa	00-2511 612354
Fiji: London Em	0171-584 3661
UK Em, Suva	00-679 311033
Finland: London Em	0171-838 6200
UK Em, Helsinki	00-3580 22865100
France: London Em	0171-201 1000
UK Em, Paris	00-331 44513100
UK Con, Marseille	00-334 91157210
Gabon: London Em	0171-823 9986
UK Em, Libreville	00-241 762200
Gambia: London HCom	0171-937 6316
UK HCom, Banjul	00-220 495135
Georgia: London Em	0171-937 8233
UK Em, Tbilisi	00-99532 955497
Germany: London Em	0171-824 1300
UK Em, Bonn	00-49228 9167
UK Em, Berlin	00-4930 201840
UK Con, Frankfurt	00-4969 1700020

Ghana: London HCom	0171-235 4142
UK Em, Accra	00-23321 221665
Greece: London Em	0171-229 3850
UK Em, Athens	00-301 7236211
Grenada: London HCom	0171-373 7809
UK HCom, St Georges	00-1809 4403222
Guatemala: London Em	0171-351 3042
UK Em, Guatemala City	00-5022 321601
Guinea: UK Em, Conakry	00-224 442959
Guyana: London HCom	0171-229 7684
UK Em, Georgetown	00-5922 65881
Haiti: UK Em, Port au Prince	00-509 573969
Honduras: London Em	0171-486 4880
UK Em, Tegucigalpa	00-504 325429
Hungary : London Em	0171-235 5218
UK Em, Budapest	00-361 2662888
Iceland: London Em	0171-730 5131
UK Em, Reykjavik	00-354 5515883
India: London HCom	0171-836 8484
UK HCom, Bombay	00-9122 2830517
UK HCom, Calcutta	00-9133 2425171
Indonesia: London Em	0171-499 7661
UK Em, Jakarta	00-6221 330904
Iran: London Em	0171-225 3000
UK Em, Tehran	00-9821 675011
Iraq: London via Jordan Em	0171-584 7141
UK Em, Baghdad	00-9641 5372121
Irish Republic: London Em	0171-235 2171
UK Em, Dublin	00-3531 2053700
Israel: London Em	0171-957 9500
UK Em, Tel Aviv	00-9723 5249171
Italy: London Em	0171-312 2200
UK Em, Rome	00-396 4825441
UK Con, Milan	00-392 72300330
UK Con, Naples	00-3981 663511
Ivory Coast: London Em	0171-235 6991
UK Em, Abidjan	00-225 226850
Jamaica: London HCom	0171-823 9911
UK HCom, Kingston	00-1809 9269050
Japan: London Em	0171-465 6500
UK Em, Tokyo	00-813 52111100
Jerusalem: UK Con	00-9722 828281
Jordan: London Em	0171-937 3685
UK Em, Amman	00-9626 823100
Kazakhstan: London Em	0171-581 4646
UK Em, Almaty	00-73272 506191
Kenya: London HCom	0171-636 2371
UK HCom, Nairobi	00-2542 335944
Korea: London Em	0171-227 5500
UK Em, Seoul	00-850 7357341
Kuwait: London Em	0171-590 3400
UK Em, Kuwait	00-965 24320461
Latvia: London Em	0171-312 0040
UK Em, Riga	00-371 7338126
Lebanon: London Em	0171-229 7265
UK Em, Beirut	00-9611 417007
Lesotho: London HCom	0171-235 5686
UK HCom	00-266 313961
Liberia: London Em	0171-221 1036

Libya: London via Saudia Arabian Em,	
Libyan Interests Section	0171-486 8387
Lithuania: London Em	0171-486 6401
UK Em, Vilnius	00-3702 222070
Luxembourg: London Em	0171-235 6961
UK Em, Luxembourg	00-352 229864
Malawi: London HCom	0171-491 4172
UK HCom, Lilongwe	00-265 782400
Malaysia: London HCom	0171-235 8033
UK HCom, Kuala Lumpur	00-603 2482122
Malta: London HCom	0171-292 4800
UK HCom, Valletta	00-356 2331347
Mauritius: London HCom	0171-581 0294
UK HCom, Port Louis	00-230 2111361
Mexico: London Em	0171-499 8586
UK Em, Mexico City	00-525 2072089
Mongolia: London Em	0171-937 0150
UK Em, Ulaan Bataar	00-9761 358133
Morocco: London Em	0171-581 5001
UK Em, Rabat	00-2127 720905
Mozambique: London Em	0171-383 3800
UK Em, Maputo	00-2581 420111
Namibia: London HCom	0171-636 6244
UK HCom, Windhoek	00-26461 223022
Nepal: London Em	0171-229 1594
UK Em, Kathmandu	00-9771 410583
Netherlands: London Em	0171-590 3200
UK Em, The Hague	00-3170 4270427
UK Con, Amsterdam	00-3120 6764343
New Zealand: London HCom	0171-930 8422
UK HCom, Wellington	00-644 4726049
Nicaragua: UK Em, Managua	00-5052 780014
Niger: UK Em, Niamey	00-227 732015
Nigeria: London HCom	0171-839 1244
UK HCom, Lagos	00-2341 2619531
Norway: London Em	0171-591 5500
UK Em, Oslo	00-4722 552400
UK Con, Bergen	00-4755 944705
Oman: London Em	0171-225 0001
UK Em, Muscat	00-968 693077
Pakistan: London HCom	0171-664 9200
UK HCom, Islamabad	00-9251 822131
UK HCom, Karachi	00-9221 5872436
Panama: London Em	0171-493 4646
UK Em, Panama City	00-507 2690866
Papua New Guinea: London HCom	0171-930 0922
UK HCom, Port Moresby	00-675 3251643
Paraguay: London Em	0171-937 1253
UK Em, Asuncion	00-59521 444472
Peru: London Em	0171-235 1917
UK Em, Lima	00-5114 334735
Philippines: London Em	0171-937 1600
UK Em, Manila	00-632 8167116
Poland: London Em	0171-580 4324
UK Em, Warsaw	00-4822 6281001
Portugal: London Em	0171-235 5331
UK Em, Lisbon	00-3511 3924000
Qatar: London Em	0171-493 2200
UK Em, Doha	00-974 421991

Romania: London Em	0171-937 9666
UK Em, Bucharest	00-401 3120303
Russian Fed. London Em	0171-229 3628
UK Em, Moscow	00-7503 9567200
Saudi Arabia: London Em	0171-917 3000
UK Em, Riyadh	00-9661 4880077
Senegal: London Em	0171-937 7237
UK Em, Dakar	00-221 237392
Seychelles: London HCom	0171-224 1660
UK HCom, Victoria	00-248 225225
Sierra Leone: London HCom	0171-636 6483
UK HCom, Freetown	00-23222 223961
Singapore: London HCom	0171-235 8315
UK HCom, Singapore	00-65 4739333
Slovak Republic: London Em	0171-243 0803
UK Em, Bratislava	00-427 364459
Slovenia: London Em	0171-495 7775
UK Em, Ljubljona	00-38661 1257191
Somalia: UK Em, Mogadishu	00-2521 20288
South Africa: London Em	0171-451 7299
UK Em, Cape Town	00-2721 4617220
UK Em, Pretoria	00-2712 433121
UK Con, Jo'burg	00-2711 3378940
Spain: London Em	0171-235 5555
UK Em, Madrid	00-341 3190200
UK Con, Barcelona	00-343 4199044
UK Con, Malaga	00-345 217571
Sri Lanka: London HCom	0171-262 1841
UK HCom, Colombo	00-941 437336
Sudan: London Em	0171-839 8080
UK Em, Khartoum	00-249 70760
Swaziland: London HCom	0171-630 6611
UK HCom, Mbabane	00-268 42581
Sweden: London Em	0171-917 6400
UK Em, Stockholm	00-468 6719000
Switzerland: London Em	0171-616 6000
UK Em, Berne	00-4131 3525021
UK Con, Geneva	00-4122 9182400
UK Con, Zurich	00-411 2611520
Syria: London Em	0171-245 9012
UK Em, Damascus	00-96311 3712561
Tanzania: London HCom	0171-499 8951
UK HCom, Dar es Salaam	00-25551 29601
Thailand: London Em	0171-589 0173
UK Em, Bangkok	00-662 2530191
Trinidad: London HCom	0171-245 9351
UK HCom, Port of Spain	00-1809 6222748
Tunisia: London Em	0171-584 8117
UK Em, Tunis	00-2161 341444
Turkey: London Em	0171-393 0202
UK Em, Ankara	00-90312 4686230
Uganda: London HCom	0171-839 5783
UK HCom, Kampala	00-25641 2570541
Ukraine: London Em	0171-727 6312
UK Em, Kiev	00-38044 4620011
UAE London Em	0171-581 1281
UK Em, Abu Dhabi	00-9712 326600
United States: London Em	0171-499 9000
UK Em, Washington	00-1202 4621340
UK Con, Chicago	00-1312 3461810
UK Con, Dallas	00-1214 5214090

GIBRALTAR: Standing guard over what has been designated a British territory since 1704

UK Con, Los Angeles	00-1310 4773322
UK Con, Miami	00-1305 3741522
UK Con, New York	00-1212 7450200
Uruguay: London Em	0171-584 8192
UK Em, Montevideo	00-5982 623630
Uzbwkistan: London Em	0171-229 7679
UK Em, Tashkent	00-73712 406288
Vanuatu: UK HCom, Vila	00-678 23100
Venezuela: London Em	0171-584 4206
UK Em, Caracas	00-582 9934111
Vietnam: London Em	0171-937 1912
UK Em, Hanoi	00-844 252349
Yemen: London Em	0171-584 6607
UK Em, Sanaa	00-9671 264081
Yugoslavia: London Em	0171-370 6105
UK Em, Belgrade	00-38111 645055
Zaire: London Em	0171-235 6137
UK Em, Kinshasa	00-24312 34775
Zambia: London HCom	0171-589 6655
UK HCom Lusaka	00-2601 251133
Zimbabwe: London HCom	0171-836 7755
UK HCom, Harare	00-2634 793781

DEPENDENT TERRITORIES

The UK's Dependent Territories (DTs) are the last remnants of the British Empire. A century ago, Britian ruled 400 million people on a third of the planet. Today there are 180,000 people living in the 13 remaining colonies, fragments of land whose governors are still appointed by the Queen, and whose government is the responsibility of the Foreign and Commonwealth Office (FCO). Much of the old empire now forms the Commonwealth, an association bound by affinity rather than treaty. It comprises 54 states with 1.6 billion people, a quarter of the world's population. Several of the DTs play military, telecomms or strategy roles for the UK. The FCO may rename the DTs the Overseas Territories. The FCO's West Indian and Atlantic Department is responsible for Caribbean and neighbouring territories, marked with an asterisk (*).

Foreign & Commonwealth Office

Main number	0171-270 3000
West Indian & Atlantic Dept	0171-270 2643
Press	0171-270 3100
Information dept	0171-270 6052
Website	www.fco.gov.uk

Anguilla*
Small eastern Caribbean island. 35 sq miles, 8,960 population.
Governor, Anguilla — 00-1809 2643312

Bermuda*
West Atlantic group of 100 small islands, 20 inhabited, 600 miles off North Carolina. 60,100 population. 21 sq miles in total.
Governor, Hamilton — 00-1809 2923600

British Antarctic Territory
Uninhabited section of Antarctica, including South Orkney and South Shetland islands. Run from London.
FCO Antarctic Dept — 0171-270 2742

British Indian Ocean Territory
Large group of the small Chagos Archipelago islands in central Indian Ocean, south of India. Uninhabited, except for joint UK/USA military base on Diego Garcia.
Port Louis — 00-230 2111361

British Virgin Islands*
Eastern Caribbean group of 46 islands, 11 inhabited, near Anguilla. 16,100 population.
Governor, Tortola — 00-1284 42345

Cayman Islands*
Three tax-free, wealthy Caribbean islands south of Cuba. Home of 33,600 people and nearly as many companies, dodging everything. 100 sq miles.
Governor, George Town — 00-1345 9497900

Falkland Islands
Largest islands in South Atlantic, off southern Argentina. 2,200 population, plus military.
FCO — 0171-270 2749
Governor, Stanley — 00-500 27433

Gibraltar
2.5 sq mile promontory of southernmost Spain, captured 1704. 28,000 population.
FCO — 0171-270 2975
Governor — 00-350 55934

Hong Kong
Ceased being a dependent territory from 1 July 1997.

Montserrat*
Eastern Caribbean volcanic island, 38 sq miles. 9,000 population.
Governor — 00-1664 4912688

Pitcairn Islands
Eastern group in Pacific, midway between north New Zealand and Peru. 1.9 sq miles, 54 population, all Seventh Day Adventists.
FCO — 0171-270 2955
Governor — 00-644 726049

St Helena
Island in the middle of the South Atlantic, 1,100 miles off Angola. Former prison of Napoleon. 5,650 population, with dependencies.
FCO — 0171-270 2749
Governor — 00-290 2555

St Helena dependent: Ascension Island
700 miles north-west of St Helena.
Administrator — 00-247 6311

St Helena dependent: Tristan da Cunha
Island group 1,850 miles west of Cape Town.
Administrator — 00-871 1445424

South Georgia and South Sandwich Islands
Scattered islands east and south-east of Cape Horn. South Georgia is military, South Sandwich uninhabited volcanic.
Commissioner, Stanley — 00-500 27433

Turks and Caicos Islands*
Caribbean group of 30 islands, north of Haiti. 19,000 population.
Governor, Grand Turk — 00-1809 946 2309

INTERNATIONAL BODIES

Commonwealth Secretariat	0171-839 3411
Federal Trust	0171-799 2818
International Coffee Organisation	0171-580 8591
Int. Fed. for Info & Documentation	00-3170 3140671
Int. Fed. of Newspaper Publishers	00-331 47428500
International Grains Council	0171-513 1122
International Labour Organisation	0171-828 6401
International Maritime Organisation	0171-735 7611
International Mobile Satellite Org	0171-728 1000
International Sugar Organisation	0171-513 1144
International Whaling Commission	01223-233971
*NATO	00-322 7074111
United Nations UK Info Centre	0171-630 1981
World Bank Group	0171-930 8511

Disasters and emergencies

In public, Whitehall defines disasters and emergencies as being floods, serious accidents, building catastrophes and storms. These are handled by "emergency planning" schemes, also known as "civil protection". In private, the government includes civil disorders, strikes and riots under the heading of emergency, and these come under "contingency plans".

At national level, there is an **emergency government** administrative structure kept in readiness for the most serious catastrophes. It can be activated either as a whole or in part, and is most likely to be used during a foreign attack, general strike or mass civil unrest. The top layer consists of the prime minister, key ministers and civil servants, and chief military and police officers. In the most extreme emergency this would become the UK government, operating from a hardened communications centre. This national disaster system is not advertised, and enquiries are seldom answered. The Cabinet Office is responsible for policies, the Home Office for admin.

The Cabinet Office is the home of the **Civil Contingencies Committee** (CCC), known as the Civil Contingencies Unit until disaster plans were rethought in 1997. The CCC has the main responsibility for co-ordinating the state's response to emergencies. The committee comprises civil servants and some ministers, chaired by the Home Secretary. It decides the state's approach to serious threats, appointing a government department (the "lead" department) to put plans into effect.

The Home Office **Emergency Planning Division** (EPD) runs the disaster system day-to-day on behalf of the CCC. The Division sets and maintains standards, represents the UK in an international context and initiates central government arrangements. At the core of the EPD is the **Central Government and International Section** (CGIS), playing crucial policy and operational roles. It runs the unique **Emergency Operations Suite**, which is maintained in a constant state of preparedness for

any major disaster. The Suite has specially trained staff, supported by the latest high-tech equipment, supervised by another EPD unit, the **Telecommunications Group** (TG).

The TG runs the **Emergency Communications Network** (ECN), a resilient, heavily-protected network, linking key elements of central government with local emergency services, via its own telephone system. It is designed to ensure that Whitehall will maintain contact with, and therefore control of, all UK civil and military forces in the worst possible disasters. The creation of the ECN in the 1980s and '90s rendered redundant the postwar regional underground bunkers that were designed to set up a devolved form of government in emergencies, especially the Cold War. The days of subterranean government are far from over, however: the MoD is in the final stages of rebuilding its enormous basement, with underground communications links with the rest of the government.

Home Office	0171-273 4000
Press	0171-273 4610
Emergency Planning Division	0171-273 3212
CGIS	0171-273 3310
Telecommunications Group	0171-273 3195
Research Group	0171-273 2865
Emergency Planning College	01347-821406

THE LEADERS

The next level of emergency planning below Whitehall is the **lead government department**. In an emergency, a specific department takes the lead in co-ordinating affected departments in their handling of regional and local issues. The lead acts as the focal point for communications between central government and any local Strategic Co-ordinating Group (see below). Individual departments are named in advance as being responsible for handling certain disasters, as listed here:

Flooding - MAFF or equivalents in Scottish, Welsh and Northern Ireland Offices.
Gas clouds - (DETR).
Marine and coastal pollution - DETR.
Marine: offshore installations - DETR.
Military - MoD.
Miscellaneous (building collapse, dam failures, earth-

quakes) - DETR or Scottish/Welsh/N Ireland Office.
Overseas disasters - FCO.
Radiation inside UK - Civil installations: DTI & Scottish Offices. Civil in transit: DETR. Military: MoD.
Radiation from outside UK - DETR.
Rivers, water services - DETR or Scottish/Welsh/N Ireland Offices.
Satellites - Home Office.
Search and rescue - Civil shipping: DETR (Coastguard Agency). Military shipping and aircraft, and civil aircraft at sea: MoD. Civil aircraft on land: DETR.
Sports accidents - DCMS, Scottish/Welsh Offices.
Transport accidents - DETR.
Weather - DETR or Scottish/Welsh/N Ireland Offices.

LOCAL PLANS

Local authorities have emergency planning duties. Each county-type authority has its own **emergency planning officer** (EPO), drawing up management plans. The EPOs are grant-aided local limbs of the Home Office EPD. The EPO is the starting point for inquiring about proposals for dealing with local disasters. Contact via the county councils, listed in this book under Local Government.

In the front line handling any disaster are the four emergency services, with the military in special reserve. All operate emergency procedures day-to-day, and have press offices for handling queries. They also have their own schemes for dealing with major incidents.

These services and the EPOs operate within a three-level, Home Office-agreed management framework. At **operational** level - on arrival at the disaster scene - all agencies run their own command system. If any co-ordination is necessary, the police play that role. Next is the **tactical** level of management, introduced to determine priority in allocating resources, to plan tasks and to obtain other resources if needed. This level is also co-ordinated by the police. The **strategic** level handles the most serious emergencies. A Strategic Co-ordinating Group (SCG) would be set up and run by the police, with members only from statutory bodies. SCGs would provide the focus for communication with the lead government department, and thereby the Home Office and CCC if necessary.

Many volunteer agencies help the official services, including the WRVS, RNLI, Red Cross, St John Ambulance, Raynet (a network of radio amateurs) and mountain rescue.

INFORMATION

As the police normally take initial charge at a disaster, the Home Office says they should set up as soon as possible a **media liaison point** run by an experienced press officer. Media access to the disaster site would be controlled. If media relations are difficult, the regional office of the Central Office of Information can send a press officer. A media centre could also be set up, supplying working accommodation for the media, plus a news conference area and telecoms equipment.

There is no single guidebook covering all contingency planning. The nearest is the official handbook *Dealing with Disaster* (Brodie Publishing 0151-707 2323, 3rd edition 1997). The Home Office publishes the quarterly magazine *Civil Protection*. Some Home Office publications, is available on Internet, along with some background material on the EPD.
Website   www.homeoffice.gov.uk/epd

EMERGENCY BODIES

Air Accidents Investigation, DTI	01252-510300
BASICS (British Association for Immediate Care)	01473-218407
British Airways Crisis Team, Gatwick	0181-513 0917
British Divers Marine Life Rescue	01634-281680
British Safety Council	0181-741 1231
British Telecom Emergency Policy Unit	0171-356 8866
Casualties Union	0171-278 6264
Emergency Planning College, Easingwold	01347-821406
Emergency Planning Society	0181-937 4984
International Rescue Corps	01324-665011
London Emergency Planning	0171-587 4048
Marine Accident Investigation, DTI	01703-395500
National Chemical Emergency Centre	01235-463060
National Voluntary Civil Aid Service	0181-977 2806
Royal Life Saving Society	01789-773994
Royal Society for the Prevention of Accidents	0121-248 2000
Search & Rescue Dog Assoc: Wales	01492-622195
England	0702-0960970
Lake District	01768-772463
Southern Scotland	01835-822211
Highlands	01721-721998
Underwater Search Unit	0171-275 4488
WRVS	0171-793 9917

The military

The UK armed forces are run by the Defence Council of Ministry of Defence (MoD) ministers and leading officers, including the Chief of the Defence Staff, the top militarist. Whitehall says the goal of its military policy is to "maintain the freedom and territorial integrity of the UK and its Dependent Territories, and the ability to pursue its legitimate interests at home and abroad".

At the heart of this policy is **NATO**, to which most British forces are committed. NATO was set up in 1949 to unite Western Europe and North America in the anti-Soviet Cold War. This came to an end around 1990. In 1994 NATO adopted a more global perspective because of problems of instability, extremism and nationalism. A Combined Joint Task Force was set up to carry out a wider range of missions around the world. In mid-1997 military ties between NATO, all Europe, Russia and central Asia were created. The multinational Allied Command Europe Rapid Reaction Corps (ARRC) has 55,000 UK troops and is commanded by a UK general.

Britain's pre-Cold War NATO policies had a major reshape in the **Strategic Defence Review**, published in July 1998. It firmly commits the UK to a worldwide role with the ability to send large expeditionary forces to any kind of trouble spot. Anticipating significant changes in the methods of warfare by 2015, the review states: "Operations will no longer be characterised as land, sea or air. There will instead be a single battlespace."

The strength of the UK armed forces is: Army 119,000, RAF 56,000, Royal Navy 46,000, plus 120,000 civilians, totalling 341,000. The budget for 1999/2000 is £22.8 billion, with £9 billion going on military equipment, including £1.6 billion on aircraft .

The MoD's administrative HQ is the **Main Building** (known by staff as "The Building"), halfway along Whitehall. At its core is the underground nuclear-proof bunker called the Joint Operations Centre, linked to other government services. All day-to-day military action is run from the new **Permanent Joint Headquarters** (PJHQ) in another bunker, next to the Navy's headquarters at Northwood, north-west London. Since mid-1996 PJHQ has been the overall control centre for national military operations, superseding many former single-service bodies. It is also the control point of another new organisation, the 5,000 strong **Joint Rapid Development Force** (JRDF). This military fire brigade is designed to "strengthen the UK's ability to project military Forces quickly worldwide in support of our interests". Specially trained National Contingency forces are assigned to the JRDF.

The Army's own operations centre is the Land Command, sited in (and under) the village of Wilton, just west of Salisbury. This is the hatching ground for any Army direct action inside the UK. The Royal Navy is run from Northwood and the Portsmouth Naval Base. The RAF is controlled by its HQ Strike Command at High Wycombe and the HQ Logistic Command at Huntingdon.

The UK also now has little-publicised **Special Forces**, which the MoD says have "four primary roles: reconnaissance, offensive action, the provision of support to indigenous forces and counter-terrorism". Journalists are warned that operations are so sensitive that the MoD "will pursue all appropriate legal options to prevent the publication of information about the Special Forces which it considers to be potentially damaging".

Inside the UK troops have three roles, jointly called **Military Aid to the Civil Authorities**. Military Aid to the Civil Power (**MaC-P**) is providing armed forces to help the police during violent civil challenges to state authority, as in Northern Ireland. Military Assistance to Civil Ministries (**MaC-M**) involves using troops to carry out specialised services for government departments, especially during strikes, such as Liverpool firefighters in 1995. Military Aid to the Civil Community (**MaC-C**) is arranging for service personnel to help the public during emergencies like bad weather and floods.

MINISTRY OF DEFENCE

Director of Information & News	0171-218 7900
Press office: Policy	0171-218 7931
Procurement	0171-218 7714
Army	0171-218 3255
Navy	0171-218 3257
RAF	0171-218 3253
Outside office hours	0171-218 7907
Secretary of State	0171-218 2111
Permanent Under-Secretary	0171-218 2839
Chief of Defence Staff	0171-218 2116
Air Force: Chief of Staff	0171-218 6313
Army Department: Chief of Staff	0171-218 7873
Navy Department: First Sea Lord	0171-218 6193
Joint Force HQ (Northwood)	01923 846032

Other MoD sections

Defence Press & Broadcasting Committee (DA Notices)	0171-218 3820
Defence Intelligence Staff	0171-218 2407
Magazines: Navy News	01705-826040
RAF News	01452-712612
Soldier Magazine	01252-347355
Meteorological Office	01344-856655
Ministry of Defence Police	01371-854000
Overseas forces: Cyprus	00357-5263919
Falkland Islands	00500-74204
Germany	004921-61472392
Gibraltar	003505-4231

Army

HQ Land Command (Wilton)	01722-336222
HQ Northern Ireland (Lisburn)	01846-609261
HQ Scotland (Edinburgh)	0131-310 2092
London District	0171-414 2396
Second Division (York)	01904-662433
Third Division (Wilts)	01980-672946
Fourth Division (Aldershot)	01252-347011
Fifth Division (Shrewsbury)	01743-262252
Infantry HQ (Warminster)	01985-214000

Royal Navy

Commander-in-Chief Fleet (Northwood)	01923-837635
Naval Home Command (Portsmouth)	01705-723737
Surface Flotilla HQ (Portsmouth)	01705-722351
Aviation Command (Yeovilton)	01935-455548
Royal Marines (Plymouth)	01752-554558
Naval Bases: Devonport	01752-554344
Faslane	01436-674321

RAF

Strike Command (High Wycombe)	01494-461461
Logistics Command (Huntingdon)	01480-52151
Air Warfare Centre (High Wycombe)	01522-727837
No 1 Group (Benson)	01491-837766
No 11 Group (Bentley Priory)	01494-496130
No 18 Group (Northwood)	01494-496130
No 38 Group (High Wycombe)	01494-461461
USAF HQ (Mildenhall)	01638-543000
Military Air Traffic Operations (Uxbridge)	01895-276009

Intelligence

Britain's three main intelligence agencies are MI5, MI6 and GCHQ. Parliamentary supervision of them comes from the all-party **Intelligence and Security Committee**, commonly called the Oversight Committee. This has to "examine the expenditure, administration and policy" of the trio. It meets in secret and publishes an uninformative annual report. Chairman is veteran Tory MP Tom King. The Cabinet Office's Joint Intelligence Organisation (JIO), run by John Alpass, adminsters the **Joint Intelligence Committee** (JIC) which oversees MI6 and GCHQ, but not MI5. The JIC sets the UK's national intelligence priorities and produces regular assessments of raw material gathered by MI6 and GCHQ. The committee is made up of officers from many departments and meets weekly. MI5 is monitored by another part of the JIO,

called the **Sub-Committee on Security Service Priorities and Performance** (SO-SSPP), set up in 1996 following a review of the intelligence agencies. They had been suffering an identity crisis since the ending of the Cold War in the late 1980s. Working alongside MI5, MI6 and GCHQ is the military's **Defence Intelligence Staff** (DIS), part of the MoD. It analyses information from a "wide variety of sources", and passes it on as necessary. The DIS is buried deep within the MoD, and virtually impossible to contact.

MI5

Britain's internal counter-subversion organisation is officially called the **Security Service**, otherwise known as MI5. It was set up in 1909 and currently holds 440,000 files opened since then, 290,000 relating to suspicious individuals. Only 13,000 of these people are "under current investigation", says MI5

Its main role is: "The protection of national security and, in particular, its protection against threats from espionage, terrorism and sabotage, from the activities of agents of foreign powers and from actions intended to overthrow or undermine parliamentary democracy by political, industrial or violent means" and to "safeguard the economic well-being of the UK" (1989 Security Service Act). In 1996 MI5 was given a wider remit, allowing it to intervene in areas unrelated to "national security". MI5 now joins the police in fighting "serious crime", the definition of which takes in "conduct by a large number of persons in pursuit of a common purpose", a catch-all description. The activities of environmentalists are one of its areas of operation. MI5's police contact point is the Special Branch (SB). All 55 police forces have their own SB, but in practice they all come under that of Metropolitan Police.

MI5 comes under the **Intelligence and Security Liaison Unit** (ISLU) of the Home Office. Stephen Lander was appointed Director-General of MI5 by the Home Secretary in April 1996. His deputy (and likely succesor) is Eliza Manningham-Buller. The Service has about 1,900 staff, 54 per cent aged under 40, and is run on an official budget of "less than £140 million". Two-fifths is spent on terrorism, 12 per cent on espionage and 7.5 per cent on "protective security". This is MI5's most sensitive work, protecting the core structure of the State from any form of disruption. In March 1998, MI5 for the first time ever made public one of its phone numbers, but only for informants. MI5 also went on Internet. It also publishes regularly a descriptive guide called *MI5: The Security Service* (3rd edition July 1998).

MI5 (for informants only)	0171-930 9000
Website	www.mi5.gov.uk
Home Office press contacts	0171-273 4610

MI6

The **Secret Intelligence Service** (SIS, or MI6) is Britain's overseas spying agency, gathering information discovered covertly in foreign countries. The 1994 Intelligence Services Act put MI6 and GCHQ on a statutory footing for the first time and widened MI6's role. It operates "in the interests of national security or of the economic well-being of the UK, or in support of the prevention or detection of serious crime", where "persons outside the British Islands" are suspects. The MI6 Chief is David Spedding. The annual budget is £140 million. Both MI5 and MI6 in 1994 took over expensive new London headquarters buildings almost facing each other across the Thames. MI5 is on the west side, at Thames House, Millbank, near Parliament, and MI6 is next to Vauxhall Bridge. MI6 has 2,000 staff.

Foreign Office press contacts	0171-270 3100

GCHQ

The **Government Communications Headquarters** (GCHQ) is Britain's most powerful intelligence gathering agency. This secret eavesdropping centre, with 4,500 staff, is based in Cheltenham. Its role, like MI6's, is defined by the 1994 Intelligence Services Act. Its primary work is providing government departments and the military with signal intelligence (Sigint) and eavesdropping on all types of communication, including Internet. This is in support of Whitehall's security, military, foreign and economic policies, and "the prevention or detection of serious crime" (1994 Act). GCHQ works with its US equivalent, the **National Security Agency** (NSA), which together with Britain runs UKUSA, a worldwide intelligence operation. The NSA is the largest intelligence agency in the world. Its main listening post is on 560 acres of Menwith Hill, near Harrogate. With nearly as many staff as all of MI5, Menwith intercepts all European phone, fax and e-mail communications. GCHQ, responsible to the Foreign Office, has an annual budget of £440 million. Its director since July 1996 is David Omand.

GCHQ, Cheltenham	01242-221491

Police

The UK has 55 **police forces**: 42 in England, four in Wales, eight in Scotland and one in Northern Ireland (the Royal Ulster Constabulary - RUC). London has two separate forces: the Metropolitan (the "Met"), based at New Scotland Yard on Victoria Street; and the City of London, responsible only for the City, with its headquarters close to the Guildhall. There are about 127,000 police officers in England and Wales, 14,500 in Scotland and 8,500 in the RUC. The Met is the biggest force, with 27,000 officers.

In England and Wales, all forces except the Met are maintained by local **police authorities.** By law, these must have 17 members: nine local councillors, three magistrates and five "independents" (chosen by the other members from a short-list supplied by the Home Office). The Home Secretary directly controls the Met, acting as its authority. In Scotland, the police authorities are the new unitary councils. The RUC is controlled by an authority appointed by the government.

Each police force is run by a chief constable, who is only nominally responsible to the police authority. The Home Office provides just over half the finance for the forces, giving it more power than the authorities. This means Britain has a national police force in many respects, but one that is not acknowledged or controllable as such.

The **Home Office** oversees policing through its Police Policy Directorate. Much of the Home Office was reorganised in 1995/6 to give it a more business-like structure, to tune it in more closely with new technology and to make policing more capable of responding to unpredictable internal security problems, such as the environment movement. The Home Office has also played a prominent role in setting up and running Europol, the European police service which is outside the authority of the EU parliament.

The key police organisation is the Association of Chief Police Officers (**ACPO**), the professional body for ranks above chief superintendent. In practice, ACPO is the unofficial equivalent of the government's Cabinet, making strategy and policy decisions. The Police Federation represents the interests of the other officers.

Several police **national services** are provided by either the government or through co-operation between forces. An important body is the **Police Information Technology Organisation** (PITO), a Home Office section created in 1996. This oversees many operations, including the **Police National Computer** (PNC). The PNC provides all forces with 24-hour on-screen essential material, especially the Criminal Justice Record Service (Phoenix) of all criminal records. Another PITO unit is the **Police National Network** which gives a full range of telecommunications to all forces.

The **National Criminal Intelligence Service** (NCIS) plays a central role in collecting and analysing criminal intelligence. Set up in 1992, it supplies the PNC with much of its information. The NCIS's London head-quarters and regional offices gather, store and analyze a wide range of material. It also liaises with the International Criminal Police Organisation (Interpol). The 1997 Police Act gave more authority to the NCIS and put it on legal footing. In addition, the Act replaced the regional crime squads with the new independent **National Crime Squad** (NCS), launched in April 1998. The 1,450-strong NCS will try to solve the crimes the NCIS detects. Both also work on the Euro front.

There was much public concern over the passing of the 1997 Police Act. It increased the strength of the police by authorising chief constables to carry out covert "intrusive surveillance" of the public in cases of "serious crime". This power to bug homes and offices was seen by some as a major infringement of civil liberties. Criminal records are now made available to employers.

Official **statistics** show the police in England and Wales were informed of 4.59 million crimes in 1997, down 8.8 per cent on

1996, although critics say many members of the public have just given up reporting crime. Of these, 350,700 were violent, an increase of 1.7 per cent on 1996. The Met had the most offences - 790,302 - and Dyfed-Powys the least - 18,098. The Met was also the most expensive police force, costing £215 per head of population, with the national average being £109. The average police officer solved 9.4 crimes per year, with the top rate being in Gwent, 15.5, and the lowest in Surrey, 5.8.

The percentage of all crime solved varied widely between forces, from the West Midlands with 15 per cent, to Dyfed-Powys at 52 per cent; the average was 24 per cent. Dyfed-Powys was the best solver of household burglaries (32 per cent) and Leicestershire the worst (8 per cent), only just behind the Met (9 per cent); the average was 15 per cent.

The leading annual directory of the police and related services is the *Police and Constabulary Almanac: Official Register* (R Hazell & Co, 01491-641018), only available directly from the publisher.

GOVT. DEPARTMENTS

Home Office	0171-273 4000
Press offices: Main	0171-273 4600
Prisons	0171-217 6633
Directorates: Criminal Policy	0171-273 3183
Immigration & Nationality	0181-686 0688
Organised & International Crime	0171-273 2830
Police Policy	0171-273 3601
Immigration Service Intelligence & Investigation	
Unit	0181-745 2400
Website	www.homeoffice.gov.uk
Northern Ireland Office	01232-520700
Police Division	01232-527547
NI Police Authority	01232-230111
Scottish Office: Home Dept	0131-556 8400
Press	0131-244 2661
Crime Squad	0141-302 1000
Criminal Record Office	0141-532 2777
Inspector of Constabulary	0131-244 5614

NATIONAL POLICE ORGS

Action Against Drugs Unit	0171-273 2185
Crime Prevention Agency	0171-273 2548
Crown Prosecution Service	0171-273 8000
Outside office hours	0171-273 8341
Press office	0171-273 8106
Public enquiries	0171-334 8505

Forensic Science Service	0121-607 6800
HM Inspector of Constabulary	0171-273 2116
HM Inspector of Probation	0171-273 3906
Intelligence & Security Liaison Unit	0171-273 2991
Interpol	0171-238 8600
Missing Persons Helpline	0181-392 2000
National/Regional Crime Squads: HQ	0171-238 2500
Midland	0121-626 4052
North East	01924-293665
North West	0161-848 5050
South East	0171-238 8499
South & West Wales	01222-222111
South West	01454-628301
National Criminal Intelligence Service	0171-238 8000
Press office	0171-238 8431
Enquiries	0171-238 8610
National Identification Service	0171-230 2780
National Police Training, Bramshill	01256-602200
Operational Policing Policy Unit	0171-273 2593
Parole Board (E&W)	0171-217 5314
Police Complaints Authority	0171-273 6450
Police Information Technology Org	0171-217 8179
Police National Computer	0181-200 3200
Police Science & Technology	0171-217 8609
Police Staff College, Bramshill	01256-602100
Policing Organised Crime Unit	0171-273 3244
Serious Fraud Office	0171-239 7272

POLICE FORCES: ENGLAND

Metropolitan Police, London	0171-230 1212
24-hour press bureau	0171-230 2171
Voicebank	0891-900099
Facility requests	0171-230 4094
Area headquarters:	
1 Central (at Cannon Row)	0171-925 1212
2 North West (at Colindale)	0181-205 1012
3 North East (at Edmonton)	0181-807 9332
4 South East (at Sidcup)	0171-853 1212
5 South West (at Kingston)	0181-541 1212
Flying Squad	0171-230 4094
Intelligence	0171-230 4094
Specialist Operations Dept	0171-230 1212
Met Police Committee	0171-271 8350
Website	www.met.police.uk
Avon & Somerset	01275-818181
Voicebanks: Bristol	01426-957011
Taunton	01426-950441
Bedfordshire	01234-841212
Voicebank	01426-925682
Berkshire	see Thames Valley
Buckinghamshire	see Thames Valley
Cambridgeshire	01480-456111
Voicebank	01426-950160
Cheshire	01244-350000
Voicebank	01426-955487
Cleveland	01642-326326
Voicebank	01426 979651
Cumbria	01768-891999
Voicebank	01426-972830

Derbyshire	01773-570100
Voicebank	01426-955020
Devon & Cornwall	0990-777444
Voicebank	01392-452198
Dorset	01929-462727
Voicebank	01426-932345
Durham	0191-386 4929
Voicebank	01426-984458
Essex	01245-491491
Voicebank	01426-925680
Gloucestershire	01242-521321
Voicebank	01426-955884
Guernsey	01481-725111
Hampshire	01962-841500
Voicebank	01426-932024
Herefordshire	see West Mercia
Hertfordshire	01707-354200
Voicebank	01426-934068
Humberside	01482-326111
Voicebank	01426-978223
Isle of Man	01624-631212
Jersey	01534-612612
Kent	01622-690690
Voicebank	01622-683932
Lancashire	01772-614444
Voicebank	01772-618194
Leicestershire	0116-222 2222
Lincolnshire	01522-532222
Voicebank	01426-957180
London, City of	0171-601-2222
Manchester, Greater	0161-872 5050
Voicebank	0891-335559
Merseyside	0151-709 6010
Voicebank	0891-557725
Norfolk	01603-768769
Voicebank	01426-952342
Northamptonshire	01604-700700
Voicebank	01426-952401
Northumbria	01661-872555
Voicebank	01426-979793
Nottinghamshire	0115-967 0999
Voicebank	01426-957125
Oxfordshire	see Thames Valley
Shropshire	see West Mercia
Staffordshire	01785-257717
Voicebank	01785-232525
Suffolk	01473-613500
Voicebank	01426-932403
Surrey	01483-571212
Voicebank	01426-953808
Sussex (East & West)	01273-475432
Voicebank	01273-479221
Thames Valley (Berks/Bucks/Oxon)	01865-846000
Voicebank	01426-932012
Warwickshire	01926-415000
Voicebank	01426-952404
West Mercia (Hereford/Salop/Worcs)	01905-723000
Voicebank	01426-913005
West Midlands	0121-626 5000
Voicebank	01426-952009
Wiltshire	01380-722341
Voicebank	01426-961045

Worcestershire	see West Mercia
Yorkshire - North	01609-783131
Voicebank	01426-979568
Yorkshire - South	0114-220 2020
Voicebank	01426-952018
Yorkshire - West	01924-375222
Voicebank	01426-979656

POLICE: SCOTLAND

Central Scotland	01786-456000
Clackmannanshire	01259-723255
Falkirk	01324-634212
Stirling	01786-456000
Dumfries & Galloway	01387-252112
Fife	01592-418888
Grampian	01224-639111
Lothian & Borders	0131-311 3131
Borders	01450-75051
Edinburgh	0131-311 3131
Midlothian	0131-663 2855
West Lothian	01506-31200
Northern	01463-715555
Command areas: Badenoch	01479-810222
Caithness & Sutherland	01955-603551
Inverness & Nairn	01463-715555
Lochaber	01397-702361
Orkney	01856-872241
Ross, Cromarty & Skye	01349-862444
Shetland	01595-692110
Western Isles	01851-702222
Strathclyde	0141-532 2000
Dunbartonshire	01389-822000
East Ayrshire	01563-505000
Glasgow	0141-532 2000
Inverclyde	01475-492500
North Lanarkshire	01698-483000
Paisley	0141-532 5900
South Ayrshire	01292-664000
South Lanarkshire	01698-483300
Tayside	01382-223200
Divisions: Eastern (Angus)	01307-302200
Western (Perth & Kinross)	01738-621141
Central (Dundee City)	01382-223200

POLICE: WALES

Dyfed-Powys	01267-222020
Divisions: Ceredigion	01970-612791
Eastern (Carmarthenshire)	01554-772222
Pembrokeshire	01437-763355
Powys, north	01686-625704
Powys, south	01874-622331
Gwent	01633-838111
Voicebank	01633-642219
Divisions: Blaenau Gwent	01495-350999
Caerphilly	01222-852999
Newport	01633-244999
Torfaen	01495-764711

North Wales	01492-517171
Voicebank	01426-950443
Divisions: Anglesey	01286-684950
Conwy	01492-411314
Denbighshire	01492-511336
Flintshire	01978-294710
Gwynedd	01286-684800
Wrexham	01978-294600
South Wales	01656-655555
Voicebank	01656-869292
Divisions: Bridgend	01656-655555
Cardiff	01222-222111
Merthyr Tydfil	01685-722541
Neath & Port Talbot	01639-456999
Rhondda Cynon Taff	01443-485351
Swansea	01792-456999
Vale of Glamorgan	01446-734451

POLICE: N IRELAND

Royal Ulster Constabulary	01232-650222
Belfast Region	01232-650222
North Region:	
Ballymena, Antrim	01266-653355
Coleraine, Londonderry	01265-44122
Londonderry	01504-367337
Enniskillen, Fermanagh	01365-322823
South Region:	
Armagh	01861-523311
Dungannon, Tyrone	01868-752525
Newtownards, Down	01247-818080
Portadown, Armagh	01762-334411

SPECIALIST POLICE FORCES

British Transport Police	0171-388 7541
PR officer	0171-830 8854
DoT Security Division	0171-271 4999
Military	
Ministry of Defence Police	01371-854000
RAF Police	01452 712612
Royal Marines Police	01752-836372
Royal Military Police (Army)	01980-615653
Royal Naval Regulating Branch	
(RN police)	01705-727243
Ports: Belfast	01232-553000
Dover	01304-216084
Falmouth	01326-212100
Liverpool	0151-949 1212
London (Tilbury)	01375-846781
Tees	01642-468129
Royal Botanic Gardens Constabulary	
(Kew)	0181-332 5121
Royal Parks Constabulary	0171-298 2000
Scotland	0131-668 8735
UK Atomic Energy Authority Police	01235-463760

OTHER ORGANISATIONS

Assoc of British Investigators	0181-546 3368
British Security Industry Assoc	01905-21464
BT Security & Investigation	0800-321999
Common Agricultural Policy Anti-Fraud	
Unit	0118-958 3626
Customs & Excise Investigation Service	0171-283 5353
Data Protection Registrar	01625-545745
Dept of Social Security Benefits Agency:	
Organised Fraud Units	0113-232 4419
Federation Against Copyright Theft	0181-568 6646
Federation Against Software Theft	01753-527999
Gaming Board	0171-306 6200
ICC Counterfeiting Intelligence Bureau	0181-591 3000
Immigration Service Intelligence and	
Investigation Unit	0181-745 2400
Inland Revenue Special Compliance	
Office	0171-234 3702
Institute of Professional Investigators	01254-680072
Jockey Club Security Dept	0171-343 3261
MAFF Food Investigation Branch	0171-270 8364
Medicines Control Agency	0171-273 0607
Personal Investment Authority	0171-538 8860
Post Office Investigation Dept	0181-681 9876
Radio Investigation Service (DTI)	0171-215 5961
Road Haulage Assoc Security	01932-841515
Sea Fisheries Inspectorate (MAFF)	0171-238 5798
Security Industry Inspectorate	01905-773131

STAFF BODIES

ACPO (Association of Chief Police Officers):	
England, Wales, N Ireland	0171-230 7184
Scotland	0131-311 3051
Assoc of Chief Officers of Probation	0171-377 9141
British Assoc of Women Police	01543-276165
Fingerprint Society	0121-236 5000
International Police Association	0115-981 3638
International Professional Security	01803-554849
Police Federation: England and Wales	0181-399 2224
N Ireland	01232-760831
Scotland	0141-332 5234
Police Superintendents Association:	
England & Wales	0118-984 4005
Scotland	0141-221 5796
N Ireland	01232-700500
Charities: National Police Fund	0171-273 3684
Police Dependents Trust	0171-273 2921
Police Foundation	0171-582 3744

MONITORING GROUPS

Justice	0171-329 5100
Lesbian & Gay Police Assoc	01426-943011
Liberty (NCCL)	0171-403 3888
Missing Persons Bureau	0181-392 2000
Police Complaints Authority	0171-273 6450
Police Review (magazine)	0171-440 4700
Statewatch	0181-802 1882
Website	ww.poptel.org.uk/statewatch

Fire services

Fire services in England are run by Fire and Civil Defence Authorities (FCDAs) in London and the six metropolitan areas, and elsewhere by county councils, reorganised with new unitary authorities if necessary. In Wales, all eight county brigades merged into three combined fire authorities in 1996. Fire services in Scotland and Northern Ireland remained unchanged during the unitary shake-up. Overseeing services in England and Wales is the Central Fire Brigades Advisory Council, part of the Home Office's Fire Services Unit, with a same-named council in Scotland under the Scottish Office Home Department. There are 34,000 full-time fire officers in the UK. The annual cost is around £1,400 million.

ENGLAND

Avon	0117-926 2061
Bedfordshire	01234-351081
Berkshire	0118-945 2888
Buckinghamshire	01494-786943
Cambridgeshire	01480-444500
Channel Islands - Guernsey	01481-724491
Jersey	01534-37444
Cheshire	01606-868700
Cleveland	01429-872311
Cornwall	01872-273117
Cumbria	01900-822503
Derbyshire	01332-771221
Devon	01392-872200
Dorset	01305-251133
Durham	0191-384 3381
Essex	01277-222531
Gloucestershire	01242-512041
Hampshire	01703-620000
Hereford & Worcester	01905-24454
Hertfordshire	01992-507507
Humberside	01482-565333
Isle of Man	01624-673333
Isle of Wight	01983-823194
Isles of Scilly	01872-273117
Kent	01622-692121
Lancashire	01772-862545
Leicestershire	0116-287 2241
Lincolnshire	01522-582222
London	0171-582 3811
Greater Manchester	0161-736 5866
Merseyside	0151-227 4466
Norfolk	01603-810351
Northamptonshire	01604-797000
Northumberland	01670-513161
Nottinghamshire	0115-967 0880
Oxfordshire	01865-842999
Shropshire	01743-260200
Somerset	01823-337222
Staffordshire	01785-813234
Suffolk	01473-588888
Surrey	01737-242444
Sussex - East	01273-406000
Sussex - West	01243-786211
Tyne and Wear	0191-232 1224
Warwickshire	01926-423231
West Midlands	0121-359 5161
Wiltshire	01380-731100
Yorkshire - North	01609-780150
Yorkshire - South	0114-272 7202
Yorkshire - West	01274-682311

WALES

Mid & West Wales	01267-221444
North Wales	01745-343431
South West Wales	01443-237777

SCOTLAND

Central Scotland	01324-716996
Dumfries & Galloway	01387-252222
Fife	01592-774451
Grampian	01224-696666
Highland & Islands	01463-222722
Lothian & Borders	0131-228 2401
Strathclyde	01698-284200
Tayside	01382-322222

NORTHERN IRELAND

NI Fire Brigade HQ (Lisburn)	01846-664221
A Division (Belfast)	01232-310360
B Division (Bangor)	01247-271906
C Division (Portadown)	01762-332222
D Division (Derry)	01504-311162
E Division (Ballymena)	01266-43370
F Division (Omagh)	01662-241190

ORGANISATIONS

Home Office:	0171-273 4000
Press Office	0171-273 4600
Fire Services Unit	0171-217 8749
Fire Services Inspectorate	0171-217 8728
Chief Fire Officers Association	01827-61516
Fire Brigades Union	0181-541 1765
Fire Research Station	01923-664000
Northern Ireland: Environment Dept	01232-540540
Fire Division	01232-540845
Scottish Office Home Dept	0131-556 8400
Press Office	0131-244 2718
Fire Service	0131-244 2184
Fire Services Inspectorate	0131-244 2342

Ambulances

Most ambulances in England and Wales are managed by NHS trusts (quangos), whose names are in brackets below if responsible for more than one county. Overseeing the services is the Department of Health's NHS Executive, based in Leeds. All Scottish ambulances are run by the Scottish Ambulance Service, with its headquarters in Edinburgh. Northern Ireland has four Health Boards of the Department of Health operating services. There were 16,330 ambulance staff in 1996.

ENGLAND

Avon	0117-927 7046
Bedfordshire	01234-408999
Berkshire	0118-977 1200
Bucks (Two Shires)	01908-262422
Cambridgeshire (East Anglian)	01603-424255
Channel Islands: Guernsey	01481-725211
Jersey	01534-622343
Cheshire (Mersey Trust)	0151-260 5220
Cleveland	01642-850888
Cornwall (Westcountry)	01884-259563
Cumbria	01228-596909
Derbyshire	01332-372441
Devon (Westcountry)	01752-767839
Dorset	01202-896111
Durham	0191-386 4488
Essex	01245-443344
Gloucestershire	01452-395050
Hampshire	01962-863511
Hereford & Worcester	01886-834200
Hertfordshire	01234-408999
Humberside	01482-561191
Isle of Man	01624-642642
Isle of Wight	01983-821655
Kent	01622-747010
Lancashire	01772-862666
Leicestershire	0116-275 0700
Lincolnshire	01522-545171
London	0171-928 0333
Greater Manchester	0161-231 7921
Merseyside (Mersey Trust)	0151-260 5220
Norfolk (East Anglian)	01603-424255
Northants (Two Shires)	01908-262422
Northumbria	0191-273 1212
Nottinghamshire	0115-929 6151
Oxfordshire	01865-740100
Scilly Isles	01884-254565
Shropshire	01743-364061
Somerset (Westcountry)	01823-278114
Staffordshire	01785-253521
Suffolk (East Anglian)	01603-424255
Surrey	01737-353333
Sussex	01273-489444
Warwickshire	01926-881331
West Midlands	01384-215555
Wiltshire	01249-443939
Yorkshire: North	01904-666000
South	01709-820520
West	01274-707070

WALES

Mid-Glamorgan	01443-217005
North Wales	01745-585106
South & East Wales	01222-552011
West Wales	01792-562900

SCOTLAND

Scottish Ambulance Service HQ	0131-447 7711
North Region:	
HQ: Aberdeen	01224-662244
Inverness	01463-236611
Dundee	01382-817171
South East Region:	
HQ: Edinburgh	0131-447 8746
Motherwell	01698-276441
West Region:	
HQ: Glasgow	0141-353 6001
Ayr	01292-284101
Paisley	0141-848 1434

NORTHERN IRELAND

Dept of Health	01232-524309
Eastern (Belfast)	01232-246113
Northern (Antrim)	01849-428911
Southern (Limerick)	01612-28177
Western (Derry)	01504-348063

OFFICIAL ORGANISATIONS

Department of Health Press:	0171-210 5221
NHS Executive	0113-254 5000
Welsh Office Health Dept Press	01222-825647
Scottish Office Press	0131-244 2656
DoH Northern Ireland	01232-520500

SUPPORT ORGANISATIONS

Assoc of Ambulance Personnel	01749-344044
British Red Cross	0171-235 5454
Patients Association	0171-242 3461
Royal Life Saving Society	01789-773994
St Andrews Ambulance Assoc	0141-332 4031
St John Ambulance	0171-235 5231

Hospitals

The National Health Service (NHS) employs 950,000 staff, occupies 46,000 acres of land and oversees 1,600 hospitals with 270,000 beds. It spent £42,383 million in 1996/7. Since 1991 self-governing trusts (quangos) have taken over most services, including hospitals, on a contractual basis. The trusts in England are monitored by the NHS Executive and its eight regional offices. These replaced the 14 regional health authorities (RHAs) in 1996. At the same time the district health authorities and family health services authorities below the RHAs were superseded by 100 all-purpose health authorities in England and five in Wales. About 82 per cent of the cost of the health service is met through general taxation, with National Insurance providing 12%. About 560 million prescriptions, worth £5 billion or £87 per head, are dispensed annually

Below are the hospitals with an accident and emergency department and some acute hospitals in larger towns without an emergency hospital.

ENGLISH HOSPITALS

Avon
Bath (Royal United)	01225-428331
Bristol (Frenchay)	0117-970 1212
Bristol (Royal Infirmary)	0117-923 0000
Bristol (Southmead)	0117-950 5050
Weston-super-Mare	01934-636363

Bedfordshire
Bedford	01234-355122
Luton & Dunstable	01582-491122

Berkshire
Ascot (Heatherwood)	01344-623333
Slough (Wexham Park)	01753-633000

Buckinghamshire
Aylesbury (Stoke Mandeville)	01296-315000
High Wycombe (Wycombe)	01494-526161

Cambridgeshire
Cambridge (Addenbrookes)	01223-245151
Huntingdon (Hinchingbrooke)	01480-416416
Peterborough	01733-874000

Channel Islands
Guernsey (Princess Elizabeth)	01481-725241
Jersey General	01534-59000

Cheshire
Chester (Countess)	01244-365000
Crewe (Leighton)	01270-255141
Macclesfield	01625-421000
Northwich (Victoria)	01606-74331
Warrington	01925-635911

Cleveland
Hartlepool	01429-266654
Middlesborough	01642-850850
North Tees	01642-617617

Cornwall
Penzance (West Cornwall)	01736-362382
Truro (Treviske)	01872-274242

Cumbria
Carlisle (Cumberland)	01228-523444
Furness, Cumbria	01229-870870

Derbyshire
Chesterfield	01246-277271
Derby (Derbyshire Royal)	01332-347141

Devon
Barnstaple (North Devon)	01271-322577
Exeter (Royal Devon)	01392-411611
Plymouth (Derriford)	01752-777111
Torbay	01803-614567

Dorset
Poole	01202-665511
Weymouth	01305-760022

Durham
Bishop Auckland, Co Durham	01388-454000
Darlington, Co Durham	01325-380100
Durham (Dryburn)	0191-333 2333
Shotley Bridge	01207-583583

Essex
Basildon, Essex	01268-533911
Chelmsford (Broomfield)	01245-440761
Epping (St Margarets)	01992-561666
Essex	01206-853535
Harlow (Princess Alexandra)	01279-444455
Harold Wood, Essex	01708-345533
Rochford/Southend	01702-435555

Gloucestershire
Cheltenham	01242-222222
Gloucester (Glos Royal)	01452-528555

Hampshire
Basingstoke	01256-473202
Portsmouth (Queen Alexandra)	01705-286000
Southampton	01703-777222
Winchester (Royal Hampshire)	01962-863535

Hereford & Worcester
Hereford	01432-355444
Kidderminster	01562-823424
Redditch (Alexandra)	01527-503030
Worcester Royal Infirmary	01905-763333

Hertfordshire
Hemel Hempstead	01442-213141
Stevenage (Lister)	01438-314333
Welwyn (Queen Elizabeth II)	01707-328111
Watford	01923-244366

Humberside
Bridlington	01262-606666
Grimsby	01472-874111
Hull (Royal Infirmary)	01482-328541
Scunthorpe	01724-282282

Isle of Man
Douglas (Nobles)	01624-642642

Isle of Wight
Newport (St Marys)	01983-524081

Kent
Ashford (William Harvey)	01233-633331
Canterbury (Kent & Canterbury)	01227-766877
Dartford (West Hill)	01322-223223
Gillingham (Medway)	01634-830000
Maidstone	01622-729000
Margate (Thanet)	01843-225544
Tunbridge Wells (Kent/Sussex)	01892-526111

Lancashire
Blackburn (Royal)	01254-263555
Blackpool (Victoria)	01253-300000
Burnley	01282-425071
Bury	0161-764 6081
Lancaster	01524-65944
Leigh	01942-672333
Ormskirk	01695-577111
Preston (Royal)	01772-716565
Southport	01704-547471

Leicestershire
Leicester	0116-254 1414

Lincolnshire
Boston (Pilgrim)	01205-364801
Grantham	01476-565232
Lincoln (County)	01522-512512
Louth (County)	01507-600100
Stamford	01780-764151

London - Emergency
Acton (Central Middlesex)	0181-965 5733
Ashford	01784-884488
Barnet	0181-440 5111
Bromley	0181-289 7000
Camberwell (Kings College)	0171-737 4000
Carshalton (St Helier)	0181-644 4343
City (St Bartholomews)	0171-601 8888
Ealing	0181-574 2444
Edgware	0181-952 2381
Edmonton (North Middlesex)	0181-887 2000
Enfield (Chase Farm)	0181-366 6600
Euston (University College)	0171-387 9300
Fulham (Charing Cross)	0181-846 1234
Greenwich	0181-858 8141
Hammersmith	0181-743 2030
Hampstead (Royal Free)	0171-794 0500
Harrow (Northwick)	0181-864 3232

Highgate (Whittington)	0171-272 3070
Hillingdon	01895-238282
Homerton	0181-919 5555
Ilford (King George)	0181-983 8000
Isleworth (West Middlesex)	0181-560 2121
Kingston	0181-546 7711
Lambeth (St Thomass)	0171-928 9292
Lewisham	0181-333 3000
Leytonstone (Whipps Cross)	0181-539 5522
Newham	0171-476 4000
North Kensington (St Charles)	0181-969 2488
Paddington (St Marys)	0171-725 6666
Roehampton (Queen Marys)	0181-789 6611
Romford (Oldchurch)	01708-746090
Sidcup (Queen Marys)	0181-302 2678
Southwark (Guys)	0171-955 5000
Thornton Heath (Mayday)	0181-401 3000
Tooting (St Georges)	0181-672 1255
Wembley	0181-903 1323
Westminster, SW1	0181-746 8000
Whitechapel (Royal London)	0171-377 7000
Woolwich (Queen Elizabeth)	0181-858 8141

London - Non-emergency
Brompton Heart, SW3	0171-352 8121
Eastman Dental, WC1	0171-915 1000
Eliz. Garrett Anderson, NW1	0171-387 2501
Gt Ormond St Childrens, WC1	0171-405 9200
London Homeopathic, WC1	0171-837 8833
Maudsley, SE5	0171-703 6333
Middlesex, W1	0171-636 8333
Moorfields Eye, EC1	0171-253 3411
National Orthopaedic	0181-954 2300
Neurology, WC1	0171-837 3611
Royal Marsden, SW3	0171-352 8171
Throat, Nose & Ear, WC1	0171-837 8855
Tropical Diseases, NW1	0171-387 4411

Greater Manchester
Ashton-under-Lyne (Tameside)	0161-331 6000
Bolton	01204-390390
Bury	0161-764 6081
Manchester Royal Infirmary	0161-276 1234
North Manchester	0161-795 4567
Royal Oldham	0161-624 0420
Rochdale Infirmary	01706-377777
Salford (Hope)	0161-789 7373
South Manchester (Withington)	0161-445 8111
Stockport	0161-483 1010
Wigan (Royal Albert Edward)	01942-244000
Wythenshawe	0161-998 7070

Merseyside
Liverpool (Alder Hay Childrens)	0151-228 4811
Liverpool (Broadgreen)	0151-282 6000
Liverpool (Royal)	0151-709 0141
Liverpool (Walton)	0151-525 3611
Whiston	0151-426 1600
Wirral	0151-678 5111

Norfolk
Gt Yarmouth (James Paget)	01493-452452
Kings Lynn (Queen Elizabeth)	01553-766266
Norfolk & Norwich	01603-286286

Northamptonshire
Kettering	01536-492000
Northampton	01604-634700

Northumberland
Ashington, Northumberland	01670-812541
Hexham, Northumberland	01434-606161

Nottinghamshire
Mansfield	01623-622515
Newark	01636-681681
Nottingham (City)	0115-969 1169
Nottingham (University)	0115-924 9924
Worksop	01909-500990

Oxfordshire
Banbury (Horton)	01295-275500
Headington (John Radcliffe)	01865-741166

Shropshire
Shrewsbury	01743-261000

Somerset
Bridgwater	01278-451501
Minehead	01643-707251
Taunton (Musgrove)	01823-333444
Yeovil	01935-475122

Staffordshire
Burton-upon-Trent (Queens)	01283-566333
Stafford	01785-257731
Stoke-on-Trent(North Staffs)	01782-715444

Suffolk
Ipswich	01473-712233
West Suffolk	01284-713000

Surrey
Ashford	01784-884488
Chertsey (St Petrs)	.01932-872000
Camberley (Frimley Park)	01276-604604
Epsom	01372-735735
Guildford (Royal Surrey)	01483-571122
Redhill & Dorking (E Surrey)	01737-768511

Sussex - East
Brighton (Royal Sussex)	01273-696955
Eastbourne	01323-417400
Hastings (Conquest)	01424-755255

Sussex - West
Chichester (St Richards)	01243-788122
Haywards Heath (Princess Royal)	01444-441881
Worthing	01903-205111

Tyne & Wear
Gateshead (Queen Elizabeth)	0191-487 8989
Newcastle	0191-273 8811
Newcastle (Royal Victoria)	0191-232 5131
North Tyneside	0191-259 6660
South Tyneside (South Shields)	0191-454 8888
Sunderland	0191-565 6256

Warwickshire
Nuneaton (George Eliot)	01203-351351
Rugby (St Cross)	01788-572831
Warwick(South Warwickshire)	01926-495321

West Midlands
Birmingham (Dudley Road)	0121-554 3801
Birmingham (Hartland)	0121-766 6611
Coventry & Warwick	01203-224055
Dudley (Russells Hall)	01384-456111
Solihull	0121-711 4455
Sutton Coldfield (Good Hope)	0121-378 2211
University Hospital	0121-627 1627
West Bromwich (Sandwell)	0121-553 1831
Wolverhampton (Royal)	01902-307999

Wiltshire
Salisbury	01722-336262
Swindon (Princess Margaret)	01793-536231

Yorkshire -North
Harrogate	01423-885959
Northallerton (Friarage)	01609-779911
Scarborough	01723-368111
York	01904-631313

Yorkshire -South
Barnsley	01226-730000
Doncaster (Royal Infirmary)	01302-366666
Rotherham Hospital	01709-820000
Sheffield (Childrens)	0114-276 1111
Sheffield (Northern General)	0114-243 4343
Sheffield (Royal Hallamshire)	0114-271 1900

Yorkshire - West
Bradford (Royal)	01274-542200
Dewsbury	01924-465105
Halifax	01422-357222
Huddersfield (Royal Infirmary)	01484-422191
Keighley (Airedale)	01535-652511
Leeds (General Infirmary)	0113-243 2799
Leeds (St Jamess University)	0113-243 3144
Pontefract	01977-600600
Wakefield(Pinderfields)	01924-201688

SCOTTISH HOSPITALS

Borders
Melrose (Borders General)	01896-754333

Central
Falkirk (Royal)	01324-624000
Stirling (Royal)	01786-434000

Dumfries & Galloway
Dumfries (Royal Infirmary)	01387-246246

Fife
Dunfermline (Queen Margarets)	01383-623623

Grampian
Aberdeen (Royal)	01224-681818

Highland
Inverness (Raigmore)	01463-704000

Lothian
Edinburgh (Eastern General)	0131-536 7000
Edinburgh (Royal Infirmary)	0131-536 1000
Edinburgh (Western General)	0131-537 1000
Livingston (St Johns)	01506-419666

Orkney
Kirkwall (Balfour) — 01856-885400

Shetland
Lerwick (Gilbert Bain) — 01595-695678

Strathclyde
Airdrie (Monklands) — 01236-748748
Ayr — 01292-610555
Carluke (Law) — 01698-361100
East Kilbride (Hairmyres) — 01355-220292
Glasgow (Royal Infirmary) — 0141-211 4000
Glasgow (Sick Children) — 0141-201 0000
Glasgow (Southern) — 0141-201 1100
Glasgow (Stobhill) — 0141-201 3000
Glasgow (Victoria Infirmary) — 0141-201 6000
Glasgow (Western Infirmary) — 0141-211 2000
Greenock (Inverclyde) — 01475-633777
Kilmarnock (Crosshouse) — 01563-521133
Paisley (Royal Alexandra) — 0141-887 9111

Tayside
Brechin (Stracathro) — 01356-647291
Dundee (Royal Infirmary) — 01382-660111
Perth (Royal) — 01738-623311

Western Isles
Stornoway (Western Isles) — 01851-704704

WELSH HOSPITALS

Clwyd
Rhyl (Clwyd) — 01745-583910

Dyfed
Aberystwyth (Bronglais) — 01970-623131
Carmarthen (West Wales) — 01267-235151
Haverfordwest (Withybush) — 01437-764545
Llanelli (Prince Phillip) — 01554-756567

Glamorgan - Mid
Bridgend (Princess of Wales) — 01656-752752
Merthyr Tydfil (Prince Charles) — 01685-721721
Pontypridd (East Glamorgan) — 01443-218218

Glamorgan - West
Swansea (Singleton) — 01792-205666

Gwent
Abergavenny (Neill Hall) — 01873-852091
Newport (Royal Gwent) — 01633-234234

Gwynedd
Bangor (Gwynedd) — 01248-384384
Llandudno — 01492-860066

N IRELAND HOSPITALS

Antrim
Ballymena (Wavney) — 01849-424000
Belfast City — 01232-329241
Belfast (Musgrave Park) — 01232-669501
Belfast (Royal Victoria) — 01232-240503
Belfast (Ulster) — 01232-484511
Larne (Moyle) — 01574-275431
Lisburn (Lagan Valley) — 01846-665141
Newtownabbey (Whiteabbey) — 01232-865181
Newtownards (Ards) — 01247-812661

Armagh
Craigavon — 01762-334444

Down
Newry (Daisy Hill) — 01693-65511

Fermanagh
Enniskillen (Erne) — 01365-324711

Londonderry
Coleraine — 01265-44177
Derry (Altnagelvin) — 01504-45171
Magheragelt (Mid-Ulster) — 01648-31031

Tyrone
Dungannon (South Tyrone) — 01868-722821
Omagh (Tyrone County) — 01662-245211

MILITARY HOSPITALS

Army
MoD Hospital Unit (Frimley Park) — 01276-604320
Duchess of Kent, Catterick — 01748-832521

Navy
Haslar, Gosport — 01705-584255
Derford, Plymouth — 01752-777111

SPECIAL HOSPITALS

Ashworth, Merseyside — 0151-473 0303
Carstairs, Lanark — 01555-840293
Broadmoor, Berkshire — 01344-773111
Rampton, Notts — 01777-248321

OFFICIAL ORGANISATIONS

Department of Health (Press office — 0171-210 5221
NHS Executive: HQ (Leeds) — 0113-254 5000
  Anglia & Oxford — 01908-844400
  Northern & Yorkshire — 0191-301 1300
  North Thames — 0171-725 5300
  North West — 01925-704000
  South Thames — 0171-725 2500
  South & West — 0117-984 1750
  Trent — 0114-263 0300
  West Midlands — 0121-224 4600
Welsh Office — 01222-825111
Scottish Office DoH — 0131-244 2410
DoH Northern Ireland — 01232-520500
Health & Safety Commission — 0171-717 6000

The sea

HM Coastguard is responsible for **Search and Rescue** (SAR) operations in the seas and shores around the UK. When accidents occur, the Coastguard can call on RNLI lifeboats, and military and civilian aircraft, helicopters and ships, to provide assistance. There are about 500 professional Coastguard officers managing the service. In addition, over 3,000 volunteer Auxiliary Coastguards carry out rescues on cliffs and beaches.

Seafarers **in distress** make radio calls on Channel 16, the distress and safety channel monitored by Coastguard control centres. In 1997 the Coastguard handled 11,667 incidents, assisting 11,667 people and actually rescuing 5,084. Coastguard officers need to have an international view of life; in 1997 they rescued off the Shetlands ten members of the crew of a ship which was registered in the Bahamas, managed from Norway, run by Croation officers and crewed by Filipinos.

The UK is divided into five **Search and Rescue Regions**, each of which is overseen by a large Maritime Rescue Co-ordination Centre (MRCC). Every region has subsidiary Maritime Rescue Sub-Centres (MRSCs). There are currently 21 of these MRCCs and MRSCs (listed below) around the UK coast, staffed 24-hours a day. Each has a Publicity Liaison Officer who can talk to the press. The five regions have their coastlines divided into a total of 64 sectors, each run by one Sector Manager, who co-ordinates the work of the Auxiliaries in the area.

A five-year **strategy plan** for the Coastguard was unveiled by the government in July 1998. A programme of substantial investment in new digital technology was announced, with many improvements. But it also included closing four of the 21 co-ordination centres: in 2000 Oban and Pentland; in 2001 Tyne Tees and Liverpool. Two south coast MRSCs at Portland and Lee-on-Solent would be merged in 2003. The 17 co-ordination centres that resulted from this would run 136 remote VHF radio sites with enhanced levels of staffing.

Auxiliary Coastguards are volunteers who are officially part of HM Coastguard. Some other volunteers in the mid-1990s formed the unofficial National Coastwatch Institution. Usually known as Coastwatch, the charity in certain places provides a coastal surveillance service to the Coastguard.

HM Coastguard operates the **Channel Navigation Information Service** (CNIS), a traffic separation scheme operating in the eastern English Channel. The Channel is the busiest shipping lane in the world, and CNIS is the world's most sophisticated radar surveillance and monitoring system. HM Coastguard hopes to revolutionise all ship rescue operations with the new Global Maritime Distress and Safety System. This is a complex new-technology satellite communications system for ships, due to be completed by early 1999.

The work of HM Coastguard is administered on behalf of the Department of Transport by the **Maritime and Coastguard Agency** (MCA), a quango based in Southampton. The MCA was created in April 1998 by the merger of the Coastguard Agency and the Marine Safety Agency, which both started in 1994. The annual budget is £90 million.

The MCA has several other roles alongside the SAR carried out by HM Coastguard. Its **Marine Pollution Control Unit** (MPCU) deals with major spillages of oil and other hazardous substances, and maintains the National Contingency Plan which sets out the responsibilities of government departments and other organisations. In major events the Unit works in the Marine Operations Emergency Room in the Coastguard HQ at Southampton. The MPCU has equipment stockpiles at Aberdeen, Stirling, Ipswich, Southampton and Milford Haven. It has aircraft for aerial spraying and remote sensing at Inverness, Lydd and Coventry. The MCA also runs the **marine safety** services of the former Marine Safety Agency. It carries out vessel survey work for the Register of Shipping and Seamen. The Receiver of Wreck, investigating the ownership of items found in the sea, is also based in the Coastguard building.

COASTGUARD AGENCY

Spring Place, 105 Commercial Road, Southampton
SO15 1EG.   01703-329400
Press   01703-329401
HM Coastguard   01703-329100
Marine Emergency Operations Room   01703-329445
Marine Pollution Control Unit   01703-329415
Receiver of Wreck   01703-329474
Dept of Environment, Transport and
    Regions   0171-271 5000
    Press   0171-276 0888
    Duty Officer   0171-276 5999

HM COASTGUARD CENTRES

North & East Scotland Region
MRCC, Aberdeen   01224-592334
MRSCs: Shetland   01595-692976
    Pentland   01856-873268
    Forth   01333-450666
Northern North Sea, from Scottish border to Shetlands
and then west to Cape Wrath, including oil and gas
installations.

Eastern Region
MRCC, Yarmouth   01493-851338
MRSCs: Tyne Tees   0191-257 2691
    Humber   01262-672317
Southern North Sea, from Scottish border to Aldeburgh,
including oil and gas installations.

Southern Region (east)
MRCC, Dover   01304-210008
MRSCs: Thames (Walton)   01255-675518
    Lee-on-Solent   01705-552100
South East coast from Aldeburgh to Bournemouth, includ-
ing eastern English Channel. The CNIS system is run from
Dover.

Southern Region (west)
MRCC, Falmouth   01326-317575
MRSCs: Portland   01305-760439
    Brixham   01803-882704
Southern Region Controller   01425-271700
From Bournemouth to Bude Bay, South West Atlantic
approaches. The controller for the whole region
(Aldeburgh to Bude Bay) is based in Christchurch.

Western Region
MRCC, Swansea   01792-366534
MRSCs: Milford Haven   01646-690909
    Holyhead   01407-762051
    Liverpool   0151-931 3341
Bristol Channel from Bude Bay, Irish Sea to North Channel
(excluding Northern Ireland coastal waters) and West
Atlantic approaches.

West of Scotland & Northern Ireland Region
MRCC, Clyde   01475-729988
MRSCs: Belfast   01247-463933
    Oban   01631-563720
    Stornoway   01851-702013
Northern Ireland, west of Scotland coast, North West
Atlantic approaches.

LIFEBOATS

The Royal National Lifeboat Institution
(RNLI) is a voluntary body supported entirely
by public donations. It has saved 131,000 lives
since it was set up in 1824. There were 6,777
launches in 1997, saving 1,420 lives and
assisting 5,288 other people. The RNLI runs
222 lifeboat stations around the British Isles.
It has a total of 300 operational boats, 128 of
them all-weather vessels. The largest class is
the 17-metre long Severn. In addition there
are 130 relief boats. Each lifeboat station is
run by a voluntary committee, whose hon-
orary secretary authorises the launch of the
boat, usually on the request of the local
Coastguard. Larger lifeboats may have a paid
mechanic or coxswain-cum-mechanic; otherwise nearly all the crews are volunteers.
During rescue operations the lifeboat is controlled by the coxswain, in liaison with the
local Coastguard MRCC. The RNLI likes all
press enquiries to go to the press office at its
headquarters in Poole, Dorset. Out of hours,
contact the central operations room.

RNLI headquarters, Poole   01202-663000
Central operations room   01202-668222

RNLI BOATHOUSES

Listed below are all the UK and Irish Republic
stations with a large lifeboat (which is defined
as being over 10 metres, and capable of off-
shore work). The numbers are mainly for the
boathouses themselves, rather than officers:
Aberdeen   01224-591658
Aith, Shetland   01595-810276
Aldeburgh, Suffolk   01728-452552
Alderney, Channel Islands   01481-823456
Amble, Northumberland   01665-712460

Angle, Dyfed	01646-641204	Longhope, Orkney	01856-701460
Anstruther, Fife	01333-310526	Lowestoft, Suffolk	01502-573757
Appledore, Devon	01237-473969	Lytham St Annes, Lancs	01253-736316
Arbroath, Tayside	01241-873235	Mallaig, Highland	01687-462579
Arklow, Wicklow	00-353402 32850	Margate, Kent	01843-221613
Arranmore, Donegal	00-35375 21580	Moelfre, Clwyd	01248-410367
Ballycotton, Cork	00-35321 646903	Montrose, Tayside	01674-674341
Ballyglass, Mayo	00-35397 82072	Mumbles, West Glamorgan	01792-390424
Baltimore, Cork	00-35328 20174	Newcastle, Down	01396-725138
Barmouth, Gwynedd	01341-280274	Newhaven, East Sussex	01273-514143
Barra Island, Western Isles	01871-810307	North Sunderland, Northmblnd	01665-720370
Barrow, Cumberland	01229-820941	Oban, Strathclyde	01631-563733
Barry Dock, South Glamorgan	01446-735678	Padstow, Cornwall	01841-520667
Beaumaris, Gwynedd	01248-810260	Penlee, Cornwall	01736-369246
Bembridge, IoW	01983-872201	Peterhead, Grampian	01779-473331
Berwick upon-Tweed	01289-306217	Plymouth, Devon	01752-662623
Blyth, Northumberland	01670-352201	Poole, Dorset	01202-665607
Bridlington, Humberside	01262-672450	Port Erin, IoM	01624-832154
Broughty Ferry, Tayside	01382-779956	Port St Mary, IoM	01624-835015
Buckie, Grampian	01542-831289	Porthdinllaen, Gwynedd	01758-720241
Calshot, Hants	01703-893509	Portpatrick, Dumfries	01776-810251
Campbeltown, Strathclyde	01586-552414	Portree, Highland	01478-613610
Clogher Head, Louth	00-35341 22600	Portrush, Antrim	00-353265 823201
Courtmacsherry, Cork	00-35323 46111	Pwllheli, Gwynedd	01758-612200
Cromer, Norfolk	01263-512237	Ramsey, IoM	01624-812169
Donaghadee, Down	01247-888556	Ramsgate, Kent	01843-583594
Douglas, IoM	01624-621367	Rhyl, Clwyd	01745-344040
Dover, Kent	01304-204280	Rosslare, Wexford	00-35353 33249
Dun Laoghaire, Dublin	00-3531 280 2667	St Davids, Dyfed	01437-720215
Dunbar, Lothian	01368-863966	St Helier, Jersey	01534-24173
Dungeness, Kent	01679-320317	St Ives, Cornwall	01736-796422
Dunmore East, Waterford	00-35351 83268	St Marys, Scilly Isles	01720-422347
Eastbourne, East Sussex	01323-722648	Salcombe, Devon	01548-842158
Exmouth, Devon	01395-263579	Scarborough, North Yorks	01723-360520
Eyemouth, Borders	01890-750293	Selsey, West Sussex	01243-602833
Falmouth, Cornwall	01326-374177	Sennen Cove, Cornwall	01736-871222
Fishguard, Dyfed	01348-873231	Sheerness, Kent	01795-664866
Flamborough, Humberside	01262-850947	Sheringham, Norfolk	01263-823212
Fleetwood, Lancs	01253-874000	Shoreham, West Sussex	01273-462670
Fowey, Cornwall	01726-832156	Skegness, Lincs	01754-763011
Fraserburgh, Grampian	01346-515162	Stornoway, Western Isles	01851-703339
Galway Bay, Galway	00-35399 61166	Stromness, Orkney	01856-850204
Girvan, Strathclyde	01465-714454	Sunderland, Tyne & Wear	0191-567 3536
Gt Yarmouth, Norfolk	01493-662508	Swanage, Dorset	01929-423237
Hartlepool, Cleveland	01429-266103	Teesmouth, Cleveland	01642-486636
Harwich, Essex	01255-502258	Tenby, Dyfed	01834-842197
Hastings, East Sussex	01424-425502	Thurso, Highland	01847-893433
Holyhead, Gwynedd	01407-762583	Tobermory, Strathclyde	01688-302250
Howth, Dublin	00-3531 8393311	Torbay, Devon	01803-853136
Hoylake, Merseyside	0151-632 2103	Troon, Strathclyde	01292-314414
Humber	01964-650228	Tynemouth, Tyne & Wear	0191-259 6673
Ilfracombe, Devon	01271-863771	Valentia, Kerry	00-323667 76100
Invergordon, Highland	01349-853915	Walton, Essex	01255-675650
Islay, Strathclyde	01496-840242	Wells, Norfolk	01328-710230
Kilmore Quay, Wexford	00-35353 29690	Weymouth, Dorset	01305-785817
Kirkwall, Orkney	01856-875201	Whitby, North Yorkshire	01947-602216
Lerwick, Shetland	01595-693827	Wick, Highland	01955-603723
Lizard, Cornwall	01326-290451	Wicklow	00-353404 67163
Llandudno, Gwynedd	01492-875777	Workington, Cumberland	01900-604124
Lochinver, Highland	01571-844513	Yarmouth, IoW	01983-872201

Businesses

Britain has about 3.6 million businesses. Many are very small, with around 97 per cent employing less than 20 people. At the other extreme, roughly 250 companies have an annual turnover of more than £500 million, with 16 of them among the top 25 European companies in terms of profitability. In the UK, HSBC Holdings is the company with both the highest annual profits (£4.52 billions) and the most capital employed (£26.95 billion). Shell has the highest turnover (£82.01 billion) and BT is the largest employer (129,600 people).

COMPANIES HOUSE

The main source of raw material when carrying out company research is Companies House. This is the official title given to the Department of Trade's company registry (and, confusingly, to its office block). Its three statutory functions are: incorporating and dissolving companies; examining and holding company documents required under legislation; and making this information available to the public. All the 1.17 million registered companies must submit annual returns and other data to the registrars in the Companies House head offices in Cardiff (for England and Wales), Edinburgh (for Scotland) and Belfast (for N Ireland). Also on record are 250,000 recently dissolved companies.

The public can carry out personal research into this information in these offices, and in the heavily-used London office in City Road. The City Road lease expires in the autumn of 1999 and new premises must be found and moved into by then. Search facilities are also available in the satellite offices in Birmingham, Manchester, Leeds and Glasgow.

Certain basic information about companies can be viewed free of charge on computer network screens in the Search Rooms at these offices. More detailed data comes in the "standard search", a microfiche of the documents received by Companies House from the company secretary over the last three years. The standard search costs £3.50 when bought in person, or £5 by post. Other information is available, at a variety of prices, and in a range of ways, including phone orders. The key is the company registration number which identifies which of the businesses is being researched. Numbers can be found on the Public Access Systems in the Search Room. All the offices are open 9-5 Monday-Friday.

The basic company data is also available online via Companies House Direct Internet service. Customers can access information in the public databases, but not as much as in the standard search. Orders for microfiche or hard copy documents can be made from the PC. The one-off registration fee is £50, monthly sub £7.50. The basic non-standard data is also on the Companies House Directory CD-ROM, updated monthly. Single copies are £30, an annual sub for 12 is £300. Companies House managers want electronic products like these to replace the microfiches, but there has been public opposition.

A new European Business Register was created in 1998, giving access to 14 national registers. Details from Cardiff.

Companies House: main offices

Cardiff Registry	01222-388588
Crown Way, Cardiff, CF4 3UZ	
All general enquiries	01222-380801
Search room	01222-380124
Edinburgh Registry	0131-535 5800
102 George Street, EH2 3DJ	.
Belfast Registry	01232-234488
64 Chichester Street, BT1 4JX	
London Search Rooms	0171-253 9393
55 City Road, EC1Y 1BB	
Website	www.companies-house.gov.uk
Companies House Direct	0345-573991

Satellite offices

Birmingham	0121-233 9047
Glasgow	0141-221 5513
Leeds	0113-233 8338
Manchester	0161-236 7500

Other company registries

Alderney	01481-822817
Guernsey/Sark	01481-725277
Isle of Man	01624-685233
Jersey	01534-603000

OTHER COMPANY INFO

Quoted companies usually produce glossy annual reports. These can be obtained from the company itself, or consulted in London's City Business Library, the best public library of its type in Britain. It has many reference sources, including the Extel Financial UK Quoted Companies Service, providing up-to-date financial data on computer, and the FT McCarthy files, containing all newspaper stories about many companies. Most other public libraries only stock some annual directories with details of the bigger companies. Company data is also available on a variety of on-line computer and CD-ROM services. Financial Times Information is one of the world's leading suppliers in these and other formats; its titles include Extel, FT Discovery, FT Profile and FT McCarthy. The Office for National Statistics runs a Business Statistics Data Analysis Service drawing on its huge supplies of material. Electronic specialists are:

Bloomberg	0171-330 7500
Business Statistics (ONS)	0800-731 5761
Dash	01494-422299
Economist Intelligence Unit	0171-830 1007
Euromonitor	0171-251 1105
FT Information	0171-825 8000
ICC Information	0181-783 1122
Knight-Ridder Information	0171-930 7646
Lexis-Nexis	0171-464 1300
Reed Business Info (Kompass)	01342-335649
Reuters Business Briefing	0171-250 1122
RM Online	0171-729 1234

Other company views

All the national media covers the ups and downs of corporate life, but there is only one UK publication focusing on global capitalism with an openly critical perspective. This is *Corporate Watch*, the non-profit occasional magazine which "aims to provide information to grass roots campaigners about the environmental, social and ethical behaviour of big business". It hopes to "reform corporations and ultimately to end corporate dominance". Contact on 01865-791391.

BUSINESS LIBRARIES

British Library Business Information Service
25 Southampton Buildings, Chancery Lane, London WC2A 1AW.　　　　　　　　　0171-412 7454
City Business Library (Corporation of London)
1 Brewers Hall Garden, London EC2V 5BX
Enquiries　　　　　　　　　0171-638 8215
Recorded details　　　　　　0171-480 7638
Fee-paying research service　0171-600 1461
The most comprehensive of the business libraries.
Open weekdays 9.30-5.00.
Export Market Information Centre (DTI)
66-74 Victoria Street, London SW1E 6SW
　　　　　　　　　　　　　　0171-215 5444

DIRECTORIES

Directory of Directors
Annual. Reed Information
Details of 50,000 directors and the 14,000 companies they control.
Industrial Trade Names
Annual. Kompass (Reed Information)
Listing of 100,000 trade names and the 25,000 companies that own them.
Kelly's Directory
Annual. Kompass (Reed Information)
Comprehensive trade directory, detailing over 110,000 companies.
Key British Enterprises
Annual. Dun & Bradstreet
Six volumes covering the top 50,000 companies, with trade name sections.
Macmillan's Unquoted Companies
Annual. Macmillan
20,000 unquoted companies, turnovers above £3m.
Major UK Companies/Smaller Companies
Annual. Extel
Specialise in financial information.
Price Waterhouse Corporate Register
Quarterly. Hemmington Scott Publishing
Data on decision-makers in stockmarket companies.
Stock Exchange Yearbook
Annual. Macmillan
A profile of 4,100 companies and securities listed on the London and Dublin Stock Exchanges.
The Times 1000
Annual. HarperCollins
Assets, turnover and profits of the top 1,000 companies.
UK Kompass Register
Annual. Kompass (Reed Information)
CBI-backed, five volumes, giving a wide range of data.
Who Owns Whom
Annual. Dun and Bradstreet
Who's Who in the City
Annual. Macmillan
Handy biographies of the business people.

KEY CONTACTS

Whitehall is replacing many of the regulatory bodies listed below with the new Financial Services Authority, due to take over in 1999.

ACAS	0171-210 3613
Association of British Insurers	0171-600 3333
Bank of England	0171-601 4444
Press	0171-601 4411(-5)
Bankruptcy Association	01524-64305
British Bankers Association	0171-216 8800
British Chambers of Commerce	0171-565 2000
British Institute of Management	01536-204222
British Standards Institution	01908-220022
Building Societies Association	0171-437 0655
Business in the Community	0171-224 1600
CBI	0171-379 7400
Chamber of Shipping	0171-417 8400
Corporation of London	0171-606 3030
Dept of Trade & Industry	0171-215 5000
Press	0171-215 5970
Company Law Directorate	0171-215 0403
Ethical Investors Group	01242-604550
Export Credits Guarantee Dept	0171-512 7000
Federation of Small Businesses	0171-928 9272
ICOF (Industrial Common Ownership Fund)	0121-523 6886
ICOM (Industrial Common Ownership Movement)	0113-246 1737
IMRO (Investment Management Regulatory Organisation)	0171-390 5000
Industrial Society	0171-262 2401
Inland Revenue - main number	0171-438 6622
Press office	0171-438 7356
Insolvency Service	0171-637 1110
Inst of Chartered Accountants	0171-920 8100
Institute of Taxation	0171-235 9381
Lloyds of London	0171-327 1000
London Chamber of Commerce	0171-248 4444
London International Financial Futures Exchange	0171-623 0444
London Metal Exchange	0171-264 5555
Low Pay Unit	0171-713 7616
Monopolies and Mergers Comm.	0171-324 1467
National Assoc of Pension Funds	0171-730 0585
Office of Fair Trading	0171-211 8000
Patent Office	01633-814000
Personal Investment Authority	0171-538 8860
Rural Development	0171-340 2900
Securities & Investments Board	0171-676 1000
Serious Fraud Office	0171-239 7272
Eves	0171-239 7050
Stock Exchange	0171-588 2355
Takeovers & Mergers Panel	0171-382 9026
HM Treasury - press	0171-270 5238
TUC (Trades Union Congress)	0171-636 4030
UK Co-operative Council	0161-829 5290

TOP COMPANIES

Abbey National (banking)	0171-612 4000
Aegis Group (communications)	0171-838 9393
Alfred McAlpine (construction)	01565-756200
Alliance & Leicester (BS)	0171-629 6661
Alliance Trust (Investments)	01382-201700
Allied Domecq (alcohol)	0171-323 9000
Allied Irish Bank	0171-629 8881
AMEC (construction)	01606-883885
Amerada Hess (fuel)	0171-823 2626
Amersham International	01494-544000
Amstrad (electronics)	01277-228888
Anglia Television	01603-615151
Anglian Water	01480-443000
Argos (retailing)	01908-690333
Arjo Wiggins Appleton (paper)	01256-723000
Asda (supermarkets)	0113-243 5435
Associated British Foods	0171-589 6363
Associated British Ports	0171-430 1177
B&Q (DIY)	01703-256256
BAA (airports)	0171-834 9449
Balfour Beatty (construction)	0171-216 6800
Bank of China	0171-282 8888
Bank of England	0171-601 4444
Bank of India	0171-628 3165
Bank of Ireland	0171-236 2000
Bank of Japan	0171-606 2454
Bank of Scotland	0131-442 7777
Barclays Bank	0171-699 5000
Barratt Development (building)	0191-286 6811
Bass (alcohol)	0171-409 1919
BAT Industries (tobacco)	0171-222 7979
Benetton UK (clothing)	0171-495 5482
Bernard Matthews (food)	01603-872611
BFI (waste disposal)	01753-662700
BG (ex-British Gas)	0118-935 3222
BICC (electrical)	0171-629 6622
Birmingham Midshires BS	01902-302000
Blue Circle (building)	0171-828 3456
BOC (chemicals)	01276-477222
Body Shop (retailing)	01903-731500
Boots (retailing)	0115-9506111
BP Mobil (oil)	01908-853000
BPB	01753-898800
Bradford & Bingley BS	01274-555555
Brent Walker (leisure)	0171-465 0111
Britannia BS	01538-399399
Britannic Assurance	0121-449 4444
British Aerospace	01252-373232
British Airways	0181-759 5511
British Bakeries	01753-857123
British Land (property)	0171-486 4466
British Nuclear Fuels	0171-222 9717
British Petroleum (oil/gas)	0171-496 4000
British Railways Board	0171-928 5151
British Shoe Corporation	0116-280 6000
British Steel	0171-735 7654
British Telecommunications	0171-356 5000
BSkyB (media)	0171-705 3000
BTR (conglomerate)	0171-834 3848

Budgens (supermarkets)	0181-422 9511
Burmah Castrol (oil/gas)	01793-511521
Burton (retailing)	0171-636 8040
Cable & Wireless (telecomms)	0171-363 2000
Cadbury Schweppes (food)	0171-409 1313
Calor (oil/gas)	0118-933 2363
Carlton Communications (TV)	0171-663 6363
Central Broadcasting (TV)	0121-643 9898
Channel 4 (TV)	0171-396 4444
Channel 5 (TV)	0171-497 5225
Chase Manhatten Bank	0171-777 2000
Cheltenham & Gloucester BS	01452-372372
Chevron (fuel)	0171-487 8100
Christian Salvesen (food)	01604-662600
Christie's (auctioneers)	0171-839 9060
Ciba-Speciality Chemicals)	01625-421933
Clydesdale Bank	0171-626 4545
Co-operative Bank	0345-212212
Co-operative Retail Services	01706-713000
Co-operative Wholesale Society	0161-834 1212
Coats Viyella (textiles)	0161-728 5100
Comet (retailing)	01482-320681
Commercial Union (insurance)	0171-283 7500
Conoco (fuel)	01926-404000
Cookson (industry)	0171-766 4500
The Co-operative (retailing)	01244-520900
Costain (construction)	0171-705 8444
Courtaulds (chemicals)	0171-612 1000
Coutts & Co (banking)	0171-623 3434
Dalgety (food)	0171-486 0200
De La Rue (printing)	0171-836 8383
Debenhams (retailing)	0171-408 4444
Deutsche Morgan Grenfell (banking)	0171-545 8000
Diadgeo (ex-Grand Met, food)	0171-518 5200
Dixons (retailing)	0171-499 3494
Do-It-All (DIY)	01384-456456
Dow Chemical (oil)	0181-848 8688
Dowty (engineering)	01235-559999
Dunhill Holdings (consumer)	0171-838 8000
East Midlands Electricity	0115-926 9711
Eastern Group (electricity)	01473-221331
Elementis	0171-711 1400
Engelhard (metals)	0171-456 7300
English China Clays (building)	0118-930 4010
Enterprise Oil	0171-925 4000
Esso (oil/gas)	0171-834 6677
European Bank	0171-338 6000
Eurotunnel (transport)	0171-872 5496
Ferranti (air systems)	0161-946 3600
First National Bank of Chicago	0171-240 7240
Ford (vehicles)	01277-253000
Forte (leisure)	0171-301 2000
Gallaher (tobacco)	01932-859777
GEC (electronics)	0171-493 8484
General Accident (insurance)	0171-626 8711
George Wimpey (building)	0181-748 2000
Girobank	0171-843 3000
GKN (engineering)	01527-517715
Glaxo Wellcome (household)	0171-493 4060
GMTV (TV)	0171-827 7000
Granada (media/leisure)	0171-451 3000
Grand Metropolitan (Diadgeo, food)	0171-518 5200
Great Portland Estates	0171-580 3040
Greenalls (leisure)	01925-651234
Greycoat (property)	0171-379 1000
Gt Universal Stores (retailing)	0161-273 8282
Guardian Insurance	0171-283 7101
Guinness (aka Diadgeo, alcohol)	0171-486 0288
Halfords (retailing)	01527-517601
Halifax BS	01422-333333
Hambros (banking)	0171-480 5000
Hammerson (property)	0171-887 1000
Hanson (conglomerate)	0171-245 1245
Hill Samuel Bank	0171-600 6000
Hillsdown (food)	0171-794 0677
Homebase (DIY)	01933-679679
House of Fraser (retailing)	0171-963 2000
HSBC Holdings (banking)	0171-260 8000
Hyder (water)	01222-500600
IBM (computers)	01705-561000
ICI (chemicals)	0171-834 4444
Imperial Tobacco	0117-963 6636
Inchcape (transport)	0171-546 0022
John Laing (construction)	0181-959 3636
John Lewis (retailing)	0171-828 1000
John Menzies (retailing)	0131-225 8555
John Mowlem (construction)	0181-568 9111
John Swire & Sons (transport)	0171-834 7717
Kingfisher (retailing)	0171-724 7749
Kleinwort Benson (banking)	0171-623 8000
Kvaerner (mixture)	0171-766 2000
Kwik Save (supermarkets)	01745-887111
Ladbroke (leisure)	0181-459 8031
Land Securities (property)	0171-413 9000
Lasmo (oil & gas)	0171-892 9000
Legal & General (insurance)	0171-528 6200
Liberty Int (property/finance)	0171-222 5496
Littlewoods (retailing)	0151-235 2222
Lloyds TSB Group	0171-626 1500
London Electricity	0171-242 9050
London Regional Transport	0171-222 5600
London Weekend Television	0171-620 1620
Lonrho (conglomerate)	0171-201 6000
Lucas Varieties (engineering)	0121-627 6000
Magnox Electric (electricity)	01453-810451
Marks & Spencer (retailing)	0171-935 4422
Marley (building materials)	01732-455255
McCarthy & Stone (building)	01202-292480
McDonalds (fast food)	0181-700 7000
MEPC (property)	0171-911 5300
MFI (furnishings)	0181-200 8000
Midland Bank	0171-260 8000
Milk Marque	01905-858500
Mirror Group (media)	0171-510 3000
Morgan Crucible (industrial)	01753-837000
Morgan Grenfell (banking)	0171-588 4545
Mothercare (parenting)	01923-241000
National Bank of Canada	0171-726 6581
National Grid (electricity)	01203-537777
National Power (electricity)	0171-454 9494
National Westminster Bank	0171-726 1000
Nationwide (BS)	01793-513513

Nestle (food)	0181-686 3333	Severn Trent (water)	0121-722 4000
News International (media)	0171-782 6000	Shell UK (oil/gas)	0171-257 3000
Next (retailing)	0116-286 6411	Siebe (engineering)	01753-855411
NFC (transport)	01234-272222	Signet Group	0121-554 3871
NFU Mutual Insurance Society	01789-204211	Sketchley (miscellaneous)	01455-238133
Nortel (communications)	01628-812000	Slough Estates (property)	01753-537171
North West Water	01925-234000	Smithkline Beecham (health)	0181-975 2000
Northern Foods	01482-325432	Smiths Industries (engineers)	0181-458 3232
Northern Rock (BS)	0191-279 4405	Somerfield (supermarkets)	0117-935 9359
Northern Telecom	0171-291 3000	South West Water	01392-446688
Northern Trust (banking)	0171-628 2233	Southern Electric	01628-822166
Northumbrian Water	0191-284 3151	Southern Water	01273-606766
Nuclear Electric	01452 652222	St Ivel (food)	01793-848444
P&O (transport)	0171-930 4343	Standard Chartered (banking)	0171-280 7500
Paragon (loans)	0171-726 4054	Storehouse (retailing)	0171-262 3456
Pearson (media)	0171-411 2000	Sunblest Bakeries (food)	01784-451366
Pentos (retailing)	0171-281 6236	Superdrug (household/health)	0181-684 7000
Peugeot (vehicles)	01203-884000	Swiss Bank Corporation	0171-329 0329
Pilkington (glass)	01744-28882	Syseca	0161-946 1001
Post Office (communications)	0171-490 2888	T&N (engineering)	0161-955 5200
Powell Duffryn (transport)	01344-666800	Tarmac (construction)	01902-307407
Powergen (electricity)	01203-424000	Tate & Lyle (food)	0171-626 6525
Press Association (media)	0171-963 7000	Taylor Woodrow (building)	0171-629 1201
Prudential (insurance)	0171-334 9000	Telewest (media)	01483-750900
Racal Electronics	01344-481222	Tesco (supermarkets)	01992-632222
Railtrack (transport)	0171-344 7100	Texaco (oil/gas)	0171-719 3000
Rank Organisation (leisure)	0171-706 1111	Thames Water	0171-636 8686
Rank Xerox (electronics)	01895-251133	Thomson Corporation (media)	0171-437 9787
Rechem (waste treatment)	01628-810011	Thorn EMI (leisure)	0171-355 4848
Reckitt & Colman (household)	0181-994 6464	3i Group (investments)	0171-928 3131
Redland (building materials)	01306-872000	TI Group (engineering)	01235-555570
Reed Elsevier (media)	0171-222 8420	Tomkins (engineering)	0181-871 4544
Rentokil (chemicals)	01342-833022	Total Oil	0171-629 1111
Reuters (media)	0171-250 1122	TSB (banking)	0121-600 6000
Rexam (paper)	0171-584 7070	Unigate (food)	01892-534424
Rhone Poulenc Rorer	01477-537112	Unilever (food/household)	0171-822 5252
RMC (building materials)	01932-568833	United Biscuits (food)	01895-432100
Rolls-Royce (engineering)	0171-222 9020	United Utilities (water)	01925-285000
Rosehaugh (property)	01463-811205	Vauxhall (vehicles)	01582-21122
Rothmans (tobacco)	0171-491 4366	Vickers (engineering)	0171-828 7777
NM Rothschild (banking)	0171-280 5000	Vodafone (telecomms)	01635-33251
Rover (vehicles)	0121-475 2101	Waitrose (supermarkets)	01344-424680
Royal Bank of Scotland	0131-556 8555	Waste Management	0181-563 7000
Royal Sun Alliance (insurance)	0151-802 8000	Welsh Water	01874-623181
RTZ Corporation (mining)	0171-930 2399	Wessex Water	0117-929 0611
Rugby Group (building)	01788-542666	WH Smith (retailing)	0171-404 4242
Saatchi & Saatchi (advertising)	0171-636 5060	Whitbread (alcohol)	0171-606 4455
Safeway (supermarkets)	0181-848 8744	Witan Investment	0171-638 5757
J Sainsbury (supermarkets)	0171-695 6000	Wittington Investments (food)	0171-589 6363
Salomon Brothers (financial)	0171-721 2000	Wolseley (building materials)	01905-794444
SBC Warburg (banking)	0171-606 1066	Woolwich (building society)	0181-298 5000
Schroders (banking)	0171-658 6000	Woolworths (retailing)	0171-262 1222
Scottish & Newcastle (beer)	0131-556 2591	WPP Group (advertising)	0171-408 2204
Scottish Hydro-Electric	01738-455040	Yorkshire Electricity	0113-289 2123
Scottish Investment Trust	0131-225 7781	Yorkshire Water	0113-234 3234
Scottish Mortgage	0131-222 4000	Zeneca (health)	0171-304 5000
Scottish Nuclear	01355-262000		
Scottish Power (electricity)	0141-568 2000		
Sears (retailing)	0171-200 5999		
Securicor (miscellaneous)	0181-770 7000		
Sentrica	0118-935 8222		

Charities

England and Wales have 187,000 registered charities. Of these, 160,00 are "main" charities and the other 27,000 subsidiaries. Their total annual income in 1997 was £18,347 million. Seventy per cent have an annual income below £10,000, while 5 per cent receive over 85 per cent of the total income, with the largest 248 attracting two-fifths of it (£7,435 million). The charities with the biggest fund-raising incomes in 1995/6 were the National Trust with £151.0m and Oxfam with £129.4m. The biggest corporate donors were BT, giving £14.9m, and Glaxo Wellcome with £10.7m.

Charities come under the umbrella of the **Charity Commission**, which gives administrative advice to trustees and ensures they comply with legal rules. The Commissioners' powers were tightened up in the mid-1990s to stop malpractice and make charities accountable. The Commission, established in 1853, is based in central London, with regional offices in Liverpool and Taunton. These three offices together form the **Central Register of Charities**. They hold the public records of all charities, which can be inspected free of charge. Much of the archive material is held by the Greater London Record Office, in Clerkenwell. In Scotland, charities are supervised by the Scottish Charities Office on behalf of the Lord Advocate. In Northern Ireland charities do not need to register, and are monitored by the DHSS Charities Branch.

The **Charities Aid Foundation**, an independent body, is one of the main organisations that help the flow of funds to charities from companies, individuals and trusts. It publishes the annual *Directory of Grant-Making Trusts*, the best-known handbook on how to raise money for a charity. The **National Council for Voluntary Organisations** (NCVO) is the leading co-ordinating body for charities and other public-spirited bodies. Its wide-ranging annual is the *Voluntary Agencies Directory*. Another reference annual is the *Charities Digest*, launched in 1882, published by Waterlow.

The **National Lottery** Charities Board distributes the portion of the proceeds of the National Lottery allocated to charities. The Lottery is the largest in the world, with about 70 per cent of adults regularly buying tickets from the 35,500 retail outlets. Camelot Group plc, a private sector consortium, has the franchise to run the Lottery until 2001. It is regulated by the Office of the National Lottery.

CO-ORDINATORS

Charity Commission	0171-210 4477
Press office	0171-210 4433
Liverpool	0151-703 1500
Taunton	01823-345000
Website	www.charity-commission.gov.uk
Charities Aid Foundation	01732-520000
Card Aid	0171-794 9835
Community Matters	0171-226 0189
Directory of Social Change	0171-209 5151
Inst of Charity Fundraising Managers	0171-627 3436
London Metropolitan Archives	0171-606 3030
National Lotteries Charity Board	0171-747 5300
NCVO	0171-713 6161
N Ireland Charities Branch DHSS	01232-522780
Scottish Charities Office	0131-226 2626
Waterlow Information	0171-490 0049

MAIN CHARITIES

Actionaid	0171-281 4101
Action research	01403-210406
Afasic	0171-236 6487
Age Concern England	0181-679 8000
Alzheimer's Disease Society	0171-306 0606
Arthritis Research Campaign	01246-558033
Arts Council	0171-333 0100
Baring Foundation	0171-767 1348
Barnardo's	0181-550 8822
BBC Children in Need Appeal	0181-735 5057
Blue Cross	01993-822651
Bridge House Estate Fund	0171-332 3710
British Council	0171-930 8466
British Diabetic Association	0171-323 1531
British Film Institute	0171-255 1444
British Heart Foundation	0171-935 0185
British Library	0171-412 7000
British Museum	0171-636 1555
British Red Cross Society	0171-235 5454
CAFOD	0171-733 7900
Cancer Relief Macmillan Fund	0171-351 7811
Cancer Research Campaign	0171-224 1333
Cats Protection League	01403-221900
Charity Projects	0171-436 1122
Christ's Hospital	01403-211293
Christian Aid	0171-620 4444

Church Commissioners	0171-222 7010	National Canine Defence League	0171-837 0006
City & Guilds of London	0171-294 2468	National Trust	0171-222 9251
City Parochial Foundation	0171-606 6145	Natural History Museum	0171-938 9123
Consumers Association	0171-830 6000	NCH Action for Children	0171-226 2033
Construction Industry.Training Board	01485-577577	NSPCC	0171-825 2500
Distressed Gentlefolk's Aid Assoc	0171-396 6700	Nuffield Foundation	0171-631 0566
Dogs' Home Battersea	0171-622 3626	Order of St John	0171-253 6644
Donkey Sanctuary	01395-578222	Oxfam	01865-311311
English Churches Housing	0181-203 9233	Parkinson's Disease Society	0171-233 5373
Foundation for Sport and Arts	0151-259 5505	Peabody Trust	0171-928 7811
Garfield Weston Foundation	0171-589 6363	Prince's Trust	0800-842842
Gatsby Charitable Foundation	0171-410 0330	Quantum Fund	0171-925 2555
Great Ormond St Children's Hospital	0171-405 9200	RAF Benevolent Fund	0171-580 8343
Guide Dogs for the Blind	0118-983 5555	Rank Foundation	0171-834 7731
Help the Aged	0171-253 0253	RNLI	01202-663000
Henry Smith's (Kensington Estate)	0171-242 1212	Robertson Trust	0141-352 6620
Imperial Cancer Research Fund	0171-242 0200	Royal British Legion	0171-973 7200
Independent Living Alternative	0181-906 9265	Royal College of Surgeons	0171-405 3474
Institute of Cancer Research	0171-352 8133	Royal Horticultural Society	0171-834 4333
Institute of Child Health	0171-242 9789	Royal National Institute for the Blind	0171-388 1266
Institute of Psychiatry	0171-7035411	Royal National Institute for Deaf People	0171-296 8000
International Planned Parenthood	0171-487 7900	Royal Opera House	0171-240 1200
Jewish Care (UJIA)	0181-922 2000	RSPB	01767-680551
Jewish Philanthropic Assoc.	0181-446 1477	RSPCA	01403-264181
JNF Charitable Trust	0181-204 9911	Salvation Army Trust	0171-332 0022
John Ellerman Foundation	0171-930 8566	Save the Children Fund	0171-703 5400
Joint Israel Appeal	0181-446 1477	Scope	0171-636 5020
Joseph Rowntree Foundation	01904-629241	Soros Global Research	0171-451 2000
JW Laing Trust	01225-310893	Stonham Housing Association	0171-401 2020
Leonard Cheshire Foundation	0171-802 8200	Stroke Association	0171-490 7999
Leverhulme Trust	0171-822 6938	Tear Fund	0181-977 9144
Ludwig Institute of Cancer Research	0171-878 4000	UNICEF-UK	0171-405 5592
Marie Curie Foundation	0171-235 3325	Variety Club Children's Foundation	0171-387 3311
MENCAP	0171-454 0454	Wellcome Trust	0171-611 8888
Methodist Homes for the Aged	01332-296200	Wolfson Foundation	0171-930 1057
Monument Trust	0171-410 0330	WWF UK	01483-426444
MS Society	0171-610 7171	YMCA	0181-520 5599
National Association for the Care and Resettlement of Offenders (NACRO)	0171-582 6500		

Communications

The UK has over 28 million phone lines, using 7,500 local exchanges and 69 main switching exchanges. All 17 million listed phone numbers are available on a CD-ROM (the Phone Disk) and in 170 local phone books, 22 million of which are printed annually. But the percentage of numbers which are ex-directory has risen from 24 in 1991 to 37 in 1998. There are 136,000 BT public payphones. BT handles an average of 103 million calls a day. It has invested more than £27,000 million since 1984 in expansion.

Charges

Phone charges vary according to the time when calls are made, the distance of the call and the service used. For UK calls using BT services, the three different **times** are:

Weekdays, 8am-6pm: daytime rate
Weekdays 6pm-8am: evening rate
Saturdays and Sundays: weekend rate

The three **distances** are:

Local - using local call code: low rate
Regional - non-local calls up to 35 miles: medium rate

National - over 35 miles: high rate
But a payphone only has two charge bands: local and national, at any time of day. International call charges vary according to the country dialled. There are many different **services**, with a wide variety of charges, the only clue to which is often the initial code.

Codes

BT's ordinary UK codes, as used by nearly all customers until the invention of the mobile phone, are known as "geographic" and they start "01". Other services (BT and non-BT), being non-geographic and not starting 01, have their own special charges, usually higher. So remember this simple poem at all times: *I could be done If it's not 01.*

The main BT codes with charges different from calls made on 01 are:

Free: 0321, 0500, 0800 (but not free on mobiles)
Local rate: 0345, 0645
National rate: 0990
Premium (expensive): 0331, 0336, 0338, 0660, 0839, 0870, 0891, 0894, 0897, 0898, 09911

Mobile phones

Mobile phones never have 01 codes. They charge a confusing variety of rates - always high, often very high - not only for outgoing calls, but for incoming ones, even from an 01 BT line. The common mobile codes are:

0370, 0378, 0585, 0589, 0802, 0831, 0850, 0860, 0881, 0973, 0976

Mobile phones were first used in the UK in 1985. By mid-1998 there were 8.5 million people using mobiles, which seemed to have an unstoppable momentum. By 2007 it was estimated 70% of the population would have one - provided charges were less extortionate and signing-up conditions not so baffling. Just before Oftel director-general Donald Cruickshank retired in March 1998 he said the mobile industry "ripped off" its customers. He said costs were too high, and people calling mobile numbers were often unaware they were being charged premium rates.

Code changes

In recent years BT has begun meeting the mushrooming demand for new phone numbers by changing codes. The biggest change so far was in April 1995, when the initial "0" had "1" added to it for nearly all geographic codes. Since then the government has anounced more numbers are needed, and that the existing complicated code system needs rationalising as soon as possible. The changes listed below are planned for the next few years, reorganising much of the existing system outlined above:

01   Ordinary geographic numbers
02   Ordinary geographic numbers
03   Reserved for future geographic use
04   Reserved for future services
05   Corporate numbering range
06   Reserved for future services
07   Mobile/personal/paging nos, incl:
    071 & 072 paging
    077, 078 & 079 mobiles
08   Specially tariffed services, incl:
    080 freephone
    084 local rate
    087 national rate
09   Premium rate services (expensive)

At Easter 2000 six areas will have their geographic codes changed. London will abolish 0171 and 0181, instead starting as 020 followed by either 7 or 8. Northern Ireland will use the single code 028, Cardiff will become 029, Coventry 024, and Portsmouth and Southampton 023.

BT service numbers

* = free of charge.

100*	Operator (UK calls)
141*	Withholds number dialled from
150*	Customer services (residential)
151*	Fault reporting (residential)
152*	Customer services (business)
153	Directory enquiries (international)
154*	Fault reporting (business)
155*	Operator (international calls)
190*	Message services
192	Directory enquiries (UK/Eire)
1471*	Calling Line Identification

BT DIRECTORY

Advisory Comm. on Telecoms	0171-634 87743
Billing queries: Home/work	0800-800192*
Public payphone	0800-115511*
Chargecards	0800-345144*
British Telecommunications	0171-356 5000
Administrative enquiries	0800-382011*
BT Archives	0171-492 8792
BT Internet	0800-800001*
Business Connections	0800-800800*
Cable Information	0990-111777
Customer Communications and Telemarketing	0800-373 543*
General enquiries	0800-309409*
ICSTIS	0171-240 5511
ISDN	0800-181514*
Malicious calls adviceline	0800-666700*
Mobile communications	0113-272 2000
Oftel	0171-634 8700
Phone Disc	0800-919199*
Press office	0171-356 5369
Pricing information	0800-800891*
Telephone preference service	0800-398893
Yellow Pages	0118-959 2111

MOBILE OPERATORS

Cellnet	0800-214000
One 2 One	0500-500121
Orange	0800-801080
Vodafone	0800-101112

Consumer watchdogs

There are four breeds of consumer watchdog in business to snap at many corporate heels:

1) Regulatory bodies
2) Ombudsmen
3) Advisory committees
4) Pressure groups

REGULATORY BODIES

These are official or semi-official organisations ensuring that legal regulations are complied with by suppliers. The Office of Fair Trading (OFT) is the non-ministerial government department which safeguards shopping consumers by administering these regulations and monitoring competition. The OFT ensures all laws are enforced, especially the two most important ones, the 1979 Sale of Goods Act and 1968 Trades Description Act. Individual consumer problems are taken up by Trading Standards Departments in county councils., whose officers are the consumer defenders most often seen at ground level.

Problems for finance consumers have been handled until now by a wide range of individual agencies. The main ones have been the Building Societies Commission, IMRO, OPRA, PIA, SFA and SIB. In a big shake-up announced in mid-1997, these are to be replaced in 1999 by a new statutory body, the Financial Services Authority (FSA) Set up in June 1998, the FS has 2,000 staff and major new powers. It could become a dynamic regulatory machine or, as widely feared, simply a quagmire of bureaucracy.

All Whitehall's consumer policies are supervised by the Consumer Affairs Directorate of the Department of Trade and Industry. Also listed below are the two government auditing departments: the National Audit Office, which audits accounts of government departments and public bodies; and the Audit Commission, which examines the accounts of both the local authorities and the NHS. In March 1998 the government published its green paper on utility regulation.

Adjudicator's Office	0171-930 2292
Audit Commission:Press	0171-930 6077
British Standards Institution	0181-996 9000
Broadcasting Standards Commission	0171-233 0544
Broadcasting Standards Council	0171-233 0544
Building Societies Commission	0171-663 5000
Copyright Tribunal	0171-438 4776
Data Protection Registrar	01625-545700
Dept of Trade & Industry	
Main number	0171-215 5000
Trade	0171-215 5960
Corporate & Consumer Affairs	0171-215 5971
Science & Technology	0171-215 5962
Industry & Employment	0171-215 5965
Gaming Board	0171-306 6200
Investment Management Regulatory Organisation (IMRO)	0171-390 5000

Investors Compensation Scheme	0171-628 8820
Lands Tribunal	0171-936 7200
Monopolies & Mergers Commission	0171-324 1467
National Audit Office	0171-798 7000
Occupational Pensions Regulatory Authority (OPRA)	01273-627600
Office of:	
Electricity Regulation (OFFER)	0121-456 2100
Scotland	0141-331 2678
Northern Ireland	01232-311575
Fair Trading (OFT)	0171-211 8000
Gas Supply (OFGAS)	0171-828 0898
National Lottery (OFLOT)	0171-227 2000
Passenger Rail Franchising (OFPRAF)	0171-478 4470
Rail Regulator (OFRR)	0171-282 2000
Social Security Commissioners	0171-353 5145
Standards in Education (OFSTED)	0171-421 6800
Telecomms (OFTEL)	0171-634 8700
Water Services (OFWAT)	0121-625 1300
Personal Investment Authority (PIA)	0171-538 8860
Police Complaints Authority	0171-273 6450
Press Complaints Commission	0171-353 1248
Securities & Investment Board (SIB)	0171-676 1000
Security and Futures Authority (SFA)	0171-378 9000
Office for the Supervision of Solicitors	01926-820082
Press	01926-822043

OMBUDSMEN

Ombudsmen answer complaints about specific areas of consumerism. Most ombudsmen are government officers, appointed to help enforce legal regulations. But some are not Whitehallers; they are PR specialists privately employed by industry sectors to give the impression that their businesses are well-behaved and publicly accountable, when in reality they do little to help customers. One example: Over 6,000 people complaining to the Building Societies Ombudsman in 1997/8 were told he was powerless to help them. Eight different ombudsman schemes are likely to be merged in 1999 by the new Financial Services Authority. All entries below are ombudsmen, eg Banking Ombudsman.

Banking	0171-404 9944
Building Societies	0171-931 0044
Estate Agents	01722-333306
European Union	003388-172313
Funerals	0171-430 1112
Health Service: England	0171-276 2035
Wales	01222-394621
Scotland	0131-225 7465

Independent Housing	0171-836 3630
Insurance	0171-928 4488
Investment	0171-796 3065
Legal Services	0161-236 9532
Scotland	0131-556 5574
Local Government:	
SE England	0171-915 3210
North of England	01904-663200
Rest of England	01203-695999
Wales	01656-661325
Scotland	0131-225 5300
Northern Ireland	01232-233821
Parliamentary	0171-276 2130
Press	0171-276 2082
Pensions	0171-834 9144
Personal Investment Authority	0171-538 8860
Prisons	0171-276 2876

ADVISORY COMMITTEES

These are the officially sponsored bodies giving consumers' views of industries and services to government ministers before decisions are made. The National Consumer Council (NCC) conducts research, lobbies policy makers and publishes reports. The NCC also helps run the Consumer Congress, the forum for consumer bodies, and publishes the annual *Consumer Congress Directory* with details of 150 organisations.

Advisory Committees on Telecomms	0171-634 8700
Air Transport Users Council	0171-242 3882
Assoc of Community Health Councils	0171-609 8405
British Standards Institution Consumer Policy Committee	0181-996 7390
Central Rail Users Consultative Cttee	0171-505 9090
Electricity Regional Consumers Cttees	0121-456 6359
Gas Consumers Council	0171-931 0977
General Consumer Council for NI	01232-672488
London Regional Passengers Cttee	0171-505 9000
Meat & Livestock Commission Consumers' Committee	01908-677577
National Consumer Council	0171-730 3469
Scottish CC	0131-556 5574
Welsh CC	01222-255454
Post Office Users National Council	0171-928 9458
Rail Users Consultative Committees	0171-222 0391
Telecomms Advisory Committees	0171-634 8774
Water Customer Service Cttees	0345-023953

PRESSURE GROUPS

The largest of the independent pressure groups is the Consumers Association, which has 700,00 members. It publishes the advertisement-free magazine (one of the few in existence) *Which?*, a wide-ranging source of independent information on products and services with a big circulation, plus many books. Local Citizens Advice Bureaux can give information and support to consumers suffering problems; see phone books.

Buswatch	01705-863080
CAMRA (Campaign for Real Ale)	01727-867201
Consumer Credit Trade Assoc	0171-636 7564
Consumers' Association	0171-830 6000
Consumers in Europe Group	0171-881 3021
Consumers International	0171-226 6663
Ethical Consumer (magazine)	0161-226 2929
Fed of Independent Advice Centres	0171-489 1800

Food Commission	0171-837 2250
Institute of Consumer Affairs	01908-694655
Institute of Safety & Public Protection	01252-542164
Institute of Trading Standards Admin	01702-559922
Local Authorities Co-ordinating Body on Trading Standards	0181-688 1996
Money Advice Association	0171-236 3566
National Association of Citizens Advice Bureaux	0171-833 2181
National Debtline	0121-359 8501
National Federation of Bus Users	01705-814493
National Federation of Consumer Groups	0113-264 8341
National Food Alliance	0171-837 1228
Research Institute for Consumer Affairs	0171-935 2460

Education

Britain has 29,400 state schools, 1,600 specials and 2,400 independents. They have over half a million teachers and 9.8 million pupils. About 93 per cent of pupils attend publicly-funded (grant-maintained) **state schools**. These are primary schools for 5-11 year olds and secondary schools for 11-16. Most are controlled by Local Education Authorities (LEAs), part of the county councils or unitary authorities. Exceptions are: grant-maintained schools which have opted out of LEA control and are overseen by the DfEE; and schools receiving public funds but run by voluntary bodies. **Independent schools** are not publicly-funded, charging fees to pupils. They have 600,000 pupils and are called: boarding, private, preparatory and public (in Scotland and most of the world "public" schools are actually publicly-funded schools); details from Independent Schools Info Service. About 70% of pupils continue studying beyond the age of 16. About 764,000 become full-time students in further education colleges. These are mainly vocational, with exams to GCE Advanced level. Other exams here are GCSE and NVQ. Beyond "further" education is "higher" education, the shorthand for universities examining above GCE A level. There have been about 90 universities since 1992, when polytechnics changed their titles and status.

DIRECTORIES

The Education Year Book
Pitman   Tel 0171-379 7383
Details of every educational organisation, official and unofficial.
The Student Book
Macmillan   Tel 01256-302699
Descriptions of life at each university and college.
UCAS Handbook
UCAS   Tel 01242-222444
The official guide to university and college entrance.
Which Degree/Which University
Hobsons Publishing   Tel 01223-354551
Also publishes Postgraduate: The Directory of Graduate Studies, with Media and Communications details.

CENTRAL BODIES

Convention of Scottish Local Auths	0131-474 9200
Council of Local Education Auths	0171-235 9554
Dept for Education & Employment	0171-925 5000
Press	0171-925 5615
Independent Schools Info Service	0171-630 8793
Local Government Assoc	0171-834 2222
National Curriculum Council	0171-229 1234
N Ireland Dept of Education	01247-279279
Office for Standards in Education (OFSTED)	0171-421 6800
Qualification & Curriculum Auth	0171-387 9898
School Curriculum and Assessment Authority	0171-229 1234
Scottish Office Education	0131-556 8400
Society of Education Officers	0161-236 5766
Welsh Joint Education Committee	01222-265000
Welsh Office Education Dept	01222-823207

TEACHING UNIONS

Assoc of Teachers & Lecturers	0171-930 6441
Assoc of University Teachers	0171-221 4370
Headmasters Conference	0116-285 4810
National Assoc of Head Teachers	01444-472472
NAS/UWT	0121-453 6150
NATFHE	0171-837 3636
National Union of Teachers	0171-388 6191
Prof Assoc of Teachers	01332-372337
Secondary Heads Assoc	0116-299 1122
Society of Independent Heads	01352-78112

UNIVERSITIES

Aberdeen	01224-272000
Abertay Dundee	01382-308000
Anglia Polytechnic	01245-493131
Aston (Birmingham)	0121-359 3611
Bath	01225-826826
Birmingham	0121-414 3344
Bournemouth	01202-524111
Bradford	01274-733466
Brighton	01273-600900
Bristol	0117-928 9000
Brunel (Uxbridge)	01895-274000
Buckingham	01280-814080
Cambridge	01223-337733
Central England in Birmingham	0121-331 5000
Central Lancashire (Preston)	01772-201201
City (London EC1)	0171-477 8000
Coventry	01203-631313
Cranfield (Bedfordshire)	01234-750111
De Montfort (Leicester)	0116-255 1551
Derby	01332-622222
Dundee	01382-223181
Durham	0191-374 2000
East Anglia (Norwich)	01603-456161
East London (Dagenham)	0181-590 7722
Edinburgh	0131-650 1000
Essex (Colchester)	01206-873333
Exeter	01392-263263
Glamorgan	01443-480480
Glasgow	0141-339 8855
Glasgow Caledonian	0141-331 3000
Greenwich	0181-331 8590
Heriot-Watt (Edinburgh)	0131-449 5111
Hertfordshire (Hatfield)	01707-284000
Huddersfield	01484-422288
Hull	01482-346311
Humberside (Hull)	01482-440550
Keele (Staffs)	01782-621111
Kent (Canterbury)	01227-764000
Kingston (W London)	0181-547 2000
Lancaster	01524-65201
Leeds	0113-233 2332
Leeds Metropolitan	0113-283 2600
Leicester	0116-252 2522
Liverpool	0151-794 2000
Liverpool John Moores	0151-231 2121
London Guildhall (Whitechapel)	0171-320 1000

University of London	0171-636 8000
Birkbeck College	0171-631 6000
Courtauld Institute	0171-872 0220
Goldsmiths College	0181-510 7171
Imperial College	0171-589 5111
Kings College	0171-836 5454
London School of Economics	0171-405 7686
Queen Mary College	0171-975 5555
Royal Holloway	01784-434455
Royal Veterinary College	0171-468 5000
School of Oriental Studies	0171-637 2388
Senate House	0171-636 8000
University College	0171-387 7050
Wye	01233-812401
Loughborough	01509-263171
Luton	01582-734111
Manchester	0161 275 2000
Manchester Metropolitan	0161-247 2000
Middlesex (London N17)	0181-362 5000
Napier (Edinburgh)	0131-444 2266
Newcastle-upon-Tyne	0191-222 6000
North London (N7)	0171-607 2789
Northumbria (Newcastle)	0191-232 6002
Nottingham	0115-951 5151
Open University	01908-274066
Oxford	01865-270000
Oxford Union	01865-241353
Oxford Brookes	01865-741111
Paisley	0141-848 3000
Plymouth	01752-600600
Portsmouth	01705-876543
Queens (Belfast)	01232-245133
Reading	0118-987 5123
Royal Agricultural College	01285-652531
Royal College of Music	0171-589 3643
Salford	0161-745 5000
Sheffield	0114-222 2000
Sheffield Hallam	0114-272 0911
South Bank (London SE1)	0171-928 8989
Southampton	01703-595000
St Andrews (Fife)	01334-476161
Staffordshire	01782-294000
Stirling	01786-473171
Strathclyde (Glasgow)	0141-552 4400
Sunderland	0191-515 2000
Surrey (Guildford)	01483-300800
Sussex (Brighton)	01273-606755
Teeside	01642-218121
Thames Valley (Ealing)	0181-579 5000
Ulster (Coleraine)	01265-44141
UMIST (Manchester)	0161-236 3311
University of Wales	01222-382656
Aberystwyth	01970-623111
Bangor	01248-351151
Cardiff	01222-874000
Lampeter	01570-422351
Swansea	01792-205678
Warwick	01203-523523
West of England (Bristol)	0117-965 6261
Westminster (Central London)	0171-911 5000
Wolverhampton	01902-321000
York	01904-43000

Religion

The UK's largest religion is Christianity, primarily the Anglicans, Presbyterians (including the Church of Scotland), Roman Catholics and Free Churches. The second biggest is the Muslim religion, followed by the Sikhs, Jews, Buddhists and Hindus.

In the **Anglican** Communion group, the Church of England is the leading body. It has been the established church since the mid-16th century. The country is divided into the two provinces of Canterbury and York, each run by an archbishop: George Carey (Canterbury) and David Hope (York). There are 44 dioceses within the provinces, with 13,000 parishes. The Church of England is governed by its General Synod, with 574 members, meeting twice a year under the presidency of the archbishops. There are about 10,000 staff and 16,000 churches.

The other main Anglican churches in the UK are the Church in Wales, the Episcopal Church in Scotland and the Church of Ireland. They are independent, but have strong links with the Church of England, along with the other Anglican churches around the world.In Scotland, the leading religious body is the non-Anglican Church of Scotland, the national church also set up in the 16th century. It has a Presbyterian structure, with 47 districts and about 750,000 members. It is governed by its General Assembly.

Every ten years all Anglican bishops meet for the international Lambeth Conference to discuss common issues, although without any policy-making formal power. The most recent conference was in July 1998, when a *Sunday Times* survey said the Anglican Communion's active membership had fallen to an all-time low of 23 million. In a league table of Protestant faith membership, Anglicans have been overtaken by the Lutherans (70 million), the Methodists (60 million) and the Baptists (40 million).

Roman Catholics form by far the world's largest Christian movement, with nearly a bil-lion members. The Roman Catholic Church is the global organisation run from the autonomous Vatican City State in Rome. The leading figure is the Pope, currently John Paul II. In England and Wales the governing body is the Bishops Conference, headed by the President, Cardinal Basil Hume, Archbishop of Westminster. In Scotland there is a similar Bishops Conference. The UK has about 12,800 staff and 8,600 churches.

The **Free Churches** are Protestant churches which, unlike the Church of England and Church of Scotland, are not established, ie, officially recognised by the State. The largest of the Free is the Methodist Church. Others include the Salvation Army, Baptists and United Reformed Church.

Muslims are followers of the Islam. Many Muslims have come to Britain since the late nineteenth century, and there are now over 600 mosques. There is no central organisation, but the most influential bodies are the Islamic Cultural Centre (the London Central Mosque) and the Imams and Mosque Council. **Sikhism** grew up in the Punjab four centuries ago, coming to Britain in the 1950s. It has no central body, but the Sikh Missionary Society has an information service.

Christianity has been overshadowed by many new religious movements, often called cults. These include the Church of Scientology and the Unification Church (the Moonies). Paganism has revived in England, especially in the form of Druidism. Many new pagans are members of the environmental movement that has shaped the more radical political undercurrents since the late 1980s. The UK government helped set up the Information Network Focus on Religious Movements (Inform) to provide objective information to the public.

The main relgious directory is:

Religions in the UK - A Multi-Faith Directory
University of Derby and the Inter Faith
  Network   Tel 01332-622222
Current edition published May 1997. £29.50.

ANGLICAN

Church of England
  General Synod (main CoE contacts)   0171-222 9011
  Archbishop of Canterbury   0171-928 8282
  Archbishop of York   01904-707021
  Church Commissioners   0171-222 7010
  Record Centre   0171-231 1251
Church in Wales   01222-231638
Episcopal Church in Scotland   0131-225 6357

ROMAN CATHOLIC

Bishops Conferences: E&W   0171-630 8220
  Scotland   0141-221 1168
Archbishops: Westminster   0171-798 9033
  Liverpool   0151-724 6398
  Glasgow   0141-226 5898
Media offices: London   0171-828 8709
  Glasgow   0141-221 1168
  Dublin   00-35312 885043
Catholic Enquiry Centre   0181-455 9871

OTHER CHRISTIAN

Baptist Union   01235-512077
Church of Jesus Christ of Latter-day
  Saints (Mormons)   0121-712 1200
Church of Scotland   0131-225 5722
Churches of Christ   01842 810357
Congregational Federation   0115-911 1460
Council of Churches for Britain   0171-620 4444
Eastern Orthodox Churches: Greek   0171-723 4787
  Russian   0181-742 3493
  Serbian   0171-727 8367
  Other nationalities   01986-896708
Free Church of England   0151-638 2564
Free Presbyterian Church of Scotland   0131-229 0649
Independent Methodist Churches   01942-223526
International Churches of Christ   0171-713 6028
Jehovah's Witnesses   0181-906 2211
Lutheran Council   0171-383 3081
Methodist Church   0171-222 8010
Moravian Church   0181-883 3409
Pentecostal Church bodies:
  Apostolic   01792-473992
  Assemblies of God   0115-9811188
  New Testament   01604-643311
Presbyterian Church in Ireland   01232-322284
Presbyterian Church of Wales   01222-494913
Religious Society of Friends (Quakers)   0171-387 3601
Salvation Army: E&W   0171-236 5222
  Scotland   0131-443 4740
Seventh Day Adventist Church   01923-672251
Unification Church   0171-723 0721
Union of Welsh Independents   01792-467040
Unitarian Churches   0171-240 2384
United Reformed Church   0171-916 2020

OTHER RELIGIONS

Aetherius Society   0171-736 4187
Baha'i Community of UK   0171-584 2566
Buddhist:
  Buddhist Society   0171-834 5858
  Friends of Western Buddhist Order   0171-700 3077
  London Buddhist Vihara   0181-995 9493
  Network of Buddhist Orgs   0171-582 5797
Church of Christ, Scientist   0171-371 0600
Church of Scientology   0171-580 3601
The Family (formerly Children of God)   01455-209172
Hindu:
  Int Soc for Krishna Consciousness   01923-856269
  National Council of Hindu Temples   01923-856269
  Swaminarayan Hindu Mission   0181-965 2651
  Vishwa Hindu Parishad   0181-552 0143
Jain Centre   0116-254 3091
Jesus Army   0181-992 0100
Jewish:
  Board of Deputies of British Jews   0171-543 5400
  United Synagogue   0181-343 6301
  Jewish Care   0181-922 2000
  Jewish Policy Research   0171-935 8266
  Jews for Jesus   0171-431 9636
  Reform Synagogues   0181-349 4731
Muslim:
  Imama & Mosques Council   0181-993 7168
  Islamic Brotherhood   01203 222169
  Islamic Cultural Centre & London Central
    Mosque   0171-724 3363
  Muslim Council of Britain   0181-903 9026
  Muslim Information Centre   0171-272 5170
  UK Action Cttee Islamic Affairs   0181-974 2780
  World Ahl Ul-Bayt, Islamic League   0181-954 9881
Pagan Federation   01787 238257
Sikhism:
  Missionary Society   0181-574 1902
  Network of Sikh Organisations.   0181-540 4148
Theosophical Society   0171-935 9261
Transcendental Meditation   0990 143733

OTHER RELIGIOUS BODIES

Christian Research Assoc.   0181-294 1989
Church Army   0181-318 1226
Church Commissioners   0171-222 7010
Church House Bookshop   0171-340 0280
Church Missionary Society   0171-928 8681
Council of Christians & Jews   0171-388 3322
Cult Information Centre   01689-833800
Evangelical Alliance UK   0171-582 0228
Fellowship of Reconciliation   01832-720257
Inform (Information Network Focus on
  Religious Movements)   0171-955 7654
Inter Faith Network for the UK   0171-388 0008
Lesbian and Gay Christians   0171-739 1249
Spiritualists National Union   01279-816363

Shopping

Britain has 290,000 shops, employing 2.38 million people. 141 businesses have 100 or more outlets, totalling 46,500, with 1.1m staff and a turnover of £86 billion, over half the total value of retail trade (£160 billion). The top 775 firms account for fourth-fifths of all retail sales. Four supermarket groups have 47 per cent of the grocery market: Tesco (profit: £866m) Sainsbury (£735m), Asda (£404m) and Argyll/Safeway (£410m). Tesco displaced Sainsbury as Britain's biggest retailer in 1998. The top 10 retailers take almost £4 of every £10 we spend in shops. Boots has the most stores (almost 2,500), M& S the most profit (£871m in 1997) and Harrods the biggest store (800,000 square feet). Biggest sellers in 1996 were Coca-Cola and Walkers Crisps.

TRADE ASSOCIATIONS ETC

Alliance of Independent Retailers and Businesses	01905-612733
Booksellers Association	0171-834 5477
British Assoc of Toy Retailers	0181-993 2894
British Council of Shopping Centres	0171-222 1122
British Frozen Food Federation	01476-515300
British Retail Consortium	0171-647 1500
British Shops & Stores Association	01295-712277
Consumers Association	0171-830 6000
Credit Card Research Group	0171-436 9937
Food & Drink Federation	0171-836 2460
National Association of Shopkeepers	0115-947 5046
National Federation of MeatTraders	01892-541412
National Fed of Retail Newsagents	0171-253 4225
National Pharmaceutical Assoc	01727-832161
Office of Fair Trading	0171-221 8000
Retail Motor Industry Federation	0171-580 9122

LARGE RETAILERS

Allders	0181-9295500
Allied Bakeries	01784-451366
Argos	01908-690333
Argyll (Safeway)	0181-848 8744
Asda	0113-243 5435
Associated British Foods	0171-589 6363
B & Q	01703-256256
BhS	0171-262 3288
Booker Belmont Cash & Carry	01933-371000
Boots	0115-950 6111
Budgens	0181-422 9511
Burton Group	0171-636 8040
Co-op (CRS - retail)	01706-713000

Co-op (CWS - wholesale)	0161-834 1212
Comet	01482-320681
Debenhams	0171-408 4444
Diadgeo (ex-Grand Metropolitan)	0171-518 5200
Dixons	0181-499 3494
Focus DIY	01270-501555
Forte	0345-404040
Freemans	0171-735 7644
Gateway	0117-935 9359
Great Universal Stores	0161-273 8282
Habitat	0171-255 2545
Halfords	01527-517601
Harrods	0171-730 1234
House of Fraser (Harrods, Army & Navy, Rackhams)	0171-963 2000
Iceland	01244-830100
John Lewis	0171-828 1000
John Menzies	0131-467 8070
Kingfisher (Comet, Woolworth, B&Q)	0171-724 7749
Kwik Save	01745-887111
Littlewoods (mail order)	0151-235 2222
Lonrho	0171-201 6000
Marks & Spencer	0171-935 4422
McDonalds Restaurants	0181-700 7000
MFI	0181-200 8000
Next	0116-286 6411
Owen Owen	0151-707 4000
Signet	0121-554 3871
Sainsbury	0171-695 6000
Sears (Freemans, Selfridges, Olympus)	0171-200 5999
WH Smith	0171-404 4242
Somerfield	0117-935 9359
Storehouse (Bhs, Habitat, Mothercare)	0171-262 3456
Superdrug	0181-684 7000
Tesco	01992-632222
Texas Homecare (Homebase)	01933-679679
EMI Group (HMV, Radio Rentals)	0171-355 4848
Toys R Us	01628-414141
Waitrose	01344-424680
FW Woolworth	0171-262 1222

LARGE SHOPPING CENTRES

The biggest are:

Lakeside, West Thurrock, south Essex, M25. 350 shops, 1.3m sq ft.

MetroCentre, edge of Gateshead, Tyneside. 320 shops, 1.5m sq ft.

Trafford Centre, outskirts of Manchester. 300+ shops, 1.3m sq ft.

Meadowhall, on outskirts of Sheffield. 270 shops, 1.2m sq ft.

Merry Hill, Dudley, West Midlands. 225 shops, 1.8m sq ft.

Cribbs Causeway, near Bristol.
140 shops, 725,000 sq ft.
Two other big centres are being built:
Bluewater, near Dartford, Kent, M25/A2 junc.
300+ shops, 1.6 m sq ft, opens March 1999.
Braehead, Renfrew, near Glasgow.
100 shops, 600,000 sq ft.
Braehead will be Scotland's first out-of-town shopping centre. Bluehead will be Britain's largest, with nearly a fifth of the UK's population living within an hour's drive. It is only two miles from Lakeside. Below are centres with parking space for more than 1,500 cars.

Basildon (Eastgate)	01268-533631
Basingstoke (Walks)	01256-326022
Belfast (Castle Court)	01232-234591
Birmingham (One Stop)	0121-344 3697
Birmingham (The Fort)	0121-386 4442
Bournemouth (Hampshire)	01202-516131
Brent Cross	0181-202 8095
Brighton (Churchill Square)	01273-327428
Bromley (Glades)	0181-313 9292
Crawley (County Mall)	01293-611975
Croydon (Whitgift)	0181-688 8522
Dartford (Bluewater Park)	01322-388989
Dudley (Merry Hill)	01384-481141
Edinburgh (Gyle)	0131-539 9000
Ellesmere Port	0151-357 2118
Gateshead (Metro)	0191-493 2040
Gillingham (Hempstead Valley)	01634-387076
Glasgow (Clyde)	0141-952 4594
Glasgow (Forge)	0141-556 6661
Hartlepool (Middleton Grange)	01429-861220
Hatfield (Galleria)	01707-278301
Leeds (White Rose)	01132-291234
Leicester (Fosse Park)	0116-263 0603
Livingston (Almondvale)	01506-432961
Luton (Arndale)	01582-412636
Milton Keynes (Central)	01908-678641
Milton Keynes (Kingston)	01908-282707
Nottingham (Broad Marsh)	0115-950 7133
Nottingham (Victoria)	0115-912 1111
Peterborough (Queensgate)	01733-311666
Redditch (Kingfisher)	01527-61355
Runcorn (Halton Lea)	01928-716363
Sheffield (Meadowhall)	0114-256 8800
Stockport (Mersey Way)	0161-480 2839
Swindon (Brunel)	01793-525857
Telford	01952-230032
Tunbridge Wells (Royal Victoria)	01892-514141
Warrington (Golden Square)	01925-655053
Washington (Galleries)	0191-416 7177
Watford (Harlequin)	01923-250292
Welwyn Garden (Howard)	01707-320026
West Thurrock (Lakeside)	01708-869933
Woking (Peacocks)	01483-750263

Sport

About 29 million British adults regularly take part in sport or physical recreation. Sport provides jobs for almost 500,000 people and generates £10 billion of business. The Department for Culture, Media and Sport (DCMS) oversees sport and recreation from Whitehall, but most of the work is devolved to the four national **Sports Councils**. They support the governing bodies of individual sports, manage the National Sports Centres and distribute National Lottery Sports Funds. .

Working with the Sports Councils are advisory and co-ordinating bodies. The **Central Council of Physical Recreation** (CCPR) represents the views of English sporting organisations to the Sports Commission, its main funder. The CCPR is the largest sport and recreation federation in the world, representing 68 English and 209 British associations. Equivalent bodies are the Scottish and Welsh Sports Associations and the Northern Ireland Council of Physical Recreation. The CCPR set up the Institute of Sports Sponsorship, and the Institute of Professional Sport, to protect professional sportspeople. The **British Olympic Association** organises British participation in the four-yearly Olympics Games (next: Sydney, Australia, 2000). In the 1996 Olympics, Britain won only 15 medals, with just one gold. The **British Sports Forum** represents non-governmental sports bodies.

The National Playing Fields Association promotes recreation and play facilities, especially playing fields. The Sports Aid Foundation raises funds to help train talented sportspeople. The Football Licensing Authority is responsible for ensuring football grounds comply with legal requirements, including the all-seating policy for top clubs. The Football Trust, set up in 1990 by pools companies, provides funds to improve football grounds. The 1998 World Cup was a disappointment for the Scotland and England teams, and host country France unexpectedly defeated Brazil 3-0 in the final. The next World Cup is in Japan and Korea in 2002.

SPORTS COUNCILS

UK Sports Council	0171-273 1500
English Sports Council	0171-273 1500
East Midlands	0115-982 1887
Eastern	01234-345222
London	0181-778 8600
North West	0161-834 0338
Northern	0191-384 9595
South East	0181-778 8600
South Western	01460-73491
Southern	0118-9483311
West Midlands	0121-456 3444
Yorkshire	0113-243 6443
Sports Council for Wales	01244-822600
Scottish Sports Council	0131-317 7200
Sports Council for N Ireland	01232-381222

NATIONAL BODIES

Assoc of Sports Historians	0181-295 0188
British Blind Sport	01926-424247
British Deaf Sports Council	01943-850214
British Olympic Association	0181-871 2677
British Paralympic Association	0181-681 9655
British Sports & Allied Industries Fed	01203-414999
British Universities Sports Fed	0171-357 8555
British Wheelchair Sports Foundation	01296-395995
Central Council of Physical Recreation	0171-828 3163
Commonwealth Games Fed	0171-383 5596
Dept of Culture, Media & Sport	0171-211 6000
Disability Sport England	0171-490 4919
Foundation for Sport & Arts	0151-259 5505
Institute of Groundsmanship	01908-312511
Institute of Leisure Management	01491-874222
Institute of Sport and Recreation	01664-565531
Institute of Sports Sponsorship	0171-233 7747
National Coaching Foundation	0113-274 4802
National Council for Schools Sports	01287-631013
National Lottery Charities Board	0345-919191
National Play Information Centre	0171-584 6464
National Playing Fields Assoc	0171-584 6445
Physical Education Assoc	01732-875888
Sports Aid Foundation	0171-387 9380
People with Learning Difficulties	0171-250 1100
Ulster Sports Trust	01232-381222
Womens Sports Foundation	0181-697 5370
Youth Clubs UK	0171-242 4045

NATIONAL SPORTS CENTRES

Bisham Abbey, Bucks	01628-476911
Crystal Palace, South London	0181-778 0131
Cumbrae & Inverclyde, Ayrshire	01475-674666
Glenmore Lodge, Aviemore	01479-861256
Holme Pierrepont, Notts	0115-982 1212
Lilleshall, Shropshire	01952-603003
Plas Menai. Gwynedd	01248-670964
Plas y Brenin, Gwynedd	01690-720214
Welsh Institute, Cardiff	01222-300500
Tollymore, County Down	01396-722158

SPORTS BODIES

Royal Aero Club	0116-253 1051
Aircraft Owners & Pilots Association	0171-834 5631
British Microlight Aircraft Assoc	01869-338888
British American Football Assoc	01205-363522
National Federation of Anglers	01283-734735
Scottish Anglers National Assoc	0131-339 8808
National Fed of Sea Anglers	01626-331330
Wales	01646-600313
Scotland	0131-317 7192
Grand National Archery Society	01203-696631
Scottish Archery Centre	01620 850401
Amateur Athletic Assoc	0121-440 5000
Scotland	0131-317 7320
N Ireland Sports Council	01232-381222
British Athletic Federation	0121-440 5000
Gaelic Athletic Assoc	0181-841 2468
Athletics Assoc of Wales	01792-456237
Badminton Assoc	01908-268400
Scottish Badminton Union	0141-445 1218
British Balloon & Airship Club	01604-870025
British Baseball Federation	01482-643551
English Basketball Assoc	0113-236 1166
Scottish Basketball Assoc	0131-317 7260
English Civil War Society (battle re-enactment)	01430-430695
Sealed Knot (battle re-enactment)	01295-278122
World Professional Billiards & Snooker Assoc	0117-974 4491
British Bobsleigh Assoc	01985-850064
British Crown Green Bowling	0151-648 5740
English Bowling Assoc	01903-820222
Wales	01446-733747
Scotland	0141-221 8999
Northern Ireland	01247-469374
English Bowling Federation	0114-247 7763
English Indoor Bowling Assoc	01664-481900
Wales	01656-841361
Scotland	01294-468372
Ireland	01232-794869
English Womens Bowling Fed	0191-413 3160
English Womens Indoor Bowling	01604-494163
Wales	01443-771618
English Bowls Council	01603-427551
Amateur Boxing Assoc	0181-778 0251
Wales	01222-623566
Scotland	01382-508261
Ireland	003531-4543525
British Boxing Board	0171-403 5879
Camping & Caravanning Club	01203-694995
British Canoe Union	0115-982 1100
Veteran Car Club (pre-1919)	01462-742818
Vintage Sports Car Club	01608-644777
Caravan Club	01342-326944
National Caving Assoc	01225-311364
British Chess Federation	01424-442500
Clay Pigeon Shooting Assoc	01536-443566
Crafts Council	0171-278 7700
England & Wales Cricket Board	0171-432 1200
Marylebone Cricket Club (MCC)	0171-289 1611

Scottish Cricket Union	0131-317 7247
Womens Cricket Assoc	0121-440 0567
Croquet Assoc	0171-736 3148
National Crossbow Federation	01902-758870
English Curling Assoc	01923-825004
Royal Caledonian Curling Club	0131-333 3003
British Cycle Speedway Council	01508-493880
British Cycling Federation	0161-230 2301
Northern Ireland	01266-48774
Welsh Cycling Union	01222 577052
Cyclists Touring Club	01483-417217
Scottish Cyclists Union	0131-652 0187
Scottish Darts Assoc	01224-692535
British Equestrian Federation	01926-707700
British Fencing Assoc	0181-742 3032
Fitness Ireland	01232-651103
English Folk Dance & Song Society	0171-405 2206
Football Assoc	0171-262 4542
Wales	01222-372325
Scotland	0141-332 6372
Northern Ireland	01232-669458
Football League	01253-729421
Scotland	0141-248 3844
Football Supporters Assoc	0151-737 2385
Football Trust	0171-388 4504
Womens Football Assoc	01707-651840
Scotland	0141-353 1162
National Gardens Scheme	01483-211535
British Gliding Assoc	0116-253 1051
English Golf Union	01526-354500
Wales	01633-430830
Scotland	0131-339 7546
English Ladies Golf Assoc	0121-456 2088
Ladies Golf Union	01334-475811
Royal & Ancient Golf Club	01334-472112
Professional Golfers Assoc	01675-470333
National Greyhound Racing	0171-267 9256
British Amateur Gymnastics	01952-820330
Scotland	01324-612308
Irish	01232-383813
British Hang-Gliding Assoc	0116-261 1322
Scottish Official Board of Highland	
Dancing	0131-668 3965
Hockey Association	01908-544644
English Hockey	01908-689290
Scottish Hockey Union	0131-650 8170
British Horse Society	01926-707700
British Horseracing Board	0171-396 0011
Jockey Club (horse racing)	0171-486 4921
Racecourse Assoc (horse racing)	01344-625912
Horse Riding for the Disabled	01203-696510
Royal Horticultural Society	0171-834 4333
British Field Sports Society/Countryside Alliance	
(hunting)	0171-582 5432
Scotland	01339-88641
British Ice Hockey Assoc	01202-303946
Scotland	01292-266203
National Ice Skating Assoc	0171-613 1188
Jousting Assoc	01271-861200
British Judo Assoc	0116-255 9669
British Ju-Jitsu Assoc	0114-266 6733
English Karate Governing Body	01225-834008
Welsh Karate Federation	01834-813776
Keep Fit Assoc	0171-233 8898
English Lacrosse Assoc	0121-773 4422
British Microlight Aircraft Assoc	01869-338888
Motor Caravanners Club	0181-893 3883
British Automobile Racing Club	01264-772607
British Racing & Sports Car	01732-848884
RAC Motor Sports Assoc	01753-681736
Auto-Cycle Union (motorcycling)	01788-540519
British Motorcyclists Federation	0181-942 7914
British Mountain Bike Federation	0161-230 2301
British Mountaineering Council	0161-445 4747
Scotland	01738-638227
Council for National Parks	0171-924 4077
Central Council for Naturism	01604-620361
All England Netball Assoc	01402-442344
Wales	01222-237048
Scotland	0141-570 4016
British Orienteering Federation	01629-734042
Outward Bound	01753-731005
British Parachute Assoc	0116-278 5271
British Petanque Assoc	01203-421408
Modern Pentathlon Assoc	01734-9817181
Hurlingham Polo Assoc	01869-350044
English Pool Assoc	01922-635587
National Quoits Assoc	01947-841100
Ramblers Assoc	0171-582 6878
British Federation of Roller Skating	01473-401430
National Rounders Assoc	0115-978 5514
Amateur Rowing Assoc	0181-748 3632
Wales	01600-714244
Scotland	0141-775 0522
Henley Royal Regatta (rowing)	01491-572153
British Amateur Rugby League	01484-544131
Rugby Football League	0113-232 9111
Rugby Football Union	0181-892 2000
Wales	01222- 390111
Scotland	0131-346 5000
Salmon & Trout Assoc	0171-283 5838
Camanachd Assoc (shinty)	01397-772772
British Assoc for Shooting and	
Conservation	01244-573000
Scotland	01350-723226
Wales	01686-688861
National Rifle Assoc (shooting)	01483-797777
British Show Jumping Assoc	01203-698800
Showmens' Guild	01784-461805
British Ski Federation	01506-884343
English Ski Council	0121-501 2314
Wales	01222-619637
Scotland	0131-317 7280
World Professional Billiards & Snooker	0117-974 4491
British Softball Federation	01254-678838
Squash Rackets Assoc	0181-746 1616
Scotland	0131-317 7343
British Sub-Aqua Club	01992-621042
British Surfing Assoc	01736-360250
Amateur Swimming Assoc	01509-618700
Wales	01222-488820
Scotland	0141-641 8818

English Table Tennis Assoc	01424-722525	British Water Ski Federation	0171-833 2855
Wales	01495-756112	Inland Waterways Assoc	0171-586 2556
Scotland	0131-317 8077	British Weightlifters Assoc	01865-200339
Tennis & Rackets Assoc	0171-386 3448	Scotland	0131-556 4116
Lawn Tennis Assoc	0171-381 7000	British Amateur Wrestling Assoc	0161-832 9209
All England Club	0181-944 1066	British Federation of Sand & Land Yacht	
Wales	01222-452000	Clubs	01509-842292
Scotland	0131-444 1984	Royal Ocean Racing Club (yachting)	0171-493 2248
British Ten-Pin Bowling Assoc	0181-478 1745	Royal Yachting Assoc	01703-627400
British Trampoline Federation	0181-863 7278	Wales	01248-670738
Tug-of-War Assoc	01494-783057	Scotland	0131-317 7388
English Volleyball Assoc	0115-981 6324	Northern Ireland	01232-381222
Northern Ireland	01232-667011	British Wheel of Yoga	01529-306851
Long Distance Walkers Assoc	0113-264 2205	Youth Hostels Association	01727-855215

Think tanks

Adam Smith Institute
23 Great Smith Street, London SW1P 9XX
Fax 0171-222 7544   Tel 0171-222 4995
Chairman: Dr Madsen Pirie
The Bow Group
92 Bishopsbridge Road, London WC2
                             Tel 0171-431 6400
Centre for Policy Studies
52 Rochester Row, London SW1P 1JU
Fax 0171-222 4388   Tel 0171-222 4488
Director: Tessa Keswick
Conservative 2000 Foundation
2 Wilfred Street, London SW1E 6PH
                             Tel 0171-630 6400
Demos
9 Bridewell Place, London EC4V 6AP
Fax 0171-353 4481   Tel 0171-353 3479
E-mail martin@demos.demon.co.uk
Director: Geoff Mulgan
Employment Policy Institute
Southbank House, Black Prince Road, London SE1
7SJ
Fax 0171-793 8192   Tel 0171-735 0777
Director : John Philpott
Fabian Society
11 Dartmouth Street, London SW1H 9BN
Fax 0171-976 7153   Tel 0171-222 8877
General Secretary: Michael Jacobs
Henley Centre for Forecasting
9 Bridewell Place, London EC4V 6AY
Fax 0171-353 2899   Tel 0171-955 1800
Chairman: Paul Edwards
Institute of Economic Affairs
2 Lord North Street, London SW1P 3LB
Fax 0171-799 2137   Tel 0171-799 3745
General Director: John Blundell
Institute for Employment Studies
University of Sussex, Falmer, Brighton BN1 9RF
Fax 01273-690430   Tel 01273-686751
Director: Richard Pearson

Institute for Fiscal Studies
7 Ridgmount Street, London WC1E 7AE
Fax 0171-323 4780   Tel 0171-636 3784
E-mail mailbox@ifs.org.uk
Director: Andrew Dilnot
It promotes research and understanding of the
economic and social implications of existing taxes and
different fiscal systems.
Institute for Public Policy Research
30-32 Southampton Street, London WC2E 7RA
Fax 0171-470 6111   Tel 0171-470 6100
E-mail ippr@easynet.co.uk
Director: Gerald Holtham
Established in 1988 IPPR provides the main centre-left
alternative to the free market think tanks of the Right.
Nexus
Fax 0171-353 7171   Tel 0171-353 4141
Director: Neil Lawson
Established 1996 to develop centre-left thought. It is
formally independent though in close contact with
Labour and the Lib Dems.
Policy Studies Institute
100 Park Village East, London NW1 3SR
Fax 0171-388 0914   Tel 0171-468 0468
Director: Pamela Meadows
Politeia
28 Charing Cross Road, London WC2H 0DB
Fax 0171-240 5095   Tel 0171-240 5070
Director: Sheila Lawlor
Social Affairs Unit
314 Regent Street, London W1
Fax 0171-436 8530   Tel 0171-637 4356
Social Market Foundation
20 Queen Anne's Gate, London SW1H 9AA
Fax 0171-222 0310   Tel 0171-222 7060
Chairman: Professor Lord Skidelsky
A non-libertarian free market think tank.

Travel

TRAINS

Britain has 15,000 kilometres of passenger track, 2,500 stations and 40,000 bridges, tunnels and viaducts. The number of passenger journeys in 1996/7 was 776 million, travelling 38,900 million kilometres and spending £2,437 million on tickets. Britain's busiest station is Victoria, with over 300,000 passengers daily. London's Underground in 1996/7 had 772 million passenger journeys, using 164,500 seats on 3,912 carriages, along 392 kilometres of track (171 subterranean), stopping at 245 stations.

The railway was nationalised in 1948 and then denationalised following the 1993 Railways Act, splitting British Rail into more than 90 separate businesses. The passenger services were divided into 25 regional units, which were franchised to private comp-anies in 1996/7, bringing to an end nearly 50 years of publicly-owned and run railways. BR's operational infrastructure was sold to Railtrack plc. They own and manage all track, signals, stations, bridges, tunnels and depots. Railtrack has seven infrastructure companies, each responsible for a geographic zone. Three companies franchised all British Rail's 11,000-strong rolling stock of passenger trains and carriages, which in turn were leased to the 25 passenger service operators. Freight services were split into seven components, which are now run by four companies, the largest being EWSR.

RAIL TRAVEL ENQUIRIES

All national rail enquiries, 24-hour	0345-484950
International (Victoria)	0171-834 2345
Channel Tunnel: Le Shuttle passengers	0990-353535
Recorded information	0891-555566
Eurostar info/reservations	0345-303030
London Transport/tube, 24-hour	0171-222 1234
Travel Check (recorded)	0171-222 1200
TBC (Train, Bus, Coach) Hotline	0891-910910
Timetables: Printed, on sale	01904-634814
Internet	www.rail.co.uk

RAIL ORGANISATIONS

Assoc of Train Operating Companies	0171-928 5151
Press	0171-214 9941
British Railways Board	0171-928 5151
British Transport Police	0171-388 7541
Central Rail Users Consultative Cttee	0171-505 9090
Scotland	0141-221 7760
Wales	01222-227247
DETR	0171-890 3000
Railways Directorate	0171-271 5238
Office of Passenger Rail Franchising	0171-940 4200
Office of Rail Regulator	0171-282 2000

RAIL OPERATORS

Passenger train companies

Anglia	01473-693333
Cardiff	01222-430000
Central	0171-930 6655
Chiltern	01296-332100
Connex South Central	0181-667 2780
Connex South Eastern	0171-928 5151
Cross-Country (Virgin)	0121-654 7400
Eurostar	0345-303030
Gatwick Express	0171-973 5005
Great Eastern	0171-928 5151
Great North Eastern	01904-653022
Great Western	01793-499400
Heathrow Express	0181-745 0578
InterCity West Coast	0121-643 4444
Island Line (IoW)	01983-812591
LTS (London, Tilbury, Southend)	01702-357889
Merseyrail Electrics	0151-709 8292
Midland MainLine	01332-221125
North Spirit	01904-653022
North Western	0161-228 2141
ScotRail	0141-332 9811
Silverlink (North London)	01923-207258
South West	0171-928 5151
Thames	0118-908 3678
Thameslink	0171-620 5760
Wales & West	01222-430400
West Anglia Great Northern	0345-818919

Freight companies

Freightliner	0171-214 9491
Loadhaul	01302-345400
English, Welsh & Scottish Railway	0171-713 2422
Railfreight Distribution	0171-922 9311

Railtrack plc

Company HQ	0171-344 7100
East Anglia	0171-295 2524
Great Western	01793-499500
London North Eastern	01904-522825
Midlands	0121-643 4444
North West	0161-228 8500
Scotland	0141-335 2424
Southern	0171-344 7292

BOATS

Britain's Merchant Navy was once the biggest-commercial fleet in the world, but is now among the smaller. This, in part, results from the transfer of legal registration to countries which allow their vessels to run to a somewhat lower standard, and therefore more cheaply. From 1987 to 1996 the number of UK-owned merchant trading ships over 500 gross tonnes fell from 657 to 514. Total gross tonnage in 1996 was 8.3 million (11.3 million in 1987), deadweight tonnage 11.6 million. The biggest single type was the tanker, with 129 vessels of 2.96 million gross tonnes.

In 1996 there were 531 million tonnes of traffic through **British ports** (457 million in 1987). There are about 80 ports of commercial significance, plus several hundred smaller ones handling local cargo, fishing vessels, ferries and recreation. The largest are (in descending order): London, Grimsby plus Immingham, Forth, Tees plus Hartlepool, and Sullom Voe. Dover is Britain's main port for roll-on roll-off traffic. The 1991 Ports Act allowed the privatisation of ports that were then owned by trusts, a fate which befell seven. Britain's largest port owner and operator is Associated British Ports, with 23 under its control, handling nearly a quarter of traffic.

The **Port of London Authority** (PLA) is organising "the biggest maritime festival ever!" in late May 2000 to celebrate Britain's island heritage and look forward to the next millennium. The West India and Millwall docks will be the main venue. The PLA is responsible for 96 miles of the tidal Thames downriver from Teddington, and incorporating 82 operational wharves and terminals. It handles over 50 million tonnes of cargo a year, including 24 million tonnes of oil and fuel products.

WATER ORGANISATIONS

Associated British Ports	0171-430 1177
British Ports Association	0171-242 1200
British Waterways	01923-226422
Inland Waterways Assoc	0171-586 2510
Register of Shipping, Seamen & Fishing Boats	01222-747333
Westminster Passenger Services Fed	0181-977 5702

PORTS AND HARBOURS

Aberdeen, Grampian	01224-597000
Ardrossan, Strathclyde	01294-463972
Belfast	01232-554422
Bristol, Avon	0117-982 0000
Brixham, Devon	01803-853321
Cardiff	01222-471311
Clyde Ports	0141-221 8733
Cowes, Isle of Wight	01983-293952
Dover, Kent	01304-240400
Dundee, Tayside	01382-224121
Falmouth, Cornwall	01326-211376
Felixstowe, Suffolk	01394-604500
Fishguard, Dyfed	01348-404453
Fleetwood, Lancs	01253-872323
Folkestone, Kent	01303-220544
Forth Ports	0131-554 4343
Gt Yarmouth, Norfolk	01493-335500
Harwich, Essex	01255-243030
Heysham, Lancs	01524-852373
Holyhead, Anglesey	01407-762304
Grimsby, Humberside	01472-359181
Hull, Humberside	01482-327171
Immingham, Humberside	01469-571555
Ipswich, Suffolk	01473-231010
Isle of Man	01624-686628
Larne, Antrim	01574-872100
Lerwick, Shetland	01595-692991
Liverpool	0151-949 6000
London:	
Port of London Authority	0171-265 2656
Chief Harbour Master (Gravesend)	01474-562200
Duty Officer (Woolwich)	0181-855 0315
Port Controller (Gravesend)	01474-560311
Website	www.portoflondon.co.uk
London: Tilbury	01375-852200
Londonderry	01504-860555
Lowestoft, Suffolk	01502-572286
Manchester	0161-872 2411
Medway Ports, Kent	01795-561234
Milford Haven, Dyfed	01646-693091
Newhaven, East Sussex	01273-514131
Peterhead, Grampian	01779-474281
Poole, Dorset	01202-440200
Portsmouth, Hants	01705-297395
Ramsgate, Kent	01843-592277
Rye, East Sussex	01797-225225
Scarborough, North Yorks	01723-373530
Shoreham, West Sussex	01273-598100
Southampton, Hants	01703-330022
Stornoway, Western Isles	01851-702688
Sunderland, Tyne & Wear	0191-553 2100
Swansea, West Glamorgan	01792-650855
Tees & Hartlepool	01642-877000
Tyne	0191-455 2671
Weymouth, Dorset	01305-206421
Whitby, North Yorks	01947-602354
Workington, Cumbria	01900-602301

FERRY COMPANIES

Brittany Ferries:
Portsmouth	01705-892207
Plymouth	01752-227941
Caledonian MacBrayne Ferries	01475-650100
Condor Ferries	01305-761555

Hoverspeed:
Belfast/Stranraer	0990-523523
Dover	01304-240101
Folkestone	01303-221281

Irish Ferries:
Dublin	00-3531 855 2222
Holyhead	01407-760223
Liverpool	0345-171717
Isle of Man Steam Packet Co	0345-523523
Isles of Scilly Steamship Co	01736-362009
Mersey Ferries	0151-630 1030
North Sea Ferries (Hull)	01642-431400
Orkney Ferries	01856-872044

P&O:
All European ferries	0181-575 8555
Head office	0171-930 4343
Aberdeen	01224-572615
Cairnryan	01581-200276
Dover	01304-212121
Felixstowe	01394-604040
Fishguard	01348-404404
Larne	0990-980777
Portsmouth	0990-980555
Scrabster	01847-892052
Red Funnel Ferries (Southampton)	01703-333042
Holyman Sally Ferries	0171-401 7470
Scandanavian Seaways (Harwich)	01255-240240

Stena:
All reservations	0990-707070
Harwich	01255-243333
Holyhead	01407-606666
Stranraer	01776-702531
Swansea Cork Ferries	01792-456116
Wightlink (Portsmouth)	01983-882432

PLANES

Britain has 142 licensed civil aerodromes and airports. A fifth of them have over 100,000 passengers a year each, with 16 handling more than 1 million. There were 137.3 million passengers in 1996. The busiest airports were: Heathrow with 55.7 million passengers, Gatwick 24.1 million, Manchester 14.5 million and Glasgow 5.5 million. Heathrow is the busiest airport in the world for international passengers, and fourth for all passengers, after Chicago, Atlanta and Los Angeles. Seven British airports, including Heathrow and Gatwick, are owned by BAA plc, and together handle 71 per cent of all passengers and 81 per cent of air cargo traffic in Britain. British Airways is the largest airline in the world in terms of international scheduled services. It has 309 aircraft, a turnover of £8.5 billion and 60,000 staff. Britannia Airways is the world's largest charter airline.

The **Civil Aviation Authority** (CAA) oversees all non-military flying and enforces all regulations, on behalf of the Civil Aviation Division of the DETR. The CAA subsidiary **National Air Traffic Services** (NATS) controls day-to-day all air traffic and safety over Britain and its surrounding seas, in collaboration with the Ministry of Defence. At the heart of NATS is its **air traffic control centre** at West Drayton near Heathrow. In the late 1980s the government decided to replace out-of-date West Drayton with a new technology operation based at Swanwick, near Fareham in Hampshire. But this has been severely delayed because of computer software problems, with completion unlikely before 2000, raising many fears about public safety.

FLIGHT ENQUIRIES

Aberdeen (Dyce)	01224-722331
Barra, Hebrides	01871-890283
Belfast (Aldergrove)	01849-422888
Belfast (City)	01232-457745
Benbecula, Outer Hebrides	01870-602051
Biggin Hill, Kent	01959-571111
Birmingham International	0121-767 5511
Blackpool, Lancs	01253-343434
Bournemouth (Hurn), Dorset	01202-593939
Bristol (Lulsgate), Avon	01275-474444
Brize Norton, Oxon (RAF)	01993-842551
Cambridge	01223-361133
Campbeltown (Strathclyde)	01586-553797
Cardiff	01446-711111
Carlisle	01228-573641
Channel Islands: Alderney	01481-822888
Guernsey	01481-37766
Jersey	01534-492000
Coventry, West Midlands	01203-301717
Culdrose, Cornwall (RAF)	01326-574121
Dundee, Tayside	01382-643242
East Midlands	01332-852852
Edinburgh (Turnhouse)	0131-333 1000
Exeter, Devon	01392-367433
Gatwick	01293-535353
Glasgow	0141-887 1111
Gloucester-Cheltenham	01452-857700
Heathrow	0181-759 4321
Inverness (Dalcross), Highland	01463-232471
Ipswich	01473-720111
Isle of Man (Ronaldsway)	01624-824313
Kent International (Manston)	01843-823333
Lands End	01736-788771
Leeds/Bradford (Yeadon)	0113-250 9696
Liverpool (Speke)	0151-486 8877
London: Battersea Heliport	0171-228 0181
City, Docklands	0171-646 0000
Gatwick, West Sussex	01293-535353
Heathrow, Middx	0181-759 4321
Stansted, Essex	01279-680500
Luton, Beds	01582-405100
Lydd, Kent	01797-320401
Manchester (Ringway)	0161-489 3000
Newcastle (Woolsington)	0191-286 0966
Northolt, Middx (RAF)	0181-845 2300
Norwich, Norfolk	01603-411923
Orkney: Kirkwall	01856-872421
Penzance Heliport, Cornwall	01736-363871
Plymouth, Devon	01752-772752
Prestwick, Strathclyde	01292-479822
St Mawgan, Cornwall	01637-860551
Scilly Isles: St Marys	01720-422646
Tresco Heliport	01720-422970
Shetland: Lerwick	01595-840246
Shoreham, West Sussex	01273-296900
Southampton (Eastleigh)	01703-629600
Southend, Essex	01702-340201
Stornoway, Western Isles	01851-702256
Teeside	01325-332811
Tiree, Argyll	01879-220456
Wick, Caithness	01955-602215

AIRLINES: BOOKINGS

Aer Lingus	0181-899 4747
Air Canada	0990-247226
Air France	0181-742 6600
Air New Zealand	0181-741 2299
Air UK	0990-074074
Alitalia	0171-602 7111
American Airlines	0181-572 5555
Britannia Airways	0990-502555
British Airways	0345-222111
British Midland	0345-554554
British World Airlines	01702-354435
Cathay Pacific	0171-747 8888
Gulf Air	0171-408 1717
Icelandair	0171-388 5599
Japan Airlines	0345-747777
KLM	0990-750900
Lufthansa	0345-737747
Northwest Airlines	01293-561000
Qantas	0345-747767
Sabena	0181-780 1444
SAS	0171-734 4020
Singapore Airlines	0181-747 0007
South African Airways	0171-312 5000
Swissair	0171-434 7300
TWA	0181-814 0707
United	0845-844777
Virgin Atlantic	01293-747747

AIR ORGANISATIONS

Airport Operators Assoc	0171-222 2249
Air Transport Users Council	0171-242 3882
Assoc of British Travel Agents (ABTA)	0171-637 2444
British Air Line Pilots Assoc	0181-476 4000
British Air Transport Assoc	0171-930 5746
Civil Aviation Authority	0171-379 7311
DETR	0171-890 3000
Civil Aviation Division	0171-271 4890
International Air Transport Association	
(IATA) (Geneva)	00-4122 7992525
London	0171-240 9036
Passport enquiries	0990-210410

ROADS

Britain has 241,800 miles of roads. The 2,000 miles of motorways and 3,000 of trunk roads carry a third of all traffic. Travel by car and van rose 35 per cent between 1985 and 1996 and the amount of freight by 45 per cent. There are 36.5 milliion drivers and 26.3 million licensed vehicles, 21.1 million of which are cars and 413,000 heavy goods vhicles. There are 52,000 licensed taxis, 18,700 of them in London. All motor vehicles on public roads must be registered, currently licensed and covered by a valid test certificate, and the drivers must be licensed to drive and have valid insurance; details on all this available from the DVLC in Swansea.

There are 75,900 buses and coaches, almost all owned by private companies. The 1979-97 Conservative government deregulated and privatised the bus service, and between 1987/8 and 1996/7 the number of local bus passenger journeys fell from 5,292 million to 4,355 million. A handful of big companies now dominate the industry. The top four bus groups are Arriva (£1,421m turnover), Stagecoach (£1,374m), National Express (£1,134m) and FirstBus (£795m) Most dynamic of all is Stagecoach, almost monopolising large areas of the country. The largest coach operator is National Express, with 14 million passengers.

Below are the main bus and coach groups, plus London Transport (LT), which is not anowner but a statutory corporation, responsible for providing public transport in London. Its day-to-day operations on all 700 bus routes are provided under contract by over 30 private companies, contactable via LT itself.

MOTORING ORGANISATIONS

AA: HQ	0990-448866
24-hr breakdown	0800-887766
AA Roadwatch	0990-500600
British Motorcyclists Fed	0181-942 7914
British Parking Assoc	01273-846455
British Roads Federation	0171-703 9769
Department of Transport	0171-271 5772
DVLA Vehicles	01792-772134
DVLA Drivers	01792-772151
Greenflag: HQ	0113-239 3666
Breakdown service	0800-400600
RAC: HQ	0181-417 2500
24-hr breakdown	0800-828282
Live road news: Website	www.rac.co.uk
Retail Motor Industry	0171-580 9122
Road Haulage Association	01932-841515
Road Operators Safety Council	01865-775552
Soc of Motor Manufacturers	0171-235 7000

COACH/BUS COMPANIES

Arriva	0181-800 8010
Blazefield Holdings	01535-611606
EYMS Group	01482-327142
FirstBus	01224-650100
Go-Ahead Group	0191-232 3123
London Transport	0171-222 5600
National Express Group	0121-625 1122
Southern Vectis	01983-522456
Stagecoach Holdings	01738-442111
Yorkshire Traction	01226-202555

Women

There are more women than men in the UK, and they live longer - but they are paid less and are more likely to be unemployed. Official figures show there are 29.95 million women and 28.86 million men. A baby girl can now expect to reach the age of 79.4, while a male toddler can only manage 74.1. At age 89 there are around three women to every man. The average male earns £408.70 a week, but females are only given £297.20. Among part-time workers women out-number men by four to one. Women spend more than twice as much time as men on caring for children and adults, and more than three times as much on cooking. Men devote more hours to tuning in to TVs and radios, and doing gardening and DIY. Over 80 per cent of all crimes are committed by men.

WOMEN'S ORGANISATIONS

Abortion Law Reform Assoc	0171-637 7264
Action for Sick Children	0171-833 2041
African & Caribbean Women Assoc	0141-942 5762
Amnesty International - Women's Action Network	0171-814 6200
Army Families Federation	01980-615525
Ash Women & Smoking Group	0171-314 1360
Asian Women's Adhikar Advice Assoc	01902-29414
Associated Country Women of the World	0171-834 8635
Assoc of Catholic Women	0181-399 1459
Assoc of Greater London Older Women	0171-281 3485
Assoc for Improvements in the Maternity Service	0181-960 5585
Assoc of Radical Midwives	01695-572776
Assoc for Teachers' Widows	01322-663833
Assoc for Women in Science & Engineering	0171-935 3282
Assoc of Women Solicitors	0171-320 5793
Baha'i National Womens Committee	0171-584 2566
Black Women & Europe Network	0181-802 0911
Breast Cancer Care	0171-384 2984
British Assoc of Women Entrepreneurs	0171-935 9455
British Assoc of Women Police	01543-276165
British Fed of Women Graduates	0171-498 8037
British Housewives League	0181-546 3388
British Pregnancy Advisory Service	01564-793225
Brook Advisory Centres	0171-713 9000
Catholic Women's League	0171-738 4894
Change	0171-430 0692
Co-operative Women's Guild	0181-804 5905
Conservative Women's National Cttee	0171-222 9000
English Collective of Prostitutes	0171-482 2496
Family Planning Assoc	0171-837 5432
Farm Women's Club	0181-652 4927
Fawcett Library	0171-320 1189
Fawcett Society	0171-628 4441
Feminist Library & Information Centre	0171-928 7789
Gingerbread	0171-336 8183
Girls Friendly Society	0171-589 9628
Guide Assoc	0171-834 6242
Justice for Women	0181-374 2948

League of Jewish Women	0171-387 7688	Society of Women Writers and	
Lesbian & Gay Police Assoc	01426-943011	Journalists	0181-529 0886
London Lesbian Line	0171-251 6911	Soroptimist International	0161-480 7686
Marriage Counselling Scotland	0131-225 5006	Suffragette Fellowship	0171-222 2597
Maternity Alliance	0171-588 8583	The 300 Group	01403-733797
Medical Women's Federation	0171-387 7765	Townswomen's Guilds	0121-456 3435
Merched Y Wawar	01970-611661	UK Asian Women's Conference	0181-946 2858
Mothers' Union	0171-222 5533	Victim Support	0171-735 9166
Muslim Women's Helpline	0181-908 3205	Wales Assembly of Women	01267-267428
National Abortion Campaign	0171-923 4976	Watch? (What About the Children?)	01386-561635
National Alliance of Women's		WATCH (Women & the Church)	01763-848822
Organisations	0171-242 0878	Welsh Women's Aid	01222-390874
National Assembly of Women	0161-205 5920	West Indian Women's Assoc	0181-521 4456
National Assoc for Maternal & Child		Womankind Worldwide	0181-563 8608
Welfare	0171-383 4117	Women Against Sexual Harassment	0171-405 0430
National Assoc of Widows	0121-643 8348	Women in Film and TV	0171-379 0344
National Assoc of Women's Clubs	0171-837 1434	Women in Journalism	0171-274 2413
National Childbirth Trust	0181-992 8637	Women in Management	0171-382 9978
National Childminding Assoc	0181-464 6164	Women in Music	0171-978 4823
National Council for One-Parent		WomenAid International	0171-925 1331
Families	0171-267 1361	Women's Advisory Council (UNA)	01395-263688
National Council of Women of GB	0171-354 2395	Women's Aid Federation	0117-944 4411
National Federation of Women's		Women's Environmental Network	0171-247 3327
Institutes	0171-371 9300	Women's Farm & Garden Assoc	01285-658339
National Free Church Womens Council	0171-387 8413	Women Overcoming Violence & Abuse	01274-385234
National Group on Homeworking	0113-245 4273	Women & Practical Conservation	0171-278 4294
National Women's Network for International		Women in Prison	0171-226 5879
Solidarity	0181-809 2388	Women Through the Millennium	0171-730 0533
One Parent Families Scotland	0131-556 3899	Women United Against Racism	0171-729 3500
Pay Equity Project	0171-242 1975	Women Working Worldwide	0161-247 1760
Positively Women	0171-713 0444	Women's Health	0171-251 6580
Pro-Choice Alliance	0171-636 4619	Women's Health Concern	0181-780 3916
Rape Crisis Centre	0171-837 1600	Women's Inter-Church Council	0171-387 8413
Refuge	0990-995 4430	Women's Liberation (Lesbian Line)	0171-837 8602
Relate	01788-573241	Women's Local Authority Network	0161-237 5077
Rights of Women	0171-251 6577	Women's National Commission	0171-712 2443
Roman Catholic Feminists	0181-886 0779	Women's Resource Centre	0171-729 4011
Royal College of Midwives	0171-872 5100	Women's Royal Voluntary Service	0171-793 9917
Royal College of Nursing	0171-409 3333	Women's Sports Foundation	0171-831 7863
Scottish Co-operative Women's Guild	0141-429 1457	Women's Therapy Centre	0171-263 6200
Scottish Women's Aid	0131-221 0401		
Scottish Women's Rural Institutes	0131-225 1724		

The workers

Nearly 8.1 million people were members of trade unions and staff associations in 1995, a fall of 5.2 million since 1979. The number of unions dropped from 453 to 238, with many merging to cope with the effects of fewer members. Only about 30 per cent of employees are now union members. 1994 saw the lowest number of stoppages since records began in 1891, with 278,000 working days lost, compared with 29.5 million in 1979. In the first half of the 1990s the number of union members fell four times faster than the overall fall in jobs, while the number of non-union jobs rose. Many of these are temporary or part-time.

The UK workforce is just under 29 million adults, but the number actually working is unclear because of the ways in which Whitehall has manipulated the figures. Labour in opposition condemned the Tory government for adjusting statistics and definitions 31 times, so in April 1998 Labour in government started producing them in a new way. This is based on the internationally recognised Labour Force Survey, using its definition of unemployment as being people out of work who have looked for a job in the last four weeks. Until then Whitehall counted the number of people claiming benefit. The first of the new statistics showed there were 1,835,000 unemployed. But in June 1998 it emerged that Labour was also massaging figures when it was revealed that anyone working for just one hour a week is now classified as employed. New Labour is introducing a national minimum wage of £3.60, for certain types of people, starting April 1999.

Seventy three unions, with 6.76 million members, are affiliated to the TUC (Trades Union Congress). The largest unions are:

Unison	1.37 million members
TGWU	891,000
AEEU	725,000
GMB	718,000
MSF	425,000

Founded in 1886, the TUC belongs to the International Confederation of Free Trade Unions, based in Brussels, with members from 124 countries.

The Royal Society for Arts warned in April 1998 after two years research that unemployment will worsen dramatically and divisions between rich and poor will widen further by 2020. The Office for National Statistics published a special report Social Focus on the Unemployed in July 1998. This found that a quarter of the working age population had claimed benefit between 1990 and 1995, a third of the unemployed are under-25 and 40 per cent of the unemployed have been so for more than a year.

One of the reasons for the decline in trade unionism in the 1980s and 90s has been the reshaping of their legal environment. The Certification Office for Trade Unions and Employers Associations is the statutory body overseeing many of the legal criteria and rules applying to unions. The Commissioner for the Rights of Trade Union Members helps trade unionists take legal action against their own union.

There are three main employers organisations. The CBI (Confederation of British Industry) has 250,000 companies as members. It is based in Centrepoint, very near the TUC in Great Russell Street. The BCC (British Chambers of Commerce) represents 196 chambers, with their 200,000 local businesses. The IoD (Institute of Directors) looks after 35,000 company directors

EMPLOYERS AND OFFICIALS

Advisory, Conciliation and Advisory Service	
(ACAS)	0171-210 3613
British Chamber of Commerce (BCC)	0171-565 2000
British Standards Institute	0181-996 9000
CBI	0171-379 7400
Central Arbitration Committee	0171-210 3737
Certification Office for Trade Unions &	
Employers Assocs	0171-210 3734
Commissioners for the Rights of Trade	
Union Members /Protection Against	
Unlawful Industrial Action	01925-415771
Dept for Education & Employment	0171-925 5000
Press	0171-925 5132
Dept of Trade & Industry	0171-215 5000
Press	0171-215 6424
Business in Europe	0117-944 4888
Innovation Enquiry Line	0171-215 1217
Employment Appeal Tribunal	0171-273 1041
Engineering Employers Federation	0171-222 7777
Federation of Small Businesses	0171-233 7900
Industrial Injuries Advisory Council	0171-962 8065
Industrial Society	0171-262 2401
Industrial Tribunals HQ	0171-273 8666
Help desk	0345-959775
Institute of Directors	0171-839 1233
Monopolies & Mergers	0171-324 1467
Office of Fair Trading	0171-211 8000

UNIONS AND ASSOCIATIONS

Amalgamated Engineering & Electrical Union	
(AEEU)	0181-462 7755
Associated Metalworkers Union (AMU)	0171-317 8600
Associated Society of Locomotive Engineers &	
Firemen (ASLEF)	0171-317 8600
Assoc of First Division Civil Servants	0171-343 1111
Assoc of Teachers & Lecturers	0171-930 6441
Assoc of University Teachers (AUT)	0171-221 4370
Bakers, Food & Allied Workers Union	01707-261570
Banking, Insurance & Finance Union	0181-946 9151
British Airline Pilots Assoc (BALPA)	0181-476 4000
British Assoc of Journalists	0171-353 3003
British Assoc of Social Workers	0121-622 3911
British Medical Assoc (BMA)	0171-387 4499
Broadcasting, Entertainment, Cinematograph &	
Theatre Union (BECTU)	0171-437 8506
Ceramic and Allied Trades Union	01782-272755
Civil & Public Services Assoc (CPSA) - now	
part of PCS (see below)	0171-924 2727
Communication Managers Assoc	0118-934 2300
Communication Workers Union	0181-971 7200
Community & Youth Workers Union	0121-244 3344
Engineers & Managers Assoc	01932-577007
Equity (British Actors Equity Assoc)	0171-379 6000
Fire Brigades Union	0181-541 1765
GMB	0181-947 3131
Graphical, Paper & Media Union	
(GPMU)	01234-351521
Institute of Journalists (IOJ)	0171-252 1187
Institution of Professionals, Managers &	
Specialists (IPMS, ex-IPCS)	0171-902 6600

International Transport Workers Fed	0171-403 2733
Iron & Steel Trades Confederation	0171-837 6691
Managerial & Professional Officers	01279-434444
Manufacturing Science Finance (MSF)	0171-505 3000
Musicians Union	0171-582 5566
NATFHE - Lecturers' Union	0171-837 3636
NAS/UWT	0171-379 9499
National Farmers Union (NFU)	0171-331 7200
National Union of Insurance Workers	0171-405 6798
National Union of Journalists (NUJ)	0171-278 7916
National Union of Marine, Aviation & Shipping	
Transport Officers (NUMAST)	0181-989 6677
National Union of Mineworkers (NUM)	01226-215555
National Union of Rail, Maritime & Transport	
Workers (RMT)	0171-387 4771
National Union of Students (NUS)	0171-272 8900
National Union of Teachers (NUT)	0171-388 6191
Police Federation	0181-399 2224
Prison Officers Assoc (POA)	0181-803 0255
Professional Footballers Assoc	0161-236 0575
Public & Commercial Services Union (merger in	
1998 of CPSA & PTC)	0171-924 2727
Royal College of Nursing	0171-409 3333
Royal College of Midwives	0171-872 5100
Society of Authors	0171-373 6642
Society of Radiographers	0171-391 4500
Society of Telecom Executives	(0181-943 5181
Transport & General Workers Union	0171-828 7788
Transport Salaried Staffs Assoc	0171-387 2101
Union of Construction, Allied Trades &	
Technicians (UCATT)	0171-622 2442
Union of Shop, Distributive & Allied	
Workers (USDAW)	0161-224 2804
Unison (ex-NALGO/NUPE/COHSE)	0171-388 2366
United Road Transport Union	0161-881 6245
Writers Guild	0171-723 8074

WORKERS' FEDERATIONS

Centre for Alternative Industrial Technological	
Systems	0114-266 5063
Confederation of Shipbuilding & Engineering	
Unions	0171-703 2215
Council of Civil Service Unions	0171-834 8393
European TU Confederation	00-322 224 0411
European TU Institute	00-322 224 0470
Federation of Entertainment Unions	01962-713134
General Federation of Trade Unions	0171-387 2578
Institute of Employment Rights	0171-738 9511
International Confederation of Free Trade	
Unions (ICFTU)	00-322 224 0211
International Federation of Chemical, Energy, Mine &	
General Workers Unions (ICEM)	00-322 626 2020
International Fed. of Journalists	00-322 223 2265
International Labour Org	0171-828 6401
Labour Research Dept	0171-928 3649
Media & Entertainment International	00-322 223 5537
Public Concern at Work	0171-404 6609
Tolpuddle Martyrs Museum	01305-848237
Trades Union Congress (TUC)	0171-636 4030
Brussels	00-322 224 0478
Website	www.tuc.org.uk
Unions 21	0171-278 9944

Action

ANIMALS, FARMING & FOOD

Animal Aid Society	01732-364546
Animal Concern	0141-445 3570
Animal Health Trust	01638-751000
Animal Rights Coalition	01902-711935
Animal Welfare Trust	0181-950 8215
Arboricultural Assoc	01794-368717
Bat Conservation Trust	0171-627 2629
Beauty Without Cruelty	0171-254 2929
Breach-Whale Wars	01405-769375
British Assoc for Shooting & Conservation	01244-573000
British Beekeepers Assoc	01203-696679
British Dietic Assoc	0121-643 5483
British Trust for Ornithology	01842-750050
British Union for Abolition of Vivisection	0171-700 4888
Butterfly Conservation	01206-322342
Cats Protection League	01403-221900
Compassion in World Farming	01730-264208
Country Landowners Assoc	0171-235 0511
Donkey Sanctuary	01395-578222
East Kent Animal Welfare	01304-363071
Earthkind	0181-889 1595
Farm Animal Welfare Council	0181-330 8022
Farm Animal Welfare Network	01484-688650
Farmers Union of Wales	01970-612755
Farming & Wildlife Advisory Gp	01203-696699
Food & Drink Federation	0171-836 2460
Game Conservancy	01425-652381
Glutamate Information Service	0171-631 3434
Henry Doubleday Research	01203-303517
Hunt Saboteurs Assoc	01273-622827
International Dolphin Watch	01482-643403
International Fund for Animal Welfare	01892-601900
International Whaling Commission	01223-233971
Kennel Club	0171-493 6651
League Against Cruel Sports	0171-403 6155
London Animal Action	0171-278 3068

London Wildlife Trust	0171-261 0447
Mammal Society	0171-498 4358
National Anti-Vivisection Soc	0181-846 9777
National Canine Defence	0171-837 0006
National Farmers Union	0171-331 7200
National Fed of Badger Groups	0171-498 3220
National Organisation Working Against Live Exports	01869-345243
National Society of Allotment & Leisure Gardeners	01536-266576
Orkney Seal Rescue	01856-831463
Otter Trust	01986-893470
Passports for Pets	0181-870 5960
Peoples Dispensary for Sick Animals	01952-290999
Pesticides Trust	0171-274 8895
PETA (People for the Ethical Treatment of Animals)	0181-785 3113
Rare Breeds Survival Trust	01203-696551
Royal Agricultural Society	01203-696969
Royal Horticultural Society	0171-834 4333
RSPB (Birds)	01767 680551
RSPCA (Animals)	01403-264181
Scottish Landowners Federation	0131-555 1031
Scottish Wildlife & Countryside Link	01738-630804
Scottish Wildlife Trust	0131-312 7765
Soil Assoc	0117-929 0661
Sportsman's Association	01743-356868
Sustainable Agriculture (SAFE)	0171-837 8980
Ulster Wildlife Trust	01396-830282
Uncaged	0114-253 0020
Urban Wildlife Trust	0121-666 7474
Vegan Society	01424-427393
Vegetarian Society	0161-928 0793
Veggies Catering Campaign	0115-958 5666
Whale & Dolphin Conservation	01225-334511
Wildfowl & Wetlands Trust	01453-890333
Wildlife Trusts (ex RSNC)	01522-544400
Womens Farming Union	01203-693171
Wood Green Animal Shelters	01763-838329
Working for Organic Growers	01273-476286
World Society for the Protection of Animals	0171-793 0540
World Wide Fund for Nature	01483-426444
Zoo Federation	0171-586 0230
Zoological Society of London	0171-722 3333

CLAIMANTS

Bootstrap Enterprises	0171-254 0775
Industrial Common Ownership Movement (ICOM)	0113-246 1737
Low Pay Unit	0171-713 7616
New Ways to Work	0171-226 4026
Public Concern at Work	0171-404 6609
Rural Development Comm.	0171-340 2900
Unemployed Workers Charter	0181-459 7146
Unemployment Unit	0171-833 1222

COMMUNITY ACTION &WORK

Advice Services Alliance	0171-247 2441
Assoc of British Credit Unions	0161-832 3694
Centre for Alternative Industrial & Technological	
Systems	0114-266 5063
Charities Aid Foundation	01732-520000
Child Poverty Action Group	0171-253 3406
Childline-info	0171-239 1000
Citizen Organising Foundation	0181-981 6200
Community Development Foundation	0171-226 5375
Community Service Volunteers	0171-278 6601
Construction Safety Campaign	0171-537 7220
Direct Action Network	0181-889 1361
Directory of Social Change	0171-209 4949
Drinkline	0345-320202
Everyman Centre	0171-737 6747
Gamblers Anonymous	0171-384 3040
Inter-Action Trust	0171-583 2652
Law Centres Federation	0171-387 8570
Letslink UK	01705-730639
London Advice Services Alliance	0171-377 2748
London Hazards Centre	0171-267 3387
Low Pay Unit	0171-713 7616
Missing Persons Helpline	0500-700700
National Assoc of Citizens Advice	
Bureaux	0171-833 2181
National Council for Voluntary Orgs	0171-713 6161
National Fed. of Community Orgs	0171-226 0189
National Group on Homeworking	0113-245 4273
Rotary International	01789-765411
Samaritans	0171-734 2800
Saneline	0345-678000
Scottish Council for Voluntary Orgs	0131-556 3882
Scottish Crofters' Union	01471-822529
Small World	0171-272 1394
Undercurrents Productions	01865-203661
Unions 96	0171-278 9944
Victim Support	0171-735 9166

DIY CULTURE

Activists Networking	0181-341 3794
Advance Party Network	0181-450 6929
Cannabis Hemp Information Club	0181-888 9277
Conscious Cinema	01273-679544
Dance Information Network	0171-729 5252
Festival Eye (annual festival guide)	01568-760492
Freedom Trail	01935-863349
Frontline Magazine	09762-36216
Glastonbury Festival (late June)	0870-607 7380
Green Events	0171-267 2552
Justice	0171-329 5100
Notting Hill Carnival	0181-964 0544
Paganlink Network	01322-288110
Reclaim the Streets	0171-281 4621
Red Pepper Magazine	0171-247 1702
SchNews Magazine	01273-685913
Squall Magazine	0171-561 1204
The Land is Ours	01865-722016
Undercurrents Videos	01865-203661

DRUGS AND ADDICTION

Alcohol Concern	0171-928 7377
Alcoholics Anonymous	01904-644026
ASH (Action on Smoking and Health)	0171-224 0743
Assoc for Nonsmokers Rights	01344-426252
Cannabis Hemp Info Club	01458-835769
Gamblers Anonymous	0171-384 3040
Institute for the Study of Drug	
Dependence	0171-928 1211
Legalise Cannabis Campaign	01603-441178
Libra Trust	01273-480012
Mainliners	0171-582 5434
Medical Council on Alcoholism	0171-487 4445
Narcotics Anonymous	0171-251 4007
Release	0171-729 9904
Scottish Council on Alcohol	0141-333 9677
Standing Conf on Drug Abuse	0171-928 9500
Transform	0117-939 8052

EDUCATION AND FAMILY

Abortion Law Reform Assoc	0171-637 7264
Active Birth Centre	0171-561 9006
Advisory Centre for Education	0171-354 8321
Age Concern	0181-679 8000
Assoc of Radical Midwives	01695-572776
Baby Life Support Systems	0171-831 9393
Baby Milk Action	01223-464420
Barnardos	0181-550 8822
Birth Control Campaign	0171-580 9360
British Pregnancy Advisory Service	01564-793225
Brook Advisory Centres	0171-833 8488
Campaign Against the Child Support	
Act	0171-482 2496
Campaign for State Education	0181-944 8206
Carers National Assoc	0171-490 8818
Child Poverty Action Group	0171-253 3406
Child Rescue	01273-692947
Childline	0171-239 1000
Childrens Legal Centre	01206-872466
Childrens Society	0171-837 4299
Divorce, Mediation & Counselling	
Service	0171-730 2422
EPOCH (End Physical Punishment of	
Children)	0171-700 0627
Exploring Parenthood	0171-221 4471
FACE (Fight Against Cuts in Education)	01203-311013
Families Need Fathers	0171-613 5060
Family Caring Trust	01693-64174
Family Planning Assoc	0171-837 5432
Family Rights Group	0171-923 2628
Family Welfare Assoc	0171-254 6251
Gingerbread	0171-336 8183
Guides Assoc	0171 834 6242
Independent Schools Information	
Service	0171-630 8795
Inter-Action	0171-583 2652
International Planned Parenthood	
Federation	0171-487 7900
Marie Stopes International	0171-574 7400

Mary Ward Centre	0171-831 7711
Message Home	0500-700740
Mothers Union	0171-222 5533
National Abortion Campaign	0171-923 4976
National Childbirth Trust	0181-992 8637
National Childcare	0171-405 5617
National Childrens Bureau	0171-843 6000
National Council for One Parent Families	0171-267 1361
NCH Action for Children	0171-226 2033
NSPCC	0171-825 2500
National Youth Agency	0116-285 6789
One Parent Families in Scotland	0131-556 3899
PAIN (Parents Against Injustice)	01279-656564
Parent Network	0171-735 1214
Pensioners Voice	01254-52606
Pre-School Learning Alliance	0171-833 0991
Relate (Marriage Guidance)	01788-573241
Save the Children Fund	0171-703 5400
Socialist Teachers Alliance	01203-332320
Watch? (What About the Children?)	01386-561635
Woodcraft Folk	0181-672 6031
Workers Educational Assoc	0181-983 1515

ENVIRONMENT & ECOLOGY

Action with Communities in Rural England	01285-653477
Advisory Committee on Protection of the Sea	0171-799 3033
Agenda 21 Network (London)	0171-296 6599
Assoc for Energy Conservation	0171-359 8000
Assoc for the Protection of Rural Scotland	0131-225 7012
Black Environment Network	01286-870715
British Assoc of Nature Conservationists	01604-405285
British Earth Sheltering Assoc	01993 703619
British Ecological Society	0181-871 9797
British Mountaineering Council	0161-445 4747
British Society of Dowsers	01233-750253
British Trust for Conservation Volunteers England	01491-839766
British Unidentified Flying Object Research Assoc	0181-449 5908
Campaign for the Protection of Rural Wales	01938-552525
Centre for Alternative Technology	01654-702400
Civic Trust	0171-930 9730
Wales	01222-484606
Scotland	0141-221 1466
Clean Rivers Trust	01636-892627
Climate Action Network	0171-836 1110
Common Ground	0171-379 3109
Communities Against Toxics	0151-339 5473
Community Recycling Network	0117-942 0142
Conservation Foundation	0171-591 3111
Council for Environmental Education	0118-975 6061
Council for National Parks	0171-924 4077
Council for the Protection of Rural England (CPRE)	0171-976 6433
Docklands Forum (London)	0171-377 1822

Earth First!	0161-224 4846
EarthAction Network	0171-865 4009
Earthwatch Europe	01865-311600
Environment Centre	0131-557 2135
Environment Council	0171-836 2626
Environmental Information Service	01603-871048
Environmental Investigation Agency	0171-490 7040
Environmental Law Foundation	0171-404 1030
Farming & Wildlife Advisory Group	01203-696699
Fauna & Flora International	01223-571000
Freedom Trail	01935-863349
Friends of the Earth	0171-490 1555
FoE Scotland	0131-554 9977
FoE Cymru	01222-229577
Frontline Magazine	09762-36216
Georgian Group	0171-387 1720
Global Witness	0181-563 7779
Green Alliance	0171-836 0341
Green Events Magazine	0171-267 2552
Green Left	01904-672489
Green Party	0171-272 4474
Green World Magazine	01252-330506
GreenNet	0171-713 1941
Greenpeace (London)	0171-837 7557
Greenpeace UK	0171-865 8100
Groundwork Foundation	0121-236 8565
Gypsy Council	01708-868986
Historic Churches Preservation Trust	0171-736 3054
Institute of Public Rights of Way	01535 637957
League Against Cruel Sports	0171-403 6155
Local Agenda 21 Steering Group	0171-296 6600
London Ecology Unit	0171-267 7944
London Green Party	0171-272 4474
London Greenpeace	0171-837 7557
Marine Conservation Society	01989-566017
Marine Society	0171-261 9535
Media Natura	0171-253 0880
Mountaineering Council of Scotland	01738-638227
National Council for the Conservation of Plants & Gardens	01483-211465
National Energy Action	0191-261 5677
National Federation of City Farms	0117-923 1800
National Pure Water Assoc.	01924-254433
National Recycling Forum	0171-248 1412
National Small Woods Assoc	01743-792644
National Society for Clean Air	01273-326313
National Trust	0171-222 9251
National Trust for Scotland	0131-226 5922
Noise Abatement Society	01322-862789
Noise Network	0181-312 9997
N Ireland Environment Link	01232-314944
Nukewatch UK	01703-554434
Oilwatch	0171-435 5000
Open Spaces Society	01491-573535
Oxleas Wood Hotline	01426-921900
Permaculture Assoc	01654-712188
Pesticides Trust	0171-274 8895
Planning Exchange	0141-248 8541
Plantlife	0171-938 9111
Rainbow Centre	0115-958 5666
Ramblers Assoc	0171-582 6878

Reclaim the Streets	0171-281 4621
Reforest the Earth	01603-611953
Reforesting Scotland	0131-226 2496
Royal Entomological Society	0171-584 8361
Royal Forestry Society	01442-822028
Royal Scottish Forestry Society	0131-660 9480
Royal Society for Nature Conservation: Wildlife	
Trusts Partnership	01522-544400
Royal Town Planning Institute	0171-636 9107
Save Britains Heritage	0171-253 3500
Scottish Conservation Projects Trust	01786-479697
Scottish Crofters Union	01471-822529
Scottish Green Party	0141-571 1215
Scottish Native Woods	01887-820392
Scottish Wildlife & Countryside Link	01738-630804
Sea Action	01273-620125
SERA (Socialist Environment & Resources	
Assoc)	0171-263 7389
Society for the Protection of Ancient	
Buildings	0171-377 1644
Squall Magazine	0171-561 1204
Surfers Against Sewage	01872-553001
The Land is Ours	01865-722016
Tourism Concern	0171-753 3330
Town & Country Planning Assoc	0171-930 8903
Tree Council	0171-828 9928
Trust for Urban Ecology	0171-237 9175
UK Environmental Law Assoc	01491-671631
Undercurrents Productions	01865-203661
Urban Pollution Research	0181-362 6374
Wales Green Party	01970-611226
Waste Watch	0171-248 0242
Waterway Recovery Group	0171-586 2510
Wild Flower Society	01509-215598
Wildfowl & Wetlands Trust	01453-890333
Womens Environmental Network	0171-247 3327
Woodland Trust	01476-581111
World Conservation Monitoring	01223-277314

ETHNIC GROUPS

Black Environment Network	01286-870715
Civic Trust (Community Action)	0171-930 9730
Commission for Racial Equality	0171-828 7022
Confederation of Indian Orgs	0181-928 9889
Gandhi Foundation	0181-981 7628
Gypsy Council	01708-868986
Immigration Advisory Service	0171-357 6917
India Assoc (UK)	0181-597 5389
Indian Workers Assoc	0181-574 6019
Institute of Race Relations	0171-837 0041
Irish Campaigns Network	0961-361518
Joint Council for the Welfare of	
Immigrants (JCWI)	0171-251 8706
Kurdish Cultural Centre	0171-735 0918
Legal Advice for Travellers	01222-874580
Migrant Resource Centre	0171-233 9868
Minority Rights Group	0171-978 9498
National Assembly Against Racism	0171-247 9907
National Group on Homeworking	0113-245 4273
National Gypsy Council	01928-723138

Newham Monitoring Project	0181-555 8151
Pakistan Welfare Assoc	0181-679 0924
Refugee Council	0171-820 3000
Refugee Legal Centre	0171-827 9090
Runnymede Trust	0171-600 9666
Scottish Asian Action Committee	0141-341 0025
Scottish Crofters Union	01471-822529
Searchlight Magazine	0171-284 4040
Standing Conference of West Indian	
Organisations	0171-928 7861
Survival	0171-242 1441
Youth Against Racism in Europe	0181-533 4533

HEALTH

Age Concern	0181-679 8000
Alzheimers Disease Society	0171-306 0606
Arthritis Research Campaign	01246-558033
ASH (Action on Smoking & Health)	0171-224 0743
Body Positive	0171-287 8010
Breast Cancer Campaign	0171-404 3955
British Deaf Assoc	0171-588 3520
British Dental Health	01788-546365
British Heart Foundation	0171-935 0185
British Holistic Medicine Assoc.	01743-261155
British Homeopathic Assoc	0171-935 2163
British Kidney Patient Assoc	01420-472021
British Lung Foundation	0171-831 5831
British Medical Assoc	0171-387 4499
British Organ Donor Society	01223-893636
British Psychological Society	0116-254 9568
British Wheel of Yoga	01529-306851
Cancer Relief Macmillan Fund	0171-351 7811
Cancer Research Campaign	0171-224 1333
Casualties Union	0171-278 6264
Clic (Cancer and Leukaemia in	
Childhood)	0117 924 8844
Crusaid	0171-833 3939
Dial UK (Disability Information and Advice	
Lines)	01302-310123
Diet Breakers	01869-337070
Direct Action Network	0181-889 1361
Disability Alliance	0171-247 8776
Disability Wales	01222-887325
Downs Syndrome Assoc	0181-682 4001
Festival for Mind, Body, Spirit	0171-938 3788
Food Commission	0171-837 2250
Foundation for the Study of Infant	
Death	0171-235 0965
GLAD (Greater London Assoc of Disabled	
People)	0171-346 5800
Haemophilia Society	0171-380 0600
Health Rights	0171-501 9856
Health Unlimited	0171-582 5999
Hearing Dogs for the Deaf	01844-353898
Help the Aged	0171-253 0253
Herpes Assoc	0171-609 9061
Hospice Information Service	0181-778 9252
Imperial Cancer Research Fund	0171-242 0200
Inquest	0181-802 7430
Institute for Complementary Medicine	0171-237 5165

Leonard Cheshire Foundation	0171-802 8200
Leukaemia Research Fund	0171-405 0101
London Lighthouse	0171-792 1200
Migraine Action Assoc	01932-352468
ME Assoc	01375-642466
MENCAP	0171-454 0454
Mental After Care Assoc	0171-436 6194
Mental Health Foundation	0171-580 0145
Mental Health Media	0171-700 8173
Migraine Trust	0171-831 4818
MIND (National Assoc for Mental Health)	0181-884 5000
Multiple Sclerosis Society	0171-610 7171
National Aids Trust	0171-814 6767
National Asthma Campaign	0171-226 2260
National Autistic Society	0181-813 8222
National Schizophrenia Fellowship	0181-547 3937
Natural Medicines Society	01773-710002
NDT (learning disabilities)	0161-228 7055
No Panic	01952-590005
Outset	0181-692 7141
Overeaters Anonymous	0161-865 8634
Parkinsons Disease Society	0171-931 8080
Patients Assoc	0181-423 8999
Pregnancy Advisory Service	0171-637 8962
RADAR (Royal Assoc for Disability & Rehabilitation)	0171-250 3222
Re-Solv (Society for the Prevention of Solvent Abuse)	01785-817885
Royal National Institute for the Blind	0171-388 1266
Royal National Institute for the Deaf	0171-296 8000
Royal Society for the Prevention of Accidents (RSPCA)	01222-762529
Samaritans	01753-532713
Sane	0171-375 1002
SCODA (Standing Conference on Drug Abuse)	0171-928 9500
Scope	0171-619 7100
Scottish Council on Alcohol	0141-333 9677
Socialist Health Assoc	0171-490 0057
St John Ambulance Assoc	0171-235 5231
Tenovus Cancer Helpline	0800-526527
Terence Higgins Trust	0171-831 0330
Voluntary Euthanasia Society	0171-937 7770

HISTORY

Ancient Monuments Society	0171-236 3934
Architectural Heritage Fund	0171-925 0199
British Assoc of Friends of Museums	01276-66617
British Records Assoc	0171-833 0428
British Society for History of Science	01367-718963
Council for British Archaeology	01904-671417
English Civil War Society	01430-430695
Folklore Society	0171-387 5894
Historical Assoc	0171-735 3901
Rescue (British Archaeological Trust)	01992-553377
Society for Folk Life Studies	0113-275 6537
Subterranea Britannica	01737-823456
Victorian Society	0181-994 1019

HOUSING

Advisory Service for Squatters	0171-359 8814
Alone in London Service	0171-278 4486
Big Issue Magazine	0171-418 0418
Building Industry Link Up	0181-534 5352
Centrepoint (Youth Homelessness)	0171-629 2229
Centrepoint's Education Team	0171-629 2229
Crisis (ex Crisis at Christmas)	0171-377 0489
Girls Alone Project	0171-383 4103
Homeless Information Project	0171-277 7639
Homes for Homeless People	01582-481426
Housing Centre Trust	0171-251 2363
Housing Law Practioners Assoc	0171-233 8322
Institute of Housing	01203-694433
London Connection	0171-766 5544
London Housing Unit	0171-428 4910
National Assoc for Voluntary Hostels	0181-286 2727
National Homeless Alliance	0171-833 2071
National Housing Federation	0171-278 6571
National Housing & Town Planning Council	0171-251 2363
National Missing Persons Helpline	0500-700 700
New Horizon	0171-388 5560
Piccadilly Advice Centre	0171-437 1579
Rural Housing Trust	0171-793 8114
Scottish Crofters Union	01471-822529
SHAC (Housing Advice Line)	0171-404 6929
SHAC: Edinburgh	0131-229 8771
Shelter	0171-505 2000
Shelter Nightline	0800-446441
Simon Community	0171-485 6639

HUMAN RIGHTS

Action for Southern Africa	0171-833 3133
Amnesty International	0171-413 5500
Anti-Racist Alliance	0181-422 4849
Anti-Fascist Action	0161-232 0813
Anti-Nazi League	0171-924 0333
Anti-Slavery International	0171-924 9555
Article 19	0171-278 9292
British Humanist Assoc	0171-430 0908
British Irish Rights Watch	0171-405 6415
British Red Cross Society	0171-235 5454
Burman Action Group	0171-359 7679
Call for Peace (NI)	0181-372 6789
Campaign Against Asylum Bill	0171-247 9907
Campaign Against Racism & Fascism (CARF)	0171-837 1450
Campaign Against Racist Laws	0181-571 1437
Campaign for Freedom of Info	0171-831 7477
Campaign for Press and Broadcasting Freedom (CPBF)	0171-278 4430
Canon Colins Educational Trust for Southern Africa	0171-354 1462
Central America Human Rights	0171-631 4200
Charter 88	0171-833 1988
Christian Aid	0171-620 4444
CIIR (Catholic Institute for International Relations	0171-354 0883

Cuba Solidarity Campaign	0171-263 6452
Cymdeithas yr Iaith Gymraeg	01970-624501
European Dialogue	0171-713 5723
Fourth World	0171-286 4366
Freedom Press	0171-247 9249
Howard League for Penal Reform	0171-281 7722
Human Rights Watch	0171-713 1995
Innocent	0161-476 6405
Intermediate Technology Development Group	0171-436 9761
Interights	0171-278 3230
International Alert	0171-793 8383
International Assoc for Religious Freedom	01865-202744
Iraqi National Congress	0171-629 2960
Irish Peace Initiative	0181-372 6789
Justice	0171-329 5100
Kashmir Freedom Movement	0181810 0104
Kurdistan Solidarity Campaign	0171-586 5892
Labour Campaign for Travellers Rights	0113-248 6746
Latin America Bureau	0171-278 2829
Law Centres Federation	0171-387 8570
Legal Action Group	0171-833 2931
Liberty (NCCL)	0171-403 3888
Minority Rights Group	0171-978 9498
New Internationalist Magazine	01865-728181
Nicaragua Solidarity Campaign	0171-272 9619
Oxfam	01865-311311
Palestine Solidarity Campaign	0171-700 6192
Peru Support Group	0171-620 1103
Philippine Resource Centre	0171-281 4561
Prisoners Abroad	0171-833 3467
Public Law Project	0171-467 9800
Redress	0171-278 9502
Release	0171-729 9904
Returned Volunteer Action	0171-278 0804
Scottish Council for Civil Liberties	0141-332 5960
Statewatch	0181-802 1882
Survival International	0171-242 1441
Third World First	01865-245678
Tibet Information Network	0171-814 9011
Tibet Society of the UK	0171-383 7533
Tools for Self Reliance	01703-869697
Travellers Support Group	01458-832371
Troops Out	0961-361518
War on Want	0171-620 1111
WaterAid	0171-793 4500
World Development Movement	0171-737 6215

ROADS AND TRANSPORT

Alarm UK Alliance Against Roads)	0181-983 3572
Capital Transport Campaign	0171-388 2489
Cyclists Public Affairs Group	01483-414320
Environmental Transport Assoc	01932-828882
Freedom of the Skies	01570-493576
Freedom Trail	01935-863349
Friends, Families and Travellers Group	01458 832371
Heritage Railway Assoc	01233-712130
London Cycling Campaign	0171-928 7220
London Lorry Control Scheme	0171-582 0852
Motorcycle Action Group	0121-459 5860
No M11 Link Road Campaign	0181-530 7577
PACTS (Parliamentary Advisory Committee for Transport Safety)	0171-922 8112
Pedestrians Assoc	0171-490 0750
Public Transport Campaign	0161-839 9040
Reclaim the Streets	0171-281 4621
Road Alert	01635 521770
Save Our Railways	0171-582 6060
South Coast Against Road Building	01273-324455
Streetlife	0171-713 7331
Sustrans: Paths for People	0117-926 8893
Third Battle of Newbury	01635-550552
Trainwatch	0171-582 6505
Transport 2000	0171-388 8386
Travellers Support Group	01458-832371

SCIENCE

Assoc for Science Education	01707-283000
Assoc for Advancement of Science	0171-973 3500
British Astrological & Psychic Society	01634-827259
British Society for History of Science	01367-718963
Centre for Alternative Technological	01142-665063
Centre for Alternative Technology	01654-702400
Centre for Exploitation of Science	0171-354 9942
Institute for Social Inventions	0181-2082853
Royal Society	0171-839 5561
Science Policy Research Unit	01273-686758
Scientists for Global Responsibility	0181-871 5175

SEX

Albany Trust	0181-767 1827
Campaign Against Pornography	0171-263 1833
Campaign for Homosexual Equality	0171-833 3912
English Collective of Prostitutes	0171-482 2496
Gay Employment Rights	0171-704 8066
Gay London Policing	0171-704 2040
Lesbian & Gay Christian Movement	0171-739 1249
Lesbian Employment Rights	0171-704 8066
Lesbian & Gay Switchboard	0121-622 6589
Lesbian Information Service	01706-817235
London Bisexual Group	0181-569 7500
London Lesbian Line	0171-251 6911
London Rape Crisis Centre	0171-916 5466
OutRage (against homophobia)	0171-439 2381
Sexual Compulsives Anon	0181-914 7599
Stonewall	0171-336 8860
Terence Higgins Trust	0171-831 0330

WAR AND PEACE

Amnesty International	0171-814 6200
International Secretariat	0171-413 5500
At Ease	0171-247 5164
Bertrand Russell Foundation	0115-978 4504
Call for Peace (N Ireland)	0181-372 6789
Campaign Against Arms Trade	0171-281 0297
Campaign Against Militarism	0171-269 9220
CND	0171-700 2393
Children and War	0171-424 9444
Clergy Against Nuclear Arms	01243-372428
Council for Arms Control	0171-873 2065
Faslane Peace Camp	01436-820901
Housmans Peace Resource Project	0171-278 4474
Institute for Law and Peace	0171-267 2153
International Institute for Strategic Studies	0171-379 7676
Labour Action for Peace	0181-467 5367
Landmines Working Group	0171-281 6073
Medical Action for Global Security	0171-272 2020
Moral Re-Armament - Initiatives for Change	0171-828 6591
National Peace Council	0171-354 5200
Non-Violent Resistance Network	0171-607 2302
Nukewatch UK	01703-554434
Pax Christi	0181-800 4612
Peace Brigades International	0171-713 0392
Peace Education Project	0171-424 9444
Peace News	0171-278 3344
Peace Pledge Union	0171-424 9444
Quaker Peace & Service	0171-663 1000
Royal British Legion	0171-973 7200
Scientists for Global Responsibility	0181-871 5175
Scottish CND	0141-423 1222
Statewatch	0181-802 1882
Troops Out Campaign (out of Northern Ireland)	0171-609 1743
War Child	0171-916 9276
War Resisters International	0171-278 4040
Working Party on Chemical & Biological Weapons	01579-384492
World Court Project	01323-844269
World Disarmament Campaign	0171-729 2523
World Peace Movement	01276-24353
Youth Action for Peace	01903-528619

HELPLINES

Organisations providing help and general information.

Advice Services Alliance	0171-377 2748
Advisory Service for Squatters	0171-359 8814
Age Concern	0181-679 8000
Aids Helpline	0800-567123
Alcoholics Anonymous Helpline	0171-352 3001
British Pregnancy Advisory Service	01564-793225
ChildLine	0800-1111
Cruse Bereavement Line	0181-332 7227
Disability Helpline	01302-310123
Drinkline National Alcohol Helpline	0171-332 0202
Eating Disorders Assoc	01603-765050
Environment Agency Emergencies	0800-807060
Federation Independent Advice Centres	0171-489 1800
Gamblers Anonymous	0171-384 3040
Gingerbread (lone parents)	0171-336 8183
Health Information Service	0800-665544
Hearing Concern Helpline	01245-344600
Legal Advice for Travellers	01222-874580
Lesbian & Gay Switchboard	0121-622 6589
London Marriage Guidance	0171-580 1087
Missing Persons Helpline	0500-700700
Money Advice Association	0171-236 3566
Narcotics Anonymous Helpline	0171-730 0009
National Aids Helpline	0800-567123
National Association of Citizens Advice Bureaux	0171-833 2181
National Debtline	0121-359 8501
NHS Helpline	0800-665544
NSPCC Helpline	0800-800500
Parent Network	0171-735 1214
Parentline	0181-689 31316
Rape Crisis Centre	0171-837 1600
Rape & Sexual Abuse Helpline	0181-239 1122
Release Emergency (drugs)	0171-603 8654
Rights of Women Advice	0171-251 6577
RSPCA	0990-555999
Samaritans	0345-909090
SaneLine	0345-678000
Shelter Nightline	0800-446441
Smokers Quitline	0171-487 3000
Womens Aid Helpline (violence)	0345-023468
Womens Health	0171-251 6580
Young Minds	0345-626376

Media Guide index

The <u>unindexed</u> sections of this guide are: